Prevail

The Inspiring Story of Ethiopia's
Victory over Mussolini's Invasion,
1935–1941

JEFF PEARCE

Foreword by Richard Pankhurst

Skyhorse Publishing

CONTENTS

DEDICATION

There are some writers who are so good that you wish you knew them. I have never dedicated a book before to someone deceased, but in working on this project I came to deeply admire the brilliant prose, the scrappy courage, and the natural integrity of George Steer. So this book is, in part, respectfully dedicated to his memory.

It is also dedicated to the Ethiopian Patriots.

And it's offered respectfully to the Ethiopian people, in the hope that I have done right by their history.

LIST OF ILLUSTRATIONS
AND PHOTO CREDITS

Maps

Maps designed by Dennis Chan.

Photos

The Modern Caesar: Mussolini reviews his troops. *Courtesy CriticalPast.*

The Hunted Lion: Haile Selassie. From *Ethiopia Under Haile Selassie*, Sandford, J.M. Dent & Sons (Orion Publishing Group).

Sidney Barton, British Minister, at Addis Ababa, Ethiopia, from 1929 to 1936. *Photo courtesy of George Steer.*

Ethiopian Imperial Guard. From *Italy's Conquest of Abyssinia*, Newman, Thornton Butterworth, 1937.

Ethiopian village. From *Italy's Conquest of Abyssinia*, Newman, Thornton Butterworth, 1937.

The Defenders: Ras Imru, Ras Seyum, and Ras Kassa. From *Ethiopia Under Haile Selassie*, Sandford, J.M. Dent & Sons (Orion Publishing Group), 1946.

Diplomacy's Galahad: Anthony Eden goes into 10 Downing Street in early 1935. *Courtesy CriticalPast.*

The Brave Front: Delegates for the Stresa Conference. *Courtesy CriticalPast.*

Hands Off Ethiopia: Part of the Harlem protests on August 3, 1935. *Courtesy CriticalPast.*

Harlem Recruitment. PARA signs up volunteers to fight for Ethiopia in July, 1935. *Courtesy CriticalPast.*

The Black Eagle: Hubert Julian. *Courtesy CriticalPast.*

The Brown Condor: John Robinson. From the *Harold Hurd Collection.*

Pietro Badoglio. From *Italy's Conquest of Abyssinia*, Newman, Thornton Butterworth.

Rodolfo Graziani. From *Italy's Conquest of Abyssinia*, Newman, Thornton Butterworth.

Haile Selassie Gugsa. From *Italy's Conquest of Abyssinia*, Newman, Thornton Butterworth.

Herbert Matthews at Ende Yesus. *Courtesy Eric Matthews.*

Correspondents at Ende Yesus. *Courtesy Eric Matthews.*

Italian tanks break through a stone wall and climb a hill to clear the way for an advance, November 6, 1935. Photo by Laurence Stallings. *Courtesy private collection of Martin Plaut.*

Herbert Matthews at Senafe, February 1936. *Courtesy Eric Matthews.*

After the bombing of the British Red Cross on the Korem plain on March 4, 1936. *Courtesy National Archives of Sweden, Stockholm, Swedish Red Cross (Svenska Röda Korset).*

Examining an Italian poison gas bomb after an attack on Irgalem, March 1936. *Courtesy National Archives of Sweden, Stockholm, Swedish Red Cross (Svenska Röda Korset).*

The Dutch Red Cross camp at Dessie. *Courtesy private collection of Borre Winckel.*

Dr. Belmonte of the Dutch Red Cross in gas mask at cave entrance. *Courtesy private collection of Borre Winckel.*

General Badoglio with officers and reporters before the Battle of Enderta. *Courtesy Eric Matthews.*

The Cheerful Saint: Dr. John Melly. *Courtesy private collection of Borre Winckel.*

Marcel Junod with Sidney Brown in Addis Ababa. *Courtesy private collection of Benoit Junod.*

The Emperor visits a field hospital in Dessie. *Courtesy private collection of Borre Winckel.*

The Crown Prince having target practice near Dessie. *Courtesy private collection of Borre Winckel.*

British ambulances bring casualties to the Dutch field hospital at Dessie. *Courtesy private collection of Borre Winckel.*

"The Al Fresco Wedding," May 4, 1936: groom George Steer and bride Margarita de Herrero. *Photo courtesy of George Steer.*

"God and history will remember your judgment." Haile Selassie speaks to the League of Nations, June 30, 1936. *Courtesy CriticalPast.*

The Face of Occupation: Mussolini's stone bust put up at Adwa. From *Diario AOI*, Poggiali, Longanesi, 1971.

Mass arrests after the assassination attempt on Graziani. From *Diario AOI*, Poggiali, Longanesi, 1971.

A tukul destroyed during the Graziani Massacre. From *Diario AOI*, Poggiali, Longanesi, 1971.

Victims of the Graziani Massacre lie dead in a street in Addis Ababa. From *Diario AOI*, Poggiali, Longanesi, 1971.

Collection and disposal of bodies. From *Diario AOI*, Poggiali, Longanesi, 1971.

Another view of the massacre victims. From *Diario AOI*, Poggiali, Longanesi, 1971.

Souvenir shot kept by Italian soldier of Italians posing with four severed heads. *Courtesy private collection of Richard Pankhurst.*

Another souvenir shot. "An Italian soldier standing guard over a mass of dead Ethiopian civilians after the Graziani Massacre . . ."—George Steer. *Courtesy private collection of Richard Pankhurst.*

Ethiopian Patriots tied to trees and blindfolded before they were shot dead. *Courtesy private collection of Richard Pankhurst.*

Italian soldier poses in front of a gallows of hanged Ethiopians. *Courtesy private collection of Richard Pankhurst.*

Severed head of Ethiopian Patriot. *Courtesy private collection of Richard Pankhurst.*

Italian soldiers smile for the camera as one holds up a "spoil of war." *Courtesy private collection of Richard Pankhurst.*

Haile Selassie with Captain George Steer, June 3, 1941. *Courtesy Nicholas Rankin,* Telegram from Guernica, Faber and Faber, 2003.

The Boy General: Jagama Kello. *Courtesy private collection of Jagama Kello.*

Success: Patriots escort the Emperor as Debra Markos is retaken. From *Ethiopia Under Haile Selassie,* Sandford, J.M. Dent & Sons (Orion Publishing Group), 1946.

Officials of the Ethiopian Orthodox Church waiting for the Emperor's entry into Addis Ababa. From *Ethiopia Under Haile Selassie,* Sandford, J.M. Dent & Sons (Orion Publishing Group), 1946.

America's Champion of Diplomacy meets the "Elect of God": Haile Selassie and Franklin Roosevelt on the *USS Quincy* at the Suez Canal, February 13, 1945. *Courtesy CriticalPast.*

The Tireless Crusader: Sylvia Pankhurst in the post-war period with Haile Selassie. *Courtesy private collection of Richard Pankhurst.*

Three Heroes: Patriots at the burial ceremony for the Emperor on November 5, 2000. *Courtesy Andrew Hilton,* The Ethiopian Patriots, *Spellmount, 2007.*

The Survivor: Imru Zelleke at age 16 and modern day as a retired and respected diplomat. *Courtesy private collection of Imru Zelleke and Adey Makonnen.*

The Emperor's former palace, now the Institute of Ethiopian Studies for Addis Ababa University. *Author's photo.*

The oldest hotel in Addis Ababa, the Taitu Hotel. *Author's photo.*

Washa Mikael, outside Addis Ababa. *Author's photo.*

One of the rock-hewn churches of Lalibela. *Author's photo.*

The past endures: people leaving market day near Blue Nile Falls, south of Gonder 2013. *Author's photo.*

Legacy restored: The stelae field in Aksum, with the Aksum Obelisk back in its proper home. *Author's photo.*

FOREWORD

Mussolini's unprovoked invasion of Ethiopia (then widely referred to by foreigners as Abyssinia), the only African member of the Geneva-based League of Nations; Fascist Italy's use of poison gas in defiance of international convention; the duplicity of the League in banning the import by the aggressor of goods it could easily do without, while refusing to close the Suez Canal to the invaders; Emperor Haile Selassie's journey from far-off Addis Ababa to Geneva by train, boat and plane, followed by his eloquent appeal to the conscience of the world—and "to history, to remember its judgement . . ."

These are memorable events of an earlier age: an age of duplicity, violence and aggression, which many of that time seem to have forgotten and later generations have never known. Many of the readers of my mother, Sylvia Pankhurst's, pre-war pro-Ethiopian weekly newspaper, *New Times and Ethiopia News*, were among those who remembered.

Yet the story of those times is still alive in Ethiopia, as well as in Italy. In both countries voices of shock, sorrow, and remembrance have once again been heard.

Ethiopians and friends of Ethiopia learned in 2012 of a most alarming and extraordinary event. This was the erection in Italy of a monument to the notorious Italian Fascist commander, Rodolfo Graziani, at Affile, his birth place. He was one of two Fascist commanders in the Italian invasion of Ethiopia in 1935–6, the other being his rival and nominal superior, Pietro Badoglio. Both men ordered the use of poison gas in Ethiopia, but Graziani was also responsible for the shooting of Ethiopian prisoners-of-war in cold blood. He earned an even more terrible reputation for his policy of "indiscriminate terror" against the "natives" of both Ethiopia and Libya (which was also in its day under Italian military rule).

Many of us believe that events such us these are too important, and indeed too terrible, to be ignored or forgotten, let alone concealed. Humanity should learn from the crimes no less than the noble happenings of the past.

That is where Jeff Pearce's writings on the Italo-Abyssinian War of 1935-1941 are invaluable, for they describe the workings of politicians and soldiers against the backdrop of international morality and justice.

Honoring Graziani, Mussolini's henchman, today is tantamount to honoring the Duce himself. Graziani gave his full support to Mussolini's infamous racial laws of 1938, and when the dictator was overthrown in Italy towards the end of the European war, Graziani became the Duce's principal commander in the Fascist so-called Salo Republic. If we ignore the Graziani monument, the next thing may well be a statue to Hitler or Mussolini—and the next thing after that will be for people to seek to emulate these criminals' handiwork.

It is with fears such as these that the articulate Ethiopian Diaspora community in London, Washington, New York, and elsewhere recently demonstrated, together with other victims of Italian Fascist and colonial rule. Rita, my wife, and I chose to demonstrate in front of the Italian Embassy in London, where we had twice earlier protested against the Italian Government's undue delay in returning to Ethiopia the ancient Aksum obelisk that Mussolini had taken to Rome in 1937—and has since been duly repatriated.

Graziani was never tried for any of the many war crimes he committed in Ethiopia—or in Libya. After the war, in 1948, he was, however, sentenced in Italy to nineteen years imprisonment for crimes carried out in collaboration with the Germans against the Italian people—but he was speedily released.

The post-war case of Badoglio was no less amazing. After Mussolini's fall from power, Badoglio surrendered to the Allies. He persuaded them to retain him as Prime Minister as a way of preserving a right-wing government in postwar Italy. Since it was evident that he could not be both Prime Minister and be tried as a war criminal, the trials were "judiciously" abandoned—and the British Ambassador in Rome was officially instructed to provide Badoglio protection against arrest by the new government. The result was that while many Germans and Japanese were prosecuted as war criminals, not one Italian was ever charged for any of the many war crimes known to have been committed in Ethiopia. The honoring of Graziani, the murderer of 1936–38, is thus the culmination of a series of events, the beginnings of which Jeff Pearce touches upon in this brilliant and unique study. There *inter alia* he formulates a revealing critique of the two European democracies, Britain and France, for denying help to Ethiopia in the mis-founded hope/belief that they could thereby alienate Mussolini from his principal ally and soul-mate, Hitler.

Richard Pankhurst

PREFACE TO THE
PAPERBACK EDITION

When many of the events of *Prevail* took place, Richard Pankhurst was a little boy in the 1930s and early 1940s, playing with his Brownie camera in England as Hitler, Stalin, Mussolini and Franco cast their sinister shadows across Europe. It's a bitter irony that just as this book is released in paperback, we are returning to a time when extreme right-wing organizations with unapologetically racist messages are on the rise—not only in Europe, but in America—and can longer be dismissed as "fringe" elements. I mention this, because no work of history should be read without considering the context of the times, not only of the era which it covers, but in which it was written.

But if our skies are steel-gray, forbidding and grim—and they may darken even more—it's worth remembering that the boy with the camera saw that storm pass. He not only survived these "sterner days" (as Winston Churchill preferred calling them) and had his own cameo role in them, he would later be their first and most insightful chronicler regarding East Africa.

We lost Richard Pankhurst in early 2017. Having been in frail health for some time, he died from pneumonia. He was eighty-nine. That means we lost not only one of the remaining eyewitnesses to events, but the greatest historian Ethiopia has ever had. He was a giant in a field he virtually created himself in collaboration with his wife, Rita. There was no "Ethiopian Studies" before Richard Pankhurst. Sure, there were books about Ethiopia: some brilliant, some frankly terrible, a few bizarrely racist. Richard's books brought a new caliber of insight and depth to examining the country's history and culture. He formalized Ethiopian history as an academic field and then became one of its most prolific contributors—and its most prestigious. So it's certainly appropriate that I also mark this new paperback edition by paying tribute to him. He helped so much in bringing the original book to life.

I was first introduced to him though a kind email by the other great historian of Ethiopia, Ian Campbell, and from the very beginning, Richard and Rita showed me the greatest kindness in helping my work on *Prevail*. Who was I? I was nobody! I couldn't boast impressive professional credentials. But Richard, with a signature modesty, kindly pointed out that he himself originally had only a degree in economic history from the London School of Economics (as if that were a minor achievement!). It was clear he was a gentle, patient man of strong ethics and quiet conviction. This is the age of shouting, of noise, but Richard Pankhurst was from a politer generation, one that preferred to make its point quietly with evidence and facts and eloquent persuasion.

There is a great little story from his and Rita's memoir, *Ethiopian Reminiscences: Early Days*, in which three years after World War Two, some unapologetic Fascists belonging to a "British-Italian society" in London began agitating to try to get Ethiopia back into Italy's fold. Richard and his famous suffragette mother, Sylvia, were among those who showed up, and they weren't having it. Sylvia spoke up and Richard asked some very pointed questions, which irritated the organizers. When he began passing out pamphlets on Italy's war crimes, they ejected him from the meeting. But nothing more was ever heard again from that noxious little group.

Cut to decades later, and how from a wheelchair, he was still fighting for the country's heritage, protesting back in London and working with the campaign to return the Aksum Obelisk, a story that is briefly referenced in the final chapter of *Prevail*.

We corresponded for something like a year or so, and to have his seal of approval in terms of his Foreword filled me with awe. I am still in awe. It's only when I got my hands on my own copy of *Ethiopian Reminiscences* that I learned of this other gem of a story: he and his mother once went around to the London flat of Orde Wingate, who had just come back from fighting in Ethiopia. Wingate offered "a vivid account of the campaign" and Richard "was much impressed by his pent-up energy, which as he walked backwards and forwards in his small room, reminded me of a lion or tiger in the zoo at feeding time." Wingate even outlined for the mother and son his strategy to capture Libya, and he very briefly loaned his official campaign report to Sylvia!

Imagine having this kind of access to one of the main actors in the drama. I had asked Richard by email if Sylvia had ever had much dealings with Anthony Eden and what she thought of him (his answer in part was that his mother didn't discuss Eden much, but had never had a high opinion of him). Yet it had never occurred to me that he and Wingate had ever crossed paths. I am the fool for not considering the possibility. After all, Richard had conversed with an emperor and counted the great artist Afewerk Tekle among his many friends.

When I finally got to visit Ethiopia, I would end up in cabs, riding around Addis Ababa (when I couldn't do any more marathon walks in the hot sun to save my cash), and in idle conversation with drivers, I would end up talking about why I was here and mentioning the great retired professor. "Richard Pankhurst!" people always softly exclaimed. They spoke about him the way you'd talk about a rock star.

I remember the day when Ian Campbell kindly drove me out to see Richard and Rita. Richard's voice was soft, practically a whisper. He had been suffering for some time, of course, from Parkinson's disease, but the great mind was of course still sharp, and he still answered my questions thoughtfully and like a master. It's my deep regret that I never had the chance to go back and visit him. But he will live on in his books, and I am very glad that part of his legacy rests in these pages.

*   *   *

And now about these pages. . . This is a good-versus-evil story with a happy ending, and I chose my title, *Prevail*, quite deliberately. The word has special significance for many Ethiopians, but it also resonates with us. I wanted to combat an attitude that you still find with a few writers today, who pick and choose aspects of the war to treat it as if it were a political farce happening in a developing world backwater. Aside from this view being patronizing and offensive, it's incredibly inaccurate. In 1935, the eyes of the world saw the war for what it was—a confrontation worthy of big headlines, a test battleground in the fight against dictators threatening the whole world.

I have also hoped that this book makes people recognize that Africa has more than fifty countries, and they all have far more to offer—both in their past and today—than the convenient narrative of famine, civil war, corruption and radicalism. There are uplifting stories, inspiring stories to be found on the continent, and this is one of them.

And I have hoped that readers enjoy this story as I intended it, a Technicolor epic that you can almost see springing to life between these covers, but one that is true, that defies the old Hollywood conventions of say *Zulu* or *Khartoum*, because in this case, the underdog heroes were the African men and women fighting for their country.

In *Prevail*, I uncovered some new findings, but the book is built mainly on the pioneering work of others. And scholarship over the war and liberation is still progressing wonderfully. Ian Campbell, whose kind assistance and his book, *The Plot to Kill Graziani*, were so crucial to this volume, has already written two more remarkable works: *The Massacre of Debre Libanos* and *The Addis Ababa Massacre*. Keith Bowers has written an invaluable book that focuses on Haile Selassie's years in Britain, *Imperial Exile*. In fact, there hadn't been a reliable full-scale biography of Haile Selassie in many years, but Asfa-Wossen Asserate, a prince of the Imperial House and a bestselling author in German, has finally filled that vacuum with *King of Kings*, which is now available in English translation. His fair and balanced chronicle helps to undo the outrageous fiction that has persisted, much of it due to the work of a charlatan named Kapuściński, whom I discuss in the second last chapter. And Imru Zelleke, an important eyewitness to the Graziani Massacre and a survivor of an Italian concentration camp, has at last released the chronicle of his own amazing life, *A Journey*.

Research on the Italian-Ethiopian War is a labor of love that's even passing down to the next generations. In *Prevail*, you'll meet Daniel Sandford, who played a key role fighting with the Ethiopian Patriots to counter the occupation. As of this writing, his great-granddaughter, Rebecca Dixon, is hard at work on a master's thesis about the Patriots. She has made the remarkable achievement of tracking down and interviewing several of the surviving fighters, as well as relatives of those involved in the struggle.

It's encouraging, too, that in February of 2015, the American ambassador to Ethiopia dedicated a reading garden at the US embassy to the memory of John Robinson, the "Brown Condor." I wonder what this quiet, unassuming hero would make of such an honor, especially given how he once told off an embassy staffer for sticking his nose in Robinson's business. I like to think he would chuckle at the irony.

There has been much made of the fact that the Great War, the Second World War and the Holocaust are passing quickly from remembered experiences into history, but little attention seems to be paid to how we're also losing witnesses to influential conflicts that shaped Africa and Asia. In April of 2017, for instance, we lost Jagama Kello, retired general of the Patriots, whose daring adventures I describe in the chapters on the liberation. Will there, for example, be someone from the West who keeps alive the survivors' memories from the brutal regime of the Derg in the 1970s? For the Derg were to Ethiopia what Pol Pot's Khmer Rouge were to Cambodia, slaughtering thousands, and you can go view literal boxes of bones and skulls on display in the Red Terror Museum in Addis Ababa. If we do not record precious testimonies, we run the risk of the pernicious "Holocaust denial" over these events that some pro-Fascist revisionists have tried to bring to the Italian-Ethiopian War.

This is why the work of historians such as Ian Campbell, Andrew Hilton, Keith Bowers, Rebecca Dixon, Asfa-Wossen Asserate, Nicholas Rankin, William R. Scott, the late and greatly missed Christopher Duggan, and the man who inspired many of us, Richard Pankhurst, is so vital and so indispensable.

The extremists usually start by rewriting history. Consider this book a response to their efforts. It was written with the hope that the truth, like Ethiopia, will prevail.

Jeff Pearce
Toronto, June, 2017

NOTE ON NAMES

The Amharic language presents a minefield of transliteration for the hapless Western writer stepping into Ethiopia's history. It's compounded by the different ways that journalists and scholars spelled names and places in the 1930s. My one rule in struggling for consistency is to use what is most familiar to general readers and what would be best for reading flow. Hence: "Haile Selassie," *not* "Haylä Sallasé." "Djibouti" is still more familiar than "Jibuti."

For Ethiopians, a surname in most cases comes first. For example, the ras known as Seyum Mangasha was known as Ras Seyum. But the traitor, Haile Selassie Gugsa, is best known as "Gugsa." There are cases where some prominent Ethiopians became known in the West by English versions of their name, so for example it will be easier for a reader to follow on second reference "George Heruy" rather than his proper name of Faqada Selassie Heruy. Similarly, purists might object, but I refer to Warqenah Eshate most often by the name that Britons knew him best: Charles Martin. But I don't want to take things too far—in this book, it's "Emperor Tewodros" *not* "Emperor Theodore" as he's been referred to by some historians.

I have tried to keep titles to a minimum to reduce confusion (*Blattengeta, Blatta*), but some, of course, are necessary, particularly military commander ranks, such as *dejazmach* and *fitawrari*). For Britain, I see no need to litter pages with "Sir So-and-So" or "Lord Huff-n-Puff," and so I use these sparingly. Hence: "Samuel Hoare," not his viscount name, "Templewood." But the lord, E. F. L. Wood, was best known as "Halifax," so he is the exception. Traditionalists in the UK are free to blame all this on my being Canadian.

Today, the term, "Galla," is considered pejorative for the Oromo people, so it is only used in direct quotations.

For places, I have tried to err on spelling locales so that readers can find them in Ethiopia's modern geography, but this isn't always possible, given what the ages and the wars have done to these points on the map, once familiar in another era, now often obscure, at least to us in North America and Europe. And while several maps have been included to help the reader, they can never be an exhaustive resource for all the many spots featured in the narrative.

Hopefully, the reader will forgive me my trespasses.

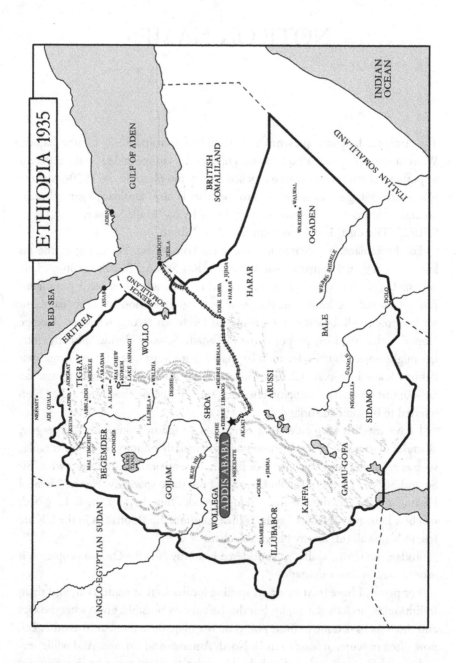

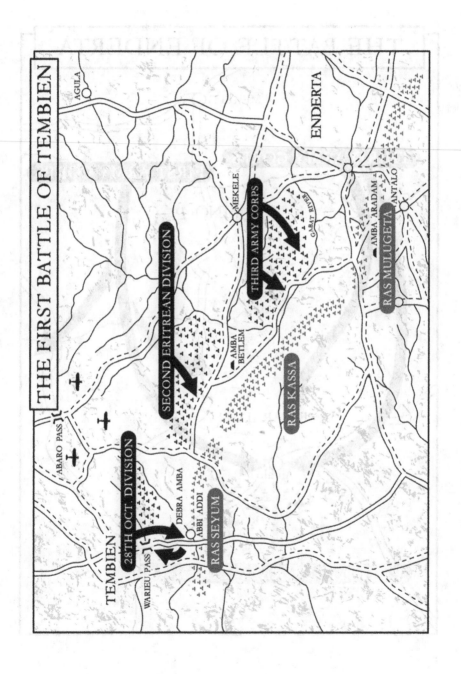

THE FIRST BATTLE OF TEMBIEN

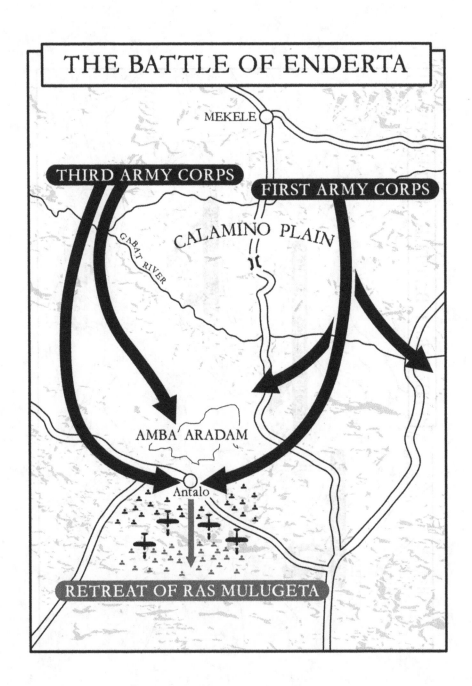

THE BATTLE OF ENDERTA

MEKELE

THIRD ARMY CORPS

FIRST ARMY CORPS

CALAMINO PLAIN

GABAT RIVER

AMBA ARADAM

Antalo

RETREAT OF RAS MULUGETA

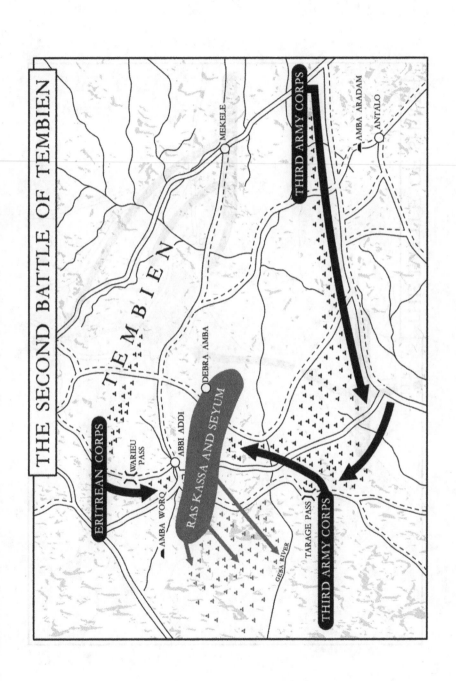

THE SECOND BATTLE OF TEMBIEN

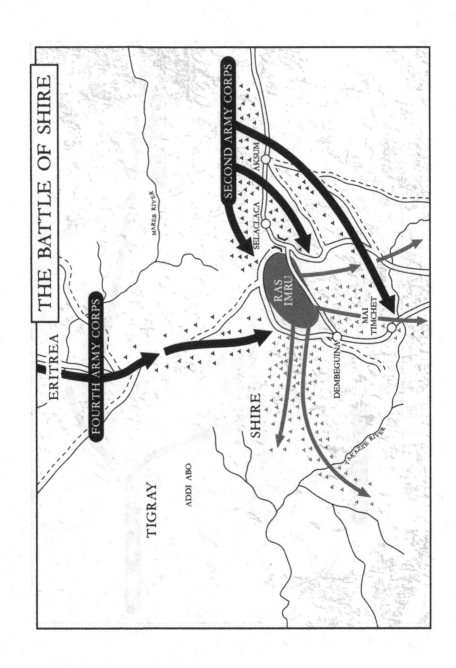

THE BATTLE OF SHIRE

ERITREA

FOURTH ARMY CORPS

SECOND ARMY CORPS

MAREB RIVER

AKSUM

SELACLACA

RAS IMRU

MAI TIMCHET

DEMBEGUINA

TAKAZZE RIVER

TIGRAY

ADDI ABO

SHIRE

PART ONE

RESIST

Amazon Fullfillment Svcs
172 Trade Street .
Lexington KY 40511

- "New"

~ $ 14.99
  $ 0.00
  $ 0.90

$ 15.89

- ord: 1/6/22
- rec : 1/11/22

INTRODUCTION

"The Lion of Judah has prevailed."
—Slogan associated with Haile Selassie and with Ethiopia

They scrambled down into the pass, their thickly-callused bare feet ignoring the bite of the rocks and stones, their swords and spears held high. If they didn't have swords or spears to carry, they would wield sticks and clubs. Some were armed with rifles, but these were often old, practically relics—their saving grace was the fact that they took a variety of cartridges. The buffalo-hide shields would do nothing to stop bullets, but they would block the bayonets slammed forward by the fierce *askaris*—native soldiers brown like themselves, born like themselves in the Horn of Africa, but now serving a colonial master. Unlike the askaris, most of the Ethiopians wore the traditional *shamma*, a toga-like garment that their ancestors had donned for generations. You could have painted the whole scene in oils like a war mural hung in London's National Gallery, or preserved it in a sepia photograph . . .

Until the tanks rolled in.

And then it was no longer a vintage scene of colonial warfare; it was a grotesque tableau of anachronism. This was not a page out of the Book of Empire from the eighteenth or nineteenth centuries. This was December 1935.

At first, the more ignorant warriors took these strange, lumbering metal *things* for monsters and ran. But one of them, fearless and proud, circled around and jumped onto a tank, pounding on its tin shell casing. Machine guns were blazing away and slicing men in half, and still the Ethiopians swarmed and flooded their numbers into the narrow gorge of what is called Dembeguina Pass, overwhelming the enemy. When it was finally dusk, the men and their brilliant commander, Imru, would slip away with fifty captured machine guns.

Miles away—beyond the frontier with Sudan, beyond Egypt and Libya and across the Mediterranean—the original Strongman of Europe sat behind the desk in his cavernous office in Rome and fumed, his eyebrows knit in frustration below his stolid dome. Benito Mussolini was furious. This was *not* how his grand campaign was supposed to go. It wasn't so much that the Ethiopians were winning—so far, overall, they weren't. But they were *not* clearly losing. And the world watched and was amazed at the defiant courage of "savages."

Hadn't his armies practically strolled into enemy territory, easily taking towns in the north? And when his general in charge had vacillated, hadn't he moved to act, replacing the old codger with his army's chief of staff? But still the war was not the continuous triumph he longed for. A month before, a skirmish at a place called Ende Giorgis had made headlines around the world because the Ethiopians had gotten the upper hand there, too. They were *not* supposed to do well! They were only supposed to fight and bleed and *die*, and let the glorious new Roman Empire be born.

But a tiny man of five foot four—as self-contained as Mussolini was wildly expansive—said no. Haile Selassie, the Emperor of Ethiopia, the Lion of Judah, insisted that the age of white colonialism was past. His warriors were only fighting now because it was a last resort, and he would not break his faith in God and the assertion that men of noble stature should keep their word and play by the rules. African monarchs had said no before—and been ignored—but this king had such presence of dignity, such gentle eloquence, that he could not be so easily dismissed. He said no.

But more importantly, most of the world was listening and, for the very first time, was also saying no.

In London, outraged liberals tangled with Oswald Mosley's Blackshirts, who naturally supported the invasion. Demonstrators in Toulouse, France, attacked a group of Italian sailors who wanted to go home to serve. Down in Accra, the capital of the British-held Gold Coast, about five hundred black citizens wanted to sign up to go fight for Ethiopia; in Cape Town, South Africa, six thousand black citizens turned up at a government office, wanting the same, to fight for distant comrades. Muslim Arabs in French and Spanish Morocco put together a small mercenary army, intent on crossing the Sahara and winding their way along the Upper Nile to go fight. Sympathetic Communists wreaked havoc in Mexico City, brawling with police armed with rifles. The Ethiopia Crisis could be felt as far away as South America and even touched Asia. The news was everywhere, inescapable, and the word was going out that Haile Selassie's soldiers would not simply roll over and accept the inevitable.

In America, support was arguably at its highest. On a hot afternoon back in August, an estimated twenty thousand people had poured into the streets of New York's Harlem neighborhood for the cause. Many of those in the throng had taken to calling themselves "African" in a remarkable show of black power before the term had even been coined. Here were African Americans marching in an age of barefoot children going to school, a time of "Whites Only" drinking fountains and back entrances at hotels, long before Black Panthers and the pride of *Roots,* before Marley and Mandela.

"This is no time to eat ice cream or peel bananas!" a speaker had shouted from the huge wooden platform. People were told to "listen to the speeches and donate as much money as possible." Cheers went up as the Ethiopian tricolor of green, yellow, and red was waved in the crowd. Then came the shouting, the chanting: "Death to Fascism!" and "Down with Mussolini!" At the height of the Depression, it was no surprise that one poster read: SIXTEEN MILLION UNEMPLOYED WANT BREAD, NOT BULLETS. The founder of the organization Pioneers of Ethiopia, F. A. Cowan, told the sea of faces that as far as Mussolini was concerned, "We will show him that the American Negro is going right over into his backyard!"

It was a good line, a line that would make the papers. And many African Americans in the crowd would surely have believed it. They could picture themselves on Ethiopian soil, each with a rifle in his hands, fighting for their distant brothers. This same hope was shared by many in West Africa, and a collection of earnest radical expatriates in London and Paris. All of them, whether American or British, Jamaican or Kenyan, could not possibly have a clue what forces would be brought to bear to prevent them or anyone else from coming to Ethiopia's aid.

* * *

For more than a year, the crisis would dominate Western headlines. Ethiopia was a member of the League of Nations, and under the League's Covenant, members were supposed to defend the African country if it was attacked. The United States, however, was not a member of the League. Still, Franklin Roosevelt was finding it increasingly difficult to stay neutral, as riots broke out between blacks and Italians in New York. As diplomatic overtures would fail and tensions escalate, Great Britain would send its fleet into the Mediterranean, and Mussolini would respond by sending two army divisions to Libya to threaten Egypt.

It would prompt comment from great political leaders of the day, from Winston Churchill to Mahatma Gandhi to Leon Trotsky. Celebrities would weigh in, from George Bernard Shaw to Josephine Baker. It inspired poets, motivated a world-famous inventor, and was turned into a Broadway play that provoked controversy and US government censorship. The war would become business news when secret negotiations were uncovered between Ethiopia and Standard Oil. It would spill into the sports pages with a prize fight between Detroit's Joe Louis and Italy's Primo Carnera, becoming a symbolic showdown between black and white. For, in the end, this was how many blacks in America, as well as other parts of Africa—along with some whites in the United States and Europe—chose to see the conflict. For them, this would be *the* race war. It was a war that would change the world.

Across the Atlantic, more than a month before the mass protest in Harlem, the League of Nations Union had published its survey of more than eleven million people in Great Britain, a poll that eventually became famously known as the "Peace Ballot." Among its five questions, it had asked if nations should use economic means to compel an aggressor nation from attacking another. Today, our shorthand for this is "sanctions." More than ten million people had answered yes, and more than six million were willing to back up the economics with military measures. Every respondent had to know what example was being implied by a question of one nation attacking another: Italy versus Ethiopia. The results of the Peace Ballot clearly indicated that yes, the British public wanted peace, but not at any price. British citizens were willing to defend an ally.

But their government would eventually allow Mussolini to have his war. So would France. Roosevelt, anxious about the coming election in 1936, would refuse to involve the United States. Alone, Ethiopia would fight to defend itself, and against all odds, it would hold its own—for a while. Italian planes would drop poison gas on its soldiers and bomb Red Cross hospitals. Italian soldiers would commit atrocities that would never be deemed worthy of a war crimes tribunal. After 1945, the conflict was considered "another war," distinct from World War Two, and not worth going back to investigate.

And the world would forget.

* * *

The war once mattered. To cite a superficial but interesting measure of its impact, consider *Casablanca*. In the film, both the French police captain, Renault, and the freedom fighter, Victor Laszlo, remind Bogart's hero, Rick Blaine: "You ran guns to Ethiopia." Everyone in the audience at the time knew what they were talking about. Laszlo asks rhetorically, "Isn't it strange that you always happen to be fighting on the side of the underdog?" Ethiopia is mentioned in the same breath as the fight against the Fascists in Spain, raising it to the status of a romantic crusade.

The war did indeed once matter. For a brief time, it captured the world's attention, stirring feelings of rebellion in Egypt and worrying the colonial masters of South Africa. The conflict would be the real beginning of the decline of the League of Nations that led to World War Two. Some people know this or were given fleeting references to the war in history classes. It's presumed that the war's only relevance is to the League of Nations. What many people don't know is that an arguably far more significant development involving Roosevelt and America also affected events—and it, too, hinged on Ethiopia.

So the war is an important turning point in world history. It is African history, and not just because Ethiopia is in Africa. The war shaped the political mind of a continent in ways that so many of us have hardly noticed but that are crucial to understanding our events today. "I was seventeen when Mussolini attacked Ethiopia, an invasion that spurred not only my hatred of that despot but of fascism in general."

Those words belong to Nelson Mandela.

In his autobiography, *Long Walk to Freedom,* he wrote: "Ethiopia has always held a special place in my own imagination and the prospect of visiting Ethiopia attracted me more strongly than a trip to France, England, and America combined. I felt I would be visiting my own genesis, unearthing the roots of what made me an African. Meeting the Emperor himself would be like shaking hands with history."[1]

Africans elsewhere felt the same way. They quite deliberately called the nation "Ethiopia," using the Greek word, and not "Abyssinia," a Latin corruption of an Arabic label, "Habesha." Whites—Europeans and European-descent Americans—used that term more often. Ethiopia was a fountainhead of legendary culture, where the obelisks and monasteries of Aksum rose in the same era as the Romans and ancient India. As a leading professor of Ghana would later put it, "If Ethiopians were the brothers of all black people then their historical achievements could be represented as the achievements of all."[2]

It's little wonder then that thousands of African Americans felt the same, and so the war is a crucial chapter in their history as well. For New York, Chicago, Pittsburgh, and Detroit, the capitals of black consciousness in 1935, Ethiopia indeed mattered. It held a spiritual significance for black Americans as an African kingdom where Christianity had flourished since the fourth century. And it was defiantly independent, smack in the middle of the colonial map. The great black historian, John Hope Franklin, wrote in his landmark work, *From Slavery to Freedom*: "Almost overnight, even the most provincial among American Negroes became international-minded. Ethiopia was a black nation, and its destruction would symbolize the final victory of whites over blacks."[3] Thousands of African Americans signed up with ad hoc militias to try to keep it that way.

Above all, this war is the story of a courageous people who, despite antiquated weapons and overwhelming odds, held their own against the Italians for as long as they could and came close to invading the Italian-held frontier of Eritrea. They were cheated out of the inheritance of a generation. Mussolini's generals ruthlessly exterminated men trained to lead the country into the twentieth century, and the history of Ethiopia might have been quite different had they lived.

Which brings us to Haile Selassie, still held in far more esteem sometimes by foreigners than by his own people, and even the foreign view is often harsh in its judgment. He is overdue for a reappraisal, a task that is for the most part beyond the scope of this narrative. Still, some points regarding him will need to be made, because the war had far-reaching effects into the modern age and how the West treated Africa after the Second World War. Western opinion of Haile Selassie today is often based on now-discredited news reports and on the aftermath of a brutal Derg regime, while the reality of his character at the time was far more complex.

We are no better served by some historians today. In an aggrandizing chronicle of the adventures of an Italian cavalry officer in East Africa, *Amedeo*, Sebastian O'Kelly writes: "At the end of 1934, the Ethiopians and the Italians clashed over the wells at Walwal in the Ogaden desert on the border with Italian Somaliland. In spite of dark suspicions on both sides, the incident does not appear to have been orchestrated by either Rome or Addis Ababa."[4] This statement is inaccurate to the point of being ludicrous. The incident was indeed orchestrated by Rome, and as will be shown, the Italians were looking for a fight.

O'Kelly goes on to say:

> It was serious, but it was not unprecedented; a month earlier the Ethiopians had killed a French officer on the border with Djibouti. But Haile Selassie's decision to complain to the League of Nations turned the dispute into an international crisis . . . He may have already calculated that a clash with Fascist Italy was unavoidable at some time, and he might as well make the issue Walwal as any other, and milk the sympathy of the other powers as Italy was revealed as the aggressor.[5]

Such is the way modern writers can still blame the victim. As we'll see, Haile Selassie wasn't intent on "milking sympathy" and had very little choice but to appeal to the League. The Walwal incident was not a case for diplomatic opportunism on Ethiopia's part; it was a response to Italy seeking a pretext for invasion.

About twenty years ago, Richard Lamb struck a disturbing chord right from the acknowledgments of his *Mussolini and the British*. He claims the period as "in part the history of my own times," telling how he was "enthusiastic for the Peace Ballot and hostile to the Hoare-Laval Pact which I now consider sound diplomacy."[6] He criticizes Ethiopia for its slave trade while ignoring Haile Selassie's efforts at reform, which have been well documented. "The proper course for the League . . . would have been to create a mandate for Abyssinia, and either divide it between Great Britain, France and Italy . . . or give the whole mandate to Italy as spoils due to her as a victor of the First World War . . . Such a mandate would have been in the interests of the inhabitants of the area."[7]

The note of White Man's Burden is jarring, but not exceptional, especially when the pervasive view of hopeless, unsalvageable Africa still infects Western reportage. Many correspondents have reflexively portrayed wars in Africa as tribal conflicts, but the bloodshed in Sierra Leone was about diamonds, and the killing in the Congo about coltan, the precious mineral used in microchips. Bill Clinton's troops went to Rwanda and then abandoned it, and nothing is new under the sun. We have the more recent example of the "Kony 2012" debate, in which many critics pointed out distressing Western ignorance over the nuances of African politics.

There has not been a new comprehensive history in English about the Italian invasion of Ethiopia for thirty years. By this, I mean a history that covers all the aspects: Ethiopia, Italy, the long diplomatic squabbles in Geneva, the interest of African Americans and other black populations, all of it. Scholars have written about *aspects* of the conflict, and I am deeply indebted to many of them for allowing me to rely on their works, but there still hasn't been a general work that encompasses the vast canvas of the war, nor one that details just how powerfully it changed the world. So, a new one is needed.

Whether my own particular effort is needed, the war itself still matters. The story told here is about a missed opportunity. In 1935, Britain, France, and America could have united to save an African nation. In doing so, they might have demonstrated to black people everywhere that at least a few whites were capable of a new enlightened consciousness, that they could change their ways and merited a new trust. It would have been something truly remarkable. Even with the contradictory nature of colonial nations such as Britain and France and the all-too-recent debacle of American slavery for the United States, white troops could have been allies to Africans.

The British would be liberators in 1941, which is not the same thing. In Khartoum, Major Orde Wingate was furious when Haile Selassie's advisers managed to procure for him a traditional state umbrella and war drums, calling them ridiculous in a modern campaign. He insisted they be left behind.[8] He could insist because Haile Selassie was an emperor who had been reduced to living in exile in Britain.

The world is now closer to 2035 than it is 1935, but the conflict of black versus white is, of course, still with us. Meanwhile, the United Nations' peacekeeping efforts are viewed in many quarters as orchestrations of Great Powers, even as its predecessor, the League of Nations, was often considered a puppet theater of Great Britain and France. It would be overreaching to consider the war a mirror of our own times. Instead, it is a window looking out on the era that helped shape our own period, and indeed, the war still matters, as the United States is governed under its first elected African-American president and Ethiopia still struggles to find its way as an independent nation.

Chapter One

THE DUCE AND THE
ETERNAL CITY

The man who promised to recapture the glories of ancient imperial Rome began his life with all the overt signs of being a sociopath. As a boy of ten, Benito Mussolini got himself expelled from a boarding school for stabbing a classmate with a knife. As a young man working as a substitute teacher at an elementary school in Gualtieri, he carried a metal knuckle-duster and once knifed his girlfriend. Boastful over his liaisons with women, he casually referred to committing rape in his autobiography.

Like Hitler, his past as a petty thug and indigent (he lived for a while in an abandoned packing case under a bridge) never really hampered his political rise. At heart he was a bully, and remained so throughout his political career, and like most bullies, he expressed his physical violence only in circumstances of the least risk. For his famous "March on Rome," he had fewer than thirty thousand men to confront garrison troops in the capital, and while his hooligans destroyed printing presses, burned books, and looted shops, he bided his time until he could safely enter Rome. He gained power through bluff. King Victor Emmanuel III was misinformed that his army couldn't match the Blackshirt numbers and backed down over signing a decree of martial law. Instead, he invited the Fascist leader to form a new government. So Mussolini didn't march on Rome at all, but chose to arrive by train. Since soldiers had ripped up the tracks outside the capital, the king obligingly sent him a car for the remainder of the trip.

For anyone looking carefully into Mussolini's evolution of political opinions and stances, the only pattern of consistency was in his opportunism. His blacksmith father had named his son after Benito Juarez, the Mexican revolutionary. Having taken on his father's atheism, Mussolini the parliament member would label Christianity as "detestable" and demand the Pope leave Rome for good. As a revolutionary, he condemned Russia's lack of free speech. As a dictator, he made Italy a state in which foreign correspondents were regularly harassed, and the only newspapers allowed to operate toed the government line. As a socialist, he was critical of Prime Minister Franceso Crispi's ambition to move into Ethiopia; it was "the dream of a jingoist minister." Once he became the Duce, the Horn of Africa was soon deemed practical and desirable.

His own personal vanity was boundless. He enjoyed being photographed in bathing trunks or in the company of athletes. He wrestled with lions for film cameras—lions that had been de-fanged beforehand. When rumors circulated that he was ill, he arranged for reporters to watch him horseback ride with wild abandon over hedges in the gardens of his Villa Torlonia. After this bizarre demonstration, he leapt off his horse and told them, "Now you can say that Mussolini is sick!"[1]

Mussolini, a man who in his youth loafed and hated working for others, paradoxically put in long hours as his nation's leader. But he toiled within elegant surroundings—inside the Palazzo Venezia, a Renaissance palace that used to be an embassy for the Venetian republic. Visitors to see the Duce passed through a gauntlet of heavy security and were led into the splendor of Mantegna murals on the walls, while a polychrome chandelier hung from the ceiling. When the Duce received a group of foreign correspondents, as he did once in 1931, he strutted up and down in front of them like an officer inspecting a company of soldiers.

One of those foreign correspondents was not impressed. He was David Darrah, a reporter in his forties working for the *Chicago Tribune*. Darrah would have preferred that Mussolini stick to Italian, instead of trying to address the reporters in clumsy English, and the Duce's famed magnetism had no effect on him. But Darrah did believe there was:

> Something profoundly disturbing, tumultuous and intense about his personality, and about that face with its tawny, yellowing Tartar-like tint, and the short square figure . . . pacing back and forth as he swaggered and talked. One couldn't help being aware of the fanatical religious patriotism that exuded from him. Afterwards I used to visualize him in memory as seated there at his work table with the bust of Caesar at one end; and I could think of him as a workman having the peninsula of Italy in miniature on his table and toiling and tinkering at it to change and transform it, with something of a scrupulous mania.[2]

Mussolini's vision of Italy was ultimately another stage set. Unlike Hitler, he was not a benefactor of an "economic miracle" for his nation. Italy, especially in the south, stayed poor under Fascism. The trains ran better but, contrary to legend, did not always run on time. The Balila car, a cheap export for Europe, was not a credit to Fascist engineering, but Fiat's. The regime's grasp of economics seemed quite pitiful. Under Mussolini, a new ministry of corporations was created, and by 1934, it had declined into an ill-conceived muddle of twenty-two umbrella corporations for major industries.

To the *Chicago Tribune's* David Darrah, the strategy boded something sinister:

> In all my studies of the process of changing Italy's economic system, which went on during the years I was there, of the transforming of it into state socialism and a national control of everything, it was never clear to me whether the ultimate purpose was to lead gradually to a form of state socialism and synthesize a new economic order which would be adaptable to normal times, or whether it was all a face to hide industrial mobilization and preparation of the country for war.[3]

* * *

David Darrah was one of those reporters who fell into his job. An Ohio native, he'd worked after high school in steel mills and rubber factories, and he served as a sailor aboard iron ore ships on the Great Lakes. After his service in the Great War, he became a correspondent in Paris by simply showing up at the *Chicago Tribune's* office and asking for a tryout. By the time he was sent to Rome, he was a seasoned correspondent but, by his own admission, was naïve in assuming it would be business as usual in collecting news in Mussolini's Italy. He wrote:

> I wondered whether one could live in Italy and work in accordance with the principles that Cezanne proposed for impressionist painting—"to propose nothing, to impose nothing, just to expose." That is to say, I was ignorant of Italy and I was not long in discovering that what I thought to do was not only impossible but illegal.[4]

Like Mussolini, Darrah also had a view to the heart of Rome from his office window, only his was from rooms two floors above the Galleria Colonna, an arcade where prostitutes and policemen, shopkeepers and petty thugs, actresses and businessmen all mingled and gossiped. The piazza was evolving into a miniature Italian Fleet Street. The editor of the Turin *Gazzetta del Popolo*, who was a sympathetic Fascist, kept his office in the Galleria instead of running his paper from his own town. The correspondent for the Hearst wire service was based down the hall from Darrah. The Press Association was located in the nearby Piazza San Silvestro.

Sitting at his typewriter, Darrah could watch the square of the Piazza Colonna, where meetings of Blackshirts were often held and where Mussolini spoke from the balcony of the Piazza Chigi before his move to the Palazzo Venezia.

> It always seemed to me that could I have made a film of what went by my window there, I would have had a fair exterior record of seven years of Mussolini's regime, for all the various manifestations of Italian life, as it was being shaped by Fascism, passed by in the innumerable parades that Mussolini proclaimed.[5]

For all its charms, Rome in 1935, to David Darrah, had only meager pretensions as a world capital, with more of the atmosphere of a large provincial town. "Its life went on in restricted circles and behind closed doors, for the most part, among the upper cliques. It was not exteriorized as was Paris or Vienna."[6] Baedecker's guide to Rome and central Italy around this period informed its readers that Rome still had a considerable number of horse-drawn cabs. And throughout the Eternal City, casting spiritual and physical shadows everywhere, were the images of the Duce and Fascism. Mussolini's face was plastered on thousands of posters and was even sported on women's swimsuits. The Fascist emblem even appeared on manhole covers. Baedecker's tactfully suggested the foreign traveler "should refrain from airing his political views" or taking photographs of beggars.[7]

Police and government operatives were everywhere. Agents could be restaurant waiters, landlords, hotel concierges, civil servants, or any number of coworkers who served as *delatori*, informers, for the police. And there were multiple police forces, from the uniformed ranks of *Carabinieri*, *Metropolitani*, and *Militzie* to the anonymous plain-clothes operatives of Italy's own version of the Gestapo, OVRA. The acronym translated roughly to the "Voluntary Organization for the Repression of Anti-Fascism"—but the name hardly mattered, since authorities denied its existence.

Darrah writes of OVRA in 1936 with a degree of wary respect, calling the network of agents in cities such as Rome and Milan "so far as humanly possible, perfect."[8] An assistant told the American point-blank: "Of course, you are watched. All the correspondents are watched. But they try to do it nicely and unobtrusively."[9] There were occasions when it wasn't so nice—deliberately so. The *Tribune's* bureau in the Piazza Colonna was a regular target for break-ins, and correspondents for Paris and London were also harassed.

And the support or even silent compliance of Italians was not absolute. Anti-Fascists carried on bombing and terrorism campaigns in the middle of the decade, though the serious leaders of the movement were in exile in France.

Mussolini didn't brazenly announce his intentions of war in a book like Hitler's *Mein Kampf,* but when he addressed the Chamber of Deputies in May of 1926, he actually announced that the next world war would be in 1935, and that Italy would have to be prepared.[10] By late December of that same year, he was telling a *New York Times* reporter that Italy's colonies were "insufficient for our needs." Banging his fist on a table, he warned that "the day will come when Italy . . . will demand her place in the sun!"[11]

"In my walks about the country I saw the youth in the small towns being organized," remembered David Darrah, "and the hills about the towns resounded with the rifle and machine-gun practice as the piazzas echoed with war-like speeches."[12] By his own reckoning, Darrah estimated that Mussolini's plans for Ethiopia began in earnest around 1932.

It was a shrewd guess, and one close to the mark. That year, Mussolini sent a special emissary to inspect Italy's colonies in Africa. This was General Emilio De Bono, an elderly man with a white goatee whose career as a soldier had been less than spectacular. De Bono, however, was loyal, an officer who had thrown in his lot with Mussolini before Fascism became popular among the military, and who had helped lead the March on Rome. He went on to hold the office of Director of Public Safety, making the title a sick joke after organizing the torture and execution squad for the Fascists' archrival, the Socialist deputy Giacomo Matteoti. In 1924, when the Matteotti case threatened to unravel the Duce's power, Mussolini dismissed De Bono but managed to orchestrate his friend's acquittal after a lengthy trial.

So by 1932, De Bono, having been restored to the inner Fascist circle, could return from Eritrea and report to his master that "if the Mother-Country was to derive the desired advantage from her two colonies, it would be necessary to abolish the vital inconveniences . . . To this end a careful and decisive political action was required."[13] The inconvenience was Ethiopia. The political action was war. De Bono's report was for Mussolini's benefit, but the world could take its own signs in 1932. Italy's foreign minister at the time, Dino Grandi, called on the world to let Italy have an empire. And King Victor Emmanuel decided to pay a visit to Eritrea and Italian Somaliland.

By the autumn of 1933, De Bono was nudging his boss to have the top job for the Roman conquest. He reported in his memoirs:

> One day I said to the Duce: "Listen, if there is war down there—and if you think me worthy of it, and capable—you ought to grant me the honor of conducting the campaign."
>   Mussolini looked at me hard and at once he replied: "Surely."
>   "You don't think me too old?" I added.
>   "No," he replied, "because we mustn't lose time."
>   *From this moment, the Duce was definitely of the opinion that the matter would have to be settled no later than 1936,* and he told me as much . . . It was the autumn of 1933. The Duce had spoken to no one of the forthcoming operations in East Africa; *only he and I* knew what was going to happen, and no indiscretion occurred by which the news could reach the public. [original italics][14]

De Bono even suggested the idea they could exploit the "unruliness of the Rases" to incite a civil war, which would offer the pretext for Italy to intervene. (*Ras* was a title of Ethiopian nobility, often equated with a duke.) Of course, the strategy might backfire, De Bono realized, and chieftains on the Italian border could attack. So he wanted his forces prepared to withstand this and then be able to "go right in with the intention of making a complete job of it, once and for all." According to De Bono, "The Duce thought as I did, and ordered me to go full speed ahead. I must be ready as soon as possible."

"Money will be needed, Chief," De Bono warned him, "lots of money."

"There will be no lack of money," replied Mussolini.[15]

Months passed, and then on the morning of May 24, 1934, with Blackshirts cheering him on, the Duce rode a white horse to the Piazza Venezia to make one of his rallying speeches. Wearing his iron helmet, he stopped to pose in front of statues of Caesars, and photographers were instructed to capture them in the background of any portrait shot. Then he headed off for his usual roost of the balcony in his office to address the people.

"The Italian infantry is now so developed that it can contend against any infantry in the world," he told the crowd. "Better to live a day as a lion than a century as a sheep. Italy wishes peace but is ready for an eventuality. Are you all ready?"

"*Yes!*" the throng shouted back to him.[16]

Two days later, he famously informed the Chamber of Deputies, "War is to men what maternity is to women." No, he did not believe in perpetual peace—the very idea depressed him. Italy needed to build up its naval and air fleets. The people had to forget about the idea of the good old days of prosperity. Sacrifices had to be made.

Then on December 7, 1934, David Darrah heard about a border skirmish between Italian and Ethiopian soldiers. "Somehow or other," Darrah wrote in his memoir of Italy, "one seemed to sense immediately that here was the spark that was to set off a great chain of events."[17]

* * *

It was supposed to be settled over a couple of beers.

In the beginning, there were representatives of the British, the Italians, and the Ethiopians all in a tent beneath a waving Union Jack with its flag pole stuck in a can.[18] Here they were, trying to keep a lid on trouble, which was threatening to break out in the middle of nowhere. "Nowhere" that day was a place called Walwal, an oasis in the Ogaden region of Ethiopia, a massive expanse of scrubland and brush that forms a triangle in Ethiopia's east.

For those who grow up and live in country like this, a flat landscape has a beauty all its own, but beautiful does not make it kind. *Water* is the key element for survival in this harsh territory, and wells are precious. Nomadic Somali tribesmen, their hair coppery red from the whitewash used to prevent lice, would step down an ingenious wooden frame that served as a set of steps into the deep hole of a well, dip their clay pots into the pool, and then pass them up the chain of hands. They would sing to their cattle, "Come and drink sweet water."[19] Somalis had been watering their camels and cattle like this for generations. It was far more important which family or clan owned a cluster of wells than where a line was marked on a map.

But because the Ogaden rested near British Somaliland, an Anglo-Ethiopian Commission was set up to map the frontier and survey the common pasture grounds. There was the small British contingent, led by a tall, blond lieutenant colonel, E. H. M. Clifford, who knew Ethiopia well. His tiny group had an escort of about six hundred Ethiopian troops, some in khaki uniforms with gray hats, others in *shammas*, the long white Ethiopian garment that resembles a toga. Many of the uniformed troops were barefoot, but all the soldiers carried rifles. The man in charge of them was a *fitawrari* (commander) named Shifferaw, who was governor of the region, but since he ran his administration from the town of Jijiga, he hadn't seen this countryside for years.

The commission was actually on its way home. It had spent two years demarcating the territory, and it was slowly making its way back to Dire Dawa, where it could board a train that would mercifully chug along the last leg of their journey to take them back to Addis Ababa. There, a treaty would be signed that settled things between Britain and Ethiopia, at least as far as the Ogaden was concerned. When Shifferaw and Clifford showed up on the morning of November 23, 1934, they wouldn't have been surprised to discover tribesmen from Italian Somaliland at the cluster of almost 360 wells. Ethiopia's treaty with Italy from 1928 even mentioned Walwal by name, granting them access, because they were the only wells around for miles.

What they *didn't* expect to find was a group of two hundred native militia soldiers, for Italy also camped there. The militia soldiers were known as *bande*.

When Italy began shopping around for a pretext to start the war, it created the *bande*. Their official purpose was to guard the frontier and police any bandit raiders making incursions into Italian Somaliland. An Italian officer usually commanded sixty Somali *dubats*, who each wore a white turban, a white Somali skirt, a colored sash, and a bandolier. The *bande* had begun a campaign of creeping occupation into Ethiopian territory, building their huts near the watering holes and then trying to restrict the use of the wells by the neighboring tribes.

When Haile Selassie decided enough was enough, fifteen thousand Ethiopian soldiers had marched down from Jijiga and the city of Harar to push them back. But at a place called Tafare Katama, near Mustahi, the Italians had already established a garrison. The governor of Harar, Gabre Mariam, was a practical fellow who knew he didn't have enough men and that the timing was bad for a showdown with a European force, one that was likely better equipped. The Ethiopians had made their point, and so off they went. But Italy now had its boot firmly planted in the country. With this success, the Italians grew bolder. By August of 1934, a *commandatore* was assigned to Walwal to build up the outpost there. What had once been a modest military presence was now to be a fort.

So here was a big problem for the boundary commission, its men weary for water and just wanting to get on with their business of surveying. The Ethiopian government had already made a point of telling Rome that the commission would be doing its work close to the border and would appreciate cooperation from the Italians. Some historians suggest that Haile Selassie was giving the Italians another loud hint that they were unwelcome guests in his empire and should go home. If he was, the Italians chose not to listen. Accounts differ, but at some point Shifferaw apparently had a quiet showdown with a Lieutenant Mousti or another one of the dubats in charge. He told them, in so many blunt words, to get lost, to leave Ethiopian soil. The alternative versions have the dubats refusing to let the Ethiopians have access to the wells.

However the discussion went, it was a stalemate, and the atmosphere was tense. The six hundred Ethiopians outnumbered the *bande*, and both sides were piling up thorn bushes outside their camps, making barriers that were usually meant for keeping out hyenas, but that were now the Ogaden's answer to barbed wire. Then Clifford got a message from a Captain Roberto Cimmaruta, asking to talk over the situation. Clifford agreed, and arrangements were made to meet at ten in the morning the next day.[20] The two men weren't strangers to each other—in fact, Cimmaruta was a guest at the formal ceremony for laying the last stone marking the boundary between Ethiopia and British Somaliland.[21] When Cimmaruta came, he wasn't alone—he brought reinforcements from his base in Warder, bolstering the Somali contingent to 250 men.

By mid-morning, the Ethiopians, British, and Italians all stepped out of the hot sun and into the large British tent, where armchairs were seated around a camp table and beer was served.

The sociable mood didn't last long. The Ethiopians on the border commission made the point that the Italians had no right to be at the oasis. Cimmaruta, however, had come to play the injured party. He claimed the Italian troops were only there to protect the Somali tribesmen from *their* colony. What's more, their forces had been at the oasis for years. The talks dragged on well into the afternoon, and Clifford, who was doing his best to play peacemaker, noted in a formal report how Cimmaruta was "unconciliatory" and "disobliging" throughout the whole discussion, repeating several times the same phrases, "Take it or leave it" and "Just as you please." The Ethiopian commissioners would leave it. Cimmaruta decided to close the negotiations with a threat: he would send for "several hundred soldiers."[22]

At that very moment, about four o'clock, two Italian planes buzzed the camp several times. They were flying so low that Clifford and others could see machine guns trained on them. The British colonel finally lost his patience. He knew a provocation when he saw one, and he promptly announced the British mission would withdraw to the town of Ado. The Ethiopian commissioners would accompany the British, but their military would stay put. Cimmaruta took what men he had and returned to Warder, but there was still a sizable number of dubats in Walwal to trade ugly looks with the Ethiopians. He allegedly told the dubats before leaving: "If a fly comes, you must first do this—" he pantomimed a wave to drive away an insect. "If it will not leave you, you take it in your hand—" now he crushed his fist "—and the fly dies."[23]

From Warder, the captain decided to pour gasoline on the fire, sending Shifferaw a note two days later that mentioned casually how he'd given a previous message to "a Chief Shifta of yours." *Shifta* was the Ethiopian term for bandit— Cimmaruta could only insult the man worse by calling him the son of a whore. He also demanded to know: "1) What you intend to do with all these armed men; 2) Whether you intend to remain in the positions where you are now and beyond which I would advise you not to go."[24]

It was Clifford and one of the Ethiopian border commissioners, Lorenzo Taezaz, who took offense. Now in Ado, they cosigned a note that was quickly sent to Warder, scolding the captain over "an expression which is not used this way in an international communication." They were taking the matter to their respective governments in London and Addis Ababa.

The stakes, of course, were higher than merely drawing water and saving face. For Italy, Walwal was as good a place as any to pick a fight, but the timing and geography couldn't be worse for Ethiopia. Besides settling boundaries, it had been trying recently to negotiate a land exchange with Great Britain. Ethiopia wanted—had always wanted—access to the sea, and it was close to getting it with the port of Zeila on the Gulf of Aden in British Somaliland. In trade, the British would gain a strip of territory that would include Walwal. Italian military squatters at the oasis were a complication Haile Selassie didn't need.

Late that night, the Emperor took a phone call at his palace in Addis Ababa and learned the Italians were refusing to withdraw. The Emperor consulted his advisers and decided Shifferaw and his soldiers had better not leave Walwal either.

The stalemate went on for days. Reinforcements came for both sides. On the afternoon of December 5, as the men in each camp sat bored and restless, an Ethiopian by a small fire allegedly threw a bone towards the dubats.[25] The mocking gesture was obvious. What still isn't clear is exactly who fired first. Some heard a whistle blast, and then the shouted words, "*A terra!*" and "*Fuoco!*" There was a shot, and suddenly the stretch of Ogaden plain erupted with gunfire from both sides.

Many Ethiopians standing out in the open were easily cut down, including another fitawrari, Alemayehu Goshu. For ten minutes, neither side had the upper hand, but the Ethiopians had unfortunately made a tactical error. They put their two machine guns between Shifferaw's tent and the ammunition storage tent, where they couldn't be fired. Then three Italian planes showed up to drop bombs on them. Two armored cars suddenly plowed through the protective thorn bush to mow them down with machine gun fire. Ethiopians were falling under the deadly spray, their outdated rifles having little effect against the armored plating. Shifferaw, a man who would rather sit behind a desk than run with a rifle, decided on the spot to take his wounded and a large contingent of men "to bury the dead in consecrated ground."[26]

The battle was left to a brave Muslim named Ali Nur, an ex-soldier of the King's African Rifles who had once been the interpreter for the British consular service. He kept the fight going after nightfall, his men rushing the armored cars in the dark. But they were cut in half by machine guns or forced back, their spears no match for bullets. At last, after midnight, he took his surviving troops to catch up to Shifferaw's men on their way to Ado. The Ethiopians had lost 107 men and had forty-five wounded. The Italians won the day with only thirty dead and one hundred men hurt, none of them white, all native soldiers.

News traveled slowly in Ethiopia. What couldn't be accomplished by tele-graph often had to be done by messenger. One from the border commission covered an impressive five hundred miles from Ado to Addis Ababa in two days to provide the Emperor with a full report on the initial confrontation at Walwal. But on December 5, Haile Selassie still didn't know his soldiers were fighting for their lives miles away. He was consulting his advisers and drafting a protest to be delivered to the Italian legation in the capital.

Ethiopia's foreign minister, Heruy Wolde Selassie, was a respected author and diplomat, a man with a white beard and portly frame who reminded one American observer of Santa Claus, minus the twinkle in the eye. Now he had to suffer the humiliation of delivering his note and having the Italians tell him the news about the battle and its outcome. Out in the Ogaden, they had wireless— the Ethiopians didn't.

* * *

On the other side of the world, readers of the *New York Times* flipped through their newspapers on December 8 and saw a story not much bigger than a postage stamp on page eleven. It was a file from the Associated Press bureau in Rome, and the headline told them that Italy was protesting—for the *second* time—against an Ethiopian attack at "Ualual [Walwal] in Italian Somaliland."[27]

The AP bureau chief in Rome made sure to attribute his facts to the Stefani News Agency, but he didn't bother to mention that the agency was, in fact, govern-ment controlled. Nor did he check the geography. Nor did the story explain why the Italian protest was "the second in two months." It was an oblique reference to a minor incident in Gonder weeks before Walwal, when Ethiopians—some fac-tory workers, plus other workers for the Italian commercial agency—apparently quarreled over a woman and ended up attacking the Italian legation. But Haile Selassie's government had already offered to make reparations for that.

Whenever David Darrah wanted the official Ethiopian perspective, it was readily available to him a block around the corner from his own apartment in Rome. There, in a Florentine villa surrounded by a high wall, with balconies and a garden of mimosa trees, was the Ethiopian legation. Darrah was regularly escorted in by a "grim and unsmiling"[28] servant to the red plush salon of Haile Selassie's representative in Italy, who was none other than Ethiopia's first novelist and one of its greatest writers, Afawarq Gabra-Iyassus.

Afawarq had his own personal reasons for war to be avoided. Darrah, of course, knew nothing about the inner workings of Ethiopian nobility and court life, and he also seemed forgivably unaware of the diplomat's literary reputation. But he easily picked up that the man detested the idea of returning to his homeland. Afawarq had been educated in Italy and had taken an Italian wife, and his mixed-race son happily rode his tricycle up and down the sidewalk as his father wrestled with questions of diplomacy in the garden.

"I often thought," wrote Darrah, "that behind his dark countenance, many an intricate idea was being hatched that winter and that he would not let his loyalty to the Emperor prevent his working well with the Italians."[29]

The reporter was bang on the money. Afawarq didn't have loyalty to Haile Selassie or to anyone else. Twenty years before, when the great Emperor Menelik had died, Afawarq wrote obsequious poems to get in good with his successor; the successor didn't last long, and Afawarq made sure to write an ode that suitably condemned him.[30] It was hardly a secret in Addis Ababa that Haile Selassie had thought this troublesome writer could do the least amount of damage in Rome. Shamelessly obsequious, Afawarq wrote articles that actually suggested Italy was a pacifist nation, and much later, he was accused of walking around with two separate passports, one Ethiopian and one Italian. He had no sense of diplomatic security either. Blaming a shortage of funds, he sent his cables to Addis Ababa through—believe it or not—Italy's Ministry of Foreign Affairs.[31] That the Italians perused them was common knowledge among reporters in Rome.

To David Darrah, Afawarq had an attitude of "sullen and silent perplexity."[32] If he enjoyed life in the Eternal City, it was no thanks to the hospitality of Italian officials. A detail of *caribinieri* police guarded the embassy like a fortress against student demonstrations, and plain-clothes operatives recorded every visitor. In the end, any cooperation mattered little to his hosts.

The world's first reaction to Walwal was a loud yawn. But while the skirmish was over, a diplomatic war was slowly intensifying that would push Ethiopia all the way to the front page.

* * *

Anthony Eden first heard about the Walwal Incident when France's delegate to the League of Nations rang him up at his Geneva hotel. He wanted Eden to come down to the Palais des Nations complex—urgently. The Frenchman wouldn't explain on the phone, but it was important.

The sprawling set of neo-classical buildings at Ariana Park serve today as the European headquarters for the UN, but the League of Nations in December of 1934 was a very different animal. It had no official flag or symbol, and had no peacekeeping forces of its own—any military strength behind its admonitions needed to come from its members, and especially from the Great Powers of Britain and France, the two heavyweights that dominated the League's Council. While several British Tories openly expressed their contempt for the League, Eden was a believer.

He was a rising star in the coalition National Government, and he was still in his thirties. He was handsome and something of a fashion icon with his stylish suits and his trademark Homburg hat. The world of British politics then was an inbred and insular one; in his second time running for office, Eden's opponent was his sister's mother-in-law. But although he could be painfully shy and was never a natural public speaker, in so many ways he was the best man for his job.

These were the years of looming war clouds, and Eden, at least, was one of the few in the Cabinet who knew how horrible *modern* war was. He had fought in the trenches of France as an officer in the King's Royal Rifle Corps, suffering a gas attack and earning himself a Military Cross. He hated "the death, muck, and misery, the pounding shell-fire and the casualty clearing stations."[33] Later, in March of 1935 at a state dinner, he and Adolf Hitler would discover they were on opposite sides of each other in battle; together, they sketched a map of the Western Front on the back of a dinner card. Eden kept it as a souvenir.

Born into a landowning family, he naturally went to Eton, and after the war to Oxford, where he graduated in what was then called "Oriental languages." He spoke Persian and Arabic, as well as French, German, and Russian, making him a natural choice to be Britain's League of Nations delegate. There were whispers and grumbles among his political colleagues. He dressed too smartly to have any *real depth*, didn't he? Not much commitment there. All of this was unfair. Eden would show a profound depth of conscience as he worked on the issue of Ethiopia, and the experience would leave such a powerful effect on his psyche that it influenced his judgment two decades later and cost him his political career.

Back on that day in December of 1934, however, he only knew that his French counterpart wanted to see him as soon as possible. When Eden arrived at the League headquarters, he discovered René Massigli in earnest conversation with Ethiopia's representative, Tekle Hawaryat Tekle Mariyam. The Frenchman asked Tekle to brief Eden on the border dispute, and then drew his British counterpart aside to complain: "It smells bad to me, like Manchuria."[34]

Eden knew what he meant. Japan had used the flimsy pretext of a blown-up section of railway to invade the Chinese province (the sabotage was actually perpetrated by soldiers of the Japanese army). In 1932, Japan bombed Shanghai, and a short and bloody war ensued. League delegates managed to broker a ceasefire, but the agreement meant humiliating terms for China and spoke more to the economic interests of Europeans than to the security of the inhabitants.

Eden was inclined to agree with Massigli; history was repeating itself. This sort of thing needed the attention of Massigli's boss, and France's foreign minister happened to be in town for the League session. Time to bring him down. Into the mix came the gnomish figure of Pierre Laval, a short man with heavily oiled black hair, a bushy mustache, and bad teeth. Though his previous post had been minister of France's colonies, Laval had barely any knowledge of Ethiopia and had expressed childish amusement over the name of its capital, reciting it over and over. *"A-bé-ba. Que c'est chic, ça. A-bé-ba."*[35]

Still, Laval agreed they should meet with their Italian counterpart, Baron Pompeo Aloisi. For Eden, this was as much as he could do for now—simply convey to London their concerns. "Thus began the first of interminable negotiations," Eden wrote in his memoirs. "For the moment we could do no more than alert London to our misgivings."[36]

* * *

On December 9, Ethiopia's foreign minister, Heruy Wolde Selassie, sent a note to the Italians that stated his government sincerely wanted to reach a settlement. The Italians had other ideas. On December 11, they replied with a note to the Foreign Ministry in Addis Ababa. It claimed that "there can be no doubt that Walwal and Warder belong to Italian Somaliland . . ." which the Italian government would "show in due course." The language was blunt, and there were no requests, simply demands:

> 1) The [provincial commander] Gabre Mariam, Governor of the Harar [Mariam was, in fact, only deputy governor] will proceed to Walwal, where he will present on behalf of the Abyssinian Government, a formal apology to the commander of the Italian post, while an Abyssinian detachment will render honors to the Italian flag
> 2) The Abyssinian Government will pay to the Royal Italian Legation at Addis Ababa a sum of two hundred thousand (200,000) T.M.T. [Maria Theresa thalers, the Ethiopian currency] as compensation for the heavy losses in dead and wounded sustained by our troops, as

separation for the damage caused to our fortified posts and as a refund of the expenditure which the Government of Somaliland has had to incur as a result of the act of aggression committed against it

3) The persons responsible for the attack must be arrested and deprived of their respective commands; after having been present at the honors rendered to the Italian flag in accordance with local usage, they must as soon as possible undergo suitable punishment . . ."[37]

The terms demanded by Rome would be humiliating for any foreign government, and since the Italians refused arbitration, Emperor Haile Selassie sent a telegram on December 15 to the League of Nations Secretary-General Joseph Avenol. It summarized the events at Walwal and drew the League Council's "attention to gravity of situation."[38]

In Geneva, European and American reporters focused on the telegram's contention that Walwal was "situated about 100 kilometers [62 miles] within the frontier." It was hard to imagine that Italy would establish a military base so far inside another country's borders, but the boundary had never been officially demarcated. Italy still denied Ethiopia's assertion in its latest salvo, a note sent to the League on December 16.

Four days later, a reporter in the press room of the League of Nations Permanent Secretariat Building in Geneva finally looked at a map of Africa. And most embarrassingly for the Italians, it was a map issued by their own Geographical Institute in Bergamo. There it was, Walwal, sixty-two miles within the Ethiopian border, as set out by a treaty back in 1897.

When Italy's man in Geneva, Baron Pompeo Aloisi, learned about this hanging indictment, he insisted it be removed because the map was out of date (some minor changes had been made by the treaty signatories in 1908). The reporters had initiative. Off they went to the north wing of the Secretariat Building, where they dug through the League library, and lo and behold—found another map of Ethiopia issued by the Italian Colonial Office in 1925. Once again, Walwal stood sixty-two miles within the Ethiopian border.[39]

This glaring truth should have been enough. All reporters had to do was spread the word of this simple geographical fact, and the case for Italy should have been thrown out then and there. It would have shamed the leader of almost any other European nation and would have severely damaged his country's international reputation. But Mussolini was the new Caesar, and he was not about to let facts get in his way.

Chapter Two

THE NEGUS AND THE NEW FLOWER

When a Swiss professor traveled to Ethiopia and talked with a group of students before the war, they were confident in victory. The professor pointed out that the Italians had a formidable air force, but the students were dismissive: "Oh, planes don't frighten us. Our priests know certain words; they say them, and the planes will crash." They had absolutely no doubt that their forces were superior. "Ah! We are strong! Our warriors are brave! No European army can defeat ours! Adwa has proved it."[1]

And when Italy's small tanks made of cheap tin (and built by Fiat) roared at last over Ethiopian soil, many had a single word painted on the side: ADWA.

What happened at Adwa? Why did it have such cultural power for both sides? And it did, indeed, for *both* sides. It's easy to think of the Ethiopian soldiers of this time as naïve and ignorant of technology. But it can't be underestimated how much the nineteenth century, with all its racial attitudes and colonial mythology, still had an almost gravitational pull on the European consciousness. It was as if the men and women who led the world into the era of radar and nuclear weapons had Victorian statues looming over their shoulders.

Cecil Rhodes was still a hero for schoolboys in Britain. In the United States, Confederate and Union soldiers of the Civil War still met for occasional anniversary reunions right through the 1930s, and there were still elderly black men and women living who could recall their days of slavery. Edith Piaf sang popular songs about heroic French foreign legionnaires defending themselves against "Salopards," a derogatory term for tribespeople in the Sahara. Later, in 1939, when the Hungarian-born Korda Brothers made their version of *The Four Feathers*—the rousing adventure tale of British soldiers fighting the Mahdi in Sudan—the Kordas shot on location and used actual warriors from the *original depicted battle* as extras in their action sequences.

Back when real British soldiers and not actors fought the Dervishes of Sudan, they needed the Ethiopians, so the two sides cut a deal. The Ethiopians would provide aid and safe passage to Britain's garrisons on the Sudan frontier, and in return, Ethiopia would get back some real estate occupied by the Egyptians and have free passage through the port of Massawa in what is today Eritrea. In less than a decade, however, Britain no longer wanted the job of port landlord. Massawa needed a subsidy of £20,000 a year, and for what? Its small export trade hardly justified London keeping it on its books. But the accountants behind the huge corporate machine that was the British Empire didn't like the idea of a Red Sea port falling into the hands of a main competitor: France.

By this time, the Scramble for Africa was full on, and upper-class Englishmen weren't inclined to think of African nobles and diplomats as equals. Just before Edward VII was about to be introduced to the sovereign of Tonga, he asked, "Is she a real queen or just another damned nigger?"[2]

So in 1884, the British government went behind Ethiopia's back and arranged for Rome to take Massawa off its hands.

Settlers for the new Italian colony of Eritrea were soon pushing out the locals, already struggling with the effects of a disease killing their cattle (a disease the Italians likely brought with them).[3] In America, the motto had been "Go West," and the white expansion decimated the lives of Cherokee, Choctaw, and Creek Indians. This was shaping up to be the Italian version. Even though the Italians were the enemy for Ethiopia as a whole, they could still play one provincial faction against another, and they supplied guns and ammunition to the man who became the next emperor, Menelik II. When Menelik ascended the throne, they assumed they had a willing dupe. They were wrong. They tried sneaking a treaty by him, which had benign phrasing in the Amharic draft and language in the Italian version that made Ethiopia a protectorate. That didn't work either.

Menelik is an intriguing personality in Ethiopian history. A man with a high forehead, thick lips, and cheeks scarred by a bout of smallpox, he never had any formal education, but he was intelligent and had an impish delight in new gadgets like lightbulbs. He knew politics. And in a patchwork quilt of different cultural groups and languages, nothing unified better than a war to defend the homeland. "I am black, and you are black," he told Muslim Dervishes. "Let us unite to hunt our common enemy."[4]

He relied heavily on his cousin and righthand man, Makonnen Walda-Mikael. Educated by a French priest, Makonnen was shrewd and had the charm and elaborate manners befitting an aristocrat. All these characteristics would be handed down to his son, who was born as Tafari, but who would become known to the world as Haile Selassie.

On March 1, 1896, Ethiopia's Emperor finally settled the score. Italy's bald, austere general, Oreste Baratieri, promised to bring back Menelik in a cage. He took with him fewer than twenty thousand Italian soldiers and fifty-six artillery guns. That should be enough, shouldn't it? Because what were they facing, really? Savages armed with spears and a few with guns, dragging along some French artillery—and after all, these were men who allowed their women and children to accompany their force like a bedraggled caravan of refugees. It was pathetic.

But Menelik commanded a host of *one hundred thousand men.* And he was fighting a defensive war on his own home ground.

It's not until you stand on a mountaintop in northern Ethiopia, looking over the vast green stretches of ambas, forests, and valleys—the summits occasionally wreathed in curls of white mist—that you begin to comprehend how much geography has determined the fate of this country. And that's only one part of a huge nation that offers a rich variety of landscapes. It's not difficult to pity the damn fool who would dare blunder into this natural fortress and try to use conventional warfare on its people. But that's just what Baratieri did, and disaster followed.

Battle trumpets and gunfire deafened the ears as the Ethiopians fearlessly ran through curtains of black smoke with their shields of buffalo hide and rifles. Across the divide were disciplined ranks of askari troops and Italian soldiers trained to fire in volleys. This would have worked well, but there were far, far too few of them. It's estimated that more than four thousand Italians were killed, with close to two thousand captured and almost fifteen hundred wounded. And this did not include askari casualties, which also numbered in the thousands. Many Italian officers lost all hope as they saw a charge of Ethiopian cavalry; a couple used their revolvers to kill themselves on the spot.[5]

A grisly fate waited for many of the askaris captured alive, for they were all considered traitors. The Italians killed you for treason. The Ethiopians let you live, but chopped off your right hand and left foot. Men stood in line, *knowing* they were about to be mutilated, while a mound of severed limbs piled higher in the background. And during the battle, many Italians, still alive and suffering from wounds, had been stripped naked and castrated. Menelik objected strongly to both these practices. He had given orders against castrations, but they were ignored. As for the askaris, there was a lot of political pressure—some of it from his own wife and empress—to make them pay for their service to Italy. Later, a British reporter challenged the Emperor over the amputations, but Menelik proved he was more statesman than politician. No apologies were made. Instead, he fired back that the askaris had looted churches and sacked villages; they were thieves, and so were treated like thieves.[6]

It had never happened before, a black African nation beating a white one in the developed world—not for a single battle, but decisively, for the climax of a war. Italy's prestige plummeted in Europe. Only two weeks after the defeat, Franceso Crispi's government was driven from office. The war had bled the Italian treasury, and the bill kept hemorrhaging after the battle. Italy was forced to pay ten million lire to cover the maintenance of its prisoners, who began to sail home less than a year later and were warned by authorities not to talk to reporters.

For Italy, Adwa was an embarrassment. For Ethiopia? Validation. Historian Raymond Jonas, who has written the definitive book *The Battle of Adwa*, rightly sums it up as "a national epic, the founding event in the modern life of the nation . . . Adwa deserves to be ranked among the great military campaigns of modern history."[7]

* * *

So much for treating the Ethiopians the way the rest of Africa was handled. In London and Paris, officials took one look at reports on the complete shellacking of Italy, cleared their throats, and decided, *ahem*, diplomacy might be the better way to go.

The British and French, along with the Italians, set up individual legations in Addis Ababa, and Britain signed a new Treaty of Friendship with Ethiopia in May 1897. In 1906, an American diplomat made a fascinating effort to win influence—President Theodore Roosevelt was rather taken with Ethiopia's exoticism—but he didn't get much for his trouble except goodwill and some zebras to take back to the Washington zoo.[8] Too bad, because as it turned out, the powers of Europe were only playing the long con, waiting for whoever would be the Emperor's successor. And by then, Menelik was in poor shape. He suffered a stroke that year and was sliding ever closer to his end, thanks to complications of syphilis.

So Britain, France, and Italy decided to divide up the pie. Their Tripartite Agreement of 1906 piously claimed that none of them would "infringe in any way the sovereign rights" of the Emperor—unless they could get away with it. They reserved the right "in the event of rivalries or internal changes in Ethiopia to intervene to protect their nationals and to act always in concert to safeguard their respective interests." The authors of this tidy bargain failed to remember one minor detail. The Emperor was still alive, and as bad as his health was, he didn't appreciate the foreign powers carving up his empire. When he got wind of the deal, he summoned diplomats from all three countries to explain themselves. Their response amounted to: Who, us? Oh, no, no, no—this is all *hypothetical*,

sir. He let them off with a tongue-lashing about Ethiopia's sovereignty and territorial integrity.

It was the last growl of a tired and sickly lion. When Menelik died in 1913,
Ethiopia was once again embroiled in court intrigues and succession politics—
perfect circumstances for the European deal. But none of the foreign powers
could swoop in and take advantage. The First World War was coming, and the
years of slaughter in faraway trenches would buy a little more time for Ethiopia.
Yet the war's aftermath provided a new pretext for Italy to claim a share of African
spoils.

It happened like this. Italy signed the secret Treaty of London in 1915 that
promised it "equitable compensation" for joining the fight against the Kaiser—
compensation, as in certain European territories and African colonies. The war
was an utter disaster for Italy when it came to economics and any dividends of
prestige. By the summer of the 1919 peace talks in Paris, the Italian government had a crushing $3.5 billion debt owed to the Allies. There was disgust, too,
over Rome's swift land grabs along the Adriatic to ensure it got the promised
European spoils. There were reports of Allied food shipments held up in Trieste
by Italian authorities and deportations of Slav nationalists from Dalmatia. When
America's Woodrow Wilson, France's Georges Clemenceau, and Britain's Lloyd
George refused to give in to Italy's demands, Prime Minister Vittorio Orlando
actually broke down and wept before abandoning the talks.

Italy kept pressing its claims, and as early as 1920, it was hassling a very young
League of Nations. "To those privileged states which enjoy a monopoly with
regard to raw materials," argued its representative, "and to those whose wealth has
permitted them to acquire a monopoly outside their territories, I say . . . declare
yourselves ready to support the cause of international solidarity."

Now here was a peculiar rationale. Italy was making its case for empire to
a body dedicated to the idea of the equality of states. But nothing came of it.
Twelve years later, with Walwal, Italy had its excuse to take on the battlefield what
it couldn't buy at a conference table.

On his deathbed, Menelik allegedly had the remaining strength to weep
mournful tears and whisper: "My poor people."[9]

*   *   *

In London and Paris, you expect chauffeured black sedans to whisk diplomats and ministers off to palaces to meet with heads of state. But in the Addis
Ababa of December 1934, it wasn't unusual for Ethiopians to see the leader of
the British legation—an innocuous-looking man who favored a bowtie in civilian

dress—wearing a formal white uniform as he rode through the streets of their capital on horseback. This is the way Sir Sidney Barton preferred to arrive at the Emperor's palace, and he liked even more having an escort of a small unit of turbaned Bengal Lancers.

Barton's ride was a ceremonial one, but a horse mount was useful when most of the roads were only mule tracks. When a policeman directed traffic in the street, he did it with a rhinoceros whip. The capital of Ethiopia was very much a place of historical anachronisms. As far as the rest of Ethiopia went at the time, it was a modern city, with a population of 130,000 people in a remote spot in the middle of the mountains, eight thousand feet above sea level. Menelik founded it because his formidable wife, Taitu, had never liked their original base at Ankobar. And so they had come here, to this spot dubbed "The New Flower." It had phones and telegraphs and (partial) electricity, and Menelik had even gone to the trouble of importing eucalyptus trees from Australia to decorate his turn-of-the-century capital. Different nobles, wanting to be as fashionable as their emperor, built impressive compounds of their own near his palace.

But aside from a small collection of stone and brick buildings, this was a land-scape of motley *tukuls*, traditional thatch huts, and an ever-growing collection of shantytown homes with tin for the roofs and mud-caked walls. When the British minister and his Lancers rode through town, they passed huge heaps of trash in nearby streets because the city had no sewage system. European visitors also soon discovered that the city shut down by nine in the evening. In hotels, water for their morning baths was fetched from hot springs in a gas can.

As Britain's man in Ethiopia, Sidney Barton was high in the pecking order of the resident expats, and his wife was a personal friend of the empress. East Africa had to be a very different world for him when he arrived in 1929, especially since he spent his career until then in Shanghai and the Asia-Pacific region. Barton didn't suffer fools, and he liked efficiency. He admired the Japanese for first having wandered all over this exotic land to check markets and make a thorough investigation of prices and practices before they got down to business. "Why don't we do that?" he asked with rhetorical exasperation.[10]

But his duties were probably light in a posting that was considered a back-water by the Foreign Office. Each week, the Bartons went to the city's racecourse to watch polo matches, and when the British ambassador wanted an escape, he could sit in the Imperial Club and read a copy of *The Illustrated London News*, which invariably arrived by mail a month out of date.[11] For years, he'd kept his own careful watch on the Italians' encroachment near British Somaliland, but he had his orders from home: make it clear to the Emperor that he shouldn't count on any open support from the British, who had pressing reasons to stay on good terms with Italy. Instead, the Emperor should work out a direct settlement with the Italian government.

To come speak with the Emperor, he had to pass a gate where on any given day, hundreds of ordinary Ethiopians in traditional shammas might wait eagerly to catch a brief sight of their sovereign, not unlike today's royal watchers at Buckingham Palace in London. The grounds held three separate courtyards, with the Imperial Palace, the *gibbi*, built by Menelik. Haile Selassie decided to build a new palace, one that was called the "Little Gibbi" and was fashioned in the style of an English country house. To go with the English architecture, one of his advisers, the Swedish general Eric Virgin, made over the manners of the Ethiopian court with the etiquette protocols of Europe. Just as foreign guests waited for their bath water in their hotel rooms, so the parched gardens in the dry season needed two hundred palace staff to fetch water from the hot springs as well. And for all the pomp of military drill and the uniforms borrowed from European styles, many soldiers of the imperial guard in their smart caps and tunics went barefoot.

But any visitors to the palace would be reminded they were still in Africa by the lions in cages kept on the grounds. A pair of them used to lazily sprawl out and pant in the heat near the door to Haile Selassie's study. Virgin was once confronted by a lion on one of his earliest visits to the library. Startled, he stepped cautiously past the animal and didn't mention it to the Emperor, but he sensed that Haile Selassie would have enjoyed him bringing it up.[12] Many newcomers heard a taller tale about the lions and Sidney Barton. The story went that when Barton came upon one of the animals, he promptly drew his pistol and shot the big cat dead, promising the Emperor that he'd do it again if he ever ran into another one. It seems highly implausible that Haile Selassie would stand for this, but whatever prompted the change, the Emperor now only played with cubs in the open, while the full-grown mascots were kept locked up.

Ethiopia's Emperor couldn't have been more of a contrast to Benito Mussolini in background, character, and physical presence. The Italian dictator was born a peasant; Haile Selassie claimed a lineage back to King Solomon. Mussolini, the once-avowed atheist, bragged of his womanizing and affairs. The Emperor, fiercely devout to the Ethiopian Orthodox Christian Church, was faithful to his wife and was grooming a son to replace him. The Duce of Rome was famous for his boisterous theatrics and his pose of athleticism. Haile Selassie was referred to in countless news reports as "tiny" at five foot four, with Western observers remarking on his high forehead, aristocratic features, and brown eyes that they often described as "melancholy." He had grown his thick black beard to offset his obvious youth when he was still trying to make a name for himself at the imperial court.

For all his life, he would have a reputation for his dignified, sometimes icy composure. Tantrums might be the response—even a conscious tactic—of a Fascist dictator, but it was impressed upon Haile Selassie at an early age that dignity was the default posture of a king. He was a man of shrewd intelligence with a competent knowledge of English, but who preferred to converse with Westerners in French. He never acted impulsively, but always weighed his options, consulted others, and didn't betray his line of thinking until he was ready to announce a decision.

Days before his troops were getting cut to pieces by Italian machine gun fire, the Emperor was already mulling over the option of a complaint to the League of Nations. He wondered if simply changing the troops for fresh ones might be interpreted as provocative. Barton was blunt. Never mind that, he explained in so many words, you have to supply the soldiers *properly*, instead of letting them rely on the resources of the neighboring tribes, many of which were nomadic and protected by British forces in Somaliland.

The Emperor thought it best to end the meeting then and there.

Eventually, the grim details of Walwal reached the palace and then, later, Italy's imperious demands for reparations. When Haile Selassie met again with Barton, the British minister was still trying to sell quiet, direct negotiation. But the Emperor had other advisers he could rely on. Two of them, a Swiss named Auberson and a retired American diplomat, Everett Colson, composed a telegram that was wired to the League, asking it to step in.[13] Colson was an old Wilsonian Democrat from Maine who once held a desk in the Philippines and put in a brief stint in China. "Here they tell you So-and-so's a very intelligent man," he once commented dryly, "and that means he can speak French."[14]

The pressure on Haile Selassie had to be enormous. He didn't need foreign enemies—he had plenty at home. He kept a Swiss cook on staff as a taster of his food to defend himself against poisons. When he toured the country, he rode in an armored car. There were always those waiting to challenge his position. And unlike Adwa for Menelik, this second imminent war with Italy was not guaranteed to be a great unifier.

Not long after the Walwal incident, a one-time provincial chief, Balcha Safo, now an elderly man, turned up in Addis Ababa without a retinue and putting his weight on a priest's staff as he walked along. Balcha was a walking museum exhibit for Ethiopia's medieval past. He was an Oromo eunuch who rose through the offices of power, and when Menelik rode to the Battle of Adwa, Balcha was given the honor of gripping the reins that led the mule of the empress. Then, in 1928, Balcha pressed his luck by showing up at the capital with five thousand warriors and acting belligerently on the palace grounds. Even his officers put some distance between them and his rude behavior. Haile Selassie wasn't Emperor yet, but he had an impressive power base as prince regent, and he took the implied threat seriously. Balcha Safo found his camp on the outskirts of the city surrounded. He had to carry a stone of penance through the streets and then serve a prison sentence, and after he was finally let out, he went off to live in quiet obscurity—until this visit.

"Janhoy," he called the Emperor, which served as the Ethiopian equivalent of *Your Majesty.* "I am done with the past! I have kept trust, and I do not see why I should ever break it. I heard of the attack on your soldiers at . . . Walwal . . . and I cannot stay shut up in my monastery when I know that they are going to battle. I fought by the side of Menelik at Adwa, and I demand my place by you!"[15]

The Emperor was moved by this devotion, but told the old warrior gently, "Thank you, Balcha, for being prepared to die for your country. It was good of you to return in your old age to lead your men to war, but times have changed since Adwa, and the war of today is no longer the war of Adwa. It is no longer enough to have courage and patriotism; today tactics and strategy are required. Your place is here, Balcha, I can make good use of you, and for the actual fighting I have younger generals."[16]

It was a lesson Haile Selassie would try to impress upon his commanders again and again for the next several months. He was well aware of the havoc that Italy's air force and its modern tanks could rain down on an army of men with spears and obsolete rifles. Months after he had neutralized Balcha back in 1928, he had put down another rebellion of ten thousand soldiers. A French pilot had flown over them in a biplane to make three bombing runs, scattering the rebel warriors and cavalry.[17] But too many Ethiopians were like Balcha, with a vision of the glorious past battle stubbornly blinding them to the metal and steel death that was coming.

* * *

Ethiopia was an African nation, but it had palace intrigues and feudal politics to rival the Borgias and Ottomans.

When Makonnen died of typhoid in 1906, Emperor Menelik brought the young Ras Tafari from Harar to be a gentleman-in-waiting at his court. Tafari was fourteen years old. Only two years later, this teenager was given responsibilities as a governor of a sub-province while he continued his education. There were key lessons to pick up outside the classroom, too. Lesson one: *Nobles and bureaucrats accept gifts.* Lesson two: *They like to line their pockets from trade deals.* This was how things got done. After Menelik suffered his stroke, certain nobles from Shoa schemed to have Empress Taitu step down because of her influence. Lesson three: *Know who your friends and enemies are, and don't change sides in a crisis.* Tafari wouldn't go along with the plot. He wouldn't give up the names of the conspirators either, carefully threading his way through the complicated alliances.[18]

He had a talent for politics. When he became governor of Harar, the province his father once ruled, he investigated the crushing taxes that were ruining the peasants and instituted reforms, making himself popular. When he married for the second time, he made sure it was to a woman with an imperial lineage and family ties to the crown prince (his first wife would die giving birth to his first daughter). He was lucky in that his second wife, Menen, was an intelligent, good-looking older woman of strong piety like himself, and there's no reason to doubt that he sincerely loved her.

He also got along reasonably well with the crown prince, Lij Iyasu, but the two were very different in temperament. Tafari's early education had been from a French priest and an Ethiopian Capuchin monk, and as a teen, he was a pensive scholar. Iyasu, Menelik's grandson and the heir to the throne, was an emotionally unstable party boy who visited brothels and already had doubts that Christianity should remain the state religion. His short reign was a disaster from the beginning. On the very night that Menelik died in 1913, he had Taitu kicked out of the palace. He then decided to play up to the country's Muslim population, alienating the Christian aristocracy. He backed Germany and Turkey in the Great War. Fine, said Britain and France, and they promptly slapped an arms embargo on Ethiopia. All this put a good and proper scare into Ethiopia's nobles. Iyasu was off his hinges. Iyasu was a traitor. Iyasu had to *go*, and they excommunicated him. When his father went to battle in 1916 to put his son back on the throne, Tafari sent an army to Segale to decisively put him down. In the aftermath, Iyasu fled into the desert.

But Ras Tafari's time still hadn't come. Menelik's conservative daughter, Zewditu, became empress, while he had to settle for the role of regent. Fortunately, Zewditu was a sickly diabetic who cared more about building churches than affairs of state. Ras Tafari was nothing if not patient. He kept slowly, quietly centralizing his power while bringing in his reforms. And he wasn't above amassing his own wealth to secure his base. He sent promising young men abroad to get a wider education, protégés who would become known as the "Young Ethiopians." Yet at every turn, while he was regent and then later as emperor, he was met with steady resistance from ministers, nobles, and church officials.

When the Allies won the Great War, Tafari knew it would be a smart move to congratulate the victors and strengthen ties. He liked Woodrow Wilson's vision for the League of Nations, and he would have loved to go to Paris himself to head a delegation for the talks in 1919. But he couldn't afford to leave the capital to the machinations of "the priests and the women" who wanted to block his reforms at every turn. Timing was everything. Soon, he would be strong enough politically. Soon, he could campaign in earnest for Ethiopia's place among the members of the League.

And he would get last-minute support for membership from a most unlikely ally: Benito Mussolini.

*   *   *

From the balcony of the royal Quirinal Palace in Rome, Ras Tafari and Italy's King Victor Emmanuel waved to a crowd cheering: "Long live Italy! Long live Ethiopia! Long live His Highness Crown Prince Tafari!" Since Tafari and his wife Menen arrived in the middle of June in 1924, Mussolini and the king had pulled out all stops to be gracious hosts. A royal train was sent for their guests at the border, and at a state dinner, Victor Emmanuel made a toast of friendship and blessings for Ethiopia.[19]

What a change this made from the treatment Ethiopia received from other countries! When it applied for membership to the League of Nations the year before, Britain opposed it. The argument? Ethiopia still had slavery. Then it came out that the British ambassador at the time kept several slaves himself as domestics. Ethiopia still won its vote to be included in the League. And to everyone's surprise, Italy was on its side. *Italy.* The country beaten so badly at Adwa. Why would Mussolini bother?

The truth was that Mussolini had *never* wanted Ethiopia in the League. One week after Ethiopia applied, in fact, he cabled his men in Paris and Addis Ababa to say he was opposed to it.[20] But then he thought it over and realized he ought to step carefully. France was backing the bid for admission. Britain resented France over this, assuming its old rival wanted to widen its sphere of influence in East Africa and cause mischief. And Britain was appalled that such an "uncivilized" nation should dare ask for admittance to the League and quite possibly hurt the young organization's prestige.

The British grumbled about all this carelessly to the Italians, so that a diplomat could send a telegram to his Duce, assuring him that the British "will try at Geneva to make admission practically impossible."[21] In Mussolini's view, why risk causing offense when you can get others to make your complaints for you?

The British, however, couldn't get others onboard their blocking bandwagon, and in the end, they gave up the effort. After the Italian delegate stood in the League Chamber to make an effusive speech, the assembly made a unanimous vote to admit Ethiopia. Mussolini's tactics had failed, but he had lost nothing for his trouble.

So in 1924, it was smiles all around when the Lion of Judah was welcomed into the Duce's own den. Part of the substance Tafari hoped to gain from his European tour was a port for Ethiopia. The French had built their railway from Djibouti, and it was to the French that Tafari had turned first. But France's prime minister at the time, Raymond Poincaré, had given him a "hopeful reply" and then left Tafari to wait . . . and wait . . .

He decided to try his luck with Mussolini in Rome.

When the two sat down to discuss matters, Tafari was impressed with Mussolini's "powerful face, his enormous eyes, his projecting jaw, his voice with its always changing inflections." He found the dictator "theatrical."[22] Of course, Italy was willing to grant Ethiopia access to the sea. In fact, he had come to their meeting prepared with a draft treaty. Tafari, being Makonnen's son, knew to be careful. No, he didn't want to sign it right now, he told his host. It needed some careful study back in Addis Ababa. This short visit in Rome would be the first and last time the two leaders would ever come face-to-face.

Mussolini's treaty was for a ninety-nine-year lease on the port of Assab, but it had the same kind of hidden tricks as previous Italian offers, and in the end Tafari rejected it. But the dictator had shown him more courtesy than he received at the other stops on his European tour. In Paris, the French were happy to take him around to all the tourist sights. By all means, go look at the Eiffel Tower. See the Louvre while you're here . . . and then they refused to talk business. And before he even crossed the Channel, the British demonstrated their contempt. The *Manchester Guardian* noted that the regent received a kiss from a little girl and decided, "A kiss for a Negro king is more than all the wealth of England can afford."[23]

George V had no more respect for Africans than his royal ancestors, and he refused to allow Tafari and his wife to stay at Buckingham Palace. No, he would not bother to greet the regent at Victoria Station, which was only a few minutes' drive away; that duty fell to the Duke of York (later George VI) while the Prince of Wales was off in Paris for the Olympics. Things went from awkward to worse when Prime Minister Ramsay MacDonald chose to lecture Tafari on nomads raiding Somaliland and Ethiopia's slow progress in justice reform.

So Ras Tafari left Europe, having impressed a few diplomats and the more liberal newspapers like London's *Observer*, but with very little else to show for his trouble. A bit of time passed, and it was as if all the diplomatic overtures had never happened. There was an exchange of notes between the Duce and the British ambassador to Rome, Sir Ronald Graham. Mussolini would back London's bid to get a concession on Ethiopia's Lake Tana, including construction of a road from Sudan, if Italy could get help securing a railway from Eritrea to Italian Somaliland—which would have to run right through Ethiopia. Of course the two sides hadn't consulted Ethiopia at all, and they were carving up a nation on paper that only two years before had been granted status as one of their equals. Tafari did his best imitation of Menelik: patient, indulgent, and, in private, furious.

But now things were different, and membership has its privileges. He took his case to the League of Nations in June. "We are greatly distressed about this agreement being concluded by the two governments among themselves alone without them informing Us, and then simply sending Us joint notifications . . ."[24] There were more smiles, more declarations of peace, and the Duke of Abruzzi presented Ras Tafari with the Grand Order of the Annunziata, the highest Italian order of chivalry, even while the Italian colonial official, Alberto Pollera, and others offered arms and covert help to Ras Gugsa Wale, the governor of Begemder, for a revolt against the government.

This was the revolt that Tafari put down in 1930 with the help of a biplane dropping bombs.

* * *

As it happened, Ras Gugsa Wale was Zewditu's husband, but this hardly mattered, as Tafari had gained so much power by then that she could hardly stand against him, having already crowned him *Negus* ("King" in Amharic). In 1930, sick with typhoid and already weak from fasting for Lent, her priests decided to dunk her in holy water as a desperate cure, and she lapsed into a coma and died with a dutiful regent at her bedside.

Whatever Tafari felt over Zewditu's passing, he was now the unquestioned Emperor of Ethiopia, and for his whole life, he considered his reign ordained by God. He took as his new imperial name *Haile Selassie*, which in Amharic means "the Power of the Trinity." Invitations went out to heads of state and representatives around the world to celebrate his coronation, and reporters and dignitaries arrived at a cleaned-up Addis Ababa decorated by triumphal arches and new lighting for its main streets.

On hand for the coronation were two young Englishmen with very different reactions and attitudes to the spectacle.

One was the son of a British minister from years past, and he had been born in the mud tukul that once served as Britain's legation. As a boy, he delighted in sightings of vultures and lions and hyenas, and at six years old, he was a witness to the procession of the victorious Shoan army of the regent. At twenty, Wilfred Thesiger had yet to make his mark, and his legendary travels through the Arabian Empty Quarter were years away. But he was the only guest to receive a personal invitation from Ras Tafari, and he had come as the Honorary Attaché of the Duke of Gloucester, who would represent his father, the king of England.

To young Thesiger, all the pomp was in some ways pitiful, and yet in others, he was spellbound by the grandeur. But he resented the creeping taint of Western influence, the noise of automobiles and the palace secretaries wearing tailcoats and top hats. He would remain a frequently absent yet lifelong loyal friend to the Emperor, and when the impressionable young man gushed about how glad he was to be back in the country, Haile Selassie told him: "It is your country. You were born here. You have lived here for half of your life. I hope you will spend many more years with us."[25] After his audience with the Emperor, Thesiger received two elephant tusks, a fancy gold cigarette case, a large, impressive carpet, and the Star of Ethiopia, Third Class.

There was no swag for the other young Englishman, who regarded all the pageantry with open contempt. This was Evelyn Waugh: seven years older than Thesiger, he took great delight in cataloging others' hypocrisy while often ignoring his own. As a novelist, he had already secured his reputation with parodies of the upper classes, such as *Decline and Fall*, and he was in Addis Ababa as correspondent for the *Graphic*. But Waugh was far out of his element. He was humiliated when the nieces of Sidney Barton laughed at him for failing to book a hotel room in advance, and he was offended that he didn't get an invitation to one of the major functions. Waugh complained about Barton as a "half-baked consul" and took his revenge by skewering the family in caricatures for *Black Mischief*.[26]

Thesiger spotted Waugh at one of the receptions and was put off instantly by the author's affectations and his entourage that hung on every *bon mot*. He also got wind of the nasty insults Waugh was dishing out over Sidney Barton and his wife. For Thesiger, the couple had turned into valued friends, which was natural, as they were all products of the Foreign Service establishment. He would not forget Waugh's slights.

"I disapproved of his gray suede shoes, his floppy tie, and the excessive width of his trousers," Thesiger remembered. "He struck me as flaccid and petulant and I disliked him on sight. Later he asked, at second-hand, if he could accompany me into the Danakil country, where I planned to travel. I refused. Had he come, I suspect only one of us would have returned."[27]

The Ethiopia Crisis and the war would turn out to be full of meetings like this, run-ins between the famous and the notorious, with dramatic moments you wouldn't believe if they were fiction. Thesiger would not go to fight for Ethiopia in 1935, conscious that he "should have achieved nothing, beyond retaining my self-respect."[28] He would fight for it later with the British Army. For Waugh, however, Ethiopia was useful as a target for his satires, starting with *Black Mischief.* And when the Crisis escalated, he would be back.

Interestingly enough, both young men took little notice of an incident that marred the festivities. There was an aerial show at the coronation dress rehearsal to demonstrate that Ethiopia could master the skies like developed nations. The colonel of the tiny Ethiopian Air Force and trainer of its cadets was a black pilot named Hubert Julian, who had made a name for himself with parachute and barnstorming stunts in Harlem. He had managed to ingratiate himself with the regent, and in one precoronation display, thrilled the crowd with stunts performed in one of the country's few aircraft. Then from five thousand feet high, Julian dived out of the plane and parachuted within a few yards of the stands.

An impressed regent awarded Julian the Gold Order of Menelik, a substantial sum of money, his new commission as colonel, and even a villa on Mount Entoto. It should have been enough glory for any man, especially one eager to make a name for himself in an exotic land.

But on the day of the dress rehearsal, the new Emperor had expressly ordered Julian *not* to fly. This was supposed to be the Ethiopians' show, their moment to shine. The colonel, however, couldn't help himself. He hopped into the Emperor's brand-new Gypsy Moth—actually bought through Selfridges department store in London (you could buy practically anything from Selfridges back then, even planes)—and taxied to the runway. After buzzing the royal canopy, Julian lost control of the engine and the Moth went into a loop, smashing into a nearby set of eucalyptus trees.

Had the arrogant pilot been an Ethiopian, Haile Selassie probably would have tossed him into a jail cell. There were some at court who wanted him executed. Instead, the punishment for him was to be banished, and a small escort took Hubert Julian to the newly fixed-up train station and put him on the next coach for Djibouti. The matter was settled. No one expected that in five years, Julian would be back in Ethiopia, seeing the African nation's desperate peril as another chance for his own personal glory.

* * *

By December 18, 1934, Haile Selassie was looking for help over Walwal from the American chargé d'affaires, William Perry George. George was a fixture of the capital's diplomatic clique, quite ready to man the bar in the Imperial Club when there were parties, but now events at his sleepy post made things awkward for him. Washington sent him a flurry of telegrams, demanding news, but he had none to offer. Then, suddenly, he *did* have something to report.

Summoned to the palace, George spoke with Haile Selassie in French. The Emperor wanted the United States to help decide things, which probably came as a complete surprise to George. Here was Haile Selassie, talking in vague terms about how America could make "some gesture"—*something*—that could push the situation toward a peaceful resolution.[29] The Emperor was astute enough to recognize that after the Great War, America was a new superpower of great influence.

Unfortunately, it was a superpower that wasn't interested. A couple of days later, in the stack of the daily telegrams George received from Washington, Secretary of State Cordell Hull pointed out that "since the incident has been brought to the attention of the League of Nations and since it is the intention of the Ethiopian Government to pursue the matter before the Council, this Government considers that it could not usefully or properly take any action."[30] Instead, Hull and the State Department would follow events with "sympathetic interest." There would be no gesture and no open support.

But America would end up playing a crucial role in the drama, whether it wanted to or not, even if it refused to raise its voice. Its position on Ethiopia would ultimately help decide the fate of the world.

Then Italian troops attacked a new target, Gerlogubi, about thirty miles southwest of Walwal. Italy rejected arbitration, flouting the terms of the 1928 Friendship Treaty, and Haile Selassie had had enough. On January 3, he sent another telegram to the League of Nations. Only this time, his government asked in no uncertain terms that his fellow members apply Article 2 of the League's Covenant. This stated, "Any war or threat of war, whether immediately affecting any of the Members of the League or not, is hereby declared a matter of concern to the whole League, and the League shall take any action that may be deemed wise and effectual to safeguard the peace of nations."

This was not what Mussolini wanted; backroom discussions among the principal players, yes, sit downs and consultations and more mutual assurances, but *not* the legitimacy of international proceedings. Britain's Anthony Eden would consider them "interminable negotiations," but what he didn't know yet was that Mussolini wanted them to be interminable. The Duce was counting on it. Two weeks after Walwal, he composed a secret memorandum entitled "Directive and Plan of Action for the Solution of the Italo-Abyssinian Question." Only five copies of it were issued, one that naturally went to his first commander for the invasion, General Emilio De Bono, who refers to it in his memoir.[31]

"Time is working against us," declared Mussolini, and his solution for the problem was the "total conquest of Ethiopia" and destruction of its military.[32] His forces, he wrote, would have to be in Eritrea by October of 1935, which would put the campaign after the rainy season in Ethiopia. He estimated one hundred thousand Italian soldiers and sixty thousand askari troops would be needed for the job, with the support of at least 250 airplanes in Eritrea and fifty in Somalia.

And what would Britain and France have to say about that?

"The more rapid our military action, the less will be the danger of diplomatic complications," Mussolini reasoned. He ordered his general to Eritrea to assume the post of High Commissioner for East Africa. *"No one in Europe will raise any difficulties for us if the conduct of military operations rapidly creates an accomplished fact* [emphasis added]. It will be enough to declare to England and France that their interests will be recognized."[33] So Mussolini wasn't thinking in terms of a last-minute invasion, but a last-minute peace.

*   *   *

As Pierre Laval's train crossed the Italian border, Fascist militia offered salutes at regular close intervals, and crowds in Turin, Genoa, and other stops seemed always ready to give him an enthusiastic greeting. Being a former newspaperman, Mussolini knew how to throw a media spectacle, and it helped, of course, that he controlled a good share of the Italian press anyway. When Laval stepped onto the station platform in Rome on January 4, Mussolini shook his hand and kissed him on both cheeks in the French tradition, and Italian Undersecretary for Foreign Affairs Fulvio Suvich offered a bouquet of roses to Laval's daughter, Josée, in the Duce's name. At a banquet the next evening, Laval called Mussolini "the writer of the most beautiful page in the history of modern Italy."[34]

Having made nice for the cameras, the two men talked the next day with their advisers at the Palazzo Venezia. Laval was about to become one of the chief architects of Ethiopia's betrayal.

He was an unusual politician. Laval was a peasant son from Puy-Guillaume in France's mountainous Auvergne, and he had the table manners to show it. The young Laval studied his way out of his home backwater, letting the family horse navigate its way to complete vegetable deliveries as he kept his nose in his books. Armed with a law degree, he started out as a hardcore Socialist, but decided he preferred to be rich, and his business connections soon earned him a fixer-upper of a castle in Châteldon. He made the most telling remark about his personality and ethics in 1930: "I believe that people can best be cared for without consulting their wishes."[35]

To Laval and most of his Cabinet colleagues in 1935, the best way to care for the people of France was to keep Nazi Germany in check.

The Great Powers had good reason to be worried. Their intelligence services confirmed that Hitler was secretly re-arming after he had pulled out of the League of Nations. What we remember today is Hitler's successful encroachment on Austria. What we forget is that, back in 1935, Austria was considered to be very much in Italy's sphere of influence, a "buffer state" to its north. While Hitler patterned himself after Mussolini in several ways, they were not fast friends, and their alliance lay in the future. In fact, the Duce called the German Fuehrer a "clown."

So it was reasonable in the beginning for the politicians of Britain and France to turn to Italy, their ally in the Great War, to maintain the peace. The problem was that Mussolini knew how important he was on the strategy board. All this factored brilliantly into his plan to steam ahead and have fewer "diplomatic complications." Back in early October, he had baited his hook and suggested in a speech that an entente with France would be "useful and fruitful."

The way to get Italy's help with Germany, reasoned Laval, was to strike a bargain over pieces of French Africa. This would be a quick way to solve that leftover migraine from Versailles, the broken promise that Italy would get a few colonial spoils out of the Great War. In French-controlled Tunisia, a vocal minority of Italian nationals, encouraged by Rome, had been insisting recently on annexation to Italian Libya. But Mussolini was willing to trade them in for different parcels of real estate, including some forty-four thousand square miles of useless desert that French Somaliland could give away without a sigh of regret.

Thousands of Italian nationals in the colony were shocked to discover their Duce had forfeited their citizenship. Even Laval heard the squawking of angry Italian officials, who said without any sense of irony, "If we had a parliament, Mussolini would be overthrown." The French governor in Tunisia later told him that in Italian schools, teachers tossed portraits of Mussolini on the floor, and children freely spat on them.[36]

Laval knew Mussolini's price for Tunisia. He admitted later that Ethiopia had been discussed, and claimed he "urged Mussolini not to resort to force . . . He started war against my will and despite my solemn protest."[37]

This was disingenuous. He was abdicating France's role right then and there as one of the protectors of the League on collective security. Why was he "urging" and not *warning* Mussolini to back off? He had to know that Mussolini would not sacrifice Italy's Tunisian subjects unless he was given a "free hand" in Ethiopia, an expression that came into use around these negotiations.

Pierre Lazareff of *Paris-Soir* learned a telling anecdote from a reliable colleague. Mussolini had apparently asked Laval: "Supposing Italy wanted to deal

with Ethiopia as France has already dealt with Morocco—what would the attitude of France be?" Laval replied: "I'll see to it that France will look on without
saying a word. We won't have any trouble on that score."[38]

Having already drawn up a systematic program for his campaign, Emilio De
Bono took the regular steamer that left Naples for Eritrea on January 7, the same
day Laval and Mussolini announced their agreement on the African colonies.

*   *   *

Less than a week later, the League of Nations began its new session in Geneva,
but the British and French managed to persuade Ethiopia's delegate, Tekle
Hawaryat, to delay putting the arbitration request on the formal agenda. They
assured him a solution could be found in quiet talks, away from the main council
chamber.

It says much about Britain's Foreign Office of the 1930s that its "expert" on
Ethiopia, Geoffrey Thompson, who was Anthony Eden's age, had never set foot
in the country. Before he tunneled his way through the files to study up, the
African nation "had never previously been anything but a name to me."[39] The
good news: Thompson was highly intelligent and brought a keen sense of insight
to his work. The bad news: Both he and Eden were undermined at every turn in
Geneva by their own boss, the foreign secretary.

Sir John Simon was the kind of Tory politician that moderates and leftists hated; he earned the eternal loathing of ordinary workers by declaring the
General Strike of 1926 illegal. His own Cabinet colleagues disliked him, with
even Neville Chamberlain feeling repulsed and Harold Nicolson calling Simon a
"toad." Simon was not a friend, let alone an objective, neutral figure during the
Crisis. He'd written a preface for a book by his wife criticizing Ethiopian slavery.

One late night in Geneva, Thompson was drafting up crucial telegrams to be
sent to Addis Ababa and Rome. When he brought the drafts to Simon's hotel
room, his boss scribbled some revisions, and as Thompson headed for the door,
Simon called out his name.

"Yes, sir?" asked Thompson, turning around.

"You realize, don't you," said Simon, "that the Italians intend to take Abyssinia?"

Thompson was "surprised and disconcerted," almost dumbstruck by his superior's cynicism.[40]

It wasn't merely that Simon knew the Italians' intent. He was quite willing to
let them have what they wanted. His telegram to Barton in Addis Ababa gave a list
of suggestions for the Emperor, all of them proposing concessions on Ethiopia's
part. None of that mattered; Mussolini's reply to all this was already a blunt *no*.

He kept Britain's ambassador to Italy, Eric Drummond, cooling his heels for two weeks before granting an appointment, and when Drummond mentioned that the Emperor was prepared to make his case before the League, Mussolini shrugged and replied that if he did, "the consequences might be very serious."[41]

Back in Geneva, Anthony Eden was also getting frustrated. Italy charged that companies were supplying arms to the Ethiopians through the port of Aden; cases marked "Machinery" but known to hold weapons were on their way to Berbera, but British Customs officials had allegedly redirected them to Djibouti. Eden was flabbergasted and checked with London. The "suspicious" cases didn't have arms at all. They held furniture for the new palace at Addis Ababa and had been diverted only so they would arrive in time for a visit by the Crown Prince of Sweden. No one apparently had the presence of mind to demand how the Italians could know what was going on with inspections out of a British-controlled port.

Tired of these games, Eden advised the Foreign Office to let things take their course. They normally would. Haile Selassie turned down the British proposals, and Ethiopia's League delegate formally lodged the application to be heard at the current Council session. The problem was that both Britain and France wanted to keep Italy happy. Italy would stay happy if it got what it wanted, but short of that, Britain and France could at least oblige Mussolini by making sure there were no diplomatic embarrassments. And how to do that? Well, the Italians didn't want the dispute aired publicly on the Council floor. It was lucky, then, that there was still the Treaty of Friendship of 1928, and it set out methods for arbitration. In early January, both sides declared their "readiness to pursue the settlement of the [Walwal] incident in conformity with the spirit" of the treaty.

But aside from platitudes, there was no firm deadline for arbitration—and still no hearing for Ethiopia's grievance on the Council floor.

"The result was acclaimed by press and public in many lands, but all we had gained was time," Eden wrote in his memoirs.[42]

Time is relative even in diplomacy, and it wasn't Britain that needed it. Less than two weeks later, Mussolini ordered the mobilization of about thirty thousand soldiers.

Chapter Three

A SILENT ROOM IN STRESA

For Mussolini, all was going according to plan. Though confident in his strategy, he was prudent enough to write De Bono in Asmara: "Even in view of possible international controversies (League of Nations, etc.) it is as well to hasten our tempo. For the lack of a few thousand men we lost the day at Adwa! We shall never make that mistake. I am willing to commit a sin of excess but never a sin of deficiency."[1]

It was only a minor inconvenience to him that Ethiopia didn't oblige his war by starting hostilities first. "The bulk of the indications and the messages intercepted allow us to suppose that the Negus does not wish to take the initiative of the encounter," he told De Bono on February 26.[2]

No matter. If provocation wasn't real, it could be manufactured. Two days later, the Foreign Ministry in Rome claimed that ninety thousand Ethiopian troops were deploying on the frontier of Italian Somaliland. In the international press corps of 1935, objective journalism dictated that you go seek a rebuttal from the Ethiopian legation, if one was available and forthcoming. Far more useful would have been if someone had tried to figure out if it was true. But then how could they? The Somali border was far away, far from where even a correspondent in Mogadishu—if by some miracle there was one—might be bothered.

De Bono went on with his preparations. Troops and laborers were arriving, barracks were to be built for hospitals and food stores, sheds were to be made for animals, and then there was the steady transfer of air forces. While some planes could be flown over, others were required to be passed disassembled through Cairo and Khartoum, where British and Egyptian authorities subjected them to strict inspection. De Bono found the British officials "uncivil," but they couldn't interfere with him, and soon the aircraft delivered to a camp at Otumlo could be assembled at a rate of six planes every forty-eight hours. By mid-March, the Italians had forty-three planes, both scouts and bombers, ready for their offensive.

In Rome, David Darrah estimated that by the end of March, a million Italians had been called up to serve.

* * *

The Ethiopia Crisis happened in the 1930s, and this was a decade that was far more interesting and vibrant than it's become in our popular imagination. Millions were unemployed, millions struggled, but newspapers still sold, many stores stayed open, music played on. In spite of their problems at home, people *cared* about what was happening in Ethiopia. This was the age before Bolshevism was bankrupt, when ideas very much mattered, when they were worth long and heated arguments, and maybe worth dying for—perhaps more so than the petty nationalism that had bequeathed nightmare visions of trench warfare and carnage.

In 1935, Christopher Isherwood published his take on Berlin decadence in *Mr. Norris Changes Trains*, one of the two books that would inspire the musical *Cabaret*. Robert Graves aired the dirty laundry of the Caesars for a second time in another unlikely bestseller, *Claudius the God*, while John Steinbeck made a name for himself with *Tortilla Flat*. In the 1930s, you had a wealth of movies to go to, each for a nickel—and many were far more risqué than we would expect from the era. In 1934, *Tarzan and His Mate* showed the Ape Man's lover, Jane, swimming underwater in the nude. In 1932, before Paul Muni was cast as sainted versions of Louis Pasteur and Emile Zola, he was an escaped convict in a searing indictment of southern prison laws, *I Am a Fugitive from a Chain Gang*.

Yet in the midst of all the exciting cultural changes of movies and books, most of the men shaping British foreign policy in 1935 were born in the 1870s and 1880s, and they came of age as the Empire was at its zenith. Despite the extent and sheer staggering size of geography under British control, the public life of these decision makers took place in only a few blocks of central London, in the length from Trafalgar Square to Westminster Hall. It's not difficult to see how, in high-ceilinged rooms with wingback leather chairs and gilt frames, complacency set in.

Ramsay MacDonald, the pacifist who once fought hard to keep Britain out of the Great War, led the coalition government. He was now prime minister only in name, and was widely considered to be senile. Winston Churchill thought he belonged in a rest home. The figure really manning the controls was Stanley Baldwin, who would take over as PM in a few months. Baldwin was the son of an industrialist and had been a successful lawyer in private life, but his meager gifts didn't equal his own craving for power. Nicknamed "Dear Vicar" by his Tory female admirers, he wanted "peace at any price."[3]

Many other Britons also wanted peace. In 1933, the Oxford Union debated the resolution "that this House will in no circumstances fight for its King and Country." It passed 275 to 153. But refusing to fight for king and country didn't imply that Britons wouldn't fight for ideals. And as 1934 had come to a close, a revealing legislative step had been taken in the British Parliament. The Foreign Enlistment Act already made it illegal for a British citizen to enlist in a foreign army, but anyone could reasonably wonder: how do you enforce *that?* So an Order in Council was introduced to make sure a Briton couldn't act on his conscience for Ethiopia.

Then in February 1935, as Ethiopia climbed higher on the front pages of newspapers around the world, there were voting surges in Great Britain for an interesting national referendum. The poll was conducted by the League of Nations Union, a peace lobby run out of offices in London's Grosvenor Crescent. While it started out with the ponderous title, "National Declaration on the League of Nations and Armaments," it soon came to be known as the Peace Ballot. There were only five questions asked, the first one being, "Should Great Britain remain a Member of the League of Nations?" But from the beginning of the year all the way to June when the results were announced, conservatives and liberals would debate its wording and its intent. The last question particularly caught the public's attention:

> Do you consider that, if a nation insists on attacking another, the
> other nations should combine to compel it to stop by
> (a) economic and non-military measures?
> (b) if necessary, military measures?[4]

Everyone, right-wingers *and* peace advocates, now interpreted this as meaning Ethiopia.

* * *

Tekle Hawaryat Tekle Mariyam submitted a fresh appeal to the League of Nations on March 17 in a letter addressed to Secretary-General Joseph Avenol. The Italians, argued Tekle Hawaryat, were not engaging in the spirit of "real negotiations." But his thunder was stolen by Germany. The day before, Hitler had reintroduced compulsory military service, hoping to bulk up the *Wehrmacht* by more than half a million men. It was a clear violation of the Versailles Treaty. Britain fired off a protest, but then undermined its own effort. It cravenly asked the German government if it still wanted London's representatives to come visit for scheduled talks in late March.

The answer was yes, and why not? Hitler, who once called the Reichstag (before it burned down) a "talking shop," knew the reassurances he would offer would be completely worthless. He looked on with amusement as Britain, France, and Italy contradicted each other, trying to respond to his game. France didn't like how Britain acted alone without consulting it. Mussolini stressed the threat of Hitler gobbling up Austria and reminded Britain and France of collective security talks coming up in its country.

Meanwhile, Anthony Eden was stuck defending the inconsistencies of his government. It was all well and good for the Labour Party and Opposition Liberals to talk of disarmament. He saw a wolf that wouldn't be run off with harsh words. At a speech in Swindon, he compared membership in the League to belonging to a fire brigade: "Would you be wise to rely upon it exclusively in an emergency if some of the members had already given notice that they would not come to play their part when sent for?"[5] Eden went on a juggernaut tour of Europe to keep the house from burning down. There were talks in Paris with Pierre Laval, who, with his signature mischief, claimed that Stanley Baldwin had confided to him that Eden was to become foreign secretary. Eden knew better; this "was not like him [Baldwin]."[6] But he might have wondered by then why he didn't have the job. John Simon didn't seem very interested in it. In Berlin, Eden and Simon both fenced with Hitler, who was "fertile in excuses,"[7] and as events demonstrated later, lied through his teeth about his interests in Austria and Czechoslovakia.

After a visit to Poland, the weather was so terrible with snow flurries and high winds that his plane suffered severe turbulence. After it put down, it was clear Eden had suffered a mild heart attack. Hitler actually offered him the use of his private plane to get him home, but in the end, doctor's orders put him on a train. When he did finally manage to get home, the king arranged for his own heart specialist to look after Eden, and it was decided that the young, overworked diplomat needed six weeks' bed rest.

So the one diplomat who could have put his foot down at a crucial turn wasn't on the stage when the moment came. And that moment was coming in April, in a small resort town in Italy called Stresa, where an international conference was to be held.

* * *

The viewpoint on the Ethiopia Crisis in mainstream newspapers naturally depended on what you read. Those who bought the *Evening Standard* on February 13, for instance, were told that Ethiopia was "still a barbarous country." The writer was Evelyn Waugh. "In the matter of abstract justice, the Italians have as much right to govern; in the matter of practical politics, it is certain that their government would be for the benefit of the Ethiopian Empire and for the rest of Africa."[8]

Like today's conflicts that prompt invasions of TV crews, the Ethiopia Crisis was now big enough that reporters and special correspondents made the long, arduous voyage to the Horn of Africa. One of the best and most perceptive of them was the Hungarian journalist Ladislas Farago, who was working at the time for a Berlin newspaper. In March, Haile Selassie granted his request for a personal interview, and after a drive up to the palace, the reporter was ushered into the Emperor's study and allowed to wait. Through the windows, he spotted General Eric Virgin and other Swedish officers drilling Ethiopian troops. As for the Emperor, he was strolling pensively in the garden with a couple of lion cubs. Farago thought of Haile Selassie as an African Don Quixote, fighting a triple threat of the church, petty nobles, and the Italians. For this interview, the Emperor chose first to give his answers in Amharic, but he soon switched to French and waved away his interpreter.

At one point, Farago asked Haile Selassie what he thought would guarantee peace, not only for Europe, but Africa as well (he was sure that Africa wasn't as advanced as the Emperor imagined, even though Farago had only been on its soil for a matter of weeks). Haile Selassie's answer shocked the journalist so much he reminded readers that he was quoting the Emperor verbatim. He may not have realized it, but in the response, he was hearing one of the earliest expressions of Pan-Africanism.

"If the European powers were to renounce their political and economic interests in Africa," promised the Emperor, "the half-independent native peoples would enact modern laws that would eventually make them independent and responsible members of the League of Nations. Then peaceful cooperation would be possible in Africa. The League of Nations has the necessary organization for guaranteeing safety and for supplying help to the member states."[9]

While Farago was being surprised by African self-determination, a competitor was out getting an alternative view. Geoffrey Harmsworth was another special correspondent to East Africa, but he was working for London's *Daily Mail*, and his first stop was Massawa, Eritrea's capital. Despite being the nephew of *Mail* founder Lord Northcliffe and a product of the privileged Harrow school, he seemed to want to make it on his own. He once felled logs in Newfoundland and served as the ghostwriter on a tell-all autobiography that landed his actress client in a couple of libel actions. But Harmsworth wasn't "roughing it" in Africa—not many foreign correspondents travel with a valet.

Harmsworth spent several bored days in Asmara, passing by the Government House that "looked like a small and rather dowdy colonial cousin of Buckingham

Palace, guarded by two native sentries in their scarlet tunics."[10] While he waited in vain for an interview with General De Bono, he noticed the endless convoy of loud trucks along the Corso del Re; planes droned above the city day and night, which seemed at least to impress the locals.[11] Finally, Harmsworth moved on to Aden. He had just left the telegraph office, having sent off a dispatch to his editor, when he spotted a familiar face on the quay, a tall man sporting a sombrero. It was George Bernard Shaw; playwright, contrarian, fervent Socialist. Harmsworth had met him once before. Shaw chatted amiably with him and then asked what he was doing in Asmara.

"Looking for a war," answered Harmsworth. Either he didn't ask, or Shaw didn't volunteer what *he* was doing there.

"You're a bit too soon," Shaw told the young reporter. "But it's bound to come. Mussolini means blood. Don't forget if it is white versus black, we shall have to come in with the Italians."[12]

* * *

Stresa sits on one of the Borromeo Islands off the western shore of Lake Maggiore. With snow still on the mountains, April was the off-season for the sleepy town, but the streets were decorated with flowers and flags.

American reporter David Darrah made sure he got in the day before the conference. He was used to traveling Italy and sharing it with the sycophantic national press, but now an army of new press arrivals descended on Stresa. It was a media circus that resembled those of modern day. The pressmen booked rooms in one of the large hotels that faced the lake, while diplomats stayed at another. The Duce himself was to stay in the Villa Borromeo, a medieval castle on Isola Bella, a small island in the lake about a five-minute rowing trip from the shore.

Outnumbering all the foreign delegations and newspapermen was an army of police. Darrah estimated about twelve hundred special plain-clothes operatives, a hundred motorcycle cops, and even airplane police "watching the skies to prevent any anti-Fascist planes from coming down over the lake by way of Switzerland to scatter pamphlets from the sky."[13] Blackshirt squads patrolled while police were dispatched at hundred-yard intervals along the railway tracks from Stresa to the end of the Simplon Tunnel. On April 11, a hydroplane dramatically flew onto the lake near the island, and Mussolini arrived with his son-in-law, Count Galeazzo Ciano, and his Foreign Affairs minister, Fulvio Suvich. Except for greeting his diplomatic visitors and attending the banquets at the officials' hotel, the Duce stayed bunkered within the Villa as the hordes of reporters lay a quiet siege, staring pointlessly through their binoculars at the castle. Mussolini stayed in a room once occupied by Napoleon.

The conference was to last four days. Press briefings were held twice a day with handouts that offered little information, and Darrah and his colleagues were left to interpret what little they knew was going on. They flitted from one delegation to another to collect viewpoints. "First we would listen to what Sir William McClure had to say then rush to M. Commert's conference on the French viewpoint; finally to hear Signor Grazzi read what the Italians had to announce about the day's negotiations. It was very much like hurrying from one class to another."[14]

The real story, however, wasn't going on at the negotiating table in the villa's music room, but in a suite at the Borromeo Hotel. While Ethiopia was never on the official agenda, the Italians had suggested to the British that they bring along their Africa expert, Geoffrey Thompson—who was then given strict instructions from the Foreign Office not to talk about Ethiopia's quarrel with Italy. In fact, if he was going to talk at all, it could only be with Italy's representative, Giovanni Guarnaschelli. So on the day that Mussolini flew in, Thompson met with Guarnaschelli and Leonardo Vitetti from the Italian embassy in London. Thompson was concerned about widespread rumors of a possible invasion of Ethiopia by September. He was looking for reassurances that it wouldn't happen. Instead, he was bluntly told that the "possibility of an offensive could not be entirely dismissed."[15]

Up until that moment, Thompson had been getting what he called "constant lip service" over the desire for a peaceful settlement, but now Guarnaschelli was almost blasé in laying out Italy's intentions. He rattled off a list of grievances and threats: "The Ethiopian question would *not* be settled by Conciliations Commissions [original italics]; at the same time, the necessity for a settlement was daily becoming more urgent." The Ethiopians were backward, they had slavery, they had no development—they couldn't resist the march of progress. Italy had been denied "opportunities for constructive labor" with desert areas and arid coastlines. "Something would have to be done to remedy this situation, and he could only see one way of doing it, either sooner or later."[16]

If he wanted to put a scare into Thompson, he succeeded, and the Englishman frankly told him that his comments were disturbing. He could also forget about any cooperation from Britain over a war. Thompson was overstepping his authority here, since he didn't make policy, only advised on it. But he felt compelled to inform Guarnaschelli that moving against Ethiopia was not only "extremely dangerous" and "inordinately expensive in blood and money," but it didn't bode well for relations with Great Britain. What's more, Thompson informed him, Britain "had a very vocal and humanitarian element in our public opinion who would not conceal their feelings." Guarnaschelli poked a big hole in this argument. Public opinion, he pointed out, hadn't done a thing to prevent the British government from letting Japan have its way with propping up a new vassal state in Manchuria.[17]

With nothing settled out of the argument, Guarnaschelli suggested that Ethiopia might be brought up during the official talks—*might*.

Thompson, thoroughly rattled, went off to report to Sir Robert Vansittart, the Permanent Undersecretary of the Foreign Office, who said he would talk to Fulvio Suvich. That left Ethiopia a subject only for backroom parlay, but Thompson was told to warn Guarnaschelli again about a military incursion, and this time that it could lead to "grave complications"—whatever those were.

Vansittart wasn't a politician; he was a career civil servant, a career that stretched back close to the start of the twentieth century, when he began working in the Foreign Office as a humble clerk at the age of twenty-one. Now he was distinguished and respected and relied upon for his advice, and while his job lifted him, in theory, above the partisan ebbs and flows of politics, he had strong views of his own. He was particularly suspicious of Hitler, but he didn't trust the Germans no matter who was in charge. When it became clear that the Fuehrer was going to be trouble, Vansittart would suggest buying Hitler off with African colonies. Later, when London was shoveling its rubble from the Blitz, he came out with a book that suggested they had been militaristic since the days of Huns fighting Romans.

The next afternoon, after Thompson had another tense talk with Guarnaschelli, Vansittart made him put it all down in a memo. What Vansittart was doing to resolve the issue remains a mystery. If he had spoken to Suvich as he'd indicated, Ethiopia still wasn't on the official agenda. It was beginning to look like Thompson was the only British diplomat near Lake Maggiore who gave a damn about the issue. Then there was a glimmer of encouragement. John Simon sent a message that he wanted to have breakfast with him the next morning. Surely, Simon must want to be briefed before he took the matter of Ethiopia to the conference table.

So at eight o'clock sharp the next morning, a hopeful Thompson sat down at the table in Sir John Simon's hotel suite. Five minutes later, as he sat listening to his top boss make an opening comment on his memo, Simon's chief private secretary breezed in and made a remark that Thompson couldn't hear. Now the foreign secretary and his aide were in a hushed conversation, and Thompson only knew that it couldn't be about Ethiopia. He went on eating his breakfast, and a half hour later, Simon told him he had to get ready for the latest negotiations. "It was indeed a sad anti-climax," Thompson wrote of the meeting later. ". . . From the moment that I had left the Secretary of State's suite after my unrewarding breakfast, I had no work of any kind."[18]

*   *   *

An old veteran by now at covering foreign affairs, David Darrah picked up early on the alliances that had formed. "It was evident that the Italians and French were working together."[19] While Farago and Harmsworth were still waiting for war in East Africa, Darrah and others now waited for an announcement over how to avoid it.

On the very last afternoon of the conference, April 14, in the Hall of Medals at the Borromeo Villa, the negotiators were wrapping up their agreement. Mussolini, as host of the talks, read out the joint communiqué to be issued. It included the key sentence: "The three Powers, the object of whose policy is the collective maintenance of peace within the framework of the League of Nations, find themselves in complete agreement in opposing, by all practicable means, any unilateral repudiation of treaties which may endanger the peace and will act in close and cordial collaboration for this purpose."

Mussolini paused at this, looked down both sides of the table and suggested, "Let us say, 'which may endanger the peace of *Europe*.'"

No one else said anything.

Mussolini prompted them once more. Shouldn't the agreement read "of Europe?"

France's Prime Minister Pierre Étienne Flandin expected the British would speak up now over Ethiopia. "But neither Mr. MacDonald nor Sir John Simon moved a muscle. M. Laval and I, and without doubt Mussolini as well, had the impression of a tacit acquiescence given by the British government to the Italian ambitions in Ethiopia."[20] Flandin, of course, could have cleared his throat and offered a few well-chosen words, but didn't. As for the British, Robert Vansittart turned to Ramsey MacDonald and muttered the obvious: the phrasing left a gigantic loophole for Mussolini's tanks to roll through East Africa. MacDonald wasn't interested.

"Don't be tiresome, Van," he replied. "We don't want any trouble. What we want is an agreement that we can put before the House of Commons."[21]

This remark gives the impression that MacDonald was lucid at Stresa, and perhaps he had his moments. But Mussolini apparently called him "an old dotard" behind his back, while during one of the main talks, an interpreter found MacDonald so incoherent he couldn't pass on a sensible translation.[22] Whatever the circumstances of the PM's mental state, the British weren't objecting. The

French weren't objecting. The silence lengthened in the room, and the communiqué was issued with Mussolini's revision.

Then representatives of the three powers faced the press, declaring triumph. "I'm glad this conference is over," MacDonald told reporters.[23] The *Manchester Guardian's* correspondent, Alexander Werth, asked him if there had been any discussion of Ethiopia. MacDonald was dismissive. "My friend, your question is irrelevant."[24]

The rest of Europe was already treating rumors about the desert tradeoff by Pierre Laval as a confirmed fact. But even Suvich later pointed to Britain as more culpable than France in allowing his country's African ambitions. David Darrah was inclined to give them the benefit of the doubt. "The British had gone to Stresa with the hope of bringing about a discussion, possibly an understanding, over the Ethiopian war question, and Mussolini's pending assault on the King of Kings . . . But Mussolini refused to be drawn into talks about his war in East Africa. He avoided British suggestions that it would be a good time to settle this problem, too. He did not really think that he had to count on British opposition to his pending campaign. He felt secure in his new French friendship."[25]

This wasn't a judgment of decades later; Darrah's indictment of the French was published a little over a year after the Stresa conference, and had he known all the facts and been inside the room, he would have likely revised his lenient verdict of the British. But what was clear to him and many others was that the Great Powers were failing to prevent Italy's steady momentum.

It was very clear to a troubled Geoffrey Thompson, who went home to London and decided to consult a friend, Hastings "Pug" Ismay. Ismay had worked his way up from being a cavalry officer in India to handling intelligence at the War Office; he was a few years away from being one of Winston Churchill's inner circle of advisers, and after the Second World War was over, the first Secretary-General of NATO. Thompson rang up Ismay for one of their regular lunches at the Travellers Club in Pall Mall.

The young diplomat asked the wise Pug a hypothetical question: if there was an invasion, could the Italians take Addis Ababa? Ismay was confident they could, especially with their modern machine guns and planes and "perhaps gas as well." Thompson went back to work at the Foreign Office, mulling the scenario over. He also wondered about the safety of the British legation in Addis Ababa, with its modest guard of cavalrymen. "Should the guard be strengthened, and if so, to what extent?"[26] Better to go with an increase, for safety's sake.

He knew his suggestion would probably be criticized or tossed out if he made it himself. The idea, he realized, would have to come from Barton. Thompson went so far as to send him a ciphered telegram, which was to have "no distribution, no copies."[27] Barton had probably come to the same conclusion about security. In early April, he'd heard from a British businessman who saw firsthand the preparations for war during a five-week stay in Mogadishu. "They are pouring troops into the country in thousands. Whilst I was there, twelve thousand Italian troops arrived, to say nothing of guns and tanks."[28]

The unidentified businessman had the chance to have dinner a couple of times at a friend's house with Roberto Cimmaruta, the captain at Walwal, whom he found to be "a very decent chap." Cimmaruta showed the dinner guests a telegram of congratulations from Mussolini. A captain in the Ogaden, he had now been "promoted on the field" to major—presumably for services rendered at Walwal.

So a formal request was made for a fully armed and equipped infantry company for the British legation. Whoever deserved the credit for asking, whether Thompson, Barton, or both, it was a decision that would turn out to save almost two thousand lives—*before* any Italian guns were even pointed in the embassy's direction.

Then Ethiopia gained an unusual ally, one that must have surprised the civil servants in Whitehall and the Tory politicians in the House of Commons—all except Geoffrey Thompson, who had predicted it. A growing portion of the British public didn't like what was happening to the African nation.

Was it so strange that English people in Nottingham, or Scots in Edinburgh, should sympathize with the Ethiopians? With every report on Italy's soldiers being mobilized, the point was sinking in that Haile Selassie's kingdom was the underdog. Voters in Britain had never liked a bully. And in recent years, they had been forced to recognize that their own government could be the bully. Mohandas Gandhi had come on a visit to Britain in 1931, dressed in his humble white loincloth and robe, and he had charmed textile workers in the north and cockneys in London. While the government still didn't want to let India go, many across Britain were now wondering why not.

Then there was the quiet charisma of Haile Selassie himself, which did a lot to persuade many Britons that he could govern Ethiopia quite well without Italian interference. Meanwhile, votes were still being taken for the so-called Peace Ballot.

* * *

When 1935 began, the burning issue for African Americans wasn't distant Ethiopia, but how to make the winter less bleak in the middle of the Depression. But in a year of pervasive despair, of still too many job lines, it shouldn't have surprised anyone that blacks became more politically active.

Harlem was undeniably the capital of black culture, the place where African-American sympathy for Ethiopia's plight would raise its voice the loudest. Seventh Avenue was the boulevard to be strolling and to be seen on a Sunday, with the poor and better-off alike sharing the promenade, from women in dresses lined with fur to hired maids wearing their employers' hand-me-downs. But even here, blacks couldn't get away from the prejudice of the times. The impressive Theresa Hotel on Seventh Avenue, as stately as the Waldorf, wouldn't admit them. White shopkeepers would take a black man's money for groceries, but they wouldn't think of hiring him to work behind the counter. When the law arrived, it came in a blue uniform, and its face was invariably white. Harlem was only a refuge because of one comfort—this was where your own kind lived in greater numbers. Sure, whites may like Duke Ellington and Count Basie, but the movies still had Bing Crosby performing a number in black face, and the biggest comedy show on radio was *Amos 'n' Andy*—two white men playing Negro tradesmen as buffoons.

For white Americans hit hard by the Depression, their political awareness would be channeled into militant trade unions and parties with socialist ideals. But trade unions were often closed to blacks. Many African Americans considered it pointless to even bother with these options. Why should they? The mainstream had shown them time and again that it didn't want them. It was natural, then, that their hopes would turn to another country, a very different country, one with an African face.

The cultural connection had always been there, for those who bothered to look. Right in the Book of Psalms, you could find the prophecy, "Princes shall come out of Egypt, and Ethiopia shall soon stretch forth her hands unto God." Wasn't Ethiopia a Christian country with a sophisticated heritage? One that could supposedly trace its lineage back to Solomon and the Queen of Sheba? From Frederick Douglass right through to Marcus Garvey, activists and intellectuals knew Ethiopia meant something to black Americans.

The irony was that Ethiopians at this time knew next to nothing about blacks in the United States. African Americans would probably be shocked if they heard the comments Menelik gave to a Caribbean activist who made the long journey to Addis Ababa. Benito Sylvain wanted to get the Emperor's support for a new society for blacks, but Menelik—the leader who once reminded Dervishes that they were all black—had told him, "I wish you the greatest possible success. But in coming to me to take the leadership, you are knocking at the wrong door, so to speak . . . I am not a Negro at all: I am a Caucasian."[29]

But now Ethiopia was in trouble. The NAACP mailed off strongly worded letters to the State Department and to Geneva, and it talked over the idea of sending a delegation to Washington to meet personally with Franklin Roosevelt and Secretary of State Cordell Hull. In the end, the details never gelled. The NAACP and its affiliates, already the staid black establishment, accomplished a startlingly effective imitation of the lame-duck League of Nations. Other groups, however, were about to step forward with more radical notions to help. Ethiopia, they reasoned, needed guns. It needed men, soldiers. And these new groups were determined to offer them. If Ethiopia needed an army, there were African Americans ready to serve.

And sympathy for Ethiopia was already reaching the youngest of black citizens. One ten-year-old boy growing up on Fifth Avenue above 130th Street sat in a darkened movie theater and watched Haile Selassie. This was a revelation for the boy—a *black* emperor. The monarch, he recalled years later, "was pleading vainly with the West to prevent the rape of his country. And the extraordinary complex of tensions thus set up in the breast, between hatred of whites and contempt for blacks, is very hard to describe. Some of the most energetic people of my generation were destroyed by this interior warfare."[30]

In those newsreels, Italian tanks were contrasted with African soldiers on horseback and men with pitiful spears. The boy in the audience was James Baldwin.

* * *

One African American had already decided to go and serve. His name was John Charles Robinson, a man with a handsome round face who sported a pencil-thin mustache and who appeared in photographs as if always ready to smile. The press would dub him "The Brown Condor."

Robinson was born in Carabelle, Florida, in 1903, and his mother and stepfather soon moved the family to Gulfport, Mississippi. For some children, there are moments that define their lives when a career or personal passion comes into focus. Maybe the moment for young Johnny Robinson was when he spotted a Navy flying boat in 1916, a rare sight that he talked about for days.[31] Flight was a new technological miracle; it was a glamorous and gentlemanly pursuit. With the good common sense of a child, it hadn't occurred to John that his skin color would have anything to do with technical skill.

Robinson showed aptitude as a mechanic, and his parents enrolled him in one of the best and most prestigious educational centers for African Americans, the Tuskegee Normal and Industrial Institute—later Tuskegee University— in Alabama. According to a profile on him later by the *Tuskegee Messenger*, Robinson, a major in automotive mechanics, was so "quiet and retiring that few except his teachers . . . knew of his presence on the grounds."[32] At eighteen, the fresh graduate ended up in Chicago, where he eventually opened an auto repair shop, but he never forgot the potential of the skies. This meant overcoming those who wanted to keep him down. The director of the Curtiss-Wright Aeronautics University in Chicago, Anson Charbuck, took one look at Robinson and told him that other students wouldn't tolerate a Negro in their ranks.[33]

Robinson had an ingenious strategy around this. He got a job at the university as a porter, and when he wasn't performing his menial duties, he was able to fiddle with engines, talk to students, and even help them with their schoolwork. The university couldn't help but be impressed, and Robinson would be not only its first black student, but also one of its instructors. He's credited with opening the door for twenty-five more black men and women to gain enrollment at Curtiss-Wright. When local air fields barred them from flying, Robinson and others personally financed a private airport to be built in the all-black town of Robbins near Chicago—the first accredited airfield owned and operated by African Americans. He also formed his own flying school. With his close friend, Cornelius Coffey, he founded the Challengers Air Pilots' Association for black Americans who wanted to fly. His achievements made him in demand as a speaker, and at a meeting in 1934 sponsored by the Associated Negro Press, he had a chance encounter with just the right Ethiopian at the right moment to plant a new inspiration.

This was Malaku Bayen, a distant relative of the Emperor. He was an interesting young son of the century, born in 1900. A man with a slightly oval face and pensive eyes who sported a mustache, he was a true believer in Pan-Africanism, and he didn't need ideology to tell him it was a good idea. While studying in India, a teacher had pompously declared in front of him that it was inevitable the British Empire would one day include Ethiopia. Malaku soon decided that "America was the only country that would never try to rob us of our country."[34] In the United States, he wanted to be among people of his own race, so he studied medicine at Howard, and he believed what he preached about black solidarity. He even broke off his engagement with the daughter of Ethiopia's Foreign Affairs minister to wed an African-American woman.[35] Besides his medical studies, he was serving as a kind of talent scout for Haile Selassie, hoping to win over specialists and technicians badly needed back home. Now the priority wasn't development, it was defense.

He and John Robinson had lost touch, but after Walwal, Claude Barnett, the founder of the Associated Negro Press in Chicago, helped them reconnect.[36] Robinson went to Washington, D.C., to meet Malaku, who found the pilot to be a modest, self-effacing young man with impeccable credentials. It impressed the Ethiopians immensely that Robinson could not only fly, but like a 1930s black "MacGyver," could build an airplane from the ground up with what was available to him.

In April, Robinson got a telegram from Emperor Haile Selassie, offering an officer's commission in his army. Robinson, Malaku, and Haile Selassie all knew they were breaking American laws with this arrangement, so a cover story was needed. A combat pilot? Of course not. He was just going over for business, to sell civilian aircraft to the Ethiopians.[37] It was a rather transparent fiction, but it did the trick. The Brown Condor would be flying over Africa.

* * *

As Johnny Robinson packed his bags and prepared to leave, the haggling went on in Europe. It had been all through May. Italy had picked its two arbitrators for the dispute and then objected to Ethiopia's choices—on the logic that they weren't Ethiopian. Haile Selassie's government had selected two professors, one French and one American, as impartial judges of an "equitable and speedy outcome." Meanwhile, British Labour MPs had come up with a clever—and, in hindsight, rather obvious—solution to keeping Italy in line.

Why not simply close the Suez Canal?

The idea haunted Mussolini enough that he wrote to General De Bono in Eritrea: "You must make sure beforehand of victuals and munitions for at least three years, and also, however absurd it seems, because there are formal conventions in existence relating to the passage of the Suez Canal in peace and war, one must expect difficulties in respect of its passage."[38]

British Labour MPs would keep on raising the issue, and the coalition government, trying to dampen criticism, took the step of at least banning arms exports to *both* sides, Italy and Ethiopia. All this did, however, was punish Ethiopia, since Mussolini's preparations had been in high gear for months.

Talks between Foreign Secretary John Simon and Italy's ambassador to London, Dino Grandi, were still going nowhere, and as Anthony Eden recovered from his heart attack, he grew ever more disillusioned with his boss and his team. But having returned to Geneva on May 19, he couldn't claim any better results than Simon. Over a dinner that night with Pompeo Aloisi, the baron told him flatly that his Duce had 600 million lire, and he wasn't about to change his mind just because the League of Nations asked him to. "More than a colony was at stake for Italy," he told Eden in so many words. "There was the whole prestige of the regime." The defeat at Adwa "must be washed out in blood." It was unfortunate, he said, that the whole matter hadn't been raised at Stresa.[39]

Britain's man in Rome, Drummond, reported that a meeting with Mussolini "could not have been of a more disquieting nature," which is a beautiful example of British understatement. It sounds very much like the dictator subjected him to one of his famous tantrums. The League Council, fumed the Duce, was only supposed to note Italy's nominations for the conciliation commission and wish it success! *That* was supposed to be the limit of its participation, he argued. In other words, stay out.

Drummond replied gently that if the dictator forced Britain to choose between friendship with Italy and support for the League, Britain might well choose the League. Mussolini already had a fall-back strategy: if the League supported Ethiopia against Italy, he would abandon the League, never to return. This should have been enough for any League member to drive the message home: you threaten one of us, you threaten us all. Yet instead of giving a counter ultimatum, the British still thought in terms of offering a deal. Eden got to work on a proposal. Unfortunately, that meant working again with Pierre Laval.

Mussolini must be mad, said Laval when he arrived in Geneva. He was full of reassurances that France hadn't encouraged Italy to go through with its military campaign (Grandi, of course, backed this denial to John Simon). *"Vous avez le mains fortes,"* he claims to have told Mussolini half-jokingly.[40] For years he would keep insisting that he had told the Duce, "Henceforth you have a free hand, but a free hand in the path of peace." Nor was Laval alone in being an accomplice. During this same month, Italy's Propaganda Minister Count Galeazzo Ciano was in Paris, and as he recounted later in his diary, Pierre Étienne Flandin gave him "some advice about the best method of starting the war. He suggested stirring up a revolt of the [rases] against the Negus, which would have given us a pretext to intervene."[41]

If Eden was suspicious of French officials, he didn't have much choice but to work with them, and perhaps they weren't as complacent as everyone thought. Preparations were being made to reinforce their troops in French Somaliland.

Eden and Laval agreed on terms for a resolution to go before the Council, one that called for a time limit to be set on a deal and demanded no hostilities during the conciliation process. The next morning, May 23, the Italians responded with a counter-proposal that immediately got on Eden's nerves. The Italians wanted only Walwal to be settled *and* the Council to be excluded from the process. Worse, nothing stated that Italy could not go ahead and use force.

A long night followed in Geneva at the League of Nations, and at two-thirty in the morning, the Council unanimously voted to pass what became two draft resolutions to hold Italy in check and ensure the conciliation process went ahead. There was an acknowledgement of the right of the Council to keep tabs. Resorting to force was ruled out. There was acceptance of arbitrators already named, plus the planned naming of a fifth arbitrator—it was all there. Eden felt that this was as good as they could get on paper, and was better than the world expected.

"Perhaps," he speculated, "Mussolini was impressed by the closeness of Anglo-French accord and the strength of feeling against him in both countries over the dispute, or maybe he thought it best to accept for the present, meaning to break these new engagements also when the time came. Whatever the motive, he gave way."[42]

Mussolini gave way for the exact reason Eden offered in his memoirs—it was wonderful on paper. For *him*. There was a huge loophole in the resolutions that put his war right back on schedule for attack after the summer rains. If a fifth arbitrator was not accepted by either side by July 25, the Council would meet once more to examine the situation, and if the arbitration process didn't wrap up by August 25, the Council . . . well, the Council would have another meeting for yet another post-mortem.

By then, it wouldn't matter at all, as tanks rolled across the Eritrean border.

Chapter Four

BLUSTER

Every war has its opportunists, and it was around this time that one of the most improbable characters in black history decided to make another bid for fame and attempt to salvage his reputation. It was the pilot who had smashed Haile Selassie's prized Gypsy Moth into a eucalyptus tree at the coronation in 1930, and who had been literally run out on a rail: Hubert Julian.

Julian was a tall black man who sported a monocle, dressed in foppish suits, and twirled an ivory-handled walking stick. When he first turned up in Harlem, he liked to strut around in full aviation regalia, wearing a whipcord uniform and polished cordovan boots, even carrying a riding crop.[1] He claimed to have been a lieutenant in the Canadian air force, and on his chest was an impressive set of military decorations. People believed him and backed him financially. In 1924, he thought he would seal his place in history by making a nonstop flight from New York to Liberia. This was three years before Charles Lindbergh became a household name for landing in France, and Julian's boast of flying solo to Africa guaranteed him a lot of attention and press coverage. It would have been an achievement for any pilot, but a black pilot who made the crossing would be a legend.

So on a hot Fourth of July, about twenty-five thousand curious onlookers came down to the 139th Street pier in Harlem to see Julian take off in a Boeing seaplane he had named "Ethiopia 1." But everyone was in for a long wait. At the opening ceremony, the Black Eagle spent five hours trying to raise the five hundred dollars he still owed on the plane. When at last Ethiopia 1 took off, at five o'clock, something went wrong—a damaged pontoon was ripped away, and the plane went plummeting into a nosedive. Within seconds, it crashed into the mud flats of Flushing Bay, leaving its pilot with a broken leg.[2] It would not, of course, be Hubert Julian's last public humiliation in the air.

At this point, some Harlemites might have wondered: where did this guy come from, and where the *hell* did he learn to fly?

Hubert Fauntleroy Julian was born in Port of Spain, Trinidad, in 1897 and allegedly spent some of his formative years in London, where he acquired his British accent, which he exaggerated after he came to the States. From there, it gets murkier. He claimed he was in the Canadian air force, but there's no record of him serving. He claimed he hung around St. Hubert airdrome in Montreal in 1918, where the most famous flying ace in the world at the time, the Canadian Billy Bishop, took him on as a student. But Billy Bishop wasn't even *in* Canada for most of 1918, and the St. Hubert airdrome didn't begin operating until 1928. In an age before computerized credit checks and data records, of course, a man with the right talent and guile could often pass himself off as whatever he wanted.

He had managed to con Malaku Bayen into buying his act (to the young Ethiopian's eternal regret), and after Malaku brought him to Ethiopia, there was the coronation crash. Now Ethiopia was under the threat of invasion, and Julian figured he had another shot at glory. He somehow bluffed his way through passport control in New York, and by the time he got to Aden, he managed to talk a sum of money out of an employee of a British firm so he could sail on to Berbera in British Somaliland. When he arrived at Ethiopia's railway town of Dire Dawa, the authorities apparently put up only a minimal effort to keep him out.[3] The Black Eagle was back in Ethiopia, whether Haile Selassie wanted him there or not.

Reporter Ladislas Farago, still waiting in Addis Ababa for the outbreak of war, glimpsed Julian from time to time in the streets. The Ethiopians hadn't forgotten him, and they were astonished that he had dared to come back. Julian even still used his rank of colonel, but the Ethiopians had another name for him: *Shankala Nrs*—"Nigger Eagle."[4] When Haile Selassie's green Rolls-Royce drove through the capital, the Emperor pretended not to see him.

In about a year's time, Julian's behavior would make him one of the most hated men in both Ethiopia *and* America.

*   *   *

Ladislas Farago got the chance to meet another minor celebrity, only this time, it was an Ethiopian. Led by a servant with an oil lamp through the dark streets of the capital, the reporter had to walk an hour and a half to reach the tukul of Agegnehu Engida, a modern painter. When Haile Selassie first sent young, smart Ethiopians abroad to be educated, he also sent Agegnehu, who had impressed him with his talent, and soon the young painter found himself studying in Paris in the late 1920s at the École des Beaux-arts, right in the Saint-Germain-des-Près. Agegnehu learned the new thriving styles at the time—expressionism, abstract, surrealism—but he blended them into something that was uniqely his own and of his own people.

Farago was intrigued by the artist, and he was even more taken with Agegnehu's beautiful wife, who doubled as the artist's model (on a shamelessly bold whim, he even asked Agegnehu if he would have her disrobe, so the reporter could appreciate her aesthetically—which she did). As they talked in the modest house full of finished canvases, the painter announced that he'd been commissioned to design the new uniforms of the soldiers. He told the reporter how his people were morally prepared to fight, but worse than a shortage of arms was the lack of sympathy for the Ethiopian cause.[5] Farago felt that the painter had drifted into a tirade and asked him if he actually wanted war.

"I and my servants, like all Abyssinians, will go to war, fighting shoulder to shoulder, to the death. And mark my words, we are all going out to die. If we are hit, we are lost, for we have no doctors to bandage our wounds, or stretcher-bearers to bring the injured out of the field to the hospital. We bleed to death if we are hit, but in spite of that, not one solitary soul will be left behind!"*

At one point in their conversation, Agegnehu noted the anxiety some of his countrymen felt that Britain might even join the Italians, though they recognized that the British were more enlightened as colonial overseers and would probably help their nation's development. But a more benevolent conquest would still be intolerable to Ethiopians, who had enjoyed independence for centuries.

"Don't you think that we have enough troubles of our own without this foreign conflict?" asked Agegnehu, summing up the exasperation that many felt. "A revolution is going on behind the scenes. There is a strong group of young men who have been abroad, and have seen for themselves that the world does not stop at the Abyssinian frontier. They are planning revolution, and the Emperor is on their side. There are also others who will always be discontented, and who will make war on the Emperor as well as Italy, and hope to be rewarded by a permanent return to the 'good old times.'"[6]

Agegnehu was deeply perceptive of the shifting loyalties to the past and the future that were fighting for his country's soul, even as these two sides prepared to fight the Italians. The young men who were supposed to be the country's destiny as educated, newly sophisticated teachers, engineers, and jurists now had to become soldiers.

Farago also had a chance to see Ethiopia's defenders. Four thousand soldiers of the garrison at Addis Ababa, the pride of the imperial guard, conducted a military parade as a goodbye to one of their Belgian instructors. After a whiskey

---

* Agegnehu didn't die in battle. He survived the war and became an assistant director of the Ministry of Education's Department of Fine Arts. Two of his portrait paintings hang today in the National Museum of Ethiopia.

with the major, Farago conducted his own modest inspection of the troops, and he noticed that their caps sported genuine lion's mane fur, and their tunics were made of Japanese khaki—but most of the soldiers were barefoot. They were also young; the average age of the Ethiopian soldier was between twelve and twenty. But life expectancy in the country back then was in the forties.[7]

A military academy had been operating since January at one of the Emperor's summer residences in Holeta, about twenty-five miles outside the capital. The school was run by five Swedish military men whose leader had merely responded to an ad in a local newspaper. And their cadets made up an army mostly without arms. Their rifles were obsolete, their bullets few. Haile Selassie had purchased ammunition with his own funds, and he eventually had to impose a tax to bring in additional supplies because it was getting more difficult every day. The British and French could claim with high-mindedness that their arms embargo punished both sides, but the Italians had Massawa; the Ethiopians had to rely on Aden and Djibouti for imports.

One day, a mock battle was held with the Emperor in attendance, holding a pair of binoculars from his vantage point at the commander-in-chief's mound. For half an hour, he looked on as shots were fired and clusters of combatants stealthily moved to gain ground. Farago suspected the Emperor was bored. The display was so anticlimactic that one of the European training officers had to announce when it was over and who had won. The officer then explained patiently to Haile Selassie and his courtiers that this was modern warfare—the winner was most often the one who disguised his positions well before he pounced. But how could the Emperor and his nobles understand? The Europeans were trying to impart the lessons of the Somme, the horrors of Passchendaele and Verdun. But no Ethiopian had ever seen those distant trenches, let alone the mechanized treachery in Flanders Fields.

"War is war," scoffed one of the indignant courtiers, "and not blind man's bluff. Only cowards sneak away from the enemy." An Ethiopian, he said, fights more chivalrously, "man to man, and will never fire at his enemy from an ambush."[8]

Weeks later, the Italians were shipping containers of poison gas through Massawa.

*   *   *

It was in May that Ethiopia had its first traitor. Haile Selassie Gugsa was a man who had been simmering and stewing in his own spite for years. When his drunk of a father finally succumbed to cirrhosis in 1933, Gugsa expected to take over as governor of Tigray. He had been married to the Emperor's young daughter, Zenabe Worq, but it was rumored that he mistreated her, and she died of influenza that same year, plunging the Emperor into inconsolable grief. Haile Selassie, always shrewd and careful in his political appointments, struck a deal with Gugsa's uncle, Seyum Mangasha, who would govern Tigray and allow the Emperor to keep centralizing control of the province's financial affairs. Gugsa couldn't stand this slight. He had been passed over, and he wouldn't forget it.

Fast forward to May 11, 1935, and an imperial decree placed more territory under his control, though still not the kind of real estate his father had ruled. Gugsa wasn't mollified. While still in Addis Ababa, he went around to the Italian legation to see Count Luigi Vinci, and on May 28, he boldly visited Asmara to see the governor of Eritrea and throw in his lot with the future invaders.[9] Gugsa was eager for the Italians to go ahead now, and steamroll across the border—he even had a plan of action to recommend to them. They could swarm down to Korem in Tigray. If the invasion had to wait until October, he would attack Adwa himself, to slaughter his hated rival, Ras Seyum. By his own reckoning, he could provide the Italians with thirty thousand men (but only half would be armed with rifles) and fourteen machine guns. He also offered his personal assessments of other commanders and their troop strengths.

The Italians gave Gugsa a bribe of a million lire and told him to sit tight. In his memoir on the campaign, Emilio De Bono wrote that Gugsa had sent him letters, complaining about his lack of recognition from Haile Selassie "and asking me for instructions as to his mode of conduct."[10] De Bono didn't consider Gugsa to be very smart, and knew he was a pawn to keep in reserve for the time being. "We were still too far from the moment when action would be possible . . . hence I had to discourage any impulsive act, any premature move, which would have broken the egg before we were ready to make the omelet."[11]

Gugsa was told to "keep quiet," to play along and look obedient. The general would have instructions for him later.

De Bono could take this casual course of action because he never had to rely on Gugsa alone. Since February, Italian forces had been busy elsewhere in Ethiopia. Agents and operatives had been cozying up to chiefs in different regions and building modest networks of informers. An explorer and rich baron, Raimondo Franchetti, had proved particularly useful in forming alliances with the Danakil, but he would die in an airplane crash over the Egyptian desert later that year.[12]

Months later, in September, the Crown Prince's tutor at Dessie rushed to Addis Ababa to let the Emperor know of Gugsa's betrayal. Here was proof! He'd brought along copies of bank receipts. But Haile Selassie was unconvinced. "Most of my rases take money from the Italians," he said. "It is bribery without corruption. They pocket Italian money and remain steadfast to Ethiopia."[13] It had been this way for ages, after all; even Menelik had taken weapons from the Italians. The Emperor fully expected Gugsa to be on his side when war broke out.

* * *

In London, Stanley Baldwin was ready to take over as prime minister of the National Coalition government from Ramsay MacDonald. Historian William Manchester once called the short, stocky, pipe-smoking Baldwin an evangelist of political mediocrity and wrote, "If Churchill's symbol is the hand forming the *V* for victory, Baldwin's was the wetted forefinger held up to test the wind."[14] Baldwin's first step was naturally a Cabinet shuffle. And Anthony Eden, coming back to London on May 26, had every reason to believe his star would rise higher. The latest headlines over the League of Nations had made him popular at home, and he seemed to be a shoo-in for foreign secretary.

There was already a lobby campaign at the Foreign Office for him to replace John Simon, and Eden himself spoke to Baldwin in mid-May about his own ambitions. He could understand if Baldwin thought he was too young, so he was willing to work in another department. What he *didn't* want was to keep serving at the Foreign Office under somebody else. This, he told Baldwin, wasn't a matter of pride—he didn't think he'd be useful as second fiddle when his views on foreign policy were widely known by the British public and foreigners.

Baldwin kept him cooling his heels for days. Then after Question Period in the Commons on June 5, Baldwin tapped him on the shoulder and said, "Come to my room, please, after this." Eden obediently followed him out of the House behind the Speaker's Chair into the Lord President's room. Before the door was even closed, Baldwin announced, "Sam is to go to the Foreign Office and I want you to stay on and help him there."

"Sam" was Sir Samuel Hoare.

Eden, bitterly disappointed, pointed out that this was exactly the situation he had asked not to be placed in. Baldwin claimed that conditions were so difficult and the workload so heavy that he'd decided the Foreign Office needed two men. Eden would get the special title of Minister for League of Nations Affairs while Samuel Hoare would mind general foreign affairs.

League affairs *are* foreign affairs, Eden argued. It would be impossible to separate them. It wouldn't work. The danger of conflicts was obvious.

The new prime minister, ignoring every objection, told Eden to go see Hoare to talk it over. "Sam is most anxious to have your help." Baldwin considered Eden unreasonable and even ungrateful. "After all, it isn't everyone who has the chance to be in the Cabinet before he is thirty-eight."[15]

Eden didn't learn until later how close he was to actually getting the job. Baldwin had chosen him, but he had been talked out of it by Neville Chamberlain, who had nothing against Eden at the time except his youth, and Geoffrey Dawson, a close friend of Baldwin's and the conservative editor of *The Times*. Both men backed Hoare. Wounded professional ego aside, Eden pegged Baldwin correctly when he wrote later: ". . . The uncertainty he felt on international questions encouraged him to accept excuses for not facing unpleasant facts."[16] The appointment, as Eden saw it, was another compromise.

And Samuel Hoare was another tired old man whose formative years had been in the last century. It was assumed he was qualified for the job because he managed to navigate the Government of India bill around the obstinate, arch-imperialist bulk of a defiant Winston Churchill. Work on the legislation had taken its toll on Hoare, who at one point was laid up for several days after collapsing from the strain. "Hitler had appeared on the scene when I was thinking of Gandhi," he confessed in his memoirs. From the Ethiopian perspective, he was a disaster. Even twenty years after Walwal, Hoare was so careless of the facts that he claimed in his memoirs that the wells were "situated in what had been recognized in fact as a part of the Italian colony" of Somaliland.[17]

Meanwhile, Eden was trying his best to defend government policy in the House of Commons. "It is alleged we have encouraged the Ethiopian Government for our own end to adopt a hostile attitude toward Italy," he told the House on June 7. "The story is as mischievously absurd as the suggestion that our colonial football fields are aerodromes in disguise."[18]

Spearheading the attack that day was Deputy Labour Party leader Clement Attlee, who demanded the government make a clear statement to Italy. "We want to tell Signor Mussolini that this government, like other governments, upholds the Covenant against an aggressor state, that it believes it a matter that affects our honor and our vital interests . . ."

This was a reversal for Attlee and Labour. Everyone in the House knew him as the champion of disarmament who had criticized "nationalist and imperialist delusions." Now he was actually calling for Britain to defend the League Covenant by force if necessary. Moreover, if Italy was intent on its war, said Attlee, it "ought to be told frankly that in that event that she would not have the use of the Suez Canal."

Anthony Eden found himself ironically defending the man he knew in his heart couldn't be trusted. Mussolini, he replied, had accepted Article 5 of the Treaty of 1928, which banned use of force. "It is a cardinal principle of British law that a man is innocent until proven guilty."

The Suez Canal would stay open.

* * *

The *Chicago Tribune's* man in Rome, David Darrah, was doing his best that summer to outfox the Italian censors. He seemed to have a fairly reliable barometer on how far he could try their patience, but he was about to seriously miscalculate.

Chicago wanted to know economic conditions in Italy and why there was no political terrorism in response to the war. Darrah had studied the financial part, "which was not difficult," and as far as the terrorism angle went, well, that was nonexistent. He didn't have to imagine, as Orwell would put it later, a big boot stamping on a human face—Italy's repressive police measures were well known. So he sat down at the typewriter in his office in the Piazza Colonna and tapped out his lead. "Economic experts declare that Fascist Italy's financial position, which already gave cause for anxiety, is becoming increasingly untenable, with the budget, in deficit now for five successive years, aggravated by the costs of Mussolini's East African military expedition."[19] In his assertion, Darrah was on solid ground. The Fascist government had been surprisingly candid over its own failure to economically perform, and Darrah was armed with a full report on finances that Finance Minister Thaon di Rival had made to the Chamber of Deputies in May.

Darrah then wrote up a second article, an analysis of public opinion towards the war. He zeroed in on Sardinia, where Fascist sympathy was low and there were reports of resistance to mobilization. Mussolini himself had flown over to tour the island and to address Sardinians in the Carlo Felice Square of Cagliari. With complete faith that he was reporting the factual truth, Darrah typed out his piece at around five o'clock in the afternoon on June 8, and after a dinner party at his house, phoned in his dispatch to London. He expected grumbling from the Propaganda Office, but no significant complaint, and went off that Sunday with his wife to enjoy the glorious sunshine of the Ostia beach.

In retrospect, he was naïve about government reaction, but for seven years he'd been able to convey an accurate picture of what was happening inside the Fascist regime. True, there was surveillance. Sometimes there were dispatches that got conveniently lost, with the reporter being told the most ridiculous excuses, such as the time when his copy allegedly got "caught in pneumatic tubes." But this was the job. If you cooperated with authorities or let yourself be intimidated, you were worthless as a foreign correspondent.

"Why should American readers be led to believe that Italy was taking Mussolini's military expedition as a carefree, gay, and reckless adventure, when I knew that to large sections of the country it was not that at all," he would complain in his memoir a year later. "When I knew that the press and propaganda bureau was deliberately, with studied effort, seeking to delude foreign opinion, especially in America, with posed photographs, suppressed facts, and untrue accounts. Besides, I was sending my dispatch to America, for American readers four thousand miles away from Italy."[20]

At a cocktail party on a Sunday evening, he chatted with Italians about the situation in Sardinia and was told, "Your story is true, but that makes it all the worse for the Fascisti."

One guest offered a more grim summation. "These Fascisti are devouring their own patrimony."[21]

For a newspaperman like Darrah, factual accuracy was the gold standard, and that should have been enough. He had no idea of the trouble his latest story would cause.

* * *

In Addis Ababa, the *Daily Mail's* Geoffrey Harmsworth could find no great anticipation over the coming war. People milled about the shops and complained that the "little rains" that should have started six weeks ago had failed to appear. Like his fellow correspondents, Harmsworth got to the front too soon, and now had to dig up copy when the battle was still a diplomatic one.

He did manage to interview Sir Sidney Barton in a walk around the gardens of the British legation. The British minister was exasperated and defensive over the latest events, especially after Harmsworth told him that he had seen enough in Eritrea and Italian Somaliland to convince him that Mussolini had always been out for blood and not peace. Barton was sorry to hear that. In Ethiopia, at least, the British relationship with the local Italians was "like a big family."[22] His elder daughter was married to Baron Muzzi, the Italian Consul at Debra Markos.

He expected Mussolini to think twice before ordering his troops across the frontier—if England and France stood firm. World opinion, he warned, would be against the Duce. Making his only prescient remark in the interview, he warned, "It seems then that we shall presently witness the collapse of the League of Nations . . . That will be a terrible calamity. We must strive our utmost to prevent that. If there is no League of Nations every country will make a mad rush to rearm. Fear will stalk through the world, and it is fear that makes war."[23]

Barton had apparently forgotten what was going on in Germany.

Back in the center of town, Harmsworth watched Ethiopians dance and enjoy the short rain that made mud of the streets. He passed a tin shed that served as a recruiting office. "It was quite pathetic to watch these undisciplined natives forming fours and two deep, some in white shammas, grey sombreros, and patent leather shoes, others in faded khaki tunics and white jodhpurs, laughing and talking, and interpreting the words of command according to their own inclinations."[24]

No imperial order had been given yet for general mobilization, but Harmsworth saw boys as young as fourteen hoping to be accepted as soldiers. "By the time they have reached the age of twenty-five they have passed their prime," he learned. "Disease takes its toll in Abyssinia." A Swedish doctor informed him that widespread syphilis and blindness was decimating the general population. Haile Selassie had spent a considerable portion of his own wealth on hospitals, but money "has now been swallowed up in buying munitions."[25]

Daniel Sandford, a British colonel who would be involved in the Liberation years later, casually chatted with Harmsworth about the military situation. He told the reporter that Addis Ababa had once been full of arms speculators and agents—Belgian, German, French, Swiss, and Czech—but most had left empty-handed because the Emperor couldn't afford to pay them.

"What arms have the Abyssinians got?" Harmsworth asked.

"An obsolete tank presented to the Emperor by the Duke of Abruzzi," said Sandford. "Four or five thousand machine guns . . . a few old cannon captured at Adwa, and two or three dozen light mountain guns." Ethiopia, he stressed, needed a Red Cross organization. "These Abyssinians are as tough as nails, but the wounded will just be left on the battlefields to be devoured by the hyenas."[26]

Over in Berbera, in British Somaliland, customs officials were rigorously following the letter of the law that month in terms of the arms embargo. They seized more than two hundred boxes of rifles and ammunition that had come through the port and declared them illegal.

A French correspondent, watching all this, complained, "I believe you overstep your authority." He quickly cited a French treaty with Ethiopia that allowed passage of arms.

The customs official didn't appreciate the challenge. "That's true, but such consignments need several licenses and permits and invariably one or the other is missing."[27]

Four thousand rifles that could have gone to Ethiopia's defense stayed in a locked warehouse.

* * *

The Wise Men in London's Whitehall weren't thinking of outdated cannon, tin shack recruitment centers, or impounded rifles. They had been busy preparing a document that considered Ethiopia with the bloodless detachment of an accountant's bottom line.

Back in March, the Cabinet had enlisted Sir John Maffey, Permanent Undersecretary for the Colonies, to lead an inter-departmental committee to examine Great Britain's interests in Ethiopia. Now he was about to hand in its report. As far as an Italian invasion was concerned, "we took no account of the wider moral issues involved." In thirty-one neatly typed, single-spaced pages, its overall verdict was brutal: Britain had no vital interests in Ethiopia except for Lake Tana, which fed the Blue Nile snaking its way into British-held Sudan. An Italian conquest would be good for Britain in some ways, bad for it in others.

Maffey and his inter-departmental committee made sure to cover themselves by writing, "It must not be assumed that because we refer in the report to possible future arrangements with Italy . . . we are suggesting that His Majesty's Government should condone, or should connive at, an Italian absorption . . ." A few pages later, they do exactly that—recommending that certain measures of conniving are "essential" once absorption has happened. The government must take steps to protect British interests over Lake Tana and other tributaries of the Nile "in the event of the establishment of Italian control over Ethiopia." Even more telling was one of their conclusions that suggested Italian recognition should be obtained for the protected tribes in British Somaliland over traditional grazing lands "in what will become Italian territory."[28] Maffey and the others presumed that the conquest, let alone the invasion, was inevitable.

The report was stamped *Secret*, but its findings weren't terribly significant at the time. After all, Britain had already staked its protection claim on a point of honor for the League. All the report did was show that Britain had nothing to lose except honor if it changed its mind. This was the sort of thing the Cabinet would definitely *not* want Benito Mussolini to know.

And it's all but certain that he got his chance to read the report personally, word for word.

Maffey submitted his report on June 18, and Samuel Hoare didn't even bother to circulate it to his Cabinet colleagues until mid-August. In the meantime, the Foreign Office sent a copy of it to the British embassy in Rome, probably to help Anthony Eden when he met with Mussolini for negotiations in late June. It would be eight months before anyone suspected serious trouble, and it only happened after the report's conclusions turned up in *Il Giornale d'Italia*. Leaks to journalists happen all the time, of course, but the Austrian foreign minister, Guido Schmidt, warned that the details must have come directly out of the British embassy—and he was right.

The British, however, didn't want to hear it. When they woke up to discover Maffey's confidential words under an Italian headline, they assumed it was a one-off. Thieves in the night. Having failed to see how deeply their legation was compromised, they did nothing to fix the problem. As astonishing as it sounds today, right up until the start of the Second World War, the Foreign Office kept no security officer or even a security department.[29] Robert Vansittart was the most conscientious top official, but he worried about Germans lurking under the British bed, not Italians. He decided early in 1935 to perform his own amateur checks on the home front—which consisted of simply walking along Downing Street to the India Office with his private secretary. He found at least five exits where anyone could slip out.[30]

Not that this would help in any way, because the problem was in Rome. Britain's embassy had a spy.

Valentine Vivian, the deputy head of Britain's Secret Intelligence Service (MI6), had even figured out early on who it was. It was an Italian working as chief messenger, Secondo Constantini. But Britain's ambassador, Eric Drummond, wouldn't accept the word of the man whose job it was to protect the government's intelligence interests. Instead, less than two years later, Drummond invited Constantini and his wife to attend the coronation of King George VI.[31]

* * *

David Darrah's newspaper now wanted him to accompany the Italian army in Eritrea for two or three weeks to cover the preparations for war. So on June 10, Darrah went down to the Propaganda Ministry in Rome's Via Veneto to make arrangements and waited an hour just to see a middle-tier official, one Signor Stranio, who decided to give the reporter an impromptu scolding about his coverage.

"Why did you write that correspondence and send it through London?" demanded Stranio.

For Darrah, this was confirmation that the press bureau and its operatives were eavesdropping.

A raging Stranio told him he misinterpreted things. "Why do you write about our finances? Foreign financial papers often write about our finances and even they are all wrong."

"But what facts, specifically, are wrong and what are the misinterpretations?" asked Darrah. "I can't control interpretations. As a matter of fact, I made none. I simply related facts and let the reader of my article make his own interpretation."

The argument got nowhere. Finally, Darrah raised the issue again of joining the army in Africa.

"No," snapped Stranio. "You can be sure of that. In the first place we are not allowing any correspondents to go with the army yet. Not even Italians. Later perhaps. But it is doubtful whether *you* would be allowed to go."[32]

Darrah left to have drinks with a friend from the Associated Press at a café in the Via della Mercede. He figured the incident wasn't that serious, but still, he was uneasy. He had a lease on a Roman apartment and a "considerable amount" of furniture in it. Days passed, and he assumed the flap was over. On June 12, he went off to enjoy the sulfur baths of Acque Albule and spent a couple of hours reviewing the Italian newspapers back at his desk. As the crowds of the Galleria Colonna moved below his window, his phone rang, and a voice that didn't identify itself asked, "How long will you be in your office?" Only ten minutes later, an "unctuous" representative from the *Questura*, the central police station, walked in and demanded the reporter come with him.[33] Darrah always packed to be on the go; his briefcase was stocked with his passport and documents. So he took it along as he was brought around to the Piazza Collegio Romano.

After more than half an hour's wait, he was taken in to see a police chief who dealt with foreigners, a man named Pedace whom Darrah had met before. He described him as "a stocky, cynical man with lips that closed completely to form a straight narrow line, and he speaks with a professional snappy snarl." Pedace announced bluntly that the American was expelled from the Kingdom of Italy. He had been cordial to Darrah in the past and seemed to hold no bias, but he was also determined to follow his orders. Gesturing to the file on his desk, he remarked, "That's your dossier. What a character!"

"You mean that's the collection of seven years' spying and censoring?" Darrah shot back. "May I see it?"

Pedace was incredulous. "No! No! No!"

Darrah did manage to see in Pedace's hand a written order—one with Ministry of the Interior letterhead—that claimed he was to be expelled for writing articles damaging Fascist prestige and for being persistently hostile to the regime. No, he couldn't go home, and no, he couldn't have the customary forty-eight hours to get his affairs in order. He had to leave Italy that very night. Darrah considered this a personal vendetta rather than an enforcement of regulations. The one mercy was that he could phone his wife—speaking only in Italian—to arrange for her to bring a bag of clothes to him at the railway station for the 10:10 train to Turin. If Darrah hadn't been in the habit of keeping a couple of hundred dollars in traveler's checks on him for the sake of emergencies, he would have found himself exiled on third-class or sent on a freight train.

In Paris, he was free to write about conditions in Italy without interference, but back in Rome, his wife was constantly under surveillance as she wrapped up their affairs. Meanwhile, the Italian Press and Propaganda Bureau told other foreign correspondents that Darrah "had gone to Vienna—that it was news to them to hear that I had gone to Paris." In the Italian version, Darrah was offered a phone call to the American embassy, of which he mysteriously (and rather implausibly) didn't avail himself.

No one in the foreign press corps believed a word of it, and the day after Darrah's arrival, his deportation was reported in newspapers across America. His own paper, the *Chicago Tribune*, ran a full-page ad on July 6 with the banner headline: "The *Tribune* will not be gagged!" Under a portrait photo of a faintly startled-looking Darrah, it reminded its readers how its correspondent had been chucked out of a country where the press was routinely intimidated and censored. Insisting it wouldn't be muzzled, the *Tribune* decided nonetheless that it wouldn't send another reporter to Rome—it had made the same choice when the Soviet Union expelled its correspondent there. Still, the paper vowed it would keep on getting the news out of Italy.[34]

As for Darrah himself, he was reassigned to running the *Tribune's* bureau in London. He would have to settle for watching events unfold from across the Channel.

* * *

It had been quite an arduous journey for a young man from Mississippi, but now here he was in Ethiopia. And John Robinson had always assumed he would be the first of many. The goal was for him to lead a whole unit of highly skilled black pilots, technicians, and mechanics, and before he'd left America, he had played the role of recruiter. Some of the men he wanted belonged to the Challengers Air Pilots' Association back in Chicago. "I told my fellow pilots," he recalled later, "that I would do everything I could to get them in the air force here."[35]

In Addis Ababa, he was reduced to playing tourist for a while, and with so many foreign correspondents hanging about, he also had to keep up a cover story. He informed people that he was an Ethiopian tailor who had grown up in the United States. "All the people believe it because I look just like an Abyssinian," he wrote in a letter to his friend, Claude Barnett. "Mr. Bayen told me to say this to the people so they wouldn't know my purpose here."[36] It was a small revelation to him that in this African capital, there was a rainbow of foreigners who ran the shops and businesses and a colorful collection of Europeans who were advising Haile Selassie's military. "The white influence over here is very, very strong. They have poisoned the minds of the Abyssinians against American Negroes."[37]

But he could help change that impression, and he eventually started his duty of training Ethiopian pilots. None of his students spoke a word of English, and none had anything close to his own educational background or technical training. Robinson would need to be patient and rely on an interpreter.

For the Ethiopians, he had to be a refreshing change from the arrogance of Hubert Julian, who was making a nuisance of himself around Addis Ababa again. Robinson was already hearing anecdotes about the Black Eagle, and they were *not* flattering. Julian allegedly boasted to anyone within earshot about a $60,000 bank account back in the United States and claimed he would open a school for the poor once he got in to see the Emperor. And the Black Eagle seemed to be intent on undermining him. "Julian is telling everybody I am an American aviator, and he sent for me to come here. You would be surprised at the lies he tells."[38]

At one point, Julian tried to talk to him, but Robinson put him in his place. ". . . I told him I had never seen him before and never heard of him before in America."[39]

* * *

What happened next on the diplomatic front had nothing to do with Italy directly, but the implications gave its war machine a hard push of encouragement. Two weeks before he took over as prime minister, Stanley Baldwin opened negotiations with German Ambassador Joachim von Ribbentrop to allow Hitler to have an increased naval force. *Why* is a mystery, since Britain didn't have to bargain at all—it gained nothing in allowing Hitler more ships on the high seas.

But there were many in Britain's upper classes who felt more natural closeness to the Germans than to the French, and who were almost apologetic over the humiliating terms imposed on Germany by Versailles. There was admiration, too, for Adolf Hitler, and the dictator's fans included the Prince of Wales, the man who would briefly sit on the throne as Edward VIII. Most Britons didn't know that while Edward carried on an affair with American divorcée, Wallis Simpson, his future bride was also sleeping with Joachim von Ribbentrop.

It's possible, of course, that Stanley Baldwin and most of his Cabinet simply wanted peace at any price, haunted by the specter of the stalemated carnage of the Great War. Most of the Cabinet may have wanted it, but not all. John Simon couldn't stomach the deal and stormed out of talks with German naval officers and diplomats. The ships the Germans were building were *brand new*, and Hitler now had permission for twenty-one more cruisers and sixty-four more destroyers—from the country that would end up its most likely target. The pact also allowed Germany to match Britain's U-boat strength.

And sitting on the sidelines, angered and fretting, was renegade Tory Winston Churchill. He warned everyone about the deal, but was ignored. "What a windfall this has been for Japan!" Churchill sneered in the House of Commons, recognizing it left the British Empire vulnerable to more than one potential enemy. "The British Fleet, when the [German] program is completed will be largely anchored in the North Sea." But Churchill was smugly dismissed. Ol' Winston was a paranoid, a warmonger, out of touch with public opinion. Churchill, in fact, understood the repercussions better than anyone else, even many of those in the War Ministry. A secret network of patriotic civil servants and intelligence operatives, all frustrated by the appeasement policy, were regularly feeding him crucial information on German rearmament.

Long before any guns went off, the first casualty of the pact was Britain's diplomatic reputation. Baldwin's government had basically said, "To hell with the Treaty of Versailles, and while we're at it, to hell with the Stresa Front and the League of Nations." Worse, the move legitimized what Hitler was doing and put Britain's closest ally at risk. France had a substantial navy that had no reason at all to welcome more German submarines. But Baldwin didn't bother to consult his allies as he made his end-run around "collective" security.

Anthony Eden hadn't played a part in the negotiations, but he was the one sent out to take the heat. Heading to Rome, he made a stop in Paris, where he listened to the "sharp" reproaches of Pierre Laval, now back in the saddle as France's prime minister. Why, he asked Eden, shouldn't other powers go off and make their own separate deals with Germany? Eden found it galling to have to listen to this, especially from a man who always talked out of both sides of his mouth. "These were fine arguments," he remembered, "but it was doubtful whether Laval, in view of the dubious bargain I suspected he had made with Mussolini over Abyssinia, was the man to put them."[40]

No sooner was Eden gone, in fact, than Laval had his ambassador to Rome, Comte Charles de Chambrun, deliver a message on June 22 to Under-Secretary Fulvio Suvich. France would "adhere faithfully" to the bargain Laval and Mussolini made back in January. And what, wondered Suvich, about the League of Nations? Chambrun replied smoothly that his prime minister was sure the Ethiopian question would be settled without any trouble from Geneva . . . and even if there was trouble, France would keep its private bargain with Italy.[41]

* * *

London was embarrassed over the naval pact. The last thing it needed was to get bogged down in the Ethiopia Crisis, and it needed a deft, discreet way out of it. Thanks to Samuel Hoare chatting things over with Robert Vansittart, someone at the Foreign Office went to the file cabinets, pulled out an old idea, and dusted it off. Britain would carve up a strip of territory from its Somaliland colony leading to the coastal town of Zeila, giving Ethiopia what it had always wanted— a seaport. In exchange, a large piece of the Ogaden would go to the Italians. *The Times* of London would dub it a "corridor for camels."

When the Ethiopia expert, Geoffrey Thompson, heard about the plan, he spouted in disbelief, "But Mussolini will never accept!"

Both Anthony Eden and his Foreign Office adviser, William Strang, "looked rather pained."

"Don't you think so?" asked Eden.

Strang, not waiting for Thompson's answer, said, "Well, we've got to put it to him anyway."[42]

No one had stopped to consider politely asking Ethiopia what it thought.

Eden was sent out to play real estate agent, but he wasn't a welcome face in Rome. By now, Mussolini considered him to be personally siding with the Ethiopians, and the Italian press had vilified Eden in various articles. Mussolini's daughter was visiting London around this time, and at a reception just before Eden left, she demanded, "What are you going to do in Rome, Mr. Eden? Don't you know that my father doesn't like you?"[43]

Just as he'd done with Drummond, Mussolini kept Eden waiting for more than an hour for their first talk on June 24. And just in case the Englishman didn't get the message, he wore casual clothes: an open-neck shirt, sports jacket with elbow patches, white linen trousers, and sneakers without socks. In contrast, Eden wore one of the elegant suits that were his signature style. Drummond and Pompeo Aloisi were on hand for preliminary remarks, but the two men soon withdrew, and Eden was left alone with Mussolini and Fulvio Suvich.

Rumors followed that Eden and Mussolini had a bitter quarrel, and Eden made a point of including most of his original notes in his memoirs, just to dispel "so many legends" about the hour-long conversation. The two spoke in French, and Eden claimed that "there was no bluster of any kind," and that Mussolini even looked ill and depressed. But he also admitted that "there was a gloomy fatality" about Mussolini's temper, which implies that the Duce lost it, however briefly, at some point along the way.[44]

The talk started with the subject of the Anglo-German Naval Agreement, and Mussolini gently skewered the British government over its hypocrisy. He told Eden he was preparing a note of protest to London; he never did send it. Both men knew the real reason why Eden was here: it was time to settle Ethiopia. Britain backed the League, Eden told Mussolini. If the dictator wanted his nation to become a rogue state within Europe, London would have support for war from British voters.

Then Eden put Zeila on the table: "If Abyssinia were willing to open up any part of their country to foreign settlers, we would wish that Italians should have a fair share."[45] Mussolini wasn't interested—from a practical view, the Ogaden parcel wouldn't connect Italian Somaliland to Eritrea. But most of his objections were based on prestige. Ethiopia could claim a victory with the seaport and argue that its concessions were made out of friendship to Britain and not to Italy. He found the proposal "positively dangerous."[46] The answer was no.

Eden had shot his bolt, the only one that Whitehall had given him. He wanted Mussolini "not to reply to me now." Mussolini didn't need to do any more thinking, especially when his spy at the British embassy had possibly forewarned him of the offer. He would not change his mind.

No, if Ethiopia wanted to avoid war, it would have to surrender territories it had conquered within the last fifty years, and that weren't inhabited by Ethiopians; the acquisitions made by Menelik. "In saying this," Eden recalled, "Signor Mussolini made a circular gesture, which I took to mean that he regarded such territories as existing on all four sides" of Ethiopia.[47] The central plateau could remain under Ethiopian sovereignty—but only if it was under Italian control. If Ethiopia said no, Italy would go to war. Mussolini swept his hand in a flourish, which conveyed to Eden that the dictator meant to take it all.

But there was virtually no difference between what would be handed over in quiet surrender and the "whole" taken by force.

It must have been here that there were heated exchanges, though Eden always insisted the discussion remained cordial. Suvich—who apparently hadn't talked much so far, and kept such a low profile that he almost faded into the mosaic tile—now put in a word. He smugly brought up France. After all, France was a member of the League, but it couldn't care less what happened to Ethiopia. Eden replied that Laval had told him personally that he was anxious and asked him to convey this at the meeting.

Mussolini, of course, knew better, and decided to educate the young Cabinet minister on his special understanding with Laval, the one that gave him a free hand in Ethiopia.

"Economically," snapped Eden.

Mussolini replied that this might be the way it was on paper. But he had given up the future of one hundred thousand Italians in Tunis to France, and for his trouble, had gotten half a dozen palm trees in one place and a strip of desert—which didn't even have one sheep—in another. He was quite clear on the implication. Eden was adamant and went over the details given him by Laval in Geneva, quoting the phrase Laval had used: *"Vous avez les mains fortes. Faites attention."*

He watched as Mussolini listened and then "flung himself back in his chair with a gesture of incredulous astonishment."[48]

Eden left minutes later to go back to the British embassy. He had to make his notes on the meeting, and then it was on to a lunch given in his honor at the Hotel Excelsior. After the Englishman left, Mussolini remarked, "I never saw a better dressed fool."[49]

When Italian foreign ministry official Mario Pansa came to escort the Duce over to the Excelsior, he was surprised to find him still in his casual clothes.

"But we shall be late for the lunch, Your Excellency," said Pansa. "You can't possibly change in five minutes."

Mussolini laughed contemptuously. "Do you think I'd change for that fellow? The idea never occurred to me. Let's go." And as he rode through the Via del Tritone on the way to the banquet, he burst out: "That frozen tailor's dummy! I may be a blacksmith's son, but I do know how to hold my own."[50]

*　*　*

To an astonished Eden, it was a completely different Duce on the afternoon of June 25 at the hotel, no matter how informally he was attired. He "was transformed, jaw thrust out, eyes rolling and popping, figure strutting and attitudinizing."[51] When the call came for lunch, Mussolini made an imperious gesture at Eden and marched into the banquet room as the British Cabinet minister hung back and waited, "English style," for the ladies.

Mussolini avoided talking with him, but when Eden persisted, the Duce lectured him on Adwa. It needed to be avenged. Eden argued that nobody could re-fight old battles—if the British tried that, they'd have to start with Bunker Hill. The single mercy of the afternoon was that Mussolini was willing to hold another round of talks.

The next day, there was another lunch, this one in Ostia and given by Galeazzo Ciano and his wife. Eden caught a second performance of Mussolini machismo. There was a moment where the conversation hit a lull, and Eden and the Drummonds heard the Italian guests chanting, "Il Duce, il Duce!" As they looked out to sea, Mussolini was in the stern of a speedboat racing over the waves, standing tall, his chin thrust out. Eden half-expected him to dive into the water and swim up to their lunch party.[52] There was no breakthrough accomplished when they met later. Mussolini tried to cast Italy in the role of the wounded victim, claiming Ethiopia had half a million men ready to pounce if there was a distracting European crisis. Eden didn't buy any of it. His information, he insisted, reported that it was the Ethiopians who feared an attack.

With Eden's departure, Mussolini must have thoroughly enjoyed his next step. Laval was in his pocket, and he could keep the diplomatic dithering going on. On his return leg through Paris, Eden got more reproaches from the French prime minister and his secretary-general to the Foreign Office, Alexis Léger.

Britain, complained Laval, had nearly played a trick on France with its Zeila offer. If Ethiopia accepted, France would have to declare Djibouti a free port, and the whole deal threatened the economic survival of the Djibouti railway, which was the cash cow funding French Somaliland. Laval also raised an idea that sounded suspiciously as if it came from Rome. He wanted to know whether Mussolini had considered the possibility of a protectorate. Eden replied coldly that he hadn't asked. When the talk circled back to French complaints over Zeila, Laval wondered out loud how it would be possible to start the idea of an Italian protectorate, one that guaranteed Haile Selassie his throne (but presumably nothing else, and leaving him entirely disposable at the Italians' whim). Eden was sure the Emperor would rather fight than be cut down to a figurehead in an occupied nation.[53]

Off in Eritrea, General Emilio De Bono received a summary of Eden's proposals in a letter from his boss dated June 25. "You can imagine my reply," wrote Mussolini. ". . . The English attitude has helped instead of injuring." The Duce was so confident that his enemy would be crushed "from the very first blows" that he informed De Bono he would come to Eritrea himself as the campaign got underway. "You have, then, only 120 days in which to get ready."[54]

Chapter Five

COLORS OF CONSCIENCE

"They put a heavy weight on my 20-year-old shoulders. Now, not only did I have to beat the man, but I had to beat him for a cause."[1] This was boxer Joe Louis, cast in the role of avenger for Ethiopia, whether he wanted it or not. And on the night of June 25, he stepped into a ring at Yankee Stadium against the fighter who was the hero of Italy, Primo Carnera.

Louis was an Alabaman sharecropper's son who spent some of his early years in Detroit's Black Bottom neighborhood—his family moved there to literally flee the KKK. You lived hard in Black Bottom; factories or breadlines, your choice. But Louis found boxing. At his professional heavyweight debut, he knocked out his opponent in the first round. Sure, he'd met seasoned fighters before, but Primo Carnera was a giant, a former circus strongman and wrestler who weighed 270 pounds. Carnera was the perfect public relations tool for Mussolini. He was on Italian stamps, and the Duce ordered him up a special Fascist uniform.

What these two young men thought about Ethiopia didn't matter at all. It was what they represented: Italy versus Ethiopia, white versus black. Cartoons didn't hesitate to portray Carnera and Louis as the nations. On the day of the fight, the *Washington Post* ran one with Mussolini and Haile Selassie as the looming shadows for the two boxers, poised to start their own match. The political heat became so intense that at one point, the Hearst Milk Fund, sponsoring the fight, wanted to cancel it.

Sixty thousand fans filled Yankee Stadium, fifteen thousand of them African Americans. More than Harlem was represented—blacks had come from Chicago, Boston, Philadelphia, and Washington. Duke Ellington was there. So were Bill "Bojangles" Robinson and Fritz Pollard of the Chicago Black Hawks, the first African American to be a head coach in the NFL. Italian Americans from their Manhattan enclave and points beyond had come out to cheer on Carnera. New York's mayor, Fiorello LaGuardia, had come to watch. So did the owners of the New York Giants and the Yankees, and leading figures from Tammany Hall.

Ed Sullivan was in the audience, still a newspaperman, for this was years before his variety television show.

There was no radio broadcast allowed, since it would obviously hurt ticket sales. But many African Americans who couldn't get ringside seats were waiting for the word, so the Savoy Ballroom became an impromptu headquarters. Twenty thousand people showed up. For those who wanted to be stompin' at the Savoy, assuming the news would be good, it was seventy-five cents for admission.

Back at the stadium, in an effort to defuse the political tension, announcer Harry Balogh walked over in his tuxedo to the microphone and resorted to platitudes. "Tonight we have gathered here to watch a contest of athletic skill. We are Americans. That means that we have come from homes of many different faiths, and we represent a lot of different nationalities. In America we admire the athlete who can win by virtue of his skill. Let me then ask you to join me in the sincere wish that regardless of race, color, or creed, the better man may emerge victorious."[2]

That raises an interesting point. About a year later, Jesse Owens would win four gold medals at the Summer Olympics in Berlin and utterly destroy the Nazi thesis of the superior master race. Owens would go to Berlin to represent America, and even many white Americans would stake a claim of patriotic pride in his victory. In stark contrast, here was Joe Louis, a year earlier in 1935, a native son on his own home ground, and few whites there seemed willing to celebrate an *American* fighting a *foreign* contender.

Louis had been coached to whittle away at Carnera, to chop him down like a tree.[3] It was more like he took a sledgehammer to the walls of a house. By round six, a right to Carnera's jaw knocked him down, and as he staggered back up, Louis punished him with a couple of combinations. The referee decided Carnera had had enough.

Black pride, black jubilation. "Bojangles" Robinson rushed to get to a phone so he could call the Savoy. After he raced his Duesenberg to the ballroom to join the revelers, he declared, "I'm so happy I could eat a mud sandwich."[4] When the news reached Chicago and Detroit, African Americans went cheering through their streets. In Detroit, one woman was so exuberant in her jumping up and down that she fractured her leg.

Louis himself was tired and had to be coaxed to appear at the Savoy to hear the cheers of his fans. He showed up at two-thirty in the morning, and any words of thanks he offered couldn't be heard because the microphone was dead.[5] It didn't matter. The celebrating throng wanted just to see him, to catch a glimpse. "Ethiopia" had won.

* * *

On June 27, the sirs and lords who ran Britain got an annoying reminder that they were in a democracy. The League of Nations Union, busy canvassing public opinion in the UK for months, now published its findings for the Peace Ballot. Five questions were asked of more than 11.5 million people polled, and millions replied in the affirmative to each:

1. Should Great Britain remain a member of the League of Nations?
2. Are you in favor of an all-around reduction of armaments by international agreement?
3. Are you in favor of an all-around abolition of national military and naval aircraft by international agreement?
4. Should the manufacture and sale of armaments for private profit be prohibited by international agreement?
5. Do you consider that, if a nation insists on attacking another, the other nations should combine to compel it to stop by
   a) economic and non-military measures?
   b) if necessary, military measures?

Stanley Baldwin said the results were misleading. "Terribly mischievous," was the verdict of Neville Chamberlain, the Chancellor of the Exchequer. Robert Vansittart declared it a "free excursion into the inane." Geoffrey Dawson of *The Times*, whose editorials recommended allowing Hitler to rearm, considered the Peace Ballot "a deplorable waste of time and effort."[6] "The question of war and peace," declared John Simon, "is not one on which the opinion of the uninstructed should be invited."[7] The response to the Peace Ballot from those in power was a collective harrumph. How *dare* anyone ask the ordinary people what they thought of foreign policy?

* * *

The American chargé d'affaires in Addis Ababa, William Perry George, no longer had cause for complaint that "nothing was happening." He was getting bombarded with telegrams from Washington, and on July 3, Haile Selassie invited him for another discussion at the palace.

The US government, of course, still used the excuse that the League of Nations should decide things. This was convenient—the United States didn't belong to the League. But the Emperor wanted to invoke another treaty dating back to 1929 to which the United States was very much a signed member, and one of its own past Secretaries of State had his name on it: Frank Kellogg. The Kellogg Pact's very first article stated that its members "condemn recourse to war for the solution of international controversies, and renounce it as an instrument of national policy in their relations with one another."

The Emperor now gave George a letter that asked the United States to consider applying pressure on Italy. If the British wouldn't honor their commitments, maybe the Americans would. George took the letter and went off to the telegraph office to wire its contents to the State Department.

Thousands of miles away in Washington, Secretary of State Cordell Hull knew that every morning he arrived at his office, he would "find at least one telegram from any one of half a dozen capitals relating to Italian troop movements and military preparations."[8] Back in January, he'd heard the rumors about Pierre Laval's deal on the side with Mussolini, as well as the indignant denials. Then in late February, Italy's ambassador, Augusto Rosso, had given the State Department assurances that his nation's troop movements were purely defensive. "He stretched our credulity," Hull wrote in his memoirs, "beyond the point of elasticity."[9]

Two months later, Rosso was back on Hull's doorstep. Hull was on friendly terms with Rosso, and he "liked his personality." Rosso was married to an American woman Hull knew from his home state of Tennessee, and the secretary of state was also aware that Rosso was popular among his fellow diplomats. This time, Italy's man in Washington wanted a favor; he hoped the US government would use its influence to stop American trucks from being shipped to Ethiopia. Hull was incredulous. His staff officials pointed out that trucks could hardly be considered arms, and Washington couldn't interfere with private export business anyway.[10]

Rosso either didn't get the message, or Mussolini thought the Americans might change their minds. In June, Italian officials approached the US embassy to make the same request. They got the same answer back.

Hull had no interest in stepping into the deep mud of Italy's colonial misadventure. He'd made up his mind long before he finished the five pages of carefully worded appeal from Haile Selassie. In the end, he decided, "There was still no point in taking any step that might impede the action of the League."[11] To his annoyance, Mussolini's propaganda writers quickly jumped all over this as evidence that the United States was on Italy's side. That wasn't what he'd meant at all. He summoned Rosso in for what sounds like a mild scolding. He had "increasing concern," as well as an "earnest hope" the two sides could find a peaceful solution.

"A war started anywhere would be awfully dangerous to everybody," he told Italy's ambassador.[12]

With limp sentiments like this, there was bound to be a disappointing answer sent to Addis Ababa. Franklin Roosevelt, with only few modifications to Hull's carefully prepared draft, informed the Emperor that "my government would be loath to believe that either [Italy and Ethiopia] would resort to other than pacific means as a method of dealing with this controversy or would permit any situation to arise which would be inconsistent with the commitments of the [Kellogg] pact."[13]

And yet the US government *did* believe the two sides would go to war—it put this view right on the record. Only a few days before William Perry George offered the fresh response at the palace, Hull gave notice to the 123 Americans living in Ethiopia that they should get out of the country while it was still safe. As Haile Selassie had waited in his study, pinning faint hopes on the chance of American support, George was managing the evacuation of US citizens who chose to leave the country.

* * *

Back when the Great War was sputtering to its bleak end, an English spy at the relatively new MI5 station in Rome jotted down a question in Italian: *"Chi é questo Benito Mussolini?"*[14] The English operative didn't know, but he was anxious to find out. His name was Samuel Hoare.

Hoare had a baronet and was an elected MP, the only MP to ever serve as an operative for the British Security Service. He had been a head of station in Petrograd, where, among other things, he sent London a dispatch on Rasputin's assassination. He was a lot like Vansittart in his obsession with Huns hiding under the blanket, sometimes when none were there (he thought the future Pope Pius XII thoroughly pro-German). And in Rome, Hoare had his work for counterintelligence cut out for him. In the First World War, the Battle of Caporetto was a disaster for the Allies, as the Austrians and Germans broke through the Italian front. Besides inspiring a young Ernest Hemingway to put its futility into *A Farewell to Arms,* it prompted waves of deserters and a tide of anti-war feeling. Part of Hoare's job was to keep Italy in the war.

Then one of his staff mentioned that a certain mob agitator in Milan might prove useful, and he got in touch. As it turned out, why, yes, the young Mussolini would be happy to create a movement that would put down peace activists. "Leave it to me," he told Hoare through his contact. "I will mobilize the *mutilati* in Milan, and they will break the heads of any pacifists who try to hold anti-war meetings in the streets."[15]

Hoare found him "true to his word," and having got permission from London, he subsidized Mussolini for more *agent provocateur* work to the tune of £100 a week, the equivalent of £6,000, or more than $10,000 US, today. After Mussolini gained power, he liked to wax nostalgic whenever he ran into Hoare about his head-cracking exploits in the war years.

Now here they were in July of 1935, with Samuel Hoare as Britain's foreign secretary, and Hoare hoped to use this chumminess to his advantage. "I lightly flattered myself with the feeling that my past associations with the Duce might still have some effect on him," he wrote in his memoirs.[16] The ploy yielded mixed results. Hoare wrote to Mussolini, mentioning their past work together, and the dictator sent him back long, rambling letters. One message was so strange that Italy's ambassador to Britain, Dino Grandi, dismissed it as "a psychological and not a diplomatic document."[17]

Hoare voiced his frustration when he sat down to talk with the US ambassador, Robert Bingham, on the morning of July 9. While the Americans didn't want to get involved in Ethiopia, they would keep an eye on how things developed. The situation was grave, Hoare admitted to Bingham. In Hoare's view, Bingham cabled to Washington, "Mussolini has now put the issue in the shape of a contest between the black and white races, which has had already unfavorable effects in Egypt, in Great Britain's African colonies, and in British dominions where there is a population of blacks."[18]

It was not only Britain that felt threatened by stirrings of black support in colonies. Only days before in Geneva, Portugal's foreign minister, Armindo Monteiro, felt it necessary to warn both Pierre Laval and Anthony Eden that the Crisis could spark a wave of nationalism across Africa.[19] The Portuguese didn't want rebel blacks in their colonies of Mozambique and Angola any more than Hoare wanted them in South Africa.

*   *   *

In the United States, blacks had already lost patience. There were reports of thousands enlisting in ad hoc armies to fight for the African motherland. The stepladders and soapboxes of Seventh Avenue in Harlem, so often used to ask passers-by to come to Jesus, were now demanding they come to Ethiopia instead. With portraits of Haile Selassie and books on black history for sale, these recruiters—sometimes wearing pith helmets or turbans—could attract crowds "varying in number from fifty to as many as a thousand."[20]

African Americans in other parts of the country didn't know how to get started, so many wrote to Washington for advice. A Henry Kimble of Cincinnati, Ohio, asked, "Can I get permission . . . to open a recruiting office of enlisting men for service in Africa."[21] For Orville Worster, a 49-year-old unemployed construction worker in Tampa, Florida, the chance to fight for Ethiopia was his last one. Having lost his home and been abandoned by his family, he confessed, "I believe that after the Relief appropriations are spent, conditions will be much worse."[22] Ethiopia meant redemption to Worster. In Oklahoma, a high school teacher named Shellie Nelson announced, "I am the representative of an organization of Bartlesville Negroes who are desirous of entering the conflict."[23] In Tucson, Arizona, the leader of the Association for Ethiopia's Independence claimed that "50,000 Americans of African descent" were prepared to go to fight.[24]

To most of these appeals, each one infused with a touching urgency, the State Department replied with perfunctory letters that said *no*. They quoted Title 18, Section 21 of the United States Code that barred citizens from exercising a commission or serving a foreign country against a people with whom the United States was at peace, risking a fine of two thousand dollars and three years in prison. Enlisting others carried a one thousand dollar fine, a three-year prison term, and the stripping of American citizenship.

Most African Americans had little choice but to comply. The people who wrote wanted to help, not wind up in jail. Some appealed to the State Department because they clearly lacked the resources to reach Ethiopia on their own. The policy prompted a blistering attack by a group in West Virginia, the International African Progressive Association, which wrote to Cordell Hull. It argued that the black man in America was "carried away by violence into the American Continent" and had "never sworn allegiance to the New World."[25]

The argument is a penetrating one—the US government was threatening to take away what had never been asked for or truly given in the first place. "It doesn't seem to me that we have any citizenship rights in this country," argued George Terry of Masontown, Pennsylvania, in a letter to the editor of the *Pittsburgh Courier*. Black people were routinely lynched, mobbed, barred from countless stores and restaurants, and turned away from jobs. "If this is what citizenship means, where is the loss?" He was willing to "go and fight to the last to assist our people in this battle."[26]

The cause also brought out its share of con men, cranks, and self-proclaimed holy men. George Baker, who had reinvented himself as "Father Divine," made sure his followers attached themselves to protests. And then there was the bizarre figure of Sufi Abdul Hamid, whose background was a shadowy one. Some historians portray him as coming from Lowell, Massachusetts, others from Pennsylvania. Wherever he came from, Hamid cut a high profile in Harlem and liked to dress in outrageous costumes of turbans, capes, and sometimes

Fascist-style uniforms. The *Daily News* called Hamid "The Black Hitler."[27] Now he latched onto the cause of Ethiopia, writing to one of the Emperor's emissaries in New York that Haile Selassie should act as the worldwide leader of blacks willing to "die for him and his cause."[28] He promised he had a training camp in upstate New York for blacks willing to fight, and he even claimed credit for sending Hubert Julian, the Black Eagle, off to Ethiopia.

Samuel Daniels was less flamboyant, but his credentials were just as shady. He apparently came from Tanganyika (now Tanzania) to the States, and he formed his own organization, the Pan-African Reconstruction Association (PARA). It kept offices on Lenox Avenue and allegedly had four thousand members.[29] Daniels had a wider vision than blacks merely going over to fight. He wanted to see skilled technicians working in an African country, helping it to develop. He talked big over how after Ethiopia beat Italy, African-American veterans could *stay on*. They could build new lives for themselves in the country they'd fought for! He'd even negotiated a parcel of land from Haile Selassie's government where they could settle!

Sounds wonderful. And as the saying goes, if it's too good to be true . . . Historian William R. Scott of Lehigh University has looked for the evidence, but found none that Daniels ever approached Haile Selassie's representatives, whether in New York or Addis Ababa, let alone struck a deal for land where veterans could make new homes.[30]

Did it matter? Was there land waiting? For many, the first thing they had to do—that they felt they ought to do—was go *fight*. News footage survives of a large crowd of black men on a street, huddled around a modest table for one of PARA's recruitment drives. The men stood in line to sign up under a large placard that read, "Ethiopian Volunteers Register Here!" In Washington, officials were grimly taking notes. As far as Daniels went, the authorities decided the PARA leader was "engaged in a petty racket." Both he and Sufi Abdul Hamid had been on the FBI's watch list for a while. Given "the violent nature of the social propaganda" at recruitment rallies, however, it was decided that hauling Daniels in for an interview would only help his cause and make him a martyr.[31]

On July 14, at one of PARA's rallies, Samuel Daniels grandly announced a new major recruitment drive for black soldiers. One of his organizers, a Reverend Harold Williamson, Jr., told the crowd, "Let's get right up and tell why we want to knock out Mussolini like Joe Louis did Carnera."[32]

There were those in the audience who wanted to be heard as well. Covering the event, the *New York Times* felt it necessary to quote them by using slang punctuation. One young man, according to the *Times*, argued, "Ethiopia is the country of our forefathers an' I feel somehow that if we can help them now, that some day they'll help us." Another man in the crowd spoke up. "I don't see why Ethiopia should just be another nation of slaves for the white man. An' I'll fight for Ethiopia an' give my life an' my blood."[33]

Less than a week later, the *Pittsburgh Courier* suggested that Daniels had managed to draw almost a thousand black recruits and that thousands of others had gotten word and were ready to come from other cities to enlist.[34] But so far, the activists weren't being harassed very much. If there were any training camps in places like upstate New York or elsewhere, officials didn't seem to be terribly alarmed, which is interesting in itself. We have no sensational reports of police raids sent to shut them down. In racially-charged America—where blacks were forbidden to eat in certain restaurants, barred from public toilets in the South, and kept from high-paying jobs—it's inconceivable that officials wouldn't panic over growing militias of black men, all learning how to use rifles and preparing to shoot them for a foreign country.

The urge to enlist ran all the way down to Texas, where a local district attorney warned it was against the law, but a black veteran of the Great War, Walter J. Davis, organized a meeting anyway for potential recruits in Fort Worth willing "to spill their blood on behalf of their native land."[35]

So African Americans kept adding their names to the lists of those willing to fight. Ethiopia would have another army, one from America. These patriots to the ancient motherland were sure of it.

* * *

More foreign correspondents were arriving in Addis Ababa every day. When Australian freelancer, Noel Monks, and South African reporter, O'Dowd Gallagher, got off their train, they saw a "short, slight man with an impish face" come up to them.

"I'm George Steer of *The Times*," he said. "Welcome to Sheba's land." Then a joke: "Did you bring your bibles?"[36]

Monks asked if there was going to be a war. Steer clearly identified with the underdog. "There's going to be a massacre unless the League of Nations get off their bottoms and stop Mussolini. These people are still living in the spear age. That's all they've got, spears."[37]

George Steer was only twenty-five years old, but he was already being deferred to as the local veteran. One of the first to arrive, he would be one of the last to leave, and he was the perfect storyteller for Ethiopia's plight. Though born in South Africa, he grew up with a liberal conscience that could treat black people as individuals, and he didn't take for granted the exotic backdrop where he spent his childhood. In his rooms in Christ Church at Oxford, he draped the sofa with the skin of a lion his father felled with a bow and arrow.[38]

He admitted later that he was "never in love with the Italians," though he tried his best "to give them a fair start in life."[39] Like other young men with left-leaning politics, he "learned to whistle and to raspberry when the revolting chin under the ludicrous plume or in the effeminate toque (officially called the Fascist Fez) obliterated the grander sights of Rome on the screen of the Oxford Super Cinema."[40] When he gave Fascism a thought at all, he despised "a system which castor-oiled people who did not agree with it and then murdered them or sent them to desert islands."[41] On a visit to Italy, he resented the busybodies and police who hassled him when he was forced to spend a night on a train after his passport and cash were stolen.

He was short enough that everyone who mentioned him commented on his height, and others described him as "fox-faced." But there was a small-dog scrappiness to him as well. He liked shooting and the outdoors. And he learned just enough Amharic to talk his way into a special correspondent's job at *The Times* of London. The editor at his Yorkshire paper was willing to be one of his references but called the young man's political judgment "quixotic."[42] *The Times* hired him anyway, and close to the end of June, he was heading for Addis Ababa.

On July 16, Steer got the first big story of his posting. Emperor Haile Selassie was willing to be interviewed at the Little Gibbi, and the young reporter had to borrow a proper white shirt and a morning coat from staff at the British legation. After being led past the guard houses and granted access to the Emperor's study, Steer was impressed with the "man of great intelligence, completely controlled by himself."[43] Haile Selassie wanted to tell the world what he thought of Britain's offer of the port of Zeila in exchange for a piece of the Ogaden desert for Italy. Since Britain hadn't thought to come to him first with the deal, it was only fitting that Whitehall would learn his opinion by opening the pages of *The Times*.

Now Steer was in the same room where Ladislas Farago had sat months ago. Sitting under his black cloak with his cocker spaniels lying quietly at his feet, the Emperor explained, "I have in view only an exchange of territory. If the Zeila offer is maintained, I am willing to surrender to Italy an equivalent."[44] He was adamant that Ethiopia would not give up any of its northern provinces, and only a portion of the Ogaden would be parceled away. Impatient over Mussolini's claims of a civilizing mission, he added, "I insist that the main factor barring Ethiopia from civilization is the lack of a seaport, and if Italy's motive for the conquest of Ethiopia is to civilize the country, I find in her resistance to the Zeila offer reason for some sarcasm."[45]

Two days later, when the interview ran in *The Times*, Haile Selassie's Rolls-Royce drove through the streets of Addis Ababa on his way to Ethiopia's Parliament. People called out to him, chanting, "Li-li-li-li," but their ruler was protected by officers of the guard, who jogged alongside the car, some in silver-buckled sandals and others barefoot. The streets were packed. Ordinary citizens knew that something was up, something important. There would have been other cars prowling the muddy mule tracks to be there on time, with more modest retinues of servants running along for ministers and officials. Soldiers in full dress uniform and priests in their robes hurried to fill the seats in the visitors' gallery.

Though it was called a parliament, there were never any debates, and Haile Selassie never had to respond to questions across a Commons floor. Instead, he used this place to make announcements. The Emperor had hand-picked the members of the Senate, and the Chamber of Deputies was stacked with land-owning nobles. Tekle Hawaryat, Haile Selassie's man in Geneva who wrote the Constitution, had once suggested, "Democracy has caused too much bloodshed even among the civilized nations." Reporters from these "civilized" nations, in fact, mostly approved of the paternalistic theater the Emperor mounted in his capital. They deplored the hypocrisy of certain powers willing to let Italy have a free hand in "backward" Ethiopia, but in the same breath, the white correspondents implied that the Africans were still too backward to vote.

Finally, at noon, a silk handkerchief floated from a draped balcony, framed by green curtains. The handkerchief indicated that the Emperor had taken his place, because etiquette dictated that he shouldn't be seen rising or sitting like a commoner. The curtains parted, and the Court Chamberlain, wielding a silver-topped staff, moved to his spot in the center of the chamber. Haile Selassie began to speak to his people, summarizing in an almost academic manner how Italy's plotting had brought them all to this crossroads. He didn't raise his voice. He made no gestures or rhetorical flourishes.

"When the Italian people, which has turned oppressor, arrives with the weapons of aggressions which the modern age has produced and claiming that it is to teach us civilization, the Ethiopian people, which is prepared to die for its Emperor and its country, will await the invader mustered in unity." Now he began a theme to bring his countrymen together, knowing that political divisions would only help the Italians. "Soldier, trader, peasant, young and old, man and woman, be united! Defend your country by helping each other! According to ancient custom, the women will stand in defense of their country by giving encouragement to the soldier and by caring for the wounded. Although Italy is doing everything possible to disunite us, whether Christian or Muslim, we will unitedly resist."

He promised that he would be in their midst, prepared to shed his blood as well for his country. His ministers kept their reserve, but those below were electrified by the words. Their excitement was so great, they lost track of the exits, and in their confused milling about, the impatient Court Chamberlain hit men with his staff to keep order. The crowd filed out onto the steps and into the streets, where the charged atmosphere infected the throng.

George Steer was on hand to cover the event, and he was unusually perceptive. Talk of dying for one's country and shedding blood on the line was all well and good, but he already knew the Emperor favored a guerrilla approach. And when Steer came to write his book on the war, which was out as early as December of 1936, he astutely summed up the Emperor's thinking. He even put it in italics to drive the point home: *"Haile Selassie never thought of his army as anything but a delaying force."*[46]

He was one of the very few who recognized the truth. The Emperor wasn't arming with the fatalism of some African samurai—his appeals to the League were always his first line of defense. If he could just buy time for League members to finally come around and do the right thing, to come to the rescue. . . .

As cheers and renewed chants of "Li-li-li!" went up among the happy crowds, the Rolls-Royce threaded its way back to the Little Gibbi, carrying its troubled Emperor.

* * *

Some valuable arms did manage to make it to Ethiopia, and from the unlikeliest source of all—Nazi Germany.

Back in March, the German embassy denied vigorously to Britain that it had offered the Emperor pilot instructors or armored cars. And yet a Junkers monoplane somehow found its way to Ethiopia with a German, Ludwig Weber, in its cockpit. The plane was to be kept for Haile Selassie's personal use. Now, almost three months later, a representative for Ethiopia came to Berlin, asking for a loan of three million Reichsmarks to buy arms. The Fuehrer was briefed and was happy to oblige. Hitler—who was repulsed by black people in general and thought they were "primitive"—was certainly no friend to the Ethiopians, so what was going on? He'd decided that any white soldier killed in Africa from a German machine gun was one less Italian that could keep him from gobbling up Austria.

Ethiopia would get ten thousand Mausers, ten million cartridges, hundreds of machine guns, several thousand hand grenades, and thirty anti-tank guns, along with field dressings. The weapons were sometimes smuggled in piano crates through the port of Djibouti, and there were rare occasions when they were brazenly flown across. All the while, Germany's man in Addis Ababa feigned innocence to Count Luigi Vinci of the Italian legation. Germany smuggle in weapons for Ethiopia? The idea was absurd! The Third Reich was strictly neutral, claimed the Fuehrer's representative, and besides, their two nations ought to close ranks against people of color.[47]

As it happened, the Great Powers of Europe had an equal cynicism over the use of chemical weapons. Despite the horrors of gas in the Great War, Winston Churchill thought it should be used during a revolt in Iraq, then under British mandate. "I do not understand this squeamishness about the use of gas," he grumbled. To Churchill, it was ridiculous to go ahead with bursting shells but be timid over chemical weapons. "I am strongly in favor of using poisoned gas against uncivilized tribes." By 1935, there were others who agreed with him, even after major nations signed the Geneva Protocol barring its use; Britain and France went ahead with importing poison gas into their colonies through Mombassa and Djibouti.

And Mussolini wanted gas used for his conquest of Ethiopia.

About 680 tons of it were shipped in for the sake of the campaign, with containers stored in a couple of warehouses near Asmara and another facility near Nefasit.[48]

Haile Selassie and his court already had several competent European military advisers who anticipated the horror. Besides gas, everyone worried about bombs. They could expect air power to be a crucial factor. And yet when Ladislas Farago had asked Eric Virgin about defenses, the Swedish general confided that he'd talked Haile Selassie out of buying a squadron of planes. He saw no point without skilled pilots to fly them, and the Walwal Incident forced him to shelve his plans for a flying school.

It was a strange perspective, this attitude of a sky marshal who thought an Ethiopian air force "superfluous." Virgin argued that there "are no large bombers with a minimum range of eight hundred miles," and that the country had "no emergency landing places." He was quick to remind Farago that the Ethiopian Highlands were to the north, with some mountains climbing more than fourteen thousand feet high. Besides, according to Virgin, there were no towns to bomb. There were no industrial centers, no arsenals, no railway junctions, none of the targets that lured planes to the bombing raids and dog fights of Europe during the Great War.

"If the Italians destroyed a village, it would be rebuilt the next morning," said Virgin, "and it would be a pointless butchery to work with undependable explosives which would probably only kill women and children. I cannot imagine a civilized power making war on these helpless creatures."[49]

* * *

Virgin couldn't, but others could, so much so that it apparently led to one of the strangest insurance investments in history. According to United Press, a group of Jews "referred to as a Semitic syndicate," approached French underwriters in Paris about actually insuring the Ark of the Covenant.[50]

If you aren't Ethiopian, you can be forgiven for thinking the great chest of acacia wood plated with gold, the container for the original Ten Commandments, would be in Israel or Egypt if it was anywhere on Earth. So goes the lore in Spielberg's *Raiders of the Lost Ark*. But for the devout of Ethiopia, the Ark rests in the land's holiest city, Aksum, where it's kept away from the public and carefully protected in the Church of Our Lady Mary of Zion. The country's national chronicle, the *Kebra Nagast* ("Glory of Kings"), tells how Menelik I—the love child of Solomon and the Queen of Sheba—went to visit his father in Jerusalem, but on his journey home, he discovered his attendants had smuggled out the Ark. Menelik, being a practical young man, decided that if God wasn't going to smite him for taking away the Ark, then God must want him to keep it. Legend has it that he brought it to the highlands of Tigray, and there it had stayed ever since.

Now this mysterious "Semitic Syndicate" worried the Ethiopians would take the Ark out of their church and carry it before one of their armies, much as the ancient Israelites had done in battles. But as United Press reminded its readers, it was one thing to face chariots and arrows, and quite another to bring the holy relic in front of modern tanks and machine guns. Whether or not the Ark had supernatural powers to shoot lightning or lay waste to armies as it did in the biblical legends, the syndicate at least wanted to safeguard a precious artifact. But what sum could the underwriters put on it? How would anyone verify a claim if one was made? It's not as if you could check a photograph of what it looked like. No one, in fact, had seen it outside the little chapel in Aksum. And the reporter who filed the story didn't have the answers to such questions, or else couldn't get them.

While some investors worried about bombs falling on a holy relic, one holy man was concerned with what the bombs would do to people. Mohandas Gandhi resented Mussolini's recent "outbursts against the darker races."[51] For India's saint, the reaction was less predictable than one might think. When Gandhi went on his European tour in 1931, he made a stop in Rome, met with the Duce, and reviewed a Fascist honor guard. The dictator was "a riddle" to him, he wrote to a friend at the time. "Many of his reforms attract me. He seems to have done much for the peasant class. I admit an iron hand is there. But as violence is the basis of Western society, Mussolini's reforms deserve an impartial study."[52]

By 1935, the view through the Mahatma's little round spectacles was clear and his ambivalence gone. Now he urged his people to raise money for a Red

Cross unit to go over to Ethiopia. "Although India is under British rule, she is a member of the League of the Nations. She is entitled fully to assist another nation even though she is a noncombatant."[53] Indians, however much they sympathized, didn't feel strongly enough to follow Gandhi on this one, but it's interesting that he expected there to be war.

Off in London's Beaumont Crescent, Marcus Garvey read the news on Ethiopia closely, frustrated over his lack of influence. He was away from the action, deported from the United States and in exile, reduced to humble digs in what is now White City in Hammersmith. He'd started *The Black Man*, a monthly magazine that was a revival of *The Blackman*, an earlier, successful periodical in Jamaica, and now that Ethiopia was in peril, he used his new publication in its defense. England's right-wing papers were still lauding Italy's dictator that July, with *Saturday Review* actually calling Mussolini "benevolent."[54] This was more than Garvey could stomach. He had found a new cause.

Once upon a time, of course, he didn't need to look elsewhere; he had been his own cause. When his Universal Negro Improvement Association was at its height, it had its own conventions and uniformed brigades, its own parades through Harlem in which Garvey himself wore fringed epaulets and plumed headgear. He even took credit for Mussolini's methods. "We were the first Fascists . . . When we had 100,000 disciplined men and were training children, Mussolini was still an unknown." The Duce, claimed Garvey, "copied our Fascism. But the Negroes sabotaged it."[55]

Many had believed in Garvey's dream to sail back to Liberia aboard ships of his Black Star line, but the FBI had checked out the pathetic, poorly maintained ships and charged him with mail fraud. His best days were behind him, but now the cause of Ethiopia seemed to reinvigorate Garvey. If he couldn't be a king himself in Africa, he would at least try to save its last Emperor. "Mussolini may not know this," he warned readers of *The Black Man* in June, "but there are millions of Western Negroes, if the powers of Europe would only allow them, who would make minced-meat of the Italians in Abyssinia if they dared to invade the lone independent black nation in the ancient Fatherland."[56] In July, Garvey told his readers that the Duce was "a tyrant, a bully, an irresponsible upstart whilst [the Emperor] is a sober, courteous, and courageous gentleman."[57]

Leon Trotsky wasn't interested in the personalities involved; what mattered to him was class warfare and exploitation. He expected *everyone* to be dragged into war. Having worn out his welcome in France, one of the leading minds of the Russian Revolution had jumped at an invitation to spend his exile in Norway. He would wind up spending most of his time in a quiet house sixty miles outside Oslo, trying to stay relevant to the world while drafting his book about his persecutor, Stalin, *The Revolution Betrayed*. But he could take a few minutes to warn about Africa.

"It is very difficult to prophesy," Trotsky told the Norwegian labor newspaper, *Arbeider Bladet*, "but I believe an eventual Italo-Ethiopian war is in the same relation to a new world war as the Balkan war of 1912 was to the World War of 1914 . . . It is impossible to say whether a world war will break out in three or five years, but we ought to focus rather on a short than a long time."[58]

* * *

Indians for ambulances, Marxists predicting darkness over the world . . . That same week, the *Sunday Times* of London wasn't concerned with either of those things. It was worried about blacks getting dangerous ideas: "As the European power ruling the greatest number of African subjects, we have quite a special interest in the matter. An Italo-Abyssinian war would be a war between black and white." The paper thought it would be bad for business in colonialism if the Italians lost. On the other hand, it would be bad as well if they won. "Reverses to the Italians, if such occurred, would excite the most dangerous feelings. Speedy victory for them won by mass bloodshed would be very unsettling, too; and equally so would the prolonged guerrilla warfare with the rumors of atrocity inseparable from it."[59]

It was only a brief walk from the *Sunday Times* offices to Northcliffe House, where the publisher of the *Daily Mail* was not so squeamish over bloodshed. "Armchair critics of Italy's action in Abyssinia are trying to make fools of the British public," grumbled Lord Rothermere in a signed editorial on July 24. "There is no basis for the moral indignation they profess. The claim that Abyssinian independence concerns the League of Nations is fallacious."[60]

It didn't surprise anyone that the *Mail* backed Italy. The lord in charge, Harold Harmsworth, was a personal friend of both Mussolini and Hitler. The *Mail's* "Youth Triumphant" headline, heaping praise on the Nazis in 1933, had been followed the next year by open support of Oswald Mosley's own home-grown British Fascists. But the paper's support had abruptly stopped after there was violence at a rally in Kensington Olympia in 1934. Now Lord Rothermere was insisting that the "League is an association of civilized states. Abyssinia is a semi-barbaric country, characterized by cruelty, slavery, and feudal anarchy."

Samuel Hoare—worried so much about Pan-Africanism—probably thought the same thing, but as Britain's foreign secretary, he had to appear more moderate. Having failed to get anywhere with Mussolini, Hoare kept busy during July, sounding out his fellow statesmen. Each of his sounding boards urged him to appear united with the French. "Go as far as the French will go," Winston Churchill told him. "Take them with you, but remember their weakness and don't make impossible requests to Laval. It is doubtful whether the French will go as far as economic sanctions, but that is no reason for not pressing them."[61] As for Ethiopia, Churchill actually considered it a "wild land of tyranny, slavery, and tribal war." He was shameless about the open bigotries of his generation, and years later would walk out on the movie, *Carmen Jones,* because, he grumbled, he didn't like "blackamoors."[62] But he also put his own faith in the League of Nations, and he was a man of principle. He would back the League—if others would.

So on July 30, Anthony Eden was sent on another trip to Paris, but his mission was doomed from the get-go. Britain's man in Rome, Eric Drummond, was now recommending an Italian protectorate over part of Ethiopia to save the rest. The Foreign Office had drafted up a memo for the ambassador to France, Sir George Clerk, to present to Laval, but the memo didn't take a hard line—it simply noted that if the League caved in, it would fall into everlasting contempt. The document wound up on Laval's desk on the morning Eden arrived in Paris, and Laval quickly spotted wriggle room. He had little hope, he confided to Eden, of stopping the war now, and didn't know what practical solution could be found. The memo, after all, didn't call for a specific action.

"This was the kind of uncertainty in which Laval reveled," Eden wrote in his memoirs. "He could only be kept to a narrow path if there were no gutters in which to drag his feet."[63]

* * *

That same month, Ethiopia's new ambassador to Great Britain was wading gently into the diplomatic waters, trying to feel his way. He had only just arrived when he managed to have a "long conversation" with Samuel Hoare, who was all pleasantries. "He ordered that [Ronald] Campbell and another officer in the FO should communicate with me and help me in every way."[64]

It was as nice a way as any to pawn the man off.

The ambassador this time wasn't another Ethiopian educated abroad like Tekle Hawaryat or Afawarq Gabra-Iyassus. He was, in fact, one of the most extraordinary figures in Ethiopian history—and yet he didn't even grow up there, and he spent his life speaking Ethiopian with a slight accent. He was a man of two names, two centuries, and in many ways, three worlds. All of this was because Charles Martin—who was really Warqenah Eshate—was literally scooped up from a battlefield as a child.

Years before Menelik, Ethiopia was ruled by Emperor Tewodros II. It depends on who's talking, but he was either a mentally unstable, violently unbalanced shifta turned warlord, or the middle-class boy who made good, a great unifier and reformer. He's a hero to many modern Ethiopians, and a statue of him stands today in Gonder. Tewodros took offense when he didn't get a reply to his letter to Queen Victoria (some clerk had misplaced it), so he had the British consul and, later, several other foreigners tossed into prison. London couldn't let a thing like that pass, so it sent General Robert Napier and a force of thirty thousand men on a rescue mission. As Napier's army shelled the mountain citadel where Tewodros was making his last stand, most of his men cut and run. Tewodros took his own life, ironically shooting himself in the head with a pistol that was a gift from Victoria. The natural question is why Britain hadn't taken over Ethiopia at the time. The answer was that it simply wasn't interested back then.

In the natural confusion and bedlam of the attack, a little 3-year-old boy got separated from his parents. They "had rushed down the hill for their lives," thinking their son was safe with a fifteen-year-old aunt. The girl found him too heavy to carry, and, in fear for her own life, left him on the ground.[65] Like something out of Kipling, the child was carried away by British soldiers back to India and given a new name. He earned his medical degree in Scotland, and for years, this young African, estranged from his own culture and language, practiced medicine in Burma, healing the poor under the shade of coconut palms and in the shadow of the gleaming, gold-plated stupas of Buddhist temples.

Martin's interest in his own heritage was kindled when the Italians tried to take on Menelik at Adwa. He missed the battle, but Menelik heard about him and invited him to visit the country. Three months after his arrival, he was working one day out of his medical tents in the center of Addis Ababa when he noticed an old lady with attendants pacing back and forth, staring at him. Martin sent over his interpreter. The old lady wanted to examine his arms and legs. What on Earth for? She had her reasons. Soon enough, it was confirmed that he had a long scar on his left forearm and a birthmark on his right leg, just as she anticipated.

"On finding both of these marks in the right places, the old lady and her companions went crazy with joy," he recalled later. "They informed me . . . that both my parents were dead and that my Ethiopian name was Warqenah, which meant 'thou art gold . . .'"[66]

The old woman was his maternal grandmother.

Martin ended up serving as personal physician to Menelik, but he became more than a *hakim*, a doctor. He was an administrator, running schools and advising Ras Tafari on everything from the slavery issue to the League of Nations. He was a natural choice to be ambassador.

But in London, it was soon clear to Martin that the British were stalling him. He got nowhere with Samuel Hoare at their first meeting over permits for arms exports, nor was the government inclined to give Ethiopia the £20 million loan he wanted. By July 22, he was taking his case public, admitting to any reporter who would listen that "Ethiopia badly needs money" to finance its war effort. "Ethiopia is potentially one of the wealthiest countries in the world. We are quite willing to lease mining and oil concessions on an equitable basis."[67] Days later, he was being fobbed off on officials rather than getting in to see the great man himself, and he was informed that "permits for exportation of arms from [Britain] will not be given neither to Italy nor to Ethiopia. France, it is said, is going to do the same."[68]

The Foreign Office was very good at looking as if it cared about a problem while doing nothing about it. In August, it created a whole new department for "Abyssinian affairs," but its boss was another pipe-smoking department insider who had never been to Ethiopia and knew next to nothing about the country.[69] This was Maurice Peterson, a seasoned diplomat who had spent postings in Cairo and Madrid and who "detested" the League of Nations for its "lack of realism." He would prove to be as contemptuous toward Ethiopia as Hoare and Simon and downright hostile to Ethiopia's man in London.

The polite turn-downs were the kind of thing carefully prepared for Dr. Charles Martin, adopted son and former servant of His Majesty's British Empire, who would be expected to politely accept it and please go away. Unfortunately, the civil servants of the Foreign Office were also dealing with *Hakim* Warqenah Eshate, proud Ethiopian and emissary of the Lion of Judah, and he would *not* go away.

* * *

"*Down with Mussolini!*"
"*Death to Fascism!*"
The chants went up as an army of black protesters marched in Harlem. It was a sunny afternoon on August 3, and twenty thousand people had come out to show their support for Ethiopia. They marched in two separate parades, one on Lenox Street, the other on Second Avenue, linking up to fill the square at 141st Street and Edgecombe Avenue for a mass protest. There were floats and posters. There was a contingent of white-gloved members of the Brotherhood of Sleeping Car Porters. There were young radicals and die-hard Communists. Father Divine was supposed to speak, but was a no-show, leaving support up to his followers, who were dressed in brown sashes that read: "Father Divine is God."

There had never been a demonstration like it before. Here was a protest for a foreign country, a country considered by thousands to be a cultural home. Posters in the multitude read, "Hands off Ethiopia!" and "Schools—Not Battleships!" Many white liberals had come out as well, and a few carried a poster that depicted falling soldiers, along with the line, "They fell in battle because they fell for propaganda."

Did it make a difference? Was anyone with influence paying attention and reconsidering their stance? No one could be sure. Roosevelt was still uncommitted. The furthest he would go was to issue a statement, expressing his "hope of the people and the Government of the United States that an amicable solution will be found and that peace will be maintained."[70] Black citizens and white liberals were unimpressed.

David Darrah was convinced, however, that at long last, Mussolini was having doubts about his planned invasion. Darrah and his wife were in the Big Apple that week for a visit, having sailed over on the ocean liner, *Manhattan*. The Italian people, he told the *New York Times* on August 8, were being reluctantly goaded into a false enthusiasm over the coming war, but Mussolini hadn't counted on such strong international opposition.

"If you see pictures of troops departing for Africa showing scenes with high-hearted enthusiasm, you will know they are bunk," said Darrah. "There is no feeling of gay adventure about the Ethiopian enterprise. There was grumbling and dissatisfaction in Sardinia about the departure of a troop ship, and Mussolini had to go there and deliver a pep-talk."[71]

If the colonial adventure failed, Darrah argued, it would mark Mussolini's end as a dictator. Darrah suspected that the Duce didn't anticipate how firm the British government would be, and now he was shopping for a graceful exit, one where he wouldn't lose prestige. But the reporter was wrong; Mussolini knew the British better than he did.

The Duce was also aware that African Americans supported Ethiopia, and he told them they ought to concern themselves with the lynching cases down in the Deep South. Predictably, this didn't go over well. It galvanized the massive throng in Harlem, and F.A. Cowan, founder of the Pioneers of Ethiopia, told supporters, "We will show him that the American Negro is going right over into his backyard!"

They weren't just going to show him in Harlem, they were going to show him across America. On the same day as the New York march, hundreds of African Americans in Memphis turned out for an all-night demonstration and prayer service on the downtown's historic Beale Street. Five days later, five thousand blacks and some sympathetic whites poured into Reyburn Plaza in Philadelphia to protest over Ethiopia. And a massive protest was in the works for Chicago. The spirit was spreading.

Chapter Six

THE BRINK

On August 3, while the marches were preparing in Harlem, it was evening already in Geneva, and the League of Nations Council had to consider two resolutions. The first tossed out the location of Walwal as a factor for deciding who to blame for the hostilities; it was as if it no longer mattered. Instead, the Council was satisfied that both Italy and Ethiopia were willing to stay committed to the arbitration process. The second declared that the Council would meet again on September 4 to examine relations between the two countries. Only two months were left before the rains were over and Italy's forces could invade Ethiopia.

Meanwhile, Anthony Eden and Pierre Laval explained to Italy's man in Geneva, Pompeo Aloisi, that they were ready for a three-power meeting—Britain, France, and Italy—but it had to be authorized by the League Council. Ethiopia wasn't even invited to take part. Eden knew this blatantly undermined the African nation, but perhaps he feared that time was running out and recognized that the Italians wouldn't negotiate directly with the Ethiopians. Instead of forcing Italy to recognize Ethiopia as a League equal, he played along in a maneuver that must have been inspired, at least in part, by Hoare. Hoare, in fact, telegraphed Eden personally to let him know that authorization shouldn't be the sticking point to hold up three-way talks.[1] If the League didn't authorize it, well, too bad. The talks could be held anyway.

To add insult to injury, the whole scheme relied on the secret "spheres of influence" treaty designed by the European powers in 1906 to carve up Ethiopia without its knowledge. And now pressure was brought to bear on Tekle Hawaryat and his French adviser, Gaston Jeze, to surrender Ethiopia's right to bargain for itself.

Mussolini had no intention of changing his demands. In his instructions to Aloisi over the new proposed talks, his position was that there would be no deal unless he got everything—and that included the decapitation of Ethiopia's

Emperor.[2] At this point, he made an astonishing gamble. He circulated rumors that he was capable of a "mad dog" attack on the British in the Mediterranean, with the naval base at Malta being his most likely target.

The League of Nations Council still hadn't taken any preparatory military actions, but Britain would. It sent its fleet into the Mediterranean. Britain and Italy were on the brink of war.

* * *

The admirals of the British Navy shuffled their vessels around on the great *Risk* board under the guise of "routine" deployments. An aircraft carrier, a harbor defense net-layer, and four minesweepers were sent to Alexandria, while five destroyers with four aging subs went to Aden. Four destroyers and two subs were dispatched to guard Malta. Haifa had an impressive flotilla of sixteen destroyers. What was left of the Home Fleet gathered at Portland in case it was needed at Gibraltar, and its Mediterranean counterpart left Malta for Alexandria. The China Squadron reinforced Malta's might with four modern subs.

But the reinforcements didn't stop there. For Alexandria, there were eight-inch and six-inch gun cruisers and minelayers loaned from the forces in China, Australia, and New Zealand, more gun cruisers and sloops from the East Indies, four destroyers for Egypt from China. It was buildup and more buildup. Merchant ships carried nets, anti-torpedo baffles, controlled mines, and searchlights to Alexandria.

But there were problems, disturbing ones, for the fleet. It could barely manage with the ammunition stores it currently had, and certainly not if a short conflict mushroomed into another world war. Ships needed additional anti-aircraft guns, and better ones. There were aircraft carriers that didn't have aircraft, or, for that matter, replacement pilots. Alexandria posed a strategic difficulty—its narrow harbor mouth couldn't dock a great number of ships, and there were justifiable fears that it could be blocked. Since Gibraltar couldn't dock anything larger than a cruiser, the navy would have to depend on French bases at Bizerta and Toulon—assuming, of course, that the French kept their resolve.

On August 6, the First Lord of the Admiralty gave a report on the navy's status, and despite its problems, there was still no contest when it came to Italy. Yes, reinforcements were needed, but the Royal Navy could easily beat the Italians and certainly ruin their shipping. Eden took comfort from this. "Though our military equipment was in poor shape, it was adequate for the immediate task."[3] But Hoare was defeatist, taking away from the report that the navy had only limited strength.

* * *

War broke out between blacks and Italians on August 11, but it wasn't in Ethiopia.

It was in Jersey City, where friction had been growing between the black West Side and the Italian-American East Village ever since Joe Louis trounced Primo Carnera in the boxing ring. Blacks had been rubbing it in over their prize-fight hero, and Italians were bragging over what would happen to Ethiopia when the Duce's army went on the march. The previous Saturday night had seen a small clash, but no winner. Word soon got around over a rematch set, and a suitable battlefield was chosen: the same spot as before, Railroad Avenue between Coles and Monmouth streets, under a set of elevated train tracks. It formed a natural border between the two neighborhoods.

The combatants began to gather and strut at around two o'clock in the afternoon. A few insults and threats were traded, and then it was mayhem. The blacks and Italians rushed each other with knives, bottles, sticks, baseball bats, rocks, and chains. One Italian used the butt of a shotgun like a club. Black women were swinging broomsticks at white fighters, and they nearly overwhelmed the Italians. But then reinforcements came and swelled the ranks of both sides. It was bloody. It was hateful. One black man fell, screaming from his injuries. Other combatants dropped, hit by a hail of flying bottles and rocks. Neither black nor Italian were besting each other.

At the battle's height, police swooped in to break it up. They needed two emergency trucks and three ambulances, plus five radio patrol cars, and just for good measure, six detective cars. The brawlers scattered quickly. The cops didn't have to use the riot guns or tear gas they'd brought along, but they still felt that they'd better call for back-up. In the end, they arrested eleven rioters and took five others to the Jersey City Medical Center.

Nothing was settled, but then independence for Ethiopia was never going to be decided on a dirty corner of Railroad Avenue in Jersey City.

* * *

As the Union Jack fluttered over ships crossing the Mediterranean Sea, the Italian army's chief of staff in Rome, Marshal Pietro Badoglio, handed in his report card on the strength of his own forces. Could they stand up to the superpower? Unlike the big cats in Mussolini's photo ops, the British lion had fangs—sharp ones. Bureaucrats might sugarcoat their language in euphemisms for the Duce, but Badoglio did not. He and his top officers thought the Italian army was evenly matched with British forces, but as far as the navy was concerned . . . well, it was no contest. Italy would lose, and it would lose *badly*.

More than a dozen Italian subs couldn't operate in a sea that was longer than two thousand miles. Yet British battleships and destroyers, Badoglio noted, could roam as they pleased through the Mediterranean and cause havoc along Italy's vulnerable open coastline. The nation's air defenses were in a state of crisis; the equipment was shot or out of date, and it wouldn't hold up to the intensive demand of an ongoing conflict. New squadrons were being prepared, but he expressed doubt that they would be set to go in time. British planes could land on six aircraft carriers; Italy had none. Badoglio's note on air power is especially interesting, since there were fears that Italy might send planes to bomb London (which didn't show much confidence in France to intercept these on behalf of her ally). Summing up, he warned that a struggle with Britain would bring catastrophe. Still, Badoglio assured his boss that "the country, indignant over British behavior, would follow the Duce with enthusiasm."[4]

Mussolini went ahead with his plans. The astonishing truth was that he had always been gambling on an enormous bluff.

And he was determined to hold it all the way to the end. The day after Badoglio gave his withering assessment, the three-way talks on Ethiopia began in Paris. Pompeo Aloisi, according to Eden, was "being Mussolini's echo, saying openly that he had instructions to be uncompromising."[5] Even Pierre Laval's proposals—economic concessions, the appointment of Italian technical advisers, and rights of settlement in parts of Ethiopia—were summarily rejected. The talks stayed deadlocked, and Mussolini was so sure of his position that he didn't bother to take Laval's urgent phone call on August 17.[6]

Even before he sat down with Aloisi, Eden took a harder line with Laval. Conscious that the Royal Navy was on the move, he suggested that if France wasn't going to help, Britain would pull out of its commitments to Europe's security and merely look after its own interests. British diplomatic security was as tight as ever—as in, not at all—and a British reporter passed along the gist of the talks to Theodore Marriner, the American chargé d'affaires in France. Marriner made a detailed report to Secretary of State Cordell Hull: "The dangers mentioned were a possible race riot from Cairo to the Cape; the threat to the headwaters of the Blue Nile; the threat to the routes to India; and particularly from the French point of view the danger of bolstering Nazi strength in Austria which might follow in the wake of Italian preoccupation in Abyssinia."[7] It hadn't taken much effort for Marriner to confirm details with Britain's Robert Vansittart, who gloomily confessed to him that he felt the danger of war was greater than at any time since 1914.[8]

The conference predictably achieved nothing, and the British team held a kind of "post-mortem" on their failure after dinner at their embassy. A "worried and earnest" Vansittart lectured Eden on the gravity of the situation: "Anthony, you are faced with a first-class international crisis. We've got to reinforce the Mediterranean fleet. Remember that naval reservists can be called up without a Royal Proclamation."[9]

After the wasted days of negotiation, Eden met again with Tekle Hawaryat Tekle Mariyam, who said it had to be obvious to everyone now that Italy would attack his country soon.[10] All Ethiopia wanted from the world was the right to self-defense, but even that was denied her, thanks to the arms embargo. Couldn't Eden ask his government to reconsider its stand on this? Eden, his conscience plagued by the injustice of the situation, could only promise the man that he would try.

* * *

The Brown Condor and the Black Eagle were never going to fly in formation, but when they crashed into each other, it was a huge public relations setback for Ethiopia's cause.

It likely took the Ethiopians a while to warm up to John Robinson, and it's probable that they wanted to verify whether their new young officer had genuine skills. No problem; Robinson went about his business in his usual, good-natured manner. Always shy, but amiable, he was keenly aware that he was a guest in this strange land. He had been moved by personal conscience to come and serve, so serve he would. Hubert Julian, on the other hand, showed no signs of having matured or changed his ways from his last time in the country. Decades later, Julian even suggested to his biographer that Haile Selassie's daughter, Tsehai, then seventeen, had a crush on him and supported him at court.[11] By then, the lady in question had passed on, and wasn't around to deny the ridiculous claim.

The reality is that Julian was barely scraping by as a stringer for the foreign correspondents, who, with the mounting diplomatic tension, were often forbidden to travel far from the capital and were stuck in their hotel rooms, writing up dispatches based on tips and communiqués. "Julian, the Black Eagle of Harlem, was one of my 'spies'—and, I subsequently found he was also 'spying' for half a dozen other newsmen," remembered Australian reporter Noel Monks. "He had fallen from favor now, and was relying solely on the money we paid him."[12]

But Julian still knew how to be his own press agent. The *New York Times* ran a story that he rode a white horse down the streets of Addis Ababa for a military review, which gave the journalist an excuse to speculate on "reports" that he would command Ethiopia's air force.[13] The Emperor eventually sent word that yes, Julian could serve in the war, but it would not be as a pilot. Instead, he was charged with the duty of drilling infantry soldiers. Monks recalled how Julian "used to come into our room after a drill session, flop into a chair, and say in a voice hoarse from shouting, 'I'll teach those goddamn black bastards how to drill if it's the last thing I do.' He was blacker than most Abyssinians."[14]

It would never have occurred to Julian that his own behavior had prompted his humiliating demotion. It had to be someone else's fault, and he decided to blame Johnny Robinson.

The hate flowed both ways. The Eagle's reputation was making it harder for the Ethiopians to trust the Condor. Robinson heard stories about how Julian wasn't paying his hotel bill (by then a whopping $450) and apparently beat his servants. "You would be surprised [at] the lies he tells," he wrote his sponsor and friend, the black newspaper editor, Claude Barnett. Robinson was disgusted by a man who set the worst example for blacks coming from America ostensibly to help.[15]

There's very little that's agreed upon about what followed. In one of Julian's versions, Robinson personally talked to the Emperor and persuaded him to clip the Eagle's wings—highly unlikely. Another version goes that Robinson, tired of Julian's antics, was involved with a story that ran in black newspapers back in the United States; he allegedly wrote an article for the Associated Negro Press under his pseudonym, "Wilson James," that called Julian a con artist and argued he was harming the confidence that Ethiopians had in African Americans.[16]

However he was provoked, Julian stormed into the lobby of the Hotel de France where Robinson was staying and took a swing at him. For years afterward, Julian claimed Robinson had actually attacked *him*, and came at him with a knife, slashing his arms; he allegedly defended himself by picking up a chair and cracking it over Robinson's head. Given that Julian lied about so much in his life, his account for this episode can't be trusted either. Robinson's side of the story is that Julian confronted him at his hotel over the con artist slur, and as Robinson started up the wooden staircase, Julian slapped him.

Whatever happened, reporters stepped in to make sure things didn't escalate, but it made better copy if the incident became a barroom-style brawl. Haile Selassie already had a good sense of Julian's ego and had taken Robinson's measure. The word came from the palace that the Black Eagle should pack his bags and *go*. Robinson was innocent, but still contrite. He wrote later to Claude Barnett, "I am sorry I caused you all to be razzed, and will try to redeem myself if I can."[17]

There was no embarrassment or regret on Julian's part. "Can you beat it?" he complained to Noel Monks. "This goddamned Emperor has put the finger on me. Says I've got forty-eight hours to get out of the country. Brother, no guy can do that to me and win a war."[18]

But Ethiopia was not rid of the Black Eagle. Whether Haile Selassie relented or Julian simply didn't bother to leave the country, he apparently ended up as an assistant civil administrator in Ambo, a spa town a short distance west of the capital. He was back to drilling infantry soldiers.[19]

By the middle of August, John Robinson was promoted to full colonel and put in charge of the Ethiopian Air Force.

* * *

The brawl hurt the cause—for maybe a day or so. In London, it was still going strong, and if Hoare and the British government were worried about black radicals, they were easy enough to find. Any Foreign Office worker with initiative could have tracked them down by merely jumping on an Underground train and riding up a few stops.

Right in Russell Square was a Georgian mansion that had been converted into a nonresidential hostel for students from far and wide: Student Movement House (today, it's called International Students House). Among the Greeks, Russians, and other Europeans who took tea and flipped through the newspapers in "the House" were many Africans and Indians. They were desperately broke, lonely, and far from home, but dedicated to their studies and always eager for a debate on colonial politics. One of those gravely concerned for Ethiopia's future was Jomo Kenyatta.

In 1935, the man who would one day lead an independent Kenya was a mature student of anthropology at the London School of Economics. Kenyatta, rounding his forties, lived in the grimmest poverty in a bed-sit near Victoria Station, dodging debts and the call for rent from his long-suffering landlady. If he got mail, he would peel off the stamps and sell them to buy a modest bit of bread; what the English used to call a "penny bun." His threadbare wardrobe embarrassed his friends to the point where they sometimes bought him new clothes.[20] If he was lucky, the phonetics department at University College would pay him ten shillings an hour for his knowledge of the Kikuyu language.

London, both then and now, is no place to be in grinding poverty, but he still found time for Ethiopia. He knew more than others how outmatched the underdog would be in the coming conflict. Fourteen years before, in Nairobi, British policemen had fired their rifles at point-blank range into thousands of protesters for Kikuyu agitator, Harry Thuku. Kenyatta's friend and fellow activist, Dinah Stock, would recall him "half jestingly, half seriously, quizzing a distinguished aircraft designer—who happened to be a Communist—on the most effective way of sabotaging an airplane on the ground with a spear."[21] While he made it sound like a joke, he was genuinely interested in the answer. When he later took a room in Stock's flat up in Camden Town, he painted the furniture in traditional Ethiopian colors.[22] He began wearing a fez and cloak, and he grew his beard as an imitative gesture of support for Haile Selassie.

There were things to do, of course, on a more practical level. In August, he joined the International African Friends of Ethiopia (which had quickly changed its name from "Abyssinia"). Kenyatta became the organization's honorary secretary. He would write an article the next month for *Labour Monthly*, which he titled, "Hands off Abyssinia." It summarized Italy's creeping expansionism and called Ethiopia "the last remaining relic of the greatness of an Africa that once was."[23]

His fellow member, C. L. R. James, had no such romantic illusions. James was earning his living as a cricket correspondent for the *Manchester Guardian*, but was already gathering research for his landmark history, *The Black Jacobins*. A critical thinker, he gave credit to the West when credit was due. "I didn't learn literature from the mango tree, or bathing on the shore and getting the sun of the colonial countries; I set out to master the literature, philosophy, and ideas of Western civilization."[24] But the tall landmarks in Mayfair didn't impress him as they did other Caribbean arrivals. English food was awful, and the grumbling of English men worse, especially if a white woman flirted with a black man.

James, however, was no bitter iconoclast. Frederic Warburg, the left-wing publisher who would bring out Orwell's *Animal Farm* and *Nineteen Eighty-Four*, thought he was "one of the most delightful and easygoing personalities I have known, colorful in more senses than one."[25] Even when James decided he should pick up a rifle for Ethiopia, he marshaled his arguments. He hoped to get into its army, where he would acquire real military experience. "It would have given me an opportunity to make contact not only with the masses of the Abyssinians and other Africans, but in the ranks with them I would have had the best possible opportunity of putting across the International Socialist case. I believed also that I could have been useful in helping to organize anti-Fascist propaganda among the Italian troops."[26]

James managed to meet with Ethiopia's ambassador, Charles Martin, and once again, the Crisis brought together two remarkable figures. Yet we know very little about how the two men got on, and the specifics of their conversation, only that Martin persuaded James that he could do more good for Ethiopia as an activist in London than as another anonymous soldier in the field.[27]

The group also had J. B. Danquah, who would one day help lead the fight for independence in Ghana. There was George Griffiths from British Guiana, who started calling himself T. Ras Makonnen in honor of Haile Selassie. Makonnen had dented the Fascist cause with actual evidence, not just rhetoric; he published an article publicizing the fact that Denmark was making Italy's mustard gas. For this, the authorities in Copenhagen kicked him out of university and put him on a boat to Britain.

James had for company his boyhood friend from Trinidad, George Padmore, who had lived for close to three incredible years in the maelstrom of revolutionary Germany, where he'd edited *The Negro Worker*—until right-wing thugs ransacked the publication offices and the Nazis kicked him out of the fatherland. In London, he was free to write articles for *The Crisis*, like "Abyssinia—The Last of Free Africa," which pointed out that Britain had a lot to answer for with Italy's invasion scheme. Like Kenyatta, he was practically destitute, surviving in part off tiny political lecture fees offered by colonial students.[28]

Here were the minds that set the tone for African and Afro-Caribbean political thought for the next fifty years. And they were all together, all in the same city! And they were all working *to help Ethiopia*. In its early days, the group hashed over its resolutions in a Chinese restaurant in Oxford Street—because they had no place else to go. It's amazing to think that a casual stroll into this humble dining spot would bring you face-to-face with the men who would help shape modern Africa and the West Indies.

At the time, however, the group had fierce competition for the hearts and minds of sympathetic whites and African students. Marcus Garvey still wanted to be front and center of the crusade. C. L. R. James dismissed the whole Back to Africa movement as "pitiable rubbish," and now that the UNIA had attached itself to the cause, he and the others would drop in on Garvey's rallies every so often to heckle speakers and poach supporters for their own organization.

But there was a Garvey they did respect—Amy Ashwood Garvey, the leader's divorced first wife. She was a formidable activist in her own right. Marcus, of course, had wound up in London as his Plan B, since he couldn't return to America; she had come to London by choice in 1930. From her home in New Oxford Street, she ran the Florence Mills Social Parlour and an African restaurant, where, as T. Ras Makonnen put it, "after you've been slugging it out for two or three hours at Hyde Park," you could "get a lovely meal, dance, and enjoy yourself."[29] She was the maternal militant, offering a refuge for black students, demonstrators, and sympathizers.

It's difficult to tell how effective they all were. Samuel Hoare imagined a flood tide of scary Africans overwhelming the colonies, and yet British intelligence operatives had to know Kenyatta was sponging off of friends while Padmore scribbled essays for a few pounds. How much of a threat could these men possibly be? Their good friend, Eric Williams—who would one day become the first prime minister of Trinidad and Tobago—was happy to come to meetings, hang out, and socialize when he rode the train down from Oxford, yet he never joined their organization and preferred to keep his head in his books.[30]

But people everywhere *were expecting war*. On August 25, the group held a protest in Trafalgar Square. It had nothing like the turnout for the Harlem marches, but the crowd was impressive enough, and its color was mostly white. Amy Ashwood Garvey declared that now was the hour for the black race's complete emancipation. Charles Martin was there with three of his sons. The Ethiopian flag was waved by a bizarre character who called himself Prince Ras Monolulu. With a name like that, he couldn't possibly be Ethiopian—and he wasn't. He was born Peter McKay in St. Croix, and he made his money as a horse race tipster.

C. L. R. James was there, too, to exhort the crowd. Though funds were always tight, the International African Friends of Ethiopia managed to scrape together enough to send him from Coventry to Nottingham, from Wales to Ireland, all to build support for the cause.[31]

*   *   *

Across the English Channel, they were demonstrating as well. The representative for Guadeloupe in the National Chamber of Deputies, Gratien Candace, told Pierre Laval that "France's black subjects were solidly behind Abyssinia in the event of war and would provide the strongest stimulus for promoting solidarity among all colored races . . ."[32] On the night of August 21, police in Paris broke up a small but determined group of black demonstrators who were trying to make their way up the Esplanade des Invalides to the Italian embassy. After they were told that protests were "forbidden," they went off to a hall in the Latin Quarter for a meeting. It wasn't long before they hit the streets again, where things grew more intense on the Boulevard Montmartre, and five in their ranks were carted off by the police.[33]

It was a very different scene in Cape Town, South Africa, where about six thousand blacks turned up at the Ministry of Native Affairs, wanting to know how they could go fight in the Ethiopian army; the authorities turned them all away because of the recently passed Foreign Enlistment Act. A tribal chief and a veteran of the Great War for the French, Walter Kumalo, offered to raise a regiment of Zulus to fight for Haile Selassie.

All of this frightened a man like Jan Smuts, hero of the Second Boer War and statesman of South Africa. Smuts always thought of Africans as beings who needed to be raised up to civilization (yet kept apart from whites). "If Italy becomes seriously involved in Ethiopia and is seriously crippled there by

a long conflict a very serious position may be created in Europe," Smuts told
The Times of London. He expected the war in Ethiopia to spread "all over the
continent of Africa" as "every African would sympathize with Abyssinia."[34] It
would "shake the whole system of civilization to its foundations," as far as
he was concerned.[35] Weeks later, he would tell the attendees of a dinner in
Johannesburg that if Ethiopia were annexed or dominated by a great European
power, it would mean "the training of the biggest and most dangerous black
army the world has ever seen."[36]

Africans did sympathize. But they were looking to Great Britain and France
for leadership, and both countries still refused to step up. Samuel Hoare couldn't,
suffering a painful attack of arthritis in the foot and laid up in Norfolk. He
took the time to write a long letter about his misgivings over Ethiopia to Neville
Chamberlain, who was then Chancellor of the Exchequer. "As you may imagine,
I have received little or no help from other quarters," complained Hoare. "Stanley
would think about nothing but his holiday, and the necessity of keeping out of
the whole business at almost any cost."[37]

Hoare looked for more advice after he was back in London, a diplomatic
Hamlet hobbling about with the aid of a walking stick. When he asked Lloyd
George what to do over the issue of arms, the old Liberal leader didn't hesitate.
"Revoke the embargo," he snapped. The key to the Crisis, argued Lloyd George,
was ensuring Ethiopia got its own supply of weapons, but the British government
didn't have to play an active role for that. "Just drop a hint to Vickers. They will
see to it."[38] But at a Cabinet meeting on August 22, Anthony Eden was the lone
voice calling for the embargo to be ended. Journalists waiting outside Parliament
for their lead got the usual bland assurances: peace was paramount, Britain would
meet its obligations . . . same song, one more verse.

Across the Atlantic, Cordell Hull decided that if he couldn't avoid stepping
in the mess, maybe he could tell the others how to clean up so he wouldn't have
to look at it. Roosevelt agreed to his suggestion to send a message to Rome.
But rather than a warning to Mussolini, Hull communicated "in all friendliness and in confidence" on behalf of the US president that "failure to arrive at a
peaceful settlement of the present dispute and a subsequent outbreak of hostilities would be a world calamity the consequences of which would adversely affect
the interests of all nations."[39] The American chargé d'affaires in Rome, Alexander
Kirk, delivered the telegram in person on August 19, but was quickly rebuffed by
Mussolini. Italy, the Duce informed Kirk, would go ahead with its plans.

During this same week, the Neutrality Act Bill was passed in Congress and
landed on the president's desk. Once he signed it, he couldn't take punitive measures against Italy to help Ethiopia. And to veto the bill meant a fight that would

cost him, especially in the isolationist South. By the end of the month, Roosevelt would cave in and sign the Neutrality Act into law.

* * *

The view over embargos and neutrality was naturally different from Ethiopia. "You have let us down like savages in the matter of arms," one official bluntly told George Steer. This was a man named Ambai, an Eritrean, but one who was sympathetic to the Ethiopians and who had taken over as political director in Harar. "When you give up your pious embargo, it will be too late."[40]

Steer interviewed him on a leg of his long trip into the Ogaden. With the Emperor's blessing, he'd boarded a train to Dire Dawa, and from there, got an arranged truck ride to Harar. As two boys rode on the mudguards and the truck climbed twenty-five hundred feet along a dirt road marked with spiny cacti, Steer spotted herds of camel by a dry riverbed and a troop of baboons. Topless Oromo women carrying heavy loads of leaves pressed against the rock faces—the unsteady truck had rolled perilously close by.

In Harar, Steer met the hero of Walwal, Ali Nur, who had kept fighting after his superior, Fitawrari Shiferraw, abandoned the oasis. "I am to take you all over the Ogaden for the Emperor," he promised Steer.

Harar was a place where Islam met Africa—and thrived. It thrived in spite of Haile Selassie's father, Ras Makonnen, tearing down its main mosque and putting up an Orthodox church.[41] For centuries, the city of forty thousand inhabitants was a wellspring of culture, coffee, basketmaking, bookbinding, poetry, and more. The Oromo had raided and harassed its inhabitants so vigorously that the people put up an impressive fortification wall to keep them out. But then, weary of the attacks, the townspeople eventually found ways to trade with them—then to convert the Oromo to the faith of Muhammad. The long wall survived past its usefulness, becoming merely a decorative frame for the extraordinary and unique architecture of the city.

Decaying stone lions of the old palace now guarded the telegraph station.

"Below and to the south," wrote Steer, "a brown and ancient honeycomb, lay Harar old town, built with sand, dark wall jammed against dark wall, packed with people and smelling to high heaven."[42] Steer took it all in, the beautiful women in bangles and tight muslin trousers, wearing black, crimson, and yellow; the lepers mumbling for money; the officers in perversely high-heeled sandals who bragged in liquor stores run by Greek expats.

In Jijiga, the little travel group shared a meal of sardines with a nuzzling Kudu buck, and then the truck drove into the vast stretches of the Ogaden. Steer seldom saw anything living; the occasional couple of donkeys or a string of camels led by Somali nomads. "The only population who stand still in the Ogaden are the dead."[43] Past the thorn bush of Daggahbur was sand. And more blistering heat. All of this harsh country would prove to be one of the greatest weapons the Ethiopians had against their invaders.

When Steer and his group stopped to try hunting a herd of oryx, they ran into the governor of Harar, Nasibu Zamanuel, a man in his thirties with prematurely graying hair, dressed in a silk shirt and dark shorts, and carrying around a riding crop. He was another loyal supporter of the Emperor, and he'd set up traffic police and got roads built in Harar. Over coffee in gold-rimmed cups, Nasibu expressed the same kind of fatalism that Steer had heard from Ambai.

"I am a pessimist," admitted Nasibu. "What has the League done? Why have you stopped us buying arms? Do you want to destroy the influence of the Emperor by proving to his chiefs that the League has no value? And how can we hold out against gas?"[44]

Steer had never heard an Ethiopian mention gas before. He asked Nasibu how he knew the Italians would use it.

"We know that they have gas in Somaliland at this very moment," replied Nasibu. This was true. Using his riding crop like a pencil in the sand, Nasibu outlined the defensive strategy in the Ogaden. The Ethiopians knew what was coming—planes, tanks, and "worst of all," artillery—but they would fight anyway, even while knowing it was in vain. "They will beat us, but we will hold them as long as we can. We are supposed to be brave. Our courage is our only weapon. In the end, we depend on you."

The Ethiopians were busy digging trenches all over the Ogaden, explained Nasibu, to cope with the Italian planes and tanks. "It is no use attacking any of their outposts—what can we do against their machine guns? Better for the camps in the Ogaden to hold out to the finish. Afawarq will see to that. His motto is 'Over my dead body.'"[45]

"Afawarq" was Afawarq Walda Samayat, the commander of the advanced posts in the region. Steer was on his way to interview him and get a sense of the Ogaden's mobilization.

On that note, Nasibu left, making a present of his reserves of champagne and Vichy water to Steer.

At last, Steer and his escorts reached their destination, the main camp of Gorahai, where the Ethiopians could make use of a fortress at nearby Imi; it was this same stronghold where the "Mad Mullah" and his Dervish followers had escaped the British. They drove up to a unit of ten soldiers presenting arms and a small cannon that was steered their way under camouflage. Its commander, Afawarq Walda Samayat, had "ferocious" hair and a fierce expression, with large eyes and a jutting chin. He was half Amharic and half Kafa, which was considered a "slave race," but his intelligence and courage had helped him overcome the traditional ethnic barriers.

As Steer walked up, Afawarq sat under a canopy, wearing a British overcoat and jodhpurs. "And the first thing that he did," Steer noted, "with a great courtesy I admit, was to place me under open arrest."[46]

Afawarq detested all Europeans, never doubting in the end that whatever the flavor—British, French, Swiss, German—they would all side with the Italians. But his hatred wasn't out of blind ignorance or love of tradition. He wanted Ethiopia to progress as it looked after its own needs without foreign interference. Even though his Emperor had sent a wire that Steer was coming, Afawarq presumed the reporter was actually a spy, and he lectured him on the hypocrisy of the Western powers.

"A law court for the world should be the same as the law court in Ethiopia," argued Afawarq. "In my country, no one is allowed to come to court with a stick. But while your court talked, Italy kept on sending arms to her colonies. She despises the court of the other nations. She says she is the biggest nation."[47]

Afawarq had set up his camp in three weeks. He proudly showed off the Oerlikon .37 anti-aircraft gun that was mounted in a turret of the Mad Mullah's fort. "That is mine." He could also appreciate the history of this spot. The Mullah, he told Steer, "was very powerful here and has left many sons. We wish that we could fight in the way that he did, but you cannot do that against the air."

When this little tour had started, Steer had loathed his host, resenting him for assuming he was some kind of agent. But his hatred turned to respect as he inspected all that Afawarq had accomplished in his "beautifully organized camp." The trenches, the gun placements, the attention to hygiene, and swift communications—it was all quite impressive. "Without exception, he was the most capable Ethiopian that I ever met," wrote Steer. "His reserves of energy were enormous." Steer marveled that the man had gotten all this done in less than a month. He watched Afawarq salute the Ethiopian flag at sunset with his troops and felt a growing admiration.

In his memoir of the war, Steer wrote, "And when I remember his contemptuous voice, 'The Italians can rob all my country—when I am dead. I shall not care. I shall not *know*,' I thank God that made me and Africa, and bound us together in such a bitter union, that once in my life I met this man."[48]

* * *

In Rome, the Pope had no thanks for God over bitter unions in Africa. On August 27, Pius XI gave an address to two thousand Catholic nurses from twenty countries at his summer residence in Castel Gandolfo. "The mere thought of war makes us tremble," he admitted, and he even went so far as to declare, "A war solely for conquest would indeed be an unjust war, surpassing imagination. It would be too sad, too horrible. . . ."[49] His remarks were so provocative that a top monsignor and Italy's acting ambassador to the Vatican quickly conspired to rewrite them for the Vatican newspaper, *l'Osservatore romano.*[50]

By the time that newspapers around the world were reporting his speech, it contained a muddled reasoning: "On the other hand, Italy informs us that such a conflict would be for just defense, to protect its frontiers from incessant dangers, and for the expansion of population, which is increasing day by day, and that such a war would be justified to assure the material welfare and security of the country . . . we can but hope that these difficult problems will be solved by other means than war."[51]

The revisions, of course, had to be cleared with the Pope first, who had perused the new draft of his speech and insisted, "I truly did not say it that way." But in the end, when he could have taken up an offer to have corrections made, he had relented. "No, let's leave it alone."[52] Even this tepid statement—apologist in tone, completely lacking in any conviction—still embarrassed Mussolini's officials, and the Italian government decided to spin it as the Pope supporting the invasion.

Vatican City as a state was less than six years old back then, forged by the Lateran Accords with Italy, and the long feud between Mussolini and the Pope even once had its own skirmishes and riots. By June of 1931, the Pope was condemning the Fascist regime for its "odious espionage, secret accusations, and constant threats."[53] Fascist newspapers attacked Catholic Action, a lay organization directed by bishops, accusing it of trying to revive the banned Italian People's Party. David Darrah, back when he was in Rome for the *Chicago Tribune*, followed the ongoing feud closely. "Blackshirts one night broke into the offices of the Catholic Action, smashed the furniture, destroyed papers, and tore down the picture of the Pope. In the provinces, there was rioting. The Catholics charged that churches were plundered under Fascist instigation."[54] In the end, Mussolini dissolved the Catholic youth groups entirely.

Relations between Duce and Pope had settled down by 1935, but they hadn't completely thawed. After the Pope's statement on an "unjust war," Mussolini pushed the Vatican hard to fall into line. Just over a week later, the Pope celebrated Mass at the Basilica of St. Paul's Outside the Walls for a congregation of war veterans. He had deep reservations about the war in Africa, but by mid-September, Eugenio Pacelli, Cardinal Secretary of State (and later Pius XII) "sent word to Mussolini that the Pope would not stand in the way of an invasion."[55] As Professor Christopher Duggan noted in *Fascist Voices*, "The Church provided overwhelming backing for the war, with seven cardinals, twenty-nine archbishops, and seventy-five bishops offering public endorsements to the press."[56]

Across the Atlantic Ocean, Lorraine Hansberry was in Chicago and becoming aware of the Ethiopia Crisis. One day, she would be hailed as a playwright and author of astonishing talent, giving the world the theater classic, *A Raisin in the Sun*. But back then she was only five years old, growing up with a father who took pride in African-American achievements and kept a house full of books.

"Little as I was, I remember the newsreels of the Ethiopian war and the feeling of outrage in our Negro community," recalled Hansberry. "Fighters with spears and our people in a passion over it; my mother attacking the Pope blessing Italian troops going off to slay Ethiopians. When the Pope died, that was the thought of him that came to my mind. I didn't know a thing about Spain, but I certainly did know about Ethiopia. . . . We had been saying for a long time: 'Ethiopia will stretch forth her hands!' This always meant that *they* were going to pay for all this one day."[57]

* * *

In Chicago, they would pay for having a conscience with cuts and bruises, with arrests and chaos.

They had tried to do things by the numbers. The tweedy, Boston Brahmin English professor, Robert Morss Lovett—a former editor at the *New Republic*—put in a request to hold a parade for a group calling itself the Joint Conference for the Defense of Ethiopia. But the police commissioner turned them down, claiming a demonstration might lead to disorder. Those who wanted to march decided they would march anyway: openly, defiantly, proudly, through the South Side of the City of Big Shoulders. One of their pamphlets promised that "the Negro people of Chicago cannot stand idly by while the Fascist tyrant, Mussolini, moves to enslave the last independent Negro country of Africa!"[58]

The event had interesting speakers as well, men like Oliver Law. Through the Depression, Law had been a cement plant worker, a taxi driver, a stevedore, and, in time, a Communist. Law wanted to go fight in Ethiopia, but he would never get the chance. Instead, his legend as an African-American soldier would be written in another country entirely.

Thousands showed up for the protest on Saturday, September 7, at Prairie Avenue above Forty-seventh Street, and the parade was supposed to wind its way gradually to Fiftieth Street, where a mass rally would be held. But more than five hundred police officers with a small fleet of vehicles blocked their way. And then the cops pulled out their billy clubs and began swinging. Though the demonstrators were predominantly black, there were a fair number of white sympathizers, including several young male and female students from the University of Chicago. The police seemed to single the whites out for brutality, to drive home a clear message. "In practically every case," reported the *Chicago Defender*, "the police piled their clubs heavily on the heads, shins, and arms of those they arrested."[59]

The *New York Times* reported that the police arrested three hundred people.[60] The *Defender* put the round-up closer to four hundred and fifty, but suggested that most of them were let go after "long grilling."[61]

* * *

"Fascism has been able to make Italian journalists keep within bounds," observed General Emilio De Bono in his memoir of the campaign, "but foreign journalists are accustomed to enjoy unbridled liberty in their own countries, and are unused to discipline. . . . The few who showed signs of being refractory, or were suspect, were deported without delay."[62]

Now the Italians were about to get their most ardent supporter among the foreign press. Evelyn Waugh was on his way back to Ethiopia, this time for London's *Daily Mail*. With the help of friends' lobbying, Waugh got the assignment after the paper's regular star for foreign coverage, Sir Percival Phillips, argued with its owner, Lord Rothermere, and defected to the *Telegraph*.

Flush with a good salary and fat expense account, Waugh also secured a book deal on Ethiopia for what was then a whopping sum, £950. The *Telegraph* gave him a typewriter and told him to use it. Waugh tried, but he also brought the same open contempt for reporters he'd displayed the last time he was in Addis Ababa. Writing about Stuart Emeny of the *News Chronicle*, he complained, "He never stopped working; he was continually jotting things down in a little notebook; all events for him had only one significance and standard of measurement—whether or not they constituted a 'story.'"[63]

On the Port Said leg of his trip to Addis Ababa, one of the biggest stories of the Ethiopia Crisis practically fell into his lap. He made the acquaintance of Francis Rickett, an Englishman who liked to travel in style, ordering a luxury carriage on the train out of Djibouti that he fully expected to come with a kitchen and cook. He invited a grateful Waugh to share it with him. But there was no luxury car, and the two had to travel by regular coach. Rickett clearly wasn't another reporter, and he seemed to relish the curiosity he attracted, hinting that he was on some kind of mission. Waugh wisely wrote a female acquaintance back home to check Rickett out: "I want particularly to know how he earns his living, whether he is in the British secret service and whether he is connected with Vickers or Imperial Chemicals." He needed her to leave his name out of it, adding as a joke: "Be a good girl about this, and I will reward you with a fine fuck when I get back." (The lady in question never found him attractive.)[64]

Waugh was hardly welcome in the capital, loathed by the Ethiopians while "half the European population," according to the *Evening Standard's* Patrick Balfour, was "out for his blood."[65] Many still remembered his 1932 novel, *Black Mischief*, which had transparent caricatures of Haile Selassie as well as Sidney Barton, his wife, and their two daughters. When Barton's daughter, Esmé, learned Waugh was back, she stormed into one of the capital's two shabby nightclubs, Le Perroquet, and promptly threw a glass of champagne in the writer's face.[66]

Some of the locals assumed Waugh was an Italian spy. Waugh, meanwhile, speculated that Francis Rickett was an arms dealer. Rickett disappeared every so often to meet with various figures, including the Abun and Haile Selassie's adviser, Everett Colson. Waugh still assumed something was going on, but thought it would be rude to ask. In journalism, however, rude questions are often a job requirement. Waugh went off to the Ogaden to investigate a tale of a Frenchman arrested for spying, and by the time he was on his way back, his editors at home were furious. They wanted to know the details of a certain concession granted by the Haile Selassie government, and they expected Waugh to match copy. But Waugh had been away. He knew nothing about it.

Oil. This is what had brought Rickett to Ethiopia. Any trips to the Abun were to throw off the gullible. On August 29, Rickett signed an agreement with the Ethiopian government on behalf of the African Exploration and Development Corporation, which would get an exclusive oil concession for seventy-five years that covered half the country. The company had committed itself to making a geological survey within a year and start drilling for oil within five years.

Percival Phillips, now of course with the *Telegraph*, piled on the hype in breaking the story and rubbing the *Mail's* nose in it: "A few strokes of an ordinary black fountain-pen this morning performed one of the most momentous and far-reaching acts in the history of Ethiopia, bringing her out from the Middle Ages and setting her fairly on the road of the twentieth century."[67]

For Waugh, the missed story was a humiliating embarrassment, especially for a literary star who made a point of looking down on his colleagues. "I am a very bad journalist, well only a shit could be good on this particular job," he wrote a friend back home.[68] He and the *Daily Mail* traded snipes back and forth through expensive telegrams, and with typical bravado, he used a couple of cables from the paper as an ashtray for his cigar. All his resentment and bitterness did ultimately serve one constructive purpose. Out of his time now as a correspondent, Waugh would write one of his most popular and enduring novels, *Scoop*, his satire on journalism.

The oil story was picked up by newspapers around the world. Surely there couldn't be war after this! How could Mussolini invade a country where now there were not only British interests, but American investment? Oil promised a financial boom for Ethiopia. Under the terms of the bargain, the company could erect its own telegraph, phone, and radio station networks across the land. News of the concession was an astonishing turn of events.

Then the whole thing unraveled.

* * *

Percival Phillips was missing a few facts in his story on the oil concession. Stuck in Addis Ababa, he might be forgiven for not looking very hard at the mysterious African Exploration and Development Corporation, which sounded safely generic. His editors back in London didn't look either, and Fleet Street didn't know it had just tossed a bomb in the direction of Whitehall.

Foreign Secretary Samuel Hoare was soon feverishly telegraphing Sidney Barton, wanting him to explain what was going on. Only hours after the news was out, the Foreign Office issued a statement that promised, "No official or unofficial support whatever has been given to Mr. Rickett by the British Government, who have made it clear on several occasions that they have no imperial economic interest in Abyssinia except Lake Tana. . . ."

All of this was actually true, because as it turned out, the African Exploration and Development Corporation was a front for Standard Oil. *Which* Standard Oil was unclear for a while, as there were many, thanks to the original monolith being broken up after anti-trust suits. But there was no British connection, and Rickett soon confirmed this for reporters.

Hoare, however, wouldn't leave well enough alone. Hours after his quick telegram to Barton, he sent another. As far as Hoare was concerned, it was obvious that the concession fell "under Article 2 of Tripartite Treaty of 1906. In these circumstances you are authorized, if report is true, to inform the Emperor that His Majesty's Government must for their part advise His Majesty to withhold the concession."[69]

Here was the British foreign secretary, telling Ethiopia it couldn't do what it liked with its own resources—all because the European powers had gotten together about thirty years before to decide how to steal them for themselves.

Haile Selassie lost his patience. "As a sovereign state, we have the right to do anything we please in our own territory. The United States is not a party to the 1906 treaty, in which England, France, and Italy merely pledged themselves to do nothing to encroach on the interests of others. That is one of the reasons I gave the concession to Standard Oil."[70]

Unfortunately, instead of the oil deal providing an incentive for America to come to the rescue, Washington reacted with embarrassment. The Americans had been in the dark as much as the British. Secretary of State Cordell Hull curtly told reporters that the US government "could not follow every American wherever he went through the world seeking business interests, or see what he was doing and give him advice."[71]

Hull also wanted to smother any notions that American flags would be following dollars into Africa. The isolationists were pouncing on the issue. William Borah, a Republican senator, considered the deal to be buying "an interest in war." Arthur Greenwood, a Democratic congressman from Indiana, joked to reporters that Americans who wanted to fight for Ethiopia might "enlist under Ethiopian colors and let the Standard Oil Company pay the expense."[72]

To Hull, the impression "was now created that all the efforts of the British and American Governments to keep Mussolini from plunging into Ethiopia were dictated by the greedy motive to corner the oil prospects in that country."[73]

No one, not in the US government nor in Whitehall, ever stopped to examine this creaky logic: countries that sought to reap investments through peaceful means were somehow *less* entitled to compete for Ethiopian resources—less entitled, in fact, than a nation that shouted loud and clear that it would take them by force.

Haile Selassie's gambit had been a shrewd one, and given the context of Ethiopia's political and economic development at the time, it would have suited America well. Cordell Hull was not interested. For the sake of shortsighted political expediency, he was intent on killing the deal.

It didn't take long for the government to hunt down the real brokers of the concession: Standard Oil out of New Jersey. Corporate officers were summoned to Washington on September 3 to explain themselves, and Hull sent word through his staff that he "deeply deplored" the whole thing. The oil men asked what the State Department wanted them to do. That was easy. "An immediate and unconditional withdrawal from the concession would meet the needs of the situation."[74] That is, the needs of the US government, not the oil company's.

Haile Selassie protested to no avail, insisting that he gave the concession to an American company as a gesture of friendship between the United States and Ethiopia. Hull, refusing to acknowledge that his move amounted to a change in

America's position, claimed that it was meant to be "helpful in the cause of peace" and to "strengthen the hands of those powers, including the United States, which are making strenuous and sincere efforts towards that end." The Emperor was watching his opportunity slip away, and on September 10, a formal request was made about whether the United States might be willing to act as a mediator in its dispute with Italy.

Hull's reply two days later was that this "would not appear to be practicable, coming as it does at a moment when the appropriate agencies of the League of Nations, to which the Ethiopian Government has referred its dispute, are occupied in an endeavor to arrive at a solution. . . ."[75] Thanks to Cordell Hull, the United States had graduated to Europe's level of hypocrisy.

Chapter Seven

"I HOPE THE ORGANMEN GAS THEM TO BUGGERY"

Geoffrey Harmsworth of the *Daily Mail* came home and noticed the hostility among white conservatives. "In London I found that they had a new name for people like myself who had long held the view that Italy should be restrained from her madness, not only for the sake of Abyssinia, but the security of European peace. We were called 'bellicose pacifists.'" He noticed the walls and pavements of the West End, as well as the steps to 10 Downing Street, were covered with the slogan: "Keep out of it."[1] In a restaurant, a bad comedian won big laughs with his greeting, "Walwal!" He exited with, "Well, Abyssinia."

"It was a huge joke," Harmsworth noted tartly, and he obviously found no humor in it.[2]

Left-wing radicals weren't laughing either. Britain's powerful Trades Union Congress voted on September 5, urging "all the necessary measures provided by the Government to resist Italy's unjust and rapacious act." Close to three million members were in favor, compared to a paltry 177,000 against. The Peace Ballot might be smugly dismissed, but here was the TUC, making its wrath against Italy clear. Was this enough now to show what people in Britain truly wanted? Perhaps. The easiest dismissal could be one of partisanship—most TUC members were probably never going to vote Tory anyway. But it all added up; the Peace Ballot, the TUC vote . . . millions of whites were *on the side of an African country* in a time when Britain still had the most powerful and extensive empire on Earth.

As the momentum for war kept building, it turned out that Ethiopia could have defenders—for a price. Paris became the unofficial recruiting base for mercenaries, many of whom were Belgians who had fought for their government's colonial regime in the Congo. By mid-September, Brussels would pack up and pull out its military mission from Addis Ababa, but it was willing to look the other way as its experienced veterans signed up. Their contracts were often for salaries of fifteen thousand francs a month, and if they were killed, their families would receive a death benefit of half a million francs.

Across the Channel, men regularly called on Ethiopia's ambassador, Charles Martin, to ask him how they should go about serving. London newspapers reported in early September that at least three thousand men had volunteered. At the embassy in Princes Gate near Hyde Park, there was one room "piled high with letters, hundreds of them unopened, while a special clerical staff [worked] feverishly trying to just keep pace with the daily postal deluge."[3] The British doorman was kept busy answering the doorbell while the phone jangled through the day.

There were many expatriates and exiles from other parts of Europe willing to fight, too: Turks, White Russians, Hungarians, and Czechs. Martin had to turn them all away. The Foreign Office was well aware of the steady stream of potential volunteers who came to the embassy. It reminded the good doctor that he would be breaking the law if he encouraged any of them, and it's entirely possible that the British government would have expelled Martin if it found clear evidence that he was recruiting. In fact, that would have given them the perfect excuse to abandon the country they barely treated as an ally.

On the night of September 3, he gave a speech at the Nile Society in London. "If worse comes to worse, Ethiopians would much prefer being under the just and considerate administration of Britain than that of Italy," he told the audience. "Let us have peace for twenty years, and a loan of £20 million to enable us to open schools all over Abyssinia, and I assure you that we will be as advanced at the end of that time as any nation could desire."[4]

Martin hadn't come to the reception alone. He brought along several of his children, and his son, John, only nine years old, made a splash. "Give us guns, and we'll fight!" he cried out in his thin, high voice to the Society members. Standing on a table, the boy was a natural. "I am told a naughty Italian wants to kill my people, take our country, and make us his slaves—because he is greedy and not a good Christian. Dear ladies and gentlemen, please stop this man from being so cruel. But if you won't stop him, please give us guns, and we'll fight him!"[5]

Then John joined his father and his brothers and sisters and sang the Ethiopian national anthem to the accompaniment of a phonograph record.

Days later, Martin was called on the carpet by Maurice Peterson, the head of the Foreign Office's Egypt and Abyssinia departments. "He said that Mussolini had complained about it," he noted in his diary. The Duce, it seemed, had been very offended by the line in his speech that "the Italians needed emancipation far more than [Ethiopia's] slaves." So here was Martin, an ambassador to the Court of St. James, subjected to a tedious lecture from a civil servant on how it "was against etiquette for a minister to make public speeches." Martin was well within his rights to suggest that if there was a complaint, it should come directly from Italy's own representative—and certainly not from an official below the foreign minister. He chose a different tack.

"Told him if it is so, I am sorry, for otherwise I shall be doing nothing for my country, however, if it is against diplomatic custom, I won't make any more speeches."[6]

Fortunately, he already had momentum on an international scale. From almost the day he arrived in London, newspapers across Britain besieged him for interviews, and he got requests from as far away as Canada, South Africa, India, and Australia. "Telephone going almost every five or ten minutes—people howling for interviews," he jotted down in his diary during his first few weeks in London.[7] The Foreign Office tried to muzzle him on this front, too, telling him he shouldn't give interviews "to ordinary newspaper correspondents." He didn't stop, merely growing more selective.

All the while, Martin must have been monitored by not only the Foreign Office, but also the Italian embassy. OVRA was watching him, and after a few months, its agents would approach him with sinister plans of their own.

* * *

The foreign correspondents kept coming to Ethiopia, ready for action. But there was still no action to be had.

Laurence Stallings had come, making his way along the capital's mule tracks on a cane. He had been wounded in the Great War and had managed to convince the doctors not to amputate his leg—only to lose it five years later, thanks to a fall on the ice. A critic, bestselling novelist, playwright, and screenwriter, Stallings was one of the wits of the Algonquin Round Table, and he would later co-write three of John Ford's most successful films. He showed up in Addis Ababa for Fox Movietone News with a crew of four photographers, fifty thousand feet of film packed in sawdust, a convoy of trucks and motorcycles, and a collection of flags. "The flags," joked Stallings in an article, "are to warn bullets to 'keep off, this means you.'"

Floyd Gibbons had come, the eye-patched reporter who made Americans learn the name "Pancho Villa" and whose radio delivery was as quick as a machine gun. The Hearst wire service sent H. R. Knickerbocker, a red-headed Texan who stomped around Addis Ababa in cowboy boots. Novices, too, had come. The

Australian, Noel Monks, would end up making a career out of covering war zones, including the Allied landing at Normandy. Years later, he would suffer the unique humiliation of his wife, Mary Welsh, leaving him for Ernest Hemingway. Monks had hoped to find a news operation to send him, but failed. The chief editor at the *Melbourne Herald*, Keith Murdoch—Rupert Murdoch's father—had told him in a cable, "Think your plans foolish adventure. Regret cannot help and strongly advise against."[8] Monks decided to gamble and go anyway as a freelancer.

"By this time there were seventy-five journalists in Addis Ababa and another thirty were reported to be on their way,"[9] according to Bill Deedes, who was a callow young journalist back then on his first African posting. Less than half, he informed his editor, were bothering to file. A press bureau had been set up, issuing statements and declaring itself the only official authority for news. "There was no censorship as such," recalled Deedes, "but there was nothing for a censor to do."[10] When there was eventually something to do, there was such an avalanche of dispatches that it caused a logjam of nuisance reports for the US State Department, which decided it was easier to give the legation in Addis Ababa its very own radio station. The equipment was donated by the US Navy, which sent four efficient technicians to set things up.[11]

Deedes isn't known in America, but he was famous decades later in Great Britain. He became a member of the Harold Macmillan Cabinet and took on the print unions as editor of the *Daily Telegraph*. He was also a stalwart friend of Margaret Thatcher. After becoming a life peer in 1986 and well into his eighties, he was still hopping on flights back to Ethiopia and campaigning against landmines.[12] But all this followed the rather dubious honor of inspiring Evelyn Waugh's hapless correspondent hero, William Boot, for the novel *Scoop*.

Waugh was inspired by Deedes, but took an almost instant dislike to George Steer, perhaps because, as has been suggested, the younger man had the coveted job at *The Times* and because Steer's Oxford education easily outshone his own. It didn't help that Steer hadn't recognized Waugh when the two met briefly at the train station. Steer's biographer, Nicholas Rankin, put it best when he wrote, "Their trains went in opposite directions, and so did their dispatches and their politics."[13] Later, as a weak joke, Waugh and another correspondent locked Steer in his hotel room so he would miss an important train; Steer could do without these pranks and checked out of the Imperial Hotel to move into a private house. Waugh and his accomplice then locked him in again and gave his house key to a brothel madam.

The novelist was clearly bored and starved for the usual attention he got at home. At the city's movie theater, a newsreel showed the latest Italian war preparations, and Waugh applauded them with relish, while sitting behind him were two high-ranking Ethiopian officials. Out of an impulse of novelty, he bought a baboon, but complained later that the bored animal moped and publicly masturbated. Waugh was also paranoid over the telegraph operators selling his copy to a competitor, so he sent one dispatch in Latin. The editor in London treated it as gibberish and spiked the copy.[14] Then, in a fit of pique over the latest argument with the paper, Waugh cabled his resignation. This was a reckless and premature move. War still hadn't broken out yet, and he was threatening the success of his book contract. The *Mail* sent out W. F. "Binks" Hartin to replace him, but the Ethiopian authorities demanded Waugh leave before they granted a visa for a new correspondent of the same—and obviously pro-Italian—newspaper. Waugh obstinately stayed put, while Hartin was left to cool his heels in Djibouti and suffer a bout of dysentery.

In a letter to his friend Lady Diana Cooper, Waugh confided, "I have got to hate the ethiopians more each day goodness they are lousy & i hope the organmen gas them to buggery [sic]."[15] When the war finally began, Evelyn Waugh was nowhere near the front, and like other correspondents, was bottled up in the capital. He wanted out. But he also wanted to stay put simply to spite the *Daily Mail*.

In the end, he would see nothing of the war, but that wouldn't prevent him from inflicting great damage on the Ethiopian cause.

*   *   *

Samuel Hoare, still hobbling with a cane, thanks to his bout of arthritis, was scheduled to address the League of Nations in early September. Off he went to Geneva, in a plane specially fitted so that he could spend the flight on his back. Always needing to check the weather with others, he'd talked again to Neville Chamberlain before he'd left. He talked with Vansittart. He talked to one of the colonial administrators. His go-to men pronounced the League dead and wanted to pull the sheet over its head, but Hoare thought there might still "be a chance of putting new life into its crippled body."[16] He knew he couldn't stand in a hall in Geneva and call time of death.

He had long talks with Pierre Laval, too. Like others, Hoare found Laval slightly repulsive in his hygiene, but he still admired the French prime minister's quick mind. In his memoir, however, Hoare also retroactively gave himself intuition, claiming that Laval made him uneasy.[17] If he ever did have misgivings, he didn't act on them. For now, he thought he could count on the French prime minister's support. Laval made it clear he was willing to back him up, as long as things didn't come to war. The only problem was that Britain's foreign minister was ready to announce to the world that his nation *was* prepared to go to war.

So on September 11, Samuel Hoare limped up to the podium. As Hoare made his speech, he noticed that his audience had grown very quiet. "We believe that backward nations are, without prejudice to their independence and integrity, entitled to expect that assistance will be afforded them by more advanced peoples in the development of their resources and the build-up of their national life."[18]

There were no interruptions, only a tense silence.

Hoare was aware that his audience was paying rapt attention, but he didn't know yet whether they liked what he was saying or not. He went on, reaffirming Britain's commitment, saying, "The League stands, and my country stands with it, for the collective maintenance of the Covenant in its entirety, and particularly for steady and collective insistence to all acts of unprovoked aggression."[19]

When he was done, there was a burst of applause and rave reviews the next day from London newspapers. No one doubted Hoare meant what he said; the British battleships, *Hood* and *Renown*, were now at Gibraltar, and later in the month, there would be more than 140 ships in the Mediterranean. If Ethiopians had to fight, now they knew they would be fighting alongside British soldiers.

Except they wouldn't—not in 1935. It was all a bluff. Hoare admitted this in his memoirs, but argued it was a moment that was "inescapable."[20] There was the reality of his public message, and the truth that would only be said behind the scenes. Hoare wanted to revive the idea of buying Mussolini's goodwill and cooperation with economic concessions in East Africa.[21] Two days after Hoare's address, Laval stood in front of the League Assembly, insisting that France would also live up to its commitments.

In private, however, Laval wouldn't agree to close the Suez Canal if things got worse. He wouldn't even discuss it. He was less fussed, however, over economic sanctions. "After all," he told Hoare, "you cannot make the British buy Gorgonzola and Chianti if they do not want to."[22] But when it came to backing up his words with steel, Laval flatly refused. Here was Great Britain, sending in the Royal Fleet, while "he, on the other hand, did not move a ship or an aeroplane or sanction even preliminary preparations for Anglo-French air bases."[23] Hoare was genuinely shocked that his accomplice, in lying to the League, should perpetuate the lie right to his face.

Meanwhile, the master of bluff was willing to raise the ante. Days after Hoare's speech, Mussolini famously told John Munro of the London *Morning Post*, "We have an army in East Africa which has cost us two billion lire. Do you really believe that we have spent such an astronomical sum for nothing? We are on the march."[24]

While there were grand plans for a potential attack on Egypt and Sudan, the Italian commanders didn't have much information to work with. They were depending at the time on a reconnaissance flight, and believe it or not, on what they could glean from a few *guidebooks* of the region. And what would they do about keeping a steady supply of water for their forces? The problem wasn't even solved by the time the plans were sent for the dictator's approval.

That wasn't the biggest problem. An attack on one piece was an attack on the entire British Empire, which flanked Mussolini's colonies *on all sides*. And within a couple of weeks, the Royal Navy could make the Mediterranean a British lake and cut off Italian ships from the Canal, the Red Sea, and their port of Massawa. Even the unreliable Pierre Laval would be forced to throw in France's lot with the British.

But Mussolini was going all in. "In their present mood," Britain's ambassador to Italy, Eric Drummond, wrote in a telegram from Rome, "both Signor Mussolini and the Italian people are capable of committing suicide if this seems the only alternative to climbing down. Rome today is full of rumors of an impending declaration of war on Great Britain."[25]

* * *

George Steer was on hand for the first-ever air-raid drill in Addis Ababa. It was not a resounding success. When an old piece of artillery gave the three loud blasts as the signal, there were cases of looting in the city, and some people took the practice shots for the real thing and stayed away for days.

As the rainy season petered out, the capital saw the frantic commerce expected with war fever. One shop did a booming business in khaki. Some chiefs considered owning a revolver as a status symbol, and they bought the guns more for their aesthetics than their usefulness. A used Mauser rifle could go for the equivalent of $200 US. Gas masks were in special demand, but ordinary items were moving fast, too: coffee, pots and pans, pack saddles. When he visited Harar, Steer wandered with his interpreter through the market square and noticed how the dealers' tables had boxes of mixed cartridges like assorted chocolates.

There was fear and apprehension, but also a lot of bravado. Ethiopia had its own boy scout movement, and its members wrote to their symbolic leader, the eleven-year-old Duke of Harar, asking for real rifles. Women had always been involved in the wars of Ethiopia as well, and they would play their part, too. They were expected to feed the troops and nurse the wounded, and they could also be—and were—respected fighters. But the politics over this were complicated, and as with the men, followed the traditions of feudal land tenure. Haile Selassie had issued a decree discouraging women from enlisting in the standing "modern" army, but given that wives and concubines showed up with the ordinary men who answered the call, they were always going to be in the thick of it.[26] And generally speaking, if you were a woman who owned land and a rifle, you fought; you *wanted* to fight to defend your home.

Women also did their part to coax more men into answering the call. One of their recruiting slogans went:

> Wake up men
> Protect your country
> Let alone the men
> We the women will fight[27]

At the Ethiopian Women's Work Association, Lady Barton and the Emperor's third daughter, Princess Tsehai, kept up a brisk pace, assembling the women of Addis Ababa to prepare food rations, pack clothes, fetch mattresses, and pile bandages.

The women listened and complied. There were still too many cases when the men didn't. Haile Selassie had recruited a brain trust of military veterans—Belgians, Swedes, Swiss, French—but they were almost always ignored. "The mercenaries, no matter how much they may have wished to do so, were never allowed to take command of the Ethiopian troops in action," wrote Pierre Ichac of France's *l'Illustration*. "The Ethiopians did not trust them because they were *ferengi*—foreigners."[28]

One of these *ferengi* knew this only too well. Feodor Konovalov once flew with the Tsar's Imperial Guards Squadron, but when the Bolsheviks turned Russia upside down, he became a man without a country and had to find new royalty to serve. Konovalov's job was to inspect the defenses in Tigray, where everyone knew the war would begin.

After he reached Adwa, he discovered quickly that the warriors had no idea how to conduct modern warfare. Their trenches were shallow pits, dug in the lowlands, which meant they had no protection whatsoever. The Italians would be able to pick them off as they pleased. Konovalov took the chiefs into the nearest mountain and showed them fresh spots for fortifications. "These are the positions which God himself created for you. You can see everything before you, and you remain unseen and under cover."

The Ethiopians were unhappy that all the previous work would go to waste. "This is true," said one of the old chiefs. "What do we do with these trenches below, which we made with such a cost of energy?"

Konovalov told them that if nothing else, the shallow trenches in the valley below would fool the Italians.

"What kind of war is this?" complained one of them. "We always fight in the open field. What sort of war is this—fighting behind stones?"[29]

Doubt, distrust, dismissal; it extended all the way to the top. Haile Selassie had little choice but to appoint commanders along the feudal lines of nobility, not on the basis of any modern training. Three of them—Seyum Mangasha of Tigray, Kassa Haile Darge of Shoa, and Mulugeta Yeggazu, the army's commander in chief—were older men who had never had a formal military education. Neither had Imru, Haile Selassie's cousin and childhood friend. Each was his own man, each with a different degree of loyalty, skill, and ingenuity, and each was determined to lead men with his own methods.

Feodor Konovalov got Ras Seyum's measure when he made his inspection in the north. Seyum, a bearded, portly figure—George Steer would call him a "nice, little chocolate Henry VIII"—received his new adviser graciously enough. But when Konovalov unrolled a topographical map, Seyum made it clear that he wasn't interested. Those should be left for Kassa: "Oh, Ras Kassa can study maps for hours."[30]

Meanwhile, the army's commander-in-chief was a belligerent alcoholic. Ras Mulugeta Yeggazu, his chin covered by a white beard, his lanky frame gnarled like a tree, was past seventy years old. He was a hero of Adwa who had served under Menelik as Minister of Finance. He had no patience or understanding of modern warfare, and he openly despised all foreigners. He wanted them all deported. "They are all spies and friends of Italy."[31]

Before he left Addis Ababa, claiming poor health, General Eric Virgin gave an interview to a Stockholm correspondent. The Ethiopian warrior was courageous, promised Virgin, while Italy's cause was an "impudent" grab for power. But Virgin made a distinction between Italy's people and its Fascist leaders. "I have been called an enemy of the white race. I, too, have my ideas as to how the white race will best be able to preserve its leading position—not by opportunism and excessive development of power, but by example."[32]

Virgin, however, would not be around much longer to be an example.

*   *   *

With the strutting peacock of Hubert Julian out of his hair, Colonel John Robinson could get down to the daunting task of building the Imperial Air Force. He'd been surprised himself at his own "rapid advancement," but now he had to deliver a crack flying unit. There must have been times when it all seemed overwhelming and practically impossible. Build an air force out of the lame duck junk piles he'd inherited and teach a class that couldn't speak his language?

Conditions were naturally different from what he expected; "in some cases much better and in other cases, 100 percent worse."[33]

To use the term "air force" for what the Ethiopians had at the moment was overly generous. There were only about a dozen planes, including the Potez 25 biplanes Haile Selassie had used to put down Gugsa's revolt in Anchim in 1930, and most of the sad aircraft, desperately in need of repair, were several years old. Pilots were as urgently needed as planes. The ones already flying were French, and to use them in combat would risk a diplomatic incident. In fact, "to use them in combat" was a generous way to put it, too, since none of the planes would ever have mounted guns. Some of them would stick around a while as instructors, and one luckily spoke English and could act as Robinson's interpreter. But many of them soon headed home.

That would leave a huge vacuum in skills, training, and experience, and there were few Ethiopians who could fill it. Until Robinson showed up, it allegedly took years for Ethiopians to learn what Westerners picked up in a few months, and some men with the country's air service still didn't know after five years how to inspect a plane before take-off.[34] If true, these facts said more about their white Western instructors not giving a damn than it did about the Ethiopians and their culture.

There were a few bright spots in the gloom. The Emperor donated an old single-engine Fokker, which would be piloted by an improbable character, a twenty-four-year-old Swedish count, Carl Gustav von Rosen. Von Rosen became interested in flying partly thanks to the example of his uncle—Hermann Goering. Goering had come to Sweden after the Great War to work as a taxi pilot, and this is where he met and married von Rosen's aunt, Karin. Young Carl first became a mechanic and later flew in an aerial circus, but Goering had no influence on his politics; von Rosen would devote half his flying career to thrill-seeking as he helped the underdog.

Meanwhile, the Ethiopians managed to smuggle in—probably by train—a brand-new treasure. Robinson and his French colleagues put it together the way a child would build a boxcar racer in his father's garage. It was a Beechcraft Staggerwing, which Robinson quickly adopted as his own. This would be his best friend and big dog. It could carry a pilot and four passengers and had an impressive top speed of two hundred miles per hour. It could also cover a distance of a thousand miles, making it perfect for transport runs. Robinson would use the Beechcraft more than any other plane, especially for missions to fly Haile Selassie.

In public, he doubted the Italian air force would play a significant role in battle. Quite simply, he reasoned, they would be foiled by the African geography, forced to fly at altitudes where they couldn't be accurate in their bombing.[35] He was wrong, but this was accepted wisdom at the time.

Privately, Robinson was far less confident. He wrote home to friends in late September, confiding that Ethiopia's crafts actually flew well, but were "of ancient vintage and as slow as snails in comparison with modern Italian planes."[36] He had originally hoped to bring over a few of his fellow black American pilots, but in these last critical days of peace, he was now telling them to stay away for their own good. "I shall stay here and deliver everything there is in me, but there is no reason for you to go down to death with me. It will be better for you to remain in America and carry on the good work which we have begun in interesting our people in aviation."[37]

And Ethiopia had only a few days left of independence.

*   *   *

As the world waited to see if war would break out between Britain and Italy, the Committee of Five offered its "compromise" solution to the Crisis on September 18.

It amounted to treating Ethiopia like an Italian colony. It proposed an international mandate, which would hand over the Danakil and Ogaden to Italy while allowing Italian citizens the right to settle in other regions. The Ethiopians were expected to be satisfied with League-appointed European experts and technicians to help them. The proposal was leaked to the press, and some reporters implied that this influenced Mussolini's decision to turn it down. Anthony Eden never doubted he would. Mussolini told a correspondent in Rome for the *Daily Mail*, "It looks as if the committee of the League thinks I am a collector of deserts."[38]

Before the report was ever published, Italy's Undersecretary for Foreign Affairs, Fulvio Suvich, let it be known that Mussolini would withdraw his two new divisions in Libya *if* the British and French would promise there would be no military sanctions.[39] And oh, the cause of peace would be truly helped if the British Fleet left the Mediterranean.

Instead of the superpowers of Europe laughing in Suvich's face, Britain and France treated these outrageous demands with serious consideration. Eden was exasperated yet again with Hoare, who wanted the British team to take its cues from Laval. By now, he should have known better, and Eden had to remind him in a long telegram. Eden also reached out to representatives of the Dominions, sensing that maybe their concern might stiffen his foreign secretary's spine.[40]

At the Foreign Office, the head of the Abyssinia Department, Maurice Peterson, drafted up a fresh analysis: Maybe the Committee of Five's proposals were dead, but they had "lopped away" so many of Mussolini's more "absurd" demands that "we can well afford to be generous towards what is left." Oh? And what would the Ethiopians think of that? It didn't matter. "Another idea which is overdone at Geneva just now is the conception that Italy can only be given what Abyssinia is willing to concede. There ought, if necessary, to be very strong pressure brought to bear on the Abyssinians to concede more than they may themselves be disposed to give."[41] Another official, Sir Lancelot Oliphant, considered him "absolutely right."

On September 26, the Committee of Five officially announced that it had failed to find a compromise between Italy and Ethiopia. The League Council decided the best thing to do now was to organize a *new* committee, the Committee of Thirteen. This one would report on the chronology of events and explore the question of economic sanctions, which would have no teeth either, thanks to the vacillation of Hoare and the complete indifference of Stanley Baldwin.

In Geneva, the Aga Khan warned Anthony Eden that if Italy took Ethiopia, this would pose a serious menace to the British Empire in the Near East and in India and Ceylon. Australia's High Commissioner to the United Kingdom, Stanley Bruce, told him that once war broke out, Britain and the Commonwealth would have to see it through to the end.

A dejected Eden had to agree, telling Bruce, "There is indeed no other course that I can see."[42]

* * *

The next evening, on September 26, an estimated seven thousand people poured into Madison Square Garden for a protest supporting Ethiopia. A reporter noted that one quarter of the audience was African American—which meant there were also thousands of white New Yorkers sympathetic to the cause.[43]

Before the rally, five hundred members of the Young Communist League hit Broadway and Forty-seventh Street to drum up interest for the event (back then, the Garden stood on Eighth Avenue between Forty-Ninth and Fiftieth streets). But the cops soon drove them off. Later, at the stadium, there were speeches against imperialism and a call to send a telegram to the League of Nations to condemn any economic infringement of Ethiopia. A twenty-foot high effigy of Mussolini, his cardboard arm holding a bloody knife, was hauled up on stage just so the crowd could hiss and boo and watch as it was torn to pieces. While that was going on, another couple of cardboard figures were brought on stage—a black man and a white man depicted as friends.

It was crude stuff, but there were those working on more sophisticated appeals. One of the heroes of the Harlem Renaissance, Langston Hughes, was back in town. His play, *Mulatto*, was due to be performed on Broadway later in the year (and to receive excoriating reviews, despite its long run). Hughes first came to fame in the 1920s, the era when Americans began to think in decades, not centuries, but he would outlast the time when, as he put it himself, "the Negro was in vogue." That month, two of his poems about the cause were published. "Call of Ethiopia" was printed in *Opportunity* magazine, hoping, "May all Africa arise."

With sentiments like this, why didn't Hughes go and actually fight in Ethiopia as others desperately wanted to do? Apparently he never considered it. But the headlines over Ethiopia would play through his mind, prompting more verses in the months ahead.

*   *   *

On September 29, Haile Selassie attended mass at St. George's Cathedral and then took his place on a platform set up in the square outside. Thousands upon thousands of warriors from all over the country, including the whole army of Shoa, would pass his throne, each man carrying a long pole on which dangled a Meskel daisy. Adwa veterans pantomimed their feats of courage from a bygone age, and young men in colorful outfits for war leaped about and swung their swords and spears. By tradition, the ordinary peasant was allowed to give advice on this day to his Emperor, and many chose to do so. Some told him that he "should not meddle anymore in the affairs of the outside world, but look after his own country."

More often, soldiers were telling him, "Give us guns, give us rifles." A frustrated older man stepped up and demanded, "What can I kill with this bastard of a *tabanja?*"[44] Furious, he broke his antique rifle into pieces on the spot. The imperial guard marched smartly by the review stand, as did the Boy Scouts. Ras Mulugeta Yeggazu was in peacock finery, wearing a coronet, carrying a silver-tipped spear, and looking very much like a relic of Ethiopia's glorious past. There was also a slow parade of Red Cross ambulances and trucks with mounted machine guns. The procession could have gone on longer, but suddenly great curtains of rain masked the display of men and arms, a final downpour of the rainy season.

The Emperor was at last facing the inevitable. There would be no last-minute rescue from the League of Nations. He sent off another cable to Geneva, warning the Council that he couldn't hold off any longer, and he went ahead and signed the mobilization decree. But, perhaps still clinging to faint hope, he locked it in his desk.

A short drive away, at the US embassy, Chargé d'Affaires Cornelius Engert was also dreading what was to come. He sent a telegram of his own that day to Cordell Hull in Washington: "I fear as I did in Constantinople in 1914 that we are on the eve of a grave calamity fraught with all the elements of another World War."[45]

* * *

In Paris, reporters were astonished to discover support for Mussolini's empire from an unlikely source: Josephine Baker.

In the Roaring Twenties and Dirty Thirties, Josephine Baker was the most famous woman in the world—not the most famous black woman, the *most famous woman*. Long before there was Madonna and Lady Gaga, there was Josephine, and she could match them for fashion, style, ego, and outrageous behavior any day of the week. Her legend was a literal rags-to-riches story. Once a rake-thin girl known as "Tumpy" to her family, she had to wear the same pitiful unwashed dress for days. Her clowning and funny faces had won her a part in *Chocolate Dandies* in New York, but it was her erotically-charged dancing while topless and dressed in a banana skirt in *La Revue Nègres* in 1925 that made her an international bombshell.

She made movies. She sold records. By 1935, there were souvenir Baker dolls sold in Paris stores, and Josephine strolled down the Champs-Elysées walking her pet cheetah, which wore a choker studded with diamonds. The poor little black girl from Missouri now lived in a mansion of gray and red brick with pointed turrets, trimmed hedges, and white statuary, complete with a swimming pool. Josephine called it *Le Beau-Chêne*, the beautiful oak. She had lovers day and night—literally. *La Bakaire* wasn't known for being a deep thinker, but whatever she did say was news, so reporters obediently answered the summons to a press conference at the mansion on October 1, where Josephine took questions in her music room.

"I am ready to travel around the world to convince my brothers that Mussolini is their friend," she declared. "If need be, I will recruit a Negro army to help Italy." This was a bolt from the blue for reporters, and before they could ask any follow-ups, she was adding, "Haile Selassie is an enemy of the people. He maintains slavery, which Mussolini is determined to stamp out."[46]

When her comments were printed back home, African Americans were asking themselves: *What on Earth is she thinking?* Josephine hadn't been home in ten years. She was out of touch with her own people! She should have known better! As a poor girl, eleven years old, she had stood on the west end of the Eads River watching black families fleeing from white mobs. She had been a witness as East St. Louis went up in that monstrous bonfire of 1917. She had even met the enemy—she was introduced to Mussolini almost a decade ago while on a European tour. The dictator had first banned her from performing in Italy, and then, with his signature unpredictability, had reversed his decision. But another Italian had much more influence on her: her manager and lover, the so-called "Count Pepito De Abatino," who was actually a former stonemason and gigolo.

To make things worse, her timing was awful. She made her stand only days before she was due to sail to New York for her appearance in the Ziegfeld Follies. When she arrived, many ordinary black Americans were sullen and hostile to her. It was no longer just her politics; it was her attitude, her airs, her choice not to stay in Harlem. And it didn't matter how famous she was—she could still be sent to the back entrance at hotels or turned away from fancy restaurants. Many African Americans thought she could use a little humbling, especially after her foolish remarks. By the time the Ziegfeld Follies closed in June the next year, she was homesick for Paris. She had already broken up with her no-account count, who had sailed back home and then died of kidney cancer.

But thanks in part to her support for a Fascist dictator, Josephine—ditzy, promiscuous, self-absorbed Josephine, of all people—would get the opportunity to affect the course of the Second World War.

*   *   *

On the afternoon of October 2, Italy's dictator, Benito Mussolini, made another speech from the balcony of the Palazzo Venezia. His people had heard him many times before, but this time was a special occasion. Proper attention to the Duce's words was mandatory, and restaurants and shops closed as they heard him through loudspeakers and on the radio. Sirens and whistles had already been celebrating the imminent invasion the night before, but significantly, the bells of St. Peter's Basilica didn't join in, and the Vatican only sounded whistles. When Mussolini finally addressed the crowd, Fascist organizers made sure the public square below him was impressively packed. He even had CBS and NBC radio broadcasting the speech.

"Blackshirts of the Revolution!" he shouted. "Men and women of all Italy! Italians all over the world—beyond the mountains, beyond the seas! A solemn hour is about to strike in the history of the country. Twenty million Italians are at this moment gathered in the squares of all Italy. It is the greatest demonstration that human history records. Twenty million! One heart alone! One will alone! One decision!"

The wheels of destiny were turning with an increasing rhythm, he promised, and nothing could stop them now. It wasn't only the army marching, he claimed, but the forty-four million citizens of the country because of the "black injustice" done to them. Sanctions? Italians would meet sanctions with discipline and obedience! As for acts of war, they would meet them with acts of war! But knowing his potential enemy well, he told the throng that "until there is proof to the contrary, I refuse to believe that the authentic people of Britain will want to spill blood and send Europe to its catastrophe for the sake of a barbarian country unworthy of ranking among civilized nations."

Wire services reported that Mussolini got "thunderous applause," though it's difficult to tell how much of it was sincere. The centurions for Mussolini's new Roman Empire were mostly conscripts—they outnumbered volunteers five to one.

Carlo Levi wasn't in Rome to applaud. Having been arrested for anti-Fascist activities, he was in *confino* first in one remote village, Grassano, and then sent in handcuffs in a rattling train car to another, Aliano in Basilicata. The poverty of southern Italy in 1935 rivaled anything depicted in today's charity commercials for Africa. Levi saw children with swollen bellies in a region where malaria and trachoma were prevalent. A doctor turned writer and Fauvist-style painter, Levi went back to doctoring and tried to make the best of things.

Here, a lieutenant in the militia from a liberal family was convinced that Mussolini's African adventure was the nation's "last chance." Levi noted that the ordinary people of Aliano were less convinced. "If they have money enough for a war, why don't they repair the bridge across the Agri?" asked one man. "They might make a dam or provide us with more fountains, or plant young trees instead of cutting down the few that are left. We've plenty of land right here, but nothing to go with it."[47] Levi listened and wrote it all down for his classic published years later, *Christ Stopped at Eboli.*

There were pockets of doubt and occasional quiet criticism elsewhere. A young schoolgirl in Treviso wrote in her diary, "The teacher has said that the Duce wants to give the Italians a place in the sun. It seems to me that we have got plenty of sun in my town."[48] Someone informed on a watermelon salesman in Reggio-Emilia for arguing the war was wrong, while a shopkeeper in Cremona got three years in exile for defending British sanctions and predicting the war's failure.[49] A truck driver in Gorizia made the mistake of speaking his mind: "My belly's full, and if Mussolini wants land, he can go conquer it himself; I don't want to go, nor will I." He didn't have to. Instead, he was sentenced to three years in *confino* in Matera.[50]

But while there were sullen rumblings in distant corners, there was *still* never any outright defiance within Mussolini's Italy. "It is literally true," wrote historian Angelo Del Boca thirty years later, "that apart from the anti-Fascists who lived in exile abroad, not a single Italian raised his voice to denounce the anachronistic character of the African venture. Not one of them had the courage to tell the dictator that he was acting against the interests of the country. Worse still, not one of them denounced the war for what it was, a long premeditated, patiently prepared-for naked act of aggression."[51]

* * *

In the small historic town of Adwa, the clouds were moving much too fast for the people. But they weren't clouds at all. Airplanes were descending on the town to wreak Italian vengeance. "They are coming!" shouted a servant boy as he rushed into the room of Colonel Feodor Konovalov, Ras Seyum's military adviser. "They are coming!"[52]

Konovalov stepped out on his balcony and saw angry Ethiopian men fire their rifles uselessly into the air as women screamed. And then the bombing started.

John Robinson had just flown in a Potez to Adwa from the capital on his regular mission of carrying military dispatches, and he had chosen to stay overnight. He "tumbled out of bed" when he first heard the explosions. Helpless to do anything, he watched how "large bombing planes arrived over the city . . . at break of day and began bombing. They caught the city asleep and unaware. The majority of the inhabitants grabbed whatever belongings they could and ran to the outskirts of the city."[53]

Ras Seyum, watching the destruction, cried out, "Great God of Ethiopia, what is happening?" He escaped before the planes blew his red tent to bits and took refuge with others in one of the nearby caves. From the town's gibbi, anti-aircraft guns spat flak at the Capronis zooming overhead, but the planes flew leisurely in formation three times, dropping their bombs on most, if not all, gun emplacements. Thick black smoke rose from machine gun nests.

The Brown Condor looked on in horror at the efficient carnage inflicted after only a few minutes. And within hours, the planes would return to make a second, even more devastating bombing run. Residents tried to find shelter at a Red Cross hospital, but the Italian pilots above did not spare even this sanctuary. Several nurses were wounded and killed. It would not be the last time the Italians flouted international conventions and bombed medical tents.

It was October 3, 1935. Without any formal declaration, Italy had launched its war on Ethiopia.

PART TWO

ENDURE

Chapter Eight

WAR

That same October 3, three advance columns sloshed their way over from the north bank of the Mareb River. For this grand offensive, there were one hundred thousand men: askari cavalry units, small light tanks, infantry soldiers on the march, road-building engineers, a long, ponderous line of pack mules carrying everything from cartridges to cannon barrels, and then trucks and transport vehicles bringing up the rear.

The man in charge of all this, General Emilio De Bono, had left his base at five in the morning to drive up to a battery where he could overlook the plain of Hasamo and watch the advance. But he could see nothing. "I was seized with a sort of vexation which I had never been able to suppress, even during the Great War," he recalled later. "The vexation that comes from being unable to see, from having to stand stock still, waiting on events, waiting for communications and constantly fearing that they will not come in time."[1] The foreign correspondents looking on were equally mystified by the lack of spectacle. Five hours later, De Bono decided it was useless to wait around and went back to his headquarters at Coatit, near Debbi, to check cable and phone reports from the front.

As the sun crept over the flat-topped mountains, men flew banners and blasted trumpets, and the askari soldiers wasted precious ammunition by firing into the air. It slowly sunk in that the glorious march was going to be an anticlimactic hike. The hot, empty hours passed, and conscript soldiers from the country turned into prospective farmers. Young Italians would each bend down, pick up some earth, and feel it in their fingers, making a brief evaluation of the soil. Yes, they decided, such earth would be good for two or even three crops each year.

The fact that there was no Ethiopian resistance was deliberate. Haile Selassie wanted to show the League of Nations that his country was clearly the victim. More importantly, he would let his enemy overextend its supply line, penetrating deep into the unfamiliar mountain ranges and valleys where his men could attack them as they pleased. But the lesson of guerrilla warfare was still a hard one for his commanders to learn. After getting a brief lecture on tactics in a cable from the Emperor, Ras Seyum Mangasha had telegraphed back his reply: "I am too old and too tired to become a shifta."[2]

Instead of obeying his Emperor, Seyum dispatched a small contingent of men and took up positions at Daro Takle and Gashorki Pass. It was a foolish effort, and after a few hours, they had to pull out. Spies tipped off the Italians that Seyum hoped to catch them off guard and surround them, and the ras could only watch as Adwa was bombed a second time. Seyum and his warriors had no choice but to fall back.

The Italians had their own minor humiliations. The small two-seater Fiat tanks were made of cheap tin, which the African sun made into ovens as they rolled their way into the Danakil region. At 120 degrees, the crew members inside fainted from heat exhaustion.

The next day, Adigrat surrendered, having put up no fight at all, and the day after, Adwa fell. As thrilled as the ordinary Italian soldiers were over their victories, they soon realized their captured sites were insignificant villages that had no real strategic value. After a while, the Italians began to pitch in and help the Ethiopians pick peas and beans.

* * *

That Thursday morning, George Steer was in the Bank of Ethiopia in Addis Ababa, and he wandered into the office of the bank's manager to chat with his friend, Lorenzo Taezaz. Taezaz was one of the "Young Ethiopians" educated abroad in France and Italy (though he was actually Eritrean), and he'd also been one of the border commissioners during the Walwal Incident. Now he was running Ethiopia's government press bureau, and Steer liked his impersonations of foreign correspondents. As the reporter sat on a hippopotamus skull stuffed with cleaning supplies and nicknamed "Vinci," Taezaz said through lips clamping a cigarette, "The war began this morning. They bombed Adwa and crossed the Mareb."[3]

Steer headed into the streets, where the locals were streaming towards the courtyard of the Little Gibbi. He saw five thousand soldiers squat down in front of the great war drum of the empire, made of lion skin and carried by four servants, with a fifth to beat it with a crooked club. By eleven o'clock, various nobles and chiefs were on hand, and the Court Chamberlain, Ligaba Tosso, stepped on an old kitchen chair, holding the Emperor's mobilization order. The drummer with the club yelled out, "Listen, listen, open your ears! The symbol of our liberty wishes words to be said to you. Long may he live, and the enemy within our gates may God destroy!"[4]

There was a respectful silence, at least from the center of the crowd, and then the Court Chamberlain read the words of Haile Selassie:

> The hour is grave. Each of you must rise up, take up his arms and speed to the appeal of the country for defense.
>
> Warmen, gather round your chiefs, obey them with a single heart and thrust back the invader.
>
> You shall have lands in Eritrea and Somaliland.
>
> All who ravage the country or steal food from the peasants will be flogged and shot.
>
> Those who cannot for weakness or infirmity take an active part in this holy struggle must aid us with their prayers.
>
> The feeling of the whole world is in revulsion at the aggression aimed against us. God will be with us.
>
> Out into the field. For the Emperor. For the Fatherland.

The crowd surged forward onto the steps, waving their rifles and yelling in a frenzy of patriotism. Steer heard some of them shout, "Till now we have had doubts of our Emperor, but now we know that he is with us."[5]

While soldiers were eager to fight, rushing the courtyard steps, Lorenzo Taezaz had to deal with a smaller rampage. Making his way to the palace's throne room, diplomats and foreign correspondents stampeded after him. "A secretary of the German legation trod violently on *Paris Soir's* toe," Steer remembered. "*Paris Soir* said he would hit him if he did it again. The representative of another famous French newspaper tried to wrench the communiqué out of Lorenzo's hand . . . [A Czech] was more or less hoisted up by the pressure of the journalists on his circumference."[6]

The reporters and diplomats were told about the bombings and the capture of Adwa and Adigrat, and when the news reached the crowd outside, people moved with fresh outrage to the north tower of the gibbi. On the top balcony stood Haile Selassie with the second son he favored, the Duke of Harar, along with his cabinet ministers. Below, the Emperor's American adviser, Everett Colson, stood under an oleander tree, and George Steer detected "a turn of steady ironic pleasure on the mouth beneath the gray mustache."[7] Colson had lobbied for Haile Selassie to wait; now the mobilization looked like a swift response to the attacks.

The Ethiopians in front of the tower waved their rifles and pulled out their knives, shouting up to their sovereign, "Death to the Italians! Finish it once and for all! God give you long life!"

Haile Selassie—quiet, composed, dignified—raised his hand for calm and quickly got it. As he leaned on the balcony, he told them, "I am happy to see you before me with knives, swords, and rifles. But it is not I alone who knows, it is the whole world outside that knows our Ethiopian soldiers will die for their freedom.

"Soldiers, I give you this advice, so that we gain the victory over the enemy. Be cunning, be savage, face the enemy one by one, two by two, five by five in the fields and mountains. Do not take white clothes . . . Hide, strike suddenly, fight the nomad war, snipe and kill singly. Today the war has begun, therefore scatter and advance to victory."[8]

Even as the Italian forces took Adigrat, Aksum, and Adwa, Haile Selassie stayed on cordial, even friendly, terms with Italian officials still in the city. The Emperor invited them to the formal opening of the capital's first model prison, and he also invited the prison's architect to stay on in the country. When the architect demurred, the Emperor told him, "Go if you must, but remember that the door of Ethiopia will always be open for you."

There were about a hundred Italians still left in the capital as the war began, along with a handful of other foreigners, and George Steer noted that while Haile Selassie was still in control, no serious harm ever came to one of them.[9]

*   *   *

Mussolini had at last avenged Adwa. He sent his general a telegram of congratulations that read, "Announcement reconquest of Adwa fills the soul of the Italians with pride. To you and all the troops my highest praise and the gratitude of the nation."[10] The first reports of the bombings suggested up to seventeen hundred casualties, including women and children. Haile Selassie claimed seventy bombs were dropped on Adwa alone, and that the hospital had been destroyed (it wasn't). During the second bombing run soon after, Ras Seyum counted another seventy-eight bombs dropped. An accurate death toll may never truly be known.

Haile Selassie also condemned the bombings of the Red Cross in a cable he sent to the League of Nations that very day. The Italian authorities tepidly denied the charge. First, they claimed to the League, "All that happened was that a few Italian airplanes, on a reconnaissance flight, having encountered heavy fire from anti-aircraft batteries and rifles, dropped a few bombs on parties of soldiers. It should also be pointed out that there is no Red Cross hospital or ambulance at Adwa."[11] In sending this message, Italy was conceding that it had violated Ethiopian air space. To others, they admitted that there was a Red Cross hospital, but only "in the vicinity of the frontier, which in itself shows the aggressive intentions of the Abyssinians."[12]

The denials weren't very effective—especially since the world press already knew the identities of some of the pilots. They included the Duce's son-in-law,

Count Galeazzo Ciano, plus Mussolini's two sons, Bruno and Vittorio, both lieutenants in the air force. For Vittorio, Adwa was his first combat mission, and when he couldn't find his assigned target, a bridge on the Takazze River, he simply dropped his bombs in the middle of the town. The son of the Duce didn't like the effect. "I was always miserable when I failed to hit my target," he wrote in his memoir, *Flight over the Ambas*, "but when I was dead on, I was equally upset because the effects were so disappointing. I suppose I was thinking about American movies and was expecting one of those terrific explosions when everything goes sky-high. Bombing these thatched mud huts of the Ethiopians doesn't give one the slightest satisfaction."[13]

After the war was over, Evelyn Waugh carried on the denial over the indiscriminate attack on the Red Cross hospital there, claiming he couldn't verify the information reported—or that there was ever a hospital in Adwa at all. Waugh also went so far as to provide the Italian regime with an affidavit suggesting Ethiopians were abusing the use of the Red Cross sign, even though the Red Cross itself never made this claim.[14]

There should be a simple explanation over the bombing, and there is one. Historian Rainer Baudendistel suggests that the field clinic was marked with the Red Cross emblem, but apparently only on the wall.[15] The Capronis on their bombing run wouldn't have been able to see the markings. This doesn't, of course, let the Italians off the hook. Mussolini hadn't bothered with a formal declaration of war—as such, Ethiopia didn't need to justify its practices when the aggressor ignored the most basic international convention.

And just as we know the sons of Mussolini were in the air dropping the bombs, there was also a credible witness on the ground.

"I was sitting in the Swedish hospital chatting with some of the doctors when we heard a sudden whistling sound," John Robinson told reporters when he was back in the capital. "I said, 'That's a bomb.' I was only joking at first but for some reason we all ran outside. I immediately ran toward the airdrome, and I saw terrified women and children flocking to the hospital where they thought they would be safe . . . That's why they were killed. The bombing was indiscriminate, and it also was inaccurate. I saw a squad of soldiers standing in the streets, dumbfounded, looking at the airplanes. They had their swords raised in their hands."[16]

Robinson had never seen war before. But he would soon get another terrifying taste of it. He was anxious to get back to Addis Ababa with new military dispatches and his report on the attack, but once he was up in the air, he ran into a couple of Italian planes. "I didn't mind being attacked," Robinson wrote later to Claude Barnett, "but I wish my airplane had been of a later type. I think I would have given them a wonderful lesson."[17] Fortunately, what Robinson lacked in a modern aircraft and combat experience, he made up for in knowing how to barnstorm, and he managed to slip away from his attackers.

After he got away and was safe at last on the ground, he checked out his damaged aircraft. One of its wings had ten bullet holes. But the Brown Condor would fly another day. As much as the thrill and the danger made an impression on him, the bombings had left a deeper scar on his psyche. John Robinson was getting his first sense that he was linked to a doomed cause and an abandoned people.

* * *

The invasion of Ethiopia was shouted in banner headlines around the world, from Paris to Toronto, from San Francisco to Sydney, and there were jitters on world stock markets.

In London's Soho district, which had many Italian restaurants and cafés, about five hundred Fascists gathered in Greek Street to listen to Italy's ambassador to Britain, who muffled his face in his coat collar against the chill October air. The ambassador claimed similar rallies were being held in America, Australia, and Canada. In France, the locals in some spots were far less tolerant. When fifty Italians in Toulouse wanted to go home to serve, a mob of angry demonstrators attacked them, and the police had to step in.

The Council of the League of Nations had been summoned to meet on the coming Saturday. But six Italian transport ships, carrying about fourteen thousand soldiers, were already moving through the Suez Canal, which was still open.

The threat of the war spreading to Europe still loomed. British authorities in India called up reservists in case troops were needed to go to British Somaliland. At dawn on October 3, the troop ship, *Dorsetshire*, had left Hamilton Harbor in Bermuda with eight hundred members of the Manchester Regiment, most of them bound for Egypt to keep watch on the Suez Canal. Six French submarines had already arrived at the Algerian port of Oran, France's closest base to Gibraltar. On the Rock itself, the Royal Air Force did a practice drill to check their defenses and simulated an air raid blackout for twenty minutes.

It wasn't just the military who went on alert. Tourists who boarded any Italian liner in Istanbul noticed their ship now had gun mountings fitted into the forecastle, though by October 3, the guns weren't in position yet. Insurance brokers in Athens hiked their rates for spots in the Mediterranean, while Greek ship owners cabled their liners in Asia to sail around the Cape of Good Hope instead of using the Suez Canal to return home. In Spain, sympathies were divided between Fascist and left-wing lines. Conservatives and monarchists wanted to stay strictly out of the whole debacle. Those to the left didn't want their normally pacifist stands to work to the advantage of Mussolini. "We prefer neutrality," argued the newspaper, *El Liberal,* "but not at the cost of defending fascism."[18] The talk over neutrality was dropped about a year later when both sides needed foreign allies in the Spanish Civil War.

Even Nazi Germany assumed the British lion hadn't been growling to clear its throat; it thought Britain would make good on its previous threats. Hitler's number-two man, Hermann Goering, went shooting in the Polish countryside with Prince Janusz Radziwell, one of Poland's prominent politicians. "I wouldn't like to be in the Duce's skin at this moment," remarked Goering.[19]

* * *

When war in Ethiopia broke out, Franklin Roosevelt was sailing out of San Diego harbor on the Navy ship, *Houston,* to start a three-week vacation trip that would take him to Cocos Island, Panama, and then to Charleston, South Carolina. He had spent the previous day reviewing the greatest massing of navy ships in American history, 130 in all. "The American people," he said before leaving on his trip, "can have but one concern, and speak but one sentiment. Despite what happens on continents overseas, the United States shall and must remain unentangled and free."[20]

Roosevelt was looking for calm waters, but he didn't get them. When word of the invasion was reported by radio, he cabled Cordell Hull to tell him that if he had "any official confirmation of Italian invasion and of battles and casualties well within Ethiopian border it seems to me that this constitutes war . . . This holds true even if there is no formal declaration."[21] He thought a brief statement should be made to the American public, and that Hull ought to send him a draft. His adviser, Harry Hopkins, was onboard and noted in his journal, "The President said that world sympathy was clearly with Ethiopia. His certainly are. He scanned the news dispatches and everything favorable to Ethiopia brought out a loud 'Good.' He went over the large war maps with great care—places, every important town—the railroads and the mountains and rivers."[22] Roosevelt was hoping to get around Congress to determine himself what sanctions should be imposed on Italy.

But Hull kept delaying, trying to tailor any official statement to whatever the League of Nations did, which was so far the usual—that is, nothing. Roosevelt, getting impatient, sent him a curt telegram, insisting: "The facts reported appear to establish the commencement of hostilities and the fact of actual war."[23] Back and forth went the telegrams, with Hull claiming that yes, he was for the arms embargo as Roosevelt wanted, but arguing that Italy might regard it as "a gratuitous affront in the nature of sanctions."[24] Exasperated, Roosevelt cabled back: "They are dropping bombs on Ethiopia—and that is war. Why wait for Mussolini to say so?"[25]

After a few more hours, Hull finally did as he was told and issued the proclamation of the Neutrality Act, along with the announcement of an arms embargo to the press corps in Washington. The United States would officially stay out of the conflict between Italy and Ethiopia.

* * *

That didn't do anything to cool the tempers of blacks and Italian Americans in the big cities, especially New York. On the day of the invasion, a group of black demonstrators went down to picket the King Julius General Market on Lenox Avenue above 118th Street, which had Italian butchers and a produce seller; the market also employed eight African Americans. A well-dressed black man outside the window was urging the group, "Drive the Italians out of Harlem! Drive the white man out of Harlem! The white man is a monster who preys on the black man. We're Ethiopian, and I'm proud of it. We must fight the battles of our brothers overseas!"[26]

The rabble-rousing went on for more than an hour, and a confrontation was probably inevitable. The angry crowd looked like it was going to storm the market, but they were moving in on a butcher shop—employees reached for their knives and meat cleavers. Someone had the presence of mind to call the cops, who decided to come in force: twenty-five patrolmen, fifteen detectives, three radio cars, and an emergency truck. Things could have settled down. But then a patrolman named Chalmowitz did a stupid, insensitive thing; he pulled out his gun and waved it over his head to try to make the black demonstrators leave faster. Fresh outrage. They walked down to the 123th Street Station to make their feelings known, and now the station captain was barking at them to leave *there*. They refused. A black man named Charles Linous stood on a stoop, waving the tricolor of Ethiopia in the air.

The police captain, George Mulholland, didn't like being defied. He had forty-five officers walking out for the four p.m. tour, and now he used them to disperse the crowd. Most of the protesters fled, but one was arrested. Linous was still waving the Ethiopian flag, which might as well have been a matador cape to a stampede of bulls. The cops would later claim that Linous hit one of them, breaking the bones in the officer's hand with the flag staff. The officer went to Harlem Hospital for his hand wound; Linous was also taken there—because of blows to the head. He was then carted off to the station house jail.

It was worse in Brooklyn. At Public School 178, a third of the twenty-two hundred students were black, another third Italian. One of each got into a fight after school, with the black student winning. The Italian boy decided to come back with ten of his friends, who fought five black youths. By Thursday, school officials were collecting every imaginable weapon from the two factions: lead pipes, sawed-off billiard cues, broom handles, and ice picks. Parents asked the cops for protection; teachers wanted protection as well.

When the school bells rang at three o'clock, the police tried to make sure students went home. Thirty police officers had already moved in to confiscate weapons from six young black men who had been waiting outside to settle the score. And that still wasn't the end of it. Black and Italian boys both drifted back to Dean Street near Saratoga Avenue, deciding on the spur of the moment that this would be their battlefield. As the cops broke up a number of fistfights, they considered the atmosphere to be so tense that they radioed for help. They needed five squad cars and an emergency crew to help them restore order.

The chief inspector held a quick conference at headquarters on Manhattan's Centre Street. Like a small army, the New York Police Department mobilized to keep a lid on trouble, pulling twelve hundred men from quiet sectors to what it called "danger zones," most of them in Harlem, Brooklyn, and Queens. They managed—just barely—to keep the city from becoming a powder keg.

* * *

In London on October 4, as the news of the war spread, a young schoolteacher from the Gold Coast, Kwame Nkrumah, had been looking forward to sailing to the United States. He was eager to continue his education, and he would end up at Lincoln University in Pennsylvania for his BA. But first he had to pick up his student visa. In the chill of autumn in the overwhelming congestion of London, he felt bewildered and very much out of his depth. "I began to wonder," he recalled later, "if it would not be better to give the whole thing up and return home." Just then, he heard a newsboy "shouting something unintelligible" as bundles of the latest edition were dumped on the corner from a panel van. Nkrumah read the paper's placard: "MUSSOLINI INVADES ETHIOPIA."

"That was all I needed," he wrote later in his autobiography. "At that moment, it was almost as if the whole of London had suddenly declared war on me personally. For the next few minutes I could do nothing but glare at each impassive face wondering if those people could possibly realize the wickedness of colonialism, and praying that the day might come when I could play my part in bringing about the downfall of such a system. My nationalism surged to the fore; I was ready and willing to go through hell itself, if need be, in order to achieve my object."[27]

Nkrumah did eventually reach his object, becoming Ghana's first president and one of the founding members of the Organization of African Unity.

Nor was he alone in how he felt. Had he stayed at home, he could have joined those who filed into Accra's Palladium five days later for the second session of the West African Youth League and the Ex-Servicemen's Union. There, it was announced that five hundred men had signed up, wanting to go fight for Ethiopia, including an elderly prince who had served in the British Navy.[28] The sentiment wasn't confined to only the urban elite; it stretched beyond the frontiers of the Gold Coast. "We want to know the time of enrolment as auxiliaries in the Abyssinian war with Italy," declared a Youth League branch in the Keta District of British Togoland. "We want to shed our blood for our suffering brothers of our dear Africa. Yes, we are ready. We will fight and die on the battlefield."[29]

But they wouldn't. The colonial authorities had their own version of the Foreign Enlistment Act, an Order-in-Council that blocked Protectorate "natives" as effectively as the Home Office stood in the way of passionate volunteers in London.

A short article appeared that day in *The New Leader,* the publication of the Independent Labour Party. It was written by C. L. R. James, who would help Nkrumah later and have a great influence on his political thinking in the postwar period. "Workers of Europe, peasants and workers of Africa and of India, sufferers from imperialism all over the world, all anxious to help the Ethiopian people, organise yourselves independently, and by your own sanctions, the use of your own power, assist the Ethiopian people. Their struggle is only now beginning. *Let us fight against not only Italian imperialism, but the other robbers and oppressors, French and British imperialism* [original italics]."

For James, there were no "good" imperialists like Britain versus "bad" ones like Italy. Blacks had waited with growing frustration for Britain to show better values, and now that it had failed the test, they were bitter. Meanwhile, the West Indies crackled with strikes and revolts that would last for another four years.

*   *   *

Anthony Eden had been about to head back to Geneva when he heard the depressing news about Adwa—Sir Sidney Barton had sent a telegram about the bombing of the Red Cross hospital.

Eden was already in the Quai d'Orsay with the members of his diplomatic team on the night of October 3, talking yet again with Pierre Laval and their respective aides. Laval had a new grand scheme. This time, he wanted to give away parts of Ethiopia that weren't occupied by the Amharic people, and he wanted to push it as a joint Anglo-French proposal. Eden poured cold water on this, promising only that he'd take it up with London. He strongly disapproved of rewarding the aggressor right after war had started.

As they talked about sanctions, the conversation drifted to whether Mussolini would make a formal declaration of war. Sitting in on the meeting was the Secretary General of the French Foreign Ministry, Alexis Léger, who mused whether Italy could claim belligerent rights. Laval was so shocked that it was clear to Eden that he had no idea what belligerent rights were. He became upset over the idea that Italian cruisers might interfere with French ships.

"I have put up with much from Signor Mussolini," said Laval. "I would never put up with that."[30]

Eden could take satisfaction that Laval was finally shaken up, but he didn't think the effect would last. For all of Laval's fears, the French prime minister still wouldn't stand united with Britain against Italy.

Worse, once Eden got to Geneva and telephoned the gist of the conversation, Samuel Hoare sent him cables, suggesting Laval put his ideas for land concessions to Mussolini. Eden telegraphed back to remind Hoare that "the whole world is watching to see how the League will acquit itself of its duty." He didn't believe for a moment that Mussolini could be bought off with more real estate, and as for Laval, "He will jump at any chance to delay the functioning of the League machinery, and if we give him any excuse to do so, we may have reason to be sorry for it."[31]

This led to a bizarre bit of amateur theater on October 7. Pierre Laval had come out to Geneva, and Alexis Léger asked Anthony Eden to pay him a visit at his hotel. He confessed that Laval was furious with him for agreeing with Eden that Italy was the aggressor. And he was worried about his job. Could Eden help him out? Maybe he could go to Laval and make a big show of complaining about him, say that he was "much dissatisfied with his attitude . . ."[32]

Eden didn't mind playing along and went to see Laval, putting on the act that Léger was being difficult. Laval was relieved to hear this and told Eden, "We will have a talk."[33]

Then Eden, Laval, and Léger sat down to discuss economic sanctions. The atmosphere was mildly surreal. Eden couldn't believe a word Laval was saying, while Laval basked in the fake confirmation that his own man was derailing allied ventures. And Léger, ever quiet, was realizing he had almost lost his job and could see clearly now that his superior, whom he knew to be a liar, was leading France towards disaster. But he could do nothing.

Within a matter of days, the League of Nations decided to lift the arms embargo against Ethiopia but maintain it against Italy, which would hardly be affected.

* * *

The ripples of the new undeclared war kept spreading. In Nairobi on October 6, the Kikuyu Central Association met and passed a resolution that its members should "go and fight for their Ethiopian brothers."[34]

The president of the Irish Free State, Eamon da Valera, promised that his young nation would stand by the League's Covenant. "Some people would say that what has the Free State to gain through guaranteeing to others greater freedom than we have ourselves?" But he argued that the Covenant was of special importance to small nations like his own. "A number of people think that because Britain's interests lie in a certain direction, we should act to the contrary, but our chief concern is to support the Covenant."[35]

Muslim Arabs and blacks in both French and Spanish Morocco were busy that day, organizing a small army with a caravan of four thousand camels. They planned to cross the Sahara and take a route up through the Upper Nile country—a long trek just to go fight for Ethiopia. The Moroccan tribesmen would sell their camels to the Ethiopian army. Then they planned to sell themselves as mercenaries.

And still the ripples spread. Again, on that same October 6 in Mexico City, a pro-Ethiopia group, with Communist banners waving in the air, marched over to a German club and pulled down its Nazi flag, dragging it through the streets. The protesters didn't care that Hitler had been staying carefully neutral over Ethiopia. Police had to rush out with rifles to protect the German club from the angry demonstrators.

That evening in America, an audience sat watching a newsreel at a movie theater in Islip, Long Island, when an item came on that showed Mussolini giving a speech. A local middle-aged couple, Alfred Ingold and his wife, stood up and hissed at the screen. The Ingolds got a few cheers, but also many boos and catcalls, and a scuffle threatened to turn into a riot. The Bay Shore State Police had to be called, and when two of their officers tried to take the couple out of the theater, Mrs. Ingold socked one of them in the nose. They were charged with disorderly conduct.

In Austria, ruled by its own brand of Fascism and caught between Italy's influence and its substantial German population, they knew how to deal with Ingolds. Any films or newsreels about Ethiopia were simply banned to prevent any public demonstrations or trouble.

Trouble had already happened again in London's Soho Square on October 6. Sir Oswald Mosley and his home-grown Blackshirts had been out in force, demanding Britain stay out of the conflict in Africa. They handed out thousands of pamphlets, too, some of which warned that "finance, oil, the Jews, and the Reds want war." The police had to break up fights and altercations everywhere the British Union of Fascists went.

Rome liked to fund this kind of trouble. After Mosley visited the Duce in 1934, he left with £20,000 from the Italian Foreign Ministry. MI5 was well aware of a secret account at Westminster Bank in Charing Cross run by Mosley's BUF cronies.[36] Maybe it didn't act on the information because Mosley wasn't getting great results. Italy's ambassador to Britain, Dino Grandi, grumbled, "All this money, believe me, Duce, even on the best supposition, simply goes down the drain."[37] Special Branch would find out the next year that Rome had cut its subsidy to Mosley's group from £3,000 to £1,000.

* * *

In New York City, at the corner of Madison Avenue and Fifty-Second Street, a 27-year-old unknown executive of CBS Radio was trying to sort out a mess involving the new war. "Nobody has the slightest understanding of what is going on in this whole Ethiopian business," he wrote a friend.[38]

This was Edward R. Murrow, who within a few short years would become one of the greatest names in American journalism. But in 1935, no one knew who he was. Murrow wasn't a news announcer—not yet—because CBS didn't have news announcers at the time, except for one, Bob Trout. Murrow had actually been hired as "Director of Talks to Coordinate Broadcasts on Current Issues." The Ethiopian War certainly qualified as a current issue, but now it was embarrassing the network in a flap that landed on the front page of the *New York Times.*

Murrow had been calling London and Geneva, trying to arrange a coup in terms of coverage. The two antagonists in the conflict could each give their side of the story in separate interviews; first Ethiopia, then Italy. The broadcast from Geneva would be shunted through London and then whipped across the Atlantic Ocean to an RCA shortwave station on Long Island, coming out for American listeners at around six o'clock Eastern Standard Time. The Paris correspondent for the *Chicago Daily News,* Edgar Mowrer, interviewed Tekle Hawaryat on October 9 without a hitch. The next night, it was supposed to be Pompeo Aloisi's turn, and he and Mowrer had rehearsed their questions and answers in the studio before they got the signal to go live. Then Mowrer got a frantic call from London;

New York wasn't getting their feed. "It was too late to arrange for another station," Mowrer said later, "so we had to abandon the whole thing."[39]

There was no technical difficulty. It was an act of God—God in this case being the British General Post Office (now Royal Mail), which back then was perversely charged with the responsibility for radio and television communications. And the Post Office decided in its infinite wisdom that because of the economic sanctions voted in by the League of Nations that day, it shouldn't make things convenient for an Italian speaker with British equipment.

Off in New York City, Edward R. Murrow was furious. The *New York Times* ran an Associated Press story on the scuttled interview as part of its front-page coverage of the League condemnations and sanctions. Murrow, a serious young man who wore starched collars and didn't discuss his politics in the office, privately sympathized with the Ethiopians, but "at the moment, I am anti-British."[40] A branch of a foreign government had interfered with a free and fair exchange of ideas intended for a neutral American audience. And Murrow did not like interference with the facts.

Aloisi, however, got his air time days later, thanks to a broadcast transmitted from Rome. Given the size of the Italian-American community, it was essential he get a chance to reach this audience, though its support was never at risk of wavering.

* * *

In Addis Ababa, the foreign correspondents were desperate to get to the front. The Emperor told them no—he couldn't guarantee their safety. The reporters told him they didn't want safety. Haile Selassie explained with a wry smile that "he wasn't thinking of safety from the Italians, but safety from his own warriors . . ."[41] They couldn't tell the difference between an Italian and any other white man.

Laurence Stallings, who had come to film the war for Fox Movietone News, now complained as he limped along on his prosthetic leg. "But Emperor, sir, I've spent 100,000 US dollars so far, and I haven't one shot of the war."[42]

The Emperor could only shrug. That was hardly his problem.

Stallings did manage to send back footage on the Ethiopians' preparations, and he filed a small but impressive selection of print stories for the *New York Times*. But he was frustrated and irritable, still mourning the loss of his leg and griping about "the boogies"—a pejorative for blacks—"and the dirty slaves." He had the strange outlook of being both anti-Ethiopian and anti-Fascist, and later George Steer discovered he could only calm the writer down by reciting or reading from Shakespeare.[43]

Penned up and limited in what they could do, the journalists began to turn on each other like prison inmates. They all had to share one telegraph office, which liked to play favorites and jack up its prices. "What with heavy outlay and wretched returns," wrote Steer, "we all got to dislike and suspect each other if we were keen journalists, to despise and cut each other if we were not."[44] During the regular squabbles and boredom, the reporters also felt a growing fear over the possibility of bombing runs and gas attacks. Evelyn Waugh heard about a poker game where the players wore gas masks around the table.[45]

A young officer of the Belgian military mission had been appointed Press Censor, and his tiny allotment of power went to his head. He issued a decree that confused everyone: nothing could be sent except "government communiqués or false military news," whatever that meant. The journalists organized a Foreign Press Association, but it became a small circus. Steer acted as secretary, shouting, "Order!" over and over as the group's president banged the table, but the motley group went on arguing among themselves (Americans particularly liked to target the Germans over their lack of press freedom).

Because there was so little substance or variation in official communiqués, a few of the journalists took to going around to the house of Haile Selassie's American adviser, Everett Colson, every day at six o'clock. Colson would give the reporters what scraps of information he could. His pleasant wife, a stout, white-haired woman, would serve them cakes.

George Steer was as frustrated as the others and resorted to a foolish and reckless stunt. As a result, he had to suffer the minor humiliation of becoming a brief item in the *New York Times*, where his stories were also being printed. Reuters sent an item on how Steer tried to scale a wall of the Italian legation so that he could slip inside and perhaps find something useful. But a couple of Ethiopian guards came along, and he jumped to the ground and ran off. The guards chased him, caught him, and with the short but feisty reporter resisting all the way to a telephone hut, he was slightly injured in the scuffle.[46] Luckily, Steer had endeared himself by now to the Emperor, who quickly ordered his release.

About three weeks later, Evelyn Waugh and the *Evening Standard's* Patrick Balfour saw Steer kick and rough up an Armenian spy who had broken into the telegraph office after it was closed to read and possibly steal his dispatches. Writing to his confidante, the actress and socialite Diana Cooper, Waugh referred to Steer as a "South African dwarf" who is "never without a black eye."[47]

Under the circumstances, the young Steer was handling the enormous pressure of his job pretty well. And his own personal life was about to improve immensely. Because on the very day the Italians invaded, yet another correspondent joined the press corps.

Le Journal of Paris had sent a female reporter. There were certainly woman journalists in the 1930s, but you'd be hard pressed to name one who covered war zones. In 1935, even legendary Martha Gellhorn hadn't started yet. So when a dark European beauty named Margarita de Herrero got off the train, she was a source of much speculation. Her father was Spanish, and Steer's biographer, Nicholas Rankin, suspects he might even have been Basque.[48] Margarita was born in Pau, a modest tourist spot in the French Pyrenees, but she was raised in the land of her mother, which happened to be England. Journalism back then was very much a man's world, and for a woman to succeed, she had to have a strong personality and face not only the dangers inherent in covering a war, but also put up with the coarse come-ons and sexist dismissals of her so-called peers.

Steer liked strong personalities. It comes through in his work, in his books, in how he referred to larger-than-life friends such as Lorenzo Taezaz and Afawarq, and how he wrote admiringly of the courage of the Ethiopians and later, the Basques. Margarita obviously could handle herself, and she was ten years older than him; they soon developed a rapport and an attraction.

Like so many aspects of the Ethiopia Crisis, a romance in exotic Africa torn apart by war would seem a cliché, and quite implausible if you scripted it in a Hollywood movie. Yet it actually happened; Steer and Margarita would marry months later. And as Steer got to know the woman who would be his first wife, he didn't know that he'd also met—in the very same place—the woman who would be his second.

* * *

There was a whole second front to the war that didn't get nearly as much attention in that first week of October—in the Ogaden. Mussolini wanted to keep Italian Somaliland safe while the main fighting went on in the north, and he also wanted to make sure no arms were passed on to the Ethiopians by the British through their own Somali colony (which he never had to worry about at all). The man he put in charge of this mission was Rodolfo Graziani, already a war hero, the "Pacifier of Libya." The Libyans had another name for him: the Butcher of Fezzan.

Graziani was a career military man, extremely tall for his time and considered ruggedly handsome by some. He had won Libya thanks to a page borrowed from the British in the Boer War, setting up scores of concentration camps. If he couldn't shoot or hang insurgents, he would let them drop dead from starvation and disease. He had arrived in Mogadishu in March to make preparations, and the infamous remark that sums up his attitude to the war was, "The Duce shall have Ethiopia, with the Ethiopians or without them, just as he pleases." It pleased Graziani to have as few of them as he could make possible.

After putting his road builders to work, he imported thousands of American-made cars through Mombassa and Dar es Salaam to drive on these fresh ribbons of concrete. His Duce expected him to hold the Ogaden with only one division of men, so he made up for this with firepower; he brought in some seventy armored cars and tanks, plus thirty-eight planes. Graziani never had any intention of merely "holding the line." He would push hard, ruthlessly, into the Ogaden with the objective of eventually taking Harar.

His first step was to bomb the thirty thousand men commanded by Nasibu Zamanuel in the provinces of Sadamo and Bale. By October 8, Nasibu was trying to tell anyone who would listen that Graziani's planes had "blanketed a wide area" with mustard gas, forcing soldiers and civilians alike to drop to the ground in agony. The accusation was lost at the time in stories of charges and counter-charges, since the Italians already claimed that the Ethiopians were using "dum-dum" bullets that exploded and shredded on contact. There were scraps of truth on both sides. The Ethiopians did use soft-nosed ammunition; they had little choice, since these were often the only kind of cartridges they had for their antique rifles. And Mussolini could say that he hadn't actually ordered Graziani to use gas, that his general had taken this step on his own—until three days later, when he gave him formal authorization in a telegram.

But the accusation was made again a couple of weeks later by another source. Laurence Stallings managed to talk to an American surgeon and missionary from Illinois, Robert Hockman, who was rushing back to the capital from his base in Jijiga for medical supplies. Hockman claimed there were hundreds of casualties in the region from "chlorine gas," and he was looking for antidotes for it.[49]

Haile Selassie struck a pose of being above such base accusations. "Let us try if we may to mitigate the inherent horrors of war by being frank and honest, and giving our enemies credit where credit is due. Is not war horrible enough without investing it with such horrors?"[50] As the evidence mounted over the coming months, the Emperor would change his tune over Italian atrocities.

The Butcher of Fezzan had all the subtlety of a meat tenderizer as he attacked the Ogaden. First, he sent six Caproni planes to rain bombs down on the fifteen hundred soldiers in a network of shallow trenches at Gorahai. But Gorahai was under the command of Afawarq Walda Samayat, the commander George Steer had befriended a couple of months before. Afawarq was still contemptuous of the Italians, and when he took his meals, he used a knife made out of a bomb splinter. Graziani was ready to stampede over Gorahai with six battalions of Somali troops, and Afawarq had a good sense of what was coming. When he received five hundred soldiers from Harar at the end of August, he sent them off into the bush, armed with rifles and loaded with enough food and water so they could strike the Italian column when it abandoned its trucks to encircle Gorahai.

He had done his best to try to prepare his men mentally for the loud, terrifying death that came from above, and they seemed to hold up as well as could be expected. In one raid, three hundred bombs were dropped, though one hundred of them failed to detonate. Those that did managed to kill five men and wound fifteen others in two direct hits on one of the trenches. And the next day, the planes came again. On October 11, in yet another bombing raid, the civilian telegraph operator fled in terror, but was captured and taken back to his post.

George Steer wrote movingly of the psychological effects of all this on an Ethiopian at Gorahai: "First, a belief at the back of his mind that the aeroplane was a devilish instrument, uncannily accurate when it was directly on top of you; and when you looked up it seemed always to be on top of you . . . Second, the failure of all Ethiopian arms to bring a plane down. Bitterest of all, the feeling that one could never send *one's own* planes back to strike the Italians. And then . . . the infernal explosions and someone with his guts pouring out into the trench."[51]

It has to be remembered that this kind of relentless bombardment, the kind used merely to terrorize and crush the spirit of civilians and soldiers alike, was *new*. The London Blitz was years away, the horrors of Spain still distant. And it was only decades afterward that historians and researchers bothered to report on the psychological impact on East End residents subjected to night after night of horrific pounding bombs, of cratered buildings, of fire and claustrophobic terror. Now consider that the Ethiopians had no Council flats. They had no proper air shelters in London Tube tunnels. They had ditches in dirt. Their commander at Gorahai had only a single Oerlikon .37 anti-aircraft gun, mounted on a turret in a fort where the Mad Mullah had made his last stand against the British.

Afawarq had called for reinforcements, but instead, he was saved by the rain. The on-again, off-again showers of the Ogaden, wrote George Steer, turned the pink earth into a spongy pulp. "A mechanized column sinks into the mud and sometimes remains engraven in the earth after it has dried, so quickly does the mud turn into rock again in the Ogaden."[52] The elements had conspired to petrify Graziani's army and give Afawarq a temporary reprieve. Of course, it wouldn't last, and worse was to come.

Chapter Nine

A SEASON OF BETRAYALS

As much as General Emilio De Bono was enjoying his modest victories so far, he was disappointed the enemy hadn't come out in force to confront him. And his ace-in-the-hole traitor, Haile Selassie Gugsa, wasn't living up to expectations.

Gugsa had boasted that he could bring De Bono a force of thirty thousand men, and he was supposed to switch sides at a key moment in a battle when the Italians took on the army of his hated rival, Ras Seyum Mangasha. Unfortunately, Seyum didn't oblige either De Bono or Gugsa with a major confrontation. All the while, Gugsa was promoting his own battle campaign—first to De Bono, and then to one of his commanders, General Santini—for an attack on his own provincial capital, Mekele. And despite his promised numbers, he claimed he needed reinforcements because there were seven thousand troops threatening his army. This didn't make much sense if he had the men he claimed he did.

De Bono's recon pilots had only to shrug and say there was no obvious threat, not from their view in the air. Mekele, they said, was practically deserted. De Bono didn't think it would be hard to capture the town, but holding on to it and keeping his troops supplied with water, food, and other provisions . . . well, that was a different story. "We can imagine what the foreigners, who were daily fabricating news of an Italian defeat, would have invented if we had a real setback, however quickly repaired."[1] The foreigners, in fact, were doing nothing of the kind; the captures of Adwa and Aksum were splashed all over the front pages. And this was an odd, not to mention timid, way of looking at war, especially for a general, and it was this kind of perspective that was about to get De Bono in trouble with his boss.

Meanwhile, Gugsa wasn't happy that his Mekele plan had been turned down. But he had bigger troubles coming. Ethiopia's consul to Asmara, Wodaju Ali, was still trying to prove once and for all that he was a traitor. The consul flew to Mekele on October 9 in one of the Emperor's planes. If the Emperor wouldn't accept the truth, Gugsa's own men did, and after Wodaju's soldiers spread the word, Gugsa's men abandoned him in droves. Before leaving Mekele in a hurry,

Gugsa had the telephone line cut, which broke off Ras Seyum's only connection with the Emperor in Addis Ababa.

By October 11, the commandant of the First Army Corps sent a radio message to De Bono that his star Ethiopian convert was heading for the town of Adigrat. When Gugsa finally arrived, he showed up in a tailored Western suit with a circle of his courtiers. As for the thirty thousand men he'd promised, his sad little contingent was made up of only twelve hundred men armed with rifles, along with eight machine guns.

No matter. In Rome, the propaganda writers inflated this to ten thousand men when they announced Gugsa's defection, capturing headlines around the world. It was a serious blow to Ethiopian morale, and some of Haile Selassie's generals informed him that they thought it put their efforts back by two months. They should have been encouraged by the fact that Gugsa had been literally run out of town, and with only a pathetic band of followers. The *real* coup for the Italians was that Gugsa brought along a Swiss engineer named Fernand Bietry, armed with unique plans for a road extension from Addis Ababa to Dessie, about four hundred kilometers to the north. De Bono now had an up-to-date and thorough survey of the region.[2]

He had to figure out what to do with Gugsa. Mussolini had decided to make him the civilian chief of Tigray, which De Bono considered "good business," but the title was meaningless. Aside from Gugsa being shown off like a show pony to the correspondents, he was good for little else. De Bono received him in his hut, where Gugsa immediately played the sycophant and pushed again for taking Mekele.

De Bono asked him for his impressions of the Italian army.

"One of great strength," replied Gugsa. But what actually impressed him were the roads and transport vehicles. De Bono seemed to find this pathetic, commenting in his memoir that at the time, the roads "did not yet amount to much."[3] Gugsa had fled with only a handful of soldiers, and now he was worried about their maintenance. The general reassured him they would be looked after. And he would also get a generous pay-off.

"But have you complete trust in your men?" De Bono asked bluntly.

Gugsa hesitated. De Bono found it "difficult to read a black man's face," but he had the feeling that the man had some doubts. Gugsa didn't bother to even answer in a yes or no, merely telling him, "It will be all right as I tell you. Go to Mekele as quickly as possible."

Having served his purpose, Gugsa was packed off to Adigrat, where presumably he couldn't cause any trouble. "I felt easier," admitted De Bono, "at seeing him under someone's immediate tutelage."[4]

* * *

Scores of Eritrean soldiers were busy fleeing to the Ethiopian side and had been doing so since the very first day of the war—but unlike Gugsa's defection, this wasn't widely reported at the time. As the conflict went on, the numbers increased. Even though Italy always portrayed their war as partly a settling of old scores between Eritreans and Ethiopians, many Eritreans preferred to fight and give their lives for the Ethiopian side.

The Italians also claimed that virtually the entire population in Adwa quickly returned after Emilio De Bono's forces swept in, but there were refugees who denied this to any foreign correspondent bothering to check. Many people had fled into the hills to try to find Seyum's army. The few shopkeepers who stayed or bothered to come back got a modest revenge on the Italians: price gouging. A bottle of beer in Adwa now cost twenty lire, four times what it cost in Rome (at the time, a lire equaled a little over eight cents). Champagne was inexplicably being sold for about the same price as wine, which went for forty lire a flask.

After a visit to Adwa, De Bono rode his horse into the conquered town of Aksum. He knew that the cheers of the crowds that greeted him were all for show. The ordinary people had been ordered to applaud the general. He found nothing left in Ras Seyum's bombed gibbi, except for a few chickens scratching in the courtyard and a lion cub that he sent off to Mussolini. Ethiopian clergy arrived under decorated umbrellas and carrying sacred framed portraits to pay homage to their new conquerors. De Bono gave a short speech and spoke to the acting head of the Orthodox Church's Aksum chapter—its real head had fled with the Abun.

On October 14, he issued a lofty proclamation. "People of Tigray, HEAR: You know that where the flag of Italy flies, there is liberty. Therefore, in your country, slavery under whatever form is suppressed."[5]

Mussolini and his propaganda machine had hammered away for close to a year on the slavery issue, but now De Bono discovered the realities that Haile Selassie had been contending with ever since he was regent. "I am obliged to say that the proclamation did not have much effect on the owners of slaves and perhaps still less on the liberated slaves themselves," he wrote in his memoir. "Many of the latter, the instant they were set free, presented themselves to the Italian authorities, asking, 'And now who gives me food?'"[6]

To his credit, De Bono and his men provided for them and then haggled with nobles to ensure the liberated slaves could have long-term employment as laborers and servants. Rome's new pro-consul would show more compassion to his subjects than the other generals who followed him.

De Bono seemed an able administrator, but Mussolini was growing ever more frustrated with him. His general was in no hurry to take Mekele, and Mussolini wanted him to get on with it. He had already sent a telegram, expecting his general to capture the town by October 18. Why the rush? For "political reasons," he cabled. Mussolini knew that the more territory that was captured, the stronger position he would have in settling things with the dithering leaders in Geneva.

Despite his warm congratulations, Mussolini had lost his faith in the old soldier. Three days after the victory of Adwa, he decided to send in watchers: Minister of the Colonies Alessandro Lessona and his army chief of staff, General Pietro Badoglio, the man who had written such a critical memo on Italy's chances for taking on Britain. He warned Lessona that De Bono would resent his old enemy, Badoglio, showing up to inspect his efforts, "hence your presence is required to prevent any friction."[7] This wouldn't do much good. De Bono loathed Lessona almost as much as he did Badoglio. Both men had backstabbed each other regularly to curry favor with their boss.

No sooner had Mussolini ordered them to Eritrea than he sent a cable to De Bono. "By the middle of November, all Tigray, to Mekele and beyond, ought to be ours."[8] But after a few days, he decided that wasn't strong enough and ordered De Bono in yet another telegram to start his advance by November 5. De Bono cabled back to say his army wasn't prepared yet to take Mekele. Back and forth it went. The elderly pro-consul would argue with his Caesar all through October over when to advance.

De Bono was surprised to find his two rivals perfectly friendly to him when they showed up on October 18 to get the lay of the land. Not that he was prepared to trust them. And he wasn't about to be rushed into his offensive, living in dread of a humiliating defeat like the Battle of Adwa. He didn't want to risk overextending his supply lines, and after summarizing all his concerns in a dispatch to Mussolini, he got in his shots at the men his boss had sent to check up on him: "This, my dear Leader, I feel it my duty to tell you in order to put you on your guard against any frivolous statements that may have been reported to you by Lessona and even Badoglio."[9]

Lessona and Badoglio actually gave every indication that they agreed with his cautious approach. Behind the general's back, it was another story. Badoglio sent word to Mussolini that De Bono had been exaggerating the problems. Yes, Mekele could be taken; any issues were tactical ones that were an easy fix. As Blackshirts fought with Ethiopians, the Fascist leaders intrigued and tried to topple each other.

* * *

In Addis Ababa on the morning of October 17, Haile Selassie reviewed Ras Mulugeta's army of eighty thousand warriors before they headed north to Dessie.

An open tent with a vividly red lining had been set up below the old gibbi, and carpets had been laid out over the dirt. Wearing a khaki field uniform for the occasion, the Emperor sat in his throne while his cabinet ministers knelt on the rugs, all of them clutching rifles except for the foreign minister. For thousands of troops on their way to the front, there were thousands of spectators. It was a bright, sunny day, with hawks and ravens flying overhead.

At ten-thirty, the review finally got started. Barefoot soldiers of the imperial guard marched by, and then a mule train carrying Vickers guns. There were peasants armed only with sticks and empty cartridge belts, boasting and capering, kicking up clouds of dust. When they took too long with their grand displays, one of the palace guards flogged them with a rhino whip to move them along. There were skilled swordsmen, flashing their blades with acrobatic skill. There were warriors who rushed up to the dais, begging for arms—always the call for more arms, for better weapons than the pitiful ancient rifles. Drummers in scarlet turbans rode on mules, their faces glazed with sweat, their eyes staring ahead with fierce concentration as they beat their instruments. The review would last four long hours.

At noon, horn blowers announced the entrance of Ras Mulugeta Yeggazu, Haile Selassie's cantankerous old war minister. Mulugeta drew his sword, struck it to the ground in a feudal gesture of loyalty, and then proceeded to lecture his king again on how to conduct his war. He gave Haile Selassie a needless reminder that he'd been killing Italians on the battlefield when the Emperor had been a child.

"Do not interest yourself over-much in politics," said Mulugeta. "Your weakness is that you trust the foreigner too much. Kick him out. What are all these fools of the press doing here? I am ready to die for my country, and you are, too, we know. War is now the thing, and to conduct it, you had better remain in the city of Addis Ababa. Send all the foreigners packing. I swear to you perfect loyalty."[10]

Haile Selassie listened to this harangue with his usual patience. Mulugeta was a walking, talking relic, and relics deserved proper respect. But this did not mean they should be elevated above their place. The Emperor deflected the old man's comments, telling the multitude before his tent that his general had the confidence of the Ethiopian people, and then he lectured the soldiers again on wearing earth-tone colors and using guerrilla tactics.

"Every man who dies for Ethiopia will be a holy saint and a martyr," promised Haile Selassie. "Comrades, I shall be with you on the battlefield to shed my blood freely with yours in defense of our common fatherland. We shall accept no such peace terms as those France proposes." While Haile Selassie could be criticized for putting too much faith in the British, he clearly knew that Pierre Laval couldn't be trusted. "I shall die with you, if necessary, rather than submit to such humiliation."[11]

The parade went on. Most of the soldiers weren't leaving for Dessie yet and were actually heading for the outskirts of the capital, where tents and food had already been prepared for them. Mulugeta wouldn't head out until the coming Saturday, but the army's vanguard would march ahead the next day. These details hardly mattered. There were men who wanted to go fight *now*. They rushed up to the throne, and knowing about the bombing of women and children in Adwa, declared, "We will drown the baby-killers in their own blood! We are going to our death, and we are unafraid!"[12]

Others were more solemn in their determination. Men slung rifles around their necks and carried tent poles, from which dangled sandals and packs. Their wives dragged along mules, and their children did their best to bring up the rear with smaller loads of supplies. One warrior approached Haile Selassie and told him, "I have a boy. If I am killed, call him to the army."

The Emperor wept.

*　*　*

Some reporters had already decided to go home. The Emperor's policy of barring them from the front for their own safety was a disastrous miscalculation. Laurence Stallings managed to get footage of casualties at Harar, but he complained to Noel Monks, "I want shots of a battle. And all I get is goddamned *Ishe Naga*." The correspondents had learned that "Ishe Naga" was the Ethiopian equivalent of the Spanish *mañana*. It could mean either "tomorrow" or was a polite way to say, "Don't hold your breath." Stallings was fed up. "Brother, I've got two hundred thousand bucks worth of *Ishe Naga* since I came to this country."[13]

Now Stallings decided to take his film crew and leave. "This is the greatest massacre since Custer was jumped at Little Big Horn, and if the Emperor doesn't want the world to see it, then he's throwing away the only goddamned weapon he's got in his locker—propaganda."[14]

Monks agreed with him and was equally frustrated. Over the next two weeks, he hitchhiked three times to the front, but was caught each time by Ethiopian soldiers and escorted back to the capital. If war was hell, purgatory seemed to be Addis Ababa. One time, he even managed to catch a glimpse of Italian guns blazing in the night, though he was still far away from where the shells were bursting on Ethiopian positions. Italian reporters were sending back dispatches about heroic battles, while he "could only pick up scrappy accounts of what was going on from our side, and these told only of retreat."[15]

* * *

Haile Selassie's man in London, Warqenah Eshate—better known to the British as Dr. Charles Martin—was too busy with work on October 17 to see his sons off at Victoria Station. Two of them, Benyam and Yosef, both in their twenties, were leaving to go join the Emperor's army, and secretaries of the embassy joined a large crowd to cheer the young men on. Before the train left the station, their sister and three younger brothers dashed up the platform to say goodbye. One of the youngest boys declared in a shrill voice, *"I* want to go to war!" The crowd laughed.[16]

Benyam and Yosef had both trained as engineers, and they had learned to fly at the Brooklands Aerodrome in Surrey. They were apparently hoping to enlist in Ethiopia's modest air force, but their father must have known about the few, decrepit planes that made up the miniscule fleet. For Martin, his sons' commitment was a source of both pride and dread. They had kept at him, trying to persuade him to let them go, and in the end, he gave in.

Only a week prior, Martin had watched in gratitude as two thousand men and women marched in support of Ethiopia up to his embassy near Hyde Park. The crowd had been an eclectic mix of intellectuals, workers, tradespeople, peace activists, and leftists. They carried banners and chanted, "End War! Down with Fascism!" After a formal address of support was read, Martin thanked the demonstrators and promised to pass their message on to Haile Selassie. "This is not the only expression, for the British Government had done a great deal for Ethiopia."[17] In private, Martin was less complimentary towards the Baldwin Cabinet, and he was growing ever more impatient with Anthony Eden's comments on events.

But the ordinary British people were obviously sincere. How then could he speak in public about the sacrifices of his fellow countrymen yet bar his own sons from going off to fight for their country?

So Benyam and Yosef left. Charles Martin would never see them again.

* * *

Martin's sons were free to fight, but it was becoming clearer by the day that African Americans were not.

The State Department sent out warning after warning over black recruitment drives, but what decisively crippled the enlistment efforts was the policy on passports. It was "deemed advisable not to issue passports in general to persons who decide to proceed to Ethiopia."[18] Then, as now, few Americans actually held passports, and even of those who did, only a tiny minority would have been African American. Just for good measure, the government warned John H. Shaw, Ethiopia's honorary consul general, that he should stop any recruitment campaigns in the United States.[19] Like Martin in the UK, he was helpless to act on the wave of support and interest from eager volunteers. Worse, the State Department made no distinction between those who wanted to go fight and those who might offer medical assistance under the neutral auspices of the Red Cross. Newspapers had reported back in August that the Ethiopian government was ready to welcome black medics, but by then the US government had already pulled the gangplank away from ships in the harbor.

Italian Americans, too, were supposed to be barred from foreign enlistment, and Italy's ambassador, Augusto Rossi, told those who wrote or showed up at his embassy that he couldn't help them break the law. Rossi's help, however, was never really needed. No injunction against heading off to Italy was imposed, despite the one for Ethiopia. By the outbreak of the war, the papers had reported several times on the modest stream of Italian-American volunteers who had gone over to train. Hundreds would make it, including an ambulance unit of Italian-American doctors.

*   *   *

War was supposed to be good for business. But halfway through October, the Bank of Italy had already burned through 226,000,000 lire in gold reserves (which worked out to more than $20,000,000 U.S. at the time). Its coverage of bank notes by gold and foreign exchange had plunged to 29 percent. Foreign bonds and exchange holdings increased to 413,000,000 lire, and the Duce's regime thought it could get itself out of trouble by printing more money.[20] The war was good business, however, for another European country: Germany. German exports of coal had likely doubled during the first eight months of the year (the Third Reich wasn't in the mood to tell). According to a spokesman, Hitler's regime didn't export any arms to Italy because the *Wehrmacht* needed the arms for itself.

Even before sanctions could have any financial impact, they were already having political ones—just not anywhere that really mattered to the conflict. Far away in Buenos Aires, outraged Italian residents decided they would boycott British goods and made a grand announcement in an Italian newspaper. The paper had the right war fever—it just picked the wrong opponent. The Argentine government didn't take kindly to an editorial calling its delegate in Geneva "a fool" and started a legal action. Over in São Paulo, Brazil, Italians made a bigger splash, but still had mixed results. They went around plastering walls, taxis, and trucks in the city with posters urging a British boycott, what they considered the "duty of every Italian in São Paulo." Brazilian police had the tiresome duty of seizing thousands of the posters and arresting several Fascist agitators.[21]

In London, British cooks and waiters decided that sanctions were a good cue to protest the employment of Italians in the city's smart hotels and restaurants. "War on the Soho Front" read a banner for a Tuesday march through the district, where there were many Italian shops and eateries. But trying to get an immigrant waiter or two sacked wasn't going to accomplish very much, and shunning macaroni wouldn't stop the slaughter in Ethiopia. In fact, as the war clouds darkened in September, imports of Italian wine were seven times what they were for the same month in 1934.

At that moment, the world cared less about Chianti and more about oil. On October 11, the League of Nation's new Committee of Eighteen met for the first time and began to hammer out a set of economic sanctions against Italy. With its delegates working through the weekend, it finally came up with a list of raw materials it would do its best to keep out of the hands of the aggressor: rubber, nickel, copper, iron ore . . . but not oil, not yet. The committee wouldn't even start to talk about an oil embargo until eight days later.

If oil did make the list, it would infuriate certain executives in the "City," London's famous business district, before it ever enraged Mussolini. British businessmen helped run Royal Dutch Shell and the Anglo-Iranian Oil Company, both of which provided substantial supplies of oil to the Italian navy, as well as to Italian merchant ships. Together, the two companies "laundered" their product through a proxy firm they jointly owned, Consolidated Petroleum, but Anglo-Iranian also used its base in Aden to send oil to Eritrea and Italian Somaliland.

All this time, the League privately kept the US government in the loop over the sanctions issue, which was one of the worst-kept secrets in Geneva anyway. League delegates were anxious over how the Roosevelt administration and the US Congress would react, and they were right to be concerned. In Washington, as in London and Paris, everyone assumed that economic sanctions could only lead to a bigger war happening in Europe.

The isolationists were crying "slippery slope" and wanted nothing to do with the League's list. "While these programs are dedicated in high nobility to peace," said a Michigan Senator, Arthur Vandenberg, "it would be absurd to blind ourselves to the patent fact that they are also intimately related to the self-interest of major European powers." North Dakota's Gerald Nye, one of the fathers of the isolationist movement with his investigation of war profiteering, argued, "By all means we must keep our hands out of that foreign war, and we cannot possibly do that by joining in League sanctions."[22]

That suited America's industry barons just fine. They wanted business as usual, and according to the Department of Commerce, the United States was already "supplying a major part of a large increase in Italian imports of four classes of products easily made into munitions." Italy could get its copper from America, as well as its scrap iron, steel, benzol, and cotton waste, which could be chemically altered into gun cotton. None of the items were on Roosevelt's own list of embargoed materials. And neither was oil.

The world's biggest petroleum company, Standard Oil of New Jersey, was chaired by the formidable Walter Teagle. Standing six foot three and weighing 250 pounds, the cigar-smoking, abrasive Teagle was used to getting his own way. And he saw no reason to stop doing business with Italy. The firm had already lost a valuable concession in Ethiopia, thanks to politics. So in a public statement issued on October 18, he explained that Standard's subsidiary, Società Italo-Americana del Petrolio, had been operating in Italy for forty years, and it intended to keep on doing so. Nor had the US government made any objection or asked it to stop.

Days after Teagle made his sentiments clear to American newspapers, he thought he'd better clarify his opinions to Secretary of State Cordell Hull on November 6. In a letter to Hull, Teagle explained that his company's subsidiary furnished "only about one-fourth of [Italy's] domestic consumption of petroleum," yet if they cut off supplies, "Italy might initiate reprisals against our subsidiary, going even to the point of taking over its property and business."[23] This was disingenuous, to say the least. Mussolini had nothing to gain from suddenly nationalizing the oil works that Standard Oil kept there.

So the oil would keep flowing. Walter Teagle lost no sleep over doing business with Mussolini, nor did he hesitate to become chairman of the American subsidiary of I. G. Farben, the notorious chemical firm that made the death camp gas, Zyklon B, for the Nazis. Throughout the mid-1930s, the firm also made sure that Nazi airplanes had tetraethyl lead for their gasoline. Teagle and Farben's Hermann Schmitz also hired Ivy Lee, the Rockefellers' public relations genius, to spread anti-Semitic propaganda in the United States and to help improve American perceptions of Hitler's regime.

* * *

By mid-October, thirty ships were steaming from Alexandria to Port Said for the biggest naval maneuvers ever held off the shores of Egypt. As the ships kept watch on the north end of the Suez Canal, things were not so secure on land. True, the Egyptian press was pro-Ethiopia, and it was ecstatic that the British were allowing the country's native army to raise more men; four regiments of two thousand soldiers each were being added to the force of twelve thousand. But a crusade to keep another African country independent only reminded Egyptians that they were under the thumb of a European power. A substantial portion of Egyptians didn't want their country to participate in sanctions, and they thought their premier, Muhammad Tawfiq Nasim Pasha, was a British stooge. There were violent protests.

Italy, meanwhile, was sending another fifteen thousand men off to Libya, and its colonial governor, Italo Balbo, had soldiers stretching barbed wire for close to 250 miles along the Egyptian frontier. When the beautiful aristocratic journalist, Lady Grace Drummond-Hay, interviewed him in Tripoli, Balbo lied to her face, saying that his nation "has never even dreamed of invading and conquering Egypt" and was only increasing its defenses because the British were stirring up the Muslim Senussi who lived in the region. [24] Drummond-Hay challenged this, pointing out that the Nile was Egypt's lifeline—and part of it sprung, after all, out of Ethiopia.

Balbo could read a newspaper like anyone else. Maybe he could stir the pot a little. "Egypt is the most civilized country in the Near East, yet it is not enjoying the complete independence which is the privilege of backward countries. And Egypt is not even admitted at Geneva."[25]

It was a clever misdirection, but the issue was never enough to erode the sympathy Egyptians had for Ethiopians. A prince and cousin of King Fuad stepped off a liner in Djibouti on October 19 with fifteen thousand Egyptian volunteers, greeted by a grateful envoy of Haile Selassie. The prince, however, wasn't too clear on how he and his men would serve. "I must first see what we can do."[26]

Back in Europe, the Hadfield munitions factory in Sheffield was reported to be turning out shells and bombs by the thousand for storage. Hawker Aircraft allegedly couldn't keep up with a flood of orders for fighter planes and had to award subcontracts. In Italy, the port of Naples had an air raid practice, with the streets going dark at eight o'clock on a Wednesday evening.

It's difficult today to convey the atmosphere that made a world war look inevitable; we can't count the world wars that *didn't* break out, only the two that did. Yet from Argentina to Tokyo, from Vancouver to Prague, the world was holding its breath in the autumn of 1935. Newspapers kept likening events to the tense summer of 1914 before the Great War.

* * *

The conflict continued to touch on aspects of life and news coverage that were sometimes novel, sometimes perverse.

There was a touch of the former century in the announcement that Italian blacksmiths in the military classes of 1905 through to 1910 were called back into service. The Italian army had brought tanks, but it needed its cavalry even more, and a cavalry needs horseshoes. There was a touch of the future when Guglielmo Marconi, famous for his innovations in radio, told the world that he was conducting experiments with microwaves. His goal was to send beams at enemy aircraft to bring them down. Marconi was an enthusiastic Fascist who expected to have his new weapon on the front in Ethiopia fairly soon. Nothing came of it, but you can find microwaves, of course, in every modern kitchen around the globe today, and yes, in military applications.

The most popular song for Italy that season—a tune that was relentlessly played on the radio and in restaurants, heard in the streets, and inescapable—was *Faccetta Nera*. The title translates as "Little Black Face," and its first verse and chorus are this:

> If from the hills, you look down at the sea,
> Little black girl who is a slave among slaves,
> Like in a dream you will see many ships
> And a tricolor waving for you
>
> Little black face, beautiful Abyssinian
> Wait and see the hour coming
> When we will be with you
> We will give you another law and another king

The song goes on to promise that the girl will be taken back to Rome, where she'll be free to be kissed by both the Italian sun and a Blackshirt. De Bono's soldiers liked to sing it as they trudged along, and they bragged about teaching it to the native villagers who submitted.[27] As a tool of propaganda, it fit in well with the new boom in sleazy pornography that featured African women.

The problem was that it was too successful. *Faccetta Nera* implied happy mixed-race couples, which was way "off message" for the new Roman conquest. Abolishing slavery was fine, but not all this poetic talk of Ethiopian girls living as Italian matrons on the streets of Rome. It wasn't long before the Fascist regime had to discourage the smash hit.[28] But *Faccetta Nera* stubbornly lasted the whole next year and was played and sung into the year after that, getting at least two new recordings in 1938.

* * *

On October 15, Samuel Hoare sent his ambassador to France to go see Pierre Laval with a blunt message: Great Britain was no longer crossing its fingers and hoping France would come in with it against Italy—it fully *expected* its ally to live up to its military obligations in case Italy attacked.

To this, Laval, the ever-slippery lawyer, had an unconventional counter-argument. With so many ships of the Royal Fleet now in the Mediterranean, the Duce could claim this went beyond what the League Covenant allowed! Laval suggested the British call back some of its ships, and then Mussolini would feel obliged to make a gesture of withdrawal in turn. London's ambassador, Sir George Clerk, replied on the spot that a withdrawal would be the same as the British government abandoning the League's effort at sanctions. Moreover, it could be seen as condoning Italy's treaty violations.

But Britain's stern pose didn't last long. The very next day, when Laval seemingly caved and promised unconditional support to London, he got exactly what he asked for: Clerk was sent back to the Quai d'Orsay with the promise that Britain would recall the battleships, the *Hood* and the *Renown*. The British hadn't even asked for any concessions. Then Mussolini announced he would throw them a bone, one that had no marrow at all. He would withdraw the bulk of his forces from Libya. It was a completely empty gesture—and it was brilliant. He knew only too well that Italy couldn't win against the British. Nothing was lost, and his armies could keep up their advance into Ethiopia. No wonder sources in Rome told reporters that the Duce was "ecstatic" over the recall of the two battle cruisers.

On that same day, the League of Nations Committee of Eighteen passed resolutions for prohibiting the import of Italian goods and the export of raw materials to Italy. It decided to meet again on November 1, when it would decide exactly when these decrees would come into force. And more time was allowed to crawl by.

On October 22, Hoare rose in the House of Commons to talk about the chances for keeping the peace with Italy. The chamber was packed, with the gallery for distinguished foreign visitors completely filled as representatives of the Commonwealth and ambassadors from France, Italy, Germany, and the United States waited to see if he had a breakthrough to announce. He didn't. But that didn't stop him from suggesting there could still be one.

"There is still a breathing space before economic pressure can be applied. Can it not be used for another attempt at such a settlement?" When it came to military sanctions, he told the House, "This is clearly a delicate matter and much harm has been done by ignorant talk on the subject. I shall say frankly that, in my view, the precondition for the enforcement of military sanctions—namely collective agreement at Geneva—has never existed." Not only was this a blatant contradiction of the League Covenant, but it was a complete reversal of the stern line he gave in his speech in Geneva back in September.[29]

At one point, someone from the Labour benches yelled out, "Close the Suez Canal!"

A few of the Tories roared back, "War monger!"

Hoare dismissed the issue of the Canal neatly by asking his critics if they meant for Britain to do this alone. "There is already too much inflammable material lying about Europe," said Hoare. "No wise man will wish to throw a spark into it by threats that cannot be collectively carried out, or if they were carried out, would turn an Abyssinian into a European war."

*   *   *

Off in the town of Mulhouse, in France's Alsace region, a young surgical resident was taking care of patients and ignoring the headlines. He had his cases, and there were always journals to keep up with. Then he got a call from an old friend in Switzerland—he had a job for him. His friend knew that when Marcel Junod was only eighteen, he had organized a relief movement for Russian refugee children back in Geneva. It was that kind of compassion and initiative that the International Red Cross was looking for; it wanted Junod to accompany a medical team going to Ethiopia.

Junod was a slightly stocky figure with brown hair and rather Gallic features for a Swiss. He was fluent in French and German and knew a smattering of English. With his language skills, his past relief efforts, and his experience at the hospital in Mulhouse, he was well qualified to go. When he informed his boss, his chief gave him six months leave on the spot and told him to go see the world.[30]

In Geneva, he met the tall, handsome delegate to Ethiopia for the International Red Cross Committee, Sidney Brown. The name was English, but Brown was not; he was raised in the family that led the Brown-Boveri engineering company, and his parents were die-hard Anglophiles. Brown had spent the past seven years traveling the globe to visit Red Cross societies, which gave him the chance to catalogue how the Japanese bayoneted Chinese in their beds while the Manchuria Crisis was on. He was often charming, but just as frequently determined and passionate. He was also gay—a fact that would come back to haunt the Red Cross at a critical moment.

Brown cheerfully introduced himself when he found Junod in the modest library of the committee's headquarters, reading up on the history of the Red Cross. He told Junod not to bother, that out in the field he would have to "fall back on [his] imagination."[31] But Ethiopia would test Brown's own imagination—and his experience—as never before. When he and Junod reached Addis Ababa, they discovered that the headquarters for the Ethiopian Red Cross was a primitive barracks with just an unvarnished table and a few chairs inside. There was not even a typewriter, but someone had thoughtfully brought a stack of paper with letterhead. At the first meeting of the fledgling organization, Brown asked a Greek doctor what medical service was available to the Ethiopian army.

The Greek offered a rueful smile and replied, "At the moment, it doesn't exist at all." He would know. His name was Argyropolus, and he also served as a colonel in the army's medical corps. "The troops of His Majesty have gone to the front without any doctors, without any nurses, and without even bandages." He and a tiny collection of European volunteers and Ethiopians had bought some supplies, and so far, were able to equip ten ambulances—barely.[32]

Junod and Brown soon discovered as well that there were no Ethiopian doctors, not unless they wanted to turn to native sorcerers relying on herbs and other dubious remedies. Fortunately, a polyglot collection of Greeks, Germans, Dutch, Norwegians, Egyptians, and British were either on their way or arriving in medical units, all well stocked, and Junod got to work assigning the staff to ambulances. A thin, bearded little Indian doctor, a devout Muslim, "had the awkward habit of leaving his patients to look after themselves, and even abandoning the operating table, when the moment arrived for his religious devotions."[33]

Junod realized he would have to make do. Later, he and Brown had the honor of meeting Haile Selassie, whose dogs played around their feet. When Junod bent down to pet one of them, the Emperor smiled. Junod found the ruler melancholy. He and Brown had the awkward duty of correcting the Emperor when he asked whether they had been in touch with the League of Nations. Did they have any information for him? It was clear that he presumed the Red Cross was an agent of the League of Nations.[34]

As the International Committee's delegate, Sidney Brown had to deal with a more blackly comical problem of misunderstanding. A red cross was the standard emblem for brothels in the country, and he needed to persuade the Ethiopians to let him have a monopoly on the symbol.

* * *

In Rome, Benito Mussolini was still waiting for his general in Africa to give him a fresh victory. He needed something to distract Italians from their real problems: inflation, chronic unemployment, and the growing scarcity of goods. Prices for butter, meat, and other food items had shot up by 30 to 40 percent. Italians had to pay dearly now for soap and coal. So on October 31, he gave another fiery address when he opened a new University of Rome campus about a mile away from the Villa Borghese. Off in Geneva, he told his audience, "a coalition of egotism and plutocracy is attempting in vain to bar our path of our young Italy of the Blackshirts."[35]

That night, student mobs—backed by uniformed Fascists and supporters—threw their weight around the Via del Corso, shouting anti-British slogans and tearing down signs in English for shops that sold foreign goods. The proprietor of the Hotel d'Anglaterre, scared out of his wits, climbed out a window with a poker and did his best to pry the offending name out of the stone of the hotel's façade. As it happened, it turned out that a stonemason was available at this late hour to help out. Meanwhile, mob justice decided that stores and businesses needed rechristening. The Prince of Wales had to change; so did a tourist trap for Americans in the Piazza di Spagna, Miss Babington's Tea Shop.

The mob felt reckless and brave enough to go attack the British Consulate, but a large force of carabinieri drove them off.

There was no riot that evening in London, but there were thousands out in support of Ethiopia. About six thousand people filled the Royal Albert Hall for a rally by the League of Nations Union. At this late date, the Union was still pushing the measures of collective security and following the Covenant, despite every sign that League members would sit on their hands. But then what else could the Union do? It was a kind of sales team for an idea. Unfortunately, their product was breaking down in front of the customers, who were too polite to speak up.

The most stirring and eloquent speech that night was made by Violet Bonham Carter, the activist and Liberal politician who was Asquith's daughter, Churchill's friend, and some day in the future, the grandmother of famous actress Helena Bonham Carter. She warned the audience about "one law for the strong and another for the weak, one law for the white and another for the black, one law for ex-allies and another for ex-enemies. We cannot make licensed brigandage in Africa the price of peace in Europe. We cannot toss backward peoples into the expansionist maw to save our own skins."[36]

*   *   *

On November 2, the Capronis soared over Gorahai again, this time in force. Twenty planes kept up a steady onslaught on the Ethiopians' camp, which was only about 150 yards wide. And when they were finished one run, they needed only half an hour to start the bombardment all over again.

As usual, Afawarq Walda Samayat was behind the Oerlikon, doing his best to shoot bursts of flak to hold them off. When he promised "over my dead body," he meant it. A splinter of bomb shrapnel sliced into his leg, but he needed to hide his wound from his men. There would be no going for help, no leaving his post. The nearest medical aid was 140 miles away at a Red Cross hospital in Daggahbur. The standard practice of the Ethiopians was to break off the fight if their chief was wounded or killed, and if he were dead, they would be duty-bound to take his body to consecrated ground.

He did have a wireless message sent to Nasibu, confiding that he was wounded, but promising that he would hold on to Gorahai. Reinforcements were urgently needed, along with a good man to lead them. In the meantime, he stayed in his tower of the Mad Mullah's fort, manning his anti-aircraft gun. His vigil went beyond duty. His wound turned gangrenous, and as Steer put it, "he could scarcely crawl."[37] Ali Nur and a few servants knew of his condition, but they obediently kept it to themselves.

On November 3, the twenty planes were back for yet another bombardment. A waterhole near the fort was hit, killing Somali women who had gone there only to water their cattle herds.

And the next day, the planes were back.

Ali Nur told George Steer later that "it could no longer be borne. The whole earth heaved about and rocked under explosions which seemed to break the ears. One could not see to shoot under the deep pall of sand. Nothing but sand, flashes of red lightning, thundercrack explosions, more sand, groans and shrieks of wounded men, the earth heaving in foul yellow obscurity, and a noise like the falling of mountains."[38]

Through it all, the Oerlikon kept firing back. Then the lone figure in the turret slumped against the gun, unconscious.

They rushed his broken, diseased body from behind the big gun and put him in a truck to drive to the hospital. No sooner was the vehicle speeding through the dust than another officer disobeyed Afawarq's orders to hold the line. The Ethiopians retreated. There were twelve dead and perhaps seventy others either dying or seriously wounded. Afawarq likely died in the truck on the way to the Red Cross post at Daggahbur, and when word reached his men, they broke into sobs.

The Italians rolled into Gorahai on November 7, finding nothing but a few grass huts burned to the ground. Six tanks, eleven armored cars, and a force of up to three hundred Somali soldiers were sent on to take Daggahbur. "The dry bush and hard dusty earth rolling sweetly to Daggahbur and Jijiga gave easy passage to the mechanized arm," wrote Steer. "It was like sending a toy tank over carpet."[39]

But the Italians were in for a rude shock. As they pursued the Ethiopians through a valley to a dry riverbed near Anale, they ran into the reinforcements coming to rescue Afawarq and his camp. As the sun beat down, the Ethiopians had stopped because the tires on some of their vehicles were flat and the radiators were sending up plumes of steam. When they heard distant rifle fire, they split into two units to flank the road. A vicious battle started, with the small, two-seater Fiat tanks rolling into the Ethiopian ranks. The warriors had never seen a tank before. Some men took it for a great beast, but their commander was already asking himself how to kill the men inside. He noticed the slits in the metal and told his men to aim for the openings.

There were heavy casualties, as the tanks had trouble moving for better positions, and as the Somalis jumped out of their trucks, they were mown down by Ethiopian rifle fire. Yet the Italian machine guns also racked up a heavy death toll for the Ethiopians. The Somali troops eventually broke out of their trap, and both sides withdrew.

Graziani claimed later that this encounter was a win for the Italian side. What he neglected to mention was that the battle was such a severe blow, he held off pushing further into the Ogaden for months.

* * *

There was no Internet, of course, in 1935. There *was* television, but it was in its infancy, and about a year later, the Olympics would be broadcast live to Germans in small viewing parlors scattered around Berlin. An even smaller handful of crude TV sets in London showed the coronation of Britain's George VI about a year after that. You can get an idea of the pace of news for that time from a convenience offered by the *Daily Express* in central London. Clusters of people who strolled by its black glass, art deco building in Fleet Street would huddle around a map in a window labeled, "Abyssinia Day by Day."[40]

If you really wanted to know what was going on *at that moment*, there was only one medium: radio.

And if you tuned in to the CBS network at five in the afternoon Eastern Standard Time on Thursday, November 6, you heard a foreign ruler make an appeal in a thin, somewhat high tenor voice all the way from his besieged empire in Africa. The Lion of Judah was talking directly to Americans from thousands of miles away. Without guards or ceremony, Emperor Haile Selassie had taken his limousine out to the primitive station in the suburb of Akaki. Weeks before, he had tried to use radio to win sympathy from the French, but the Laval government kept refusing to allow his broadcast; when he did at last get to speak to them, it had little effect. He was hoping he would fare better with the citizens of the United States.

He gave his speech in Amharic, and then *New York Times* reporter Josef Israels read an English translation. "I ask no one to take the sword against Italy. Methods of the sword and of force are methods of ancient ignorance." What he preferred was for Roosevelt to push the League of Nations to do its job. "No nation, even were its people wholeheartedly behind its rulers can stand before the collective will of the people of the world and of justice—the justice of God. Ethiopia will live on, her people proudly free in the hills of her liberty-loving ancestors. Thanks to God Almighty."

After his broadcast, the Emperor was bound for a visit to Jijiga in the province of Harar, where he wanted to maintain control on the western front. He got a report on the battle at Gorahai and gave Afawarq Walda Samayat the posthumous title of Dejazmach of the Ogaden. Afawarq's son was given the military rank of *grazmach*. There was another less pleasant duty to take care of. Soldiers were holding a couple of officers who had ordered the men to quit Gorahai after they learned Afawarq was fatally wounded—they were supposed to be shot. But the Emperor decided to commute their sentences. Instead, both were flogged, with one given two bayonet stabs in the back, no doubt a punishment meant to symbolize cowardice. The Emperor ordered certain redeployments and then headed to Harar, where he visited and gave presents to the wounded at a French-run hospital. He also stopped in to visit a wounded Spanish reporter.

"I burn for shame as I think of his smiling face then," wrote George Steer, "when he walked in the half-dark under the pink oleanders which framed the courtyard of the French hospital at Harar . . . When did he neglect any of the press, however humble, who came to Addis Ababa to disturb his peace and make his war complicated past bearing? What white man's request did he turn aside? Yet when they had forced him into failure, they dropped him like a stone."[41]

The next morning, Haile Selassie flew back to the capital. The Italians had intelligence that the Emperor had been in the area, and their planes circled three times over an old gibbi that had been converted to a radio station. "I stood in the tower which dominated the town and the fruit groves outside and watched them spin above," recalled Steer. [42] A nervous servant rushed up to hand him his rifle. Steer knew not to bother.

* * *

General De Bono vacillated over whether to take Mekele, and then finally gave the order, sending out three columns in a classic maneuver. On any map of Ethiopia, you can draw an almost-straight vertical line from Adigrat down to Dessie, a caravan route that the Ethiopians called the "Imperial Road." Mekele sits a few miles south of Adigrat, and while the town had little strategic importance in itself, it made for a natural advance point to bore deeper into the countryside towards Addis Ababa. This is why Mussolini was beside himself with frustration over De Bono's delays. The irony is that Haile Selassie had given orders that Mekele was not to be defended. If the Italians wanted it, they could have it.

On November 7, reconnaissance planes suggested the town was empty. At dawn the next morning, the Italians moved in cautiously, and they decided it was a chance for their traitor-stooge, Gugsa, to earn his keep. With the colors flying and an army band playing, Gugsa was sent with his twelve hundred personal recruits ahead of the main force to check things out. But there was no enemy to be found. It hardly mattered. Mussolini was jubilant, sending De Bono a telegram the same day that read, "News reconquest Mekele thrills with pride soul of the Italian people. Give greetings of the Government and self to all troops."[43] De Bono should have known his Duce's joy wouldn't last.

Three days after his congratulatory telegram, Mussolini was back to playing armchair general and prodding De Bono south. In his telegram on November 11, he demanded, "On the right, bring the Maravigna Army Corps to front on the Takazze [River], and with the native divisions march without hesitation on Amba Alagi while the national divisions remain at Mekele. Reply to me."[44]

This time, however, De Bono's notorious caution was reasonable. His forces had penetrated deep into Tigray, but now the army's whole right flank was exposed. Without road-builders securing his tenuous line from Adigrat, he expected the Ethiopians to swoop in and cut his force in two. In a long, lecturing telegram back to his dictator, he pointed out that his field guns hadn't arrived yet, and besides, Amba Alagi had "no strategic importance" and was "tactically defective because it can be completely surrounded."[45] Exasperated, he reminded Mussolini that he was "on the spot" to evaluate the operation. He hadn't come right out and defied his Duce, but it was clear he didn't intend to comply.

Mussolini decided enough was enough. On November 17, when De Bono returned to his headquarters in Adigrat at four in the afternoon, he found a pink slip in the form of a fresh telegram. "With reconquest of Mekele," wrote Mussolini, "I consider your mission in East Africa completed."[46] There were a couple of lines of insincere praise, and then the cable informed De Bono that his replacement would be a man he loathed, his hated rival Pietro Badoglio.

De Bono was furious. Mekele was to be his "swan song," as he would call it. And the gold watch for his trouble would be the title of "Marshal of Italy." Disgusted, he arranged to leave on the very day that Badoglio was due to arrive. In his memoir, he couldn't resist a last dig over the controversy of the advance. When he met his successor in Massawa, he recalled, "Badoglio himself wished to tell me at once that he had fully approved of my resolution to make no further progress southwards before the troops were completely ready."[47]

Not quite. Badoglio, in fact, had been undermining De Bono all this time in Rome. But now that *he* was in the field, he soon discovered that De Bono was, in fact, right. It would be suicidal to press on without securing their positions first.

It would be time soon for the Ethiopians to unleash a major offensive of their own. Ras Mulugeta Yeggazu was marching north, moving gradually towards Amba Alagi with his eighty thousand men. In the province of Gonder, Ras Kassa Haile Darge, the Emperor's older cousin, had raised an army of one hundred and sixty thousand soldiers and was also heading north. Ras Seyum would make his way with his army across the Tembien. And from Gojjam, Ras Imru, the Emperor's childhood friend and other cousin, had twenty-five thousand men behind him, moving to link up with the ten thousand led by a dejazmach, Ayalew Birru, near the Eritrean border.

All these forces kept on the go at an impressively swift pace, always moving forward, steadily toward the enemy.

Chapter Ten

SCHEMES . . .

"That civilized nations can sit back and without a word of protest watch Italy's blatant action, should bring a blush to every white cheek in the world. At least a black Emperor has given a lesson to the so-called Christian civilized white races on how to conduct honest, diplomatic relations and to respect treaties . . ."[1]

These words didn't fall from the lips of C. L. R. James or Jomo Kenyatta. They were written in a letter home that summer by a white, thirty-seven-year-old doctor from Liverpool who was a fervent Christian. John Melly had been trying to do the Lord's work in Ethiopia, but Mussolini's invasion got in his way. Now he was determined to defend Haile Selassie's kingdom—not with a sword, but with a scalpel.

Melly wasn't what anyone expected of a medical missionary. He would show up for night rounds at London's St. Bartholomew's Hospital in full evening dress, a gardenia in his lapel. He was known as a positive type, always upbeat, famous for charming his patients. When a burn victim resisted exercising for her recovery, he lured her into dancing the Charleston with him.

In the summer of 1934, Melly had gone to Ethiopia with the ambitious plan of opening a hospital and medical school. He made friends with the Bartons and still managed to keep his reputation as a dandy, going about the capital in a sharp blue hat and carrying an ivory fly-whisk. Barton's daughter, Esmé, was likely smitten with him, but Melly's first love was his planned medical school. It had been clear to him that war was coming, and so he hoped to organize a Red Cross unit. He could see that medically, the country was completely unprepared for war.

"There are some millions, I suppose, of what are supposed to be the bravest warriors in the world," he wrote his sister, Kathleen Nelson, "waiting to die for this country and fight and die for it they will, to the very last man. But K, they have *no Red Cross whatsoever* [original italics]. If you want a sleepless night, picture to yourself the indescribable horror and suffering behind the Ethiopian lines when Italian planes, with no danger whatsoever to themselves and no opposition, have been dropping bombs on the Ethiopians for twenty-four hours . . . we have nearly five months to do something."[2]

Melly had developed a love of polo while he was in Addis Ababa, but fed up with the political timidity in Europe, he sold his ponies and bought his passage to get home to London. He expected the fighting to break out any day, despite the rains, and he boldly, cavalierly chose to draft anti-Italian articles for the press while onboard an *Italian* ship taking him up the Red Sea—borrowing a typewriter from the captain.[3]

The new British Ambulance Service of Ethiopia was the culmination of months of effort. From an affluent background, Melly hit up his rich friends. He helped organize appeals to the public, and one over the radio brought in £27,000. By October 19, the *British Medical Journal* could run a notice in its pages: "We are asked to announce that medical officers are required immediately to serve with an ambulance unit for Abyssinia. They should not be over thirty-five years of age, and should be unmarried."[4] On the morning of November 11, at St. Thomas's Hospital in Lambeth, London, there was a small ceremony to see off the BASE, as it was called. The Archbishop of Canterbury blessed the Red Cross flag, and after checking out the vehicles, wished the men going over, "God speed." Then the surgeons and trucks sailed on the *SS Rampura*.

The British team included Dr. John Macfie, a tropical disease expert who would be far less enamored of the Ethiopians than Melly. Working from a tent near Korem against a backdrop of mountains, Macfie would complain that the wounded Ethiopians who straggled to their camp were unappreciative; they were bad-tempered and sullen, their bodies crawling with lice and fleas. Melly, on the other hand, with all the harsh conditions and chronic lack of supplies, would write home about having *fun*.

* * *

Herbert Matthews was also having fun, of a kind. Dining on terrible rations in the light of storm lanterns hung from a nearby tree, the *New York Times* reporter sipped a glass of Chianti as he sat in a camp by the Lasguddi River and thought to himself, "What more could a man want?"[5]

This wasn't his usual, preferred comfort level. Matthews, a gaunt, balding figure of thirty-five, liked tailored suits and nice hotel rooms, so much so that he and his wife would later be in severe financial trouble because of their expensive tastes. But he liked adventure. He was also an unashamed Italophile, and before he wound up in the *Times* Paris bureau, he'd studied Dante and medieval history in Italy. On the day the war broke out in October, he was on a ship for Eritrea.

The Modern Caesar: Mussolini reviews his troops.

The Hunted Lion: Haile Selassie.

Sidney Barton, British Minister, at Addis Ababa, Ethiopia, from 1929 to 1936.

Ethiopian Imperial Guard.

Ethiopian village.

The Brave Front: Delegates for the Stresa Conference. Pierre Laval (black hair and mustache) is just off center. Ramsay MacDonald (white hair, using cane) is to the left.

The Defenders: (from left to right) Ras Imru, Ras Seyum, and Ras Kassa.

Diplomacy's Galahad: Anthony Eden goes into 10 Downing Street in early 1935.

Hands Off Ethiopia: Part of the Harlem protests on August 3, 1935.

Harlem Recruitment: PARA signs up volunteers to fight for Ethiopia in July 1935.

The Black Eagle: Hubert Julian.

The Brown Condor: John Robinson.

Pietro Badoglio.

Rodolfo Graziani.

Haile Selassie Gugsa.

Herbert Matthews at Ende Yesus.

Correspondents at Ende Yesus.

Italian tanks break through a stone wall and climb a hill to clear the way for an advance, November 6, 1935. This photo was taken by Laurence Stallings.

Herbert Matthews at Senafe, February 1936.

He was diligent in trying to get his facts right. He had a good sense of story and wrote well. But at heart, he was something of a romantic who was attracted to power. "If you start from the premise that a lot of rascals are having a fight," he wrote later, "it is not unnatural to want to see the victory of the rascal you like." After the war in Ethiopia, he would admit his doubts: "I, like so many other people, am going through an evolution about Fascism which must be obtruding through my daily work."[6]

Now he was one of only two correspondents who got to accompany General Oreste Mariotti's flying column, an advance unit penetrating deeper into the south. To Matthews, Ethiopia was "no different from hundreds of such invasions in the past," and that "for all practical purposes, I might just as well have been a chronicler accompanying Caesar's legions in Gaul."[7]

The other chronicler was Luigi Barzini Jr. of the *Corriere Della Sera*. Barzini wrote sensible, objective prose about the war, rather than soaring propaganda pieces. Perhaps it was because he'd gone to Columbia University and had worked for a couple of New York newspapers. He and Matthews got along well, though "Barzini never ceased to be amused at my insistence on getting first names— something which is necessary in American journalism, but considered unimportant elsewhere." Barzini even told a story—"false in detail, but illustrative of his point"—that "at the crucial moment Matthews would say to the native girl: 'No! Not yet! Before we go any further I must know your first name.'"[8]

Matthews and Barzini had been introduced to the short, stocky general as he pored over his maps, sketching out stages of his campaign in crayon, his face impassive. His flying column had to protect the left flank of General Ruggero Santini's First Corps heading down from Adigrat, and also secure the Danakil region. As far back as April, the Italians had reached out to the Danakils to throw in their lot with them when the invasion started. A Captain Gavino De Sarno had made his headquarters at Renda Coma in the Danakil and "built up a corps of spies—askaris who risked their lives by mingling with the natives and even joining the forces of Ras Seyum and [Dejazmach] Kassa Sebat, which permitted De Sarno to keep informed of the counter-activities of the Emperor's commanders."[9]

At first, the Italians had been promised ten thousand men, but when the war started, Kassa Sebat realized the danger and kept most of the Danakils with him through bribes or threats. Now with orders to advance, Mariotti couldn't wait for native support and moved with only a few hundred Danakils to round out his force of about two thousand men, most of them Eritreans. His battery of artillery was mounted on some of the eighty camels for his supply train.

First, the Italians had to march through the punishing Danakil Desert, hot and desolate, where right into the twenty-first century, caravans of camels have still been used, each beast loaded up with slabs of salt that need to be cut by hand. The landscape is remorseless, and Mariotti made his soldiers climb for twelve hours up a massive plateau. Guards were posted ahead on ridges and hills, and Herbert Matthews noticed that "at night their fires formed a glittering chain in whose protection the camp slumbered heavily."

Despite their arduous journey, Mariotti wouldn't let his men drop their guard. He'd been tipped off to expect an attack from Kassa Sebat, and he even knew where it was likely to happen—near a small town called Azbi, where Kassa Sebat was supposed to have some five thousand warriors. The general didn't have any more precise information than that, but he did have two important advantages. He knew the enemy was moving his way, plus Mekele had already been taken, closing off one avenue of escape for the enemy if they were forced to retreat.

The Ethiopians, however, didn't want to retreat. They had chosen their ground well. At just after nine-thirty in the morning on November 12, the Italians were picking their way slowly through a narrow canyon known as Ende Gorge. At the bottom lay the dried-up bed of the En River. In what was becoming a typical move, the Italians let their askaris and Danakils take point. If there were going to be shots, let them get hit first. High above, the Ethiopians were hidden behind the rocks and cliffs, waiting. They were patient and clever, allowing the entire army-ant progression of soldiers to fill the gorge so that there was nowhere to escape when they opened fire.

"Mariotti's face was as expressionless as always," recalled Matthews. "Suddenly he stopped his mule and barked out some staccato orders" to two orderlies, sending one ahead to tell the askaris to halt, and the other to go fetch the captain commanding the battery. "We waited in tense silence, standing in the center of a gorge in a completely exposed spot. Guns were being trained on every one of us, and eager trigger fingers trembled with excitement on the heavy wooded slopes." When the captain rode up fast on his mule, Mariotti pointed ahead and told him, "Mount your guns here and train them on that ridge."

The captain saluted and went on his way, but he'd barely gone three steps before there was a *crack-crack-crack* of shots, with echoes that bounced along the ravine and terrified the soldiers. Matthews watched in "amazed incomprehension as he staggered and fell, holding his right knee and groin while his face became distorted with pain. My body stiffened as every muscle in it contracted in an involuntary start of fear. Just next to me, my orderly, who had been standing at the head of my mule, swayed and threw his arm around the animal's neck to prevent himself from falling. A bullet had smashed his left ankle."

Soldiers dove for cover. The Ethiopians didn't simply have rifles, they had machine guns. Mariotti and his men searched frantically for where the shots were coming from, but it was no good. The acoustics of the gorge were perfect for confusion. Were they on the ridge? No, from the south. No, *both*. It was almost textbook, and Mariotti had only himself to blame for wading into the ravine.

And yet the Italians were still arrogant about the enemy. "Give them a little time!" said one. "They'll soon exhaust their four rounds of ammunition. Then if they don't run away, we'll counterattack."

But the Ethiopians weren't running out of bullets. They *kept on firing*. Three gunners were killed before the heavy guns were even mounted and ready to fire. Most of the camels in the supply train were slaughtered. "For one moment at the beginning," wrote Matthews, "some of the Danakil allies became panicky and started to run, but they were quickly halted by officers with pistols before the panic could spread." All this happened in just fifteen minutes. When the Ethiopians did finally run out of bullets, they ran down into the pass with intimidating yells and shouts, ready to fight hand to hand. The askaris tried bayonet charges, but the tactic didn't work. They only managed to hold the line by using grenades. The Ethiopians threw themselves at their enemy with spiteful abandon, and the fighting went on and on, for seven hours, until a stalemate in the hot afternoon.

Then night fell. The Ethiopians were known for never fighting at night, but the Italians were pinned down. Mariotti's men were in a remote and lonely place seven thousand feet above sea level, expecting to be wiped out the next day. "It was bitterly cold with no fires and even cigarettes were forbidden," wrote Matthews. "No one had eaten all day, and there was only the water each man had carried for himself."[10] Thirty-seven men were killed, with fifty-two others seriously wounded. Matthews assumed his fellow reporter, Luigi Barzini, was dead. "Barzini," he noted later, had "been doing the same for me, even to the extent of concocting an elegant obituary on 'falling in the line of duty,' and all that sort of thing."

In the dark, Mariotti's soldiers scrambled to set up a radio to contact headquarters; the general wanted planes to come to the rescue. But his coded message got no answer. "They have abandoned us without help," said the general bitterly. "Let us hope God will not abandon us." He and his officers gave themselves the perverse consolation that at least the Ethiopians weren't like the Libyans. "If these were Arabs," Mariotti remarked, "not one of us would come out of this alive." Still, his men must have been terrified. If they didn't die in a massacre, they feared the Ethiopians might do as their ancestors did at Adwa and castrate the survivors. Matthews refused to let himself think of his wife and children, "but sleep had never seemed so impossible, and thoughts are stubborn things."

And when the sun came up, there was the awful waiting.

When his firsthand account eventually ran in the *New York Times* on November 18, Matthews summed up the battle by writing, "Even the oldest colonial officers in the columns, who had seen twenty years and more in Italian service, consider General Mariotti's feat as one of the greatest in modern colonial history. It is a story well worth telling."[11]

What had happened? How could they possibly have survived?

It was a story well worth telling, and Matthews told it extremely well. But there was no great feat, except in survival. The Ethiopians had simply left.

The Italians could scarcely believe it. They could have been obliterated, but they had been saved—by culture. In addition to not fighting at night, it was standard practice for the Ethiopian warrior to pack it in after a single day of battle. The warriors at Ende Giorgis thought they had done their job. Both sides had displayed great physical courage, but Mariotti only gained his objective afterwards thanks to the Ethiopians' lack of strategic thinking, not because of any heroic valor on his men's part.

Hours later, after another tiring march, the general and his column—reduced in numbers, but not destroyed—received a delegation from submissive locals in a spot called Mai Fahena, in the Azbi region.

* * *

Elections are all about timing, and Stanley Baldwin knew he'd never have a better moment when he called one for November 14. He could capitalize on the boost in popularity Samuel Hoare got from his speech in Geneva, plus take advantage of the squabbling within the Labour ranks over the issue of sanctions. Its leader, George Lansbury, a devout pacifist, had decided to quit. The party faithful had chosen Clement Attlee to act as "caretaker" during the election, and it would only let him have the job for keeps after the election was over.

It wasn't difficult to take the temperature of the British public that season, and the Conservative Party put "League of Nations" at the very top of the subjects covered in its election manifesto. It was "the keystone of British foreign policy." Peace was of vital interest; the Covenant would be maintained; there would be "no wavering" on Ethiopia and Italy. It all sounded very good—and it worked.

On November 14, Baldwin and his National Government won by a landslide. With 432 seats for the Tories, it was a Conservative government in all but name.

Hoare and Anthony Eden, still in the voters' good graces for trying over Ethiopia, both kept their seats with large majorities. Sir John Simon barely held on to his with little more than six hundred votes. Ramsay MacDonald, physically worn down and perpetually in a mental fog, was kicked out of his riding in the north, thanks to the anger of thousands of jobless coal miners.

His son, Malcolm, also had a miserable campaign experience, probably hoping by the time it was over that he would never hear the word "Ethiopia" again. At election time, he was secretary of state for the colonies, and as he made campaign appearances in Retford, he found himself doggedly pursued by Gold Coast activists. What about the African colonial peoples? What about Ethiopia? MacDonald was beside himself. Two days before Britons went to the polls, he complained in a letter to the governor of the Gold Coast that they might cost him at least a hundred votes: "I cannot remember a similar case in which Africans or others from the Colonies have taken a direct part like this in an election here."[12] He lost his seat and had to wait to capture a new one in a by-election in February. Baldwin had him moved into the Dominions Office.

The overall status quo would be kept, which included, naturally, Samuel Hoare as foreign secretary. Baldwin's government had also promised to take no action in isolation and to rely on the League. Only weeks after the election, the British public would discover they had been lied to, and that Hoare had broken this promise.

As far as Pierre Laval was concerned, the British election told him one thing: he could go on just as he'd done before. Soon after the election, Laval was chairing a meeting of France's High Military Committee, and he bragged to the worried council about having a secret deal with Mussolini. One of those listening and unconvinced was the commander-in-chief of France's armed forces, Maurice Gamelin. Gamelin, with his round head and white mustache framed by jowls, was the intellectuals' general, the hero architect behind the Battle of the Marne during the Great War. He was so demoralized that he went home after the meeting and sobbed. He hadn't broken down like this since his mother had passed away.

He wrote in his diary, "I wept for the destiny of my country, which up to now has always found the men it needed in the hours of crisis; not only a Joffre, a Foch, but a Poincaré and a Clemenceau. But today we have none like them."[13]

* * *

It wasn't safe anymore to be British or American in Rome. On Saturday, November 16, four members of the Manhattan String Quartet—young men in their twenties from spots in Brooklyn, the Bronx, and Yonkers—were out and about, chatting and joking among themselves. They had sailed over for a European concert tour and had already played London back in September. Now as they walked along, oblivious to what was going on around them, they happened to laugh at a private joke as they came upon a Fascist funeral procession. They didn't know either that they were supposed to salute.

A Blackshirt walked up to the Americans. "What's funny?" he asked.

None of the Americans could understand him. "We only speak English," one of them replied.

That was enough to set off the Blackshirts. They took the Americans for British citizens and beat the hell out of them. And they beat them badly enough that their victims were too scared to make a complaint to the police. They packed up and left quickly for the next leg of their tour in Paris.

* * *

Ras Mulugeta Yeggazu was old, cantankerous, and alcoholic, but he could march like a young warrior a third his age. The general would rise at dawn and cover twenty-five miles with his army until late in the afternoon, when he would finally strike camp. Seven secretaries, plus their servants, would march behind him, carrying tables and chairs, which he used to write dispatches and orders. Despite the old war horse's hatred of foreigners, he'd brought along a Cuban revolutionary named Alejandro Del Valle, a man educated in Texas who knew his way around a machine gun and acted as both a commander and a military adviser.

Out in the rolling landscape and about to face the enemy, Mulugeta was as defiant as ever, ignoring his Emperor's strict order that his men shouldn't loot the farms of peasants. Like locusts, they stripped the fields bare of corn, beans, and tef. In Wollo, the general targeted the chiefs who were holding back supplies of food and rifles and had them flogged. When he reached the territory south of Lake Ashangi, it was time for more discipline. Claiming that some of the Oromo leaders had colluded with Gugsa, he had the men flogged close to death or conscripted into his army. At Korem, he set up a large garrison to check the traffic of bandits in the area, with caves dug for disobedient shifta chiefs.

Mulugeta didn't have a field radio. If he wanted to communicate, he had to send messages by runner. It would take him more than a month to reach his objective, as he stopped and held position for a while, trying to avoid being spotted by reconnaissance planes and bombers. He had no idea if the armies would be able to link up in their grand strategy. When he reached Amba Aradam, twenty miles south of Mekele, his orders were to hold the line. This is where the Italians had stopped, and this was where he should make them stay.

On a mountain nine thousand feet high, his warriors could hide and wait in countless caves. Water wasn't a problem; there were five springs that flowed out of channels of the impressive summit, and each night, groups of fifty to one hundred soldiers climbed out to get their rations. He would send a message to Ras Kassa Haile Darge: "I am turning my mountain into a castle."[14] Pasture land lay conveniently below behind the amba for their mules and for cattle. And Mulugeta had brought along a unique prize to launch at the Italians—one of their own cannons, captured at Adwa in 1896. The general ordered it to be hauled all the way to the top of the mountain, where it could be pointed at Mekele. It didn't have a hope in hell of striking the town.

Meanwhile, Kassa Haile Darge, along with his two sons, had led his army along a caravan route to the pass at Amba Alagi. There, the big, bearded ras, always preferring traditional dress to Western khaki uniforms, had to wait. On November 17, he was joined by Ras Seyum Magasha, who brought with him fifteen thousand warriors on a march across the Tembien region. Seyum knelt down and kissed Kassa's feet, and as Kassa lifted him back up, he kissed his fellow ras on both cheeks. The two men planned their attack.

The next day, Kassa proved he was talented at deception. An Italian squadron of planes was buzzing about a stream near the pass. His men managed to stay out of sight, but obstinate, wandering mules tipped the enemy off. When the planes came back that day, they flew low and strafed the empty countryside with machine gun fire, dropping bombs for good measure. They struck nothing. Then, to the pilots' horror, eight thousand Ethiopians suddenly showed themselves and let them have it. Hit by the volleys, the planes pulled their noses up in panic and banked away. They were machine-gunning frantically now, letting their bombs loose in desperation to hit their attackers.

The antique rifles didn't send any planes careening into a mountain, but the Ethiopians did more damage than they realized. An Italian sergeant died later of his wounds. One pilot had to make an emergency landing at Hauzien. The Ethiopians were thrilled with their small victory. The Italians wouldn't fly so low next time, and their new respect for the enemy's sharpshooting would give the Ethiopians a bit of breathing room to advance.

*   *   *

That same day, the Black Eagle stepped on a morning train in Addis Ababa bound for Djibouti. Hubert Julian was leaving forever and claimed he was foregoing "a big send-off by my thousands of admirers." Reporters didn't notice any *small* send-off of admirers at the train station either; they did notice he quarreled with customs officers over his baggage.

"I'm through with Ethiopia," Julian announced with a flourish. Now that he was no longer under orders, he could let loose a long stream of grievances and criticisms. "I couldn't stand those lazy fellows any longer . . . I trained the infantry in modern methods of crawling and guerrilla warfare. Then the Emperor ordered his underlings to supply arms; but they were lazy and inefficient, and the arms were not forthcoming, so I resigned."[15]

He didn't elaborate on what qualified as "modern methods of crawling," but there's no evidence, of course, that Julian ever had any military education.

Weeks later, customs staff on Ellis Island thumbed through his passport and discovered that his US visa had expired. The proud Eagle was forced to stay in the grubby detention rooms and endure several days of hearings before he was allowed to walk the streets of Harlem again. Yes, he could be in the United States—on the condition that he either formally apply as an immigrant or use only his British citizenship.

His first order of business was a fresh round of interviews. He was no longer slinging insults at Ethiopia's military; now he was condemning the rases, the Orthodox Church, and the general poverty of the ordinary peasants. The irony is that for the first time in a long while, the preposterous liar was speaking some truth; an exaggerated, caustic version, but one still salted with facts. But he went too far, implying that Mussolini's war on Ethiopia was "an act of God in answer to the suffering cries of humanity."

He would soon find out this was definitely *not* what African Americans wanted to hear.

* * *

America's "moral embargo," as Cordell Hull liked to call it, wasn't working. In fact, exports to Italy—the kind of goods disapproved of by the Roosevelt administration—had actually *increased* through October. Cordell Hull was alarmed enough by the bump in figures that he issued a stern statement on November 15 that the government was keeping an eye on exporters. "The American people," said Hull, "are entitled to know that there are certain commodities such as oil, copper, trucks, tractors, scrap iron, and scrap steel which are essential war materials, although not actually 'arms, ammunition and implements of war' . . . This class of trade is directly contrary to the policy of this Government . . ."[16]

Even foreign neighbors could see there was no bite in Hull's bark. A day after his statement, customs officials in Canada, still a loyal part of the British Commonwealth, received new orders. They were to watch out for goods secretly bound for Italy being shipped through the United States.

Hull's statement accomplished little except to antagonize Rome, which now lumped America in with the countries imposing sanctions. His old friend, Italian Ambassador Augusto Rosso, came calling on November 22, and no sooner was he in Hull's office than he began reading a protest. The United States, claimed Rosso, had violated an 1871 treaty that guaranteed both countries "complete freedom of commerce and navigation." The arms embargo, he argued, was "bound to assume the meaning of a 'sanction' and therefore the positive character of an unfriendly act."[17]

Hull wasn't having any of this. He asked if Italy complained as much when Germany took steps over business ties with belligerents. At one point, he posed an astonishing idea to Rosso, asking "why his Government did not invest $100,000,000 in Ethiopia instead of expending several hundred million dollars in its military conquest and bringing worry and the threat of danger to the balance of the world."[18] To Hull, Italy should have bought what it was now trying to conquer.

Meanwhile, Britain's man in Washington, Sir Ronald Lindsay, looked for the administration to throw in its lot with Europe over an oil embargo. International peace had nothing to do with his motives—Lindsay thought that if America didn't join in, the entire Italian oil market would wind up going to the United States. Perhaps Stanley Baldwin was also thinking past the war to how Royal Dutch Shell and the Anglo-Iranian Oil Company would fare. Hull was tiring of it all. "We had gone as far as we could."[19]

Both he and Roosevelt still expected the League of Nations to do what they were unwilling to do: stand up to Italy.

*   *   *

Colonel John Robinson was in the thick of it now. He had built the Imperial Air Force, but in many ways, he *was* the Imperial Air Force. If he wasn't delivering messages for the Emperor, he was taking the monarch to the front. If he wasn't getting his hands black with engine grease, repairing a plane, he was training pilots. "With the war on, I worked out a . . . system to carry doctors and Red Cross and other medical supplies to the front," he recalled later.[20] And if he wasn't ferrying physicians, he was campaigning for African Americans back home to mobilize Red Cross units.

As Haile Selassie's personal pilot, his flights could involve white-knuckle moments in which both men got the chance to measure each other. On one trip, they were grimly aware that the Italians were only a couple of hours behind them in pursuit. Robinson was charmed by his royal passenger, who, like him, had been excited about flight from an early age, and who must have plied him with questions about the aircraft. He noted that Haile Selassie "is not the big warrior type of Ethiopian, but he is fearless."[21] But courtiers and advisers eventually persuaded the Emperor that it was too risky to depend on air travel.

Robinson had the most skill, and so he took the biggest risks. With so few planes in the fleet and none of them armed with guns, he had no way to defend himself, and no air support for his missions. He flew barnstorming style, diving deep if he was over the Great Rift Valley and pulling hairpin stunts to shake any Italians off his tail.

When his day was done (if it was ever really done), or when he took rare breaks, he lived well. He was given a house that would have been a mansion to ordinary Ethiopians. He was given a car, and servants were retained to look after him. But with the war progressing, it sunk in for him that he was alone. In a letter to his friend back in Chicago, Claude Barnett, dated November 21, he wrote bitterly, "I told my fellow pilots that I would do everything I could to get them in the air force here. Last Saturday, I cabled for six of them." If his old friend, Cornelius Coffey, would respond, "I would cable the fare [for the trip] at once to them. That was one week ago, and I haven't had any reply. All of these men asked me before I left there to please get them jobs here. Every one of them has failed me so far, which means the last time I will ever ask the Emperor permission to send for anyone else."[22]

Perhaps he had forgotten his own warning weeks ago to a friend to stay away and how the Ethiopian air force was in rough shape. His appraisal had been so demoralizing that one of his friends had leaked it to Barnett's own operation, the Associated Negro Press, and it was printed in newspapers like the *Afro-American* only days after the bombing of Adwa. But their opinions may not have mattered. What Robinson didn't know, what thousands of black citizens couldn't know, was that Washington was still denying African Americans passports.

Robinson was equally frustrated over obstacles to getting more aircraft. In the same letter to Barnett, he wrote, "New airplanes were ordered for the six pilots I cabled. These airplanes cost over 30,000 American dollars each. They are coming from England. I first ordered some American planes, but the order was turned down on account of the American embargo on planes being sent here."[23]

There was an obvious solution to use when the planes eventually arrived—only he wasn't allowed to pursue it. "There are many European pilots here trying to get jobs in the air service. They came here at their own expense and have been two or three months trying to get work. I am sure they will be given work now because it seems impossible to get colored Americans. There are many white American pilots that send cablegrams and many letters every day wanting to pay their way here if they are promised a job when they get here. Up to the present day, they have been turned down."[24]

To make matters worse, the few French pilots were also due to leave Ethiopia by the end of November. Robinson was clearly depressed by conditions, helpless to change them. He couldn't help but notice as well that among all the Red Cross units from different countries, America was clearly absent. Instead, the US government made itself felt in a different way—one of the embassy officials summoned the Brown Condor more than once to ask him "many annoying questions."

Robinson was deeply offended at being asked to explain himself, but wrote that he wouldn't pay any attention to these episodes. "I don't intend to be bluffed by a narrow-minded person." After one curt interrogation, he asked the official if he wanted Robinson to surrender his passport. "He at once changed his attitude and assured me that he was proud of me as an American citizen and hoped that I will always remain one [and] that the American government is behind me one hundred percent. And any time I need their help, he would only [be] too glad to help me in any way." Robinson thanked him politely, but assured the man that he didn't think he would ever need his help in any way whatsoever. "He hasn't called me anymore."[25]

In his darker moods, he could be less than generous about Ethiopian fighting skills and wrote to Barnett on November 28, "On the northeast and southeast frontier, most [of] the Ethiopians are Mohammedan, and they are putting up a good fight. The Italians are having a real hard job fighting them. It is strange to say, but is true, the Christians in the north are the worst fighters. When it comes to battle, the Italians kick them around like nothing."

This wasn't true, of course, but it's likely that Robinson hadn't heard at that time about the battle at Ende Giorgis, and he certainly wouldn't have known the full extent of the counteroffensive slowly taking shape. The Ethiopians, in fact, were a couple of weeks away from offering a stirring example of how wrong he was.

* * *

The Labour Party, having picked up more than a hundred seats in the British election, wasn't about to let the pressure up over Ethiopia. MP Hugh Dalton was once the undersecretary for foreign affairs, and he kept well-informed sources; he could see how Stanley Baldwin had exploited Anthony Eden's sincere commitment. "The Minister for League Affairs has been used in some quarters as a sort of decoy duck to attract the League of Nations Union vote at election time."[26]

Eden's public warnings about men killed and homes being shattered, Dalton pointed out, were earnest—if only the government would act on them. But homes in Ethiopia were still being "shattered by bombs dropped from Italian airplanes driven by British oil." The Anglo-Iranian Oil Company had boosted its exports to Italy during the first seven months of 1935 by 80 percent over the same period in 1934.

"The Foreign Secretary is going to Paris and is going to see Monsieur Laval," Dalton told the House. "I trust he will speak what I'm sure is the mind of this country and tell Monsieur Laval that this country is not favorable to, or even interested in, any terms of settlement of this war which will allow the Italian dictator to profit by his aggression."

Samuel Hoare wouldn't promise that. And as far as the oil embargo went, he said the League and Great Britain had already "agreed to it in principle" (but hadn't done anything about it). "The League machinery is working well," he told the House. And despite the fact that there was now a war, with casualties recorded and reports of a hospital bombed, he referred to it as a "dispute."

Hoare later blamed his muddled thinking on poor health. "It may be that I was so pulled down by overwork that my judgment was out of gear," he wrote in his memoir.[27] Anthony Eden could attest to him being in rough shape. One night, he, Hoare, and their wives were at the cinema together when Britain's foreign secretary collapsed in a corridor. Hoare was experiencing what was turning out to be a series of blackouts. His doctors insisted he rest. He could have invited Laval to come to London for a proper conference, but he opted instead to see him during a stopover in Paris before taking a couple of weeks' holiday in Switzerland.

Before Hoare left, he ran into Eden at the top of a staircase in the Foreign Office. Eden advised caution in dealing with Laval and then warned Hoare about one of their own team, Robert Vansittart. "Don't forget that in Paris, Van can be more French than the French."

"Don't worry," replied Hoare. "I shall not commit you to anything. It wouldn't be fair on my way through to my holiday."[28]

Hoare was more concerned with what his boss thought. But Stanley Baldwin showed his typical indifference to foreign affairs. "Have a good leave and get your health back," said Baldwin. "That is the most important thing. By all means stop in Paris and push Laval as far as you can, but on no account get this country into war."[29]

* * *

Emperor Haile Selassie meant it when he promised his people that he would
be in the battlefield with them. In all the talk over guerrilla tactics, it was always
suggested that the Emperor stay in the capital and not be directly in the fight. "But
a time must come when I *must* fight," he once said impatiently to Everett Colson.

Now he moved his headquarters to Dessie, a market town more than two
hundred miles north of the capital. Its name in Amharic means "my joy." He
took over the abandoned Italian consulate, and the building was not only his
base but also his temporary home, where he still lived like an English country
squire. His court still held four-course meals of European and Ethiopian dishes,
and in the front hall was a set of walking sticks. There were even stables for his
Arabian horses. The Emperor kept up a busy pace, organizing the construction
of two roads, both of which he would need months later, one to Korem and one
to Lalibela, the country's second holiest city. He made sure food caravans went
through Dessie and negotiated with local chiefs, supervised air raid precautions,
and when he found the time, wrote to his wife.

Haile Selassie also familiarized himself with the big Oerlikon anti-aircraft gun
that took up space in the building's garden. He'd been given lessons on how to
aim and fire this impressive piece of hardware. The Italians knew where he was,
and there had never been any secrecy over the fact—it was reported in the newspapers of the world. At eight o'clock in the morning on December 6, the Italian
air force decided to pay the Lion of Judah a visit.

Earlier that morning, six planes had flown over Gonder, a town in the
northern highlands that boasted royal castles going back to the seventeenth century (today, it's a world heritage site). The planes dropped more than fifty bombs
in the middle of its cobbled streets, killing four women and six children.[30] Most
of the men had already gone to fight. Then eighteen planes flew towards Dessie.

When he heard the distant roar of the aircraft, Haile Selassie put on his helmet
and made sure his teenage son and favorite, Makonnen, was bundled off to the air
raid shelter. His courtiers wanted him to join his son, but the Emperor was adamant
that he would be in the thick of the fighting. He rushed out to man the Oerlikon,
aiming its barrel at the planes droning closer to the shabby little town. There could
be nothing worth their attention here except *him*. Dessie had the usual sprinkling of
tukuls, a couple of Western buildings, and a gibbi for the crown prince. A group of
American Seventh-Day Adventists had established a mission and a Red Cross hospital.
Forty of the bombs, most of them incendiaries, hit their compound immediately.

Warriors shot their rifles pointlessly into the air while bombs exploded, boring
craters into the ground and burning tukuls. The Westerners dove for cover or
put their backs up against trees. One bomb almost hit the fuel storage for the
vehicles of the *Times* and Reuters correspondents. Servants for the reporters in

town pulled out their revolvers and fired into the sky, while the reporters themselves took quiet, spiteful pleasure in one particular casualty—the Belgian censor was wounded.

Haile Selassie, his arms shaking with the force of the Oerlikon's cannon recoils, did his best to bring down one of the planes, but he was having little luck. As if he didn't have enough to think of, his courtiers were circled around him, watching him work. "Haven't I told you not to mass?" he barked at them, losing his temper at their stupidity. "Do you want to make me a target? Take cover and let me fire!"[31]

When it was over, the Italians had killed fifty-three people, many of them burning to death in their tukuls. A mother and her two small children were blown to bits on a road. About two hundred others in the center of town were wounded. Some of the bombs weighed two hundred pounds, and they wrecked the operating theater of the Red Cross hospital and wiped out a tent for instruments. With their medical services either destroyed or in disarray, it was little wonder that the doctors on site had to perform thirty amputations.

The reporters piled into their trucks to go check out the damage in the town. The traumatized residents of Dessie, thinking they were Italians, gave them an angry burst of rifle fire, wounding the correspondent for France's Havas news agency in the knee.[32]

For Haile Selassie, the outrage of this bombing wasn't like the reports that came in over Adwa. He was *right there* to witness the suffering of his people—bleeding, crippled, losing their limbs, and mourning loved ones. Putting away his helmet and leaving the Oerlikon, its metal now very hot from use, he went to draft a telegram of protest to the League of Nations. Then he put on a cloak and took one of his walking sticks to go be among his people and visit the injured. He ordered a plane to take wounded Europeans back to the capital and made sure the radio was reserved to get the word out on the attack. The officious Belgian censor got a decoration for being wounded in battle.

It turned out the Italian planes had added insult to massacre. One of the pilots had dropped a bottle holding a note scribbled in pencil. It read:

> Long live Italy, long live the Duce, long live the king. We carry with
> our three colors the Lictor's badge [the Fascist emblem], the civiliza-
> tion of Rome. Greetings to the Negus. Ask him if he has digested his
> biscuits.[33]

By biscuits, the pilot meant bombs.

Haile Selassie ordered his men to collect all the safely unexploded examples of Roman civilization and pile them in front of the consulate building. Then he defiantly posed for press photographers with one foot perched on a large bomb. The reporters weren't completely convinced they were safe and took their shots as quickly as possible. After they left, the Emperor inspected the bombs and had the range and the depth of the shell bursts measured, recording them all in a little notebook. The next morning, when five planes returned for another bombing run, he didn't bother to man the Oerlikon, but merely sat in his air raid shelter. The people of the town had also been safely evacuated.

* * *

Dr. Marcel Junod was horrified when he received a telegram in Addis Ababa on December 6 about the bombing. "But Dessie is an open town," he insisted, "and the hospital and our ambulances are clearly marked."

The Europeans and Ethiopians told him laconically that "Fascist airmen don't take any notice of that."[34]

He and Sidney Brown left the next day with a convoy of six trucks, knowing that fresh supplies would be urgently needed. It was a long trek, and when they arrived, a Greek surgeon petulantly indicated how long they'd been waiting. One of the councilors for the Emperor took Brown and Junod on a tour of the ruins, which still gave off an acrid odor of burned remains. John Melly's ambulance unit had just arrived, and Haile Selassie invited them, along with Junod, to dine with him that evening. At a table decorated in the colors of the Ethiopian flag, the Emperor turned to Junod and mentioned the courage of the doctors of the Ethiopian Red Cross under fire. That was the last they would discuss of the raid, but Junod got the impression that Haile Selassie was deeply saddened and far more upset than he appeared.

When the Emperor asked where their ambulances were stationed, Junod went into an explanation of the problems he and Brown had getting the vehicles to the front. The road from Waldia to Korem, for instance, wouldn't be passable for trucks for about a month.

"I will send a thousand men to speed up the work," the Emperor answered promptly.

"Because of lack of transport, the Ethiopian ambulances are still being held up here," said Junod.

The Emperor understood. "I will give the necessary orders. Two hundred mules and their drivers will be placed at your disposal within three days." Junod realized that Haile Selassie had to deal with even small details in person, and he admired the Emperor's calm and methodical persistence.[35]

As he was about to leave the dinner party, the Emperor's young son, Makonnen, mentioned that his wireless no longer worked. On the spot, Junod became a radio surgeon, using a glass of rainwater to lubricate the set's accumulators. Makonnen was delighted to have it working again, and so quickly. Junod must have impressed his host.

He also had the chance to talk with John Melly, who invited him for a drink at his quarters to cap off the night. The two became fast friends, and Junod was impressed with how the always-positive Melly had quickly made his living space into a little corner of home. Melly had canvas armchairs, a small library, a work table, and a wireless that was playing a concert by a dance band thousands of miles away at the Savoy.[36] But for all the creature comforts the young Englishman had in his tent, he was also hanging onto visions that outraged his quiet Christian morality. Two days before Dessie was bombed, Melly had written home to his sister, Kathleen, "This isn't a war—it isn't even a slaughter—it's the torture of tens of thousands of defenseless men, women, and children, with bombs and poison gas. They're using gas incessantly, and we've treated hundreds of cases, including infants in arms—and the world looks on—and passes by on the other side."[37]

After Junod had his drink with Melly, he trudged back to his own quarters, passing the tents of the foreign correspondents. They were making a racket late into the night, drinking and playing cards.

Days later, George Steer came up from Addis Ababa to see the damage. Because of the winds and the geography of Dessie, he concluded that the pilots hadn't targeted the hospital. "It was not a deliberate attack on the Red Cross, like those which were to follow. It was an attempt to burn a large civilian center and a rather poor potshot at the Emperor."[38]

The Italians would claim they had only struck military targets—if civilians and the hospital were hit, they had to have been located close to them. But all the camps for the Ethiopian soldiers were north of the town, their tents spread out along the flat countryside. The planes didn't even try to hit the military camps until they made their return home.

* * *

Samuel Hoare left for Paris on Saturday, December 7, and there was a large scrum of newspapermen waiting for him when he arrived at five o'clock in the afternoon. Overwhelmed by the questions yelled at him and the pop and crackle of camera bulbs, he could hardly believe what was happening. "The mob . . .

seemed to have taken possession of the Quai d'Orsay as if it had been Versailles in 1789," he recalled later. Ignoring the press men, he went off to greet the French prime minister, who was shabby in appearance as usual.

An extraordinary meeting was about to take place, to try again to decide the fate of Ethiopia. Vansittart claimed later in his memoir that his presence was "an attempt to counter the Anglophobe press which was more venomous than usual." But what he had in mind to combat the French media was anyone's guess. If Vansittart's role was unclear, he was unsure himself about what Hoare intended to accomplish, and warned him "that the way of the peacemaker would be hard, and asked whether the Government meant to fight."[39] Hoare had his instructions from Stanley Baldwin: no war, under any circumstances. "Then you will have to compromise," said Vansittart. "That will be unpopular, but there is no third way."[40]

Hoare could also count on the advice of his ambassador in Paris, George Clerk, and the Foreign Office's Maurice Peterson, who had been working on broad strokes of a new proposal with their French counterparts. The four British delegates now sat down in Pierre Laval's study across from four representatives of France. Laval sat with a telephone next to him, and a couple of the British delegates presumed he had it there to impress them.

No one was present to speak for or act in the interests of Ethiopia. No one was in person to represent Italy either, but as it turned out, no representative was necessary.

Even before Hoare could offer a compromise, Pierre Laval wanted something taken off the table: the threat of an oil embargo. Such a move, argued Laval, would force Mussolini into a corner and prompt him to make the "mad dog" attack that everyone feared—well, almost everyone. Before Hoare left, Anthony Eden put down a rebuttal in a memo for the Cabinet, and his clear irritation rings through his phrasing:

> I confess that this danger has always seemed to me very remote, and I am quite unimpressed by the threats of such persons as the Marchese Theodoli, who has clearly been instructed to frighten us as much as possible. This maneuver is so obvious as scarcely to require comment. In calculating the likelihood of a mad dog act, the isolation of the Italian forces in East Africa should not be overlooked.
>
> Moreover, Signor Mussolini has never struck me as the kind of person who would commit suicide. He has been ill-informed about our attitude in this dispute, and while he may well be exasperated, there is a considerable gap between that condition and insanity.[41]

But in Laval's study, the French prime minister was back to acting as the Duce's front man. He insisted that an oil embargo could lead directly to war in Europe, one in which only a gloating Hitler would stand to gain, watching from the sidelines. This was a tune that Hoare and Vansittart were already humming to themselves, and the only question was whether France would stand by Britain's side. A month and a half ago, George Clerk had faced Laval, bluntly demanding support. It made world headlines when he got it. Now the two Great Powers were back to being unsure of each other. Laval refused to be pinned down over any formal preparations for war and was only prepared for the "opening of staff talks."[42]

He was determined to make Anglo-French unity depend on what more could be offered to Rome. Given that the invasion had already grabbed a fair amount of Ethiopia's north, it seemed unlikely that Mussolini would ever agree to give these spoils back. If anything, he would expect more if he came to the negotiation table. Hoare "felt that there was some force in Laval's argument," particularly because he "had been informed that the Emperor would find serious opposition from the rases who had gone over to the Italian side in the occupied districts if their territory was restored to Abyssinia."[43]

Whoever informed Hoare had misled him, and his logic didn't hold. No rases had gone over to the Italian side; true, Gugsa was highly prized as a traitor, but he was only a dejazmach. Moreover, it was a strange notion to give up pieces of Haile Selassie's kingdom on the off chance that he might face rebellion from hypothetical traitors. George Steer, as well as other correspondents in the field, had been sending back stories for weeks on how nobles were in the mountains and hills, marshalling their forces to keep the fight going. Hoare, however, only thought in terms of his own measure of territorial worth. He considered the Ogaden "mostly a sandy desert," one that "had never been under the effective control of Addis Ababa."[44] Peterson thought Italy "would make more of these territories than Abyssinia had ever done."[45]

It was late in the evening when the British and French wrapped up their first day of talks, and when they resumed the next morning, they worked on the problem of appeasing Haile Selassie with an outlet to the sea. The Emperor could have it in exchange for giving up large chunks of Tigray. Hoare's team didn't like trading away their port of Zeila in British Somaliland, while Laval and his delegates were equally obstinate over letting the Ethiopians have Assab in Eritrea. With Assab, the Ethiopians could build a railroad to the port that could compete with the French's line from Djibouti. No one picked up on the irony—they were quite willing to parlay others' land, but not their own.

After the minor squabbling, Assab ended up the chosen sacrifice. Hoare and Laval were now ready to tackle the economic monopoly the Italians wanted for the non-Amharic provinces in Ethiopia's south. Their aides had already done some measuring on what they thought would appease the dictator, but Laval thought there should be more. Hoare was willing, but wanted the monopoly placed under League supervision. All through the negotiations, Mussolini was well aware of their progress—that was the real purpose of the phone next to Laval. More than once, as Hoare sat by, Laval rang up the dictator to get his opinion.[46]

*   *   *

On Sunday, December 8, Anthony Eden was spending the weekend at home when he got a telegram from Hoare, reporting that the talks were going well and that the French appeared to be making an honest attempt to find common ground. Eden knew better than to believe this, and he "wondered how many cooks were stirring the broth in Paris."[47]

His concern was justified. Under what came to be known as the Hoare-Laval Plan, Ethiopia would have to forfeit most of Tigray, much of the Danakil region, and a substantial portion of the Ogaden. Italy would get about half the African nation, as well as the means to capture what was left through an economic monopoly. For all these spoils, Ethiopia would get Assab—but it wouldn't be allowed to link a railroad to it. As a sop, the Italians would grant Ethiopia the privilege of maintaining its church within the historic city of Aksum.

Pierre Laval was in a self-congratulatory mood as he escorted Hoare out of his office. Promising that a new chapter had opened for British and French cooperation, he said, "Now we have finished with Italy. Together, we shall tackle Germany."

To mollify the newsmen camped outside the Quai d'Orsay, the two delegations issued a joint communiqué that informed the world they had come up with a plan. "We are both satisfied with the results that have been reached."[48] The details were supposed to be withheld so that Baldwin's Cabinet, as well as the "interested governments," could review them. But as Hoare returned to the British embassy, he chose on the spot to give reporters "a very general idea of what we had been attempting." He asked them "not to comment upon it in any detail until the two governments released the actual terms," and with astonishing naiveté, he thought the "correspondents appeared ready to fall in with my request."[49]

The reporters nodded, smiled . . . and then hit their typewriters and phones as soon as they could. Two Paris newspapers, the *Oeuvre* and *L'Écho de Paris*, published the full details of the peace plan the very next day. Soon the London papers had it. René de Chambrun, in a book that was a revisionist defense of Laval, his father-in-law, alleged that the reports in London and Paris were "two obviously synchronized bombshells."[50] In de Chambrun's version, an official at the Quai d'Orsay handed over the document to a representative in the Havas news agency, who put it into the hands of André Géraud, performing double duty as the head foreign correspondent for *L'Écho* and a writer for the *Daily Telegraph*.[51] Perhaps. But neither Hoare nor Laval knew how to keep his mouth shut, and Hoare actually believed reporters would sit on their hands and obediently wait for an official announcement.[52]

Having no idea what was coming, Hoare thought his job was done. He sent a cable to Eden, asking him to put in a request for a Cabinet meeting. Then he planned to hop on the night train from the Gare de Lyon so he could at last join his wife on holiday in Switzerland. Meanwhile, Maurice Peterson headed home to London with the formal text of the bargain. Vansittart, always obsessed with Germany, tried to enlist Peterson to get another message to the government that it was high time to close ranks against Hitler. He'd congratulated Hoare on the outcome of the meetings, but privately, Vansittart was unhappy, and he recalled that "George Clerk, scrutinizing France, never thought that we could wring more out of her."[53]

Across the Channel, a puzzled Anthony Eden called Paris to find out more. He was told that Vansittart couldn't be reached at the Ritz, his usual place to stay, while Hoare was taking a nap before his trip. Peterson was on a train home. All Eden could get from an embassy secretary was that Hoare and Vansittart were "well satisfied with the day's work."[54]

Eden had to wait until the next morning to learn what was so satisfying. At a meeting over breakfast in Eden's home, Peterson passed along a letter Hoare had drafted up, urging the Cabinet to decide on the plan as soon as possible. Eden then read through the four typed pages in French, which looked to him like they had been drafted in a rush in a government office; they had been initialed "S.H." and "P.L." The polyglot Eden was completely fluent in French. He knew Hoare wasn't. As he wondered why Hoare hadn't insisted on having the document translated, his "mild reflections rapidly turned to astonishment" as he read the plan.[55]

He couldn't imagine what Hoare was thinking, and looking to his guest for answers, Peterson timidly replied, "I did not suppose that you would like them."[56] He gave Eden the impression that he hadn't played an active role in the talks. In fact, Peterson told Eden that if it been up to him, he could have won better terms. Based on the evidence of surviving Foreign Office documents, this was clearly a bare-faced lie. Peterson, after all, was the one who first suggested that the Ethiopians should be pushed into giving up more than they wanted. He was also one of the original architects of the plan.

Eden made his PM sit down for a one-on-one briefing, complete with a map as visual aid, as he tried his best to stop the deal in its tracks. And when he was done, Baldwin ventured no comment or opinion at all, the Sphinx of Downing Street. He simply asked what his minister thought. Eden assured him there was no way that Haile Selassie, or the League for that matter, would accept such a proposal.

Baldwin frowned and offered a grunt, murmuring, "That lets us out, doesn't it?"[57]

If nothing else, the absent Hoare had won his Cabinet meeting, which was set for six o'clock in the evening on December 9. In the comfortable bubble of their conference room, Baldwin and his ministers had no clue yet what storm of outrage was gathering in the world. The story was already on the front pages in America. But to Eden's dismay, his colleagues overwhelmingly approved Hoare's plan and ignored his objections. Worse, they charged *him* with the embarrassing job of trying to persuade both the Duce and the Emperor to accept it. He wanted nothing to do with the scheme and thought of resigning, and it was only thanks to the persuasion of the Foreign Office's undersecretary, Lord Stanhope, that he didn't.

Off in the village of Zuoz nestled in the Swiss Alps, Samuel Hoare was glad to be starting his much-needed holiday, but was getting a dim sense from the newspapers of the rising criticism. He was willing to cut short his vacation and return home, but Baldwin phoned to say he had the situation well in hand and that the Cabinet was on his side. Years later, Baldwin confided to Eden that this had been a mistake, and that he should have summoned Hoare back. Instead, Hoare would be left alone.

"It was at this point," Hoare wrote in his memoir, "that a cynical providence turned the scene into a medley of farce and tragedy." Despite the pompous prose, he got it right about the farce; the foreign secretary seemed to be forever sickly or injured. Hoare was an avid skater and had booked "one of the best rinks in the Engadine" to have all to himself before it was due to open to the general public. On the day after his arrival, he rushed out to the rink with a boyish delight over "blue sky, white snow and black ice."[58]

And promptly fell flat on his face.

Hoare had blacked out again, and when he smacked into the ice, he broke his nose in two places.

Chapter Eleven

. . . AND DOWNFALLS

Back in London, Anthony Eden was determined to make sure that Haile Selassie was briefed on the plan at the same time as Mussolini. He'd managed to talk the Cabinet at least into this, and he called Vansittart in Paris, charging him with the job of letting Laval know. Vansittart treated this as if Laval should be consulted, rather than informed, and predictably, when he called Eden back in the evening at the Foreign Office, the word was that Laval only wanted the Emperor given a partial briefing of the details. Eden, losing his patience, made it clear that he wasn't *asking*, he was *telling*. "This is a Cabinet decision reached after careful consideration," Eden replied. "A partial account will not do, for what is proposed goes beyond the Committee of Five's report."[1]

Eden knew this wouldn't be the end of the haggling, and he settled in for a long night. Back and forth it went into the small hours of the morning, with Vansittart playing messenger. Laval decided that if all the facts were *not* going to be withheld from the Emperor as he wanted, he ought to get a pledge from Britain that it wouldn't vote for an oil embargo when the League met again in Geneva. *No*, said Eden. France's premier was trying not only to reward the aggressor, but keep his victim blind, deaf, and mute. All while Ethiopia's Emperor was set up to look like a stubborn obstacle to peace in Europe. Eden's firmness might have had a useful effect if it weren't for the fact that Laval had briefed Mussolini in advance on the terms anyway.

Then on December 10, the prime minister of Great Britain stood in the House of Commons during Question Period and lied to Parliament over the Hoare-Laval Plan.

Stanley Baldwin first claimed that the League's Committee of Eighteen—the one that worked on sanctions—had approved the negotiations between Hoare and Laval, but the committee, except for its two leading members, wasn't even aware of them. He then told the House that the plan had yet to be submitted to either Italy or Ethiopia. Baldwin then suggested that "there were considerable

differences in the matter of substance" between what was reported and the original proposals. This fooled no one, because newspapers around the globe were
printing the actual text.

With the Opposition thundering away, Baldwin was out of ammunition, so
he fell back on bluff and made a remark that would be a barnacle on his reputation for the rest of his political life. "I have seldom spoken with greater regret, for
my lips are not yet unsealed. Were these troubles over, I would make a case, and
I guarantee that not a man would go into the lobby against us."[2]

This was perfect inspiration for the political cartoonist, David Low, whose
caricatures of Hitler earned him a place later on the Nazis' murder list. Low took
to drawing Baldwin without his signature pipe and instead with plaster across his
mouth. Years later, when the League of Nations finally collapsed, he portrayed
Baldwin standing over the corpse of the organization, with his lips still sealed by
plaster, while the caption read, "You know you can trust me!"

Anthony Eden was another target for accusations, which he must have bitterly
resented, given how he knew the truth. His defenses in the House were better
than Baldwin's, but they still weren't very convincing. If the plan was contrary to
the principles of the League, "then it is for the League to say so. If they do say so,
we shall make no complaint. We shall be ready to accept their judgment just as
we have been ready to take our part in this very unwelcome task."[3] Eden, though
disgusted by the whole sham, was still a good soldier. On this same day, he sent
two telegrams to Sidney Barton in Addis Ababa. One cable had the text of the
Hoare-Laval Plan, while the other carried a message drafted by Hoare before he'd
left on holiday.

"You should use your utmost influence," Hoare had written, "to induce the
Emperor to give careful and favorable consideration to these proposals and on
no account lightly to reject them. On the contrary, I feel sure that he will give
further proof of his statesmanship by realizing the advantages of the opportunity
of negotiation which they afford, and will avail himself thereof."[4]

*   *   *

Hoare and Eden couldn't know it, but word of the plan had reached Ethiopia
on the same day the news broke in Europe. A reporter for Havas, Christian
Ozanne, got a wire from Paris and rushed off to get a reaction from American
adviser Everett Colson. Colson was disgusted with such shoddy treatment. "We
felt that we were treated worse than the dirt," he told George Steer.[5]

But Colson had a big problem. The Emperor was more than 260 miles away,
a two-hour plane trip or a three-day drive. And he'd left his Cabinet in charge,

headed by Foreign Minister Heruy Wolde Selassie, a man who was out of his depth. Heruy was fluent in French and was respected as a minor administrator who had published a few novels in Amharic. A story circulated that when he received important memos, he would leave them on the floor next to his desk, where they'd gather dust; later he'd read them and pin them on a spike like the kind used in shops for receipts. This still didn't mean he'd *do* anything about them. This was the man who was trusted with Ethiopia's foreign affairs in his sovereign's absence.

Sidney Barton, following orders, went to Heruy to go over the plan and see what influence he could have. For Barton, the situation had to be terribly awkward. As Britain's representative, he was forced to back a scheme he must have personally found contemptible.

Heruy listened politely and said nothing. He no doubt would have left the proposal in one of his dusty piles if it hadn't been for Haile Selassie's other ministers being present. After Barton left, they vented their outrage, but couldn't come to a decision on how to respond. The younger officials knew the answer they wanted to give—a no, a defiant no. They probably would have liked to have added a more polite equivalent of "Go to hell." Heruy wouldn't commit to an answer, defiant or not. But then he didn't agree with any other suggestion, either. Nothing was being decided, nothing getting done.

Colson, his blood pressure put to the test, couldn't stand it anymore and fired off a four-page wire to Dessie, insisting he fly up immediately to brief the Emperor. It's not clear whether he received a prompt answer, but he may have reckoned there was no point in waiting for one. He flew out to Dessie that evening.[6]

* * *

After defending the plan as best he could in the Commons, Anthony Eden left for another trip to Geneva. The League of Nations Committee of Eighteen was scheduled to meet on December 12 to go over the matter of possible oil sanctions against Italy. Eden was slipping out of one hornet's nest to walk into another. Many of his fellow League delegates felt betrayed, especially the smaller countries that had been forced to apply for financial aid by toeing the line on earlier sanctions.

Portugal's delegate, Augusto de Vasconcelos, had been a staunch ally of Britain and was chairman of the Committee. He dropped by to see Eden on the morning before the meeting and didn't bother to hide his disgust. His criticisms boiled down to this: "Why have our countries been asked to put on sanctions, to suffer loss of trade and other inconvenience, if the only result is that Italy should be offered by France and Great Britain more, probably, than she would ever have achieved by herself alone?"[7]

One after another, delegates came to Eden to give a piece of their minds. Yugoslavia's representative, Bozhidar Pouritch, feared that Mussolini, having got away with it once, might try another invasion with Albania as the target. Interestingly, Pouritch thought Mussolini might also make overtures for an alliance with Hitler. When Eden addressed the Chamber later, he downplayed the importance of the generous terms in the plan, calling them neither "definitive nor sacrosanct. They are suggestions, which, it is hoped, may make possible the beginning of negotiations. If the League does not agree with these suggestions, we shall make no complaint; indeed, we should cordially welcome any suggestions for their improvement."[8]

The Hoare-Laval Plan, Eden was saying, was only a trial balloon, an opening overture. Technically, this was true, but everyone knew full well that Britain and France had gone behind their backs to sell out Ethiopia. And yet the diplomats who complained to Eden in private refused to make their grumblings public. Poland's delegate suggested that until the reactions of Italy and Ethiopia were known, the Committee of Eighteen should delay any more talk of oil sanctions.

Another crucial opportunity, come and gone.

* * *

Off in America, both isolationists and pro-Ethiopia activists now had something in common: their disgust for the Great Powers of Europe. Michigan Senator Arthur Vandenberg, an isolationist, considered the Hoare-Laval Plan a display of "moral bankruptcy." He and others like Senator William Borah took it as proof of their cause. Europe couldn't be trusted, and the United States should stay well out of what was going on. Thousands of Americans, however, still felt personally and culturally invested in what was happening across the ocean.

In New York City, the issue of the war hit Madison Square Garden again. Twenty thousand supporters of the invasion braved the winter chill on the night of December 14 to attend a fundraising rally for the Italian Red Cross in Africa. The exuberant crowd at the stadium cheered Mussolini's name, and it booed every time any reference was made to Britain and the League of Nations' sanctions. The event's speakers didn't feel any political conflict either; they included two New York Supreme Court justices, both with Italian backgrounds.

The rally's guest of honor was the city's mayor, Fiorello LaGuardia. When he was pressured by the calls from the audience to make a speech, he picked his way carefully to keep his remarks from sounding like an endorsement of Italian Fascism.

"I have seen the Italian Red Cross operate," he told the crowd, "and I have lived with them for many months during the World War. I can testify that not one penny is diverted to any other purpose."[9]

Outside, a far smaller crowd made its protest. Two thousand demonstrators had shown up, but the police—anticipating a potential outbreak of fresh violence—had come in force. Six hundred cops were at the entrances to keep a lid on trouble, and the demonstrators slowly drifted away, unable to make any impact.

* * *

In the midst of all the outrage over Hoare-Laval, the Ethiopians had seemed to achieve the impossible.

Ras Imru was on the move. He had orders from his cousin, the Emperor, to converge on Adwa, and he led his twenty-five thousand men on a punishing trek of five hundred miles from Debra Markos in his home province of Gojjam. On and on, Imru marched his soldiers, right through the region of Lake Tana, the source of the Blue Nile, into the highlands. And he was far from done. He didn't have much formal battle experience or military training, but what he did have—which other commanders didn't—was imagination. And a brilliant strategic mind.

He knew he was cut off in the west by both Man and Nature. The Takazze River was flanked by one of the deepest canyons in the world, with a depth at some points of more than sixty-five hundred feet. The Italians made sure to put troops and tanks where the river was forded, with about a thousand askaris at the major ford near a small town some forty-five miles south of Adwa. It was called Mai Timchet, "Water of Easter." There was not much else further west. It was bandit country, a dangerous route for even caravans that kept to the main road.

At Debat, north of Gonder, Imru had his first taste of trouble. Italian planes spotted his army and launched an intense bombing raid. "It was our first experience with this kind of warfare," Imru told historian Angelo Del Boca in an interview thirty years later.[10] It threw his troops into such confusion that he only realized later that several of his chiefs had deserted, taking their men with them.

To make matters worse, he was on his way to rendezvous with a dejazmach he was sure was a traitor. Ayalew Birru was supposed to be harassing the Italians and launching raids into the Eritrean lowlands. After the fall of Mekele, De Bono put out overtures to him, and since Ayalew was a seasoned and mature leader of soldiers, he would have proved far more useful than the upstart Gugsa. Ayalew

Birru didn't throw in his lot with the Italians, but he hadn't put much effort into his mission either.

"I knew I could not rely on Ayalew Birru with his 10,000 men," recalled Imru. "I was aware that he was negotiating with the Italians, and when we held our counsels of war, his attitude was invariably defeatist. By the time I reached the Takazze fords, therefore, I could only count on about half the number of men who made up my original force."[11]

A small Potez had flown into Debat December 4. It had slipped away from enemy planes in hot pursuit so the pilot could deliver urgent new orders: Ayalew was to quit his pointless raids and join Imru in attacking Mai Timchet.

Since the Italians had already spotted his army, Imru needed a ruse to throw them off. He persuaded a column of soldiers to head out in broad daylight to the northwest. Italian planes spotted them easily and bombed them, killing three and wounding another ten. The detachment limped back to camp, but two days later, they were once more on the march, again heading to the northwest. The Italian planes returned to punish them, but this time, there were no casualties. And the next time they soared over the patch of country, they couldn't even spot the column. That's because there was none. Imru had sent his army in the complete opposite direction, heading northeast by night for the Takazze.

It was a time of year when the river was low. As the dawn started December 15, Ayalew's first detachment of two thousand men sloshed across the ford and quickly, silently took out the askari defenders at a small stone fort. But as they were heading up the mountain trail that led to the main position of the Italians, they ran into a patrol, which scampered back to sound the alarm. At the same time, a column of another two thousand soldiers—men from Imru's detachments—was crossing nine miles downriver, finding no guards at their location. Imru knew the only way the Italians could withdraw was to make for a crossing called Dembeguina Pass, which was the only path to retreat to Selaclaca and Adwa. His men would get there first.

A Major Criniti, the commander of the garrison observation post, called Aksum to send air support, but the planes couldn't help. To fire on the Ethiopians meant possibly hitting their own men. Criniti, however, had also called in tanks. He would bust his way out.

When the first tank rolled out to do reconnaissance below the pass, its twin machine guns blasted away at the Ethiopians trying to sniper this strange beast through the heart. Some bolted and fled. Then one lone warrior worked his way around and, to everyone's astonishment, jumped onto the tank and began pounding on its turret, yelling, "Open!" The tank was now roaring in reverse. "Open! Open!" The soldiers inside stupidly opened the hatch and—

The Ethiopian decapitated them with his sword.

Criniti and his men watched this spectacle and were desperate to flee. Blackshirts drove trucks in the lead, but they were soon ambushed, their drivers ruthlessly fired on as they tried to scramble out of the cabs. The two Ethiopian columns chased Criniti's force along the pass, "almost at spear distance,"[12] and then the real battle started at around noon, when the heat was at its worst, near a town called Ende Selassie. The Italians were only two or three miles out from Selaclaca, but the tanks had no way to maneuver in the tight pass. The Ethiopians—no longer frightened of these lumbering tin crates—rolled large rocks to block their way. When the driver in the lead tank was killed, there was no hope for the ones behind. Their turrets couldn't even swing wide enough to fire in defense. Some of the tanks tried to lumber into grooves off the main path and got quickly stuck. The Ethiopians gathered and pushed two of them over and then set them on fire. As drivers clambered out armed only with pistols, they were shot to pieces.

A swarm of Ethiopians overran the rest of the tanks, ripping off their chains, dragging the soldiers out of their hatches. Criniti sent the askaris in a doomed bayonet charge, but while it made a brief opening, the Ethiopians had overwhelming numbers. When the day was done and the sun was down, close to half his men were dead, bleeding, or bloody close to dying.

The two sides offered wildly varying casualty figures, but the Italians were willing to concede this time that nine officers and twenty-two white soldiers were killed, as well as 370 natives killed or wounded.

Imru's brilliant offensive captured fifty machine guns and put the Ethiopians ten miles from Aksum. When Haile Selassie learned of the victory four days later, he sent a curt message to his commanders on the northern front: "Why do you not do likewise?"[13]

The invasion's new commander, General Pietro Badoglio, would later try to write off the Battle of Dembeguina Pass as a small affair, but in private, he was badly shaken. He could sneer all he wanted in public about how the enemy couldn't carry out a strategic plan, but he knew Imru's soldiers were now within striking distance of Adwa. His flank was exposed, just as De Bono had warned. He sent off a message to Mussolini, asking for two more divisions.

Against all odds, the Ethiopians were *actually turning the tide*.

He had to stop that. So he changed the entire character of the war, introducing a new viciousness and barbarity that would cause fresh outrage around the world.

* * *

As Imru was humbling Blackshirts, readers of the *Pittsburgh Courier* could read the latest adventure of their favorite pilot on page one: "Col. Robinson Stages Air Duel in Clouds with Enemy Planes!"[14]

The story went that the Brown Condor (misidentified as "William T." Robinson) was supposedly making a run to Dessie to drop off medical supplies when he spotted a bomber and "attacked it with his machine gun spitting bullets."[15] But other Italian planes, the story alleged, came to its rescue. According to the article, the Brown Condor neatly slipped away into the cloud banks, and his plane was only slightly damaged. Or so the story went, which relied by its own admission on incomplete reports. But Robinson never flew a plane in Ethiopia that had guns, and a bomber—which would have had gunners—would be faster and more than a match for his little craft.

As for the Brown Condor himself, clouds of disillusionment were settling in. His contract would be up in May, and he was already thinking of packing up and going home. He had done all that he could, hadn't he? He was sure that by then he would have done his part "to help Ethiopia and also to let the Ethiopians know that the American Negro is not at all as bad as the white race try to picture him to be."[16]

Towards the end of November, he was suspicious of a British aviation manufacturer that wanted to send its own pilots and mechanics. "They also want the director to be English. It seems to me that the same English policy that happened in Egypt some years ago is beginning to happen here," he wrote newspaper editor Claude Barnett. Like the Ethiopians, he feared a creeping British mandate. "All a person can hear now is the English people are this and is that. When I first came, it was French this and French that. Really, I often wonder what the hell they [the Ethiopians] will be saying next."[17]

The posturing and quibbling of nobles was now even harming his efforts to secure more planes. "Japan wants to send as many airplanes as they want or anything else that they might need," he wrote Barnett. "The government is afraid England won't like it if Ethiopia accepts too many things from Japan. You see how childish these officials are and how frightened their attitude is getting. I am beginning to get fed up in fighting here, because of the attitude of the officials." He wanted them to commit, to be decisive. "I think they should take a definite stand, win or lose. If we all have to die, I think we should all die like men and have it over with."[18]

And Robinson apparently kept flirting with death himself again and again. One time, while flying one of the Potez biplanes, he was ambushed by two Italian Imam fighters, which strafed his craft with machine gun fire as he tried to hide in a bank of clouds over the mountains. A bullet smashed into his left arm, but he kept his cool, sending the Potez in a deft little roll that bought him the seconds he needed to escape the fighters. After he was back on the ground in Addis Ababa, he was lucky to learn that he'd only received a flesh wound—painful as hell, since it had torn into the bone, but he'd heal and scar and fly again.[19]

It would not be the last time he would be wounded, but the enemy inflicted the most lasting damage to him when he wasn't in a plane. Robinson was caught in three bombing attacks when the Italians dropped mustard gas, which caused long-term damage to his breathing.[20] In his earlier letters to Claude Barnett, he had related his narrow escapes as thrilling adventures; now he was a veteran, his exuberance sanded down, his commitment tempered by the practical obstacles. The Ethiopians were losing, the Italians taking more and more ground.

"Really, Mr. Barnett," he wrote on November 28, "it looks like the beginning of the end for this country to me."[21]

*   *   *

On December 16 in Addis Ababa, Sidney Barton sent a telegram off to the Foreign Office about the Hoare-Laval Plan: "The Emperor and his adviser [presumably Colson] are bewildered by the association of His Majesty's Government with these proposals." Barton wasn't too thrilled with them either. Ethiopia's foreign minister, Heruy Wolde Selassie, had challenged him that very day to clarify just what the British were thinking. Barton had to do some quick verbal tap-dancing. "I drew on my imagination to paint a picture of an alternative future with war continuing for months or years."[22] He wanted Samuel Hoare to give him permission to tell the Ethiopians the truth, to be candid with them so he could salvage Britain's reputation and influence in the country.

It's difficult to imagine how this could have helped. A betrayal with an excuse is still a betrayal. That same day, Haile Selassie held a news conference in Dessie at the former Italian consulate building where he made his headquarters. He stood on the porch, holding a statement prepared with Colson's help, as the newsmen trudged up to the consulate. Haile Selassie's purpose was to give his public answer to the Hoare-Laval Plan, and to no one's great surprise, he politely but firmly declined it.

"These proposals are the negation and the abandonment of the principles upon which the League of Nations is founded," said the Emperor. "For Ethiopia, they would consecrate the amputation of her territory and the disappearance of her independence for the benefit of the state which has attacked her."[23]

Many of the reporters had come to feel sympathy for Ethiopia's plight, and now as they walked away, Noel Monks recalled that they felt "heartily ashamed of anything that had to do with European politics." A French journalist for the Havas agency, probably Christian Ozanne, growled to him, "That man, Laval. He is a pig."

Monks remembered that "ruder things were said about Hoare by us."[24]

*   *   *

On the same day Haile Selassie rejected the plan, Samuel Hoare—miserable, his face covered in bandages—flew into the Croydon Aerodrome. Public outrage had only grown worse. His telegram to Barton, demanding he push the deal, along with an embarrassing cable to Drummond in Rome, had been leaked to the press. Now his private secretary was waiting for him with "a very long face." Hoare was in no mood to fight for his political life and immediately went to bed on doctor's orders.

The next morning, he found Neville Chamberlain on his doorstep in Chelsea. The Chancellor of the Exchequer was dropping by on behalf of the rest of the Cabinet, but it wasn't to show him support. They were now willing to pitch Hoare over the side of their sinking political boat. Of course, they—through Chamberlain—couldn't come out and say this. Under the British system of government, members of the Cabinet were collectively responsible for all policy, which put them all on the hook for Hoare's disaster. They needed him to arrive at the obvious conclusion himself: to jump overboard.

But Hoare didn't think he was wrong. In fact, he considered his plan "a great improvement both on the Italian demands and Laval's first attempt to compromise."[25] Instead of admitting his mistake, he wanted to make a full explanation in the House of Commons for why the government had first backed the plan. He thought his friend agreed with him, but Chamberlain confided to his diary that if the election were held now, they surely would lose it. He also thought that if he were prime minister instead of Baldwin, the same things "would not have happened."[26] It's a stunning conceit in light of how Chamberlain would give away Czechoslovakia's Sudetenland less than three years later.

Hoare also got a visit from the prime minister, who reassured him, "We all stand together."[27] Perhaps part of Baldwin believed it. He didn't want Hoare to resign, and told him so. Having played the steadfast leader, he left it to Chamberlain to come by again with the dagger polished. Chamberlain told Hoare his proposed statement wouldn't do the trick. What was needed was for the foreign secretary to recant. Do a *mea culpa* in the House, and all might be forgiven. Hoare would rather resign than disown his own plan.

But the backlash had grown ever more intense, and there were fears it could bring down Baldwin's government. A Labour MP proposed a new sign be hung over the doors of the League headquarters: "Abandon half, all ye who enter here—half your territory, half your prestige." In a letter published in *The Times* on December 18, Conservative backbencher (and future PM) Harold Macmillan wrote that the plan would make Britain party to a conspiracy "to undermine the very structure which a few weeks ago the nation authorized us to underpin. I have never attended the funeral of a murdered man, but I take it that at such a ceremony some distinction is made between the mourners and the assassins."[28] By December 17, all the members of the British Cabinet were prepared to dump Samuel Hoare from their ranks—all except Chamberlain, who could now pose as the loyal friend after doing their dirty work for them.

Anthony Eden, meanwhile, was trying to get actual work done. He'd come home two days before Hoare, and now looked to his foreign secretary for approval on a drafted statement he wanted to give the League of Nations Assembly the next day. It was to be one of the last duties Hoare performed in his office. When Baldwin, Chamberlain, and Eden went around to visit him at his home, he was desolate.

"How do you feel?" Baldwin asked him.

"I wish I were dead," said Hoare.

Eden couldn't stay. He had a train to catch to cross the Channel for his trip to Geneva. He thanked Hoare for approving his draft statement, and Hoare told him, "Thank you so much for all your loyal help."[29]

On that same day, Samuel Hoare tendered his resignation.

* * *

Incredibly, despite a storm of protest in Paris that matched the one in London, despite Haile Selassie making it clear that he wouldn't accept such terms, Pierre Laval thought the plan he'd mapped out with Hoare *could still be a success.*

He even argued this with Eden on December 18 when the two met before the session of the League. Like a haggler in a market, Laval tried to get Eden to modify his latest statement to the Council, which was another lame defense that the proposals were only suggestions. When Eden wouldn't budge, Laval said in a depressed voice that he never seemed to have much luck negotiating with the British. At the Council session in the afternoon, Laval told the Assembly that "if this effort does not secure the consent of all the interested parties, the Council will not be relieved of its duty to explore every avenue."[30]

But one of the interested parties was there, and it was high time to let Laval have it with both barrels. Ethiopia's Wolde Mariam Ayeleu told the session that his government "cannot believe that the Ethiopian people will be abandoned and delivered over to its cruel enemy." It had followed the procedures and made every honest effort at making peace. "The government and people of Ethiopia do not ask any people in the world to come to Africa and shed their blood in defense of Ethiopia. The blood of Ethiopians will suffice for that."

But his government wanted justice; it wanted equal access to arms. As for the Hoare-Laval Plan, he wanted to know "is it consistent with the Covenant that the Covenant-breaking state should be begged by the League of Nations to be good enough to accept a large part of its victim's territory, together with the effective control of the rest under the cloak of the League?"[31]

What could the men in front of him possibly say in response?

Nothing. But the presiding president of the session, Argentina's Ruiz Guiñazú, got them quickly out of this embarrassing jam. It was as if he hadn't heard a word Wolde Mariam had spoken for the last few minutes. "Since the final attitudes of the Italian and Ethiopian Governments are not yet known, the Council will perhaps prefer to postpone consideration of this question to a later meeting." And that was that. The proposal that outraged the world would die quietly in a file in the League's archives, but even this was not enough to spur the members to action.

In London, Samuel Hoare got up the next day in the Commons to make his resignation speech, defending his actions to the last. When he got to the topic of the Italian economic monopoly, he said, "I am aware that this part of the scheme has met with the fiercest criticism. I would, however, remind Honorable Members firstly, that a free hand was left to the League to fill in this chapter as it willed, and secondly, that from all parts of the House we have heard demands for Italian colonial expansion."

This prompted a roar back from the Opposition: *"No!"*

"Let me say then from more than one part of the House," added Hoare timidly.

His remarks sounded like a cheating husband who assures his wife he'd been thinking about her the whole time. "I have been terrified with the thought—I speak very frankly to the House—that we might lead Abyssinia on to think that the League could do more than it can do."[32] And he was convinced that some day in the future, with tempers cooled, he might be proved right.

Two hours later, after Hoare had left the Commons, Baldwin had his turn. Having thrown his minister under a bus, Baldwin wanted to re-pave the road as quickly as possible. He blamed the initial support for the plan on the news leaks:

"We had to decide quickly because we knew that a storm of questions would be upon us and that the matter would be raised in this House. We none of us liked the proposals; we thought they went too far."[33]

When a Labour MP pointed out that the timeline for events didn't fit with this cover story, Baldwin claimed he wasn't trying to be evasive. "I was not expecting that deeper feeling which was manifested . . . in many parts of the country on what I may call the ground of conscience and of honor." This was a strange line of logic: in other words, things would have gone swimmingly if not for the annoying British public, which alas, had shown more principles than those who governed it.

"It is perfectly obvious now that the proposals are absolutely and completely dead," Baldwin told the House. "The Government is certainly going to make no attempt to resurrect them."

* * *

Miles away on the French Riviera, Winston Churchill was on holiday. He was staying at the house of the retired American stage actress, Maxine Elliott, who liked to treat her fashionable guests like interior decoration. She would overlook their faults and intrigues if they could play a decent enough game of backgammon. Having fled the United States and Franklin Roosevelt's New Deal, she also liked to complain how America was going to hell. "Do you know what they've got in my theater in New York now? Bolshevik plays!"

It was true that the Federal Theater Project had leased the theater named after her, but according to one guest who bothered to check, "the most 'Bolshevik' play they performed in it was Shakespeare's *Coriolanus*."[34]

Her house in Cannes was where Churchill was ducking the humiliation of being shut out of Baldwin's Cabinet. Pear-shaped and pale, he came out on the terrace over the swimming pool to greet his hostess, dressed in a red bathrobe over bathing trunks, his big bald head covered by a floppy straw hat. "My dear Maxine, you have no idea how easy it is to travel without a servant. I came here all the way from London alone, and it was quite simple."

"Winston, how brave of you!" she replied.[35]

Churchill kept busy painting by day and writing by night, but he could be a sulking lump when in mixed company, clearly missing Parliament. The atmosphere of the party—full of nouveau-riche wives and peers all trading gossip from home—was like something out of a Somerset Maugham short story. And just like a Maugham tale, the hero was a restless exile. Vincent Sheean, the novelist and reporter, was another party guest, and he noticed the Great Man didn't care about upper-class scandals. "I never pay attention to that sort of thing unless I happen to know the people," snapped Churchill.

The subject on Churchill's mind was Ethiopia. He'd read about the Hoare-Laval Plan in the newspapers and was grateful to be untainted. But his political lecturing in Cannes was wasted on the more feather-headed guests, and there were moments when Somerset Maugham lapsed into P. G. Wodehouse. One titled lady stretched out her bare legs under the sun, asking him in a piercing nasal voice, "Winston, why is it they always seem to go to *Geneva* for their meet-ings? Seems to me they could pick out a nicer place."

Churchill "looked at her benevolently from the shade of his big straw hat and said as to a child: 'Because, my dear, Geneva happens to be the seat of the League of Nations. You have heard of it, no doubt?'"[36]

The puzzle of Ethiopia clearly vexed him, and he struggled to find moral clarity for the British position. "It's not the *thing* we object to, it's the *kind* of thing," he insisted to Sheean and the other guests. They failed to see the distinction. One of them, a Frenchwoman who was smarter and better informed, argued that the British Empire had collected its territory through wars just like the one Italy was waging.

Churchill was unruffled and offered a smug reply: "Ah, but you see, all that belongs to the unregenerate past, is locked away in the limbo of the old, the wicked days. The world progresses."

This came from the man who had once called Gandhi a "half-naked fakir" who ought to be "trampled on by an enormous elephant with the new viceroy seated on its back." Some imperial animals, it seemed, were more equal than others.

"We have endeavored," Churchill went on, "by means of the League of Nations and the whole fabric of international law, to make it impossible for nations nowadays to infringe upon each other's rights. In trying to upset the empire of Ethiopia, Mussolini is making a most dangerous and foolhardy attack upon the whole established structure, and the results of such an attack are quite incalculable. Who is to say what will come of it in a year, or two, or three? With Germany arming at breakneck speed, England lost in a pacifist dream, France corrupt and torn by dissension, America remote and indifferent—Madame, my dear lady, do you not tremble for your children?"[37]

*   *   *

Back in London, as it turned out, Samuel Hoare didn't need to tremble at all over his political future. Thanks to the gentlemen's club of British politics, he would be back in the fold of the Cabinet sooner than anyone expected. In Paris, things were different. Pierre Laval wasn't so easily forgiven by France's Chamber of Deputies, which vented its outrage through late December and early January.

"You have displeased everyone without even pleasing Italy," observed Yvon Delbos of the Radicals.[38] The most scathing attack came from Léon Blum after the Chamber's Christmas recess. "We meet again. And of all that existed still ten days ago, there is nothing left but dust and ruin. No, I am wrong: you are left." The next day, Blum was on the warpath again: "You have proceeded in the great affairs of the world as we have seen you proceed in your own little business. You have tried to give and keep back. You have cancelled your words by your actions and your actions by your words. You have corrupted everything by combinations, intrigues, and second-rate cleverness. You have brought everything down to the scale of your own small talents."[39]

Perhaps by now, it was sinking in for Laval that his political posterity was in danger. According to his son-in-law, he fired off an indignant note on January 23 to Mussolini that ended, "I have never given my assent to the war that you seem to have found it necessary to undertake."[40]

He would soon have to go—for a while. He was no more finished in politics than Hoare. His return, however, would come long after the Ethiopia Crisis and would have far more sinister origins and repercussions for France.

Meanwhile, the Foreign Office carried on with business as usual. Hoare and Laval could suffer temporary eviction, but those equally responsible in the FO had nothing to fear. Maurice Peterson bemoaned in his autobiography how the debate in the House of Commons over the plan was "a sorry affair, in which sentiment took the place of reason" and how once the plan was dead, "one could do no more than watch the development of the tragedy."[41] After these crocodile tears, Peterson betrayed his own cynicism with a revealing scene. When Charles Martin came to the Foreign Office to express his anger at the plan, Peterson told him "that it was all over and that his country was now free to go on fighting as long as she felt able to do so. But she would fight alone."[42]

Historians have sometimes been far kinder to the Hoare-Laval Plan than the world was in 1935. In *The Origins of the Second World War*, A. J. P. Taylor called it "a perfectly sensible plan" that would have "ended the war; satisfied Italy; and left Abyssinia with a more workable, national territory." Taylor thought the "common sense of the plan was, in the circumstances of the time, its vital defect."[43] This "common sense" only works on two massive presumptions: one, that Ethiopia was not entitled to act for itself in its own national interests, and two, that when rewarded for their aggression, dictators won't feel encouraged to grab more.

It's difficult to fathom why any historian clings to this view. Mussolini's own words torpedo it out of the water. In 1938, he would confide to Hitler: "If the League of Nations had followed Eden's advice in the Abyssinian dispute and had extended economic sanctions to oil, I would have had to withdraw from Abyssinia within a week. That would have been an incalculable disaster for me."[44]

Chapter Twelve

THE RAIN THAT BURNS AND KILLS

On December 18—the day that Pierre Laval had moved from the "denial" phase to "bargaining" with Anthony Eden in Geneva—Benito Mussolini was playing grandmaster to another feat of early public relations. Economic sanctions were putting the squeeze on his government, but they also punished ordinary citizens living under the regime, and now it looked like the whole world was picking on Italy. The Duce needed a big gesture to appear strong, resilient, something that involved participation from the public. And so his government came up with the "Gold for the Fatherland" drive, inaugurated on a "Faith Day." The faith in question had nothing to do with Catholicism; it was faith in Italy's manifest destiny.

Faith often involves a pilgrimage. Mussolini traveled miles outside of Rome to the Pontine Marshes to dedicate a new town, Pontinia, and to host a strange new ceremony. He stood on a platform covered with flags and watched as a line of married women came forward, each loyal matron stepping up and plunking her gold wedding band into a steel helmet. For making this great personal sacrifice, she got in exchange an iron substitute ring, her token of honor. Near the Duce was a crucible, a prop to remind the audience how the gold would be melted down and used for the war effort.

"As we conquer the Pontine Marshes," he told the crowd, "so shall we fight our African battle and emerge victorious. It will take time, but time does not matter as much as victory." The residents of Pontinia served up an impressive 3,086 ounces of gold, 7,216 ounces of silver, and 1,333 pounds of scrap iron.[1]

Mussolini needed far more than that to keep the war going, but Fascism operated, after all, partly on coercion. As he returned to Rome, the typically huge throngs waited in the Piazza Venezia, with more lines of women to give up their wedding rings. Queen Elena placed her own ring, along with the matching one worn by the king, into a huge brazier that faced Italy's Tomb of the Unknown

Soldier. The army's chaplain-general blessed her iron substitute, which must have been small consolation. And no figures were given out for how much gold was raised through the mass drive organized across the country.

Mussolini gave up more than his wedding ring for the drive. He put himself on the flames—symbolically. Over the years, sculptors had presented him with an assortment of bronze busts, and he'd accepted them all, thanked each artist at the time, and then had every one of them dumped into storage at his country home. Somewhere, a furnace was waiting for this truckload of bronze portraits, though it certainly wasn't at the ring ceremony. For the sake of his civilizing mission, Benito Mussolini would be burned in effigy multiple times.

*   *   *

For much of the war, leading Fascists talked big about great victories. They saw no contradiction in sneering at the Ethiopians' lack of strategic skill and comprehension of logistics. Glory was the thing, even if it was glory over an enemy that couldn't put up a fight. They used the askaris as disposable pawns, happy to let Eritreans and Somalis rack up the body count instead of whites. But those askaris who survived became a toughened, experienced fighting force, and they were justly proud of themselves—so much so that regular Italian soldiers started to feel that these blacks were looking down on them. Regular troops already felt resentment towards the Blackshirts, who hadn't distinguished themselves yet but were treated as the elite.

"We conscripts underwent an iron discipline," one soldier recalled more than a year later (and safely in France), "but the Blackshirts weren't put through it as we were. They got far better rations than we did and higher pay as well. Naturally, this caused a lot of bad blood between us and often led to blows."[2] Historian Angelo Del Boca learned from a Blackshirt veteran that once, when regular troops and some Blackshirts had to share quarters for a while, the two factions were "never on good terms, there was no feeling of comradeship. There was even a certain coolness between their officers and ours."[3]

Morale was low. The army seemed stuck in amber, and Marshal Pietro Badoglio was surprised to learn he had a real fight on his hands. These primitives with their spears and swords might actually push his men all the way back to Eritrea! Imru and Ayalew Birru threatened his right flank, and if they got ambitious and creative, they could bypass Adwa altogether and head north, invading Italy's colonial frontier to attack the supply base at Adi Quala. The base had been left with few defenses. Kassa and Seyum were forming a wall to the south in the Tembien, preparing to launch a major assault, and Mulugeta's army was lodged in the caves of the mountains near Mekele itself—perfect for raiding parties if the Italians had to retreat from an attack by the Kassa-Seyum forces.

At dawn on December 22, the Ethiopians made a move on Abbi Addi, proving they had a sense of strategy after all. One column swept up from the south while another came at their enemy from the southwest. Six battalions of Italian and askari troops were charged with holding the line, but in the dim light of the early morning, they had to wait for air support unless they expected the planes to bomb friend and foe indiscriminately. Instead, they fired their big guns at point-blank range to drive the Ethiopians back. With courage that bordered on the suicidal, a tidal wave of warriors in shammas charged the artillery positions, forcing the gunners to fight for their lives with rifles and pistols.

When the Italians fell back towards the town, they discovered a lie in their propaganda. The ordinary residents never thought of the Italians as "liberators" and were happy to attack them.

The battle had taken nine hours, but now the Ethiopians were some twenty-five miles out from Mekele.

* * *

Before Christmas, Dr. Marcel Junod decided to visit the ambulance stations on the northern front at Waldia, a hundred miles or so from Dessie. The Emperor was keeping about ten thousand men of his imperial guard here in reserve for major battles.

When Junod arrived, he found the ambulance unit dealing with a few soldiers who weren't seriously wounded, as well as some cases of dysentery, but then he was surprised to hear bugle calls. As he watched in confusion, the workers suddenly collected their supplies, packed up their tents, and then camouflaged them with brushwood. The young Greek surgeon in charge, George Dassios, explained that after a recent bombing, he wasn't prepared to take risks with his patients and staff. "Have you already forgotten the bombing of Dessie?" he snapped at Junod.[4]

When Junod looked at the plain below the camp, he was astonished to find that the soldiers were all gone. They had melted into the landscape, knowing what was coming. But off to the right was a group of tents in a half-circle. Decoys. There was another warning blast of bugles, and then the planes appeared, zeroing in and bombing the little phantom camp. As they droned away, the Ethiopians laughed and congratulated themselves on their clever trick.

Once Junod heard the all-clear, he went off to visit the British ambulance unit stationed a mile and a half away, which was run by his friend John Melly. It was smartly organized, and days later, thanks to the Emperor's arrangements, it would have a permanent liaison from the government to make sure it got what it needed: Charles Martin's son, Yosef. John Melly was delighted with the selection, writing that he knew the young Ethiopian from London "and have seen him since in Addis Ababa. Having spent twelve years in England, he is thoroughly Europeanized and a good fellow."[5]

The British camp kept a large Red Cross flag displayed on the ground, and Melly laughed when Junod told him the story of the bait-and-switch at the Dassios unit. The Englishman refused to use the same tactics and was going to run things according to standard practices in the field. Of course, there was still a touch of the Melly personality to the camp. A large tortoise plodded about as the unit's mascot, a red cross painted on its shell.

After a few minutes, everyone heard the approach of Italian bombers.

"Those airmen are as inquisitive as monkeys," said Melly. "They come to see us every day, and sometimes several times a day."[6]

The medical staff waited. So did Junod and Melly. No one bothered to take cover. A short distance off, the planes dropped bombs, hitting nothing, and then flew off.

"Total damage, a few holes in the ground," said Melly.[7]

*   *   *

On December 23, several detachments of Ethiopians made the short trip across the Takazze near Mai Timchet. Ras Imru was personally leading them, intent on reaching forward positions so that he could swoop in on Selaclaca. When he and his men spotted planes approaching, he wasn't "unduly alarmed." Like the men Marcel Junod saw at the ambulance unit, the soldiers had learned to adjust to the threat of the Capronis, knowing to take cover as needed, camouflaging their gear if they had enough warning. But the planes flying overhead weren't dropping bombs this time. They released odd containers that broke open as they hit the earth, splashing great pools of transparent liquid.

A few seconds elapsed, and then Imru and his troops were in a nightmare. The soldiers that were splashed "began to scream in agony as blisters broke out on their bare feet, their hands, their faces." For Imru, standing helplessly by, it was a terrifying experience. "I hardly had time to ask myself what could be happening before a hundred or so of my men who had been splashed by the mysterious fluid began to scream in agony as blisters broke out on their bare feet, their hands, their faces."[8]

In excruciating pain and panic, they rushed to the river to take great gulps of water, not realizing the fiendish liquid had poisoned the stream. They collapsed on the river banks, their throats burned, their limbs seemingly on fire, and this hell would go on for hours. Soldiers and civilians from nearby villages were all victims; cattle that drank from the river suffered as well.

"My chiefs surrounded me," remembered Imru decades later, "asking wildly what they should do, but I was completely stunned. I didn't know what to tell them, I didn't know how to fight this terrible rain that burned and killed."[9]

* * *

Thousands of miles away, a normal, benign shower pelted down on Calais, and Anthony Eden—about to cross the Channel to go home again—took a message from the British Consul. The moment his boat-train arrived home, the prime minister wanted him to drive over to Number 10. There was an air of secrecy to the appointment; Stanley Baldwin didn't want him talking to anyone beforehand.

Eden was coming home to a London where the hottest toys for children that holiday season were topical. Youngsters would wake up on Christmas morning, tear open the brightly colored wrapping, and find replicas of Italian military hardware for the East Africa campaign. There were tiny tanks that fired sparks as they rolled along the battlefield of a living room carpet and toy gas masks sold for six pence each. While adults worried about the approach of a new world war, English boys badly wanted little Italian bombers and fake rifles.

As Robert Vansittart put it years later, "Anthony Eden got a lovely Christmas box, bright red and marked F.O. It was full of troubles."[10] And like all smart gifts, it came as a surprise. Eden had no idea what his prime minister wanted. He found Baldwin in the small library that overlooked Downing Street, looking agitated, pacing and snapping his fingers, a habit he fell back on when nervous. He told Eden he didn't know how he had let matters come to this. He needed a new foreign secretary, and he wanted to know whom Eden would recommend.

Not so long ago, Eden had wanted the job for himself. He'd resented it when the office was split in two, with Hoare winding up his superior. But he was in no hurry to take over when the whole world had lost so much confidence in Britain. Eden thought Austen Chamberlain would be good as foreign secretary. Chamberlain had held the job years before, and Eden would have been happy to serve under him. It was a strange choice, given that when it came to Mussolini, Chamberlain once said he would "trust his word when given." Baldwin didn't care about that. He thought Chamberlain too old. When Eden started a rebuttal, Baldwin cut him short. "Anyway, I saw him yesterday and told him so."

Eden said nothing for a long moment. Did he have any other names? Eden suggested Edward Wood, a former viceroy of India who was known simply as "Halifax," after his viscount title. Baldwin didn't like this choice either. Halifax's polices on India had been controversial, and besides, he sat in the House of Lords, not the Commons. Any others? Eden was out of names—he said nothing. Finally, Baldwin looked at him and said, "It looks as if it will have to be you."[11]

It was a hell of a tactless way to be given the job, and Eden was justifiably hurt. He told Baldwin that while six months ago, he would have been grateful to get it, he felt quite differently about it now. Baldwin was Baldwin: oblivious. He didn't hear a clear refusal, and as far as he was concerned, Eden was his new foreign secretary.

Just before Christmas, Eden headed off into the bitter winter cold to pay a visit to King George V at Sandringham, the royal family's country house in Norfolk. There was a formal ceremony to get out of the way. Eden would be handed the seals of office for his new Cabinet post. With an uncanny physical resemblance to his cousin, Tsar Nicholas II, George V was a strong personality. He was also an interesting, contradictory mixture of conservative prejudices and soft liberal sympathies. He'd refused to greet Ras Tafari when he was regent, but as a younger man, George had been shocked at the racial prejudice Indians were subjected to under the raj and pushed for change.[12] When there was a threat of unrest among coal miners in 1926, one peer (who had financial interests in coal mines) snapped that the workers were a damned lot of revolutionaries; that prompted the king to reply, "Try living on their wages before you judge them."[13] He and his young granddaughter, the future Elizabeth II, adored each other. To him, as she was to other close members of the royal family, she was "Lilibet." To her, he was "Grandpa England."[14]

Now he was seventy years old and gravely ill. A habitual smoker and a chronic invalid in recent years, he had less than a month to live. Though he was coughing painfully, he seemed in good spirits to Eden and offered to give the new foreign secretary any help he could. When Hoare had come to surrender the seals, the King had told him bluntly that his plan had been a mistake: "You cannot drive a train full steam ahead in one direction . . . and then without warning, suddenly reverse without somebody coming off the rails."[15] Like Baldwin's Cabinet, the king had done a reverse of his own. Eden could remember George pressuring him to keep good relations with Italy.

But George V wasn't finished. "I said to your predecessor: 'You know what they're all saying, no more coals to Newcastle, no more Hoares to Paris.' The fellow didn't even laugh."[16]

* * *

The day before Christmas, far off in the province of Harar, an Italian pilot, Lieutenant Tito Minniti, had been flying over the area near Dagahbur. And whatever happened during his flight has stayed controversial ever since.

It's most likely that Minniti's plane developed engine trouble, and he was forced to land in a stretch of desert. According to one account, his passenger, a sergeant named Livio Zannoni, panicked and fled into the barren waste. Since both men ended up dead, we have no way of knowing what Zannoni was thinking or why the two men would consider splitting up. The most commonly told story goes that Minniti was trying to fix his plane when a group of men rushed up and took him prisoner while killing Zannoni. The Italian propaganda writers later concocted a fabulous tale that anti-aircraft fire had damaged the plane. After it landed, the brave lieutenant held off his attackers by using the plane's machine guns until he ran out of bullets and had to surrender.

Rome never doubted that the men who allegedly attacked Minniti were Ethiopian soldiers. Ethiopia was willing to concede that Minniti had been captured, but blamed local nomads who were sick of their livestock herds being bombed and strafed from above. Whoever they were, they allegedly dragged the pilot to a small village called Bir, where they shackled his legs and tied him to a tree. First, they cut off his fingers, and as Minniti screamed in pain, they stripped him naked and castrated him. After their victim bled to death, his torturers cut his body into pieces and placed his severed head on a bayonet.

The story has many problems, the biggest being that there was only one supposed eyewitness. This was a paramedic for an Egyptian Red Crescent unit, Abdel Mohsein Uisci, who testified to the League of Nations that Minniti's head and feet were taken to Dagahbur, Jijiga, and Harar. But his own boss and the director of the Egyptian Red Crescent, Prince Ismail Daoud, practically called him a liar. And he poured cold water on other sensational tales of tortured prisoners as well. It turned out that the staff who offered up these horror stories and signed affidavits were in the middle of a dispute over pay, while some had been shipped back to Cairo before their contracts had expired.

One Red Crescent worker had another compelling story. It went like this: There was a battle. The Ethiopians demolished two tanks, and a couple of Italians were hauled in front of Haile Selassie, who was in the area on a visit. The Emperor did nothing to save these prisoners of war from grisly treatment. This was so over-the-top that even the Italian Ministry of Foreign Affairs went fact-checking. Its final verdict: no Emperor, no lost tanks in the most recent battle, and while yes, eight soldiers had been killed, none were captured. The propaganda writers ran the story anyway.

But the horror of Minniti's alleged castration and beheading made the biggest stir and has proved the most enduring. Even as the Italians shouted to the world how their soldier had been tortured, the dejazmach for the remote area went to the extraordinary effort of sending a Somali messenger, armed with a white flag, to General Graziani; the torture never happened, he claimed, and the Emperor himself had ordered that POWs be respected. Graziani didn't kill the messenger, but he did have him arrested—for the peculiar charge of illegally crossing the border back in 1934. His dejazmach waited around for a response, and when he figured it was long enough, he repeated his message over the radio. He also said that the Somali's arrest contravened "military laws and the chivalry which should be the sign of a general."[17]

Minniti proved to be a highly effective martyr. Mussolini awarded him a posthumous Gold Medal of Valor, while flags were flown at half mast in his hometown of Reggio Calabria. His hometown's airport was given his name, and the sculptor, Arturo Martini, was so moved by the story that he made a unique but arguably grotesque tribute in 1936. Minniti's headless nude is crucified in an almost horizontal yet startled pose to a tree. It's titled, "Tito Minniti, Hero of Africa."

And in the end, the story might have all been a lie.

It's likely that there never was any macabre parading of body parts or that Minniti was ever dragged off to a nearby village. That's because both his corpse and Zannoni's were eventually discovered 650 feet from their crippled, burned aircraft. By then, of course, wild animals had long since got to the bodies, and the remains had suffered further decay. There is no way to tell conclusively how they died or whether the torture ever occurred.

It didn't really matter in December 1935. General Graziani accepted the tale without a second thought, and it provided him with the perfect excuse to unleash his full rage on the Ethiopians. He wanted an "eye for eye" and promptly sent orders to the Gorahei air base: "Heroic death of our comrade in barbaric enemy land requires exemplary reprisal punishment."[18] On December 30, more than a dozen bombers took off on their mission of vengeance in the Ogaden.

* * *

A Swedish field unit for the Red Cross had left Stockholm with much fanfare and media attention, and you can still find old footage online of Dr. Fride Hylander and his colleagues smiling for the newsreel cameras, dressed in their smart uniforms. Sidney Brown, the organization's top delegate in Ethiopia, saw how Hylander interacted with the Ethiopians and adopted an attitude of condescending bemusement. To him, the Swedish unit director "loves the

Ethiopians as only a missionary can love his Negroes." He was mildly scornful of how Hylander seemed to border on sympathy for the Ethiopians' plight, when the Red Cross was supposed to affect a pose—at least in public—of neutrality. Hylander "accepts all what comes from the Ethiopian government as if it came directly from Heaven."[19]

The Swedish field unit ended up near Melka Dida by the River Genale Doria, where they expected to serve any medical emergencies for Ras Desta and his army, based about four miles away. While part of the camp was nestled in an area of palm trees and bush, providing much-needed shade, at least three tents were out in the open. From surviving photos and footage, it's clear the camp had good signage with the Red Cross emblem and its flags hung like clothes from a line.[20] Dr. Hylander had gotten used to the reconnaissance planes of the Italians making dragonfly sweeps overhead, and the pilots themselves made notes that testify they knew exactly what was below them.

On the morning of December 30, Hylander was with a couple of Ethiopian assistants in the operating tent when he heard planes. He stepped outside and spotted six of them overhead in formations of three. Within seconds, they started dropping bombs and machine gunning the camp, and Hylander's two assistants were slaughtered on the spot. Before he could dive for cover, a bomb exploded close to where he stood, its shrapnel slicing into his shoulder, back, and legs. Hylander crawled, desperate for shelter. He couldn't lay where he'd fallen, because now ten planes in all were swooping down, and the bombardment sounded to his ears like a "continuous thunder rolling."[21]

A male nurse named Gunner Lundstroem ducked into one of the ambulances, reading his bible for comfort, and a bomb fragment sheared away parts of his jawbone.[22] He would die two days later while being transported with the other wounded. Incendiaries lit the camp tents on fire, and the guns ripped them to tatters. Any wounded patients inside were completely helpless to escape. Worse, the Italians were mixing their bombs with loads of mustard gas. Both staff and patients were so traumatized, they couldn't be sure how long it lasted, but it's been estimated that the planes pulverized the camp for a solid twenty minutes.

Hylander would later describe the horror: "The sick section offered an appalling sight. A man reduced to strips, another whose flesh had been torn from the hips and the legs. A few were lying half-buried under the debris and earth thrown up by the explosions. Everywhere flesh quivered. A strip of flesh thrown onto the roof of the tent where we took our meals."[23] Twenty-eight Red Cross workers, native helpers, and wounded were killed outright, with another fifty wounded. Of those, fourteen would succumb to their injuries, bringing the final death toll to forty-two. The surviving members of the unit made use of the large bomb craters to bury some of their dead, and one was so large, they could fit six bodies into it.

*   *   *

The next morning in Dessie, Marcel Junod received a summons from the Emperor, who handed him a telegram when he arrived. The Swedish team had urgently requested that one of the Red Cross aircraft fly out to collect their wounded. As the survivors of Hylander's team had rushed to evacuate, they were allowed to use the wireless transmitter of Ras Desta Damtew, his one means of communication with the Emperor's military headquarters. Junod headed off for Addis Ababa, where Carl von Rosen took him up in his plane and off towards the southern region of Sidamo.

But first Junod had to pay a call on the army of Ras Desta, the Emperor's son-in-law. Desta was in his early forties, a tall and reserved man with the right Shoan pedigree, but who was the kind of loyal reformer Haile Selassie wanted and needed. Back in his twenties, he'd run off to become a monk at Debre Libanos. For all his independence of mind, however, Desta had a big ego and a streak of xenophobia like other high-ranking nobles; he once told guests at a function in the British legation, "The less foreigners visit Ethiopia, the better." When his Belgian military adviser died of pleurisy, his body was shipped back on a plane to the capital for a proper military funeral, and another mercenary was dispatched to the Sidamo; one Belgian lieutenant was replaced with another, with no more influence than the first.

Desta had split his army into three columns and had led them out from Negelli on a wearying trek of about 250 miles south towards Dolo. In some ways, he had planned well. He was advancing into a region that didn't have any history of the Italians making mischief before the war, not even having a consulate post where they could offer bribes to any potential spies. The countryside between the two rivers of Dawa and Ganale Doria was shaded by massive palm trees, perfect for cover, and the high ground had wild olive groves. While Desta didn't want to rely on Oromo scouts, concerned about their possible lack of discipline, his commanders thought they could trust them. And Desta insisted that no foreign reporters be allowed to tag along on his offensive. So if anything, the ras wasn't looking to hide under the tent flaps of the Swedes and their Red Cross—he was worried their camp might betray his position.

His plan was a daring attempt to threaten Italian Somaliland, but it was doomed to fail. Graziani had his wireless messages monitored and knew he was coming; it was only a question of pinning down where he was. But the Butcher of Fezzan was also concerned enough that he moved his own headquarters to Baidoa, about 160 miles north of Mogadishu, to keep a hawkish gaze on Desta's progress. The Somali spies had given him nothing to work with, so it had been up to the Italian air force. On December 6, a squadron of seven planes was conducting reconnaissance over the Genale Doria and the Kenya frontier when it spotted Ethiopians on mules. The Ethiopians quickly dismounted and ducked under the bush. Were they part of a caravan or an army baggage train? The planes deliberately swooped in to draw fire.

Desta had given orders that no one shoot up at the planes. The message didn't get through to the Oromo scouts, and they blasted into the air, giving the game away. From then on, squadrons of planes returned to the area, scattering his camel and mule trains. The Italians quickly set up barbed wire along the Kenyan frontier, along with sand-bagged machine gun nests to harass them further and hold the line.

Desta had started with a force that was fifteen thousand men strong, but now it was perhaps a third of that, bombed to bits and ravaged by starvation, malaria, dysentery, and other illnesses. The substantial herd of cattle that was supposed to feed his army had also shrunk to pitiful numbers, so much so that only three steers a day could afford to be slaughtered to feed the men.[24] The starving warriors were given only a cup of flour a week—that was if the distribution vans didn't break down or were plundered. The soldiers were down to foraging for roots and berries.

During all this time, the Swedish field hospital had offered the only medical care within hundreds of miles, and now it had been devastated.

If Desta's men were suffering, Desta was not. A ras who wore a tailored khaki uniform and smart sun helmet, he invited the Swiss doctor and the other foreign guests to lunch in his tent, where he hosted a small feast of tasty dishes and different wines, followed by toasts with champagne.[25] There was a tradition in Ethiopian nobility that hosts were expected to put on a proper feast for arrivals, but Junod and the others seemed to be a little appalled at this bounty in the midst of the army's suffering.

After lunch, Desta led Junod down to the bank of the river, where he ordered a fine carpet to be spread out. Then he pointed out a group of crocodiles sunning themselves on the opposite side of the river, about 150 feet away. He armed himself with a rifle and offered one to his guest. Firing off three shots from his Remington, Desta scared the crocs into the river and then lolled back on the carpet, fanned gently by a servant. Junod thought of it as "the relaxation of a prince in the ante-room of hell."[26]

At last, Junod tore himself away from this brief interlude of comfort and drove on to inspect the Red Cross camp. All he had to do was follow the trail of bomb craters and uprooted trees. When he arrived at what was left of the field unit, he saw that nowhere else "had been bombed with such concentrated fury." In Dessie, the army, at least, had been available to help in the aftermath. "Here, there was nothing."[27]

The raid on the Swedish Red Cross unit made a bigger international stir than previous ones. Adwa was controversial, contested. Dessie was ambiguous with the presence of the Emperor and his military headquarters. True, the bombing of the unit near Melka Dida happened in the middle of nowhere, but this time, there were several foreign nationals as victims. Sidney Brown, who considered Fride Hylander too chummy with the Ethiopians, didn't mince words. When he reported to his superiors in Geneva, he called what the Italians did a massacre.

There should have been no dispute over the deliberateness of the operation—the squadron's high commander had signed his work. Fluttering among the steel splinters and bits of flesh and debris was a light snowfall of dropped leaflets. Written in Amharic, they all gave the same message: "You have beheaded one of our airmen, infringing all human and international laws, under which prisoners are sacred and deserve respect. You will get what you deserve—Graziani."[28]

It hardly made sense for Graziani to take his vengeance out on the field hospital of a neutral organization, but in fact, it was only one of the targets of his outrage that December 30. Planes also bombed the towns of Degehabur, Sassebaneh, and Bulale.

But it was the raid on Hylander's camp that earned the most attention, and the Swedish government fired off protests immediately to Rome and to the League of Nations, where delegates would soon have the opportunity to review photos of the devastation as well as the wounded. A Universal News cameraman also flew out to get footage, which was shown in newsreels across America. Anthony Eden would look back on the bombing as a sign of things to come. "We began to hear more and more about Fascist disregard for the rules of war . . . Here was the first presage of that organized brutality which the dictators later achieved."[29]

By New Year's Day, Mussolini was cabling Badoglio over how much political fallout the raid had caused. If there were going to be future attacks like this, they had to be worth the heat he was getting. Three days later, in fact, he even cabled Badoglio to tell him that the use of gas was to be suspended until the latest talks in Geneva bore fruit. Out in the Ogaden, Rodolfo Graziani had already sensed that he'd made a serious mistake, and on the night of the raid itself, he went so far as to lie to his own commanding officer, claiming in a telegram to Badoglio that he'd been informed Ras Desta was camping in a Red Cross hospital to avoid air raids.

Desta, of course, was four miles upriver, with men who could hardly stagger, let alone march to the relative safety of a cluster of tents.

* * *

In Eritrea, about thirty miles from the border, is a hill called Mendefera, which means, "No one dared."

The Italians hadn't been able to take the hill when they had first gobbled up the territory. But they were thinking more about logistics and less about symbolism back in December; that was when truckload after truckload of prisoners of war were hauled to the nearby town of Adi Ugri (the town has since been renamed after the hill). It was as good a place as any to put defeated soldiers and troublesome civilians. And only days after the war began in October, prisoners were being shipped here and to another post at Adi Keyh.

These were the first of Italy's concentration camps for Ethiopians.

No one gave much thought to how long these detainees would be kept or even how they were to be treated. At first, only a few carabinieri guards were assigned to watch over them, but by the middle of December, there were forty-two inmates at Adi Ugri. By the end of the month, there were dozens more. A prison break was perhaps inevitable, and on December 31, more than 150 of the prisoners managed to get away. The Italians spent days trying to recapture them, managing to retake twenty and kill nine others.

And still the trucks came to unload more Ethiopians.

In the overcrowded camps, where little attention was being paid to the growing filth of people herded together, even an Italian officer complained up the chain of command that something had to be done.[30]

It's somehow grimly appropriate that the solution came from the army's quartermaster, General Fidenzio Dall'Ora, the same man who headed up the Chemical Warfare Service. Within weeks, Dall'Ora would prepare a report recommending more efficient ways of taking captured Ethiopians out of the game. It was decided that the prisoners would be shuttled from mobile detention camps to bigger, permanent ones in Adwa and Mekele. From there, they could be taken—via the mobile camps again—to their final stops. One was Nokra, a prison island in the Red Sea, and later, there was Danane, a lonely stretch of field in Italian Somaliland. Danane was pretty much unused until after the main conflict. But thousands of warriors and civilians alike would end up being interred in these two places.[31]

In Ethiopia, the camps were called Nokra and Danane. In Europe, places like these would have names that would become familiar to everyone in Europe and North America: *Buchenwald, Dachau, Ravensbrück, Bergen-Belsen . . .*

* * *

In Harlem, Hubert Julian knew who would win the war. It was plain as day to anyone, unless the League of Nations stepped in. And having decided it was better to be on the winning side, Julian wanted to say he had known it first. But he made a huge miscalculation in expecting that black sympathies would change as Ethiopia lost more battles. In talking to reporters, he acted as if Ethiopia had let *him* down. African Americans were inclined to think the reverse: at best, he was an opportunistic narcissist, and at worst, a race traitor. He was stunned to wake up and discover that among blacks, he was the most hated man in America.

Julian being Julian, he would not back off, determined to bluster it out. It would be almost a century before celebrities mastered the art of shedding tears of regret on camera and begging forgiveness from fans. He couldn't very well tell the truth—that for all intents and purposes, he had been fired and ignored—so he doubled down, announcing he'd prepared a sixty-eight-page manuscript titled, "Why I Resigned from the Abyssinian Army." Instead of submitting it to magazines or newspapers, he wanted to auction it off. It's not clear whether he had any takers. While yes, he was news, black papers would have found it hard to justify to their readers why they had *paid* to give him a platform.

Worse, his accusations sounded an awful lot like the same charges from Italian propagandists. He claimed to have seen "horrors, tortures, and massacres." He claimed to have witnessed both atrocities committed against Italian prisoners and cruel punishments against Ethiopian soldiers who made minor infractions. Some reporters asked a new question: just what was the Black Eagle living off of, now that he was no longer getting a colonel's pay in Haile Selassie's army? No one seemed to know. A story in a black newspaper in Baltimore suggested that a wealthy (and presumably right-wing) British woman in London was moved by Julian's display of integrity in quitting the Ethiopian army. She supposedly gave him sixty thousand dollars. But his patroness didn't out herself, and when the *Chicago Defender* went looking, it couldn't find her; it did learn of rumors that the Black Eagle's patron was right in Harlem, only it couldn't locate her either.[32]

As Julian ranted about rases and the Ethiopian clergy, a high-profile reporter for the *Philadelphia Tribune*, Floyd Calvin, openly called him a coward: "American friends of Colonel Julian have no grounds left on which to stand in defending him. Instead of rushing to the front to repel the Italians, Colonel Julian was hurrying back to the safety of Harlem . . . He quit cold, when the enemy guns were booming within earshot."[33]

The attacks got uglier. There were probably readers of the *Tribune* among those who filled the Berean Presbyterian Church in Philadelphia two weeks later for a meeting about Ethiopia. This is where they got to hear Willis N. Huggins, a champion of teaching African-American history in schools and a strong campaigner for the cause. Huggins denounced Hubert Julian as a "Judas," a "Benedict Arnold." The Black Eagle's betrayal could not be forgiven.[34]

Then word got around that Julian would tour across America, the bill paid for by a pro-Italian group. This was more than African Americans could stand, and an organization in Harlem led the charge that he should be deported because he was some kind of foreign operative. The State Department showed no interest in the accusation, and even if it had, the case wouldn't have gone far anyway; the United States was not at war with Italy, which was technically still an ally, and Julian had already been thoroughly checked out at Ellis Island on his return. But the Harlem group did get its wish in the end. Perhaps he was running out of funds or he sensed the overwhelming backlash, but Julian—without fanfare this time—boarded a ship in early January headed for France.

* * *

The Black Eagle left behind a very cold winter that January in New York.

In Midtown, earnest actors and dedicated stage hands braved the freezing temperatures each day to make it to the Biltmore Theatre on West 47th Street. They were preparing to make the last sixteen months of the Crisis come alive again, rehearsing *Ethiopia*. The work would be credited to playwright Arthur Arent, but it depended almost as much on the talents of journalist Morris Watson. "The performance will last about an hour, and there will be three shows each evening," stated a promotional article by playwright Elmer Rice. "The admission price will be 25 cents."

It was a short but ambitious production, with a company of three hundred cast and crew members, and it would include real Africans. Not Africans necessarily from the countries depicted, but Africans just the same, wearing lion mane headdresses and playing traditional harps. They were dancers and musicians who originally belonged to the troupe Shogola Oloba, founded by Sierra Leone's Asadata Dafora. With no scenery on stage and only a few cheap costumes and props (spears, chairs, tables), the actors would recreate the machine gun fire of Walwal and the bickering of the League of Nations. War drums beat on through the forty-five minute production as musicians played what was meant to be a "native song" that was "a sad, keening sort of air."[35]

All the actors' speeches were taken verbatim from sourced reports, because the spectacle was intended to be the first issue of a "Living Newspaper." The audience would hear the words of Mussolini, Pierre Laval, Haile Selassie, and others out of the mouths of actors playing them, with the drama changing each night according to the latest events. One scene was to have "a projection of marching feet, and the tramp, tramp, tramp is amplified on the sound system."

It was bound to be controversial, not only because of the subject matter, but because of its producer: the US government. *Ethiopia* came under the Federal Theater Project, a grand "make work" scheme for stage folk during the Great Depression. The Project's most famous production would be *The Cradle Will Rock*, mounted a year later by John Houseman and Orson Welles at the Maxine Elliott Theater a few blocks down on West Thirty-ninth Street (while its namesake in Cannes had already bemoaned how her theater was being used for "Bolshevik plays"). This was the show that was later immortalized in a 1999 film by Tim Robbins.

The energetic and idealistic Hallie Flanagan, playwright and former theater director at Harvard and Vassar College, had been hired to run the FTP. "I am asked whether a theater subsidized by the government can be kept free from censorship, and I say yes, it is going to be kept free from censorship," she declared. "What we want is a free, adult, uncensored theater."[36]

She didn't get it, not with *Ethiopia*. Morris Watson—who had a journalist's conscience for detail, but who probably needed some political antennae—wrote to White House Press Secretary Stephen Early. He wanted to get a recording of one of Roosevelt's speeches, specifically one that made a veiled attack on Mussolini and Italy. Early, of course, was put immediately on his guard. He fired back a letter on January 11 warning that "extreme care should be used in a dramatization" and that given it was a government-funded production, "we are skating on thin ice."[37]

But Hallie Flanagan thought she knew how to swim. She promptly wrote Roosevelt's adviser, Harry Hopkins, promising, "All the famous people are characterized with great respect and with no attempt at cartooning. This is particularly true of Mussolini, who is presented sympathetically and with power."[38] This was true. If the Duce was to be damned in the show, he would be damned by his own words. She also reminded Hopkins that after all, the Project was supposed to be about strong plays, contemporary subject matter.

Unfortunately, her letter—along with a copy of a script—bounced instead to Hopkin's assistant at the Works Progress Administration, Jacob Baker. Baker was not a fan of Flanagan or what she was trying to accomplish. Back it all went to Stephen Early, who still felt any depiction of foreign relations was "dangerous."

Flanagan and those involved in the production were now in serious trouble. A Broadway play was at genuine risk of being shut down simply because the US government was afraid of what it might say, even though what it would say had already been reported in newspapers around the world. And *Ethiopia* had less than two weeks before its premiere.

* * *

Ras Desta's army had one remaining thing going for it as it struggled to press on sixty miles outside Dolo. Its right flank was still protected by the border of British-held Kenya, where RAF planes were now making regular patrols. In fact, had the Italians foolishly dared to cross this territory, this would have been a perfect pretext for expanding the war. But Graziani was a butcher—not a fool. To get Desta's army to move where he wanted it to, he merely had to keep pounding the Ethiopians with cruel bombardments and multiple gassings.

Worse, Desta's commanders began deploying men and countermanding orders in a confusing mess. It wasn't really their fault. On January 9, Graziani's radio men had found their frequency, and for three days, they sent out false messages. Then dubats—the Somali soldiers in their white turbans—tried to drive out a tiny advance guard of three hundred Ethiopians from their trenches in the Ganale valley. The Ethiopians managed to hold the line for a day, but armored cars pushed them into retreat.

On January 12, Graziani dispatched three columns to engage what was left of Desta's pitiful, straggling army. The confrontation would become known as the Battle of Ganale Doria, but it's also been called a slaughter, a massacre. First came another bombardment. And for three days, tanks and armored cars, dubats and Eritrean regulars, punished the half-starved Ethiopians and sent them fleeing from their positions. His forces crumbling around him, Desta launched a hopeless cavalry charge—against tanks.

For weeks, his soldiers had been kept from wells and prevented from securing any kind of food source. Now, as they escaped, their imminent starvation and thirst overwhelmed their basic instincts for survival. The Italian reporter, Sandro Volta, who was embedded with the column under General Agostini, wrote, "The Ethiopians went mad and rushed toward certain death for a gulp of water. It was no longer a question of fighting a war, all they could think of was water, water, water. The machine gunners had only to aim a few inches above the ground to slaughter them by the hundreds."[39]

The death toll for the Ethiopians from the battle was later estimated at around four thousand men.

On January 15, Desta realized that all was lost, and with his Belgian military adviser in tow, took off in a couple of trucks with his servants and his bodyguard. When the Italians captured his base later, they found his forgotten luggage, along with cables and papers of the Belgian lieutenant. On the road, Desta ran into a Canadian Red Cross doctor in his own vehicle, Ralph Hooper, who had regularly annoyed him and his troops with his evangelical proselytizing. Now he yelled at Hooper for his own good, "Turn, turn! The whole army is broken, and they are upon us with thousands of camions."[40] Hooper wheeled around, and the small convoy made it to Negelli on January 18.

But there was no safe haven here, because Graziani wasn't through. Two days later, Italian planes bombed Negelli for forty-five minutes, despite the fact that there were no Ethiopian troops. Ras Desta had escaped to Irgalem with the remains of his forces, while some of his men had apparently scrambled into the forests of Wardara. No matter. The Italians dropped almost forty tons of explosives, virtually wiping Negelli off the map.

When Graziani's columns rolled into what was left of the town, the general ordered champagne.

* * *

The Battle of Ganale Doria had an embarrassing postscript for Graziani. On one of the nights of the ongoing struggle, more than nine hundred askaris slipped out of the column run by Colonel Agostini and deserted. They had had enough. Some of these men had given twenty years of their lives fighting for Italy in Libya, and they had boarded steamships under the impression that they were finally going home—instead, they were taken to Mogadishu, where they learned they were to be cannon fodder all over again.

The deserters eventually headed for Irgalem, where they joined Desta's battered, recovering army, while six hundred made it across the Kenyan frontier, where a British officer short on compassion threatened to deliver them right back into the hands of Graziani (who almost certainly would have had them all shot). In the end, the deserters waited out the war in prison. So many Eritreans were fleeing by then that the King's African Rifles established a detainment camp north of Mount Kenya.

Around this same time, an Eritrean in the north, a man named Andom Tesfazien, had also reached his limit with the Italians. Tesfazien had been ordered to bury the Italian dead, but the bodies of the askaris were to be left to rot on the battlefield. He protested. These black men, these brothers of his, had fought hard and died for Italy, for a land they had never seen; they had as much right to a proper burial as any white soldier. When he complained too loudly, they called it insubordination. Tesfazien took to the hills with one hundred others who felt as he did, going over to the Ethiopian side.[41]

From one hundred men, Andom Tesfazien would soon lead a unit of more than one thousand Eritrean deserters just like himself. Four years later, he was still leading guerrilla assaults against the Italians, and the Emperor promoted him to the commander rank of dejazmach. He never heard about the honor, dying in battle in 1939.

Chapter Thirteen

THE OLD MAN ON THE MOUNTAIN

In Geneva, the Council for the League of Nations met on January 20. And the Council was confronted with yet another polite but pointed reminder from the Emperor that up until now, it had done nothing to help his country. "The Ethiopian Government," wrote Haile Selassie, "is learning the cruel lesson that small peoples must chiefly rely on themselves to defend their independence and their territorial integrity."[1]

Eden wanted to get on with an oil embargo, but went along with the Committee of Eighteen's latest move: appointing a panel of experts to study the idea. When the news reached the Council the next day that Britain's King George V had died, the morning's business was canceled. As the League Council got back to work in the afternoon, it turned down a plea from Ethiopia to investigate what Eden considered "disregard for the rules of war"—the accusations of mustard gas, bombings of hospitals, and wholesale slaughter.

Eden went home to London, and as several foreign dignitaries came in for the king's funeral, they dropped by to see him. Germany's foreign minister, Baron Konstantin von Neurath, thought that Mussolini was losing confidence under the weight of the sanctions and was perhaps open to terms he wouldn't have considered before. Italy's economic situation, suggested von Neurath, was "undoubtedly grave."[2] That same day, Eden met with Pierre Étienne Flandin, who had taken over the foreign minister duties from the disgraced Laval (the office of France's prime minister was now held by Albert Sarraut). Flandin believed, like Eden, that the Fascist position was deteriorating.

"Neither of us," recalled Eden, "was prepared to make any move to restart negotiations between the parties."[3] They were gambling that Italy would be on its knees soon.

* * *

As war raged in Ethiopia, a far smaller, more contained war waged over *Ethiopia*. Here was a play "ripped from the headlines" that brought the whole Crisis into a narrative sweep of an hour. And it was proving too hot for Broadway.

The Federal Theater Project's Hallie Flanagan had even appealed to the first lady. Eleanor Roosevelt had listened with polite interest, made an even more polite phone call to try to intervene, and then withdrew quietly from the whole thing, thinking she'd done her part. It wasn't enough. Jacob Baker of the Works Progress Administration, which was playing foster parent to the Project, sent Flanagan a stern order on January 18: "This will direct that no issue of the living newspaper shall contain any representation of the head or one of the ministers or the cabinet of a foreign state unless such representation shall have been approved in advance by the Department of State."[4] With only days before the curtain was to go up, the cast and crew could hardly wait around for bureaucrats to decide theatrical merit.

Flanagan tried again with Eleanor Roosevelt, who was perfect in the role of agony aunt, but didn't perform very well as a court of appeal. She told Flanagan that her husband, the president, thought it would be "deplorable" if *Ethiopia* was dropped, but he didn't like the idea of heads of state being portrayed on stage.[5] Couldn't the news be conveyed through a secondary person? In other words, the whole heart and soul of the play, the very things that made it innovative, would have to be thrown out for it to survive.

Time finally ran out, and there was a dress rehearsal on January 22 at the Biltmore Theater on West Forty-seventh Street. There was Mussolini, thundering away about his Fascist empire, and there was Haile Selassie speaking from a desk, "his manner calm, scholarly." At the end, as the war drums beat on, spotlights came up on different actors in military uniforms of various countries.

ENGLAND: Watch Italy!
ITALY: Watch Britain!
ETHIOPIA: Fight to the death!
FRANCE: Watch Germany!
RUMANIA: Be ready!
POLAND: More bullets!

As more dialogue like this was barked out, the word "war" was passed down the line of actors while the music rose and the marching sound got louder.

Jacob Baker was in the audience that afternoon, and after the curtain fell, he had a new memo typed up that clarified his position: "No one impersonating a ruler or cabinet officer shall actually appear on the stage."[6]

Not only Flanagan was exasperated. So was the head of the Project's New York division, Elmer Rice. With his round spectacles and toothy smile, Rice looked deceptively boyish, but his first play had earned him $100,000 at the impressive age of twenty-one, and he'd been awarded a Pulitzer Prize for Drama in 1929. Theater with social meaning was meat and drink to him, and he'd already written plays about poverty and soulless mechanization, about Nazism and American expats fleeing materialism to live in Paris. The "Living Newspaper" concept was very much his baby, and he was furious with Baker's meddling.

Hallie Flanagan recalled his outrage: "Washington, he felt, never really intended to let us get a curtain up on a play which said anything; we would never be able to do anything except pap for babes and octogenarians."[7] He and Flanagan went off to confront Baker in his office the day after the dress rehearsal. Rice had threatened to quit before and had warned that if he did, he'd go to the press. But this time Baker called his bluff. He reached into a desk drawer and pulled out a letter of acceptance, one that actually suggested Rice could quote him when he ran to the papers. Baker took out his pen and signed the letter, acknowledging he'd received it. "It was one of several occasions on the project," Flanagan remembered, "when homicide would not have surprised me."[8]

Rice was going. Flanagan wondered whether to go, too, but she ultimately stayed on. In a last act of defiance, she and Rice had invited all the theater critics to the dress rehearsal. "*Ethiopia* is no masterpiece," wrote the critic, Brooks Atkinson. "But as a living newspaper account of a breach of peace that is happening under our nose it is sobering and impressive—even frightening . . . There is an abundance of first-rate talent."[9]

At the time, Atkinson had the power to make or break a play on Broadway, and with praise like this, the Biltmore should have had a hit. But aside from the critics and a few curious matinee goers, no one would ever see *Ethiopia*.

There was one other small controversy over impersonating public figures. One scene for the play dramatizes the homecoming press conference for Hubert Julian; reporters fire off questions, and Julian is naturally his inflated, egotistical self, telling the scrum on stage: "I was given a commander's uniform, and I walked around like a debutante that had been stood up by her boyfriend—all dressed up and no place to go. But I couldn't find any airplanes!"

Julian was lying again, but neither the playwrights nor the producers could know this. They were, after all, using verbatim comments. The scene was a notable success in the rehearsal, but it was a white man who played Julian. The Black Eagle was so hated by now that no African American wanted to play the part.[10]

* * *

General Pietro Badoglio, a signature beret on his stolid head and a flannel-lined cape over his shoulders, strolled each morning between the tents of his soldiers, looking every inch a son of the Piedmont Alps. He'd kept busy all this time at his base in Ende Yesus, not far from Mekele, making sure roads got built and reinforcements were deployed. It "has always been my rule," Badoglio claimed later, "to be meticulous in preparation, and therefore, able to be swift in action."[11]

So far, however, he hadn't acted at all. Ras Mulugeta's army of eighty thousand warriors was massed on Amba Aradam, and back in Rome, Mussolini was growing impatient again to the point where he was willing to re-authorize the use of gas and indiscriminate bombing. Badoglio was prepared to use both, but he wasn't ready to move. Each day, his planes bombarded the mountain where Mulugeta was entrenched, blasting it as if they meant to build a fresh railway tunnel. With so many caves and fissures to hide in, there were few casualties; only eight warriors were killed in the first week of January. Far more destructive was how the daily gas raids slaughtered the livestock below in the pasture lands, killing precious pack animals and cattle that were to feed the soldiers. The animals all died lingering, choking deaths.

For his part, Mulugeta had done little to break the stalemate. Urged on by the priests with his army, he ordered the only night raid the Ethiopians ever attempted during the war on January 9, a valiant attempt to capture the machine guns in Doghea Pass when there was an eclipse. George Steer summed it up well when he wrote that the curmudgeonly hero of Adwa "found the searchlights staring him in his face and his comrades broken by machine gun fire. Mulugeta could carry out no surprises on the Italians, who had money enough to pay for their information."[12]

Not that Mulugeta learned anything from the experience. Having come all this way, he considered himself king of the mountain. When operatives for the traitor Gugsa were found one morning camped in the middle of his army's livestock, they were captured and dragged in front of the old general. Mulugeta ordered that each man receive forty lashes and then endure the searing and permanent agony of a face brand. "Now let them go to Mekele and draw their silver."

His Cuban adviser, Del Valle, knew what the international reaction would be if word got out over the punishment. "But what will the League of Nations say?"

"To hell with the League of Nations," snapped Mulugeta.[13]

Traitors feared him. But Badoglio didn't fear him at all. He was concerned only with Seyum and Kassa. They posed genuine threats. Ras Seyum, the commander so contemptuous of maps, and Ras Kassa, the bearded and reticent cousin of the Emperor, were threatening to plow right across the Tembien province and cut the Italian army in two. If they captured the mountain passes at Warieu to the west and Abaro in the north, they could sever their enemy's supply line to Mekele and allow Imru to push on into Eritrea.

It was an ambitious plan, but their reach was further than the Ethiopians' grasp. They could be astonishing in their mobility, swift and responsive, but harassed by the Italians from the air, they had to be careful in how they approached and made gains. It didn't help that their communications were poor; they had hardly any field radios, and if Kassa wanted to alert Imru to his movements, it took a messenger fourteen days to get to Imru's base.

Haile Selassie had made Kassa his commander-in-chief for the northern campaign, but this wasn't a decision made on the man's military record. Kassa had none. His finest quality was his loyalty, and so the Emperor rewarded it, much to the annoyance of Mulugeta, who, if nothing else, could at least call himself a soldier. The old warrior's envy may have played a small part in what happened over the last tense days of January in 1936.

As Seyum and Kassa waited for their moment, Badoglio finally decided he'd better take it away from them. On January 19, he had the Third Army Corps—which held the center ground of Mekele—march ten miles southwest and hold Nebri and Negada. The idea was to keep Mulugeta, if he was so inclined, from sending any reinforcements to help Kassa, and in the larger scheme of things, distract the frighteningly long Ethiopian line from his main thrust. The next day, the Second Eritrean Division headed out of Warieu Pass in two columns to attack Kassa's right flank at Abbi Addi. A Blackshirt division, the "28 October," was to attack Kassa's left flank, but they were never intended for any heavy engagement with the enemy. As usual, the askaris were sent in to do the bloodiest fighting.

Fierce and battle-hardened, the Eritreans spent an entire day with their rifles and bayonets driving the Ethiopians off their mountain strongholds. But a day later, there was a stunning reversal, and the Italians had only themselves to blame. Four battalions under the command of General Filippo Diamanti, along with the three legions of Blackshirts, headed out from Warieu Pass to take more ground, but they took too much of it. By the early afternoon, they were on Debra Amba, and they realized their supply line was overstretched and that they were vulnerable to Ras Seyum in the west. The smart thing to do was to fall back, but this only encouraged the Ethiopians, who went after them with a vengeance. It was a frenzied counterattack, and as an Italian chaplain, one Father Giuliani, gave the last rites to a soldier, he was speared to death. The worst slaughter was in the ranks of the inexperienced Blackshirts.

Diamanti's stunned survivors managed to get back to the safe ground of their Warieu garrison, but by nightfall, the bodies were counted, and the Blackshirts had 335 men either killed or wounded.

First retreat, now they were under a siege. The Ethiopians swarmed the Italian defensive positions with hardly a care for their own safety. Screaming battle cries, rushing barefoot toward the muzzle flash and roar of machine guns, they threw their numbers against the Italians, who were shocked and horrified as bodies literally piled up in front of them. And the Ethiopians didn't care. They jumped over corpses, swords flashing, spears finding their marks. The waves of warriors rolled on, eroding Italian defenses and morale, while supplies of ammunition, food, and vital water gradually ran out. The Blackshirts were entirely surrounded.

Badoglio sent orders to the Eritreans to the west: they should fall back to their original position so they could come to the rescue. But the word didn't seem to get through. The Eritreans didn't come. Here was Badoglio's first real heavy fighting of the war, and it was turning into a disaster.

Kassa knew he could throw men at machine guns for only so long. If he actually wanted to capture Warieu, he would need his forces bolstered. No help would be coming from Imru, who, without a radio, had no idea what was going on. The logical source was Mulugeta, but *he* claimed by radio that he was in fierce fighting with the Third Army Corps—which simply wasn't true. The general had decided to spitefully leave Kassa to fend for himself.

Badoglio was now trying to disguise his inner panic, a growing fear that he would go down in history as the commander during Adwa's sequel. It was an anxiety he didn't share at all in his book on the war published afterwards, but his soldiers saw him keeping a steady vigil in the radio tent, listening to every message, intently questioning pilots coming back from bombing raids on any scrap of reconnaissance they might be able to give him. He finally told his officers to consider what only a few days ago was unthinkable—giving up Mekele. He needed an evacuation plan, just in case. The threat of his supply line being cut was so real he had to consider pulling out the thousands of men, all the armored cars and artillery and pack animals that had so casually moved in under De Bono. If he did, of course, Mussolini would surely make good on his threats to replace him—but then Mussolini might find himself being replaced, thanks to the scandal.

On January 23, the desperate Italians at Warieu Pass looked up and saw planes dropping supplies for them, all except water, which couldn't be dropped. Things were so bleak that some men used damp cotton swabs to moisten their cracked and parched lips. Badoglio had to wonder when the relief column he'd sent for would arrive to turn the tide. An Italian reporter named Paulo Monelli saw how the marshal was coping. Badoglio, he wrote, wouldn't go off to sleep, "and still wearing his cap, with his cape spread over his knees like a blanket, he sat on a stool in his tent beside the telephone. On the few occasions when it rang, he lifted the receiver and listened in silence, his face a mask of stone in the crude light of the acetylene lamp."[14]

At close to dawn, the phone rang once more, and Badoglio scooped up the receiver. He listened carefully, and others saw him smile over what he heard. Then the marshal walked out of the tent, resuming his morning habit of strolling around the camp.

The news in the call was that the relief column was pushing back Kassa's army. The Warieu Pass would not fall. But what really turned the tables were not the fresh soldiers, but the planes that relentlessly gassed the Ethiopians' rear positions. Like Imru before, Kassa was a helpless witness. Warriors dropped, screaming, their knees buckling. The gas poisoned the pasture land and bushes; it drove bleating and terrified cows and mules stampeding off the cliffs of ravines.

Perhaps up to eight thousand Ethiopians were killed or wounded in the battle, while Kassa himself estimated that about two thousand animals were slaughtered during the gas attacks.[15] The Italians had suffered far fewer casualties, but for them, it was still a devastating number, estimated at close to eleven hundred men killed or wounded, sixty of them officers. Add to this the humiliation of Mussolini's prized Blackshirts. In the end, the Ethiopians had captured Abbi Addi, but they failed to take Warieu Pass. The First Battle of Tembien was nothing for either side to brag about, but starved of any morale-boosting news, the Ethiopians and their advocates in the UK and America hailed it as an important victory. It was a mouthful of ashes for the Italians, who, having trumpeted their capture of Adwa and Aksum, were discovering their enemy could inflate successes almost as well as they could.

* * *

Haile Selassie knew better than to brag. He was commander-in-chief to an army spread so thin and so far that communications were constantly daunting and next to impossible. And his forces made constant demands. Kassa wanted more men. Mulugeta complained about the situation at Amba Aradam, where the Italians kept up their steady bombardment, gradually wiping out the herd of cattle below that was supposed to feed his restless soldiers stuck in the cliffs and caves. Mulugeta's Oromo fighters had abandoned the mountain and deserted, and the old ras was telling his Emperor it was time to either fight or pull back.

The Emperor was not an armchair general like Mussolini. He couldn't afford to be. While not a military man, he understood deployment and resources, and so his orders to Mulugeta were once again a careful mix of proper deference, yet with a tight snap of the reins: yes, you can go forward, but don't do it if you risk an open battle. If you need to withdraw, don't wait until the enemy is breathing down your neck. Kassa did, indeed, need men, so the Emperor ordered that fifteen thousand soldiers under the command of Dejazmach Moshesha Wolde —battle-hardened warriors all—detach from Mulugeta's forces and head for the Tembien. Ras Mulugeta predictably sulked in his cave on the mountain. He would not move.

As Haile Selassie considered his options as commander-in-chief, his time was also eaten away by affairs of state. Off in Paris, Tekle Hawaryat Tekle Mariyam hadn't received his regular money transfer to run his embassy. Should he close it and come home? By now, Tekle Hawaryat would have preferred to be on the fighting line, but his Emperor, still having faith in the Europeans, needed him there. There were also more frivolous matters that Haile Selassie should have left on the desk of an aide. In early February, an American minister and a Canadian missionary in Wallamo were arrested for walking around town after hours. The local authorities bound the American with a dog chain—the Canadian only escaped the same humiliation because no other shackles were available. The Emperor had to deal with their complaint.

Helping him through it all back in the capital was Everett Colson, who kept drafting correspondence, haggling with nobles, sending urgent messages. But the endless pressure of the war had taken its toll on his weak constitution. His health was failing. He was doing his best to groom a young American lawyer, John Spencer, as his successor because he knew he couldn't stay.

Meanwhile, Haile Selassie decided to go north. Though it was dangerous, he needed a better vantage point from which to direct the traffic of his forces, and he also had to restore order to the region with his presence. The Caproni planes had been dropping leaflets claiming he was dead. Shiftas had beaten one small army and were plaguing the valuable route to Lalibela, the country's second holiest city. The Emperor decided to establish a new base at Korem, on the edge of the high-lands in Tigray. It was a move that wasn't unexpected to the Italians, who would bomb the Korem plain and areas around Dessie several times.

* * *

In Geneva, Max Huber, president of the International Committee of the Red Cross, sat in his office in the Villa Moynier and composed a letter.

Huber was what they used to call an "august presence" in political affairs. Born to industrialists, he might have become one of Zurich's leading corporate magnates, but instead he went first into law, then diplomacy. His furrowed brow, full white mustache, and jowls became a familiar sight in courtrooms, university lecture halls, and international conferences. His office walls could be papered with honorary degrees. All this patrician bearing and a lifetime of legal study he used now on January 23 to write in the sternest terms to Benito Mussolini. Italy, charged Huber, had broken the Geneva Convention over and over.

The Duce must have been quite amused as he read Huber's accusations. Here was another organization that assumed the written word was magic that could beat a machine gun. The usual tactics would do—he wrote back to assure Huber that *of course* the Italians respected the Geneva Convention. And just for good measure, an officer of the Italian Red Cross muddied the waters. He claimed in a ten-page letter that Ethiopian warriors were chopping off the limbs of enemy soldiers. The letter also repeated the old lie about dum-dum bullets.[16] So far as historians have been able to tell, Huber made no effort to follow up on Mussolini's response.[17]

There was thinly-veiled contempt, too, in Addis Ababa for the International Committee's men on the ground. Sidney Brown and Marcel Junod had gotten off on the wrong foot with the foreign expat circle, and each would keep stumbling socially for the rest of their time in the capital. Brown, of course, had traveled the world, and he must have expected a certain amount of deference to his role. Before he'd even spent a month in Ethiopia, he complained about what he called "occult influences" on the part of Sidney Barton, the most prominent diplomat in Addis Ababa.[18] But Barton and the others had experience. They knew the country, and even if they disagreed privately among themselves, they had earned the confidence—at varying levels—of the Emperor.

Clacking away on a portable Remington typewriter, the young American lawyer, John Spencer, and Lorenzo Taezaz prepared their own reports each day on the bombings of ambulances and gas attacks. Spencer was peevishly wondering what these two men from Geneva actually did to make themselves useful. At least the Pittsburgh doctor, Thomas Lambie—who had been in the region for years and was the executive secretary of the Ethiopian Red Cross—was willing to help with collecting statistics and statements. Lambie also sent out reports and complained about poison gas to other Red Cross societies. He would warn the Dutch, for example, that they should "be sure to have a large Red Cross flag, dimensions fourteen (14) meter square, displayed on the field near the ambulance wherever you are. If you do not have such a flag, purchase materials and have your boys make one."[19] The Dutch complied—and were bombed anyway.

Out in the field, there were very different relations. In sharp contrast to Spencer's coldness to Junod and Brown, plus the pack of reporters behaving like jealous hyenas in the capital, the doctors and medics to the north seemed to get along reasonably well with each other for the most part, whatever their national factions. The head of the Dutch Red Cross was Dr. Charles Winckel, a portly, spectacled tropical disease specialist who greeted the mornings in a beret and a robe with stripes as loud as a barber's pole. Winckel was something of a shutterbug, taking great stocks of photos and film, and like so many others, he would soon befriend John Melly, who was happy to have their units share tasks. Junod, too, would be on good terms with Winckel both during the war and after. He would write to the Dutch doctor months later, promising to pass through The Hague for a visit and declaring his "most devoted friendship."[20]

The Emperor cultivated these doctors in a way he didn't with the journalists, but aside from political shrewdness, he was also genuinely grateful for their services. A letter survives of a court secretary inviting Winckel to introduce his staff, "and if the weather permits, you may take photos of H.M. the Emperor."[21] Haile Selassie was comfortable enough with Winckel that, over a meal, he brought up the issue of an unusual casualty—his pet dog. Rather than be put off, Winckel was quite willing to take a look at the sick animal and then peer into his microscope; it so happened he was also a rabies expert. A parasite was discovered, and the patient soon cured.

But all this friendliness had its limits. On February 9, the Italians flew over and dropped four bombs less than half a mile from the Dutch camp in Dessie. Winckel and his team members dived for their trenches, "armed with gas masks and cameras." The media in the Netherlands had shown great interest in their unit, and Winckel wanted to send a telegram back home to let his superiors and everyone else know they were all right. "We did not gain the impression that the Italians were after us," wrote Winckel in a report back to The Hague, but when he was ready to send his telegram, the official censor was conveniently "not to be found."[22] And when the man did turn up after several hours, he red-penciled out references to the Emperor being there for a visit—that would leave the impression to the world that the planes had come specifically to go after the hospital.

Maybe they had, or then again, maybe Winckel was right. From Haile Selassie's perspective, of course, there was nothing to be gained anymore in giving the Italians the benefit of the doubt. And he was quickly vindicated on this score. Only a week later, the bombers returned and began regularly harassing the Dutch and British units. And much to Winckel's annoyance, the Italians were protesting the Dutch unit's cache of hunting rifles for game shooting and standard sidearms for personal protection.

Haile Selassie's advisers had already given up on the League of Nations over the issue of conduct in a time of war. By January 20, they had sent instructions to Geneva to withdraw their request for an inquiry. Now the International Committee of the Red Cross was proving to be as apathetic and downright obstructionist as the League. Requests had been made to send Ethiopia gas masks, along with the proper instructions for them. They were all turned down. The Committee would insist and, indeed, keep on insisting: "A general appeal for gas masks on behalf of one of the parties, *without specifying for what purpose these masks were to be used*, would have caused the International Red Cross Committee to go outside its proper role [emphasis added]."[23]

If Ethiopia would not be given gas masks, it would just have to make them. Lady Barton and Princess Tsehai started organizing again, and with sewing machines *whizzing* and chittering away, women in white overalls were busy throughout the spring, making masks for the soldiers out of flannel bags. They were crude but clever jobs—there were mica slits for eyes, and you exhaled through a rubber tube. By early April, Tsehai and Lady Barton's seamstresses had created eighteen hundred of them for the men going to the northern front. If there were no gas masks to give out, the warriors would be told to urinate on their shammas and breathe through the cotton. This was an old trick learned by soldiers during the Great War.

And Sidney Brown, though he failed to impress the leading expats, was also trying to do what he could. He was genuinely dedicated to letting the world know about Ethiopia's plight and Italy's war crimes. The pitch of outrage in his accounts rose higher for each Italian attack. "It is now very clear that this little colonial affair has become a war of extermination," he would write in late February, "and that if we do not manage to have the Red Cross emblem respected by a country calling itself civilized, we will never be able to do so later if we are ever faced by a war in Europe."[24]

He was right, but he was also alienating his superiors. To them, he was strident; he was siding, quite openly and plainly, with the Ethiopians instead of walking the strict and neutral razor's edge the organization claimed to always set for itself. It was especially clear when he added his signature to formal protests from the Ethiopian Red Cross. Huber and the other officials back in the Villa Moynier began to think young Sidney needed a rest. It was high time he was back in Geneva anyway for other duties.

Within a matter of weeks, however, Brown would find himself being gently interrogated over not only his professional conduct, but his private life as well. Perhaps he should have exercised more tact. But, of course, there was no way that Sidney Brown could anticipate that the fate of his career would be tied to a mailbag in the airport in Asmara.

* * *

After representing Ethiopia at the League of Nations over the summer of 1935, Gaston Jèze had gone back to the quiet life of a law professor, ready to deliver lectures and write scholarly papers at the University of Paris. Anthony Eden had thought of him as a man who enjoyed hearing himself talk (and talk and talk . . .). But over the past few months, Jèze often couldn't hear the sound of his own voice. Too many disruptions in class. Too much hate and venom turned his way. And then there were the all-out riots. The far right in France had its own schedule for the term, and they made him its target.

Jèze had withdrawn from the field, waiting patiently for things to settle down. When he tried to get back to business on January 9, the whole controversy over his mere presence got uglier. His more radical students, along with the plants from the *Action française*, were no longer happy just to shout him down. They hurled books and bags of flour at him. Jèze tried to brave the onslaught of their catcalls and abuse for more than half an hour, and then he finally left.

But the hooligans weren't finished with him. They followed the 67-year-old professor into the faculty rooms, breaking down one of the doors to try to find him. They only left when the dean of the law school threatened to call the police.[25] That same day, the Ministry of Education ordered the law school closed indefinitely. The move amounted to a stalemate, given that the students were planning to strike anyway, hoping to drive Jèze out of the university. For seven days, the law school stayed closed, and then Education Minister Henri Guernut tried to get things back to a state of order and sanity. Students on their way to class couldn't help noticing the increased police presence in the Latin Quarter. And the university bumped Jèze's lecture up from eleven o'clock to eight-forty in the morning.

There were only supposed to be thirty-five students filing into the lecture hall on February 1, but a mob of hundreds pushed their way in—the police were out on the streets, not in the campus buildings. Once again, Jèze couldn't make himself heard over the din of shouts and insults. And when he left this time, his tormentors threw tear-gas bombs.

Guernut, exasperated and out of ideas, summoned the university council to try to figure out what to do. Jèze hadn't drawn any particular attention to himself over comments about Ethiopia, nor was he making any fresh stand. It was enough for his opponents that he once represented Haile Selassie in Geneva. The controversy would drag on through February into March.

Among the student demonstrators was a 19-year-old son of an engineer from Jarnac. One day, François Mitterrand would be president of France for the Socialists, a controversial statesman who would dominate his country's politics for fourteen years. But in 1935, he had stood in a crowd, protesting against an "invasion" of mixed-race students, i.e., Polish Jews.[26] And in 1936, he was with protesters several times over Jèze, who obliged the rightists that loathed him by being both a left-winger and a Jew.

Mitterrand never joined the extremist *Action française*, but he did belong for a while to a xenophobic youth organization known as the "National Volunteers." Historians are still sifting through Mitterrand's past, trying to figure out the jigsaw that included his work for both the Vichy regime *and* the Résistance. But he's never made things simple for them. And he wouldn't when it came to Ethiopia, either. In a speech he gave on Ethiopia to other students, Mitterrand remarked, "It is always useful to know the history of peoples at once so different and so much the same as others; because, at bottom, it is not the color or the form of one's hair which gives value to the soul."[27]

*   *   *

On February 9, a Sunday, Pietro Badoglio summoned correspondents to the mess tent of his headquarters at Ende Yesus, not far from Mekele. Most of the reporters covering the Italian side had spent a good deal of the war since December in Asmara, where they nagged and haggled with officers to be embedded with the forces—and got nowhere. Only now were most of them getting even this close to the front. And today, Badoglio was in the mood to be expansive, though his voice apparently irritated reporters because of its pedantic, monotonous rhythms.

"I have decided to attack Ras Mulugeta," he announced. Then he sketched out the broad lines of his advance, telling the correspondents, "I do not expect any enemy reaction on the first day, but this will be an action on a very large scale, indeed a tremendous scale. I shall be directing the movements of 70,000 men." Just in case the reporters didn't recognize the significance of the offensive, he would explain it to them. "You will have the privilege of witnessing a tremendous, indeed a stupendous spectacle, Gentlemen. We shall win this war with a campaign of the utmost brilliance, a campaign unequaled since the days of Napoleon. In less than two months, beneath the weight of our assault, you will see the Ethiopian empire crumble to dust."[28]

Badoglio had already inflicted what he himself called "a continuous and persistent air bombardment" that was comparable to the "pounding, harassing artillery in the Great War"—all to "affect the morale of the enemy and lower his fighting spirit." It was a strange comparison. Besides carnage, the Great War was famous for its futility, particularly when it came to barrages. The case could be made that Badoglio had Mulugeta trapped in his pockets of stone, and so the marshal didn't have to do anything at all. Why not leave him there? T. E. Lawrence, for instance, had let the Turks tie up their resources and waste their supplies on their garrison at Medina. The old ras held a rock. He still hadn't shown any signs he was willing to leave it.

But the marshal was not going to get caught with his pants down again as he was in the Tembien.

Italian planes had mapped Aradam so thoroughly that reconnaissance experts knew it better than the Ethiopians hiding in its caves. Badoglio never showed much public respect for his enemy, but now he paid Mulugeta a compliment in the form of the massive firepower he brought to the job. Seven divisions with 280 field artillery pieces and 170 planes were deployed for what was to be called the Battle of Enderta, named after the province. Before the dark follies of the French in Vietnam, it was called the mightiest force to participate in a colonial war. All this was to take on what the Italians estimated were eighty thousand Ethiopians with antique rifles, a few rusting cannons from Adwa, and several Oerlikons that could only waste flak at the bombers. In truth, because of the desertions and bombings, Mulugeta probably had thousands fewer than this.

There was nothing especially Napoleonic or particularly brilliant about the Italian battle strategy. The northern face of Amba Aradam is like a straight vertical wall of rock, making it practically impregnable. Badoglio's only option was to use a pincer movement that flanked the two sides and then to circle around to the valleys that granted southern access to the mountain, cutting off Mulugeta's retreat at a spot called Antalo.

Early on the morning of February 10, Badoglio's First and Third Army Corps each advanced south across the Calamino Plain and marched the next day under an unusually heavy downpour to take positions at Aradam. The Third was to the west, the First Army Corps to the east. Badoglio came to an observation post at nearby Amba Gadam, where he'd reserved a place for reporters to watch the coming battle like a drill exercise. They saw him give brief orders to his officers and then chain-smoke as he waited for developments, not bothering to take off the mosquito veil that covered his hair.

Then he noticed them. "Well, gentlemen, are you satisfied? Have you a good view of what's going on? You are watching a drama that will unfold itself in several acts. This is the prologue. Our troops have made excellent progress."[29]

The reporters were unimpressed. If they had a good view, it was only of a tabletop mountain in the distance with occasional blooms of smoke from shell fire and dropped bombs. Soon, however, their opinions would change. The French correspondent, Paul Gentizon, embedded for *Le Temps*, was astonished by the relentless shelling from more than two hundred artillery guns and the assembly line precision of the bombing raids.[30] Badoglio had brought a sledge-hammer to knock over an ant hill.

* * *

On February 12, the "Third of January" division of the First Army was making its way along one of the caravan roads of the Antalo plain when it ran into the advance guards of Dejazmach Wodaju, the governor of Dessie. Wodaju had an army of fewer than twenty thousand Wollo soldiers. He was loyal, but his men were more ambivalent over the Emperor, already thinking Haile Selassie was dead, thanks to the hail of Italian leaflets. Wodaju sent his men against the Italians, and they fought so ferociously that Badoglio ordered another division, the Alpine, to engage them.

The broken Wollo army fled while Wodaju, seriously wounded, had himself lifted up the mountainside so that he could report on the Italian advance directly to Mulugeta. In Badoglio's memoir of the war, he wrote that the Ethiopian defenses, "though carried out with the greatest determination, gave no sign of any homogenous plan or any efficient series of command."[31]

Others were inclined to be more charitable. The reporter Cesco Tomaselli was another correspondent on hand to see the fighting. "The Ethiopians attacked the Italians with obsolescent rifles charged with black powder and a few machine guns—hopeless. They should have hurled themselves en masse against our troops and cut them down with their scimitars; in other words, if they had fought in their traditional manner, they might have achieved much."[32]

It rained again on the night of February 13, giving the Ethiopians up on the mountain a respite, and the next day, after another aerial bombardment, sentries didn't spot any Italian or askari forces on the move. They were resting, and this was merely more of Badoglio's "prologue."

At seven o'clock the next morning, as Mulugeta pulled on his boots, "the whole mountain thundered about his ears."[33] The shelling was so severe that his men assumed that planes were making another bombing run, and they merely burrowed deeper inside their cracks and crevices. During the battle, the Italians would fire a total of twenty-three thousand shells, while their planes would drop almost four hundred tons of high explosive. Mulugeta still refused to act, thinking the landscape would accomplish all the work for him. There were shallow trenches for cover at the base . . . and then no obstacles at all to block the Italians when they came.

In the early afternoon, his mountain was being defended by a single small army belonging to one of his commanders, Bitwoded Makonnen from Wollega province. Makonnen knew if the circle was closed, all would be lost. So he took his sons and four thousand of his soldiers to make a stand against the First Army Corps coming around from the east. On one of the yellowish slopes, a whole village was being consumed by fire, sending out dense banks of smoke while green pepper bushes nearby also went up in flames. Early in the fighting, Makonnen was strafed by machine gun fire along his side, and his men carried him off the field to a nearby cave. Unaware that their leader was mortally wounded, the army courageously held back two divisions to buy Mulugeta an escape. The Italians had failed to link up their armies, and the Ethiopians could slip through this precious corridor.

As Makonnen lay dying, his wounds were tended in vain by another one of those foreign eccentrics the war seemed to attract, a retired British major named Gerald Achilles Burgoyne. Burgoyne had casually told his wife one day that he wanted to train cavalry soldiers in Ethiopia. When he ran smack into the law that prevented enlistment in foreign armies, he volunteered for the Red Cross. He claimed he was in his fifties; he was sixty-one. Then he talked his way into managing a mule transport unit—because he had absolutely no training to be a medic.

After Makonnen was dead, the men closest to him wanted only to take his body back to Wollega, where they could bury it in his native soil. So they had come to Burgoyne in the night and asked him—given that he was with the Red Cross, and must know how to do such things—to cut his body in two for easier transport. They also had to keep up the charade that he was alive for the soldiers. These were matters of conscience that Burgoyne could easily understand. Going about his duties wearing a monocle, he wouldn't dive for cover during aerial raids because "he thought it would make a poor impression if a British officer seemed afraid of Italian bombs."[34] Makonnen's two parts were packed up in a couple of war drums, and his army fought on.

Above, horns blew to sound the alarm for Mulugeta's men. Mulugeta drew his sword as he barked at messengers to run to this corner and that cliff of the mountain. For the Italians rushing up the terraces of the amba, it was a macabre version of the child's game of war—"gotcha." Machine guns blasted men racing out of caves, and when warriors hid or delayed too long to surrender, there were grenades tossed to blow them to bits. Mulugeta tried to rally his surviving men in an eastern section of the mountain, but by five-thirty, the "23rd of March" Blackshirt division was raising its flag on the amba's summit.

The old ras had squandered the time that Makonnen had died to give him. He abandoned his precious desk tables, his books, and his uniforms and hurried down the mountain with his adviser, Del Valle. Back at his observation post,

Pietro Badoglio was ecstatic. The Italian correspondent Cesco Tomaselli thought the marshal was "looking twenty years younger."[35]

Much of the blame for what happened belonged to Mulugeta; too much pride, too much arrogance. In any siege, vigilance is essential, and Mulugeta didn't even have scouts who could have warned of the Italians' approach. It was an appalling slaughter. The official casualty figures for the Italians were 36 officers, 621 regular soldiers, and 145 askaris either killed or wounded. The Ethiopians had at least six thousand and perhaps as many as eight thousand killed, with almost twice that number wounded. The Italians dragged the dead bodies out and burned them. There is nothing quite like the stench of burned flesh, a sickly-sweet odor, and it apparently *stayed* for months after, permeating the landscape as a grisly reminder of what had taken place.

And for Ras Mulugeta Yeggazu and the other survivors of the battle, the ordeal wasn't over.

* * *

It wasn't all bleakness and defeat. Miles away, the ras who was Ethiopia's one undisputed war hero, Imru, kept taking the fight to the Italians. George Steer was correct in declaring that he "was the only Ethiopian in this war who knew how to carry out an offensive with small means. His was the worst-armed of all the northern armies, but it did the most."[36]

The Italians dropped gas along the trails of the Takkaze to poison the livestock. Imru found other trails. The gas could poison and burn his men, so he urged them, "You soldiers must be always washing."[37] He was on his own, completely detached from the other forces, and yet he found ways to keep his soldiers regularly paid—in fact, it seems to have been a point of principle to do so. Incredibly, he managed to stay ahead or behind the enemy forces, his steady raids inching out from southern Shire and prompting General Pietro Maravigna to keep pulling back his outposts until he was about three miles from Aksum.

By February 11, as Marshal Badoglio's columns advanced on Amba Aradam to destroy Mulugeta, Imru was far to the northeast, with a thousand of his men raiding cattle near the Mareb River belonging to those who gave in to the Italians. The following night, they were on their way back to safe territory, slipping past lighted guard posts. Seven miles from the Mareb and close to the border, they came across Fort Rama, a stone garrison on a hill protected by barbed wire but without any lights. Imru's intelligence suggested the place was probably an ammo dump.

His men split in two, with half using stealth to cut the wire and penetrate the enclosure while the other half started a head-on assault. The Italians didn't know what hit them. When a cache of shells exploded during the battle, five of the Ethiopians were killed, forty-five Italians as well, and about a hundred others were wounded. Despite the casualties, the raid was still a great success, and Imru and his men raced off into the night, lugging rifles, machine guns, uniforms, and plenty of food.

The next night, five hundred of his men attacked a convoy along a stretch of the Adwa-Asmara road, making off with more than one hundred thousand cartridges. "All that we could carry, but there are many still in the camions," they bragged.[38] Imru was using the guerrilla tactics that his fellow rases had spurned—and he was *hurting* the enemy. It would be more than a month before Rome acknowledged his success, and when at last it did, it focused instead on one special raid to counter the bad press over Italian atrocities. A group of workers for the Gondrand transport company had been attacked in an operation site at Utok Emme, not far from the Eritrean border. There are conflicting death toll figures, but at least fifty-five and perhaps as many as sixty-eight workers, including one woman, were killed.[39] Imru, both then and three decades later, considered it just another raid.

"I felt, and still feel, that this was a legitimate act of war because all these men were armed with rifles," he told Angelo Del Boca during an interview. "Indeed, they defended themselves fiercely and inflicted heavy casualties on us. At least they had the means and defense whereas our people were unable to strike back when they were bombed and decimated by the Fascist air force."[40]

Whether Mussolini and his generals chose to think of Imru as a war criminal or—far more likely—they couldn't stand this single Ethiopian making fools of them at every turn, they marked him down as a special case. They were going to make an example of him one day.

* * *

Back at Amba Aradam, a Polish doctor from Warsaw, Stanislaw Belau, and his assistant had been waiting out the bloody battle of Enderta in a cave. Belau was in his thirties, a tropical disease specialist who had seen a fair amount of the world: Iran, India, China. He'd been working in Ethiopia since before Walwal, first with the missionary, Thomas Lambie, and then later opening a nursing home. He was so talented that even Haile Selassie tried to get him to adopt Ethiopian citizenship, but Belau wasn't interested. He was, however, willing to stay on and work for the Red Cross, and having served in Dessie, he signed his name to a protest over the bombings there. Along the way, he picked up an assistant, Tadeusz Medynski, who knew how to speak enough medical jargon to be convincing, but who was apparently a Polish journalist.

Up on the mountain, Belau had done what he could to create a makeshift hospital out of a cave. He couldn't use tents because "the Italians systematically bombarded everything displaying the Red Cross emblem."[41] Belau spent most of his time operating on Mulugeta's soldiers, seeing cases of mustard gas and the effects of other kinds of chemical gases used, but all his compassion and skill seemed to do nothing to make the general appreciate his services. When the army was close to retreating, Belau needed mules to evacuate the hospital, but he was forced to haggle for money with the stubborn old ras "at great length" so he could buy the animals.[42]

Belau was busy operating when an attendant rushed in to tell him that Mulugeta's army was gone. The doctor didn't want to believe it, but by evening, he saw for himself that the troops were making their way down the slopes. There were still more than thirty severely wounded patients, many of whom had lost an arm or a leg to their wounds. The lighter casualties had fled with the soldiers—so had the stretcher bearers, defying his orders.

Belau was feeling the toll of his work. He was ill. Still, he gave permission to Medynski to go while he stayed with his patients. His fellow Pole elected to stay. Then, early in the morning, they heard shouts—in Italian. As they stepped out of their quarters, they saw rifles trained on them. Medynski declared on the spot that he was a journalist, obviously hoping this would mean better treatment or that maybe he would be released. It didn't mean a thing to their captors.

A young Italian lieutenant was astonished to see two white men in the cave, and he began peppering them with questions over Mulugeta's retreat. Belau didn't know anything, and he wasn't inclined to give it to them anyway. The lieutenant decided to rummage through their personal things, taking away Belau's carbine rifle and slinging it over the pommel of his horse's saddle. Then the Poles were beaten and forced to kneel, and the Italians performed a mock firing squad. Belau, already ill, cracked under the psychological torture. There can be no dispute at least over the fact that they were captured, because a photograph—taken by the Italians themselves—survives to this day, and it shows the two men with Red Cross armbands on their knees.[43]

This wouldn't be the last time their guards played firing squad. All the way to Mekele, the prisoners were jeered at and suffered regular humiliation, and once they arrived, another soldier threatened them with his rifle. The soldiers hit them with rifle butts as well, and one blow sprained Belau's hand. Their Ethiopian aides, including a boy, had also been taken prisoner, but nothing is known about what happened to them, or for that matter, Belau's patients back at Amba Aradam.

In Mekele, Belau and Medynski were taken in handcuffs into a tent. Belau was gripped in another panic attack.

"We are not Boches, we are Italians," said an officer, trying to calm him down. "Don't be frightened!"[44]

Someone fetched a glass of cognac. Belau was so terrified, he couldn't bring the glass to his lips.

The questions started again over Mulugeta's army, but the doctor still knew nothing. Neither did Medynski. The Italians gave them a tent, but made them sleep on a dirty patch of earth. After only a couple of hours, they woke the Poles up again. It was time for another firing squad drill.

The next day, Belau was interrogated over the bombing of Dessie, which he could remember all too well. But to his statements of fact, an officer blandly replied, "That is not true." Belau, his nerves shattered, past sobs and prayers, pointed out that *he was there*. There was clearly a last reserve of strength in the Pole that hadn't broken yet. Then the interrogating officer slipped in front of him a carefully typed sheet of paper with room for his signature at the bottom. The Red Cross had caused Mussolini's invasion far too much trouble. It needed an apostate.

"You are an intelligent man," the officer told Belau. "You must realize what may happen to you if you refuse to sign this retraction. You will come before a military court in which you will be charged with being an enemy of Italy, and you will be shot."[45]

Belau wouldn't sign.

The next day, a truck carried Belau and Medynski on a grueling, twenty-six-hour journey to Massawa. Inside, Belau was feverish, his hand swollen from the blow of the rifle butt. When they arrived at eight o'clock at night, they were dumped into a prison with the regular criminal population. They had a cement floor to sleep on and were given only bread and water. When they protested, they were told it didn't matter and that "they . . . were Negroes."[46] Medynski pleaded for three days for proper medical care for Belau. When the doctor was finally taken to a hospital, it was clear he had malaria. Belau asked for quinine. He was told it "wasn't necessary." He was still more prisoner than patient, guarded by carabinieri as "Enemy Number 6" and instructed not to speak to any other patients.

Then his doctor came to him with a copy of the retraction. There were more threats. Weak with fever, denied medical treatment, he scribbled his name across the page. But he was still refused quinine. On board a ship with Medynski bound for Naples, he managed to get a couple of packets from the ship's sick berth attendant. His fever went down, and it was only this subterfuge that saved his life. In Naples, the two Poles were briefly dumped in a drunk tank and then taken later to Rome.

There, Belau finally received proper care, but there was an additional humiliation—the chief of police made him sign a document promising he wouldn't go back to Ethiopia. The truth was that the doctor wasn't thinking about Ethiopia anymore. He was willing to sign anything that would get him out of Italy.

*   *   *

Broken and dazed, the fifty thousand surviving soldiers of Mulugeta's army plodded in no set formation in full retreat, spreading out because they feared the planes would rain down more death. They were right to be afraid. In the early morning of February 16, the Italian planes came, dropping forty tons of bombs. Over the rest of that day and the next, they dropped a hundred tons more in what George Steer called for his time "the most intensive aerial bombardment that the world has ever seen."[47]

When the Italians weren't using bombs, they used gas. It's estimated that Mulugeta lost another fifteen thousand men who were either ripped to pieces by explosions or succumbed to the agony of the burning liquid that struck their skin and boiled their lungs. Gerald Burgoyne led a caravan with as many wounded as he and his assistants could load on mules. On top of all this, the weary soldiers were plagued by Oromo shiftas paid with Italian money and armed with Italian bullets. The bandits picked them off as they struggled south towards Amba Alagi. Part of the Wollega army, under the leadership of Bitwoded Maknonnen's second son, tried to hold them back from the trenches at their new mountain position. The Italians flew over with their gas and drove them out.

They were refugees more than soldiers, staggering on with a commander who was a ghost of his former self. Mulugeta paused at Alagi and tried to rally the fleeing warriors to make a fresh stand. This mountain had more to recommend it than Aradam; it had two formidable sides, and once upon a time, its strategic location and rugged geography made it a choice spot for battles. But that was in the age before white men came. And their point on the map was no longer the issue. The men were exhausted, beaten, and they didn't believe anymore in this wrinkled, pompous fool who had let this happen to them.

On February 19, Mulugeta sent word to another commander, Ras Kebede, who was prepared to help. But his word was to abandon Alagi. What remained of the ever-dwindling force would now try for Mai Chew, twenty miles further south. They reached it about February 24. Kebede's army met up with Mulugeta's survivors and helped drive away another band of shiftas, but the raids wouldn't stop.

They would all push on southward, ever southward, in the hopes that they could link up with the Emperor's army, which was supposed to be heading for Korem.

On the morning of February 27, Mulugeta's warriors were ahead of Kebede's men on an open road. This time, they were attacked by both planes *and* shiftas, with three bombers and another band of Oromo coming to harass them. As the planes roared past, one of the mules took a direct hit. The animal was carrying the war drum loaded with a part of Makonnen's corpse. The loyal Wollegas scrambled to bury what was left under a tree, and then pulled the mule with the other drum to a church for an abrupt funeral ceremony.

Back on the road, the warriors were trading rifle shots with the Oromo when Mulugeta noticed that he couldn't see his son, Tadessa. Tadessa, in fact, was a short distance behind, with Burgoyne at a ford. A plane dropped its bombs on Burgoyne and Tadessa, and after their corpses were strafed for good measure with machine gun fire, the shiftas moved in to strip their bodies and pick over their remains.

A messenger hurried back to tell Mulugeta, "Master, your son has been murdered and mutilated by the Galla on the edge of the mountain."[48]

With inconsolable rage and grief, Mulugeta rushed out for vengeance. He lost all sense of his surroundings, either thinking he could outrun bullets or no longer caring. Whether he was shot by the Oromo or the low-flying planes singled him out, it hardly mattered. He fell dead over the body of his son, and his bodyguard crept up afterwards and carried off his limp, gnarled frame. Ethiopia no longer had a minister of war.

Those still alive moved on toward Korem.

* * *

Halfway through February, the panel of experts retained by the League of Nations Council published its report on the idea of the oil embargo. Its final conclusion was a depressing one. Even if all the members of the League complied, it would take about three and a half months before an embargo proved effective—and that was only if the United States trimmed its exports to Italy back to the levels it shipped before 1935. It was no secret that America was doing a booming oil trade with Italy.

Eden sent off a telegram to Britain's man in Washington, Ronald Lindsay, to find out how the Americans would react to the idea. While he waited, he met late in the morning on February 20 with Ethiopia's ambassador, Charles Martin, who was anxious to make another appeal for his country, especially over the oil embargo. Martin reminded Eden of the devastating, continuous bombings and how he was personally afraid of heavy casualties because of the Ethiopians "rushing into pitched battle with the enemy."[49] Once again, he was looking for a public loan. If Ethiopia could get planes, as well as some proper arms and ammunition, he argued, it "would finish the war without any other Power being obliged to get implicated in it."[50]

The foreign secretary made sympathetic noises, but still couldn't offer a commitment. For his part, Eden noticed that Martin "seemed to be in some confusion as to the difference between a private and a public loan."[51] Finances weren't Martin's strong suit, and they would get him into trouble with others in the future.

Eden wasn't unsympathetic. In his notes on the meeting, he confessed, "I would appreciate how difficult it was for him when his country was continually asking for help, and he could show no signs that any help of any kind was forthcoming."[52] But Martin hadn't come for tea and sympathy; he was hoping for concrete action.

Martin got nowhere with Eden, and two days later, Eden got nowhere with Lindsay. When it came to the Americans, Lindsay suggested an oil embargo would bring "some expressions of shame and heartburnings in some volume and perhaps even pressure, but it would be ineffective, even if it became apparent that the United States alone were furnishing supplies."[53] The ambassador also presented a paradox. "Nevertheless, this course of action would do more than anything else to restore the League's prestige and to influence American opinion in favor of the collective peace system."[54] So even though an embargo would be useless, Lindsay thought it might still be good for the League's image.

Then came a surprising breakthrough, but it wasn't the government's idea at all. Instead, it came from the Labour Opposition, which asked: why can't Britain go it alone and impose its *own* oil embargo? Amazingly, the Cabinet adopted this on February 26, and Eden went back to Geneva to announce it to the League and the Committee of Eighteen. Then he discovered that he had offended the new French foreign minister. Pierre Étienne Flandin was beginning to quibble very much like Pierre Laval. If there were any more sanctions, he argued, Italy would abandon the League. Eden replied that this amounted to the aggressor choosing which sanctions to be applied.

"Flandin," he recalled, "continued to argue the Fascist case with blatant confidence, maintaining that the embargo would not work. I said that if the oil sanctions were not going to be effective, it was difficult to understand why Mussolini was making so much noise about it."[55]

Flandin could have made the case to Eden that Britain was throwing its weight around without first consulting its allies. But he focused instead on the tiresome notion that Mussolini would make good his threats. Eden thought the Sarraut government, just like Laval's, wanted to be a fair-weather friend. This only prompted Flandin to poison the well for the others, and he told the representative of Yugoslavia, "One of the disadvantages if Italy left Geneva would be that Britain would be left in a position of excessive preponderance in the League in future."[56]

By March 3, Flandin had managed to swing a Laval-like delay in his favor. Instead of an oil embargo promptly going into effect, one last attempt at conciliation should be made to win Mussolini back. Flandin had bought more time, and the Committee of Eighteen agreed to meet in a week to learn the results of his overture.

* * *

In Paris, Ethiopians and black activists followed the news and were naturally depressed by events, but they were also concerned about the response from America—or, rather, the lack of it. What was going on with the different support groups? A young African-American doctor, Charles Diggs, was living in Montmartre and had made connections with the Ethiopian legation. When he wrote to the *Pittsburgh Courier's* columnist George Schuyler, he reported that Ethiopians in Paris had no word that American organizations were accomplishing anything. The stakes were clear enough. "You and I know that this war is a struggle between the white and black race, and if we lose it, it is the end for us. There shall be no place on Earth where we can say is our own [sic] . . ."[57]

Diggs was looking to the black newspapers at home to provide leadership, because he thought the small organizations probably couldn't accomplish very much. And he guessed correctly that a few of them were scams. The right newspaper might be able to raise a couple of million dollars, he argued, to buy the Ethiopians planes. He'd met John Robinson in Paris on his way to Ethiopia, and the Brown Condor had explained how to buy aircraft privately. What's more, black expatriates and French leftists were already setting the bar high with their example. "There are people here who are sending two or three hundred francs each month to the Abyssinian legation."[58]

The man on the receiving end of this letter, George Schuyler, was a kind of African-American Christopher Hitchens, a columnist who started on the left and then made a hard right, skewering claptrap whenever he found it—at least as he saw it. He didn't like the Negro Renaissance. He despised traditional churches. And as for going to war for Ethiopia, he'd once dismissed the idea as ludicrous— blacks should organize an ambulance corps instead, buy small arms ammunition, raise funds to deposit in a major bank, do anything else but go fight. But even he conceded the lure of romanticism over the crusade.

Now Schuyler gave an entire column over to Diggs' letter at the end of February and offered his own appeal in his next one, gently shaming his readers. Are we standing against discrimination? Are we against inequalities? If we were *really* concerned . . . and on it went. White governments, he told them, "would be delighted to see [Ethiopia] defeated so they could fall upon her like the vultures they are and rend her limb from limb."[59] He urged his readers to open their wallets, add their names to lists, do something, do *more*—while there was still time.

* * *

Pietro Badoglio now set out to obliterate the armies of the two men he had always considered the real threat: Ras Kassa Haile Darge and Ras Seyum Mangasha. He had a vice, and he meant to squeeze. South of the rases' positions, his Third Army Corps swept across the Gheva valley below the River Geba, while to the north, the Eritrean Corps, as always, had the harder job of advancing on the stronghold of Amba Worq, a near-impregnable mountain where the Ethiopians were entrenched above the Warieu and Abaro passes.

Kassa got on his wireless and asked Haile Selassie if he could move his men, which was hardly necessary, as the Emperor had ordered him time and again to withdraw.[60] It didn't matter. Badoglio's men intercepted his message.[61] Kassa and Seyum had heard that Mulugeta had been attacked, but they had no idea of the devastation of the war minister's army, that the army was on the run, or that Mulugeta was dead. "What has happened to Ras Mulugeta?" Kassa asked in a message to the Emperor. "We have heard rumors that he has returned to his fortified position; is this true?"[62]

In the end, he and Seyum decided—for whatever reasons—that it was better to stand and fight than flee. Kassa was an intelligent man, but he belonged more in a church library than on a battlefield. He might have had a chance on his mountain if he knew or had remembered one simple fact: *Italy has Alps.*

On February 27, at one o'clock in the morning, the Italians, whose generals kept talking in terms of "scenes" and "acts," played out a sequence that belonged in an action movie. A young lieutenant, Tito Polo, led a small team of sixty men, half Blackshirts and half askari volunteers, to the northern base of the amba. Each man was traveling light for swift, silent movement—rifle, 120 cartridges, dagger, and five hand grenades.[63] They were patient as they made their way past garrison sentries, who dozed on as they planted their grenades. By five in the morning, Polo's team was at the summit, hauling up machine guns. Meanwhile, the battalions of General Alesandro Pirzio-Biroli were moving along the Warieu Pass to form a ring around the amba. And still the Ethiopians slept, with no one sounding the alarm.

When the grenades went off around dawn, the five hundred Ethiopian guards lost all discipline. They mistook the explosions for an aerial assault and, assuming the amba had been captured, fled for their lives down the mountain. George Steer, though he wasn't there, had spoken with his old sources and done his homework. The Ethiopians, he wrote, had lost the amba because of the psychological impact of carpet bombing. As usual with his unique insight, Steer looked beyond the battle and saw that a whole culture was being extinguished.

"Italian air supremacy made of the Ethiopians a rabble which could not think for itself. It demolished, in fearful explosions and vibrations of the solid earth, the aristocracy which was the cadre of their military organization. The people's support of that framework was very physical. It kissed its feet, hung on to its mule, crowded behind it in the streets, touched it when it walked, helped its limbs in every activity. The aerial supremacy of Italy abolished all these contacts in war forever."[64]

Kassa, however, wasn't going to let that framework die quietly. He was furious that the amba had been taken with such relative ease, and now he was going to make the Italians pay for it. Less than ten miles away to the southeast, Seyum felt the same way. The war drums beat, the horns blew, and a tide of Ethiopians, thousands strong, poured out of the nearby woods and hurtled themselves at the Italians on the hills of Debra Ansa. Irregular soldiers in white shammas ran forward with clubs and swords, covered by the more seasoned troops firing volleys. Blackshirts behind machine guns apparently couldn't hold their nerve, and sometimes the line almost broke, only for them to be saved again by askaris driving the Ethiopians back with bayonet charges.[65] This was the second Battle of Tembien.

The ferocity of the counterattack was so powerful that the Ethiopians managed to reach the outer parts of Warieu Pass, and Pirzio-Birolli sent in his reserve soldiers. The Ethiopians fought on for hours, from eight in the morning until four in the afternoon—aggressively, courageously, and in vain. An officer named Beyene, with medieval valor, rode his white horse into the thick of the fighting and was cut down.[66] And once again, Italian planes flew in to hammer the Ethiopians, dropping close to two hundred tons of explosives, about twice what they'd dropped on Mulugeta's wretched soldiers.[67]

As the sun went down, Seyum realized his retreat was cut off to the south, and he took his men and made for the Takkaze River, pursued by bombers. "The Ethiopians straggled along in disorder," wrote a reporter for *Corriere della Sera*, Alessandro Pavolini, who was up in one of the planes. "There was only one road open to them, and the fords were so narrow, the rocky walls of the ravines so precipitous that they were soon jammed together in a solid mass. Even though we were flying at [thirty-five hundred feet], we could see them quite plainly. Our plane swooped down, zigzagged along the defile, sowed its seeds of death, and zoomed upward."[68]

For Kassa, camped on Debra Amba above Abbi Addi, it was slowly sinking in that his position was hopeless. On February 29, he sent for his Russian military adviser, Colonel Feodor Konovalov. Konovalov, said Kassa, ought to head for Korem, where the Emperor and the last major army were supposed to be. The Russian asked what he would do, and Kassa claimed he would defend his mountain. Konovalov urged him to retreat instead, and the ras finally dispatched orders to his chiefs that they should fight until sundown and then make for a point on the Takkaze River, where their men would be supplied food. [69]

That evening, Kassa and his men left the amba, ditching their captured guns, their camp equipment, even their radios. The wounded in a Red Cross unit were allegedly abandoned as well, left for the Italians to find and promptly murder, according to an Ethiopian servant of the Irish medic, James Hickey.[70] For all his piety, Kassa might have had a streak of greed in his character. A British military attaché later wrote, "Kassa, having failed to pay his men, found he could not transport his money and is reported to have thrown a quantity of silver into the river during his retreat from the Tembien."[71]

As the Tigrayans and Shoans struggled to make their escape, they got the same treatment as Mulugeta's survivors. The planes came, and they fired machine guns, they bombed, they gassed. Konovalov was with them and wrote later that all they wanted to do was to go home. When Kassa and Seyum finally reached the base of their Emperor after two weeks, their numbers were pathetically small.

Once, there had been six huge armies with a multitude to face Mussolini's invasion. Now, there were only two great forces left: the Emperor and his army at Korem and Imru in the north. Badoglio decided he should go after Imru next, but while he might defeat the ras's army, he didn't know the measure of the man's character. Imru could not—would not—be defeated, even if he had to stand alone.

*   *   *

While the forests at last went quiet in the Tembien, Dr. John Melly was supervising the clumsy but dogged move of his British Red Cross unit at Alamata to Korem. A local commander named Legaba Tassa had sent two hundred soldiers to beat back a group of shiftas to the south. Now he was urging Melly and his people to move on for their own safety, taking along the patients brought in only a couple of days ago. Most were severe cases of mustard gas burns.[72] The *Times* correspondent, Walter M. Holmes, who had come out to tag along to Korem, counted 130 cases.[73]

It had been a long, slogging migration for Melly's unit, held up for six weeks because they needed to wait for the completion of road work. Even when on the move, they had to travel when the low cloud banks hindered bombers, and they often had to travel at night. At one point, the twelve Red Cross vehicles were stuck "in the midst of a chaotic straggling mass of irregular soldiers with thousands of pack mules and donkeys." With "tow-ropes and unloading and oaths," the convoy was on the road again two hours later.[74]

And now, finally to Korem—only the last leg wasn't easy, either. Down the steep mountain went the caravan of ambulances, split in half and spaced about an hour apart because the spiraling road was so treacherous. It took seven hours for one half to cover the twelve miles to its final destination.

On the Korem Plain, the Red Cross camp was organized in a square, with two massive Red Cross flags laid on the ground and a third, along with a Union Jack, flying from a couple of poles. The next morning, March 4, an Italian bomber circled low over the camp several times and then flew off to drop its loads on the hills and woods a couple of miles away. The doctors in the camp took little notice. As Melly started an operation at noon, he heard a plane flying over his tent and then a large bomb crashed into the ground about 150 yards away. "I thought the aviator was just being rude."[75] But a minute later, two more bombs fell into the camp, and then more.

One of the English staff blew a whistle to sound the alarm, and Melly and Dr. John Macfie dashed to the stream nearby to take cover. The plane flew over nine times, bombarding both the camp and the stream, raining forty bombs for more than half an hour. Five Ethiopians were killed and several others wounded. For Melly, there was no doubt that the attack had been deliberate. One of the two Red Cross flags on the ground took a direct hit.[76]

Chapter Fourteen

"... IF YOU THINK IT BETTER TO COME HERE AND DIE WITH US ..."

Ras Imru's intelligence gave him some idea of the behemoth coming for him. His sources in Eritrea warned of a new road being built to the Mareb frontier on his left flank, with thousands of Italian soldiers and tanks preparing for an advance. The news was a bit of a shock. He thought he was protected on this side by the pitiless, rocky Adi Abo Desert between him and the Mareb.[1] In fact, he'd already decided to take his army and retreat across the Takazze fords, but now it was clear it would be better to attack the enemy. So far, his guerrilla tactics had proved incredibly successful, and if he'd known that Kassa, Seyum, and Mulugeta had all been pushed off the board, he probably wouldn't have chosen a traditional head-on battle.[2] Still, he had a few ideas of how to put the odds more in his favor.

As usual, Marshal Pietro Badoglio went to his weapons chest, ignored the rapier, and pulled out a broadsword. It had worked for him so well in the past. Against Imru's ten thousand men, he would throw forty-seven thousand. General Maravigna's Second Army Corps, which Imru had managed to drive away from several outposts, was now given a chance to redeem itself and push down from Aksum. The Fourth Army Corps, under the command of General Ezio Babbini, would have to cross the Adi Abo Desert to attack the Ethiopians' left flank and rear—this was the army that Imru had learned about in advance.

At dawn on February 27, under a sunny cloudless sky, Maravigna sent out his men as if they were going on a training drill. The long column stretched out over the only working road, but Maravigna was so confident in their progress that he didn't bother to dispatch any patrols to scout for trouble. For hours, there wasn't a single Ethiopian in sight. Then, about noon, as Blackshirts split off to the left to take possession of the surrounding hills and another division was to forge ahead to Selaclaca, Imru sprung a surprise. His soldiers were hiding behind bushes and rocks at a point called Addi Haimanal, and now they blasted away, pinning the column in a cross-fire. They were shooting, in fact, at point-blank range, reaping the Italian soldiers like wheat as their comrades hurried to form an old-fashioned square to return fire, their artillery men frantically setting up their guns.

This was the Battle of Shire, and its first engagement went on for twelve straight hours.

Both sides would later acknowledge the courage of the other. An artillery shell would burst in a cluster of warriors, but out of the mangled, bloody bodies of the fallen, a handful of men would keep running towards their goal. For Imru's side, the prize was the convoy of trucks carrying ammunition, food, and other supplies. By midnight, Imru's men—with the exception of those in his personal guard—were down to twenty rounds each.[3] The marathon battle made such an impact that Maravigna decided he had to stop where he was. By the next morning, he was meekly asking for permission to do so from his commander. Badoglio could hardly believe what his general was telling him. Hadn't Maravigna almost five times the size of Imru's army? The man clearly gave his enemy too much credit. Badoglio didn't give them enough. When Maravigna decided at last on March 2 to move forward, Imru hit him again—hard. For four hours, they waged their counterattack on the Italians.

Where was the Fourth Army Corps to relieve the pressure on the Second? Still in the desert. Badoglio had assumed the Fourth would roll over a flat expanse, but the Adi Abo was a craggy moonscape etched with deep furrows. Badoglio couldn't put the blame for this on Maravigna; he would have to look in a mirror. You have to wonder why his aerial reconnaissance details, which presumably made trips over the region, simply didn't fly low enough to get a proper sense of the terrain. It's not as if there were any Oerlikons waiting for them out there on the rocks. And even if the photos were misleading, plain common sense should have prompted a change in Badoglio's strategy. As others have pointed out, here were soldiers of the Fourth Army Corps sent to cross fifty miles of a wasteland that was new to them, all while the Second Army Corps had to cover only *fifteen* miles over familiar ground—using a quite serviceable road.[4] They couldn't possibly link up on schedule, and Badoglio's claim later that the Fourth helped significantly at Shire was pure fiction.

The Fourth Army wasn't really needed. The broadsword was coming down, clubbing and hacking, its double-edge of artillery and bombings driving Imru's men into full retreat, and they "flooded back to the Takkaze."[5] Some took refuge in caves. When an interpreter called out that they would be spared if they gave up peacefully, the warriors in the darkness fought on until the last of them were killed.[6] In the aftermath, chemical warfare squads used flame-throwers to cremate the thousands of dead Ethiopians.

The next day, March 3, Imru and his surviving men reached the Takazze fords, encased by steep slopes, which were themselves blanketed by dense woods. It wasn't enough that the Second Army Corps had wiped out four thousand of Imru's troops. Badoglio didn't want the ras to escape into the mountain range of Tsellemti, so he sent in planes to drop eighty tons of bombs, including incendiaries to scorch the territory, and fire a hail of more than twenty-five thousand rounds of machine gun fire—all of it, in his words, "rendering utterly tragic the plight of the fleeing enemy."[7]

The marshal didn't mention in his book that in addition to the "utterly tragic" assault for which he was personally responsible, his planes also relied on gas. When Italian pilots were ordered to perform mop-up operations—strafing survivors— even they were shaken by the grisly panorama below them, a Hieronymus Bosch nightmare. Bodies lay along the banks of the Takkaze, bodies of men, bodies of cattle, thousands of bodies . . . Bodies lay along the caravan routes, decaying, rotting, and still more bodies could be spotted as the planes droned on, grotesque commas on a page of empty landscape.

Another army's back was broken, along with its spirit. Imru hoped to carry on a guerrilla war from the mountains of Tsellemti and Simien, but Ayalew Birru "would have nothing to do with it and with his brother, Admasu, made his way to Begemder. Day by day, my ranks thinned out, many were killed in the course of air attacks, many deserted."[8] Imru was nearly killed himself when a low-flying pilot spotted him in his uniform, and the ras ran for his life behind some bushes as machine gun fire tore into the ground.

But this was not the end. The Italians had broken his army, but they hadn't broken the man. Imru assigned himself a new mission, one that was a journey to reach his cousin, the Emperor. Like an African Bonnie Prince Charlie, he would cross miles and miles of potentially hostile territory to try to reach his goal.

*   *   *

The world stopped caring for a while about Ethiopia, and it was all because of Berlin. There, a very different invasion was being planned by Germany's commander-in-chief. If he'd had his way, he wouldn't have gone through with it at all. But orders were orders, especially when they came from the Fuehrer. Adolf Hitler wanted to reoccupy the Rhineland.

General Werner von Blomberg doubted his soldiers would get away with it. He expected the French would rush in and be breathing down his soldiers' necks within minutes, making quick work of them. This was not the proud Wehrmacht of the future that stormed through Europe—not yet. In fact, Blomberg had so little confidence in his forces that soldiers had orders to retreat if they even glimpsed the French coming their way.

But the Germans had nothing to worry about. At dawn on March 7, only three battalions crossed the Rhine River. They met no resistance. The French hadn't moved against them, in part, because they simply couldn't believe what they were hearing. Military intelligence finally called the army general staff in Paris at nine-forty-five in the morning to confirm the news of the reoccupation, but still not one soldier of France stood in the Germans' way. It took until the next day for Prime Minister Albert Sarraut to demand from the commander-in-chief of the French army, Maurice Gamelin, just what he planned to do about the Germans causally wading into the demilitarized zone. Gamelin only wanted general mobilization—a tedious recall of troops on leave, of redeployment of men by train—instead of a swift, decisive response. And while he expected France might do well in the beginning if the incident provoked a war, he didn't believe his army could beat the Germans in the long run if it had to fight alone without allies.

Hitler had already announced his bold move in the Kroll Opera House, which was serving as the home of the German parliament because the Reichstag had suspiciously burned to a smoking hulk three years before. The French, he claimed, had broken the Locarno Treaty by cozying up to Russia. Any excuse would serve. While hysterical Nazis screamed, saluted, and cried in a display of fanaticism that William Shirer, looking on, called "gruesome," Hitler waited for the applause to ebb and then muttered in a low voice with messianic theatricality: "We have no territorial demands to make in Europe . . . Germany will never break the peace!"[9]

When the cheering at last subsided, Shirer spotted a few generals leaving the Opera House, their fixed smiles barely hiding their anxiety. He saw Blomberg, whose "face was white, his cheeks twitching."[10]

In Paris, Pierre-Étienne Flandin waited until Sunday to send off a message of protest to the League of Nations, giving the Germans an entire weekend to dig in and secure their positions. And in the end, Stanley Baldwin decided not to back any military move by France. Hitler had pulled it off. He took the Rhineland completely by bluff, which he confirmed later. The Ethiopian War had taught him all he needed to know about how to get around the French and the British.

* * *

George Steer went around one last time to the house of Everett Colson to say goodbye. He was anxious to catch up to Haile Selassie, wherever he might be (the correspondents in Addis Ababa weren't sure). Colson was also due to travel soon, but not to the side of the Emperor. He was going home, his health past its breaking point. Steer found him in bed and was disturbed to see the American looking ghastly pale, struggling to breathe. "He was my greatest friend in Ethiopia and I was sorry he had to go," he recalled. "He looked so ill, I wondered if I would see him again."[11]

Colson knew it was all over—not for him, but for Ethiopia's struggle. He confided to Steer that the government had just received a phone call from Gonder. The Italians were a day's march out, and the Ethiopians would have to surrender because there was no one left to defend the town.

"But where are Imru and Ayalew?" asked Steer.

"That is Imru and Ayalew," Colson replied. "The other soldiers went home because they said they could not fight against gas. It's getting the Emperor under the skin, too."[12]

It was around this time that three high-ranking conservative nobles who had been at Amba Aradam surprisingly hatched a revolt. Instead of being cowed by Mulugeta's humiliation up on Aradam, the defeat seemed to push them to foolish desperation, and they wanted to replace the crown prince, as well as probably the Emperor himself, with one of their own faction. But the treachery was prevented before it could really get started, and the trio was packed off in chains down to the capital.[13]

Soon after, the Emperor composed a message to the one general left who might still accomplish a victory. He wrote to Imru, "Our army, famous throughout Europe for its valor, has lost its name; brought to ruin by a few traitors, to this pass is it reduced . . . For yourself, if you think that with your troops and with such of the local inhabitants as you can collect together you can do anything where you are, do it; if on the other hand, your position is difficult and you are convinced of the impossibility of fighting, having lost all hope on your front, and if you think it better to come here and die with us, let us know of your decision by telephone from Dabat. From the League, we have so far derived no hope and no benefit."[14]

Imru could not come die with them—because he never got the invitation. The courier with the message was captured, and Badoglio printed its text later in his war memoir.

*   *   *

John Spencer—the young American lawyer who took over Everett Colson's duties—easily grasped what France's prime minister was up to by calling one last time for the two sides to talk. The specter of Laval wasn't far from the elbow of Pierre-Étienne Flandin when it came to the issue of Ethiopia.

But the more senior members of Haile Selassie's team thought conciliation was still worth a gamble. Spencer was overruled. Assigned to write the reply to Geneva's latest overture, he had the chance to pick some carefully chosen words to at least *try* to protect their side. Spencer was also tipped off by a reliable source that if a ceasefire was called, Flandin would blame Ethiopia for any minor clash and move quickly to withdraw all sanctions, as well as any European involvement. His source was reliable—it was the German chargé d'affaires in Addis Ababa.[15]

On this matter, at least, Spencer managed to convince the others to cross out any references to a ceasefire. Within a matter of days, the opportunity—if there ever really was one—evaporated. The Committee of Thirteen, the one that was supposed to tackle the chronology of events and also broker mediation, put off its scheduled meeting as the Rhineland Crisis eclipsed all other news. And Spencer suspected that Hitler's bold gambit had pushed France further into Italy's arms. Pompeo Aloisi returned to Rome, and no amount of pleading by the Committee's chairman or indignant remarks from Anthony Eden would get him to budge. Aloisi wouldn't come to Geneva, he said, until April 15.

March was a month of intrigue. Throughout the war, and even after Italy declared it officially over, back channels were always open between the two sides. Like a counterfeit coin, Afawarq Gabra-Iyassus was always in circulation, and now the diplomat was on his way home from Rome, taking a moment out of his stop in Djibouti to visit the Italian consulate. He claimed that he could negotiate on the Emperor's behalf for peace, but nothing came of it, despite his generous terms for Italy. By late March, when the ailing Colson had reached Alexandria, he was approached about possible negotiations, too.[16] Nothing came of that either.

And as the weeks passed, neither side saw any point in a ceasefire.

* * *

The Swedish pilot and adventurous count, Carl Gustav von Rosen, put his airplane through acrobatic maneuvers as he flew through a narrow valley, playing the usual cat-and-mouse game with Italian fighters. By now, his passenger, Marcel Junod, knew that the bright Red Cross painted on the aircraft meant nothing to Italian aviators. If they were spotted, he was sure they would be instantly shot down. It was March 16, and they had braved these skies to bring medical supplies and fetch a wounded doctor of the Dutch Red Cross unit. Soon after, Junod and von Rosen were astride mules, making their way along the mountain tracks to

Haile Selassie's headquarters, when Junod picked up the distinctive horseradish smell. He was told that every day, the Italians used gas.

Once they arrived near the firefly glow of campfires, they were led into the cave for the imperial retinue, divided into chambers with heavy wall hangings. Junod found the Emperor in one of two garden chairs, looking sad and depressed. "Have you any news?" he asked the doctor. "Is there any message from the League of Nations?"

Once again, Junod had to remind him that he didn't represent the League.

"Yes, I know," answered Haile Selassie, "but I thought you might nevertheless have a message for me."[17]

Junod briefed the Emperor on the critical state of affairs of the various ambulance units. The next morning, Capronis appeared overhead and efficiently blew the Emperor's plane to bits—despite camouflage, its shape stood out against the bushes and trees. Junod and von Rosen raced to their own craft, hoping that if they pulled off its camouflage, maybe, just once, the Red Cross emblem would ward off an attack. The Italian planes were already trying to bomb it.

Soon Junod's eyes began to feel a sting. Unfortunately, an Ethiopian mechanic had accidentally carried off the doctor's gas mask when he ran for cover during the bombings.[18] The next day, when von Rosen casually touched a bush, his hand and wrist would be burned. He could also now feel the effects of the gas, the sensation of burning on his tongue and in his nostrils. But the more immediate problem as they lay flat on the ground was that the Capronis shot their plane's fuel tank full of holes and then blew it with incendiaries into charred rubble. And just for good measure, they tossed bombs at the pack mules on the airfield.

To Junod, it was obvious the pilots recognized the Red Cross emblem. He and von Rosen were now stuck about six hundred miles from Addis Ababa. It was worse for the wounded Dutch physician, robbed of a swift flight to where he could receive care in better facilities. And the planes came back later, making another bombardment.

Junod decided to head back to the Emperor's base to ask for a vehicle that could transport their patient. The others would have to wait where they were. He rushed his way along hills slippery with dried grass and pine needles, unable to stop for Ethiopians who were clearly suffering. There was a noise of a banal yet insistent drone, a chant that grew in its haunting volume.

As Junod came over the last hill, he spotted what must have been thousands of Ethiopians, each flayed by the scorching liquid dropped from the planes. He was horrified by the sight of their suppurating burns.

"Abiet," they moaned. "Abiet . . . Abiet . . ." *Have pity . . . Have pity . . .*[19]

* * *

Haile Selassie loaned Junod and von Rosen a truck to take them back to Dessie, where von Rosen could get a plane to fly them to Addis Ababa. In granting the vehicle, the Emperor told them to be careful. Junod asked him if he meant the Italian planes. The Emperor meant the shiftas.[20]

The remnants of Ras Kassa's army finally spotted the blue expanse of Lake Ashangi and the tiny center of Korem on March 20. As soldiers milled around campfires and pack mules wandered about in their sullen and cranky way, the European advisers for Kassa were led to the caves being used as bomb shelters. They had to report to the Emperor. Practically the entire staff from the imperial household had set up shop here, and servants went about their duties in a pavilion tent. As for the Emperor, the strain had made him lose weight, but not his resolve. He gently interrogated the White Russian, whose advice had all too often been ignored by Kassa.

"Are you convinced that Ras Kassa couldn't hold on to the Tembien any longer?" asked Haile Selassie. "Was he really forced to retire?"[21]

Konovalov kept his answer vague. He didn't want to depress the Emperor with the specifics in a more candid appraisal. He could have talked about the "total ineptitude of the chiefs, the complete disorganization and demoralization of their forces," but he didn't. "What do you think of the situation, Sire?"

"It's all going normally," replied the Emperor. "Up to now we have resisted as best we might and kept them back—I see nothing very dangerous in the situation." It seems a peculiar thing to say, but perhaps Haile Selassie was trying to project confidence. As wine and apples were brought, he looked to the Russian with a smile and commented, "I suppose it's been a long time since you have eaten fruit?"[22]

The interview complete, he made sure the Europeans were each given a new set of boots, a blanket, and camping gear, along with permits that allowed them to travel down to the capital with John Melly's Red Cross unit. "After all those months of privation and fatigue," Konovalov wrote later, "I was going home at last."[23]

Only he wasn't. The next day, Konovalov was about to leave when he got word that the Emperor wanted to see him again. He found Haile Selassie waiting for him, holding a notebook with decorated covers.

"I have decided to attack the Italians at their camp near Mai Chew before they have gathered in force," said the Emperor. He showed the Russian a sketch of the mountains, and with less regal confidence, he added, "I am not an engineer like you, and you'll probably think my draft plan a wretched one."

Whatever Konovalov thought of his draftsmanship, the Emperor had an assignment for him. "I want you to visit these mountains with three of our officers who were at St. Cyr* and make a complete plan of the region occupied by the enemy as well as a note of possible positions for us."[24]

With the graduates in tow, Konovalov headed out on March 21, and soon, from the vantage point of a tall mountain, he took in the spectacular sweep of the hills and valleys near Mehoni, where the Italians were preparing for their final push. Through his binoculars, he spotted a couple of observation posts and what he suspected was an artillery station. He wasn't impressed with what he found. The weather was making it tough for the Italians to lengthen their road—essential to keeping their supply line intact. And if it wasn't the rain causing problems, the earth stubbornly resisted demolition. Konovalov noted that the soldiers were digging trenches with picks and shovels, but their fortifications were modest, with barricades made out of tree trunks and without barbed wire.

So the Russian returned to base and reported to the Emperor what he had seen. The trouble was that the Italians had several opportunities to shore up their arms and position afterwards, and it seems that *no one* ordered a follow-up recon of the Italian camp.

All of this would come back to damage Konovalov's reputation down the line, and in the most bizarre fashion imaginable. Why did he give such low estimates? Had he *deliberately* played down the strength of the enemy? Why would he? All of these questions waited in the future.

For the time being, the Russian offered his encouraging picture of how bad the Italian defenses were.

* * *

Harar was beautiful in the early decades of the twentieth century, just as parts of it are still beautiful today, its old town with a kasbah-like honeycomb of stone walls and multiple mosques, now a UNESCO World Heritage site. It was considered by some to be the "fourth holy city" of Islam. But it wasn't a treasure to the world in late March of 1936, and so the first wave of bombings in the Ogaden earned little of its attention. After the obliteration of Ras Desta's army, the east had been almost forgotten.

Now it was about to become important again. This was because of another drama of rivalry and squabbling that had been playing out in the Italian military all this time. Badoglio and Mussolini, having grown more confident of winning, both began to nag and prod Rodolfo Graziani with telegram after telegram to get back in the game. The Butcher of Fezzan couldn't believe what he was reading.

---

* The military school in France

He had practically begged his Duce and Badoglio to free up men, supplies, and vehicles for *weeks* so that he could advance! *Now* they expected him to push recklessly in, away from the safety of his base in Italian Somaliland? He wouldn't be rushed, and cabled Mussolini to tell him so.

In the meantime, he would soften up enemy positions with an aerial assault. From March 21 until four days later, the planes bombed Jijiga, Harar, and the smaller towns like Birkut and Degehabur. On March 22, Jijiga was bombed for more than an hour.

Days later, on March 29, two large squadrons of Italian bombers flew over Harar in the early morning, quickly got the lay of the land in Ethiopia's second largest city, and then came back at around quarter after seven to try to pound it into oblivion. The Italians would claim Harar was a legitimate target as a military base, but there were no anti-aircraft guns to fend them off. It was an "open city," completely defenseless, while all the firepower was at the genuine base of Jijiga. For two and a half hours, the incendiaries fell, and the city burned. Beyond the sand-brown wall had been the Egyptian Red Crescent Hospital, clearly marked and just as clearly camped there not to handle any soldiers within the city, but those who streamed in from fifty miles away in Jijiga. The Italians dropped fifteen bombs on it, and for good measure, bombarded the Ethiopian Red Cross that was camped even farther off.

Once it was over, the casualty list sounded unimpressively low: about forty killed and 120 wounded. But thousands were made homeless, parts of their ancient city wiped out, never to be the same. The bombs took out the old gibbi, a French hospital and the French consulate, a radio station, a prison, even the Orthodox cathedral, which held the tomb of Haile Selassie's father, Ras Makonnen. What some considered the oldest mosque in Africa was destroyed.

Thousands of miles away, Jomo Kenyatta was walking in Hertfordshire with a friend, and he noticed headlines in the newspapers on the bombing of Harar. Its emotional impact on him was profound. This was Africa's Guernica, about a year before the bombing of the real one in Spain. But Guernica would be in the newspapers of the world for days. Guernica would have a masterpiece by Pablo Picasso. The irony is that Guernica became famous thanks to the dogged reportage of George Steer, who didn't know it yet, but would be covering Spain's civil war for *The Times* of London. Spain's torment, however, was in the future. Steer's story on the bombing of Harar was on the front page of the *New York Times* above the fold on March 30, and he tried to point out—yet again—that if open towns wouldn't be respected in Africa, there was nothing to bar them from being cherry-picked as targets in Europe.[25]

Harar landed right in the lap of Anthony Eden in London, but he had little time to wring his hands over Ethiopia. He was becoming increasingly preoccupied with the threat of Germany, and Stanley Baldwin had already told him that he wanted closer relations with Hitler than Britain had with Mussolini. Eden had asked, "How?"

"I have no idea," snapped Baldwin. "That is your job."[26]

Then on April 1, the Opposition in the House of Commons vented its outrage over Harar squarely in his direction. Hugh Dalton, a Labour MP but frequent ally of Winston Churchill's, asked Eden, "Is the Right Honorable Gentleman aware that British public opinion is increasingly stirred by these horrible atrocities which are being perpetrated, and when are His Majesty's Government going to take any further step to end it, at least by refusing to supply British oil to these murderous airmen?"[27]

Eden gave a tepid, indirect answer to this, spotting the trap of the oil question. He merely told Dalton that the government was "just as anxious as he can be to bring this war, and the miserable suffering consequent upon it, to an end." No, he had no information on whether the Ethiopians had advance warning of the bombing raid.

Another Labour MP, Reginald Sorenson, got to his feet to ask, "Is the Right Honorable Gentleman aware that considerable pleasure at the result of the raid has been registered by many supporters of the Government, who are also readers of the *Daily Mail?*" Then as now, the *Mail* was one of London's more conservative newspapers.

The question gave Eden a number of easy outs, and he replied simply, "The Honorable Member does not suppose that I like these raids any more than he does."

But it was another Labour MP who scored the sharpest point, one that was all too prophetic. The Midland radical, Geoffrey Mander, asked sarcastically, "Are these the people who are now going to police the Rhineland?"[28]

* * *

With what remained of his personal bodyguard, Ras Imru tramped through the night along detours and side roads, anxious to catch up to the Emperor. The local populations along the way had been hammered down by war, bombs, and the scavenging of deserters and shiftas. Imru knew there should be a working telephone at Dabat, but as he and his small band of men got closer, it was clear the Italians had already captured Dabat. He tried for Gonder. The enemy was there, too. It was "only by a hair's breadth," he told historian Angelo Del Boca years later, "that I escaped capture."[29]

He pressed on, trying now for Debra Markos. The journey would take him a month. Bands of rebels—well compensated by Italian agents—wreaked havoc along the mountain countryside of Gojjam, harassing and attacking Imru and his men whenever they dared raise their heads.

* * *

If the Ethiopians could hang on for a few more precious weeks, Badoglio and his men would be shut out of the interior by curtains of summer rain, the annual downpour that made sludge out of roads and mountain passes. The stalemate could prove deadly to Mussolini, more concerned with prestige than anything else. It would allow the warriors to dig in for the long-awaited guerrilla strategy, the one that Haile Selassie had urged on his men for so long and which several military experts in the West argued was their only chance.

And yet now the Emperor was going to disregard his own advice.

Haile Selassie would be going up against the might of Badoglio with less than half the number of soldiers that he'd sent off months ago under Mulugeta. He had his imperial guard, better armed than any of the other forces, with about twenty 75-mm and 37-mm guns, as well as six mortars. There were also the battle-experienced but demoralized survivors of Enderta and Tembien. And then there was the untested army of another ras, Getachew Abate, who had his position mostly because he was related to the empress. Years ago, he'd gotten himself fired as ambassador to Paris for spending the legation's money on himself like a drunken sailor on a lottery cruise.[30] As with so many others, he had faced rebellion, not modern war.

There were additional soldiers and irregulars who had been mustered as well from the areas around the capital. But altogether, these forces added up to a little more than thirty thousand men.

To top it off, Haile Selassie had few artillery pieces to start his assault and no air cover; worse, he had no radio communications. What he did have was Kassa and Seyum, who had failed. But because of their rank, they had to be entrusted with field commands again. He also hoped the Azebu Oromo—who had so ruthlessly picked on Mulugeta's survivors after Enderta—would throw in their lot with him for once. The Oromo went away with striped silk shirts and black satin capes, with Mannlicher and Alpini rifles, and with the heavy silver coins of the Ethiopian Mint. The Italians had often bribed them; he would pay them more.

He didn't need to risk a conventional last-stand battle at all. If the plan he showed Konovalov was not a wretched one, it was certainly desperate, bordering on military suicide, and yet he chose to go through with it anyway. Being the man that Haile Selassie was, his decision seems inevitable. If his reign was ordained by God, God might test him, but surely wouldn't let him fail in the end. A wireless message he sent to his wife on March 27 suggested he still believed this: "Since our trust is in our Creator and in the hope of His help, and as we have decided to advance and enter the fortifications, and since God is our only help, confide this decision of ours in secret to the Abun, to the ministers and dignitaries, and offer up to God your fervent prayers."[31]

He might also have felt that one last battle might rally his people and even prove useful to the international campaign. Newspaper photos of him manning his Oerlikon had helped, but now the world would have its confirmation that he was in the thick of it, and those of good conscience in the rain-drizzled London streets and in the corridors of power in Geneva would *know*. More importantly, *he* would know. He had promised to fight and shed his blood with his people. Everything suggests he wanted to keep his word.

He originally intended to shock Badoglio with his attack on March 24, a Tuesday, but there were delays. The Ethiopians decided to throw a feast in one of the caves, one to which both the high- and low-born could take part. The tej flowed freely, poured in little zinc containers, and traditional raw meat was served. After the meal, the Emperor debriefed Konovalov, who was back from his recon mission with the three officers trained at St. Cyr. Running a hand over his battle plans, Haile Selassie said, "Don't destroy the enemy who come over to us, but make them prisoner and send them to the rear."[32]

But there were more delays. Chiefs complained that not all of their men had arrived and assembled. There was word from the commander of the imperial guard that the offensive was waiting on delivery of a 75-mm gun. Italian planes flew overhead, and soldiers congratulated themselves as they managed to hit a couple of them. One of the planes soared so low that many in the camp feared it might fly right into the mouth of their cave. Haile Selassie watched it cut across the sky and remarked, "They are really very brave."[33]

And they were accurate, providing plenty of casualties to treat for the young surgeon, Dr. Malaku Bayen, the man who had brought Ethiopia the Brown Condor. Malaku "worked unceasingly, close to the Emperor's cavern." He stayed close, because if the Emperor was ever wounded, he didn't trust Western doctors to take good care of him.

Konovalov was getting fed up with the lack of momentum. A dejazmach had promised he'd found a good spot to dig a trench where the Emperor could observe the front line, but to the Russian's disgust, the man "had done nothing; he had not even told us that he had done nothing."[34] Konovalov took a work detail of men and had the trench dug under his orders. It took the entire evening. Yet another war council was held where the passionate voices rolled over each other, making a cantankerous din. Outside, their soldiers were so bored and restless that some fired their rifles into the air, wasting precious ammunition. They were promptly flogged for this, but it didn't drown out the argument at the council. And Haile Selassie finally acquiesced to another delay.

As the Ethiopians dawdled, the Italians were putting their time to good use. They had been tipped off on two fronts that an attack was imminent. One, Haile Selassie's telegram to Empress Menen was intercepted like all the others, and two, they heard the news from a defector, who crossed over on March 29 or 30 and apparently told the Italians that the attack was mere hours away. When the Ethiopians finally launched their offensive, Badoglio's troops were ready for them. And yet, even in this final showdown, the marshal would discover things wouldn't completely go his way.

Haile Selassie had a chance to call it off—there was a warning sign. Only the night before his men were set to head out, Italian planes dropped gas over the territory in front of their positions. But he would not be put off. He told his officers that if they smelled yperite, they ought to change direction quickly, and if hit by the gas, they should wash themselves immediately. Luckily, much of the gas had evaporated by the time they were on their way. In the hours before dawn, the warriors marched out in three designated columns, two of them led by Kassa and Seyum, and they planted their machine guns mere yards away from the trenches freshly dug by the Italians.

At about quarter to six in the morning, a Mauser pistol was fired twice.

Two red rockets shot upward, slicing into the cobalt sky of the new morning. Now there were yells: *"Mekele! Alagi!"*

With machine guns blazing cover fire, the Ethiopians hurled themselves into enemy trenches for hand-to-hand combat. As an Italian battalion commander ordered his own signal rockets to request artillery, he was shot down. The Italians couldn't replace men on the front line quick enough; no sooner was one soldier killed over his machine gun than the Ethiopians killed the next one. Mai Chew was a grim final exam for some students from a military school in Harar. There was theory, and then there was the reality of your schoolmate coughing blood. They fought on, and still the line wouldn't buckle. It was no longer the sad collection of trenches and a half-finished road promised by Konovalov. Knowing the Ethiopians were coming, Badoglio had steered his artillery into place and shored up his fortifications.

There was also a ridiculous distraction, and culture was behind it. Even as Haile Selassie gave orders and fired a machine gun, warriors abandoned their posts and rushed up to him with their spoils captured in battle, performing war songs. The Emperor had no time for this, and soon, none of the others would either.

At eight o'clock in the morning, the planes came.

The Emperor barked out an order for the Oerlikon guns to be redeployed. Instead of providing cover fire for the soldiers, they needed to fire up at the Capronis. Then he slipped behind one of the guns himself and let out a deadly burst. For the most part, the Ethiopians had seldom downed any of the Italians' planes, but at Mai Chew, thirty-six out of seventy went spinning with trails of smoke into the countryside. But was it enough? The planes still did horrific damage to both Ras Seyum's and Ras Kassa's columns.

By nine in the morning, Haile Selassie knew his tide couldn't wear down the Italian rock. He decided to hit Badoglio's left flank, and the marshal was unusually charitable in recalling the maneuver: "This time the whole of the Imperial Guard, supported by a lively fire, moved against our positions, advancing in rushes and making good use of the ground, giving proof of a solidity and a remarkable degree of training combined with a superb contempt for danger."[35]

Both sides fought with a hideous will. At one hill, the Italians for the Second Division were forced to rush forward in a bayonet charge against a hail of machine gun fire. No sooner had they taken the hill than the Ethiopians rallied, and the Italians launched another charge of bayonets to claim it a second time. Italian survivors at Mai Chew would testify to the courage of their enemy. One captured Ethiopian soldier—wounded so badly that gray matter was visible from his head wound—refused to accept the stretcher the Italians offered him. He would die standing, he told them. Impressed by his valor, the Italians urged him to lie down. What he was doing was pointless, it served no purpose. The soldier insisted on standing. Like others in his ranks, he had promised to win or die, and since they hadn't won yet . . . Leaning against a boulder, he pointed to the landscape covered in dead Ethiopians.[36]

Watching it all, Konovalov was less impressed. The Ethiopians were brave, yes, but they didn't follow through to make any gains count or to hold onto new positions. Gunners blasted away at anything and at random, sometimes hitting their own men. It didn't help that the warriors didn't wait for the artillery to soften a position—they merely charged a fortification on their own whims. The point of a tactical assault was lost on the Emperor as well. Ordering the artillery to fire, he told his adviser, "Our men must hear their artillery shooting. It will give them courage and improve their morale."[37]

Konovalov despaired. In many places, the new Italian walls were only two feet high, and only a few were built so that a machine gun nest would fit in the slapdash masonry. Perfect targets. "If anybody in the Ethiopian army besides the Emperor had known how to fire artillery," Konovalov wrote later, "they could have been shot to pieces."[38]

The final insult was when the Azebu Oromo made their last choice. They attacked the Ethiopians.

By four in the afternoon, a slate gray sky covered the destruction on the lonely stretch of Tigray. A light drizzle fell. Men died, and the machine guns and artillery roared on, and the small droplets that pattered on the ground were indifferent to all this cacophonous rage. All three columns had failed to achieve their goals, and as the night descended, the Emperor ordered his forces to withdraw. The Italians were wise enough not to pursue the retreating army. Many of the askaris, who had borne the brunt of the offensive as usual, would discover they barely had any rounds left.

Once he was back at his temporary base, Haile Selassie cabled his wife and described the day's fighting: "Our chiefs and trusted soldiers are dead or wounded. Although our losses are heavy, the enemy, too, has been injured. The Guard fought magnificently and deserve every praise. The Amhara troops also did their best. Our troops, even though they are not adapted for fighting of the European type, were able to bear comparison throughout the day with the Italian troops. The Galla [Oromo] helped us only with shouts, not with their strong right arm."[39]

For these glorious moments of honor, Haile Selassie and his soldiers would pay dearly. There was no Red Cross anymore to tend to the wounded; Melly's unit had evacuated. The supply train was late, and the men who were on their feet for hours, shooting away or slashing with their swords, were now weak with hunger. In dismay, the Emperor told Konovalov, "I fail to understand the role of the League of Nations. It seems quite impotent."[40]

The Emperor summoned what remained of his nobles and tried to lift their spirits with a long speech, suggesting they fade into the mountains around Korem to continue the fight. The younger chiefs were still willing to launch a fresh attack from their current position.

But no one beyond the mouth of the cave was in any shape for that. The mood, in fact, was one of funereal gloom, an atmosphere that wasn't helped by the droning of priests and the tedious, steady ringing of a large bell. Once-proud warriors milled about, drifting and in shock with no place to go, and when it was time for women and boys to bring the regular meal, they quickened their pace because the Italians had sent bombers to harass the retreat. The women carried baskets of *injura* and clay pots covered with a red cloth, holding *wot*, leaving these dishes by the mouth of the cave and then scampering off for shelter. They couldn't go in, not while the council was in session.

Discipline was breaking down. At one point, Haile Selassie turned to a chief with a prominent sword scar across his forehead and said, "You see that mountain covered with bush. You must occupy it with your men and stop the *ferengi* from taking it."

The man stared blankly, and Konovalov, looking on, speculated that the chief had no clue as to how many Italians might be threatening the targeted hill or, for that matter, how many soldiers he still had himself. He seemed rooted to his spot until Haile Selassie snapped, "Go on!"

But only two hours later, Konovalov spotted the chief perched on a heap of stones, talking to others "without a care in the world."[41] Of the warriors left under his command, the chief had found only fifty, and so he shooed them off to the hill while he stayed behind.

Word was trickling back that the Italians were now on the move, coming up fast to engulf what remained of the Emperor's army. The Ethiopians would head down towards Lake Ashangi and Korem. When the Emperor chose to divvy up the possessions he couldn't possibly bring along on the retreat—clothing, preserved food, liquor, cartridges—a mob filled the cave and proved so determined in their greed that guards had to clear a path for him with angry shouts and blows. As the long train of soldiers took to the road, the order was given to blow up the shells and rifle ammunition along with any drums of fuel. Better for it to burn than become useful to the enemy.

And in the crackling flames were a few remaining shirts and capes intended to be gifts for the Azebu Oromo.

*   *   *

When Stanislaw Belau was safely home in Geneva, he renounced the statement he'd signed for the Italians and told the story of his harrowing ordeal. Torture, denial of medical treatment, imprisonment of a neutral operative of the Red Cross—it was all lurid and caused a lot of controversy.

The propaganda mill in Rome did its best to shred his character: the doctor was suddenly a deserter from the Polish army—oh, and he was a deserter from the Ethiopian Red Cross, too. He wasn't Belau at all, he was Beloff. He didn't have a legal passport. He didn't have an actual medical degree. One can almost hear the panic in the formal message sent to the Council of the League of Nations. "At Massawa, [Belau] spontaneously disavowed a declaration he had signed at

Dessie," wrote Italy's Fulvio Suvich, "and today in Switzerland, he disavows the disavowal he made at Massawa . . . I beg you to communicate the present telegram to the States Members of the League of Nations."[42]

To all this, Belau sent the League a brief, dispassionate set of facts for his military background, including his passport number. Sidney Brown came to his defense, but the International Committee of the Red Cross seems to have made only tepid efforts to champion its own doctor. A series of polite requests were issued, first for an explanation, then for the property and money the Italian soldiers had confiscated back at Amba Aradam, and then for the proper return, as stipulated under the Geneva Convention, of medical supplies to the Ethiopians. The Italians ignored them all. Badoglio joked that had the Poles been soldiers instead of medical men, "there would be no need to talk about them now."[43] Mussolini wasn't in a laughing mood over the Poles. Rather than let them go home, "we should have shot them instead and thrown them into the heap."[44]

In addition to Belau's imprisonment, there were now so many horror stories of gas attacks and hospital bombings that the International Committee of the Red Cross had to do something, or at least be *seen* to do something. An investigative commission should be set up, an inquiry held—ostensibly to check violations of the Geneva Convention on both sides. But then, incredibly, the Committee decided it should consult *Rome* on how to do this. Its top men would go visit, including its president, Max Huber, who believed there were things better said in person to the Italians "that one cannot publish."[45] No such visit was planned for Ethiopia.

Meanwhile, the news reports were also forcing the hand of the League of Nations, and the Committee of Thirteen decided to pass on Ethiopian "complaints" over gas to Italy on March 23 and request answers, while politely reminding Mussolini's government that it had signed the League's 1925 protocols that prohibited gas warfare. The pressure should have been on. The very next day, Huber and his fellow Committee delegates arrived in Rome, and six days later, they were granted a visit with Mussolini for what amounted to a social call. But when Huber, his vice-president, and the others finally sat down to talk with Italian officials, Rome had already set the ground rules.

Mussolini's man in Geneva, Pompeo Aloisi, had come home to help smooth things over, and he warned Huber that if the issue of gas was brought up, the Fascist government would consider any conclusions reached by the inquiry to be a "purely arbitrary verdict."[46] Huber inexplicably complied. The only backbone he showed was to make a passing reference to mustard gas—one that everyone present chose to ignore.[47] When the meetings were over, the press were simply told that Italy never meant any harm to the Red Cross and that it would respect its emblem. In private, Mussolini got Aloisi to spread the word: the gas isn't lethal, and never mind if it was lethal or not, Italians had only used it to avenge Ethiopian atrocities.[48] What happened? Huber's outrage had dissipated into nothing, and so apparently had the influence and the credibility of the Red Cross. Historian Rainer Baudendistel suggests the Committee men didn't want to be seen as anti-Italian, and perhaps some delegates still couldn't bring themselves to believe the truth.[49]

In our own age, we've seen this same international disbelief. Initial news reports portrayed the wars in Bosnia and Kosovo, for instance, as "two sides at each other's throats" until the incontrovertible evidence piled up that demonstrated Serbian leaders ruthlessly started both conflicts. The world clucked its tongue despairingly over the genocide in Rwanda as "tribal warfare" when the national government in Kigali developed a calculated plan for the slaughter of thousands of Tutsis and their Hutu sympathizers. Huber and his team were sitting at the conference table with their own kind, men of aristocratic titles and degrees and embossed business cards, gentlemen whose words were their bond as befit gentlemen. The victims were brown and strange and far away, and no one was there to speak for them.

The day before the Committee delegates had their crucial meeting with Italian officials—the day, in fact, before the battle of Mai Chew—Mussolini sent a cable to his marshal at the front. Badoglio was granted permission to use whatever kind of gas he wanted, and as much as he wanted.

* * *

The Emperor's retreating army set out at night to avoid the bombers, but it was a long, slow, disorderly procession down a mountain that took the whole evening to cover the six miles or so to Lake Ashangi. By seven in the morning, the planes were back, and those in the baggage train who made it to the pass had nowhere to go.

They were rushing between the lake on one side and the mountains on the other, some scattering, some clumping together in their dread. Konovalov—who was trudging along with a couple of the Emperor's pages—heard explosions and turned to look over his shoulder. Men and women had abandoned one of their own dying on the ground, his legs gone. Adding to this misery, Oromo bandits from the nearby hilltops fired sniper–style down at the screaming, running members of the caravan. There was no longer an army, only a frightened mass.

And there was the gas, too. The rain that burned and killed. Haile Selassie gave his own account years later about the horror. "We could do nothing to protect ourselves against it. Our thin cotton shammas were soaked with yperite . . ."[50]

Besides the bombing and the gas attacks, there was wholesale confusion and a breakdown at times in any military discipline. A few of the soldiers who heard the Emperor had fled took to looting. But he hadn't fled—he was, in fact, taking shelter in a cave from the bombing. When Konovalov caught up to him and asked what he planned to do, the Emperor replied, "I do not know. My chiefs will do nothing. My brain no longer works."[51]

There was nothing to do but to head south, always south. As they set out, some men couldn't find their mules in the minor chaos. They hadn't traveled far before the Azebu Oromo were back, forcing them to take an alternate path. Then it was another long march through the night. They marched through the next one, too, under a steady drizzle over terrain that reached elevations of ten thousand feet. They had no provisions and made do with kosso and small balls of grilled barley flour, but eventually, when they braved the valleys, there were villagers who brought them cereals, honey, even a native beer made out of barley. The soldiers paid them in old cartridges.

When they came down for firewood, Konovalov saw a breathtaking expanse of mountain ranges bathed in the dying sunlight. "Lit up by the evening sun, they took on fantastic shapes of castles, towers, and gigantic stairways."[52] For some reason he couldn't explain to himself, he was reminded of why he had come to Ethiopia so many years before.

Along their humbling journey, chiefs pestered the Russian over the chance of last-minute help from abroad. "Do you think that Germany will come to our help? If she does, let her take all that she wishes . . . Some say that the English are on the road from the Sudan to Gonder . . . What about Japan? It seemed that they were going to help us."[53]

Konovalov had no answers. The truth, of course, was that no one was coming. As the weary survivors dragged themselves along an open plateau, Haile Selassie had also faced the bitter truth, and he would admit it to the Russian, even if he couldn't yet divulge it to his own army: "It is beyond our power to hold them back."[54]

Chapter Fifteen

A KING'S LONELY PRAYER

The survivors of Mai Chew spent the cold night of Easter Sunday on a mountaintop. Later, as they continued to make their way ever southward, bullocks and sheep were slaughtered for the traditional feast that ended the fast for Lent, but it was a somber occasion, one marked more than celebrated in a cramped tukul. The Emperor and his rases would normally be drinking mead. That night, they didn't.

The sad caravan plodded on towards Dessie, and then the Emperor decided that he, personally, needed to make a detour. To the mild consternation of his nobles, he chose to leave in the middle of the night with only a small complement of a hundred soldiers and head for the holy town of Lalibela. Their concern for his safety was justified. As it later turned out, the ever-devout Ras Kassa and his sons had made their own journey to Lalibela days before, and their caravan had been attacked, only to be saved in the end by the priests.

Haile Selassie could not be dissuaded from going. In a way, he was travelling back through time, leaving the nightmare panorama of aerial bombings and rifle snipers and tanks for a consoling visit to the twelfth century. Long ago, after Jerusalem had fallen to the Muslims and after Christian pilgrims were temporarily denied entry, King Lalibela had decided to recreate the city in the African mountains. His New Jerusalem boasted churches hewn out of soft volcanic rock, a place of elaborate trenches and dark tunnels, and it would become the second holiest place in Ethiopia. Stones here spoke to the glory of God. The river nearby borrowed its name from the Middle East: Jordan.

For his solace and his most intensely personal appeal, the Emperor chose to spend his time in what's considered perhaps the largest monolithic church ever built, Bet Medhani Alem, the "House of the Savior of the World." Here, there are massive rectangular columns, and there is a play of light and shadow in the medieval spaces to encourage humble devotion. For two days, Haile Selassie lingered, risking capture and the final destruction of his army's remnants nearby as he prayed and reflected. He didn't eat. He didn't drink. He had done all that he could, and it wasn't enough. God had to save his country. But whatever prayers or promises the last Emperor of Ethiopia made in the lonely sanctity of Bet Medhani Alem, when he emerged, the situation was no different. Konovalov noticed "his face was thinner, his forehead full of new lines . . ."[1]

Soon after the Emperor rejoined the main retreat column, the news came of betrayal by a couple of Wollo dejazmaches. This was offset by word that residents of Waldia had defied the Italians, and instead of surrendering their weapons, had gone into the mountains to fight another day. Haile Selassie gathered his guard, now reduced to a few hundred soldiers, and gently upbraided them: "Never forget what a soldier should be, especially at this present time."[2]

As they continued on, there were plenty of exhibits to drive home his lesson. Rotting corpses floated along a river, all of them once soldiers who had resorted to looting—slaughtered by villagers desperate to hold on to what they had. By now, their own column of men were viewed as looters, and they had to fire their rifles and machine guns to defend themselves. Tukuls burned. Clothes lay on the ground with shattered clay pots and spilled grain. The Emperor forbade looting, but his command wasn't always obeyed. "Our men went off to villages further away," recalled Konovalov, "and after burning the houses brought back grain, chickens, and honey." When a detachment was sent to fetch the chiefs and people of a local area, they were late in returning—and to make up for it, brought freshly looted spoils.

"It is always like that with the Ethiopians," Ras Kassa explained to him. "In the grip of his natural instincts he loots and even murders, but his Christian conscience always forces him to admit his guilt and offer himself for punishment. You have just seen a case in point."[3]

When they approached Magdala, it was probably not lost on some—as it certainly wasn't on Konovalov—that they stood in the shadow of the mountain where the doomed Emperor Tewodros had lost his own battle against modern weapons; in his case, during his conflict with the British. But the immediate threat now was from the local people, who were probably frightened, like others before them, of looters. There was news they might attack, and as the Emperor led the column ahead of schedule, rifle fire slaughtered more of his men. The soldiers burned the houses of their attackers and moved south, always south. For miles, the air stank with the odor of the rotting dead and of burned things, charred things.

* * *

While the Emperor had been praying in Lalibela, the fall of Addis Ababa looked imminent, and preparations had to be made to move the formal seat of government. His American adviser, John Spencer, thought the best place would be a river port along a tributary of the White Nile, but it was eventually decided the new capital would be Gore, on the same river of Baro. Meanwhile, Spencer got to work on a memo outlining procedures for the formal surrender of the city to the Italians. No one would ever put his arrangements into effect. Having inherited Colson's role and house, Spencer now inherited the frustrating scene Colson had put up with all too often, the maddening theater of the high nobles talking an issue to death.

Fortunately, bankers are more decisive. With the help of Ethiopian and French bank officials, Spencer had no trouble moving the bulk of government funds to Khartoum, Cairo, and London. He put them under the name of Haile Selassie in the hopes that the account would be treated as personal instead of a potential spoil of war that the Italians would try to claim.[4] It likely helped fuel the rumors later that the Emperor had smuggled a massive amount of wealth out of the country.

Italian planes swooped over the capital in regular reconnaissance missions and, with casual spite, routinely machine-gunned the airdrome. On April 27, they dropped a payload on the city, but instead of bombs, it was pamphlets. They offered a message from Marshal Badoglio to the people of Shoa: "I am the head of the victorious Italian army and will enter Addis Ababa with the help of God. The Emperor and his First Army are useless and defeated . . . We bring peace and civilization . . . But if you destroy our roads or try to oppose the advance of my army then the Italian Army will destroy and kill without pity, the airplanes will massacre from the air and destroy everything that exists."[5]

* * *

Rodolfo Graziani had pounded Harar with bombs from the air and then ignored it for two more weeks. And yet the Ogaden lay like an open road, with Harar and Jijiga practically for the taking.

In what must have felt like forever, but was less than a year ago, Dejazmach Nasibu Zamanuel had dug his riding crop into the sand while drinking coffee with George Steer. *They will beat us, but we will hold them as long as we can. We are supposed to be brave. Our courage is our only weapon.* Nasibu had only twenty-eight thousand men and the usual pathetic deficiencies in weapons and ammunition. The one bright spot: the Ethiopians managed to strip a few machine guns from tanks during the fighting in November. But Graziani's force had ten thousand more men, and more importantly, the Butcher of Fezzan would be coming with air power, artillery, and vehicles.

A lot of faith was placed then on the Turkish military advisers, more so than the Belgians (one of the Belgians had no first-hand experience with war). The Turks were led by a grizzled old general with Albanian heritage who had fought in the Balkans and at Gallilope. Sporting a zippered blue tunic made of artificial silk, Wehib Pasha "had been defending the past since the Dardanelles," as George Steer put it.[6] He boasted that he had built a "*deuxième Verdun*" at Jijiga (named after the bloody stalemate of the First World War). Spanning a stretch of more than twelve miles outside the city, a modest honeycomb of trenches had been dug over several months. But the trenches had no fire steps, no radio or phone hookups to communicate with each other, no water supply, and most vital of all, they had no parapets.

Graziani's advance was a direct, if not terribly imaginative one—another three-column attack that would ram its way north to Nasibu's headquarters at Degehabur. He would rely heavily on his battle-tested Libyans while his Blackshirts were benched, held in reserve. On April 14, the columns headed out. The western column under General Guglielmo Nasi had come up from Danane and was making its way to Janogoto, but early the next morning, it encountered fierce fire in one of the nearby gorges. On top of that, the "Little Rains" were not so little that week, making the ground a watery sludge that was only to the benefit of the Ethiopians, who were dug in at their positions. Nasi put the Libyans to work, constructing a ford and claiming a new forward position, but after two days of being literally stuck in the mud, he sent in flamethrowers and tanks to drive the Ethiopians out and make them fall back. At Birkut, there was a surprise counteroffensive and more stubborn resistance, but by April 19, it was in Italian hands.

In some spots, however, the Ethiopians were making the enemy pay for its real estate. At Sasabaneh, they launched quick, efficient raids from their garrison that proved so effective, they nearly overwhelmed the middle column. At Gunu Gadu in the east, they melted into the forbidding landscape, shooting their rifles from the blackness of caves and tree hollows until the dubats and Libyans tossed their grenades and waited for silence after the blasts—or rushed the hiding spots with their bayonets.

Off in Degehabur, Nasibu was so worried about Somali spies that each time he consulted his staff and European military advisers, he picked a new remote spot in the bush seven miles away from town. But the meetings made no difference. Wehib Pasha's second Verdun didn't last ten months, as its namesake did in 1916; it didn't even last a day. First the planes came, causing noise but little damage, and then the three columns. Under the crushing forward momentum of the Italians on April 30, the line broke after only three hours, and Nasibu and Wehib Pasha organized a retreat and fled to link up with the Emperor's army.

George Steer, who fell in love with the Ogaden, would wonder why Graziani didn't send a column to snake around to the east, cut off Nasibu's forces, and *then* move on to Harar, which was still completely undefended. He suspected the Butcher of Fezzan suffered self-doubt. But it's possible Graziani had weighed the risk; he may have thought one column wouldn't be enough for Harar, especially after the reception his armies had met. At heart he was a paranoid, and he also might have believed the propaganda from the Ethiopians that the Muslims of Harar, outraged by the bombings, would resist him with vengeful resolve.

As soon as Degehabur was captured, however, ego was a greater motivator than any anxious suspicions. Badoglio would be racing towards Addis Ababa. Graziani's star would shine brighter if he reached Harar first.

*   *   *

Janet Flanner, writing under the pseudonym "Genêt," acted as an American barometer of the French mood that spring. She wrote for the April 11 issue of *The New Yorker* that if only France didn't have to worry about being attacked by her neighbors, Europe could give up the pretense that she was a superpower. "Free for peace and to take her own shape, France could sink back into literature, fine conversation, the making of superb wines . . . In other words, France could relax with a sigh into being a second-rate power or a first-rate state of civilization."

It may have been pleasant to think so, but it wasn't going to happen. France *did* fear invasion. And the rest of Europe feared war. Ethiopia was a big part of that, but rather than face what was happening in the moment, there were those who indulged in *what-ifs*. They scribbled away about the Ethiopian conflict in the most bizarrely abstract terms. Leon Trotsky, still in exile in his house in Norway, was one of the worst offenders, and he sat down on April 22 to draft some comments for the *New International*.

Trotsky wanted to reject the notion of a few Communists that the war was little more than a fight between "rival dictators." He argued, "If Mussolini triumphs, it means the reinforcement of Fascism, the strengthening of imperialism, and the discouragement of the colonial peoples in Africa and elsewhere." A leading member of Britain's Independent Labour Party had likened Ethiopia to Belgium in the Great War. This was too much for Trotsky, who was scathing: "Well, 'poor little Belgium' has ten million slaves in Africa, whereas the Ethiopian people are fighting in order not to be the slaves of Italy. Belgium was and remains a link of the European imperialist chain. Ethiopia is only a victim of imperialist appetites. Putting the two cases on the same plane is the sheerest nonsense."[7]

At that moment, of course, the Ethiopians wouldn't have cared. Having struck a blow for deck chairs on the *Titanic*, the great revolutionary moved on in his article to the dark underbrush of Marxist conference politics, the kind of thing that didn't interest the outside world and never would.

European Communists and imperialists now had something in common: their failure to act. But Trotsky and his fellow leftists didn't have to worry. In less than three months, the Spanish Civil War would break out, and left-wing radicals could pick up their rifles without worrying over the political ambiguity of coming to the aid of an emperor.

* * *

At his base in Ende Yesus, Marshal Badoglio recounted for the correspondents his version of events at Mai Chew and Lake Ashangi, but he wouldn't let them cable it yet to their newspapers. "Evidently, the Negus's chieftans wanted to show him how to be defeated by attacking the Italian army," sneered Badoglio.[8] His army now prepared the largest convoy of modern vehicles that had ever been organized, all of it to roar its way down to Dessie and then to Addis Ababa.

For about ten thousand Italian soldiers and another ten thousand askaris, there were 1,725 vehicles that set out on April 26, many of them civilian cars mixed in with the army tanks and trucks and the eleven batteries of artillery. Badoglio dubbed this super-column "The March of the Iron Will," though it was more like a noncompetitive, slow-motion drag race. With all the Fiats, Alfa Romeos, and Studebakers pushing up the dust of the road, it resembled a bizarre *Mad Max* action sequence, slowed down and set in the 1930s. Close to two hundred horses were ferried along on trucks, because to drive into Addis Ababa in victory wasn't enough. It would be more dignified and majestic for the marshal to ride. No one besides the Italians would notice this bit of theater at the climactic moment. They would only remember the cars and tanks.

Herbert Matthews, the *New York Times* correspondent, and the Italian reporter, Luigi Barzini, Jr., were along for the trip. As Matthews sat in one of the frequent traffic jams caused by geography and rain, an Italian major ordered a radio receiver to be set up, and they soon heard the polished voice of a British announcer all the way from London. It was like the convenience of timing in the movies—the presenter was giving the latest news of the war. There were reports of Dessie's capture, but these were unconfirmed. With signature English understatement, the newsman conceded that the Ethiopian position was "rather difficult."

Matthews and the others in the vehicle made some quick calculations. "There was no doubt of it. The location of the fighting was exactly where we were, and without having the vaguest notion of it, there we sat in the midst of a saguinary battle, on the way towards a city which the Italians had not captured yet! The Italians roared with laughter, but as a newspaperman, I felt rather ashamed of my profession."[9]

Along the way, Matthews noticed a strong scent coming from the higher slopes of a valley, and he realized it was the stench of corpses, the same smell that had revolted Konovalov as the Emperor's army made its retreat. Worse would come when the trucks reached about fourteen hundred dead mules barring their way. Matthews, one of those in denial over the Italian use of gas, described them as "left in the middle of the road where they fell."[10] More plausibly, the animals probably died as they were led across the road, with their human owners fleeing dropped gas or strafing planes. Now the heavy trucks of the column drove over their carcasses as if they were speed-bumps, their weight gradually flattening them down until "even the bones were ground into dust." Here was a new "indescribably loathesome smell—a putrid, fetid, nauseating odor."[11]

Badoglio's convoy rolled on, but there was an excruciating period when it took six hours to cover sixty miles. With many of the cars showing empty on their fuel gauges, the "March" crawled its way into Dessie, and Badoglio flew into the town so that he could lead his column on the final leg of the trip. The askaris had been sent on ahead to soften up the capital's defenses.

The end was a mere handful of days away.

* * *

On April 30, the Emperor and his cortege returned to a city where the will to fight and the spirit of resistance were collapsing rapidly. By then, the Italians were about eighty miles from the capital, and a confused and pathetic defense was staged by villagers and a handful of military cadets near the foot of Ad Termaber, a ten-thousand-foot-high pass. The cadets suffered one casualty and quickly retreated back to the capital, where it's likely they dispersed.[12]

There was now nothing that stood in the Italians' way.

At one point, an enterprising German soldier who delivered thirty-six antitank guns was summoned to join a brigade at Holeta and defend the capital. But Ethiopia's prime minister ordered a convoy of trucks to transport his soldiers to the front—and the shells for the guns were in those vehicles. As George Steer noted, "Guns and ammunition cost the Emperor a million marks; not a shot was fired out of their barrels against the enemy."[13] For that matter, the prime minister's soldiers didn't even leave the capital.

Amazingly, as shiftas prowled at the ragged edges of the city and panic bubbled up in the streets over the confusing rumors and lack of gas masks, the Emperor went through with the ritual of receiving the credentials of Cornelius Van H. Engert, who had served as America's chargé d'affaires and was now the US ambassador in Ethiopia. Engert was a career diplomat who had worked in postings from Constantinople to Santiago. His wife seemed to take exotic postings in stride. "Life is simple and very pleasant," she wrote in a letter to a friend. At the time, she was arranging for new chintz for her parlor. "We have a large piece of property, and it is far more like a farm than a legation. It is a marvelous place for the children."[14] Except, of course, for the imminent threat of gunfire.

Early on, Engert had made his sympathies clear to Washington, sending Roosevelt a cable urging America to put pressure on Mussolini. Now he could see the result of his advice unheeded. "My private audience of the Emperor was a unique experience which confirmed the high opinion I had formed of him," Engert wrote in a telegram to Cordell Hull on the night of April 30. "Considering the tragic hour in his country's history, he showed remarkable *sang froid* and conducted the interview with the same gracious unhurried suavity which had always impressed me on previous occasions. His frail body seemed perhaps a trifle frailer and his thoughtful, deep-set eyes showed a profoundly perturbed soul. But his handshake had its usual firmness, and his inscrutable features were lit up by the same winsome smile."[15]

After taking Engert's credentials, Haile Selassie complimented Roosevelt over his annual message to Congress in which he condemned dictatorships. He was still baffled by the behavior of the European diplomats and realized "the stage was set" for another world war. When the audience was over, the Emperor took the diplomat's hand as he said, "Convey my greetings to your President and tell him the fate of my country may serve as a warning that words are of no avail against a determined aggressor who will tear up any peace pacts whose terms no longer serve his purpose."[16]

Engert told Hull that he was deeply moved by the experience, and that he hoped the US administration might find a way to exert its moral influence. "Having seen this nation and its ruler in their dire extremity, I cannot believe that Italy will be permitted to dictate terms based solely on her recent victories," wrote Engert. "Surely the time has come for plain speaking, for if unilateral denunciation of treaties are tolerated [sic], not only collective security but collective civilization will receive a blow from which they may never recover."[17]

Haile Selassie still refused to give up. He clung to a ragged tatter of hope that he could defend his capital with the five thousand men who belonged to Ras Getachew Abate of Kaffa province, but Getachew's heart wasn't in it. The Emperor thought that maybe he should move his government west. Imru had "not come to die with him," and so Imru was alive until he heard differently.

On the night of May 1, he sent for Sidney Barton, who thought "his usual calm dignity to be tinged with despair." Would the British be willing, Haile Selassie asked, to let him purchase arms and supplies through the Sudan if he did make the move west? "In the last resort could he be given facilities to escape by aeroplane to the Sudan[?]"[18]

By now, arms through the Sudan were out of the question, and the chance of helping an escape at some hypothetical time in the future extremely remote. Escape, if there was going to be one, had to be *now*. In London, Anthony Eden was closely monitoring the cables from Barton, and he had already offered transport for the empress and her children to Haifa via Djibouti.

The Emperor's closest advisers were pressing the case hard that he must leave the country. It was the only choice that could do any good, they said. Kassa the scholar led the case for exile. If His Majesty headed west, he would only deliver an exhausted army as targets for Oromo shiftas. Go instead to Geneva, make one final appeal there, he urged. Getachew sided with Kassa. But there were others against. *No*, argued the military governor of Addis Ababa, an older man with crooked, weak legs and suffering from the skin disease of vitiligo. *Head west*, he demanded. Fight on from there. He was so fierce in his belief that he stamped the floor with his boot.

There was another moment in the lengthy debates when the director-general of Addis Ababa, a young, mercurial individual, Tekle Wolde Hawaryat, decided to cut the issues down to the bone. A couple of weeks before, he spread optimistic rumors of army progress as he hired eight hundred volunteers for the capital's defenses. Now Tekle stuck a pistol in his mouth and marched towards the Emperor, demanding, "Janhoy, are you not the son of Tewodros?"[19] In other words, he considered it more honorable for Haile Selassie to shoot himself in the head like his predecessor, than to be captured by the Italians . . . or to run away.

Haile Selassie couldn't decide. He could be an exile or a bandit, a dead martyr or a trophy prisoner if captured. To a substantial portion of his subjects, fleeing would mark him as a coward; it was unthinkable for an Emperor to leave Ethiopia. There were those who would never forgive him. The empress wasn't going to leave without her husband, and that meant adding her own voice to the chorus that urged him to leave.

As the debates of the Imperial Council went on, Haile Selassie went to visit the stables, where the last of his beloved Arabian horses were kept. They were now few in number and badly needed some proper grooming and care. In the company of these neglected animals, he was alone to make up his own mind. Soon after, he ordered the beating of the war drums in front of Menelik's palace, a defiant noise that could be heard all over the city.

Up to these critical moments, his rases, his closest advisers—everyone—still had no idea what he would finally do.

* * *

George Steer drove over to the Little Gibbi, where several nobles and the die-hard supporters waited for the Emperor to announce his decision. He spotted Benyam and Yosef, the two sons of Charles Martin, a.k.a. Warqenah Eshate, both dressed in khaki, having ridden over on motorcycles while "all the young Ethiopians stood around, waiting, doing nothing, talking very little." Then a door to the empress's pavilion opened, and two barefoot servants rushed out to clear the way for their sovereign.

Steer watched Haile Selassie come out, and he was shocked by the man's appearance. "He was dressed in khaki as a general. His aspect froze my blood. Vigor had left his face, and as he walked forward he did not seem to know where he was putting his feet. His body was crumpled up, his shoulders drooped; the orders on his tunic concealed a hollow, not a chest."[20]

The Emperor had given instructions to his chiefs to take their men out of the capital to hold off Badoglio's column. It turned out later that the chiefs refused to go, claiming they couldn't organize their men. Steer was disgusted at how they stood behind their sovereign, "completely satisfied with their excuses."[21] To him, they had driven in the last nail of the coffin holding Ethiopia's butchered independence.

Then there was a review of the remaining handful of soldiers. Months ago, Haile Selassie had watched Ras Mulugeta leave his capital with eighty thousand men; now his impassive face showed nothing as a dozen buglers sounded, and only nine hundred marched by, carrying pistols and gas masks. When it was over, he went back inside the pavilion, and Steer glimpsed the Emperor slumped on a sofa while Menen desperately implored him to flee with her out of the country. She could reach him as no one else could, and finally, he acquiesced. He would go to Europe.

He had some final instructions for those staying behind. He charged Tekle Wolde Hawaryat with the daunting task of maintaining peace in the city after his departure, and he hoped the Abuna could help. Sidney Barton cabled London that the Emperor had ordered the Gibbi to be thrown open to the people, and that they be "allowed to help themselves." Already, "streams" of men and women were "running all directions Gibbiwards" and rushing home, laden with "clothing arms all sorts beds carpets furniture [sic]."[22]

But Haile Selassie was still conflicted over his decision up to the last minute. He didn't know it, but the city's own chief of police, Abebe Aregai, along with others, actually contemplated his assassination. The commander of the crown prince's troops, a dejazmach named Fikre Mariam, had confided to Tekle Wolde Hawaryat, "If the Emperor should flee, our honor demands that we should ambush the train at Akaki, and that he die at our hands."[23]

A few minutes after four in the morning on May 2, Haile Selassie stepped on the train that would take him and his family—along with a collection of nobles and army officers—to Djibouti. Besides the ten tons worth of baggage and documents, a Buick and Chrysler had also been loaded onto the train. Too many nobles and courtiers had attached themselves like barnacles to the retinue, and according to John Spencer, several of them were "heartlessly" told at various points to disembark—sometimes in barren spots in the desert.[24] What makes this accusation so curious is why Spencer would want to continue serving such a ruler if he'd learned about this alleged lack of compassion.

The train slipped away in the early morning, but the personal danger was far from over. For hours, the retinue dreaded the sound of airplanes that might swoop in to bomb the carriages. And if Graziani had got his way, that's exactly what would have happened. He sent a cable to Mussolini, asking for permission to bomb the train, but the idea was turned down. Italy was already becoming a diplomatic pariah; Mussolini must have recognized that this move would go too far.

There was a stop in the small town of Mieso, where Haile Selassie had an unpleasant run-in with his former ambassador to Paris and Geneva. Tekle Hawariat Tekle Mariyam was there with his soldiers, and he boarded the special carriage to ask for permission to go home to Ethiopia to fight on. But aside from the formalities, he apparently told Haile Selassie exactly what he thought of the decision to leave the country. John Spencer got the sense of the old diplomat's bitterness when he later met him on a train stop in Afdem. "Although I must have been for him an almost complete stranger, he lost no time unburdening himself to me of his thoughts about Haile Selassie, whom he denounced as a traitor to Ethiopia, a coward, and one unworthy to bear the title of Emperor after his flight into exile."[25]

Perhaps the scathing lecture from his former official was on Haile Selassie's mind when the train pulled into Dire Dawa. He made it linger there several hours, anxious to talk with Edwin Chapman-Andrews, who served as Britain's consul in Harar. When Chapman-Andrews finally arrived, he had to talk Haile Selassie out of a change of heart and the desire to join Ras Desta's army in Sidamo. "It took me some time to dissuade him, but it had to be done," recalled Chapman-Andrews.[26] Finally resolved again to go into exile, the Emperor and his entourage continued on.

Dire Dawa was the port of call for one passenger, one that had never been welcome in the royals' company. This was Hailu Tekle Haymanot, a ras now in disgrace who had been taken aboard as one of five prisoners. He was once so greedy, so corrupt, he had been nicknamed *Birru* ("Dollars") Hailu.[27] When he ran the province of Gojjam, political and church offices went to the highest bidder, and he shamelessly approached American and British envoys with his hand out, warning he'd cut off access to the Blue Nile and Lake Tana if they didn't line his pockets. It wasn't long before Haile Selassie punished him, but about two years later, Hailu came up with a preposterous scheme to work his way back into his ruler's good graces. He would organize a prison break.

Hailu's son-in-law happened to be Lij Iyassu, the deposed heir from years ago who wanted to steer Ethiopia towards Islam, and he'd been under the official custody of Ras Kassa in Fiche, north of the capital. Hailu managed to get Iyassu out (quite possibly with the help of a troublesome Italian agent provocateur).[28] Then events turned comical. His next step was to turn around and betray Iyassu, promptly snatch him back, and present him to Haile Selassie in the hopes that a grateful Emperor would say well done, there's a good fellow, and reward his initiative. But incriminating letters turned up, ones Hailu could only offer fumbling explanations for, and he found himself in front of a court. He was soon found guilty and sentenced to death, which was later commuted to life in prison.[29]

He was aboard the train because Haile Selassie knew the man's patriotism was on par with Gugsa's, and that given half a chance, he could be useful to the Italians. But what to do with Hailu now? Finally, the Emperor ordered that he be released at Dire Dawa. No sooner was Hailu a free man with the locomotive chugging along in the distance than he booked himself a ticket back to the capital—where he greeted the Italians as conquerors and offered his services.

The train, meanwhile, chugged forward on its way to Djibouti.

* * *

Back in Addis Ababa, no one had bothered to give the news to Ethiopia's press secretary that his ruler had slipped away in the darkness of the early morning. Lorenzo Taezaz decided to follow him on the next train, a revolver in his pocket in case he ran into trouble.[30] But the trouble wasn't on the rail platform; it was back in the city.

Between nine and ten, minor hooliganism gathered force and became anarchy. It was a frenzy of looting, of destruction that was casual and senseless, drunken and indiscriminate, without a thought or care as to who was the target. The Emperor was gone. Nothing could stop the advance of the Italians. So many went on a rampage, burning and taking what they could get. Station Road was covered by a rare snowfall—except it wasn't snow. All the stuffing of pillows and mattresses had been ripped out by looters, leaving a carpet of white along the main thoroughfare.

The Europeans who stayed behind barricaded themselves in their homes. They were especially at risk, as the looters didn't care about nationality, only about the *ferengi*, the foreigners. Thirteen of them would be killed in the chaos, most of them Greeks and Armenians, while it's roughly estimated that between five and eight hundred Ethiopians were killed.

Like Lorenzo Taezaz, John Spencer had been told nothing and now wandered the streets, as bewildered as other expats. At one point, the city's chief of police, Abebe Aregai, rushed up to him, wide-eyed, telling him the chaos was so bad that his own officers had begun killing each other. Just then—with machine gun fire rattling in the background—the British consul ran over and begged the chief to take control of the situation, but Abebe Aregai was too far in shock to hear him. Eventually, Spencer ended up at the American embassy, where Cornelius Engert provided him with a room in the residence quarters. In turn, Spencer offered the use of his car to the American legation officials, and it came back loaded with food, guns, his files, and his servants, who had brought along their families. Greek merchants and American missionaries now began to pour into the US legation with horror stories of their own, including accounts of police officers demanding they be paid or they'd start shooting the *ferengi* on the spot.[31]

Black smoke curled up from gutted houses as mutilated corpses lay in the streets. The shooting and mayhem went on. At the American embassy, food supplies began to run low. When Spencer accompanied Engert's wife to fetch eggs from the back of the legation compound, looters came within a short distance, blasting away at them. Later, while Spencer stood guard, Engert showed him a copy of a telegram that Cordell Hull had sent to Mussolini. The secretary of state demanded that Badoglio's forces hurry up and invade the capital so they could restore order. Spencer thought "Badoglio must have had a good laugh over such simple-mindedness."[32]

Beyond the endangered island of American sovereignty, policemen were joining the looters as they smashed their way into the capital's most popular upscale grocery—its Greek owner had fled to Djibouti. Shiftas from outside the capital already smelled blood and chaos and were taking sniper shots. George Steer spotted a bunch of tipsy Ethiopians running up a street, wearing tailcoats, top hats, and bowlers stolen from a Goanese tailor shop.

Knowing he'd better salvage what he could from his office, he scooped up his camera, binoculars, and cash and made sure to destroy messages lying around that might be useful to Badoglio's troops, "and idiotically forgot seven bottles of champagne stored there against my nuptials."[33] As he drove through the streets in an old Ford, he passed mobs breaking windows and tossing chairs through them, people drinking with abandon and unrolling the great spools of film for an imported movie.

Sitting in his car, waiting for his lover and fellow journalist, Margarita de Herrero, and their friend, Lolita de Pedroso y Sturdza, he watched the looters raid a French wine bar. Across the street, high up on the balcony of a hotel, Marcel Junod of the Red Cross was laughing at the Ethiopians shooting up the bar. "Junod disappeared for three days," wrote Steer. "He was still laughing when they set fire to the hotel underneath him."[34]

Maybe Junod laughed because he assumed the looting was more in a carnival atmosphere rather than an outpouring of frustration and violence. He was staying in the apartment of a French journalist friend, who told him dismissively, "Don't worry, the Abyssinians like firing into the air when they're excited. It doesn't mean a thing."[35] The Swiss doctor stopped laughing when bullets tore splinters out of the floor, and he saw his friend run out, lugging a suitcase to the home of Greek neighbors.

Junod spent three harrowing days defending himself, losing most of his clothes and belongings, winding up in a flea-ridden cellar, and helping to repulse yet another onslaught of shiftas, until he was at long last rescued by machine gun-toting friends in a truck, who drove him and others to the French embassy. But the cyclone of wild gunfire and arson was working its way to the various European legations. With troops from colonial Senegal, the French embassy could hold out well enough, and when it was attacked, women and children were sent into tunnels underground that led to caves—they had been reserved for just this kind of emergency.

The safest point in the city was now actually the British legation, defended by Sidney Barton's 130 Sikhs and a battalion of the Fourteenth Punjab Regiment. It was Barton's defenders who came to the rescue of the Turks and later the Americans when their missions were attacked. Barton invited the Belgians to abandon their embassy and take refuge in his. They turned him down—only to ask for help later when the shiftas came.[36]

This was Barton's finest hour. He would send a telegram to London on May 3, intended for release to the press to let them know Britain's patch in Addis Ababa stood firm and defiant: "Looters were looted this morning when taxi-load stolen goods driven into British Legation offered for sale to very people from whom taken."[37] Barton had the soldiers confiscate everything and add it to the camp stores.

Steer knew this locale was his best bet for safety. Having reunited with Margarita and Lolita, he drove along the unpaved roads, dreading that he might hit someone accidentally and be dragged from the car by an outraged mob. The rioters hit the car's roof with sticks and swords and fired haphazardly across its hood, but the car plowed on. "We thanked God when we saw the barbed wire and the fringed turbans of the Sikhs, entered the neat gateway, and climbed the cool, empty drive of the British legation, under the eucalyptus trees planted in Menelik's day."[38]

But Steer braved the streets again in the Ford to check on his house and take his interpreter back with him to the embassy. The legation was rapidly filling up: Sudanese and Somalis, Indians, even a Latvian and a Jamaican national. Close to two thousand refugees of all sorts took shelter there. Even Abun Qirillos, the highest Orthodox authority in the land, looked for sanctuary after mobs looted and burned several churches.

Other Ethiopians frantically tried to get away. One was the family of Imru Zelleke, then a boy of twelve. Young Imru's family was in a better position than many others to flee the havoc; his parents were people of nobility, influence, and wealth. His beautiful mother was a cousin of the Emperor, and his father was Bejironde Zelleke Agidew, a seasoned diplomat and cabinet minister. Young Imru had spent time learning English and getting an education from a British nanny in the home of Charles Martin, who was a distant cousin to his father. Later, his horizons had been expanded further by living with his parents as guests in the Emperor's villa in Vevey, Switzerland; Bejironde had been serving as Ethiopia's minister to France and Britain, and its representative to the League of Nations. The war had touched young Imru's life from its very first day. The fitawrari who commanded Ethiopians at Walwal, Alemayehu Goshu, had been his great uncle. Now his father was an official without a government, and worse, his health was failing badly.

They tried to escape anyway. "People were looting shops, shooting in the air," he remembers.[39] He watched the chaos as he, his parents, and his siblings made their way to the rail station, boarding an overcrowded train on its way to Djibouti. It was packed with the desperate, anxious to flee the Italians and the chaos of the capital. His family was lucky—the train made it safe and sound to the tiny neutral patch of France's empire. But his father's condition failed to improve.

"So my mother decided that we go back to Addis Ababa," recalls Imru. "Because of his condition, we couldn't travel anywhere else. Some of the other officials went to Jerusalem or migrated to Egypt, but we couldn't."[40]

Back they went to Ethiopia, where their country would be ruled and governed by others.

Young Imru's father died only a month later. And by going home, the family would lose much more in the months to come.

* * *

After all the months of inspection and travel, after all the desperate lobbying to save the Ethiopians, the top man assigned there for the Red Cross was nowhere near the capital when the flames started.

Sidney Brown had been abruptly summoned home to Geneva, and now he was watching his professional career—and then his personal life—implode in the polite stillness of a room in the Villa Moyene. Like the destruction in Addis Ababa, however, what happened to him was dragged out over days. Brown had to give a full accounting of his activities in Ethiopia to his superiors, only to be told that the International Committee wanted to let him go. Because of his past record and in deference to his well-known family, he could resign instead of being fired.[41]

When they first called Brown back to Geneva, the top brass intended to merely reassign him. But now he was an embarrassment. When Max Huber and other representatives had visited Rome, Italian officials showed them a damning piece of evidence over Brown's lack of impartiality. It was an item that soldiers could only obtain by rummaging illegally through mail bags—planes carrying mail to Djibouti would stop for refueling in Asmara. And in one of the bags was a letter meant for Brown from a friend back in Switzerland, who thanked him for a leaked report from January and for his "perseverance and determination to continue the fight against 'Mister Mussolini.'" The letter actually warned Brown to be careful in how he dealt with the International Committee, because the "swine" might give him a hard time.[42]

But the Italians didn't think one small scandal was enough, so they hedged their bets.

Maybe to save face, maybe to leave on decent terms, Brown met with Committee representatives and let them know he'd already been thinking of quitting. That should have been it, but it wasn't. At another meeting on May 1, the Committee men began asking him, seemingly out of the blue, about his sex life. All this led back to a shady smear attempt by Italian operatives. They had hired a private detective and hoped to bribe Brown months ago—before he even left for Ethiopia—but their plan fell through thanks to sloppy planning. No matter, they would dig into his personal life. Brown was gay, and though Switzerland was more progressive than some places in Europe, there was just enough shame and intolerance over homosexuality to derail his career.[43] He had to go.

Brown was badly shaken by his humiliating dismissal. He would end up working in public relations for his family's respected engineering firm, and he brought out a kind of "tell-all" book about his experiences in Ethiopia with the Red Cross. But the book came out in 1939, at a time when the world was in what we would now charitably call "compassion fatigue." The Red Cross would have even less moral authority in the grim new war zones that burst open like spider eggs.

*   *   *

On May 3, at ten o'clock in the morning, John Melly and members of his Red Cross unit were out in a convoy, collecting and treating wounded. For all the danger in the streets, they weren't being completely reckless. There were armed Ethiopian guards for the convoy. A British member of the team named Gatward was driving the ambulance with Melly when it turned down the main road, and they spotted a man wounded in the street. Gatward jumped out to take a look and then called out to Melly. Suddenly, a drunken man in khaki rushed up to their vehicle, and one of them shoved a revolver into the cab, shouting, "*Ferengi!*" He shot the doctor point-blank in the chest and then ran off.

As Gatward rushed up in horror, Melly called out that he needed to be taken back to their base quickly. The bullet had passed through his lung, and he was losing lots of blood. A pharmacist, L. J. Bunner, was riding in the second vehicle and now ran up to find his boss lying on the running board. Bleeding to death, yet still conscious, Melly told his furious colleagues not to shoot the rioters in revenge. "They're drunk," said Melly. "They don't know what they're doing. Don't cause more bloodshed than there is."[44]

After he was operated on at the hospital, it was decided he should be moved to the British legation, where he could get oxygen and would be treated by European nurses. Bunner suggested later that this was Melly's own idea, so that other patients would receive more attention: "Don't stop the good work because of this."[45] They didn't. All through the night, the doctors and staff at Melly's hospital worked on, performing operations and doing a fair number of amputations. They heard the steady crackle outside of burning buildings, and while stray bullets hit the walls, they counted themselves lucky that no one fired at them deliberately.

The next day, one of the doctors, W. S. Empey, returned to the legation to check on Melly. To Empey, the young surgeon "appeared cheerful and was bearing up remarkably well, but his actual condition did not hold out much hope."[46] He was right. John Melly was dying, but he seemed determined to go out with good manners. He asked about his hospital and sent back encouraging messages to his friends. His only moment of consideration over his own fate seemed to be when he asked a Swedish nurse to hold his hand, and yet in his last two days, he would look up at her and say frequently, "But really, you ought to go sleep."[47]

On the first day the Italians took possession of the capital, he died at nine in the evening, making the toll of Europeans killed in the riots fourteen. The legation—knowing he didn't have long to live—had sent word to his mother through its wireless, and messages had gone back and forth between mother and son. Melly's last one to his mother and family read, "I am perfectly happy."[48]

* * *

By evening, the looters were attacking the US legation, and while the embassy staff had their share of rifles and shotguns, its ambassador, Cornelius Engert, wisely decided to get help from the British. Sidney Barton promptly sent over three trucks, along with a military escort of three officers and fifteen Sikhs to evacuate women and children. Engert's young son and daughter were among them, along with their English governess. The seven-mile trip to the British legation was a harrowing journey for small children, not least because a few of them sat in the back of the truck with a cheetah, a pet that belonged to one of the war correspondents.[49]

Engert's wife, Sara, was a reluctant passenger. "I had just thirty minutes to decide what to take with me from my home which I might never see again, and in the excitement I made some pretty odd decisions. I took, for instance, the needles with which I was knitting a skirt for my little girl. But I left my grandmother's silver spoons on the dining room table."[50]

Engert stayed behind. He sent word to the State Department that the men intended to hold out and defend their embassy, because if they abandoned it and their radio station, "they would certainly be pillaged and burnt after our departure." The Americans had a long night, but came through it unscathed. Engert later received a cable from President Roosevelt, thanking him for "his courage and devotion to duty," while a Massachusetts congresswoman recommended his wife for the Medal of Honor.[51] The papers at home, always looking for a feature angle, pointed out that the Emperor's escape meant he'd broken a promise to Engert's children. Haile Selassie had pledged to give young Roderick Engert, ten years old, and Sheila, six, the next lion cub born at the palace.[52] It would have been interesting to see how long the US ambassador would have let his son and daughter keep the new family cat.

In the midst of the chaos and violence, George Steer and Margarita got married the next day, May 4. It was a simple enough ceremony, conducted "al fresco,"

as the groom himself put it. It took place on a trimmed lawn of the British legation. Margarita, a trilby on her head and a bouquet of arum lilies and oversized
daisies in her left arm, had her friend, Lolita, as her bridesmaid. A staff member
of the embassy, Don Lee, served as Steer's best man. "There was a delicate titter
in the congregation when all the worldly goods were endowed," recalled Steer.[53]
What worldly goods the happy couple still had, no doubt, were with them in
the compound. Shots cracked intermittently from all sides of the embassy as the
wedding progressed, and the bride and groom signed the necessary documents.
Afterwards, the newlyweds drove around the grounds in a pick-up, blowing on
a hunting horn.

That evening, refugee volunteers guarded the legation. The Turks proved themselves the most effective, or at least the most enthusiastic. Downing all the cups
of coffee that Lady Barton had prepared, the Turks fired off hundreds of rounds
at every noise that might mean an invader—or simply a hungry jackal sniffing
around. The real enemy, however, was not far away. Askari troops had advanced
ahead of Badoglio's mechanized column and were camped on Entoto; they were
only waiting for the marshal's vehicles to catch up. Beyond the embassy, white
flags were already hung on poles of the nearby Ethiopian houses.

Later, there were many condescending shakes of the head and sharp criticism
over the looting of Addis Ababa. When the people turned on their own capital,
it only seemed to justify the remarks of those who talked about "savages" and the
natural inferiority of the African. Only Steer recognized the failure for what it
was: a glimpse into the future.

> It was neither the breakdown of the central authority—which has
> broken down often in Ethiopian history—nor the barbarian's love of
> theft nor the black man's hatred of the white that caused the sack of
> Addis Ababa. It was the threat of gas from the air that demoralized
> the people. The crowds that gathered round Lady Barton's committee
> rooms for masks were evidence of that.
>
> Precisely the same thing will happen in the capital of any Euro-
> pean state that is defeated. War against the civilian population breaks
> it up into its warring parts.
>
> It seems to me important that our leaders should understand this.
> Ethiopia is nearer to Europe than they think.[54]

* * *

The train for the exiles arrived late in Djibouti, and Haile Selassie emerged, bareheaded, dressed in white, save for his brown cape. Empress Menen was heavily veiled and apparently overcome with emotion. Reporters noted how fatigued and thin Haile Selassie looked, and then, being professionals, pestered him with questions. "I did not desert my people," he told the *Daily Telegraph*. "It was not fear of continuing the war, but I saw the impossibility of my unarmed and brave warriors competing with modern weapons, especially gas. I therefore left to avoid further bloodshed and destruction."[55]

There were more embarrassments and humiliating complications to endure. An Italian tried to photograph the Emperor, but Haile Selassie's guards moved in to intercept the man and blows were exchanged right in front of their consulate. When the royal party wanted to send telegrams to Addis Ababa, they were refused by the Djibouti post office. The British authorities wouldn't let everyone onboard the ship heading up the Red Sea. Forty-seven of the eighty-plus Ethiopians had to stay behind.

It could have been worse. Britain's ambassador to Italy, Eric Drummond, had been lobbying to pawn off Haile Selassie and his retinue altogether on the French: "In view of high feelings against us here, I should feel considerably happier if the French could be induced to take the major part of the responsibility for the Emperor's journey to the Suez."[56] The French said no.

If it wasn't apparent before, it was becoming starkly clear that the Ethiopian royals were no longer in charge of their own fate. Bugles from Senegalese troops were sounded as the Emperor and his family got into cars to take them to the docks, and a somber crowd waited in the smothering heat for just this sad spectacle. There was the empty pomp of a gun salute, and then a launch took the imperial family out to the HMS *Enterprise*, which was to bring them to Haifa in British-held Palestine. From there, they would go on to Jerusalem.

It would be years before Haile Selassie set foot again on Ethiopian soil.

*   *   *

On May 5, the riots in Addis Ababa finally ended. Marcel Junod emerged from his last hiding spot at the French embassy and found the streets "silent and deserted," with smoke still rising from burned-out buildings and corpses among the ruins. There were carpets and other furniture debris strewn about the gardens of the Imperial Palace. "Even the [other] hospitals were empty," Junod wrote later. "The wards had been ransacked and the dispensaries rifled. The patients had all disappeared, taking material and medicaments with them."[57]

In the middle of the afternoon, the whole city could hear a long, reverberating rumble, which grew steadily louder. Marcel Junod wandered, as did others, over to the British legation, where the Bartons and a crowd of curious foreigners stood out front. From the steps of the embassy, they could see a great cloud of dust in the distance. George Steer stood near the Union Jack at the legation's gates, holding a tommy gun; he knew his way around rifles, but didn't have a clue how to handle the weapon in his hands.

The cloud of dust slowly took shape, getting ever closer, and with it, the noise of engines, sirens, and trumpets.

A fleet of small tanks suddenly burst through the massive curtain of dust, growling their menace to the waiting, apprehensive onlookers. Then motorcycles and cars. Then trucks. On the side of one truck was a sign with the words scrawled: "ETIOPIA è FINITA."

The Italian advance guard had finally arrived.

PART THREE

PREVAIL

Chapter Sixteen

TAKEN UP TO ROME

Embedded with Badoglio's army, Herbert Matthews got a firsthand look at the capture of Ethiopia's capital. The Italian columns had halted about thirty miles or so outside Addis Ababa to make their final preparations, and with no champagne or wine available, Matthews and another correspondent drank a toast with juice from a can of tomatoes.[1] Then they followed the columns in. Badoglio entered the city at four in the afternoon, and Matthews considered the few Ethiopian men left to be "a sullen and fearful lot, wondering what retribution Italy would take for the horrible orgy of the four previous days."[2] It was this fear of retribution that had kept the Italian embassy completely untouched.

At the gates of the British legation, George Steer watched the tanks lead the way of the conquering army. Then came the small herd of international correspondents and "then Badoglio and his staff looking rather big for their cars, like the necks of bookmakers overswelling their collars."[3] One of the soldiers driving a truck stuck out his tongue at the Union Jack, while others booed. Like Steer, the legation's military attaché was similarly unimpressed; he didn't attend Badoglio's parade, but he saw a large number of troops returning to camp from it. "The filthiness of the men, their clothes, and their arms," Major Taylor wrote of the victors, "the lack of discipline must be seen to be believed." During the parade, a few Italian soldiers dropped their rifles and, in one case, a machine gun; two of them broke ranks to take photos.[4] Days later, Sidney Barton would be infuriated when the Italians fired an artillery salute with blanks over the roof of his embassy.

Badoglio made the Italian legation his new headquarters, and with brief but appropriate pomp, Italy's flag was raised, a trumpet sounded, and there were shouts of *"Viva il Duce!"* Marcel Junod watched the ceremony and then paid a call on the marshal as the delegate of the International Red Cross. Badoglio greeted him with barely disguised contempt: "The International Red Cross would have done better not to interfere."

Junod didn't reply.[5]

But even the intrusion of a meddlesome doctor couldn't spoil his jubilant mood, and he soon summoned the correspondents. He felt like pontificating and told the reporters, "You have seen . . . what tenacity and force Italians are capable of. You have seen them work in the rain, make paths through mountains, drag trucks from the mud and across rivers—and all this with enthusiasm and vigor."[6]

Outside, another rain shower was pelting down, an appropriate omen of how hard it might be for the Italians to keep their new possession. The chief censor told the reporters that they had to submit their stories to him in half an hour, otherwise he couldn't guarantee they'd get filed on time. Herbert Matthews sat in an old Fiat car with a bad headache and his typewriter on his knees, tapping out his dispatch. He moved into a room at La Mascotte Hotel, "bathed in natural, hot sulfur spring water, drove round in a limousine, smoked Havana cigars, drank cocktails before meals and brandy after."[7] His assignment was over.

"So much for Ethiopia!" Matthews wrote his wife. "Some day, ten or fifteen years from now, if I'm still alive, I hope to come back and see what they've done with it."[8] Matthews didn't know it, but the story was far from over.

While one *New York Times* correspondent celebrated, another grieved. George Steer watched in disgust how some Ethiopians were shown off like spoils in a victory parade and then herded in front of the reviewing platform, where they were forced to offer a Fascist salute each time a detachment passed. "The American journalists who had come with the Italians were mightily amused; it was great fun, they said, seeing Tasfai and Kidane nearly splitting their sides with the Fascist salute."[9]

The Kidane that Steer refers to was his friend, Kidane Maryam, of the Young Ethiopians."Educated in France, Kidane had been made director of public instruction and fine arts, an outgoing young man who enjoyed jazz and dancing and liked to raise his glass with the toast, "Let the fine arts flourish."[10] As the riots had torn the city apart, he'd been trying to save it along with the rest of the country, organizing what young men remained, as well as women, into resistance cells. Now he was paraded like a show dog for the occupiers.

The Italian soldiers later took him high up in an airplane and pushed him to his death.

*   *   *

Italians didn't learn of Badoglio's victory through their state-controlled press. Instead, the word came thanks to news reports out of London, which relied on Sidney Barton's account of the Italian troops' arrival. Radio stations in Rome began announcing bulletins and playing marching tunes, while carabinieri ringed the embassies and consulates that had been the most committed to sanctions.

The chamber of deputies adjourned until the next day, and obedient Fascists went home to don their black shirts. In the massive crowd that filled the Piazza Venezia, some carried posters. Others held up a two-headed dummy; one head for Haile Selassie, the other for Anthony Eden. A gang of university students were pallbearers for an empty coffin painted with the slogan, "Here lies the Negus."

Then Mussolini shouted from his balcony what many in the throng already assumed. "I announce to the Italian people and to the world the war is finished," he declared, proclaiming that now "Ethiopia is Italian" and promising that "world peace has been re-established."[11]

The rest of the world didn't believe him for a minute. The representatives of the Balkan Entente—Greece, Turkey, Romania, and Yugoslavia—were all in Belgrade for a conference, and their negotiations were chilled by the news of Ethiopia's defeat. It was clear that "no real protection" could be expected from the Great Powers or from the League of Nations.[12] In Geneva, the normally neutral Swiss shouted "Scoundrel!" and "Assassin!" when Mussolini was shown in a newsreel.

In what was then Britain's colony of Tanganyika (modern day Tanzania), outraged locals saw dominoes in danger of falling. They set up a committee and fired off a telegram that blasted the Baldwin government for its "evasive attitude" over whether to keep its territorial mandate. "The present uncertain position is gravely retarding the economic development of the territory." In South Africa, the major newspapers warned that Britain had to stick to its sanctions and back the League, unless it wanted "strong opposition" from Cape Town. In Sudan, foreign residents still had their minds on the looting and rioting that occurred before Badoglio's arrival. They issued a plea to Khartoum, asking that British ships steam up the White Nile to protect the Gambela enclave, a foreign concession on the border with Ethiopia.

In Washington, a Massachusetts congresswoman, Edith Rogers, wanted to know why the US embassy in Ethiopia's capital had been left "practically defenseless and virtually unarmed." She argued that "the rioting and rebellion had been predicted for some time, and it seemed only reasonable to expect that the State Department should have taken some precautions to guard American lives and property."[13] As it turned out, the Americans had to fire pistols and rifles to fend off looters again on the first night the Italians occupied the city. Instead of accepting help this time from the British, US Vice Consul William Cramp had a car roar out from the legation grounds and through the mob, carrying a request to the Italians, who obliged him by sending over a guard of fifty soldiers.

Today, such a request might cause embarrassment for an administration. In the election year of 2012, in the wake of the attack on the US diplomatic mission in Benghazi, the question was what American authorities could have done better, not what better help could have been obtained from Libyans in power. But this was 1936, and Cordell Hull told the chargé d'affaires in Rome, Alexander Kirk, to find out what Mussolini's regime was doing to protect foreign nationals.

When Kirk tried to check, the news hadn't come in yet of Badoglio's arrival in Addis Ababa. He knew perfectly well that the planes far away buzzing over Ethiopia's capital were there for reconnaissance—to see if any last stand of resistance might greet them. The Italians now expected Kirk to believe the planes were there to ward off looters. The riots worked beautifully to further Italy's PR line, the idea that Blackshirts were marching in as liberators.

There were those who recognized this pose for what it was. At a party at the US embassy that night, Anthony Eden pointed out to the new Belgian ambassador that his countrymen in Addis Ababa were saved by Barton's Sikhs. Hovering nearby, the Italian ambassador realized this didn't make his country look too good. He presumed the job should have been done by Badoglio's soldiers, and he blamed delays in the army's arrival on road sabotage and the annual rains. Winston Churchill was at the party, too, and within earshot. "Mr. Mussolini must be only too glad at the present spectacle," he said to the Belgian ambassador. "It throws a rather vivid light on the reactions of a people which is today turning on even the Powers which imposed sanctions."[14]

In New York City, the police were concerned that night about reactions in Harlem. Extra police were put on duty and prepared for trouble, but the authorities misread the mood of the neighborhood. African Americans were feeling shock, grief, despair. Harlem stayed quiet that night. Black America was in mourning.

Among those who strongly felt the loss were several black left-wing radicals and organizers, men like Oliver Law and James Yates, Albert Chisholm and Alonzo Watson, all men with varying degrees of faith in Communism, simply because Communism promised an equality never offered by Democrats or Republicans. Not that Marx was always on their side. Oscar Hunter was "always in trouble" because he didn't toe the correct line of ideology, so much so that his white comrades actually gave him condescending lectures on the history of his own people.[15]

James Yates was also about action more than doctrine; he had moved from Mississippi to Chicago, where he tried to organize labor unions with Law and free the Scottsboro Boys. He'd come to New York looking for work and had fallen in with fellow radicals like the painter, Alonzo Watson. Yates felt inspired by the work and words of Phillip Randolph, the president of the Black Brotherhood of Sleeping Car Porters, recognizing how Randolph "linked the cruel, uncalled-for rape of Ethiopia to the terrible repression of black people in the United States."[16]

Yates and the others felt a spiritual bond with Ethiopia, but they saw beyond a race war to issues of class struggle. They had even tried to quell the rage of black rioters and looters who had targeted Italian shops, printing a leaflet to explain that "many Italians were against Mussolini's invasion of Ethiopia and pointing out that throughout Italy people were demonstrating against the war."[17] (In this, they were hopelessly, tragically wrong, for as historian Angelo Del Boca has concluded, regular Italians didn't object to the war, merely to their serving in it.)

Now that it was all over, Yates "slept around the clock," exhausted and trying "not to feel like the bottom was falling out of the world again." For days, his friend Watson would refuse to speak to anyone, and would stay in his loft, painting more canvases that depicted "sightless eyes and broken limbs—canvases that he seemed to reject as fast as he painted them. He was happier when he did posters of giant fists in the air."[18] What could be done? Nothing. The Emperor was on his way into exile.

In New York's Little Italy, an impromptu crowd of twenty-five hundred people hit the streets to cheer and sing about the Fascist victory. At Mulberry Street and Hester, there were fireworks—which prompted the police to hand out summonses because there was a lack of permits. No one cared. People waved a banner that read, "The Eagles of Rome Have Devoured the Lion of Judah." They tossed large, dangerous firecrackers and cherry bombs from the windows above, which exploded and cascaded in sparks, adding more percussion for the twenty-five-piece band playing in the street.

The celebrating started early in the afternoon. Little boys wearing crepe paper bandanas chased each other with pointed sticks, playing "Haile Selassie and Mussolini." Italian Americans milled around bookshops, consulting maps of Ethiopia and sticking pins of the Italian flag above Addis Ababa. As the afternoon wore on, a youth swung a dummy effigy of the Emperor from a fire escape. Dressed in a top hat, black shirt, and white trousers, it made a bizarre pendulum arc from the landing. Then people cut it down and stuffed it into a pine coffin donated by a local undertaker. Boys smeared skulls and crossbones on the box, its crushed top hat sticking out from one end. It wasn't the only stand-in for Haile Selassie. Over on East Twelfth Street, people brought out a dummy portrait of the Emperor stuffed with sawdust and dressed—for reasons that aren't quite clear—in a blue sweater and a red skirt, its neck roped with sausages.

Instead of hanging the effigy, the revelers stabbed this one in the heart.

* * *

The next day in London was all about brave faces and public relations. The Opposition, having sat in the Commons and listened politely the day before to Anthony Eden's tribute to Sidney Barton's conduct during the riots, now tore into the foreign secretary that afternoon. Ethiopia's conquest was seen as the government's failure, as well as the League's failure. Labour's Hugh Dalton led the charge again and made what, in retrospect, seem to be Cassandra-like opening remarks. "Deeply distressed and concerned as we are at what has happened in Africa we cannot put Europe, particularly Central Europe, out of our minds," said Dalton, thinking of Germany, "and there have been rumors of impending possible acts of violence towards Austria or Czechoslovakia which are persistent and plausible enough to disturb us."[19]

Then he eventually got back to his theme of Ethiopia. "The Right Honorable Gentleman opposite," he continued, meaning Eden, "seemed for one brief and fleeting hour to have assumed the leadership of the peace cause at the League of Nations and then to have ignominiously surrendered it, and not only to have ignominiously surrendered it, but to have succeeded none the less in incurring for this country the bitter hatred of the Italian dictator, which in days to come, in certain contingencies, might cost us very dear indeed."

"How?" prompted the backbenchers around him.

"Must I elaborate what I should have thought was obvious?" Dalton asked back. "Is it not clear that, with the enmity of Italy, our position in Egypt, our position in the Sudan, our position in Kenya, our position in the Red Sea, our power of passage through the Mediterranean, our communications with Australia, New Zealand, India, and with all the East—is it not clear that all these things are menaced in a new way and with a new force?"

Dalton charged the government with being responsible for the war, which only prompted laughter from the Tory benches. But he kept up the harangue, piling on his charges over the issue of oil, over the decision not to close the Suez Canal, over "having betrayed the trust of millions." Up until then, Eden had enjoyed the Opposition's faith that he had been genuinely sincere in his peacemaking efforts, and now his pride was wounded by the attack. The debate became heated, with interruptions and quibbles by different MPs over statements made in the past.

Defending himself, Eden told the House, "The truth is that while the Honorable Gentlemen opposite profess to support the League with horse, foot, and artillery, they really only mean to support it with threats, insults, and perorations. If the Honorable Gentlemen wish to take military action, I must warn them that you cannot close the Canal with paper boats. I must make clear that if His Majesty's Government, in the course of this dispute, have not pressed for military sanctions, it is due to their horror of war and not to a fear of the ultimate outcome of it."

In Washington, Secretary of State Cordell Hull was ducking questions over whether the US government would recognize an Italian regime in Ethiopia. At his press conference, he told reporters he couldn't discuss the possibilities before "ascertaining the nature of the occupation." This was evasive, and Hull knew it. Privately, it didn't seem logical or moral to him to recognize Mussolini's conquest, but for the time being, he kept such thoughts to himself. Reporters got no straight answer either from the president. When he was asked at his own press conference whether his policy of "non-recognition against territorial gains won by force would apply," Roosevelt laughed—and then refused to answer the question.

* * *

In Addis Ababa, Italian soldiers were deployed at crossroads and bridges, while their trucks parked at every open space in the city. They put up notices and posters that ordered the residents to be quiet and not to form any crowds. Any breach of the peace would be severely punished. The order came right from Badoglio, "General Commander of all Land, Sea, and Air Forces of Italian East Africa." The soldiers had nothing to worry about. Most Ethiopians stayed out of the streets and behind their shutters.[20]

In fact, for many weeks after, the soldiers would guard what still looked and felt like a ghost town. The people stayed inside. The market stayed empty. The soldiers finally had to spread the word that peasants and merchants were welcome to return, and their new conquerors would be happy to pay for any goods they wanted to sell. Eventually, some Oromo peasants ventured in with their goods, but the Italians had only lire. This was beyond the peasants' understanding—what could they do with this strange new paper? It wasn't Ethiopian thalers, it wasn't anything they knew. The Italians were forced to import what they needed.[21]

It was on the second day of occupation that John Melly was buried in a quiet corner of the British legation's gardens. His casket was lifted by an honor guard of Sikhs, and the service was well attended by the English nationals and other foreigners. One of those who mourned the physician's death was George Steer. "I liked Melly immensely," Steer wrote later. "I have heard that when he was in Abyssinia before the war, he sometimes sang hymns during dinner. But when he came out as chief of the British Ambulance Unit, his religion had discarded an earlier exhibitionism and found more exhilarating humane work to do."[22]

If this sounds somewhat tart, there's no mistake that Steer was genuinely moved by Melly's character. He felt that any sincere British commitment had seemed to start and end with this amiable, devout doctor who had cheerfully patched up Ethiopian wounds. "That was all that could be wrung out of England, who had pledged so much; I honor Melly who could do it."[23]

In the days that followed, the tributes from others poured in. The Archbishop of Canterbury spoke at a service held in London's St. Martin's-in-the-Fields. Melly was posthumously awarded a medal for gallantry by Edward VIII. Anthony Eden wrote a letter to Melly's mother, apologizing for "intruding on your grief" to express his sympathy and to call his death a "tragic loss."[24] Ethiopia's ambassador in London, Charles Martin, wanted to express how he was "humbled to think that one of my wild countrymen was the cause of the death of a real friend and benefactor of my country." He promised her that if he returned to Ethiopia, he would make sure a memorial to her son was erected.[25]

On the same day that Martin wrote to Melly's grieving mother, May 9, Benito Mussolini proclaimed that the ambassador's homeland was now a province of Rome, officially annexed. Victor Emmanuel was no longer just the king of Italy; he was now "Emperor of Ethiopia." Foreign diplomats in Addis Ababa were curtly informed that the Ethiopian imperial court no longer existed, which meant their own official statuses were now in limbo, though they would be treated as distinguished guests. Rome would soon give its colonial holdings in the region a new name: *Africa Orientale Italiana.*

An impressive multitude gathered once again that night in the Piazza Venezia, and Mussolini stood at his balcony, bathed in the glow of searchlights as if he were responsible for their illumination. "The Italian people have created an empire with their blood!" he shouted. "They will fertilize it with their work and will defend it against anyone with their men! With this supreme assurance, raise on high your ensigns, your swords, your hearts!" For this new empire, he asked the crowd below, "Will you be worthy of it?"

And the people roared back, *"Si! Si!"*

"This cry is like a sacred vow," said Mussolini—more cries of *Si, Si* interrupted him—"which binds you before God, before men, for life and for death."

Then the people began their chant of ominous blind worship, *"Duce! Duce! Duce!"*

For Benito Mussolini, the raw emotional power of this moment was his reward for years of plotting, for bleeding the Italian treasury dry, for sacrificing the lives of so many conscripts, whether they were sons of Naples or Sardinia or Eritreans left to rot on battlefields while their distant families wondered if they were alive or dead. He had won. It had never really been about empire, as he had made clear in his private communications. It had been about vengeance and glory, and now that it was over, he fully expected the world to acknowledge his victory and let him keep it.

Then, after such a delirious high, there was an abrupt let-down. If only Europe's premiers and diplomats could have haunted Mussolini's office that day during his more confidential meetings—how their eyes would have been opened. No sooner had he agreed to let Victor Emmanuel have the title of emperor than the Council of Ministers applied gentle pressure to make the title hereditary for the king's heirs. It hadn't seemed to occur to Mussolini that the glory of the title wasn't a one-time gift; it would eventually be out of his hands. And there was a worse blow to his ego that evening, because after all the chants of *Duce*, the patriotic masses were heading to the Piazza del Quirinale to chant for someone else: the king. Mussolini was furious, slamming his fist on a table as he barked, *"How does the King fit in?"*[26] He had to be talked into going to the Quirinale.

The outside world, however, still thought him invincible. As the Italians cheered their Duce and monarch, the British government ordered a massive test mobilization for its land and air defenses on Malta.

*   *   *

If they were cheering in Rome, they were puzzled in Addis Ababa. A notice was put up for all to see, but the colonial authorities didn't think to translate Mussolini's proclamation into Amharic. Feodor Konovalov was on hand when a group of residents stared curiously at one of the placards, and one of them translated the text for his friends. When the man came to Mussolini's words, "Ethiopia is Italian," he turned to the Russian.

"Why, why does he say that Ethiopia is Italian? Is it possible? Is it not a temporary occupation?" Many Ethiopians were apparently convinced that the Italians wouldn't stay long; prophecies had said so.

Konovalov didn't know how to respond. "What could I say?"[27]

For reasons that still aren't clear, Konovalov had elected to stay behind for several months rather than accompany the Emperor to Djibouti. Maybe he saw little point; his services were no longer needed. And he must have assumed that it didn't matter to the Italians that he was a military adviser. They would see him as a white foreigner, ignorant of the fact that at least on paper, he was legally an Ethiopian. They apparently never interfered with him. And how Konovalov related to the Italians would prove to be a mystery—and a minor scandal—in the years to come.

If Konovalov didn't mind sticking around, the American adviser, John Spencer, minded very much. It was an extremely nervous Spencer who boarded the train from Addis Ababa to Djibouti that week, and he tried to make himself invisible in a corner of one of its passenger cars. Bored carabinieri were ambling up and down the platform as the train squatted on its rails, destined in its own sweet time to pull out of the station.

Spencer had left behind his diaries and work files with the US embassy, but he didn't fully trust its ambassador, even though Cornelius Engert had given him sanctuary. He was sure Engert had let the Italians know he was trying to leave. Why Engert should put a fellow American in danger isn't clear, and there's nothing in his correspondence or cables to suggest he would ever do such a thing. But Spencer, his nerves shot, was clearly past trusting anyone. As the excruciating wait went on, an American missionary poked his head in one of the windows and saw him.

"Well, Spencer, what do you think you are doing here?"[28]

It was a stupid, careless remark, and Spencer rounded on him—only days before, he'd saved the missionary's life by facing down some shiftas with a pistol and the help of a US embassy guard. Now he had to get out of here, and this fool might get him locked up in a cell. There was one upside—the train cars had an escort of French Senegalese guards, whose presence warned off waiting shiftas.

Jobless, homeless, John Spencer spent a few dull days in Djibouti. He tried to escape the punishing heat by swimming in freshwater springs near the seabed and looked on as a group of juvenile French officers got their small dog drunk on absinthe. He was all set to sail home to New York when he received a telegram. The Emperor of Ethiopia, now in exile, wanted Spencer to join him in London.[29]

* * *

Meanwhile, the self-proclaimed liberators of Addis Ababa began to show their true colors. Several executions by firing squad were carried out. The official reason was usually that it was a sentence for murder committed during the riots. One exception was the case of Balahu, a giant of a man who stood seven feet, five inches tall. The Emperor had been so impressed with him that he made Balahu his official umbrella carrier. Then, during the war, Balahu was transferred to the job of drum major with the imperial band. The Italians claimed he was a spy, then put him against a wall and raised their rifles.

Word also spread that Italian soldiers were forcing their way into foreign embassies, flouting the most sacred of international laws to confiscate wireless transmitters and cut off their links to the outside world. But they didn't dare challenge Barton's Sikh guards at the gates of the little corner of Britain.

It was fortunate then that, ever since the riots, George Steer and his wife, Margarita, had stayed at the British legation. On May 13, two carabinieri officers, tipped off by a Greek informant tagging along, loitered near the embassy until they were asked what they wanted. They wanted to see Steer, but they weren't interested in stepping on what was technically British soil. Instead, they hoped to give the reporter a lift to some vague destination where they wanted to ask him some questions. Steer had no intention of going with them. Although he doesn't state it outright in his book on the war, it sounds very much as if he would never have been seen again.[30]

Having failed to lure him out, the Italians decided to throw him out. An expulsion order was delivered the next day with no grounds or explanation given. Steer and Margarita had to leave Ethiopia by train in three days. Naturally, they wouldn't be alone; the new colonial government also tossed out the Hearst correspondent and the French director of an Ethiopian newspaper. Later, the Italians announced that they were all being deported for "anti-Italian activities and espionage." Far away in London, someone at MI6 read the morning papers and checked the files—no, George Steer wasn't one of their operatives.[31]

His expulsion even turned into a question in the House of Commons; how many British subjects had been told to get out of Ethiopia? Anthony Eden replied that there was only one—"Mr. Steer," the *Times* correspondent, "who had already decided to leave."[32] This was true. Through Sidney Barton and the Foreign Office, Steer had already sent a message off to *The Times*, asking if he should book passage to Djibouti, as he had "many articles," and the paper had sent back a cable, suggesting the best thing would be to come home to London.[33]

On May 16, Steer's last few minutes in Addis Ababa were spent perched on the steps of the train car with his typewriter on his knees, whipping up recommendation letters for his servants, along with a formal statement that one of them was entitled to keep his horse, saddle, and tent. Without this permission, the man could be shot for looting. The two servants had lost what little money they had, thanks to the upheavals of war, riots, and now brutal occupation, but they still thought God would provide for them. They put out their hands to say goodbye, and when Steer offered his, they took it and kissed it. "I could have cried," wrote Steer.[34]

He and the others tried nonetheless to put up a brave front. The Emperor's Greek head of counter-espionage "smiled wearily to other Greek friends" as he took a seat in a train car with a gramophone on his lap. Margarita chatted with the wife of the French director of the Ethiopian newspaper, the couple banished after twenty-five years in the country. Then the whistle blew, and the friends and his loyal servants got smaller with the distance. Steer realized how young he had come to this exotic land, and he was going away older. He was also going away armed, in a manner of speaking. Steer was smuggling out something valuable in his luggage—Feodor Konovalov's drafted pages on his time with the Emperor's army at Mai Chew and the long retreat. Steer would publish them later in his own book on the war.

The train creaked past the old Akaki radio station, hollowed out by fire before the Italian forces arrived, and Steer spotted the wreckage of a hotel in the town of Bishoftu where he, his wife, and their friend, Lolita, used to socialize. It was burned to the ground.

"One day," Steer warned the Fascist regime in the privacy of his own thoughts, "you will get the punishment that you deserve for your impertinence to the greatest imperial race in the world."[35] With his Ethiopian friends, he had been less dark, more positive. To the former director of the country's Foreign Office, Tsafai Teguegne, he promised, "We will return, this is not the end."[36] To another friend at the stop in Djibouti, he insisted, "After all, we may have been slow, but we English do keep our word. We have solemnly signed a Covenant which guarantees, *guarantees* to you your independence and territory integrity."[37] No doubt feeling guilty, Steer noted later that his friend "really believed what I said."[38]

* * *

So much attention was naturally paid to Addis Ababa that the capture of Dire Dawa the day after went virtually unnoticed. But Italian forces here were also showing signs of what was to come. Unlike Addis Ababa, there was not even the pretense here of caring what the international legations thought. French troops had been a presence in much of the town, including the treasury. When the Italians arrived, their soldiers broke the staff of the French flag in two and hoisted their own colors. Whenever they saw the Union Jack, they tore it down, and any hanging photos of the king were immediately trampled.

According to one British observer, no woman—married or unmarried, white or black—was safe. They were routinely abducted and raped by soldiers, both Italian and askari, and if anyone moved to defend them or protest, he was promptly shot dead. A British officer of the Red Cross was allegedly thrown into prison; he escaped, was re-arrested, and was only freed after the intervention of the British vice-consul coming out from Harar. Days later, a British major and the lady with him were harassed and assaulted in a hotel. The same bullying and abuse quickly spread to Harar, where the Italians forced their way into the British consulate and took Somali soldiers prisoner.[39]

All over the land, the Italians took what they pleased—goats, sheep, fruit, and farm produce—tossing their paper lire in exchange. As in the capital, people who had only known thalers soon stopped bringing their goods to market. *Compel* them to bring their produce, the Italians told the chiefs. The Ethiopian nobles replied that they were powerless. Bread sellers would have to buy flour at high prices, their payments at pitifully low fixed rates. Vegetable sellers who flouted the price restrictions were thrown into jail. Soldiers would raid homes and farms and order that the coffee crop be sold only to Italians. The Ethiopians preferred to burn their surplus rather than let the Italians have it.

Back in the capital, one Ethiopian woman in her thirties persisted in selling her wares. Dressed in dirty clothes, she could be seen often carrying a basket of eggs along the dusty roads, but if any customer or soldier stopped her, she seemed uncommonly stupid. You could ask her a question, and she didn't seem to understand. And then she would go on her way, taking her time, walking to the very edge of town.

The woman was Shawaragad Gadle, and she was learning a new trade—not egg seller, but agent of the underground resistance. The dirty clothes were a distraction, a disguise for a daughter of the man who was grand chamberlain to Menelik. When the war broke out, she served as president of the Ethiopian Women's Association and worked at the Red Cross. When Badoglio's troops captured the capital, she cried as the Italian flag was raised. In another sign of Fascist spite, the new rulers forced her to explain herself in court. She reportedly answered, "Is my weeping alone a crime when I see my country invaded by alien people, my state collapsed, my country's flag replaced by another?"[40]

She was let go, but she wasn't about to give up the struggle. Her trips with her basket were always a ruse, her way of slipping information to rebel leaders waiting in the hills just beyond the Italian defenses.[41]

She wasn't the only one. Lekelash Bayan had already left Addis Ababa, simply walking away from her house in the neighborhood of the palace and leaving the door open so neighbors wouldn't think she'd abandoned it. She headed for the hills with her husband and a group of friends, and two weeks later organized a guerrilla cell of some forty-two fighters.

"I would not let down the memory of my father," she told historian Tsehai Berhane-Selassie in an interview decades later. "When the Emperor said that an enemy that would take our lands and defile our churches was invading the country, I took up my father's gun, put my four-month-old daughter on my back, and joined [the resistance] . . . I wore men's clothes."[42] Lekelash was involved in the regular skirmishes near the capital to harass the occupiers: "I fired many shots and killed many of the enemy, but I was not even wounded." Still, her guerrilla cell had to give ground and move further into the countryside.[43]

Women's work seemed to be fighting *and* cooking, as well as spinning thread, repairing clothes, and taking care of children. As the guerrillas kept on the move—accepting offerings of food from sympathetic peasants, keeping out of sight of convoys and patrols—there were long stretches of tedium and downtime. And then bursts of activity, of frightening danger.

Her fellow guerrillas took to calling her "*Balaw.*" It meant, "Strike him!" Lekelash used to say the word as she trained her rifle on Italian soldiers or when she encouraged the others to cut down the enemy.[44] *Strike him, strike him!*

* * *

Off in Woodford Green, in what was then the leafy suburban countryside of Essex beyond London, a team of volunteers and two secretaries had put together the first issue of a new newspaper. It was the brainchild of Sylvia Pankhurst—suffragette, one-time Communist, anti-war activist, and a force to be reckoned with.

Sylvia had already proved herself to be a headache over the years to the British establishment. She had grown up in a house full of intellectual stimulation in London's Russell Square, where Kropotkin and William Morris could be guests, and so it was no surprise she would wind up joining her radical mother and sisters on the front lines for the right to vote. She annoyed the authorities with her hunger strikes. She dabbled in Communism and visited Moscow (which won her the attention of Special Branch). But she soon parted ways with its orthodoxy and its ruthless totalitarianism. She set up "cost price" restaurants for the hungry and even founded a toy factory to create jobs. At one point, she became fascinated by India and wrote a six-hundred-page tome published in Mumbai that criticized the caste system and the lot of untouchables. And she still found time to write poetry and create interesting painting compositions. She was a woman of inexhaustible passions and energy.

And now she turned her attention to Ethiopia.

She'd already made the speaking circuit to condemn Italy's bombings of hospitals, and she had drafted countless letters of protest. But her name alone wasn't enough. Almost a year before, she'd written her local MP, and a local newspaper had reprinted her letter: "Horror has been piled on horror in the atrocious campaign without any effective step being taken by this Government or the League."[45] Her MP was unmoved, mainly because he happened to be Winston Churchill.

More than twenty years before, Sylvia had started a newspaper to help win the women's vote. She transformed it when she needed a paper to protest the Great War. Now she was back to what worked, back to publishing. At first, she thought of calling her paper *Ethiopia News*, but as a tip of the hat to Charlie Chaplin's *Modern Times*, which was out in the cinemas that spring, she christened it the *New Times and Ethiopia News*.[46]

For its first issue, Sylvia wrote that the paper "appears at the moment when the fortunes of Ethiopia seem at their lowest ebb; the greater the need for an advocate and friend." In fact, it was printed on the day that Badoglio's column drove into

Addis Ababa, May 5. "We know that the difficulties facing her are grave, but we do not falter, either in faith or determination that they shall be overcome. The cause of Ethiopia cannot be divided from the cause of international justice, which is permanent, and is not to be determined by ephemeral military victories."[47]

Sylvia understood that not all Italians should be tarred with the same brush of Fascism, and that Mussolini had brutalized his own people before he looked with hungry eyes towards Africa. "We draw a profound distinction between the Italian Fascist government and the Italian people, who are enslaved today, but whose freedom is slowly but surely being prepared by the martyrdom of thousands of heroic men and women . . ."[48] A more personal reminder of Italian freedom was her lover, Silvio Corio, an anarchist and the father of her young son, Richard. She never married him, a fact that scandalized her mother. The social pretensions didn't matter. As her son, Richard, recalled, when she first met Haile Selassie, "she told him frankly as a republican that she supported him not because he was an emperor, but because she believed his cause, the cause of Ethiopia, was a just one."[49]

Biographers and historians have made a meal out of her idiosyncrasies. She was strident, stubborn—in modern parlance, often a huge pain in the ass. She exasperated Foreign Office clerks with her endless stream of letters and her knack for getting questions asked in the Commons. They considered her a fanatic and eventually put together a special file for how to deal with her. Officials worried their responses might appear verbatim in next week's issue. A phone conversation with Sylvia Pankhurst could turn into a passionate monologue. Yet in spite of her quirks and maybe because of a few of them, she was essential to reminding the British government of its broken promises and obligations. Charles Martin could get summoned like a schoolboy for stern lectures. Haile Selassie could be treated like unsightly gift furniture, best covered up if possible. Critics in the House of Commons could be shot down with a snide remark over their party's ambitions. But Sylvia was independent. This matronly, fifty-four-year-old radical was determined to drag officials on a Grand Tour of a guilt trip to the Horn of Africa.

As with C. L. R. James's and George Padmore's crew, her paper was run on a shoestring mostly by volunteers, and Padmore, James, and Jomo Kenyatta occasionally floated in her circle. With a print run of only ten thousand copies, it somehow managed to reach beyond Britain to the United States and the Caribbean. Over time, it offered readers an impressive list of activist contributors, from anti-Fascist professor Gaetano Salvemini to Harold Moody, founder of the League of Coloured Peoples. "The Ethiopians are a superior race of men," declared Nikola Tesla in an article in July of 1936. "I am almost tempted to say a race of supermen, chiefly Caucasian Whites like ourselves."[50] Charles Martin wrote a column for it almost every week. Sylvia sometimes went to the trouble of publishing an edition in Amharic so that copies could be sent to Ethiopia's resistance fighters.

The paper's partisan tone could be shrill, overly intrusive at times. But Sylvia and her team got crucial information out of Ethiopia that no one else had, that directly contradicted the Italian line: guerrilla raids, a breakdown of who had submitted and who was still fighting, stories of Italian desertions . . . Some information she no doubt obtained thanks to Martin, perhaps even sometimes from the Emperor. More details flowed all the way from Djibouti, where a reporter named Ali Baig, kicked out of Addis Ababa by the Italians, picked up what news he could from refugees and other sources, such as Ethiopia's former consul there, Andagachew Masay.

Like Padmore and Kenyatta, Sylvia Pankhurst now had the attention once more of Britain's men in the shadows. MI5 regularly kept tabs on her. A more interesting measure of her impact was that Benito Mussolini learned of her efforts, and so critical articles about her began to appear in the Italian press. One of them made her out to be headline-hungry, and it crudely implied that she was angling for Haile Selassie's sexual attentions. "Who is this Miss Sylvia who has espoused—failing a better opportunity—the cause of the slave-driver ex-Emperor?" Sylvia reprinted it in translation.[51] All this must have flummoxed the Duce, who, like Britain's Foreign Office, wondered *how* this annoying woman managed to get herself heard? Why should she have influence at all? Ethiopia had been beaten. The whole affair was supposed to be *over*.

But it wasn't over. And the country wasn't beaten. The war was entering a new critical phase, one full of intrigue and soaked in bloodshed that would test the resolve of both Emperor and dictator.

*   *   *

Sylvia Pankhurst's articles weren't the only landmarks for the cause that month. On May 15, the *African Morning Post* in Accra, the Gold Coast (now Ghana), published an op-ed piece titled, "Has the African a God?"

It was written by I. T. A. Wallace-Johnson, whose fury over Ethiopia's downfall spoke for many. "I believe the European has a God in whom he believes and whom he is representing in his churches all over Africa," wrote Wallace-Johnson. "He believes in the god whose name is spelled *Deceit*. He believes in the god whose law is 'Ye strong, you must weaken the weak.' Ye 'Civilized' Europeans, you must 'civilize' the 'barbarous' Africans with machine guns. Ye 'Christian' Europeans, you must 'Christianize' the 'pagan' Africans with bombs, poison gases, etc."[52]

Johnson had been an irritant to British colonial authorities for some time, and he was proud of it. Born in Sierra Leone, the son of poor Creole parents, he never got to finish school, but he earned a radical's education by bouncing around from the United States to England to Russia for various jobs and political activities. He would annoy the authorities in Nigeria so much with his union organizing that academics still debate whether he left the country or was deported. The colonial powers surely paused when they learned the motto for his West African Youth League, founded in February of 1935: "Liberty or Death."

As an activist and writer, he was effective—but more for the Gold Coast than Ethiopia. When his Youth League met in Accra in March for its first annual conference, Badoglio had already bombed and gassed the rases of the north. The delegates were wasting their time in calling on the diplomats in Geneva to "denounce the aggressor." [53] Still, he was causing headaches for the Gold Coast's governor, Arnold Hodson. "I do wish that you could suggest some plan whereby I could get rid of Wallace-Johnson," Hodson wrote the Colonial Office. "He is in the employ of the Bolsheviks and is doing a certain amount of harm by getting hold of young men for his 'Youth League.' He just keeps within the law; but only just. At many of his meetings he says outrageous and criminal things, but the law officers tell me that it is almost impossible to get a conviction on the spoken word."[54]

Now in May of 1936, he gave the governor an opportunity. "Has the African a God?" attacked European civilization, Western religion, colonial business and government practices—the lot. His editor and friend, Nnamdi "Zik" Azikiwe, knew the article was a literary time bomb, and he was reluctant to print it. He was overruled by his publisher, but it was Azikiwe who suffered the consequences. The police picked him up, just as they did Wallace-Johnson, and both were slapped with charges of sedition.

Then curious negotiations went on through back channels. Wallace-Johnson got word the government was willing to drop its case if he would please go away now, and there's a good chap, here's £100 for your trouble. He smelled a set-up, the old "trying to escape" frame. In the end, the government backed out on the deal, brought him to trial, and after the inevitable conviction, fined him £50 or three months in jail. But the trial only helped recruitment for the Youth League, which soon boasted *seven thousand members* in twenty branches.[55] Wallace-Johnson appealed—and lost. The West African Court of Appeal said it didn't matter that he hadn't incited violence; he was still guilty. The British justice system, however, has always bent over backwards to at least have the *appearance* of fairness. Colonial officials must have fumed and spat when it was decided that their despised radical had the right of further appeal.

The governor was getting what he wanted. Though legal costs were daunting, Wallace-Johnson would leave Accra less than a year later, eager to take his case to Britain's Privy Council—and he would lose again. When his moment came, the Privy Council didn't buy the sedition charge, but decided he was guilty of breaching the colony's criminal code for his statements about religion.[56] Well, now he would at least have his chance to lobby and agitate, right at the heart of the enemy's camp.

* * *

That May 15, far away from Accra, Anthony Eden stood in a house on the Île Saint-Louis in Paris, having his first informal meeting with Léon Blum and envying his host's library.

The two hit it off—different in outlooks and ages, but both elegant, both appreciators of culture. With his mustache, grey commas of hair, and his shining spectacles, Léon Blum was the grand thinker behind France's moderate left, and he was his country's first Socialist prime minister. He was also its first Jewish one. He was a true believer in disarmament, without which he didn't believe collective security would work. Eden considered himself more of a realist, appreciating the value of a strong army, but he couldn't help regretting that Blum wasn't in office months ago. The French prime minister gave him a book by one of Eden's favorite authors, Anatole France, inscribed by the writer himself.

After Blum had sailed into power, thanks to the coalition tide of the Popular Front, squalls and storms followed. No sooner was he elected than an extremist member in the Chamber of Deputies spouted anti-Semitic vitriol his way on the assembly floor. And now as he chatted over literature with Eden, France was being convulsed by a general strike. Hitler's reoccupation of the Rhineland had polarized France, with right-wingers bizarrely painting the Popular Front as the party of war, while those on the left either stuck their heads in the sand or made noises about following the League.

Blum himself was already a victim of France's bipolar disorder. Back in February, he was getting a ride home with friends from the Chamber of Deputies when their Citroen got held up in traffic on the boulevard Saint-Germain. The delay was because of the funeral procession for a leader of the right-wing group *Action française*, Jacques Bainville, and the mourners wanted to make a statement with their presence. As the car tried to crawl its way through, the students and right-wingers noticed its deputy ID sticker—and then they spotted Blum inside.

They rushed up and dragged the sixty-four-year-old politician from the vehicle, beating him bloody on the cobblestones. Women looking on shouted,

"Kill him!" Two police officers tried to pull him free of the mob, but it took a group of construction workers to finally get Blum to safety on the rue de Lille. He spent his evening in bed with his head swathed in bandages, and by the next morning the journal, *L'Action française*, rewrote history to suggest the car was trying to bully its way through the street. In their version, the extremists had "rescued" Blum from an incensed mob.

Blum was now healed, in power, and, refreshingly for Eden, anxious for France to fall into step with Britain against Italian aggression. The "right man" had arrived at last.

But what could be done now? If the allies maintained their position, he expected that keeping up sanctions would lead to war. Even if Mussolini buckled under, how could things ever go back to what they were in the Horn of Africa after Haile Selassie had left his country? Eden knew the alternative was to admit that sanctions had failed, while still refusing to recognize Mussolini's conquest.

The two floated the idea of a "Mediterranean Pact." Italy couldn't take on Britain on the high seas, but it was still a formidable naval power. Maybe a pact would harden the resolve of countries in the region that had chosen sanctions; it could also renew their faith. Blum expected Britain to take the lead on this new initiative. In fact, according to him, most French expected it of Britain because "you are regarded as a sanctionist power par excellence. Clearly, therefore, I cannot take a lead in advance of what you would be prepared to do. My public would never understand that at all."[57]

This remark makes Blum look weak, but he knew politics, and he knew his own mind. He despised Fascism, and he saw well ahead of time what took others years to recognize. Mussolini and Hitler, he warned Eden, would sooner or later strike a bargain as their interests aligned. Blum thought the British were falling all over themselves to accommodate Hitler as a buffer against Mussolini. Eden did his best to reassure him that nothing could be further from the truth.

With the new treasure of the Anatole France book packed in his luggage, Eden rode the boat-train home to London and right into the stack of grim balance sheets of the anti-sanction crowd. If Italy was hurting, so in many ways was Britain; Wales, for instance, had lost a valuable market for its coal. The major flaw in any sanctions strategy is that there's always someone willing to trade with the enemy. Apartheid-era South Africa relied on Israel for military contracts throughout the mid-1970s and most of the 1980s. China and India won big by investing in Burma as it stubbornly endured sanctions from the United States and Europe. And in 1936, Germany could sit back and laugh over its arms profits from Ethiopia—because here was Italy, now a hungry market for its industrial goods.

It wasn't just a matter of trade. The British fleet had been on constant alert for months, its ships deployed and far from the safe harbors of home. Eden was told that if the situation didn't relax soon, the navy would have to call up reservists to man vessels.

There was a name that would fit the limbo they were all in, except the term hadn't been invented yet: *Cold War*. All the features were there. Instead of nuclear doom, the psychological nightmare was gas, and in a couple of months, the Home Office would announce it was working to supply every man, woman, and child in Britain with a gas mask—which they couldn't have right away, and could only get at specific centers if it became necessary. The world of espionage was just as sinister and ludicrous as it would be twenty years later. While OVRA agents slipped through London shadows, sitting in an SIS file in Malta had been a plan—scrapped due to lack of funds—for a disinformation campaign. It was to fool Italian spies and some Maltese into thinking the RAF had a secret "interference" weapon to bring down their planes.[58]

All the ambiguity of a Cold War was there, too. When the war clouds had first darkened, people in Britain, France, and their allied countries at least had something to fight for. But Ethiopia was lost, so what were the stakes now? The young foreign secretary would have to answer this because so far, Great Britain had refused to defend only a principle.

* * *

John Robinson left Addis Ababa only two days before the Emperor, knowing "the Italians might have shot me first and investigated afterwards."[59]

Or not investigated at all. By his own count, there were at least six attempts to kill him after he departed Ethiopia, the most serious one happening as he stood on the deck of the ship to Marseilles. An Egyptian had warned him, and then moments later, three men started towards him, one armed with a dagger. Robinson was lucky. Two sailors came to his rescue. He later told the attendees of a Sunday banquet in his honor that a special detail from the ship's kitchen staff was assigned to watch his food. And days after his arrival home, thugs posing as left-wing friends allegedly tried to "get him" after he finished a speech at Rockland Palace.[60]

Even without the crime thriller drama, it was a bittersweet homecoming. He was greeted as a hero, but his side had lost. An impressive crowd of two thousand supporters waited for him when his ship came into New York on May 18. Ethiopian flags were waved, songs were sung, and he was expected to say a few words to insist the fight wasn't over. This was the kind of reception he would get at every major stop on a week-long tour organized by the United Aid for Ethiopia.

"Mussolini's troubles are just beginning," he promised. "Guerrilla warfare will soon commence in the west of Ethiopia, especially in the mountain fastnesses where it will take years for the Italians to penetrate."[61] He claimed armies loyal to the Emperor were waiting for the word to strike at strategic spots. He was both right and wrong. Guerrilla warfare *had* started, but Haile Selassie was on his own ship to Britain, and the guerrilla units had no unifying single leadership.

There is a strange mystery to all the attention Robinson received. At home, he was now a legendary pilot. Yet he was never formally decorated by the Emperor for his bravery, and though his letters home bear the unmistakable seal of the Lion of Judah with Amharic script on the stationary, not one of the major chroniclers and witnesses in the war bother to mention him. *At all.* Not George Steer, who refers to Mischa Babitcheff as the Emperor's chief of aviation. Not Ladislas Farago, who names Babitcheff the Emperor's personal pilot. Not Feodor Konovalov. Not even Haile Selassie.

Racism is a tempting culprit, but it doesn't fit any of these men. Steer might not have met Robinson, and his account of the war only mentions the Ethiopian air force briefly; he obviously thought it didn't play a big role. Farago had returned to Ethiopia in the autumn of 1935, thinking he might have to update his book, but he came home to London by the end of November, "satisfied that no new book was yet required"—which is peculiar, because by then the fighting had started. He also fails to mention Robinson, and the December edition of his book still has Eric Virgin's emphatic arguments that Ethiopia didn't need an air force and that Italy posed no real threat from the skies. Perhaps part of the blame lies here; the little Potez planes were all but ignored by historians, and Robinson along with them.

Konovalov and the Emperor are the most puzzling for their omissions. Konovalov, who saw so much of the war, had to have run into Robinson at least once or twice as the pilot delivered his military dispatches, yet he doesn't mention him. And Haile Selassie, whom Robinson praised and said always treated him well, didn't bother to sing Robinson's praises in his autobiography, though many bit players in the great drama are named.

The best explanation until more information comes to light may be that John Robinson, for all the news coverage he inspired, was simply *too* modest. In a war filled with colorful, sometimes outlandish personalities, the shy pilot must have faded into the collage of anxious battle preparations, refugee caravans, and war councils. No sooner was he home than the Spanish Civil War was making him yesterday's news. John Robinson didn't really look for attention unless Claude Barnett and others nudged him to step into the spotlight for the cause.

And he soon resented being pushed. In fact, he felt very, very used. He was back only two months when friction developed with his old sponsor. Barnett and others raised an aviation fund relying on *his* name and *his* reputation, ostensibly to help the kind of initiatives for black pilots that Robinson started before the war. But he was shocked to discover when he tried to take out money to buy a plane that Barnett had refused to sign for the withdrawal. In a polite but unequivocal letter, he wrote, "That incident really hurt me very much, but it was no more than I expected, having dealt often with the leaders of the Negro race."[62]

He would not be anyone's pawn, symbol, or frontman. Instead, he would quietly get on with the job of being a pilot.

* * *

On John Robinson's first night back in New York City, he enjoyed a dinner in his honor at the YMCA on 135th Street. There would be trouble one street over and a few hours later. Even the news of a returning hero couldn't placate the bottled rage simmering and stewing in Harlem.

Reports were getting out over atrocities committed by the Italians. Sympathizers to the Ethiopian cause met that night in front of an Italian fish market on Lenox Avenue, and the meeting broke up at about twelve-thirty in the morning without any trouble. But then a gang of about twelve "hoodlums" threw a brick through the store's window and marched down Lenox, looking to hurt a certain black police officer. They couldn't find him. Instead, they turned their wrath on another Italian store, this one an all-night fruit and vegetable outlet. They smashed its windows, and soon the road was strewn with produce. That's when the cops came. It became an ugly free-for-all, and when still more officers rushed in, one of them pulled out his revolver and shot one of the black men in the leg.

The shot was the alarm for more angry locals and nervous cops. As paddy wagons roared up, their sirens wailing, and mounted police rode in to play cavalry, stones and bricks were hurled down at them from rooftops. In a macabre fashion, the riot was imitating the crude simplicity and the same unequal struggle as one of the battles in Ethiopia. Four hundred black Harlemites were challenging 110 of New York's finest, but stones and bricks couldn't beat truncheons and the charges by trained horses from the police stables. It was probably a small miracle that no one else was shot, let alone killed.

Still, the resentment lingered. It took hours to restore relative peace, and for days, outraged people rode in trucks through the streets of Harlem, shouting for their fellow residents to boycott Italian stores. Father Divine led a protest march that attracted thousands, and now it was decided that the police had to make themselves felt again in the neighborhood. Harlem was starting to *feel* like

Ethiopia. Fiorella La Guardia was Mussolini, and his mostly white police officers were the occupiers. It was reported that on a building overlooking a key intersection in Harlem, cops were deployed with machine guns.[63]

*   *   *

The *Orford* reached Southampton on June 3, but no one important in the British government was there to greet Haile Selassie.

It was the same when he arrived at Waterloo Station in London, although delegations from the Friends of Abyssinia, the League of Nations Union, and other groups were on hand to welcome him. Ordinary London residents hoped to spot the Emperor along his expected route to his embassy in Princes Gate—thousands came out to see him and wish him well. But police diverted his car, and they were robbed of their chance. Every arrangement made implied that he wasn't a head of state, merely a political embarrassment.

Anthony Eden had suggested to Edward VIII that it would be a popular gesture if the British monarch received the Emperor at Buckingham Palace.

"Popular with whom?" snapped the king. "Certainly not with the Italians."[64] Any such gesture, he argued to Eden, would offend Mussolini and push him further towards Hitler.

Edward, of course, was being less than candid. He was, in fact, an enthusiastic admirer of Hitler.

Eden didn't press the point over a visit and, because Edward didn't want him to "go away empty-handed," suggested fobbing off the duty to his brother, the Duke of York, who could pay a visit to Haile Selassie at his hotel. Edward didn't know it, but he was mere months away from going into exile himself, and his brother would soon have his job as the newly crowned George VI.

If Haile Selassie felt rejected by his hosts, he had no idea that his own behavior at Waterloo Station would prompt a new controversy in black communities around the world. Among the well-wishers at the station waited Marcus Garvey and a small band of UNIA members. But when Garvey tried to approach the Emperor, Haile Selassie apparently ignored him and went on his way. Instead of Garvey meeting his hero, he was left on a patch of concrete while one of his delegates chased after an official to deliver the UNIA's address.[65]

Garvey would pour out his hurt in a long article for the May-June issue of *The Black Man*, claiming that the royal exile "was, no doubt, advised by his Minister to receive the white delegation that waited on him . . ."[66] But Garvey also castigated the Emperor in print for a failure to rally blacks, with a rationale that betrayed more about Garvey's thinking than Haile Selassie's: "He must not be ashamed to be a member of the Negro race . . . The new Negro doesn't give two pence about the line of Solomon. Solomon has been long dead. Solomon was a Jew. The Negro is no Jew. The Negro has a racial origin running from Sheba to the present, of which he is proud. He is proud of Sheba, but he is not proud of Solomon."[67] His criticisms of the Emperor would grow more scathing in the months to come.

It's difficult to know how much Haile Selassie knew of Garvey at the time, if he knew of him at all; even if the Emperor was aware of him, Garvey would have had no standing. For Garvey, however, the snub—if it was indeed a deliberate snub, and not Haile Selassie's failure to see him—was a humiliating embarrassment. Garvey took it personally, and now he turned on his idol.

Yet one supporter did get through to the Emperor. He apparently broke through the human gate of officials around Haile Selassie and embraced him. The man who stepped forward was Jomo Kenyatta.

Once away from the chaotic London streets and inside his embassy, the Emperor accepted the consolation of old friends, receiving Wilfred Thesiger and his mother. Thesiger found him worn and tired but otherwise unchanged. "As we sat there looking on Hyde Park, he evinced no bitterness, gave no sign of the despair he must have felt. Only when he spoke briefly of the horrors he had seen was I conscious of his inutterable sadness."[68]

Chapter Seventeen

"WHAT ANSWER AM I TO TAKE BACK TO MY PEOPLE?"

Hubert Julian made news with an arrival of his own, this one in Naples on the Italian liner, *Vulcania*. He publicly announced that he'd become an Italian citizen, taking the new name, "Huberto Faunterloyana Juliano," and as usual, he had a different story for everyone.

For fellow passengers onboard the ship, he claimed he wanted to make a transatlantic flight between Rome and New York. To certain reporters, he said he was accepting an officer's commission in the *Regia Aeronautica*, with an assignment to the occupation forces. Whatever he would do, Italian officials thought this defector could be useful, but he kept them and the police waiting for an hour and a half while he dressed in a morning suit and top hat. He refused to leave his cabin until they provided him with a red carnation instead of the white one they'd given him.

In the end, there's no evidence to suggest he ever returned to Ethiopia to fly for the Italians. And the Black Eagle tried to rewrite history years later with another preposterous tall tale. In his autobiography, published in 1964, he claimed his public comments and about-face were all part of a carefully orchestrated plan with his "close friend and most loyal supporter," Malaku Bayen—who wasn't even in America for the first half of 1936. And what was the plan? To assassinate Benito Mussolini! Italian diplomats in New York had allegedly invited Julian to visit Rome to tell about his change of heart. Julian claims he went, and he eventually found himself having a private audience with Italian foreign minister, Count Galeazzo Ciano. But during the conversation, he forgot his role and began to defend Haile Selassie. Ciano then grew suspicious and canceled Julian's scheduled meeting with the dictator.[1]

Far from corroborating the tale, Bayen was scathing when he wrote later about the Black Eagle: "Another such rascal was in Ethiopia on wings for no other purpose than to gain information which he could sell to the Italian aggressors."[2]

So much for the assassination conspiracy. If the scene with Ciano ever took place, no doubt OVRA agents would have hauled Julian away for a long night of torture and questions under a bare light bulb. At the time, Julian was still defiant in proclaiming his new Italian citizenship, and in the United States, African Americans were outraged all over again. Julian's pose of disillusionment and his abandonment of the cause was one thing; this was outright treason to his own race.

Julian spent many more years as a glory hound, still trying to pin his name to events of great import, and he even challenged Hermann Goering to a duel in the air. But he would never reach the heights of celebrity he enjoyed over the Ethiopian War. There was, however, to be one last pathetic grasp for attention over Ethiopia in the future.

*   *   *

After the fall of Addis Ababa, Pietro Badoglio stayed on about two weeks and then went home, smart enough to enjoy his moment and leave. Conquering this stubborn land was one thing. Holding on to the country would be another, and Italy's Minister of Finance Thaon di Revel reported in June that the war had cost 12,111,000,000 lire.[3]

Just as in the war, there were naturally those willing to make things easier for the conquerors. The traitor Hailu was willing to submit. Ras Seyum Mangasha, who was supposed to be keeping the flame of rebellion alive in Tigray, swore an oath of allegiance a mere four days after Badoglio's arrival. Seyum, however, could not be lumped in with a Gugsa or a Hailu, and it's more likely he saw the hopelessness of the situation and decided he would fight another day. Eventually, he would get his chance.

Mussolini now dumped the thankless job of controlling Ethiopia into the lap of Rodolfo Graziani, trusting he would be utterly ruthless. It wouldn't hurt, however, to underscore his authorization. He sent Graziani an urgent telegram on June 5: "All the rebels made prisoners should be shot."[4] Days later, he granted permission for the Capronis to keep flying and drop their lethal rains of poison gas. On July 8, Mussolini cabled his viceroy: "I once more authorize Your Excellency systematically to conduct policy of political terror and extermination against rebels and implicated populations. Without the law of ten-fold retribution, one does not cure the wound in good time."[5]

Mussolini's Minister of the Colonies, Alessandro Lessona, was especially fixated on getting rid of the country's educated elites, the Young Ethiopians. To Lessona, they had a "false veneer of Europeanized culture" and were "particularly poisonous and dangerous," which meant that they should be "eliminated without mercy or pardon."[6] They had always been marked men; Mussolini had actually given Badoglio the kill order for them two days before the capture of the city.[7]

The executions were well underway; for the Europeanized ones, for the peasant rebels, for those who merely had the bad fortune to be caught. Sometimes, there was the farce of a show trial, its outcome never in doubt, so there was no need for an interpreter. A confused prisoner would stand listening to a language he recognized but couldn't understand, and then a bullet would follow; occasionally, there was the sadistic novelty of gasoline poured over the victim's head, and he was burned alive.[8] In at least one instance, Italian soldiers lined up their captives and used them for target practice. An officer decided this was too quick a way for them to die, so the Italians shot the men first in the genitals.[9]

There can be no dispute over whether such incidents took place. We know they did, not only from Ethiopian sources, but because Europeans, including one Italian, recorded them. Ciro Poggiali, correspondent for *Corriere della Sera*, watched the increasing sadism and brutality of the colonial regime and wrote about it in a secret diary that would be published by his son decades later.

According to the Hungarian doctor, Ladislas Sava, off in the ancient town of Agre Mariam near Sidamo, a group of forty Orthodox priests had fled into the hills with guerrillas to lend support, but none of them actually fought. When the Italians occupied the town, they captured the priests and machine-gunned them to death.[10] A grotesque insider expression became common usage during the occupation: "Taken up to Rome" or "He went to Rome," always "with a signifi-cant look which could not be misunderstood."[11] Certain nobles and chiefs were selected for a particularly sadistic form of execution. Like George Steer's friend, Kidane Maryam, their wrists and ankles were shackled, and they were put aboard planes. When the airplane hovered above a remote stretch of mountains, the bound prisoner was dragged to the cabin door and pushed to his death.[12]

At one point, a greater display—what the Italians called an "exhibition of pacification"—was made just outside Addis Ababa. At a radius of about eighteen miles around the capital, planes bombed and gassed the surrounding tukuls, and the flames could be seen from Addis Ababa streets. There were more scenes and smells of unburied bodies.[13]

* * *

For Anthony Eden, life in the Cabinet was becoming increasingly uncom-fortable. By the end of May, Samuel Hoare was back in the fold, now as lord of the admiralty. For some, his return from political exile was too soon; Halifax grumbled about Stanley Baldwin's decision to take him back once the PM was out of earshot. And Eden was now in a unique and unenviable position. Whenever he sat down at a Cabinet meeting, he faced not one, but two of his predecessors in the job: John Simon and, now, Hoare.

As it happened, however, he needed to worry more about someone else. On the night of June 10, Neville Chamberlain spoke to members of the 1900 Club, a Tory bastion. Intensifying sanctions, he argued, was not the answer. "That seems to me the very midsummer of madness," said Chamberlain. Sanctions meant an inherent risk of war, so what about "regional arrangements" instead? What about ones that could be approved by the League and guaranteed "only by those nations whose interests were vitally connected with those danger zones?"[14]

Eden wondered himself what the point was in continuing sanctions. He learned from French sources that thirteen nations in the League were shirking their responsibilities to keep the pressure on Italy. But in tossing out his hypothetical over port and cigars, Chamberlain jumped the gun. Eden was left to clean up the mess in the House of Commons, and as usual, Baldwin looked after Baldwin. He issued a predictable denial—no, his chancellor of the exchequer wasn't speaking for the government.

The chancellor of the exchequer, in fact, sent Eden a private apology, claiming he was overworked and had simply run out of time to show his colleague a draft of the upcoming speech. It was all a lie. "I did it deliberately because I felt that the party and the country needed a lead," Chamberlain wrote in his diary on June 17, "and an indication that the government was not wavering and drifting without a policy . . . I did not consult Anthony Eden because he would have been bound to beg me not to say what I proposed . . . He himself has been as nice as possible about it, though it is, of course, true that to some extent he has had to suffer in the public interest."[15] It wouldn't be the last time Chamberlain deliberately undermined him.

Thanks to his connection with Léon Blum, Eden was in a forgiving mood as he learned the new French government wouldn't take the lead over dropping sanctions; it was left up to Britain to tell the world that collective security was a failure. Perhaps Eden would have changed his mind if he'd known about the gale-force indignation that would blast his way from across the aisle. Just before four in the afternoon on June 18, he rose to read a statement about the government's change of heart. The House of Commons was packed, with Conservatives overflowing onto Labour benches. Chamberlain had chummed the waters, and it didn't take long for the debate to become raucous. When Eden told the House that the government had a responsibility to act with the League, the Scottish Communist William Gallacher piped up: "A responsibility in running away!"

Eden pressed on, but the heckling was breaking his stride, and he interrupted himself to say, "The Honorable Member's cheap gibes are not appropriate to the discussion." Then he finally got to his announcement: it was up to Britain to take the lead again over the League's stand. "I am quite convinced that so far from this lead, which we are going to take, embarrassing others, it will be welcomed in many quarters—"

"In Rome!" shouted some of the Opposition.

Eden ignored this and reminded the House that everyone once expected the war to last longer than it did. There were serious miscalculations, and the League had chosen certain specific sanctions because these were the ones they hoped would be effective—

The Opposition MPs pounced on this, shouting, *"Oil! Oil!"*

"Oil could not be made effective by League action alone," replied Eden.

There was some truth in this, and his opponents let this one pass for the most part. The sanctions, he went on, did not realize their purpose, and the Italian military campaign had succeeded. "To use plain language, it is plain that if the League means to enforce in Abyssinia a peace which the League can rightly approve, then the League must take action of a kind which must inevitably lead to war in the Mediterranean."

He neglected to mention the obvious: "the action of a kind" had already been explicitly set down in the League Covenant, and members were duty-bound to go to war.

Instead, he dropped his bombshell: "His Majesty's Government, after mature consideration, on advice which I, as Foreign Secretary, thought it my duty to give them, have come to the conclusion that there is no longer any utility in continuing these measures as a means of pressure upon Italy—"

Explosion from the Opposition benches: *"Shame!"*

"Resign!"

"Sabotage!"

"If the [members] will bear with me, I will give them the reasons which have brought us to take this decision," said Eden. "It cannot be expected by anyone that the continuance of existing sanctions will restore in Abyssinia the position which has been destroyed; nobody expects that. That position can be restored only by military action. So far as I am aware no other Government, certainly not this Government, is prepared to take such military action."

When Eden sat down, Labour's Arthur Greenwood fired a few salvos, but it was David Lloyd George who most eloquently expressed the Opposition's outrage. The former Liberal prime minister was one of the original architects of the League of Nations at the Versailles peace conference in 1919, and he reminded the Commons of this fact now. The League was not some "debating society," he pointed out. "Which of the nations have refused to stand by it? Which of the nations have failed to stand by sanctions? I put that question to the Prime Minister. Not one—"

Someone foolishly called out, "Germany!"

"Germany is not in the League," answered Lloyd George. There was laughter over this, and he snapped, "What a silly laugh that is. It is the sort of laugh that betrays the vacant mind." Then the old Welsh lion let out a rhetorical roar to shame the government benches. "I have been in this House very nearly half-a-century, I am sorry to say, and I cannot recall an occasion quite like this. I have never before heard a British Minister . . . come down to the House of Commons and say that Britain was beaten, Britain and her Empire beaten, and that we must abandon an enterprise we had taken in hand."

He hammered away at Eden, demanding to know whether press reports were true and that Blum's government in Paris was willing to back Britain up over any step to enforce the Covenant. What about guerrillas in Ethiopia? Would the government close imperial frontiers and stop all arms trade? Eden's answers were sincere and fairly direct, but it was clear that no policy had been worked out for this scenario.

"Fifty nations trusted us," said Lloyd George. "They will not when they see the British Empire saying it cannot go on. They will never trust this crowd." He pointed an accusing finger at the men on the front bench. "Tonight we have had the cowardly surrender, and there are the cowards."[16]

He spoke for many that day, but within four years time, the moral roles would be reversed. Eden would stand shoulder-to-shoulder with those determined to fight a Nazi invasion, while Lloyd George would be in the camp of the defeatists, advocating that Britain negotiate peace terms with Germany.

*   *   *

Rodolfo Graziani had a small ritual each weekday. He left his house in what used to be the Italian embassy and mounted a mule adorned in a caparison, leading his animal on its slow, ambling way through the streets of Addis Ababa to what was once the Little Gibbi, now known as the Governo Generale. This was where he worked on the business of the colony. He had a small military escort, at least at the beginning; only two guards riding along with him. Graziani probably doubted they were enough. The capital was only under nominal Italian control, and he knew it. His troops could make this city a garrison, but it was also a stronghold that was constantly under the threat of siege.

Still, Addis Ababa was changing practically overnight, being squeezed and crushed and molded in the great fist of the occupying power. Soldiers moved in and took over office buildings. They took over the better homes of wealthier Ethiopians as they pleased. A school run by Swedish missionaries had to be vacated, its children put out on the street, and the Swedes promptly deported. The Arada was the market center of the capital, and the Italians soon made it their own place of business and social gathering.

With their guns and their tanks, the soldiers had also brought in the racial laws imposed on Eritrea. New laws were being drafted in Rome. Alessandro Lessona, the Duce's minister of the colonies, sent a directive in early August that "the white race must impose itself through its superiority."[17] Now an Ethiopian, without knowing it, had a taste of what it was like to be black person in Jackson, Mississippi. A black woman couldn't walk into the Arada anymore as she pleased. A black man couldn't go into a cinema and sit where he liked.

It's a myth that Italy had a brand of Fascism distinct from Nazism over racial obsessions. American reporter Herbert Matthews had done an about-face on Fascism, but he was still among those who insisted that it was just the "lunatic fringe" of the party that called for measures against the Jews. In 1943, he would write, "The Italian people were simply bewildered and distressed when they were asked to hate people they considered to be just as good Italians as they were."[18] Matthews sincerely believed this, but he forgot how easy it had been to loathe and repress thousands of black citizens of the Italian colonies. Anyone surprised by the racial laws introduced in late 1938 had only to look at the laws quickly introduced in 1936. But those were for black people, out of sight and out of mind.

The hard line of white superiority had come from Mussolini himself. There could be no sexual involvement between Italians and Africans—a race of mixed-race children would prove to be "our worst enemies" who would "ruin what is beautiful in us."[19] The son of a blacksmith who spent years in poverty himself, Mussolini was brutal in his opinions that it must be the lower classes that chose to live with Ethiopian women; after all, this type had slaves as ancestors.[20]

The result should have been obvious and anticipated: a deep, simmering hatred and resentment in the black population of Ethiopia. But the regime was willfully blind to counterproductive results, and it often ignored its own flagrant displays of incompetence. A collection of elderly judges, for example, stepped off the train in Addis Ababa to preside over the new Italian courts. Working in remote Africa would double their pensions and get them closer to comfortable retirement, either back in Italy or in the colonies. But none of them bothered to learn the local language, and nobody cared if a translator wasn't fluent in Italian.

Journalist Ciro Poggiali sat in a courtroom, stunned at the official translator's nonsensical babbling: "Where are you going? The onions are. How much for hundred? I go to Florence."[21]

For some Ethiopians—those who collaborated—life was marginally better. And as Graziani rode his way to work, he was regularly joined by one of them, a lanky young black man in his early twenties who walked alongside the viceroy's mule. With a smile for his boss, he made himself so useful that he was almost "like a son to the general."[22] His name was Abriha Deboch, and he would soon become one of the most mysterious figures in Ethiopian history.

Yet he wasn't Ethiopian at all. He was a well-educated Eritrean fluent in Italian and French. Though clever enough to have earned brief schooling in Cairo, he was a habitual troublemaker, and he later spent time in prison over spying for the Italians. By all accounts, he could be volatile, secretive, and easily manipulated, yet ambitious and eager for personal glory. His prison term put him on the right side of the Italians, and he soon ingratiated himself with Graziani and the new regime. His actual duties are sketchy; he was an interpreter, but he was also valued as a political informant. It wasn't long before he was throwing his weight around town, taunting people that he could denounce them as rebels and agents, sometimes extorting them for money.[23]

He was a perfect fit for a leader like Graziani. Even paranoids have enemies, and the new viceroy was in a capital simmering with hostility against its occupiers, ruling a place where it was difficult to tell who had given in and who was working for the rebels. He was already rounding up Ethiopians who worked for foreign embassies, and he told Rome that he'd detected a resistance network. The legations protested. He didn't care. He would go on having their employees watched and opening their mail.

His darkest suspicions were over Sidney Barton, whom he knew met with nobles in his home. He also knew Barton used diplomatic mail to send along private letters from Kassa's son, Aberra, to the exiled ras in Jerusalem. Graziani was already threatening to expel diplomats, and Barton was high on his list to put on a train to Djibouti. In the end, he didn't have to. London used the excuse that Barton was due leave.[24] The truth was that his position had become impossible under the new regime.

Everyone in Addis Ababa knew the Bartons. They were a fixture of diplomatic and social life in the capital. They were people who worked to save Ethiopians and foreign expats alike from gas and shiftas and looting. Now they were being forced out. On June 19, the Bartons had to go "home."

* * *

You didn't need to be a natural-born Ethiopian or an Eritrean to be a collaborator.

Thomas Lambie, the doctor and missionary, was starting to panic. At fifty-one, he'd spent seventeen years of his life in Ethiopia, running his mission, founding two hospitals (one of them for lepers), and enjoying the personal sponsorship of the Emperor. He nominally worked under the auspices of the Sudan Interior Mission, but he'd always run his own show, and he adopted Ethiopian citizenship in 1934 just so he could work with less bureaucracy. Now the Italians had marched in with their Iron Will, and none of that seemed to matter anymore. Or maybe it still could.

He had worked with Stanislaw Belau, whose story of torture had reached the world's newspapers, and like Belau and John Melly, he'd put his name to condemnations of the Italians over gas attacks and bombings. Now he made an appalling about-face. He was desperate to keep his mission going, and as historian Rainer Baudendistel put it, "his deep religious convictions prevented him from really understanding the Ethiopians. He was so committed to his mission work that it was the only thing which mattered to him."[25]

Lambie was the kind of man who could strike a deal with the devil and quote scripture as he did it. When he submitted to Italian authorities, "I told them that although I had been against them, I was not going to oppose them, but took Paul's words from Romans 13:1 as my guide, 'Resist not the Powers.'"[26] The Italians were delighted. Lambie was so good at not resisting that he helped in the dismantling of the Ethiopian Red Cross, which, thanks to Fascist bookkeeping, meant staff members never received their proper pay. And while he was being so cooperative, the new regime would appreciate it if he would recant his criticisms of their conduct.

He did. Suddenly, his accusations didn't belong to him anymore; they were supposedly the mischief of Ethiopian Foreign Minister Heruy Wolde Selassie and Sidney Brown. As the Italians got their propaganda mileage out of his retractions, the enormity of what he'd done sank in. Now he felt a brand-new wave of panic mixed possibly with guilt and shame, and he sent off a fresh letter to the International Red Cross Committee, trying to undo the damage. But it was too late. Lambie had more to worry about than staying in the good graces of the Committee. Old friends were disgusted and turned their backs on him: Marcel Junod, Sidney Barton—and the Emperor, who wanted nothing more to do with him. The Sudan Interior Mission strongly suggested he leave Ethiopia for a short period, and while he was away, the Italians kept busy by taking over church properties and deporting foreign missionary staff.

In a memoir published three years later, he would complain bitterly about his former homeland and its people. "The Ethiopians were seldom grateful for what we did for them." He also disparaged their valor: "They did not have the requisite courage to fight a guerrilla war."[27] In this, he would be proved categorically wrong.

Lambie soon discovered he was a man without a country. He was legally Ethiopian, but under the Italians, there was no more Ethiopia; it had been absorbed into *Africa Orientale Italiana*. His surrender to the Fascists had also not escaped the eyes of the US State Department, which didn't consider him Ethiopian either. Though born in Pittsburgh, Thomas Lambie had to apply for naturalization to be an American again. And when Ethiopia was no longer under a black Fascist cloud, Lambie would still not be allowed to come back. He would never be forgiven for his betrayal.

*   *   *

In London, John Spencer paid a call at the embassy in Princes Gate. He found the Emperor sitting in an armchair, facing away from a window with an enviable view onto Hyde Park. Haile Selassie rose to greet him, and when the audience was over, his aides fell all over themselves to explain that the Emperor was so exhausted, he forgot his own protocols.[28] Spencer hardly cared. Now that he was in London, he was quickly back on the job, handling correspondence and running interference with the huge British press machine, which was fascinated by the royal exile. Spencer was astonished at the large volume of what he considered "crank" letters sent to the Emperor from the United States.

Stanley Baldwin was definitely *not* one of the fascinated. He had to contend with the greatest embarrassment for his government strolling down the avenues of Mayfair. Baldwin couldn't even bring himself to share the same air as Haile Selassie. One afternoon in June, he was taking tea with a colleague on the terrace of the House of Commons. Then, as now, the Houses of Parliament were a big tourist draw, and a small group of black people seemed to be making a beeline towards his table. It included a diminutive figure wearing a cape. The prime minister of Great Britain obviously hadn't paid close attention to the photos in the papers, because he had to ask a waiter who it was.

"Haile Selassie, the Emperor of Ethiopia, and some Ethiopians, sir."

Baldwin, flustered, looked for escape. Haile Selassie's entourage cut off his direct path out. Where to go? There weren't many options—not unless he felt like jumping in the Thames and swimming away. Instead, Baldwin shaded his face with a hand and slunk behind some tables, finding another route to hurry back to his office.[29]

The Emperor, however, had already set his sights on a far larger target than the PM and his government. He was planning to go to Geneva in a few days' time to address the League of Nations. He would shame the world with what had happened to his country.

* * *

June offered more bad news for African Americans. Joe Louis lost a rematch bout to German fighter, Max Schmelling. The *Chicago Defender* spoke for many when it asked on June 27, "Haile Selassie First, Now Louis, Who Next?"

That was the mood of the summer over politics: despair. The Harlem riot and protests back in May were the last great roars of outrage. There were other demonstrations that summer over Ethiopia, but the numbers weren't there, the feeling subdued.[30] After all, the protests before were to urge *action*. What could be done now? Black Americans, like their white counterparts and Europeans, assumed the struggle was over merely because Addis Ababa was taken. Most Americans had no idea how precarious a grasp Italy had on Ethiopia. Thousands in Harlem would march again that autumn, but it would be over rent increases and housing conditions. "Give us milk at prices we can afford to pay," would be the rallying cry for mothers that November, not only in Harlem but also in Little Italy, the Bronx, and Brooklyn. *Local* concerns, issues close to home. The Depression was still on.

America was still neutral and firmly looking inward. It was often downright nostalgic. The most popular film of the year was *San Francisco*, released that month with Clark Gable and Jeanette Macdonald playing lovers in the time of the Great Earthquake of 1906. When *The Great Ziegfield* had been released in April, it reminded moviegoers of a time with Follies long before soup kitchens and job lines.

The Macmillan publishing company was happily shocked to discover that women would part with three dollars—a hefty price back then—for a new romance novel. It was a brick of a read at 1,037 pages, but that didn't matter. The book sold all through June of 1936 and would keep on doing well for months after, reaching a million copies sold by New Year. For its portrait of the South in the aftermath of the Civil War, it described field hands set free this way: "Like monkeys or small children turned loose among treasured objects whose value is beyond their comprehension, they ran wild—either from perverse pleasure in destruction or simply because of their ignorance."

The book was called *Gone with the Wind*.

* * *

The Emperor's delegation spent four days in Geneva before his speech to the League Assembly. The Swiss Government refused to let him stay at his private villa in Vevey less than forty miles away on the flimsy and outrageous pretext that he was planning to engage in political activities. Instead, the Emperor took rooms at the Carleton Park Hotel. John Spencer, Lorenzo Taezaz, and Everett Colson (having recovered enough to rejoin the team) all got to work on a draft of the address.

They had help, too, from Gaston Jèze, the old French academic who had tried to facilitate negotiations in Geneva about a year ago. By now, after so many riots and demonstrations, Jèze was so thoroughly disgusted with the right wing and his own country's weak-willed government that he composed an acid-dripping manifesto of a speech. It laid a good portion of the blame for the Crisis at the door of the Élysée Palace.[31] It was too much in Colson's and Spencer's view, and they sanded down the harsher passages.

On June 30, the delegation arrived, the Emperor dressed in a dark cloak and wearing a fedora. There had actually been a question of whether Haile Selassie was entitled to be heard at all, with back-room maneuverings going on over credentials and protocol. It was not merely a case of Italian lobbying; Switzerland and Hungary didn't want him there either. But the world was watching, and if the League refused to let him speak, its credibility would suffer even more.

The Emperor's speech was scheduled for late on the day's agenda. Before he could be heard, he and his team had to endure the reading of a long statement from Italy that congratulated itself on its conquest: "Italy views the works she has undertaken in Ethiopia as a sacred mission of civilization and proposes to carry it out according to the principles of the League Covenant and of other international deeds which set forth the duties and tasks of civilizing powers." Then came promises. The Ethiopians could keep their languages and pray as they liked. There would be freedom of movement and communications. "Italy will consider it an honor to inform the League of Nations of the progress achieved in her work of civilizing Ethiopia, of which she has assumed the heavy responsibility."

When at last the Emperor was invited forward, he glided to the rostrum and unfolded his notes under a desk lamp. There was a sprinkling of polite applause, which was suddenly interrupted by a vulgar racket going on in the press gallery. Ten Italian journalists shouted insults and blew whistles. Down on the Assembly floor, the Rumanian representative, Nicolae Titulescu, was so disgusted that he jumped to his feet and yelled: *"À la porte les sauvages!"* ["Throw out the savages!"]

Haile Selassie waited in stoic silence at the rostrum.

The lights were switched off to quell the storm of insolence, but still the journalists kept up the racket. The lights were turned on and then turned off again.

More whistles and shouts. Police finally reached the gallery and roughly hauled the Italians out of the chamber. It turned out they were arresting a who's who of the Italian press establishment: the diplomatic correspondent for Mussolini's own newspaper, the *Popolo d'Italia*, two reporters for the *Corriere della Sera*, the editor of the *Stampa* in Turin, an official with the Stefani news agency, and the press attaché of the Italian embassy in Vienna. Two of the group were questioned and let go, while the rest spent the night in a cell.

Back in the hall, the delegates settled down, and the tiny Emperor began to speak. He was supposed to address his audience in French, but at the last moment, he relied on Amharic. "I, Haile Selassie the First, Emperor of Ethiopia, am here today to claim that justice that is due to my people, and the assistance promised to it eight months ago, when fifty nations asserted that aggression had been committed in violation of international treaties."

Those fortunate to be wearing headphones could listen to a translation in either English or French. "There is no precedent for a head of state himself speaking in this assembly. But there is also no precedent for a people being victim of such injustice and being at present threatened by abandonment to its aggressor. Also, there has never before been an example of any government proceeding to the systematic extermination of a nation by barbarous means, in violation of the most solemn promises made by the nations of the earth that there should not be used against innocent human beings the terrible poison of harmful gases . . ."

He spent several minutes summarizing the Italian atrocities, and after reviewing the Walwal pretext for war and the fruitless peace overtures, he held his audience to account. "If a strong government finds that it may, with impunity, destroy a small people then the hour strikes for that weak people to appeal to the League of Nations to give its judgment in all freedom. God and history will remember your judgment . . .

"I ask the fifty-two nations, who have given the Ethiopian people a promise to help them in their resistance to the aggressor, what are they willing to do for Ethiopia? You, Great Powers, who have promised the guarantee of collective security to small states over whom hangs the threat that they may one day suffer the fate of Ethiopia, I ask: What measures do they intend to take?

"Representatives of the world, I have come to Geneva to discharge in your midst the most painful of duties for the head of a state. What answer am I to take back to my people?"

As the Emperor stepped down from the rostrum, the microphone picked up his bitter last words: "It is us today. It will be you tomorrow."

*   *   *

Haile Selassie's speech closed the formal session that day. Maybe a few in the audience recognized this would go down as one of the greatest speeches of modern political history, but the Emperor's address failed to persuade anyone at the time. For all the shame he poured on the League of Nations, the next day in the Assembly, there was still no one who offered a proper answer to his question.

On July 3, there was a startling incident on the Assembly floor that on the surface, had nothing to do with Ethiopia—and yet it had everything to do with Ethiopia. And it spoke, if nothing else, to the general impotency of the League of Nations.

An interpreter was busy droning on with the translation of a speech by the Spanish delegate. A journalist, Stefan Lux, had somehow found his way down from the press balcony to the Assembly floor and over to a bench reserved for photographers. Lux was a Jew, born in Austria, spending most of his life in Germany, but he'd been forced to move his family and to work in Czechoslovakia. He waited for some time on the bench with the cameramen and then suddenly got to his feet and pulled out an automatic pistol, shouting in French, *"This is the end! It's all over!"* Then he shot himself in the chest and dropped to the floor.

The delegates heard a noise, but most didn't recognize it as a gunshot. Even an American woman standing next to Lux, Helen Kirkpatrick of the US Research Center in Geneva, thought it was only the distinctive *pop* of a flash bulb. Down front, Belgium's Premier Paul Van Zeeland was presiding over the session and said, "Gentlemen, let us continue."

Doctors rushed over to Lux, who was still alive but badly hemorrhaging. He would die later that evening in the hospital. "Avenol, Avenol," he gasped, calling the name of the League's Secretary General. "Briefcase . . ."[32] One of the reporters apparently heard his more coherent last words. "I want to die as a public protest to the way Germany is treating Jews. I am not sorry. My mind is completely lucid."[33] Inside his briefcase were letters addressed to *The Times* of London, the *Manchester Guardian*, Joseph Avenol, Edward VIII, and Anthony Eden.

Not long after the incident, Sweden's Kirsten Hesselgren, the first woman to ever address the Assembly, told her fellow delegates that "fifty nations are letting one small one fail. How can any small nation henceforth have any hope?"

Lux had killed himself over Germany, but in two years time, his small nation of refuge, Czechoslovakia, would be sold out as well. That July 3, 1936, Hesselgren asked the Assembly, "Why bear children into a world so hopeless and so insecure?"[34]

Three days after that, the League suspended its sanctions against Italy, and by July 15, they were lifted.

*   *   *

Now, *now* after all this time, the guerrilla war that Haile Selassie always wanted was finally happening. It grew without any central strategy or command, because now it had to. Those who were patriots of Ethiopia simply had no other methods available to them. And that is what the resistance fighters called themselves: Patriots.

They started small. The Little Rains washed out the road from Addis Ababa to Dessie, which made the rail line to Djibouti all the more crucial. Around July 2, about three thousand Ethiopians dressed in khaki swooped down from a hill east of Bishoftu—they had even dug trenches around the hill in case they were discovered. As night fell on July 5, they overwhelmed a small army outpost, killing half the Italians and scores of askaris. The surviving troops fell back to where a larger detachment was holding the capital's railway station. There was another skirmish, and the Ethiopians melted away.

But the fighting turned out to be a mere sideshow. The phone line between Mojo and the capital had been cut in several spots—about two miles of line ripped out in one spot alone. The next day, one of the regular trains was chugging a few miles out of Addis Ababa in its slow, meandering way when the Patriots attacked. Someone had "loosened" the rails so expertly that the driver didn't spot any trouble until the train was derailed. The Ethiopians managed to kill a colonel while forty other soldiers and passengers scrambled to a construction house outfitted like a bunker with slit windows. The raid became a siege, lasting thirty-six hours. The Italians managed to pick off a few of their attackers, but the Ethiopians made good use of cover. The British military attaché found an eyewitness who "stated not a few of the Italian soldiers . . . spent much of their time huddled in a corner and in tears."

The Ethiopians attacking them were a disciplined unit. They didn't bother to loot the train, and they didn't go after the stray passengers who cowered under it. "The name of the Ethiopian leader is not known, but there is no doubt that he is a man of some intelligence," wrote the British military attaché for his intelligence report.[35] It was possibly Fikre Mariam, the former commander of troops for the crown prince. Italian authorities blamed "the sons of Ras Kassa."[36]

For the Italians, this was becoming embarrassing. Though it was clear the phone lines were cut, no one thought to bring a portable wireless on their search for the overdue, missing train. One small search party went out, and the soldiers rode in a coal-car pulled by an engine. The Somali driver was afraid of getting hit by gunfire, so he crouched down while opening the throttle and driving blind. At fifty miles an hour, the engine smashed right into the derailed train. Half the search party was killed by the Ethiopians, while the others ran back to Addis Ababa. More skillful breaks in the line prevented another relief train from getting through. By then, some of the local residents grew bold and started looting what they could, while more fighting broke out near Mojo.

At last, reinforcements for the Italians arrived, and the Ethiopians had the good sense to withdraw. The British military attaché didn't know their losses but assumed "they were probably heavy." He might have been wrong. His assumption was based on what happened during the war, but the raid was cleverly thought out, its plan well executed, its targets and methods precise. The Ethiopians were at last using guerrilla warfare, and one of its first rules is *leave* when the numbers go against you. The Italians had to take 150 wounded back to the capital.

Bloodied and humiliated, the Italians couldn't catch the Patriots, so they took their fury out on the local population of the Mojo region. In the same report sent to the Foreign Office, it was disclosed that "Eritreans who comprised part of the force were given 'carte blanche' to do what they liked for eight days. Villages were burnt and looted. Any native, man, woman, or child seen in the neighborhood was shot." The military attaché made another presumption, thinking the worst of the Patriots. "What effect this massacre will have in preventing further occurrences is difficult to say . . . the fact that some thousand Gallas, for whom they probably do not care two pins, have been killed, might well not worry them."[37]

Fikre Mariam was Amhara, but even if he didn't care, those who fought in and around Mojo may well have included Oromo, and no doubt, they had lost mothers, children, fathers, sisters. But it was true that the reprisal had no preventive effect. The Patriots swooped down from the hills time and again to wreck rail sections, bomb bridges, and cut telegraph wires, and for months, the railway would never be safe. The Italians were so embarrassed by the early attacks that they went around to all the foreign legations and shut down their wireless to stop the news from spreading.

They were fighting, too, outside Harar, though the occupiers denied this. Some chiefs and nobles had of course submitted, but the Italians felt they had to litter the region with pamphlets that declared, "No foreign power can save the brigands; moreover, all nationals including those of England and France recognize the might of Italy." A senior Italian officer was far more candid in private with the British Consul in Harar, admitting that his forces shouldn't have allowed the bande to roam the streets of the city, bragging about their atrocities; it infuriated the Ethiopians and stiffened their resolve. Worse, the now-exhausted Italian troops were stuck in the city without proper transport, and they had failed to secure nearby Gara Mulata and Deder soon after taking Harar. On the night of July 12, when pistols and machine guns blasted away for a full hour, the Italians tried to claim it was practice fire.[38]

The guerrilla war evolved without even the higher nobles consciously realizing it—there were pitifully few higher nobles left who could. Ethiopia's Foreign Minister Heruy Wolde Selassie had left with the Emperor for England; so had Malaku Bayen. Tekle Hawaryat Tekle Mariyam, who had poured such scorn on Haile Selassie for fleeing, decided he would go into exile himself that year and wound up in Madagascar.[39] He had few other choices. Britain's Colonial Office had heartlessly refused him permission to live in Kenya.[40]

Ras Imru was still on the loose, but when he reached Debra Markos at last, he was a defeated man in spirit, and the last straw was the news that the Emperor had left the capital, bound for Djibouti. If he had known about the rail attacks, he might have applauded their ingenuity and daring, but they wouldn't have changed his mind. With a mere one thousand men, he had decided to cross the Blue Nile and make for Gore, the new capital of what was left of the Ethiopian state.

What he found in Gore, however, must have demoralized him further. Haile Selassie had left in charge of the city Wolde Tsadik, the ex-president of the Ethiopian Senate. Close to seventy, Wolde Tsadik was a genial dodderer, another man who wasn't up to the task of maintaining discipline. Though he had a Shoan army at his command, the whole region was in chaos and open revolt, and when he dispatched a contingent to put down a rebellion at the garrison in Jimma, his troops promptly deserted. And things got worse. The British consul in Gore was a young, arrogant captain, E. N. Erskine, with unrepentant biases who liked to meddle. He loathed "the despotic Tafari regime" and the "self-seeking treacherous smooth-spoken and bigoted Amhara officials," favoring the Oromo instead.[41] He would have liked nothing better than to have the country under London's remote control.

Erskine had cabled the Foreign Office on June 10 to announce, "A Galla delegation of chiefs would like to transmit via Khartoum to the League of Nations the request for a British mandate in Ethiopia to the west of the 36th meridian. All the Galla chiefs refuse to be represented by their enemies and oppressors—that is, the Amhara delegation now present in London."[42] If some in the Foreign Office liked the idea, Khartoum was furious; officials for Anglo-Egyptian Sudan favored the Italians taking over Ethiopia. The idea was soon turned down.[43]

In Gore, the petty feuds of diplomats were far from Imru's mind. Exhausted, he hardly cared that he was now viceroy of Ethiopia. He sent a telegram to Haile Selassie, urging surrender, and he wanted Erskine to help arrange his safe passage to Uganda. For his part, Erskine was always glad to see the back of another Amharic noble, but he genuinely respected Imru and was willing to give him safe escort. Then in early July, the ras was paid a visit by a group of 350 soldiers and cadets from the military school in Holeta. They were looking to Imru for help and leadership. Two of them were Charles Martin's sons, Benyam and Yosef, and there were about fifty Eritrean deserters as well.

The cadets were feeling quite proud of themselves after a sensational raid in the last week of June. First, the Italians had been conned with a fake invitation from Oromo leaders to come out and negotiate with them, with the long-term view of building up a garrison in Wellega in the south. The Italians, fearless and complacent, had cheerfully accepted and put several officers on three planes, including a general who was second-in-command of their air force, a colonel and former military attaché, plus Antonio Locatelli, one of the Italians' famous combat pilots. In Boneya, as soon as the officers stepped off the plane, Benyam, Yosef, and the other cadets had opened fire, killing nine of them and destroying all three aircraft. The ambush was so embarrassing that the Italian government reflexively denied it happened when reporters called to check.

Imru knew that one ambush does not a war make. He told them that to keep on fighting would be insane. They had no guns, no ammunition, no artillery, no supplies. They wanted to fight anyway. Some were mere boys who had the ranks of "major" or "lieutenant colonel" only because the battlefields were littered with the veteran dead. Their raid had managed to put Ethiopia back in the newspapers abroad, but it did little to rally immediate support at home. In fact, the local dejazmach urged them to leave because he feared Italian reprisals, which was how their tiny force had ended up in Gore.

They called themselves the Black Lions. Led by Alamawarq Bayyana, a veterinary surgeon educated in Britain, they formed a loose group fueled by youth: young energy, young confidence, new ideas, and a spirit shaped by education abroad. They had sat down and written up a rather unique constitution, and perhaps not surprisingly with this collection of intellectuals, they put the political authority above the military hierarchy. They had other bold ideas, too. Prisoners were to be given humane treatment, villagers and peasants not preyed upon, and if the combat situation was hopeless, better to kill yourself than be captured.

Ras Imru listened to their excited patriotic talk and then at last gave his answer to their pleas. The Black Lions were thrilled. He would join them and keep on fighting.

Chapter Eighteen

THE PRIDE OF LIONS

Back in the capital, a young bishop of Dessie, his face ascetically handsome and appropriately pensive in surviving photographs, was horrified by what was being done to his country. The abun, Petros, began to galvanize the local people, wanting them to fight back.

He organized a secret meeting at the Debre Libanos monastery, and men showed up to discuss strategy. There were men fighting for the old, die-hard war horse, Balcha, and for the guerrilla leader, Fikre Mariam. The former chief of police, Abebe Aregai, was there. While Kassa Haile Darge had gone into exile in Jerusalem, three of his sons (Wondosson, Abera, and Asfa Wossen) had kept up the resistance at home and would take part. By most accounts, Petros had little to do with the actual military end. He was a guiding spiritual force, encouraging the men to be bold and to win.

Their plan was to hit the capital, and they would strike multiple targets. Shawaragad Gadle sent messengers out to spread the word of when the attack should start. She'd graduated quickly from strolling along the road with her egg basket, and she recalled later that she was arrested twelve times in the early period of the occupation. If things had gone as usual with the regime, she would have been shot dead. She'd been accused of making propaganda, of even receiving letters from the Emperor, but before she faced a firing squad, a dejazmach and several priests had spoken up and secured her release.[1] Her close calls didn't sway her resolve at all.

The rebels would move in to the Arada and also go after St. George's Cathedral in the center of the city, the two gibbis, the rail station, and a new airbase. Priests had to act as messengers because the rebels had no other way to communicate with each other. They would rush off with letters to guerrilla leaders in the southwest, giving them the signal to interfere with the garrison at Ambo to stop it from sending reinforcements.

Just before dawn on July 28, the attack started. Abera Kassa's men easily made it to the cathedral, and the soldiers under Abebe Aregai even managed to penetrate the Governo Generale, putting Graziani himself in danger. Lekelash Bayan and her guerrilla cell were there, too, with Lekelash no doubt snapping the signature word that was now her nickname, *"Balaw!" Strike him!* But the forces couldn't stay in touch with each other. While Abebe Aregai was being driven off by two battalions of Blackshirts, Fikre Mariam hadn't crossed a river yet to take the Great Gibbi, and Balcha wasn't in position, either. Two commanders on the outskirts of the city didn't have a clue what was going on. They both lost heart and didn't enter the fray at all.[2]

One of the tragedies of the attack is that the rebels had inside information and didn't act on it, perhaps because it came from a most improbable source—Abriha Deboch.

Here was an apparent traitor offering help, the same young man who worked in Graziani's office. He had approached Fikre Mariam shortly before the riots and the Italians' arrival, asking to fight in his ranks. Fikre Mariam might have been aware of his prison sentence, or maybe he was simply unimpressed by the young man, but whatever his reasons, the dejazmach gave him the brush off. You'll be more useful as an informer, he was told. This turned out to be true, because Fikre Mariam couldn't imagine how high Abriha would climb. Abriha had insinuated himself quickly in the short-lived administration of Badoglio, so that by the time Abun Petros was having his clandestine meetings with rebels, he was well-placed to get key information.

And as historian Ian Campbell has uncovered, he was an active double agent. He sent letters to the top men in Petros's group, warning them the Italians would soon get reinforcements; they were planning to roll out a net of barbed wire to encircle the capital.[3] Time was *running out.* He even had the clever suggestion that the rebels should use flares to coordinate with each other.[4] But he was virtually ignored.

In the middle of the shooting that day, reinforcements came for the Italians— General Vincenzo Tessitore's forces from Dessie. The two sons of Kassa wisely withdrew before Tessitore could go after them, and Balcha, arriving too late, chose to flee early. No one was sure what happened to Fikre Mariam, and he was presumed killed in the attack.

People had a better idea of what happened to Abun Petros—he was in custody. According to Feodor Konovalov, the Italians had learned that the Abun had received a letter from Ras Desta, and that while admitting this, Petros argued that "it proves nothing."[5] An alternative story—which makes him equally heroic, but seems more plausible because of the unfolding events—is that in the midst of the fighting, he simply went down to St. George's Cathedral and presented himself defiantly to the Italian soldiers.[6] The attack was another humiliating embarrassment for the colonial regime. If Graziani needed to make an example of a ringleader, Petros was willing to sacrifice himself.

There are several versions of what happened next. When the Italians demanded that he submit to their authority, he's supposed to have famously replied, "The cry of my countrymen who died due to your nerve gas and terror machinery will never allow my conscience to accept your ultimatum. How can I see my God if I give a blind eye to such a crime?"

During the interrogation, an officer reportedly came straight from the Governo Generale. The viceroy, said the officer, deemed it "necessary" to shoot the prelate. The lawyer for the tribunal, thrown by this, sent a deferential message back: the case was still going on, and so far, he couldn't find any legal grounds for execution. Off went the officer with this news. After a while, there was a curt reply from Graziani: "Shoot the Abun at once."[7]

And so Petros was taken to a public square, where he was invited to sit on a stool against a wall. He faced the firing squad perfectly composed, holding a large silver cross in his hands.[8] His last words are supposed to have been, "My fellow Ethiopians, do not believe the Fascists if they tell you that the Patriots are bandits—the Patriots are people who yearn for freedom from the terrors of Fascism. Bandits are the soldiers who are standing in front of me and you, who came from far away to violently occupy a weak and peaceful country. May God give the people of Ethiopia the strength to resist and never bow to the Fascist army and its violence. May the Ethiopian earth never accept the invading army's rule."

Did Petros make this stirring final speech? Would he have even had the chance? His alleged final words were printed in a church newspaper in 1945 and they circulate widely on the Internet, but according to Ladislas Sava, who was living in Addis Ababa at the time, Petros didn't get that far. He only managed to tell the weeping crowd that they must endure the occupation with patience and never abandon their rights as a people and—

Then the bullets silenced him forever.

And Abriha Deboch? He went back to his job in Graziani's office and got married in August to a young, attractive woman of good family. At the Governo Generale, he was perfectly accommodating to his fellow office workers, and none was the wiser that his stew of conflicted loyalties was boiling and bubbling. He seems to have wanted to be a part of history, to be a hero to someone, but he would eventually, *clearly* have to choose a side. When he did, he stepped onto a path that led him months later to a stunning act of violence. It would be a blow against tyranny, but it would also bring about a slaughter of thousands and change the course of history in Ethiopia forever.

* * *

David Darrah's memoir of his Italian years, *Hail, Caesar!*, came out that July. If the world thought Mussolini was satisfied with his Ethiopian conquest, Darrah was not so sure. He suspected the Duce might turn his eye to Egypt, Sudan, possibly even Yemen. "European complications, that is, another European War, might help Mussolini in his project," wrote Darrah. "He thinks so, anyway. Once again, as in 1915, Italy would be able to choose the more advantageous side—for her. Mussolini has more than a million men under arms. If there were to be a war and a re-distribution of territory, Mussolini's participation would be on the side of the highest bidder."[9]

The latter half of 1936 was full of Ethiopia books. Haile Selassie managed to see a copy of Emilio De Bono's *Anno XIIII: The Conquest of an Empire*. He complained to Sir Lancelot Oliphant at the Foreign Office that "it showed how contemptuous of the League Italy had been, and how plans for the invasion of Abyssinia had been worked out more than two years ago." Oliphant, missing his point completely, replied that he'd spoken with an Italian scholar friend, and that De Bono's book was so technical with its dull chronicle of road construction that it likely wouldn't find a publisher in Britain.[10]

The Emperor likely preferred *Caesar in Abyssinia*, George Steer's book, which was released that December. Steer wanted "to show what was the strength and spirit of the Ethiopian armies sent against a European Great Power. My conclusions are that they had no artillery, no aviation, a pathetic proportion of automatic weapons and modern rifles, and ammunition sufficient for two days' modern battle. I have seen a child nation, ruled by a man who was both noble and intelligent, done brutally to death almost before it had begun to breathe."[11] Steer, while empathizing with the Ethiopians, never romanticizes them. He saw them plain; their failures, their courage.

As for Steer himself, he arranged to spend about a month covering the Spanish Civil War for *The Times*, and by late August, he was watching a firefight from his hotel in Biriatou.[12] When Steer reported on the bombing of Guernica, he assured his place in journalism's pantheon, and his reportage helped inspire Picasso's most famous masterpiece.

Herbert Matthews was there, too, befriending Ernest Hemingway and Martha Gellhorn, and Spain ironically cured him of Fascism in a way that Ethiopia couldn't. Just as Steer uncovered the Nazis helping Franco, Matthews noted clear evidence of Italian soldiers and equipment in the mix—and he deeply resented his editors in New York scrubbing his copy clean of this truth.[13]

Spain made things easy for politicians and reporters because it was about politics: left versus right. Ethiopia made it hard because it was about race and hypocrisy. But on another level, Spain represented the future of war coverage. Ethiopia was remote, geographically difficult, the last oil painting of bayonets and camels. After World War Two, reporters would watch battles as if they were fireworks. Desert Storm would be televised from rooftops, Syria's civil war agony uploaded on YouTube. George Steer was one of the first to note the surrealism of it, how war by night was "ethereal." He soon ended his short-term assignment with *The Times* to finish up *Caesar in Abyssinia* while still in Spain.

Other players from Ethiopia were there, too. Marcel Junod had come for the Red Cross, expecting to stay three weeks. He would stay for more than three years. Feodor Konovalov was there as well, only Konovalov was now a colonel on the Fascist side. Even more surprising is what happened with the Russian's memoir of the war. Steer used excerpts from it for *Caesar in Abyssinia*, but another version of it was published at around the same time—in Italian. The translation was done by an old friend of Konovalov who knew him before the war, one Commander Stefano Miccichè of the Italian navy. The final product was titled, *Con le armate del Negus* (With the Army of the Negus), and the racist subtitle gave a tip right away that the memoir had been doctored: *Un bianco fra i neri* (A White Among the Blacks).[14]

Anyone who knew Konovalov from the old days would have been shocked by the book's dedication: "To the Italian soldier who showed to the world, at first skeptical and then amazed but always hostile, that glorifying in the new Fascist climate, he has the ancient virtues of the Roman legionary." It was all downhill from there. The Italian version changed dates, dropped references to gas attacks, left out the Russian's more positive comments on Ethiopia and its effort to modernize, and told readers that when Badoglio arrived, "the population went out of their houses and hailed the new arrivals."[15]

It also included a strange "Lawrence of Arabia"–style anecdote: when Konovalov went to check the enemy's strength before the Emperor's doomed battle, he allegedly sauntered into the village of Mai Chew disguised as an Ethiopian church deacon. And readers were supposed to believe that a middle-aged, pale-complexioned former officer of the Tsar slipped out again past Italian and askari troops. If anything, this created more suspicion over the estimates of field strength that Konovalov offered Haile Selassie.

What was going on? Had Konovalov been a double-agent all this time? It's a debate for the historians, but so far, the evidence simply isn't there, though the Russian's behavior leaves many questions—and fighting for Franco doesn't help the case for the defense. Still, more than one draft of his manuscript is lying around, including versions that clearly praise the Emperor and the Ethiopians, and we know that Konovalov wrote critically about the occupation.

But *Con le armate del Negus* did its obvious job of rewriting history, and it naturally got a rave review in *Popolo d'Italia* from Italy's most important critic: Benito Mussolini. A second edition reprinted the Duce's praise when it came out in 1938.

*   *   *

Evelyn Waugh still hadn't delivered his own book. He had left the conflict so prematurely that he realized he had to go back to update his highly subjective findings. "Off to Africa full of the gloomiest forebodings," he wrote his friend Katharine Asquith. "I am sick of Abyssinia and my book about it. It was fun being pro-Italian when it was an unpopular and (I thought) losing cause. I have little sympathy with these exultant fascists now."[16]

Waugh arrived in Djibouti August 18, and on his new tour of Ethiopia, he was surprised to find the country beset by guerrilla attacks. He was dismissive of them in his book, sure that they posed no serious threat, but the Italians weren't so cavalier; neither was Waugh at the time to his diary: "Truth appears to be Wops in jam."[17] On the day he arrived, eight thousand white and askari troops were due to leave Awash railway station to capture Ankober, which had never been under Italian control. Morale was low, and Italian officers spent the day before at the hotel in Awash, consuming "vast quantities of liquor . . . to summon courage."[18]

The culture of a once-great civilization was lost on Waugh. He considered the ruins of Aksum "very ugly" and was fascinated instead by the Italian road works. When his book came out at the end of the year, sales were dismal and reviews withering. *The Times Literary Supplement* suggested the author "should perhaps temper his judgment with a little generosity."[19] Public sympathy for Ethiopia, of course, was still high. *Waugh in Abyssinia* couldn't even find a publisher in the United States after its release in Britain. Waugh never did change with the times and enraged David Niven on a visit to Hollywood in 1947 by calling the actor's black housekeeper "your native bearer" right in front of her.[20]

Waugh in Abyssinia is a troublesome book mainly because it *does* remain in print. Waugh certainly wasn't alone in writing an apologist tract for the Italian invasion, but his account is the most enduring by default of his reputation. A book that calls Ethiopians "an inferior race" and described them celebrating their victory at Adwa as "slavering at the mouth" still has fans. John Maxwell Hamilton, author of a rich history on American foreign reportage, *Journalism's Roving Eye*, wrote an introduction for a reprint of *Waugh in Abyssinia*. To Maxwell, the book is a "memoir like no other" about a "largely unknown country that lent itself to farcical imaginings."[21]

Back in Ethiopia, the land that supposedly lent itself to such imaginings, there were those who would survive the occupation and tell a different story.

* * *

Out in his house in West Sussex, the philosopher, Bertrand Russell—now sixty-four, white-haired, and bird-like in appearance, looking the way a sage was expected to look—was writing another book of his own. He lit his pipe and set his considerable mental powers to solving political tensions in the world. It didn't take him long. In three short weeks, Russell cranked out forty-eight thousand words of what he casually admitted was "a purely propaganda book."[22] It was called, *Which Way to Peace?* Peace, wrote Russell, wouldn't be found through collective security.

Russell could have always played it safe and stayed a tweedy Cambridge don and member of the Bloomsbury set. But he became an ardent pacifist during World War One, getting himself locked up in Brixton Prison for half a year and not enjoying the experience. Conservatives didn't like him because he advocated open marriage and new methods of education. Champagne socialists didn't like him because he went to Russia, saw the sadism of Lenin and the Bolsheviks, and wrote about it plainly. When he became almost unhirable for any university position, he discovered he could knock out short books of essays that became bestsellers. *Why I Am Not A Christian* is still a bible for agnostics, and *In Praise of Idleness* was the guilty pleasure of 1935.

Which Way to Peace? was rushed into print and immediately sold well in Britain. Russell considered Ethiopia to be a false crusade. "If we had gone to war with Italy on the Abyssinian question," he wrote, "it would not have been to preserve the independence of a gallant little nation, but to safeguard the route to India and the headwaters of the Blue Nile."[23] He poked holes in the presumption of those in Britain that "was it not obvious that African tribes *must* prefer us to anyone else?" The moral bankruptcy of empire was clear to him, and he believed in handing over British colonies to an international mandate. But "the destruction which such a [world] war would cause in Europe is obviously a much graver matter than a somewhat worse government of parts of Africa."[24]

Decades later, Russell admitted that his stand was "unconsciously insincere."[25] It had never occurred to him that Britain could *lose* a war, that all that he loved might be extinguished by Italian Fascists or Nazis—as usual, an emotional response prompted him to search for new logic. There were cases, he decided, when war *was* needed. But by the time he had this change of heart and change of head, he was on the wrong side of the Atlantic, teaching in New York, and unable to come home.

The book dated quickly and so it hasn't survived in print, yet it had true gems of sparkling writing, and the kernels of Russell's evolving arguments on disarmament and pacifism. "The view that the situation is hopeless, and that Western civilization is inexorably doomed to self-destruction, is one which I cannot accept," he wrote in the closing pages. "What is needed now is action by individuals, in unison, inspired by reason and passion intimately combined."

This is the fixed star he was trying to navigate to, and which he would rediscover thirty years later. "The movement in favor of war resistance is not to be viewed primarily as political, but rather as a matter of personal conviction, like religion."[26]

A peace movement.

There had been *pacifist* movements before, of course, always entangled with organizations and party dogma, but Russell was advocating something more fluid, more adaptable and responsive in its influence and its power. Could it have started there? Tracing the origins of a social phenomenon is like wrestling vapor, but the book was popular, and so this new concept was out there, at least from this one social activist. It would wait for others to develop it.

In the 1960s, hundreds of thousands would march for peace in America, in Britain, and in other parts of Europe. And a white-haired philosopher, by then in his nineties, would bring along an air cushion so he could plunk himself down on the hard stone of Trafalgar Square and take part in a sit-in. The West's failure to save Ethiopia played its own small part to inspire—on a slow-motion, circuitous route—a movement intended to save everybody.

*   *   *

Haile Selassie settled in Bath, first staying in the Spa Hotel and then moving into a six-bedroom Georgian home called Fairfield, which had impressive gardens. As writer Shirley Harrison put it, the Emperor soon charmed the townspeople of Bath and became something of a beloved figure, "striding in his knee-length cape (black in winter, white in summer) and his homburg or trilby hat . . . Local people responded to him because he liked dogs and children and raised his hat when greeted."[27]

The Foreign Office did some lobbying, and like an angry spouse with possession of the home, Italy relented and sent over some clothes and furniture belonging to the royal exile. Haile Selassie's alleged hidden wealth would become a controversial tale told throughout his life and long after, but at least in 1936, it simply wasn't true. Some money *had* been moved, but it wasn't a lot—and most of that went over time to others, such as the exiles in Jerusalem. The Emperor was in desperate straits. Municipal officials didn't bother to charge the humbled Emperor for his electricity, and neither did he have to make excuses to the tradesman who delivered coal.[28] However he managed, the Lion of Judah lived in comparatively modest comfort for his five years in Britain.*

But the money situation spelled doom for any goodwill and loyalty between him and Charles Martin. Mere weeks after the Emperor's arrival, they had a falling out. The main issue was a complicated one involving the purchases and sales of the Ethiopian embassy and another house only three numbers down in Princes Gate. Martin had dug into his own pockets for these, and he felt he ought to control the funds. For his part, Haile Selassie had quickly discovered just how close to broke he was (despite what the press said), and since his earliest days at court and as regent, he'd tried to keep a steely grip on finances. He also questioned how Martin handled donations made to the Ethiopian struggle. The friction between them was palpable, so much so that Foreign Office officials began to notice Martin was getting sidelined from discussions between the Emperor and the British government.[29] It was true, however, that Martin often didn't manage money well, and Foreign Office files show several entries noting hefty bills he owed to the British government.

Outside the corridors of Whitehall and Parliament, no one was the wiser, and both men were popular with the British public. As they grew frostier to each other, they each warmed to the energy and sincere commitment of Sylvia Pankhurst, who befriended them both. When she got sick the next year, Martin would write her a touching letter: "You are very precious, my darling, to millions of people, so please take special care of your dear self."[30] If Martin could no longer speak with confidence on behalf of his Emperor, he still had a platform to express himself in *New Times and Ethiopia News.* And for a woman whose bluntness and hardheadedness was commented on by so many, she seemed wise enough to steer clear of what was, by definition, an internal dispute.

She became a regular visitor to Bath, where she strolled the grounds of Fairfield with the Emperor. Sylvia's young son, Richard, captured them in unguarded conversation with his Brownie camera: the firebrand, godless suffragette and the tiny Emperor who clung to the idea that he was the elect of God. There were moments when he apparently chastised her—gently—for her tactlessness, but as others have pointed out, Haile Selassie always appreciated the kindness that foreigners showed him.

---

* Years later, after his restoration, he paid tribute to his time in exile by renaming his palace in Harar, "Fairfield." In 1958, he donated the Georgian mansion to the Town of Bath, and it's still there, currently the home of its Ethnic Minority Senior Citizens Association.

Three decades on, after his mother had passed away, Richard Pankhurst met the Emperor by chance in Addis Ababa. "When I mentioned to him that I was writing a history of Ethiopia, he interrupted me to say I should instead write her biography."[31] He would end up doing both.

*   *   *

While Sylvia Pankhurst and Martin mobilized the British, Dr. Malaku Bayen was sent off to America to rekindle support there. He was back in a country he knew well.

But his mission got off to an ugly start. Malaku, his wife, Dorothy, and their little boy arrived in New York on September 23, and they expected to check into their room at the Delano Hotel in Midtown. The hotel didn't care that someone had made a reservation on their behalf, and it sure as hell didn't care where the doctor was from—he was still black. Too bad for the management that it didn't know Malaku Bayen. Soon, the major newspapers, the NAACP, and the *Daily Worker*—not to mention the gale-force holy wrath of Harlem——descended on West Forty-third Street and made the Delano change its mind. By then Malaku no longer cared—he moved his family up to Harlem.[32]

He was a qualified surgeon, but he was also a phenomenal lobbyist. Only five days later, he was promising two thousand people at Rockland Palace, "Our soldiers will never cease fighting until the enemy is driven from our soil."[33] True, it was familiar stuff, and Malaku's appeal was actually meant to raise funds for refugees, not the Patriot effort. He didn't get much from wealthier blacks who may not have cared, or for that matter, from the very poor who couldn't afford to. No problem. He would just reach out farther. Malaku looked to unite black people around the world to help his country. "Fellow Ethiopians," he would address his audience when giving a speech, and he meant it. Within a handful of years, his Ethiopian World Federation had a long list of branches in the United States, as well as representatives in spots like Uganda, the Gold Coast, and South Africa.[34]

And his call to action was infused with a special pride. For those who read his newspaper, *Voice of Ethiopia*, or listened to his speeches, Malaku told them to "think black, act black, and be black."[35]

*   *   *

More than a millennium ago, at the height of their ingenuity, the architects and builders of the Aksumite Empire put up the equivalent of skyscrapers— monoliths of granite with imitation windows and doors. These massive stelae were often carted in single blocks for more than three miles to reach their final foundation spot. They were probably used as grave markers for the rich and the royal dead, but whatever they were for, they were built to impress. One of them once stood eighty-two feet high.

But during the tenth century, it was knocked over and broken into three pieces. And there it lay, down through the centuries. Stone slept.

Then the ground was disturbed by the modern noise of rubber tires and Fiat engines.

If Mussolini was going to imitate the ancient Roman Empire, he needed a monument as a prize. Hadn't the British taken what they wanted from India and Africa? Hadn't Napoleon's soldiers confiscated treasures and antiquities from Egypt? (Many of those, ironically enough, were swiped by the British Royal Navy as the loot was sailing for France; they wound up in the British Museum.)

The Duce's soldiers and engineers got to work, and though the tonnage of the ancient stones tested their vehicles and ship holds, an obelisk was carted off to Massawa. When it arrived in Rome, metal rods pierced its granite so it could be assembled and stand upright in Porta Capena square, not far from the ancient Romans' Circus Maximus. It was unveiled on October 28, just in time to celebrate the fifteenth anniversary of the March on Rome.

On the same day as the unveiling, Mussolini made an interesting speech that should have curdled the blood of European diplomats, and it gave another sign of things to come. There was a familiar rant over Bolshevism in Spain, but he also called for the Great Powers to give Germany back its African colonies, which had been stripped by the Allies after they won the First World War. The Germans had once governed places like the Cameroons and Togoland (modern Togo), Tanganyika (modern Tanzania), and what is now Mozambique, plus pieces of territory that would one day become Rwanda and Burundi.

Standing by and listening to all this with approval was an honored visitor, Germany's deputy fuehrer, Rudolf Hess.

* * *

While Aksum was losing its precious stones, Addis Ababa was getting a Fascist makeover.

Just as in Rome, Mussolini's face now grinned and glowered from portraits. On a night in October, Italian soldiers—"like cat burglars"—drove up in a van and hauled away the equestrian statue of Menelik from its place in front of St. George's Cathedral, loading it on an early train out of the city. The Hungarian doctor, Ladislas Sava, was woken up by the cries of his servant. Out in the streets, he found other Ethiopians stunned and crying over the theft of the statue. All that remained on the pedestal was the broken-off fragment of one of the horse's legs. As the locals gathered in mournful huddles over their lost symbol, the soldiers drove them away with bayonets.[36]

Journalist Ciro Poggiali traced the statue's removal to the minister of public works in Rome, Giuseppe Cobolli-Gigli. "You cannot imagine anything stupider than to remove monuments from the places where they were built," he observed in his secret diary. "They are testimonies to an indestructible history. Can anyone deny that before us Abyssinia belonged to the Abyssinians?"[37]

The regime would try. The mausoleum where the country's heroes had been laid to rest was blown to bits. The monument of an Ethiopian lion in front of the railway station was taken away. So was a bas-relief of three fishes covered in gold leaf in front of the central post office. In place of these landmarks went the garish and grotesque emblems of Fascism. And the campaign of erase-and-replace wasn't restricted to the capital. In Adwa, where Mussolini always felt the most spiteful towards history, a large idealized portrait of him was put up in the form of a bust. The statue of Menelik turned up in Rome, where the Duce posed for a photo in front of it, wearing a steel helmet.[38]

The Italians could redecorate all they wanted, but the old problems were still there. Rebels under Balcha Safo had made another attack on the capital in late August, but were driven off with the help of bombers. Outside Addis Ababa, the Patriots refused to let up—there were battles and skirmishes in Debre Sina, near Akaki, and in parts of Shoa and Harar from late August into October. Graziani casually reported in late October that twenty-five planes on one morning raid alone dropped incendiary bombs and yperite on a set of villages, where the priests at their monasteries were suspected of giving asylum to rebels. In the village of Goro, south of the capital, an Ethiopian judge later testified that Italian troops "gathered all civilians, who had no rifles at all, including mothers who carried their babies on their backs and shepherds found round there, in a hollow-place and machine-gunned them."[39] But the bloody struggle would go on.

Relations with Britain also remained strained. The consulate in Gore closed until further notice. In London, Dino Grandi bragged that this move was looked on favorably by Rome; Anthony Eden put him quickly in his place by telling him it hadn't been done to satisfy Italy. Mussolini later made things worse by giving a speech in which he claimed he was extending an olive branch—but one that grew out of a forest of eight million bayonets. Eden quipped it was hard to see the branch for the forest.[40]

The colonial regime was squeezing native peasant and expat businessman alike. Many of the Greeks and Armenians who were once the steady drivers of commerce fled the country for easier spots to run their businesses. Ethiopians on their way to market to sell their produce were roughly searched, and if they carried old Maria Theresa dollars, these were confiscated. "One person is allowed on leaving the country to take with him only 350 lire," reported *The Economist*, "and on the train to Djibouti passengers are turned inside out in search for money. They are taken down in parties to one end of the train, and there, their clothing is examined; their boots and socks are removed; sometimes they are stripped to the skin."[41] A currency black market proliferated just the same, with an exchange rate by then of 10.5 lire to one thaler. The export trade crumbled; it couldn't afford to buy in dollars and sell in lire.

And all the while, the colony was in a state of siege. By the time officials were wrestling with currency problems, one of the Emperor's entourage had snuck back into the country, thanks to the help of the British in Sudan, who preferred to play along and believe his cover story. This was the Faqada Selassie Heruy, known as "George" Heruy, the son of Heruy Wolde Selassie, the writer and the Emperor's one-time foreign minister. George Heruy had come with letters from the Emperor, encouraging rebellion. The letters also made some outlandish promises: that the Emperor was coming home, and with British military help. There were rumors, too, of impending nuptials between a British princess and the Emperor's son, the Duke of Harar (not very likely, given that Makonnen was only thirteen).

This gave the outgoing consul in Gore, Captain Erskine, a reason to vent his spleen in a note to Anthony Eden, complaining that "the return of this insignificant lying individual, George Heruy, has led the remnants of the Amhara to believe that powerful help from Europe is forthcoming."[42] He would complain bitterly to his higher-ups that all this violated the terms of the Emperor's arrangement with London not to get involved in the hostilities back home.[43]

Erskine, however, was on his way out and could do nothing about it. In his lie over British aid, Haile Selassie showed the streak of Machiavellian cunning that he once used to put down rebellions and outmaneuver his court rivals. While there were those who felt betrayed when the Emperor left the country, this was a moment when he was far more deserving of harsh criticism. He was giving his loyal subjects false hope while he stayed safe in his mansion in Bath. He was doing what was expedient. Did it even make a difference?

Maybe not. The truth was that the Black Lions and the younger generation of Ethiopians were already rising up to fight—not for the Emperor, but for themselves. The fact that they created their own constitution demonstrates they were modernists who expected to enjoy a very different Ethiopia after they clawed back their nation.

But first they would have to win it, and reality was setting in after the heady victory of that first raid. Imru and his new pride of Lions hoped to retake Ambo as a first step to capture the predictable prize, the capital. But in the province of Wollega, his men were not welcome, at least not by the local Oromo. Then they were surprised by the Italians, and they had to fight their way out. There would be worse ahead. By October 24, Graziani's soldiers had moved in force into the provincial capital and key market town of Nekemte. Meanwhile, the Italians had armed about a thousand fighters of the Sultan of Jimma, who was happy to make his struggle one of Muslim versus Christian. The tactics of the war had changed, but the old political divisions had not. And on top of all that, Graziani dispatched a mechanized column to put down the rebels.

Imru and his army melted into the forests south of Nekemte and north of Jimma. What was supposed to be a compact, mobile guerrilla team had swollen with refugees to some thirty thousand people. When Tekle Wolde Hawaryat and his men showed up after a long, arduous journey at Imru's camp, he urged the ras and his officers—in his usual blunt style—to cut the numbers down. Their force, he told them, should be trimmed to three thousand men. This made sense. A smaller army would be able to react faster, move more easily and more quickly. Imru wasn't interested. Perhaps he felt reassured by the size of the ranks under his command. A more charitable explanation would be that he didn't want to cut adrift the homeless women and children, old and injured who looked to his men for protection. But whatever the reasons, Tekle was turned down.

Tekle didn't take it well. Imru, he argued, was sure to be killed or taken prisoner—why, his army wouldn't last fifteen days! Any officer who wanted to could leave with Tekle's guerrilla band right now. Virtually all of Imru's men kept their places. Very few wanted to serve with so volatile a commander, and Imru was the one ras who had *won* against the Italians last year. Bubbling with his angry convictions, Tekle led his own men out of the camp, blasting his war trumpet defiantly. He and Imru had disagreed over tactics, and after the war, they would wind up standing on opposite sides of Ethiopia's future.

* * *

It is no longer enough to have courage and patriotism; today tactics and strategy are required. Your place is here, Balcha, I can make good use of you, and for the actual fighting I have younger generals.

Haile Selassie had offered these words to Balcha Safo many months ago as his former enemy had leaned on his priest's staff, begging to be put in the fight. His place *was* here, while, ironically, the Emperor no longer had a place anywhere, and certainly not in their homeland. Now Balcha faced one of those lumbering, composite beasts of metal and mule, an army plodding its way towards Jimma at the excruciating pace of ten miles a day. But even big creatures can be driven to distraction by insects. Balcha had about three hundred soldiers. He attacked, and while it was reported later that his force had been betrayed, his paltry army never stood a chance. A legend goes that his health was failing, and as things looked hopeless, he sent word to the Italians that he would only surrender to senior officers. After all, he was a dejazmach.

The Italians sent for their chaplain—the only man who could interpret—and then the little delegation made its way to Balcha. He sat waiting for them, wrapped in the folds of his cloak. The story goes that "a white man," no doubt the chaplain, walked up and asked simply, "Are you Dejazmach Balcha?"

"Yes, I am."

"Surrender your arms and untie your pistol [belt]."

"I am not here to surrender my arms," replied Balcha, and he opened his cloak like a curtain. He was holding a Belgian-made machine gun and began blasting away, taking as many officers with him as he could before they shot him down.[44]

* * *

Abriha Deboch was going out with friends one evening when his group tried to take in a show at the Cinema Italia. But he was in for a shock. The young man who walked to work each morning beside the viceroy himself discovered his office status meant nothing here. He was just another black subject of the Fascist Empire, and no, he and his friends could not sit where they liked—blacks go where they're told. More than anything else, this episode is what apparently convinced Abriha that he must side with the Patriots.[45]

The armies of the old rases had failed. The surprise attack on the capital had failed. Something else was needed. There had to be *some* kind of revolt, some decisive blow against the Italians. Abriha found sympathy for his outrage among his immediate collection of friends. There was Moges Asgedom, a gentle, scholarly young man of twenty-five, and also an Eritrean. Moges was working as an interpreter, too, in the same department as Abriha, but he was closer to an old friend from school, Sebhat Tiruneh, who worked as a language teacher at the German-run Hermannsburg Evangelical Mission. The three of them often met in Sebhat's house on the mission's grounds, talking animatedly while Moges, the intellectual in the group, consulted a set of precious maps he kept in a box. It would be the names of Moges and Abriha, however, that would go down in history. Moges was the undisputed brains of the operation.[46]

The conspiracy was building, with other young men joining the cell. Weeks later, Abriha and Moges were guests at the fancy villa of Letyibelu Gebre, a noble who was known for socializing and had been a commander during the war. Letyibelu came home to Addis Ababa as the Italians began their occupation, and some people presumed he was a deserter, a collaborator. But instead, he used his house as another meeting point for the resistance. To outsiders, it would have been hard to tell just whose side he was on—after all, his guests, Moges and Abriha, worked as agents of the viceroy.[47]

Moges had been staying with Sebhat and his much younger brother, Taddesse, in rooms at the German mission, but as the plot grew, Moges moved out. The German mission had begun to see frequent visits from various Europeans in military uniforms who came to call on its leader, Hermann Bahlburg—for what purpose wasn't clear. But Moges knew better than to arouse suspicion by hanging around, and he took a small cottage a short distance away from Sebhat's house. It was perfect: close enough to visit his friend, but far enough away so that he could slip out unnoticed by German and Italian eyes.[48]

Back at Letyibelu's villa, Abriha, Moges, and their trusted friends were soon meeting high-ranked nobles and former officials of the Emperor's government. Before, Moges and Abriha were lanky young men who knew nothing about weapons. They had planned and talked big, but now they would learn how to be fighters.[49] The plot now included some of the most prominent figures of Ethiopian aristocracy, and it might well have reached all the way to London.

* * *

Back in New York City, in December, sculptor Herman Wolfowitz rushed into the Greenwich Village loft he shared with his two black friends and fellow radicals, Alonzo Watson and James Yates. He was carrying groceries and five different newspapers, but the only news that mattered was that Mussolini was sending troops to fight for Franco in Spain's Civil War. Wolfowitz talked excitedly with Yates while the painter, Watson, stared silently at one of the newspapers. Then Watson announced quietly, "I'm going, I'm volunteering. The time for talking is over. You've got to put your conviction where your mouth is!"[50]

Yates had to think about it carefully. He "had been more than ready to go to Ethiopia, but that was different. Ethiopia, a black nation, was part of me."[51] In his memoir, he wrote that at the time, he was just beginning to understand the complexities of Spain's politics and its recent election, "the kind of victory that would have brought black people to the top levels of government if such an election had been won in the USA."[52] He stepped away to the back of their loft and stared out a window looking over Thirteenth Street, his mind shutting out the crowd below and the honking horns. He could imagine a bigger war on the horizon. When he stepped back to his friends, the two were talking about the importance of race versus capitalist profit and territory. Yates made his decision. Yes, he would go.

The three friends were among the first to sign up, and Yates and Watson were among the very first African Americans to go fight for Spain. Yates would have likely traveled on the same ship as his friends if not for the trouble he had getting a passport—there were no birth records for him in his native Mississippi.[53] By the time he managed to sail on the *Île de France* on February 20, his friend Watson had less than one week to live. Moving along a road between trenches on the Jarama Front on February 25, Watson was cut down by a sniper's bullet, making him the first black volunteer killed in action.[54]

Oliver Law, who played an important role in the "Hands Off Ethiopia" campaign, had already sailed over in January, and he would eventually become commander of the Abraham Lincoln Brigade. He would lead the battalion for three months before he, too, was killed in combat. For Albert Chisholm, who had joined the Communists and agitated for the cause while he worked as a bellhop on cruise ships, Ethiopia would have been his first choice, too. "I wanted to go [to Ethiopia] to fight against the Fascists. But then shortly after that the Spanish issue surfaced, and I saw there would be my best chance."[55]

It was the same for Oscar Hunter, an activist who would not only serve in Spain with the Abraham Lincoln Brigade, but who would also become one of the founders of its archives. Hunter would defy FBI harassment and go on to protest the Vietnam War. Years later, he wrote a short story that captured the sentiment many felt in 1936. His character of a black volunteer for Spain says, "I wanted to go to Ethiopia and fight Mussolini . . . This ain't Ethiopia, but it'll do."[56]

* * *

Ras Imru held out as long as he could. Having played cat-and-mouse with the Italians in raids and skirmishes near Wollega, his men had gradually run out of ammunition, and after a year of fighting, they were exhausted. Many contracted malaria. When he couldn't take them safely into British-held Sudan, he tried to beat his way back to Gojjam, but it was no good. One night, his guards and scouts simply deserted the camp, and the next morning, Imru convened the committee of the Black Lions outside his tent to decide what to do. But he had gate-crashers—an Oromo envoy from Jimma showed up with two Italian officers.

The Italians expected Imru to surrender, their offer to negotiate a mere courtesy. But the wily ras had one last trick up his sleeve. He wouldn't agree to anything until the sick and the old, the women and children, were allowed safe passage away from any battlefield. This, the Italians were willing to do, and as the exodus started, Imru was apparently astonished over how few warriors he had once the great collection of refugees was stripped away. When the ordinary people were at last gone, the Italians expected an answer. No, Imru would not give up.

The Italians felt tricked. One of the officers lost his temper and raged that they would drop more bombs and gas. "We shall be brutal and kill the civilian hostages if you do not surrender!"[57] Imru wasn't moved by this at all. Throughout the war, his enemy had been brutal towards soldier and civilian alike without provocation. How could they possibly tell the difference now?

He consulted the young Lions. They were the ones who favored surrender, worried what could happen to him if they resisted. Imru cryptically told them he would consider it. In the meantime, the Italians sent more threats, demanding a decision and warning that Graziani had given orders for a slaughter of the refugees and a gassing of the camp unless they capitulated within a few hours. Once more, Imru turned to the Black Lions committee. His concern now was for the Eritreans in their ranks. They would be ruthlessly slaughtered, whether they turned themselves in or not. Imru thought they ought to have a fighting chance. He ordered that they be given the best weapons available, and the Eritreans all managed to slip out of the camp. They eventually joined another force of Patriots south of Jimma in Gamu-Gofa, near what is today the Tama Wildlife Reserve.

Then it was just the Ethiopians. Black Lions all, their pride at bay. There was nothing left to do but to throw their guns into creeks and stroll down the hill. Imru pulled out a pistol that his cousin, the Emperor, had given him and tossed it aside. As the remaining Black Lions ambled their way into the enemy camp, an Italian officer noticed one of Imru's commanders, a man named Dejené, wearing the distinctive brown khakis of his own ranks.

"Where did you get this?" demanded the Italian.

"In battle," said Dejené.

"How?"

"I captured it while fighting for my master, Ras Imru."

"Where is the owner?"

"If I captured him, do you think he could be alive? I killed him, of course!"

As the historian, Richard Greenfield, put it, this fearless reply "eventually cost him his life." Dejené was separated from the other Ethiopians, placed in manacles, and put under heavy guard. But he went, cheeky and laughing, taunting the enemy still: "We were unarmed, and you took us as women might. Now you guard us like lions with machine guns. Will you look after me thus for the rest of my days? Then I am your king!"[58]

Despite all the threats, there was no massacre that day, and being fair, Imru would later acknowledge that the Italians took care of his sick and wounded. Graziani, of course, had no compunction about putting to death high-ranking nobles. And Imru was the noblest of them all—a skilled commander who had outwitted generals and who was Ethiopia's viceroy. His feats and his name made him the most hunted, but they also might have saved his life after his surrender. Such a prize, Mussolini decided, should have a different fate than being lined up against a wall and shot.

The man who usually had no sympathy at all for the Amhara, Captain Erskine, was now in London, and he was so moved by Imru's plight that he appealed to Anthony Eden. Erskine told the foreign secretary that "Imru was the only respectable ras among the Abyssinian leaders and begged that we should do our best for him." Eden put the Foreign Office experts to work on the issue, and they examined legalities and *locus standi* and the status of inhabitants in lands taken by conquest and . . . and . . . they didn't know what to do.

Their analysis boiled down to wishful thinking. They *hoped* that Imru would only be taken to Rome and shown off as a prize to Mussolini: "Even the Italians . . . would shrink from the deplorable impression that would be created if Ras Imru's pathway from the Palazzo Venezia led straight to the firing squad." They decided in the end that interference could do more harm than good.[59]

On December 16, at nine in the morning, Imru was taken to the Addis Ababa airport. A crowd of Italians was on hand for a spectacle of medieval hate and loathing. They screamed, "Liar! Murderer!" But instead of a pillory, there was a plane. The British had guessed right; Imru was to be spared. After a flight to Massawa, he was put on a ship to Naples, to be exported to Italy like the golden lion and the Obelisk of Aksum and other trophies. Then he was taken to Ponza, where he stayed, like an exiled senator of ancient Rome, in a little house.*

Tekle Wolde Hawaryat had given Imru odds of lasting fifteen days, and he was almost bang on the money—but he didn't last much longer. Single-minded and volatile, he never commanded the same loyalty as Imru, and as his skirmishes with the enemy thinned his ranks, he fled into the countryside. Charles Martin's sons, Benyam and Yosef, were among those who submitted when Imru gave

---

* But Imru would survive his incarceration. He would be freed by the Allies when they swept across Europe and would become a diplomat for his country after the Second World War.

himself up, and yet amazingly, they were walking around free, thanks to a rare and brief amnesty.

The mercy shown to Imru and the Martin brothers was an anomaly for the regime. Bande in the Takazze region hunted down Ras Kassa's eldest son, Wondosson, and cornered him in some caves; once he surrendered, they promptly executed him. Days later, his two brothers, Aberra and Afsa Wossen, who had fought with him in the failed attack on the capital in July, realized they couldn't elude five Italian columns bearing down on them near Fikke. They would have to submit.

Perhaps they should have suspected treachery when the traitor, Ras Hailu, showed up to play intermediary, sipping coffee with the brothers and an Italian general, Ruggero Tracchia. Hailu had done well for himself in the occupation. The Italians gave him the Star of Italy and a fat loan, let him use his car during a fuel shortage, and allowed him to keep a house in the Italian district of Addis Ababa, a privilege no other Ethiopian had. He wanted to be Negus. The colonial authorities weren't that stupid—they were sure that with such a lofty title, he could rally supporters and lead a revolt in Gojjam when the time was right.[60] Hailu would always bite the hand that fed him, and he would smile right before he did it.

Whether Hailu knew what was planned for the brothers or not, after sundown, the sons of Kassa were led to Fikke's public square and shot. Their heads were cut off and displayed in the most profane and inflammatory fashion—right in the Church of St. George.[61] Patrick Roberts, Britain's chargé d'affaires in Addis Ababa, reported later that Graziani gave a speech to Ethiopian nobles, listing off the Kassa brothers' supposed crimes, and "high Italian officials on either side raised their hands to their mouths, sniggered, and winked."[62]

Ras Kassa had now lost three sons to the Italian occupation.

But their deaths only served as new inspiration. Before Aberra Kassa and his brother turned themselves in, he wrote a letter to his wife, Kebedech, a resourceful, intelligent woman who was Ras Seyum's daughter. She had been with him when he tried to take the capital, and she had bandaged the wounds of his men and managed supplies. When things looked dire, he sent her away to Adisge to be safe. His letter arrived by messenger, explaining how he'd decided to surrender rather than risk his men getting slaughtered as punishment for his defiance. Before she received his letter or probably soon after, she must have gotten the news that he was dead. She was a widow, her father had submitted, and she was alone. And she was pregnant.[63]

But she was also a *woizero*, a noblewoman and the daughter of a ras. Her husband's army was now her army, and she would lead it. A surviving portrait photo shows her cutting a dashing figure, her beautiful face under a pith helmet and wearing a man's uniform with a Sam Browne belt, and she often wore men's clothing. Part of her legend includes the fact that she gave birth to her son out in the desert. She hated the Fascists for killing her husband, and she was now going to make them pay for it. For one Patriot leader shot dead, the Italians had created another; a woman who would make herself an avenging fury on their camps and patrols.

* * *

The crowds in Times Square braved the early rain to ring in 1937.

Reporters noticed that people spent more this holiday season than in any year since the stock market crash. The Depression was finally over. Americans knew who had pulled them out of it, so they voted to keep Franklin Roosevelt in the Oval Office, and he would be sworn in as president later that January. But a recovering United States still wasn't interested in taking sides in foreign wars, despite the big headlines over Spain. It was more pleasant to read about Howard Hughes setting a flying record for Los Angeles to New York City—seven and a half hours. If they wanted to get lost in international locales, they could go to the movies, where that month saw the premiere of *The Good Earth*, a film about China in which none of the top stars cast were Chinese (MGM offered the role of the "bad girl" character to the biggest and only Asian film star, the beautiful Anna May Wong, who tartly declined).

In Britain, it was harder to escape the news, though some tried—by moving forward in time. Two days after the New Year was rung in, a thin, spectacled pensions auditor named Arthur C. Clarke went out to Leeds for a modest social affair—Britain's first science fiction convention. Given how the shadows were darkening across Europe, it's no surprise that the country's film hit in February was *Fire Over England*, starring Laurence Olivier and Vivian Leigh, who played Elizabeth I at the time when the Spanish Armada was the nation's greatest threat. Others preferred to leave reality altogether; in the autumn, *The Hobbit* would sell out of its initial modest print run.

As for Ethiopia . . . wasn't that over? Of course, there were short items in the papers, which presumably meant there were only short rebellions, each sputtering to an inevitable end. Few realized the extent of the resistance.

True, the surrender of Imru and his men was a serious blow, but other Patriot guerrillas exacted a brutal toll on occupation forces. A British military intelligence report from the Kenyan frontier reported that Italian casualties were "considerable" and their advance "wasn't great" in their offensives along the Rift Valley and near the Sidamo Highlands. The Ethiopians, reported the officer in charge,

V. G. Glenday, were "fighting true guerrilla warfare by avoiding action with any strong Italian force, but raiding convoys, etc." as far south as Yabelo. In general, losses of white troops in the colony were prompting a desperate effort to find suitable native soldiers, but understandably, the local tribes—including the Oromo—were "[not] at all anxious to join up."[64]

Glenday reported that because the Italians couldn't recruit army prospects inside Ethiopia, they relied on their old standbys, the Somalis. And in an effort to keep their support, they encouraged Islam. This was playing with a very dangerous double-edged sword, and the Italians "allowed their soldiers to ill-treat and insult the pagan Galla as well as playing fast and loose with their women."[65]

Back in Britain, the party line for the court in exile was that *no* negotiations whatsoever would be held with the Italians. But throughout the fall of 1936, the Italians and the Emperor had remained in occasional contact, with the Italians making covert overtures to try to lure him home. In late October, OVRA agents in London hoped to make Charles Martin into a collaborator. No doubt they had kept him under surveillance for months, and since London was neutral ground, one of their operatives, a Marius Delicio, could phone the embassy or walk right into Princes Gate if he chose. Martin was curious enough to talk to him; what did Delicio want? The answer was the Italians wanted to "give me plenty of money, a good position, and all my property if I'll submit to Italy."[66] Martin didn't want their money. Instead, he haggled with them for parts of western Ethiopia to stay independent, but the talks came to nothing.[67]

When historians mention these secret discussions, especially with Haile Selassie, there is often a faint tone of disapproval over apparent duplicity. The Emperor had fled; perhaps he hoped to salvage a small piece of what he had lost? But this is highly unlikely. Having mocked and ridiculed him for close to two years, the Italians could only want him back as a puppet, a figurehead who could help stop the rebellions. Haile Selassie knew it. After all, he once sat across from Mussolini at a conference table, and he'd spent much of 1935 coping with delays, excuses, and empty promises. The Italians were trying to take his country, and now they wanted him, too. He would give them a taste of their own tactics. Delay, delay, delay.

One sign of his quiet resolve is perhaps demonstrated in what happened at Puttick & Simpson's auction rooms in London. There, four days before Christmas 1936, the news cameras snapped away and large klieg lights shone on display tables. Haile Selassie's collection of English and foreign silver went on the block. To their surprise, the regular dealers found themselves outnumbered by a large crowd of the curious. People who knew who the Emperor was from the papers wanted a keepsake of exotic royalty.

There were charming menu holders in the shape of Ethiopian soldiers, a plate inlaid with US gold and silver coins that must have been a diplomatic gift (it fetched £33). Why was the Emperor parting with these treasures? The official explanation was that he no longer had the "proper place" for them. The delicate lie fooled no one. The Emperor needed cash. The auction brought in more than £2,500.

This kept the wolves from the doors of Fairfield a little while longer, and the Emperor clearly expected a prolonged stay. Haile Selassie preferred to sell off his house possessions in Bath than accept the new landlord back home. But he might also have invested in another strategy, a daring and dangerous plan to strike a blow against the Italians.

One of his closest advisers, Beshawired Habte-Weld—intelligent, educated in economics and journalism in Ohio, fiercely loyal—had decided that month to go home and live under the Italian regime. This could be a death sentence, others told him. Beshawired didn't care; he would go "whatever the consequences,"[68] and it's inconceivable he would have left without Haile Selassie's permission and for some higher, clandestine purpose—one that even officials at the Ethiopian legation didn't know.

By the time the auction gavel was cracking in London, Beshawired was home in Addis Ababa, and days later, he stood in the ranks of a group of high-placed nobles who formally submitted. Graziani was thrilled. A snowfall of propaganda leaflets fluttered down on the adviser's home district in Shoa, proclaiming, "The right hand of the Emperor has now deserted him and has come to join us, so there is no point in continuing to resist. Give yourselves up!"[69]

Of course, Beshawired's return raised many eyebrows in London and in Addis Ababa. He had been one of the first to warn the Emperor of the looming threat of war way back in 1932. And if the Fascists knew where he'd gotten his information back then, they might not have acted so smug. While General Emilio De Bono and others were honeycombing Ethiopia with spies and collaborators, Beshawired had managed an intelligence coup of his own. He'd secured precious documents from the Italian embassy, thanks to an Eritrean operative. It's entirely possible that this had been Abriha Deboch.

Beshawired had long been friends, too, with an Anglo-Indian family that ran a trading firm with branches throughout Ethiopia. It could be no coincidence that the company arranged for a shipment of grenades to be smuggled in around the time of his arrival. Meanwhile, with the Italians convinced of his sincerity, Beshawired started turning up for low-key and furtive visits to the cottage near the Hermannsburg Mission, where Sebhat Tiruneh lived and often met with Abriha Deboch and Moges Asgedom.

Some of these facts would emerge months later, while others stayed hidden for decades. Graziani was none the wiser. The viceroy was gleefully collecting Ethiopian nobles as 1937 began. Charles Martin's sons, Benyam and Yosef, were walking around free, but their voices had already been bought—or so it seemed. They wrote a letter back to their father, one that called the resistance efforts a "hopeless fight." It was a strange letter, indeed, one that bizarrely asked the doctor to send money to help build roads.[70] If Martin didn't believe it was composed under duress, he had to know his boys were sending him a secret message.

Whatever they were trying to tell him, the fight was not so hopeless, and the resistance went on.

George Heruy, too, put on a convincing show that he had given up the struggle. Four months ago, he'd found his way to Gore to smuggle in letters from the Emperor, but now he wrote a letter to Graziani that cleverly built a rationale for why he was switching sides. Of course, younger Ethiopians like himself were Patriots in the beginning, until they saw how the country was "so easily surrendered" by the older generation and those in power, who were "corrupt, full of intrigue," and decadent.[71] It wasn't the Italians the young Patriots held in contempt, but the other nations who sold them out or merely stood by (presumably Britain and France). He had seen the light. Fascism would bring out the best in Ethiopians.

The players were assembling on the stage. Cues given, the right speeches made, the clever twist soon to be revealed.

And a grim rehearsal was conducted in the days of mid-February, likely at the Siga Wedem gorge near the Abbay River, not far from the Debre Libanos monastery.

Abriha Deboch and Moges Asgedom were learning how to throw grenades.[72]

* * *

The last of the old guard hold-outs was a surprise—Ras Desta Damtew. Though his army had been starved and ruthlessly bombed by Graziani's forces about a year before, and despite the slaughter of Ganale Doria, the ras had managed to salvage what he could in Irgalem, far to the south of the capital. For months, he frustrated the Italians by simply being on the loose. He headed north and tried to rally warriors in Gurage and got nowhere—they wouldn't follow him. Then west to Sidamo, but the real power in Sidamo was in the hands of his old rival, Dejazmach Gabre Mariam, whom Haile Selassie once pushed out to favor Desta, his son-in-law. Fortunately for Desta, Gabre

Mariam cared more about Ethiopia than old conflicts. Italian planes blanketed the region with leaflets containing a bribe: turn over the ras, submit, and you can have Sidamo. Gabre Mariam's answer was that he already had Sidamo.[73]

In mid to late October, the Italian columns came for them. Gabre Mariam was wounded in an early engagement and forced to retreat. For the next three months, a slow-motion chase drove both Desta and Gabre Mariam, along with their allies, through the Rift Valley Lakes region all the way back past Irgalem towards the mountains near Bale. The situation proved so embarrassing to Graziani that he had an elaborate explanation ready when he met with Patrick Roberts of the British legation on January 4. Desta, the viceroy informed Roberts, had met with an Italian official, an intermediary; the ras "was extremely nervous, being anxious to submit but fearing [for] his subordinate chiefs and particularly the Eritrean deserters with whom he is surrounded, and who realize they can expect no mercy." The British nodded politely to all this and marked how Graziani gave himself away with the telling comment of "no mercy."[74]

Whether Desta privately thought of submitting or not, the stalemate for him and Gabre Mariam went on. The Italians bombed them. They threw thousands of Arussi Oromo and Tigrayan bande at them. The pattern was all too predictable and familiar. Many of Gabre Mariam's pummeled men deserted, and the two former rivals had to make their last stand at a spot called Gogetti on February 19. By now, the Italians had imported battalions from Libya. When the end came, Gabre Mariam, wounded again but unable to slip away, asked an askari junior officer to finish him off instead of handing him over to the Italians.

Desta managed to escape. The news was seized upon in London by the *New Times and Ethiopia News*, but by the time the paper was heralding his bravery, he was already dead. He'd made it back to his old home in Gurage, but it wasn't safe there anymore. The Italians hunted him down to a village called Egia, where they found a wreck of a man. Desta had once worn tailored khaki uniforms and was a commander of quiet graces and intelligence; now he was an exhausted, pitiful figure, his beard unruly, his face drawn.[75] On February 24, he was tied to a tree and shot.

Those who had stayed with him also suffered. Many ended up in a detention camp at Akaki, where the women captured from Desta's army were left stark naked in the compound, "with not even a piece of cloth to hide their delicate organs day and night." Several of the dejazmaches and commanders were tortured.[76] One of Desta's commanders was executed—Beyene Merid, the Emperor's son-in-law.

And now Romanework, Haile Selassie's daughter by his first marriage,* along with her three children, were captives of the Fascists.

* * *

News was trickling out to the world that the Ethiopians hadn't given up the fight, a truth that had to be denied. Rome demanded on February 3, 1937, that all journalists in the colony sign a pledge that they wouldn't report anything that gave the impression the war was not over.[77] Months ago, Rome had sycophants like reporter Salvatore Aponte cheerfully rearrange facts on his own initiative. Now it needed to impose discipline to keep a rosy picture.

But maybe compassion would yield better results—an artificial display of compassion would do. February 19 marked the annual celebration of St. Michael, and Rodolfo Graziani was using it to celebrate the birth of a new son to the king and queen of Italy. With his officials and many of the Ethiopian clergy in attendance, he would make a great show of distributing alms to the poor. This date would famously go down in Ethiopian history as Yekatit 12.

Abun Qirillos had heard rumors of a rebel attack and had stupidly tried to "call in sick," which only raised the Italians' suspicions. They sent a doctor for him, who naturally found the cleric was fine, and now his hand was forced. Amazingly, the plot's security was so bad that the whiff of danger had blown all the way to Rome, and high-ranking military officers, including Badoglio, had sent cables of warning.[78]

Friday came. The old and the sick, the lame and the blind, shuffled their way to the Governo Generale in the early morning hours, and soon, a crowd of about three thousand Ethiopians—most of them wretchedly poor and physically afflicted in some way—began to coalesce in front of the palace steps.

Ciro Poggiali and other reporters arrived around nine o'clock, bored as journalists usually get over ceremonial functions. Qirillos tried to play the sick card again, and Graziani held up the ceremony while a car fetched the reluctant Abun. The viceroy and his officers hadn't ignored the attack warnings; far from it. On the palace's balcony over the dais, machine guns were trained on the people, while an Ethiopian police officer noticed, "Around the fence you could see those special guards fully armed with machine guns, and looking as if they were hunting elephants."[79] Despite the show of firepower, Abriha Deboch and Moges Asgedom had no trouble wading through the crowd and entering the palace, finding their way up to the front balcony (today, the building has a second story).

---

* Romanework's mother reportedly died in childbirth.

At last Qirillos arrived, and the ceremony could get underway. Graziani made a fiery speech—gesturing, yelling, demanding. He borrowed Mussolini's style, but he didn't have his Duce's charisma, and all his flourishes were wasted on huddles of sick and crippled locals. "Believe in our government and obey it— that is the motto which everyone of you ought to make his own," he told the crowd. "Only in that manner will you be able to cooperate in the work of civilization, peace, and progress undertaken by Italy in Ethiopia."[80] There were oaths of loyalty and a fly-by made by Italian planes, and then at around eleven-thirty, Graziani began his magnanimous gesture.

Not that the viceroy deigned to bring himself near any of the natives he governed. No, coins were handed out from a large table a short distance away. Graziani soon grew bored and restless with this interminable ritual, and he barked to one of his officers, "Hurry up or we will still be here until dark!"[81]

At around quarter to twelve, as Ras Hailu pointed out a group of chiefs to Graziani, everyone heard a loud explosion. Though no one understood in that moment, they soon would—it was a grenade. It seemed to hit the top of the portico. There was a pause of astonishment and terror. And then more grenades were exploding—

The bloodbath that followed would pour out of the palace grounds and engulf all of Addis Ababa, and it would last more than half a year.

Chapter Nineteen

ABATTOIR

The second grenade struck a pillar and blew its deadly pieces not far away from Graziani. Moges Asgedom and Abriha Deboch were hurling them from two windows set on each side of the front wall of the palace, behind the dais.* They might have had help from accomplices, but this still can't be pinned down decisively by historians. What seems likely is that they made their first throw to try to take out one of the machine guns on the terrace.

People began to panic, some shouting, "Bombs! Bombs!" Others were trapped against the building's façade with nowhere to escape. A third grenade was tossed and exploded right in front of Poggiali, lashing him with shrapnel fragments. Abun Qirillos, standing next to Poggiali, was wounded as well and collapsed on top of him, while his umbrella carrier was killed outright. In that crucial instant, Rodolfo Graziani, hero of the invasion, the Butcher of Fezzan, turned tail without a thought for anyone else and tried to get inside the building—but the grenade found him, too. More than 350 pieces of shrapnel lacerated his back, shoulders, and the back of his right leg. In the swirl of smoke and noise, more grenades were thrown, perhaps as many as seven, and to this day it's unknown whether Abriha Deboch and Moges Asgedom were the ones who specifically hurled them or if accomplices did.

An Italian cameraman put down his equipment and rushed to help Graziani, lifting him up. He and Italian officers took him to a car to drive him to the hospital. Poggiali, though wounded, thought the attack was the start of a rebellion

---

* For decades, it was thought the grenades were lobbed from above, but historian Ian Campbell and Professor Richard Pankhurst conducted a reconstruction in 2004 that proved this scenario was all but impossible. Campbell makes a highly persuasive case in *The Plot to Kill Graziani* (pp. 206-212) that the grenades had to have been thrown from the windows.

and went with others to collect weapons, but soon he spotted the effort to take the wounded viceroy to a car and joined to help.

In the confusion and smoke, Guido Cortese, the secretary of the Fascist Party, began blasting away with his pistol, presuming that it was the high-ranking Ethiopian guests who were responsible. His fellow Italians and the askari soldiers took that as a cue to shoot into the audience—the lame and the sick and the old who had only shown up for alms. Then the machine guns above mowed through the crowd, killing thousands.

All the while, the actual culprits, Moges and Abriha, ran through a side gate close to a school and disappeared near some woods by a mission. But within a couple of hours, Italian military intelligence knew the pair was responsible and were questioning one of their friends and fellow conspirators.[1] By then, Graziani was in surgery, but he would come through it successfully, though he was marked for the rest of his life with scars. The commander of the air force, General Liotta, was also injured in the blasts but far less fortunate, losing his leg.

The authorities immediately shut down most telephone connections and the post office, with carabinieri and soldiers demanding every store close, every citizen get off the streets and go home. But the Blackshirts weren't content with their summary executions at the palace. Now, back in the Arada district outside the Fascist Party headquarters, Guido Cortese declared to those around him, "For three days, I give you *carta bianca* [free reign] to destroy and kill and do what you want to the Ethiopians."[2] What followed always had official sanction. At six o'clock as the evening started, the massacre began.

Ciro Poggiali heard the guns of reprisal as he was treated at the hospital. He quickly hit the streets and saw Italian civilians exacting horrific vengeance. They bludgeoned any Ethiopian they found with iron bars and lashed them with whips. "Soon the streets around the tukuls are strewn with bodies," Poggiali wrote in his diary. "I see a driver who, after knocking an old Negro to the ground with a blow of a club, thrusts a bayonet right through his head."[3]

At one point in the afternoon, Italian soldiers entered a hut, supposedly looking for British hand grenades. Instead, they found thalers and a hidden picture of Haile Selassie. For this, the Italians locked the entire family in the house and set it on fire. The people inside screamed, burning to death. Ladislas Sava wrote years later, "Their desperate cries were heard around the hut, but the Italians did not move from the place till the cries had ceased; they were anxious that none should escape the fire."[4]

As night fell, Sava stood at the windows of his house and watched Addis Ababa become abattoir. Italians burst into the homes of Ethiopians, searched and looted them, beat and killed their inhabitants, and then often set the houses ablaze. They slopped oil and petrol from cans to hasten the infernos. Toka Binegid, then just twenty years old and an officer of the fire brigade, reported years later that he and others were told not to put out the fires. He saw Italians murdering Ethiopians while others "were gathering the corpses from the roads with iron rakes. Among the persons who were pulled by the iron rakes, many were alive."[5]

The Ethiopians who were not killed by dagger, truncheon, or rifle in the streets were arrested and shoved into trucks, sometimes murdered in the vehicles, sometimes taken to the Governo Generale to be killed. "Whole streets were burned down, and if any of the occupants of the houses ran out from the flames, they were machine-gunned or stabbed with cries of *'Duce! Duce! Duce!'*"[6] Sometimes the fleeing occupants were pushed back into the blaze.

The shooting went on through the night.

*   *   *

In the midst of this chaos, a feverish manhunt was underway. Italian military intelligence and carabinieri raced through the night, roaring their vehicles up to the thatched-roof cottage that Abriha Deboch had called home. It was eight o'clock. The Italians burst through the door. No Abriha, no Moges Asgedom. What they found instead was an Italian flag laid out on the floor and pierced with a bayonet, which was tied with the Ethiopian tricolor. It might as well have been a signed confession.

The soldiers and police were already trying to confirm a stunning notion, that the assassination had started with someone *right on the viceroy's staff.* As historian Ian Campbell puts it, "The news could make the Italians an international laughing-stock and would surely mean the end of Rodolfo Graziani as viceroy of the new Italian Empire." This couldn't come out. It was too humiliating, too embarrassing, and so "decisions were apparently made that were to create doubt and confusion in the minds of historians and keep the Italian nation in the dark on this matter for the next fifty years."[7]

The cover-up would start that night. The names of the suspects would be kept even from officials in Rome. Their backgrounds, especially any ties to Graziani's office, would not be documented. Abriha's cottage was set alight, as were neighboring houses, and with so many locals' homes burning to ashes, a few more wouldn't prompt anyone's curiosity.

But the intelligence officers and police *did* find one suspect in the house and took him away—Abriha's friend, Haylu Gabre-Wold, who was only there because he was sick and in bed. The astonishing thing is that he wasn't murdered on the spot, and if any Blackshirts had come along on the raid, he probably would have been.[8] Amazingly, despite the flags-and-bayonet display that implicated the pair's circle of friends and fellow conspirators, Haylu was merely put in prison. He stayed there a year. He was comparatively lucky, because death waited for others. The insult of the stabbed Italian flag was enough to send the intelligence men and police on a search for all other known associates and acquaintances.

And where, in all this, were Abriha and Moges? At seven-thirty, the pair turned up at the German Hermannsburg Mission. They were looking for help from their friend who lived and worked as a teacher on the grounds, Sebhat Tiruneh, shouting for him beyond the fence. Moges needed money, fresh clothes. Sebhat had already been questioned twice by authorities over their whereabouts, and he was anxious to send them away. Abriha and Moges thought Sebhat should skip town with them, but he felt he couldn't leave because he needed to care for his younger brother, Taddesse, who was only twelve years old. "I'll be completely safe here," he told another friend, "because I'll be protected by the Germans."[9] Abriha and Moges continued their escape without him.

Half an hour later, soldiers pounced on the German mission and came for Sebhat. Young Taddesse looked on in dread under the glow of flashlights and was forced to translate as a colonel interrogated his brother. What was he doing here? How did he know the two men? Where were they now? When the colonel finally turned to the German missionaries, one vouched for him on the spot: "I believe Sebhat, and I trust him." The other German was the head of the mission, Hermann Bahlburg, and he'd employed the young teacher for years. But he stood in the semi-darkness and snapped coldly, "Prominent people come here to meet Sebhat. He is not to be trusted . . . I am sure that Sebhat is involved in this crime."[10]

As Taddesse watched, stunned and horrified, the Italians dragged away Sebhat and the first missionary. The German would eventually be released. Sebhat would not be coming back. The next morning, the boy fled the Hermannsburg grounds and found refuge in a Swedish mission, where a friendly Orthodox priest, Badima Yelew, took him in and told him, "As of this moment, you are my son."

Sebhat was gone; the boy couldn't admit to anyone that he was his brother.

*   *   *

They came for Michael Bekele Hapte in the middle of the night, as they did for others. One day, Bekele Hapte would be a respected judge of the High Court of Ethiopia, but at the time he was just another suspect in the attack, and the Italian authorities "suspected everyone." At around midnight, carabinieri barged into his house, woke him up from his bed, and packed him off with other suspects on a train, where they tied his hands together with wire. Bekele Hepte would have to endure an excruciating, long journey with temporary prison stops where the rooms were filled with bugs. At one locale, there was a single latrine for almost two hundred prisoners.

It was a quirk of Fascist justice that food and supply packages were allowed for some lucky inmates, sent by their families (presuming the family members knew where they were). But when one man tried to share his precious goods from home, "an Italian brigadier saw the boy who brought the provisions and tied both his hands together and hanged him from the ceiling of the latrine for twenty-four hours."[11]

Bekele Hapte and others spent three days in chains in a prison in Harar, starved, desperately thirsty, at the limits of their endurance. And the journey wasn't over. Their final stop was Danane, the most notorious concentration camp in Ethiopian history. It once stood less than twenty miles southwest of Mogadishu.

About two hundred prisoners of war from Ras Desta's last stand were already kept there, but Bekele Hapte and those rounded up in Addis Ababa were tossed in with a collection of murderers and other criminals. Their daily rations consisted of hard biscuits, rotten with worms, and tea or coffee. Many became sick. The inmates complained. Bekele Hapte recalled that the jail's commander told them "he could not do anything about it, because it was ordered by his superiors. Even if we possessed a small amount of money, we were forbidden to buy any kind of food."[12] Eventually, they were transferred to the general population being held in the compounds, where Bekele Hapte considered the food to be much worse.

Though Italian Quartermaster Fidenzio Dall'Ora came up with new efficiencies, the use of concentration camps was an old method for the Fascists—and for Graziani. For the pacification of Libya earlier in the decade, multiple camps were used, and in time, forty thousand of one hundred thousand prisoners had died of similarly appalling conditions: rotten food, starvation, typhus, malaria, dysentery, and other diseases.[13]

Danane would never have close to such numbers for its population, but it would hold thousands. It began with a handful of inmates, and now its compounds were starting to fill. And smaller camps were being established back in Ethiopia.

*   *   *

On Saturday morning, homeless Ethiopians, too traumatized to even sob or cry out, wandered slowly, looking for lost relatives. Sava saw blood flowing in the water streams. Dead bodies lay both under and on top of Makonnen Bridge. Italian soldiers ordered Ethiopians at gunpoint to dispose of the people they had murdered the previous evening. Blackshirts rushed to the Bank of Italy—they needed to change the thalers they had stolen from Ethiopian homes and exchange the gold and silver ornaments they had ripped from the necks of black female victims.[14] Ciro Poggiali tried to get permission to send a story on the growing massacre. "The orders from Rome are categorical: Italy must not know about it."[15]

If Italy couldn't know, Washington would. "Not since the Armenian massacres have I seen a display of such unbridled brutality and cowardice," Cornelius Engert cabled Cordell Hull that morning. He reported "mass executions in batches of 50 or 100 all over town of wretched people who by no stretch of the imagination could have had anything to do with the incident."[16] Engert was told by the French minister that a gang of Blackshirts had rushed into his compound Friday afternoon, set fire to three huts in the servants' quarters, and chased away four Ethiopians. "He agrees with me that for the last 24 hours, the Italians have been acting like raving maniacs, which bodes ill for the future." On his way back from the French embassy, Engert saw trucks carting away victims murdered earlier that morning.

Daylight did not bring an end to the orgy of violence. David Oqbazqui, the ex-governor of Adwa, was rounded up and sent to the Ras Makonnen Bridge police station. He saw people thrown from trucks so that they rolled down to the river, only to be shot. He saw the houses and tukuls in front of the compound burn. Oqbazqui testified years later, "Some Greeks and Armenians who had found Ethiopian babies coming from the burning houses came to our compound with these children to ask if their mothers were there. I especially remember one case when an Armenian carried a little baby in her arms, asking for the mother. She was allowed to come to us with the baby and went around in the crying crowd (most of them were injured) and tried to find the mother. One woman took care of the child. Whether it was the mother or not, I do not know."[17]

The compound filled with more people until none of them could move. According to Oqbazqui, for three days, they were not given any food or water.

That same Saturday, the authorities also arrested Shawaragad Gadle. They assumed she played some role in the grenade attack, but she denied it.* A rubber band was tied around her neck, her wrists bound, and then the shocks started. "The electric shocks made my nose bleed, and I eventually lost consciousness," she recalled later. Finally, she was released.

Ladislas Sava, who had used his medical skills in the Great War and had seen death in battle, was shaken by the visions unfolding over the three major days of slaughter. He had seen "a man's head split open by a truncheon so that the brains

---

* Her retainers did visit the house of Letyibelu Gebre, so perhaps this is what aroused their suspicion, though a pretext was hardly needed.

gushed out." He heard Italian officers lament the fact that the complete extermination of the Ethiopians was "unfortunately impossible."[18] Another long night of barbaric pillage and murder was unfolding, and he knew it would get worse with the encroaching darkness. He ordered his servant to stay with him and not even show his face at the window.

A Blackshirt had his comrades take a photo of him standing in front of the bodies of some Ethiopians—a complete family slain—as he held a dagger in one hand and a severed head in another.

It would be years before Sava was free to write about what he saw in the *New Times and Ethiopia News*, and his account would be clearly partisan, an indictment of the colonial regime. But Foreign Office officials in London learned about the massacre far earlier, and if they had any doubts such horrors took place, they had only to read the cold, objective prose of a monthly intelligence report from the British Somaliland Camel Corps. For his report of March 30, Lieutenant Thorold, stationed in Burao, wrote a brief paragraph on the wholesale bayoneting and burning and then listed incidents during the massacre "reported on good authority" that he considered "illustrative of the conduct of the Italians."

> A band of eight Blackshirts were seen beating with staves, apparently to death, an Ethiopian whose hands had first been tied behind his back.
>
> A three-day-old corpse was being buried when an Italian officer came up and stopped the proceedings in order to search the body for money. He pocketed the dollar or two he found on it . . .
>
> Two thousand people were packed into a compound at such close quarters that they could not sit down and [were] kept there for two days without food or water. Later, they were moved to a bigger camp where some received bread and water in small quantities; others had nothing, for there was not enough to go round. Numbers died from exposure.[19]

Incredibly, the massacre had one African-American witness, Walter Merguson, working as the *Pittsburgh Courier's* correspondent. Had the Blackshirts discovered he was a reporter, he surely would have been stabbed or beaten to death on the spot—he ran that risk just for being a black man. Merguson wrote that he saw victims shot by Italian soldiers "who laughed in maniacal glee as they killed, with the full sanction of their commanding officers." His story home included a stunning, uncorroborated accusation. "It is common knowledge in Addis Ababa that hundreds of Ethiopians, their lives in danger on the streets of the city, stormed into the American legation, seeking refuge. American officials, apparently seeking to keep the 'peace' with Italians, drove these people out . . . There, they were shot down like dogs."[20]

It simply wasn't true—quite the opposite. Italian soldiers, Engert cabled Hull, had bluntly told members of his staff that the remaining Ethiopian houses adjoined to their compound would be burned that evening. Engert had twice gone out to make an appeal to the commandant of the carabinieri, who sent him away with an empty promise that a guard would be posted outside the legation. Night fell, and no guard was to be seen as a fresh mob appeared with their torches. Soon, about seven hundred Ethiopians were fleeing their burning huts. "As they climbed over the fences during the night in order to save their lives, I was, of course, powerless to stop them. However, even had I been able to keep them out, I should not have done so because I felt that the most elementary dictates of humanity and decency required that they be permitted to seek refuge in the only place available to them. I merely insisted that most of them be unarmed."[21]

It's interesting that Engert felt the need to justify his compassion to Hull; perhaps he thought his boss would consider that taking in the Ethiopians put the compound at risk (he was right; Hull did). "So far, the Italians are hardly aware of their existence, but should they request that they leave our compound, I shall first demand a definite assurance from the authorities that they will not be hunted down like wild beasts."[22] Why, at this point, Engert would believe any assurance is a mystery. It didn't seem to occur to him that his legation was within its rights, and the Italians had no right to request anything over how the grounds were used. Engert was not a stubborn bull like Sidney Barton, but he would do what he could.

From the second floor of his family's house, the young boy, Imru Zelleke, watched the bloody panorama playing itself out in and around Menelik Square. To think that his family had come so close months ago to escape in Djibouti! What shook him to his core now was "the extreme and indiscriminate violence inflicted on peaceful people, which even today after witnessing the unfolding of so many dramas, I find difficult to rationalize."[23] Now the violence came to his doorstep, as he, his mother, and his two sisters, one nine years old and one merely two, were all arrested.

They were kept in the basement of a villa near their house, where a group of Italian prisoners were also held. What these Italians had done to deserve arrest was unclear; they might have been criminals, or perhaps they tried to save Ethiopians. Imru Zelleke and his family had to suffer hearing their screams from being tortured and interrogated.

* * *

On February 21, a Sunday, a formal proclamation put an end to the reprisals by noon. The order came from Fascist Party Secretary Guido Cortese, but it was actually sent by Mussolini in Rome to Graziani, and it managed to end a plan for airplanes to bomb and obliterate St. George's Cathedral.[24] When Ladislas Sava ventured to go out into the streets, he spotted a poster put on different walls throughout the city. It read in Amharic, "Mussolini is mighty as God. They have the same ways. He was angry, but he is angry no more. Get home and continue your daily work."[25]

For many Ethiopians, official word of the reprisals' end meant nothing, and it would turn out to be another lie anyway. While many history books record the reprisals lasting two and a half days, the killing didn't end at all. It was simply more organized and resumed the guise of official execution. That same afternoon, Cortese realized that a highly respected Orthodox priest had lived through the massacre. He dispatched men to go kill him. At a private house, where a group of more than twenty Ethiopians were gathered, most of them women, the cleric was stabbed to death as he knelt in prayer.[26]

David Oqbazqui was one of the lucky ones who had an identity card, and so he was released from the compound at the Ras Makonnen Bridge police station. Those let out were each given a piece of bread and a little water. As he walked home, Oqbazqui saw there were houses still burning, and he noticed that the ruins of some still held the charred corpses of their inhabitants. He heard later that "a good number of [those still in the compound] died from thirst and hunger."[27]

On Monday, Cornelius Engert was driving his car through the streets of the capital when the vehicle ahead suddenly stopped. An old Ethiopian man was walking alongside the road up ahead with two women. An Italian colonel suddenly jumped out of the car in front and began striking the old man savagely with a horse whip. "I'll make you beasts crawl in the dust before me!" he yelled. He whipped his victim's face bloody, the old man thrusting up his hands, begging for mercy. The women were already on their knees beside him, and now the Italian started beating them, too. Engert blasted his horn—"as if wishing to pass his [car]." The colonel was startled. He was so embarrassed at the sight of the twin American flags on Engert's vehicle that he jumped back in his car and drove off.[28]

By the next afternoon, Engert negotiated the safe departure of the Ethiopians at his legation. Before they left, a small group of them expressed their thanks to the United States government "for saving their lives," a touching gesture that moved Engert. In Washington, Cordell Hull's reaction to the reports from Addis Ababa was to roll up the embassy; the United States had to avoid becoming involved in "embarrassing if not dangerous incidents which are not of any vital concern to this country."[29] Engert was to take his holiday, and the consular office would close its doors on March 30. Now, the United States, the last power that might have exerted moral influence in Ethiopia, was leaving. The doors were shut for good on April 8, with the US consulate in Tripoli closing as well.

Thousands had been rounded up and placed in detention centers and prisons. The fire brigade officer, Toka Binegid, and others took drinking water for the prisoners at the central police station, but "when they were struggling to quench their thirst, the Italians struck them with bludgeons and stabbed them with bayonets."[30] Thousands of others were being detained and as badly treated at the central prison, the Ras Makonnen Bridge police station, St. George's Prison, and other locations. Perhaps as many as five thousand other Ethiopians managed to flee the city. Some joined the different Patriot bands, but most would eventually decide to come back to their homes . . . or what was left of their homes.

To this day, no one can say definitively how many were killed in the Graziani Massacre. Some Ethiopians have claimed thirty thousand deaths, while some Italians have insisted on a hardly credible few hundred. Modern historians put the figure at between three and six thousand.[31] Cornelius Engert cabled Washington a conservative estimate of "at least 3,000 harmless natives" killed over the three days. The French minister in Addis Ababa estimated six thousand killed.[32] We can get another measure by going back to Britain's Lieutenant Thorold, who had fresh intelligence coming in at the time. "It is difficult to estimate the number killed," he conceded in his secret report to the Foreign Office, "but a report, as yet unconfirmed, states that three thousand, two hundred Ethiopians were accounted for by officially ordered executions alone, and it seems likely that as many again were killed indiscriminately."[33]

Though Thorold's initial estimate was a guess, it was a shrewd one, given the information he had at the time. If his preliminary estimates were even close to accurate, the death toll would be at least sixty-four hundred. But Thorold and Engert both may have forgotten something—close to three thousand Ethiopians mown down by machine guns and pistols just after the grenades went off. Historian Ian Campbell, who has made a thorough study of the different stages of the massacre and the numbers involved, puts the final death toll at a range of more than seventeen to eighteen thousand people.[34]

We may never be certain of the math. But if numbers don't persuade, there's always the power of an image: one European witness saw convoys of military trucks heading out of the city on the Ambo Road, truck after truck, each vehicle loaded with corpses. And years later, the remains of five hundred decomposing bodies were discovered dumped in various rivers and wells.[35]

* * *

Examining an Italian poison gas bomb after an attack on Irgalem,
March 1936.

After the bombing of the British Red Cross on the Korem plain on
March 4, 1936.

The Dutch Red Cross camp at Dessie. Note the large flag on the ground
intended for planes.

Dr. Belmonte of the Dutch Red Cross in gas mask at cave entrance.

General Badoglio (pointing) with officers and reporters before the Battle of Enderta. Herbert Matthews is off center to the right, holding his hat behind his back.

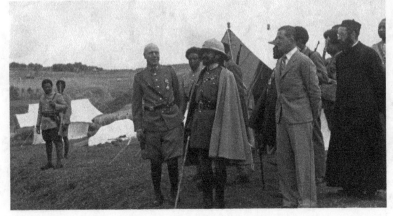

The Emperor visits a field hospital in Dessie. Dr. Charles Winckel of the Dutch Red Cross (in uniform) is to the left of Haile Selassie, while Marcel Junod (in suit) is to the right.

The Cheerful Saint: Dr. John Melly

The Crown Prince having target practice near Dessie.

Marcel Junod (left) with Sidney Brown in Addis Ababa.

British ambulances bring casualties to the Dutch field hospital at Dessie.

"The Al Fresco Wedding," May 4, 1936. The groom is George Steer (in boots), and his new bride is Margarita de Herrero (wearing hat, holding flowers).

"God and history will remember your judgment." Haile Selassie speaks to the League of Nations, June 30, 1936.

The Face of Occupation: Mussolini's stone bust put up at Adwa.

Mass arrests after the assassination attempt on Graziani.

A tukul destroyed during the Graziani Massacre.

Victims of the Graziani Massacre lie dead in a street in Addis Ababa.

Collection and disposal of bodies.

Another view of the massacre victims.

Souvenir shot kept by Italian soldier of Italians posing with four severed heads.

Italian soldier poses in front of a gallows of hanged Ethiopians.

By Thursday morning, Galeazzo Ciano—war hero, the Duce's son-in-law, and most recently, Italy's foreign minister—was performing damage control, assuring American Ambassador William Phillips that all was well and that orders had gone out to provide the US embassy with proper protection. Even after the bombs were thrown, the native population remained entirely tranquil, claimed Ciano. Still, there were hostile groups trying to make trouble, hence police measures. Phillips, a tall, Harvard-educated diplomat of quiet bearing and carefully chosen words, didn't buy any of this. He cabled Hull that "I felt that it was wise to let him know that we were fully aware of the manner in which the Italians had conducted themselves."[36]

The story of the assassination attempt and the massacre had unravelled completely out of the hands of the viceroy's loyal officials in Addis Ababa. As the chaos in the capital had unfolded, a telegram about the attack had been sent to Rome in Graziani's name. Who actually sent it remains unclear, but the wounded viceroy was hardly in any shape to dictate it himself. The telegram tried to portray the powers in Addis Ababa as being in control; they were on top of things, nothing to worry about here. Italy's minister of the colonies and master intriguer, Alessandro Lessona, knew better. He thought the news was important enough to call Mussolini while he was on a skiing holiday in Terminillo. His instincts were right, and Mussolini ordered him to drive up.

As Lessona trudged in the snow with his Duce decked out in ski gear, the two recognized the political fallout from hurled grenades. "Graziani after what has happened cannot anymore remain Viceroy," said Mussolini. "It is necessary to replace him."[37]

Graziani, however, would stay in charge of Ethiopia for several more months, giving him plenty of time to inflict a terrible vengeance. The grenade attack not only left the tattoos of shrapnel on his body, but they unhinged his mind, leaving him an unstable paranoid. While he turned his office into a fortress of guards and barbed wire, he made the bizarre connection that one of the biggest threats of sedition originated with Ethiopia's traditional soothsayers and witch doctors. He had scores of them arrested and executed.[38]

On March 1, he ordered General Guglielmo Nasi to have all the Amharic nobles and ex-military officers who had surrendered "all be shot immediately according to the directions of the Duce repeated a thousand times."[39] Almost two months later, Nasi—after having already passed on the orders for indiscriminate killing—would manage to persuade his viceroy to briefly relent, suggesting that mass executions would have "damaging repercussions." Far better, he argued, to use show trials. But mere weeks later, Graziani was back to obsessing over the elimination of Amharic chiefs.

In Gojjam, a Captain Corvo proved how efficient he could be at eliminating chiefs who once backed Imru. The chiefs were forced onto a boat, and then in the middle of Lake Tana, they were tossed over the side, each man tied to heavy stones to drag him down under the water.[40]

A few hundred nobles had a different fate. About four hundred of them were sent into exile at various locations in Italy, and often their status determined their location. Rases (excluding the notable case of Imru) wound up in Tivoli or closer to Rome, while others were incarcerated in Asinara, Sardinia. One of those sent to Asinara was Shawaragad Gadle. Her release after her torture and interrogation had meant only a few days of freedom. She was soon picked up again and taken to Massawa, one of dozens "kept for nine days, men, women and children crowded together in cells in the most terrible heat. We were then taken by ship, battened down in the holds."

After some time at Asinara, Shawaragad was in a group that was relocated to another prison forty miles outside of Naples. "It was a very hard life, and the food was very bad, made of maize and bad potatoes."[41] There was more torture. Her jailers still thought she might have valuable information, and they flogged her to try to get it. She lost her temper once and slapped an Italian officer in the face, yelling, "You are entitled to imprison me, but not to insult me!"[42]

She would spend a year and a half of her life like this.

Haile Selassie would feel a very personal cost over these exiles. His own daughter, Princess Romanework, and her three children were sent to Asinara. One of the children died, while Romanework later succumbed to illness in a Turin hospital in 1941.[43] For the exiles, life stayed harsh, with even their jailers complaining to government authorities about their small budgets to provide food, water, clothing, and heat.[44]

Mere days after the festival of bloodlust in the streets, soldiers and police zeroed in on more of the Young Ethiopians—educated abroad, groomed to govern—and rounded them up for execution. The grenade attack offered another convenient pretext for the firing squads. George Heruy was among those slain. So, too, was Beshahwired Habte-Weld, whom Graziani was convinced was involved in the plot against him. He was put in chains and interrogated, then executed.[45]

So were others, including the sons of Charles Martin, Benyam and Yosef, who had gone through so much, accomplished so much. Walking with youthful dash along a Victoria train platform on their way to war, standing in the loyal ranks of the Emperor before his exile, carrying out the first inspiring raid of the Black Lions—the pair of handsome brothers seemed heroically immortal. In a way, they would be, soon to be frozen in time in photos that celebrated their lives in the *New Times and Ethiopia News.*

*   *   *

Young Imru Zelleke and his mother and sisters had lived through the night of screams, only to be transferred to a large concentration camp in Akaki.

There, Imru met his twenty-two-year-old half-brother, once a civil engineering graduate at Montpellier University and now a fellow inmate. They were among hundreds of simple peasants and farmers from all over the country who had been rounded up and tossed in the camp without a clue as to why they should be detained. For about a week, Imru and his mother and sisters were stuck in Akaki. The camp was only a waystation, a place where the occupation forces could catalogue their prisoners and dispatch them to even further destinations. Then came the day when young Imru was put on a truck, just one more inmate in a convoy of vehicles bound east for Italian Somaliland.

The covered trucks had no sides, and they had no benches. "The trucks were so crowded that no other position but sitting or standing was possible," he remembered. "Prisoners were allowed down from the trucks for a couple of short spells a day, to relieve themselves. Otherwise they had to stay in the trucks all the time."[46] Their single meal a day would be a miniscule portion of *galletta*, a hard chunk of bread, and some tomato paste. Scores of prisoners on the trucks fell sick with malaria, dysentery, and other illnesses. At Dire Dawa, those who had money were permitted to shop with a soldier escort. Then the hell on wheels continued. As the truck passed Jijiga, a heavy rainstorm turned the primitive tracks into a sea of thick mud, and the vehicle got stuck. The Italians made their inmates get out and push their own jail. When prisoners died, the soldiers dumped the bodies by the side of the road.

"The Somali askaris . . . that were guarding us were irascible and very cruel," recalled Imru. "They did not give any help to the prisoners. They would beat a prisoner for any excuse."

At last, the convoy arrived; the journey had taken a month. Imru Zelleke was now an inmate of the Danane concentration camp.

*   *   *

As news of the grenade attack reached the rest of the world, the newspapers of America and Europe passed on the Italian version of events with little if any critical examination. Both the *Daily Telegraph* and the *Manchester Guardian* cited official sources, reporting that two thousand *arrests* were made. Blackshirts had apparently "cleaned up" a native quarter where riots supposedly broke out. Such credulity infuriated Sylvia Pankhurst, whose newspaper pointed out that not one major British newspaper kept a correspondent in Ethiopia anymore, and that all had "bowed to the Fascist expulsion of the Press."[47] Even the *Pittsburgh Courier's* Walter Merguson, who had actually been there, mistakenly told readers that Ethiopian chiefs were responsible for the attack, drawing "grenades from under their shammas."[48]

In London, Charles Martin—Warqenah Eshate—was devastated more than anyone else, having lost two of his sons. He poured out his sorrow and fury in a front page article for the March 20th edition of the *New Times and Ethiopia News* with the headline, "CRUELTY AFTER CRUELTY." He was "afflicted almost beyond endurance," and asked, "As doubtless it is thought by some that these cruelties have really not been committed, may I suggest that some impartial and honorable observers be allowed to enter Ethiopia and report on the state of affairs there?"[49] None would be allowed. The idea of international observers, let alone that of peacekeepers, would have to wait until after the Second World War.

To add insult to inconsolable loss, Martin had to weather the insults of Italian propagandists, who tried to claim Britain was behind the assassination plot, and more specifically that his sons were involved. "How does *The Times*," demanded the *Azione Coloniale*, "explain the singular fact that two of the persons principally responsible for the attempt left the British capital early in February?"[50] Martin fired back that the attempt on Graziani's life must have been committed with the help of a foreigner. True, both Abriha and Moges *were* technically foreigners— they were Eritrean. But the Italians might have been closer to the truth than Martin could ever know. It's possible his sons *were* involved. And to this day, the extent of Haile Selassie's involvement, if any, or his knowledge about the attack remains a mystery.[51]

Charles Martin wouldn't be alone that March in expressing his grief and outrage.

George Steer had been in Spain reporting on the civil war, where he'd come to identify with the Basques in Bilbao as much as he did with the Ethiopians. The love of his life, Margarita, was back in London. She'd possibly accompanied him on his first assignment to Spain,[52] but he was alone this time, while she was at home, carrying their first child. Then word came: Margarita was sick—trouble with the pregnancy, the reasons vague, but they didn't matter. She was admitted to a private hospital in Marylebone, and he had to get back.

Officials with the Basque government gave him transport with a minesweeper trawler. With precious hours crawling by, Steer feared for his wife, feared for his unborn child, while the vessel slipped through an enemy blockade to reach the safe harbor of Bayonne, in France. He must have thought he got home in time, but his presence didn't matter. After Margarita's water broke, her doctors—for reasons that aren't clear—didn't induce delivery or perform a Caesarian section. She died in the night on January 30, 1937.

Steer's anguish was near unbearable, and a bewildered secretary for Faber & Faber was on a receiving end of a call when the young reporter broke down and sobbed. "He was hysterical, completely distraught," recalled Erica Wright.[53] His crippling grief included outrage and frustration over the physicians' conduct because they "didn't do anything." He later considered suing, but was talked out of it by a lawyer friend.[54] In *The Times*'s obituary, Margarita was praised for remaining in Addis Ababa during dangerous times, having "proved herself to be a journalist of marked ability and a brave and a fearless woman."[55] Her funeral was delayed so Steer's mother could attend, sailing to London from South Africa.

Waiting for his mother to arrive, trying to keep it together and be polite as he accepted condolences, Steer kept his eye on current events. He'd never forgotten Ethiopia, and the Graziani Massacre demanded he go to his typewriter. He banged out an article for *The Spectator* magazine, an indictment of the Italians in the form of a moving requiem. It was titled, *Addis Ababa—Civilized*:

> . . . Facing the Post Office was Mon Cine, where we saw Greta Garbo in an old but satisfying Grand Hotel, and danced until the stars faded into their heavenly screen; then we walked home past dark policemen muffled nose and ears in their shammas against the dawn wind. All these houses are destroyed by war. Tasfai Teguegne was at Mon Cine and Blatta Kidane Mariam, and the British Legation and the Greek garage proprietors. The young Ethiopians drank and laughed at the little chromium bar. Now they have been murdered because they could speak French. And we have gone home . . .

From scenes of the capital in happier times, Steer moved on to recreating the horror of the three days of reprisal. "The New Flower is become a butcher's shop, where Italy hangs Abyssinian flesh on hooks every day," he wrote. "The new abattoir is swimming with blood, the price of raw meat must be low indeed with such a glut in Shoa."[56]

On March 4, Margarita's funeral was held at last, and old friends came to pay their respects: Sir Sidney and Lady Barton, along with their daughter, Esmé, once the social butterfly of Addis Ababa. As Steer's biographer put it, despite her apparent flightiness, she "could see when someone needed looking after,"[57] and with her shared experiences of the capital, she could be a comfort to him as few others could. A romance would blossom, and Steer would eventually marry Esmé.

But that came two years later. At the time, private loss still mixed with a more public bereavement over what was happening in Ethiopia. Two weeks after Margarita's funeral, Steer, the Bartons, and others filed into St. George's Church on Bloomsbury Way to mourn the thousands killed by Graziani's soldiers. The Emperor came in from Bath for the service. As Steer sat with friends, he heard his own words from *The Spectator* article quoted back to him in the sermon by the Dean of Winchester. The Dean believed their atrocities could "only be explained on the view that they have been seized by a spirit of evil of superhuman stature."[58]

On March 15, three days after *The Spectator's* issue with Steer's article hit newsstands, it was reported that London had reached a deal: Italian ships could now sail into the Gulf of Aden and anchor at the British ports of Seila and Berbera, using these locales to unload goods bound for Ethiopia. Britain still didn't formally recognize Italian sovereignty, but it didn't seem to matter. The rationale was that the deal would relieve the pressure on the congested port of Djibouti.

For those in St. George's Church and many more elsewhere, the future of Ethiopia seemed as bleak as the gunmetal-gray clouds that regularly loomed over England, which was now feeling an increasing chill all the way from Germany.

* * *

It didn't take long for young Imru Zelleke to explore his new world. Danane prison had a large compound enclosed by walls twenty-five feet high, with towers where guards could keep a vigilant eye on their prisoners. One section of the compound was reserved for administration, while three more housed the inmates in tukuls. But with sixty-five hundred Ethiopians eventually filling up the camp, open sheds were built along the perimeter of the walls, where each person had to make do with a straw mat and a space of about thirty inches. In this cauldron built in an already steaming hot climate, there were far too many bodies, not enough space, and never enough air.

"The first few months were terrible," recalled Imru. He and other inmates had to subsist on meals of boiled vegetables and gallettas that were already rotten and full of worms. The water drawn from local wells was close enough to the coast to have a salty taste. "There were only eight or ten holes in the latrines; you can imagine what it was like with hundreds of people suffering from diarrhea."[59]

Imru recalled that several hundred died during the first few months he was there, prey to a long list of diseases brought on by malnutrition and the appalling conditions: malaria, pneumonia, dysentery, scurvy, typhus, tropical sores. "After a few months they brought in a young doctor, an Italian doctor, in the infirmary, but before that, there was not even a doctor, there was nothing there."[60]

The boy, Imru, had the advantage of his youth. He was allowed, at least, to go visit his mother and sisters. "At one time I was so sick with malaria, they let me stay with my mother until I recovered." He was fortunate in that he wasn't put off in an isolated tent called Lazaretto, the last stop for the sick who could no longer take care of themselves and who were simply abandoned to die. He remembers that "a young nurse and I were the only ones that went there to give them some water and food. Few lasted more than two or three days before they passed away."

At one point, he remembers, there were about seventy prisoners dying a day, which meant more work for those still living. "[The guards] wouldn't touch them themselves. They ordered the prisoners to go and bury them, and of course, people had to dig for their compatriots and people they knew."

The walled camp was only for men. A women's camp was just beyond, an enclosure of military tents roped off with barbed wire, but there was no communication between the men's and women's prisons. After some time passed, the Italians granted a small mercy of allowing married men to visit their wives on Sunday, but they could only talk over a fence; no physical contact was allowed.

And as Danane's population grew, the Italians had to build yet more camps, put up more tents, stretch more barbed wire.

There were the odd privileges. Imru and the others were allowed to go to the beach every Sunday to bathe and wash their pitiful scraps of clothing. Some were allowed to write and receive letters. "Spirits were generally high," remembered Imru. "There was always something to laugh or cry about. People had not lost hope. They believed firmly that they would be free and that the Italian would go away someday."[61]

The men were put to work each morning, gathering wood or forced to perform some other manual labor. Imru Zelleke was too young for such tasks, so he spent many a day in the infirmary cleaning and doing odd jobs. "There, I saw more death and human agony than for the rest of my whole life."[62]

The punctuations of fear, revulsion, and grief stood out in a seemingly endless desert of crushing boredom. There were those who took refuge in reading the bible or other religious texts, and at night, Imru could hear the devout mutterings and cries of "Igziyooo!" It was a group prayer. Some became teachers, and the boy learned Italian. The Ethiopians fashioned crude game boards and played chess and *gebeta*. They debated philosophy and politics, history and faith. What they didn't do was plan an escape. Where could they go? Especially when the Somalis in the countryside were hostile.

"I heard later, though, that two men had escaped and made it home," remembered Imru.[63]

From his recollections and the testimony of other inmates, it's clear the authorities hardly cared whether their inmates lived or died. The Italians' genuine goal seems to have been incarceration, not extermination, but massive extermination happened nevertheless. Instead of shooting a bullet into an Ethiopian, all they had to do was merely guard him as he starved or expired from cholera or malaria or dysentery or another one of a collection of quite treatable diseases.

James Walston of the American University of Rome put it well when he wrote: "Despite the fact that there were officials there who did their best to render the internees' lives more bearable, the government's position was clear; on a letter which described the deaths of two internees, an official of Graziani's . . . wrote 'two less to feed.'"[64]

Most historians have settled on a figure of probably sixty-five hundred Ethiopians, as well as some Eritreans and Somalis, who were held at Danane between 1936 and 1941. The figure comes from a Michael Tassemma, who worked in the camp as a medical assistant for three and a half years.[65] The Italians had inadvertently created a future witness for any war crimes prosecution, because Tassemma had the grim job of being in charge of recording illnesses and death. And out of the sixty-five hundred inmates, roughly half died of starvation, poor food, disease, and simply due to the appalling conditions.[66]

The figures are just as difficult to pin down for the camp at Nokra, an island in the Dahlak Archipelago off Massawa. At the very least, fifteen hundred to perhaps as many as another five or six thousand were held there, and no doubt, the camp had a similar mortality rate. Smaller populations were held at various camps in Akaki, Nefassilk, Debre Birhan, and other spots.

At the Nokra concentration camp, prisoners were condemned to shifts of forced labor in stone quarries. If the malaria and dysentery didn't kill them, many dropped on their feet from sunstroke, exhaustion, and dehydration. It could get up to 122°F on the island.[67]

In the midst of all this horrible death, there were episodes of defiance and the uniquely Ethiopian sense of humor. Imru Zelleke remembers the story of Alamawarq Bayyana's incarceration. The leader of the Black Lions had managed to escape being executed outright, and the Italians put the veterinarian in charge of the infirmary at the prison of Addis Ababa Tyit-bet, despite the fact that he didn't have any medicine "to treat even a headache" and that he knew nothing about human diseases and conditions. "His only real function was to register the dead in the prison ledger," recalls Imru. So in the column that listed cause of death, Alamawarq wrote in Italian "*Morto per la Patria.*"[68] Died for the country.

It was inevitable that the Italians would get around to checking the documents, and when his impishness was discovered, they interrogated him. Alamawarq replied that he didn't know what caused their deaths, so he considered it appropriate to register the real reason for their imprisonment. According to Imru, "the Italian authorities were not amused." Alamawarq was shipped off to Nokra, where he spent five years.[69] But he would survive this second sampling of Hell to become a liaison official to the post-war British administration.[70]

Meanwhile, in Danane in 1937, the months would roll on, and young Imru Zelleke would grow another year older.

*   *   *

They could imprison them, they could shoot them and torture them, they could cook Ethiopians alive in their windowless, oven-hot trucks on the steaming roads to Somaliland, but *Ethiopia itself* still had international interest and appeal. It seemed impossible to kill, indestructible. The Fascists kept trying and looked all the more desperate for it. One example took place on the other side of the world on the Sunday the reprisals were finishing. Eclipsed by reports of the massacre, it didn't get into most Western newspapers, including Sylvia Pankhurst's, until weeks later.

It happened in Shanghai.[71] At the Isis Theater on Bei Sichuang Road on the border of the International Settlement, an audience of a thousand people sat in the dark, smoking and whispering comments to each other as a Russian-made film about Ethiopia's conquest flickered on the screen. Suddenly, a mob of two hundred Italians—some civilians, but many sailors from the anchored warship, *Lepanto*—drove up in a convoy of vehicles and barged into the cinema. The leaders forced their way into the projection booth, hitting the Russian operators with rifle butts and clubs. One of the Russians suffered a broken arm, and the other took a gash to the head. The Italians naturally stole the film. The goons below fired revolvers and tossed ammonia bombs, the noxious fumes starting a panic and making the patrons flee to the street.

It was all pointless and counterproductive. Only a month before, when the film was first shown, Italian diplomats had carped, and Chinese authorities had obliged them by ordering severe censorship. The film was being shown again that night "under special government permission." The violence merely antagonized Shanghai officials and prompted fresh headlines around the world. Just as the country couldn't be easily gobbled up, the *idea* of Ethiopia couldn't be successfully vandalized or erased. Though lower in the headlines, pushed to the back pages, it stubbornly continued to draw interest.

*   *   *

In the incredible fallout from the grenade attack, what happened to the would-be assassins? The two young men who actually tossed the grenades? Where were they?

They fled.[72] Astonishingly, Abriha Deboch and Moges Asgedom rode a chauffeur-driven *limousine* part of the way out of Addis Ababa. Any Ethiopian traveling like this ran a deadly risk, but Abriha was no doubt anxious to contact his wife, who was staying with her mother at a house near the Debre Libanos monastery. He wanted to warn her to go underground, to hide, and he was racing against time to do it because nearby was the army base of Fiche. He and Moges then had to literally head for the hills, into the rugged terrain of Shoa. Moges had a week's head start, but they both wanted to link up with a Patriot leader they greatly admired, Abebe Aregai, the former chief of police in Addis Ababa.

Moges, however, was in for a shock. When he found Abebe's guerrilla band, the leader promptly took him prisoner. What was this tall tale about grenades right in front of the viceroy's headquarters? He didn't buy it at all. But Letyibelu Gebre had slipped through the dragnet in the capital with relatives, riding on pack mules into the mountainous terrain. Picking up willing new Patriots along the way, they caught up eventually to Abebe and set him straight about the pair's involvement. Abriha soon joined them and confirmed what had happened.

Abebe was contrite over his harsh treatment of Moges, but the deed was done, and it's possible both Moges and Abriha were badly put off. Perhaps they were disillusioned by Abebe's personality or his methods, but whatever their reasons, they decided not to join his army. Letyibelu, too, chose to go and run his own resistance unit.

Graziani knew it was Abriha and Moges who had scarred him for life, and he wanted nothing more than to get his hands on them. But the intelligence on their whereabouts was poor. In May, he had the idea they were with Abebe, whose army was in bad enough shape to negotiate with the viceroy. Graziani had a deal for him, sent in a letter: Abebe could live if he was willing to give up, plus betray, the two young men. It didn't matter at all whether Abebe was tempted—Abriha and Moges were long gone.

For a while, they reportedly fought in Shoa as Patriots under the dejazmach, Zewde Asfaw, though it's unclear for how long or even if they fought under him at all. Their goal had always been Sudan, where they hoped to run a new resistance movement of their own. Then they turned up in Ginde Beret, northwest of Addis Ababa, hoping to join the Patriot leader, Mesfin Sileshi, who was cordial but wanted them gone as quickly as possible in case the Italians were hot on their trail. So they drifted.

The details of their lives at this point were forgotten and lost so badly that most history books in the West have often dismissed them as simply being killed by local tribesmen in the borderlands. Ethiopian sources say differently, and Abriha and Moges would suffer a far more dramatic fate.

*   *   *

The Black Eagle, Hubert Julian, had turned traitor. And Marcus Garvey had become an apostate, not willing to forgive the perceived slight at Waterloo Station by his African messiah.

Readers of *The Black Man* could measure Garvey's stewing contempt in each issue. By January of 1937, "The Emperor was never competent." As for the guerrillas still carrying on the fight against occupation, Haile Selassie "has no more control over the fighting patriots than Mussolini has."[73] Then in the issue for March-April, Garvey wrote, "It is a pity that a man of the limited intellectual caliber and weak political character like Haile Selassie became Emperor of Abyssinia at so crucial a time in the political history of the world." Garvey wanted the "white world" to realize that black pride hadn't surrendered in Ethiopia. "It was the disloyalty of a single man who was too silly to take pride in his race."[74]

This new stance was a bolt from the blue to critics and supporters alike. Samuel Haynes, the soldier and activist from Belize who was Garvey's national organizer in the United States, could only shake his head. He knew members of the UNIA were quitting their organization, and they were walking across the street, so to speak, to join the competition—organizations for Ethiopia's defense. "Disgrace stares us in the face," Haynes admitted publicly. "Mr. Garvey is indifferent to the matter."[75]

Mr. Garvey, in fact, made things worse by scolding one of his important fundraisers for working with old enemies like W. E. B. Du Bois on committees to help Ethiopia. Adam Clayton Powell, Sr., the pastor of Harlem's landmark Abyssinian Baptist Church, thought Garvey had "signed his death warrant," and that "The halo around St. Marcus' head is rapidly growing faint . . . The figure of Emperor Haile Selassie, commanding the intense admiration and support of all racial groups, gives the Negro his first vision of internationalism."[76]

Garvey was now shouted down at Speaker's Corner in Hyde Park, and he was a pariah to African students in London, who were eager to break up his modest rallies. At one meeting about Ethiopia, he debated George Padmore on the issue, and among those watching was a brilliant young political scientist, Ralph Bunche, who years later would be the first person of color to win the Nobel Peace Prize. Bunche had come from the States to study anthropology at the London School of Economics. He noticed how the crowd became hostile as Garvey called the Emperor a dumb trickster, and Padmore actually had to protect his opponent as Garvey called his hecklers "riff-raff" and then dismissed Haile Selassie's empire for relying on white advisers.[77]

Garvey's UNIA had been in decline for years, and it had been sailing towards irrelevancy ever since he set foot on that ship sailing out of New Orleans. But this was a foolish, self-inflicted blow to his organization. With UNIA brigades breaking up in America, his funds low and dwindling, all Garvey really had left was the force of his own personality, but he antagonized too many, too often.

Once upon a time, he crowned Haile Selassie an African Christ, but he failed to recognize that Christ was most effective as a martyr.

* * *

For African Americans like Oscar Hunter and James Yates, Spain was a stand-in for Ethiopia over the fight for freedom. And now there was a tangible link between the two crusades.

On April 3, the *Chicago Defender* told its readers about Ashebir Gabre-Hywot, who had been one of the "Young Ethiopians" studying at Lausanne University. When the Italians invaded, he went home to fight with Ras Imru's forces in the north and in Gore. Though it wasn't explained how he slipped out of his country and found his way to Valencia, he told the *Madrid Daily*, "I am fully convinced that to fight in Spain is tantamount to fighting for the independence of Ethiopia."[78]

His nation's defiance even dared to show itself in Italy. That May saw the usual pomp and ceremonies in Rome to commemorate the occupation, with both Mussolini and the king presiding over marching throngs. A 21-year-old Eritrean named Zerai Deres was selected to present a collection of trophies and spoils to officials. It must have never occurred to Zerai that he would have to make his gesture in public. Then he saw the golden statue of the Lion of Judah—stolen from its place in front of the Addis Ababa railway station—displayed like a thief's prize. He was apparently filled with a mix of shame and rage, and he knelt on the spot to pray.

He was causing a scene, and police officers went over to move him along. Furious, Zerai drew the ceremonial sword he'd been given and slashed and thrust away, going on a vengeful rampage, and he managed to give four people minor injuries before he was shot and stopped. He survived his wounds only to be packed off to a mental hospital and then eventually sent back to Eritrea.[79]

* * *

Meanwhile, the Duce's regime kept up a steady barrage of anti-British propaganda. It didn't mind a little anti-Semitism either, when it was useful, telling Islamic Somalis that the British were helping the Jews against Arabs and siding with them in Palestine.[80]

And yet the Fascists hadn't given up on London or, for that matter, the British public. One tack they used was public relations. They found a useful pawn in the form of a retired British major, E. W. Polson Newman. His first big step was to author a history of the Ethiopian War, which came out that September and told its readers that "no information of any value is available from the Abyssinian side; and my experience of Abyssinia convinces me that none will be forthcoming, except possibly in a much limited sense from European officers with the Abyssinian forces."[81] This was like writing a history of the American War of Independence with only the official reports of the British army. In other words, the African could not be trusted.

The Foreign Office had long known what he was up to and had warned its staff, "For the last few years, Major Newman has been occupied in carrying out propaganda on behalf of Italian authorities, mainly in connection with Ethiopia, and his various tours through Italian controlled territory have been made under the auspices and it is believed at the expense of the Italian government." As a result, the FO told staff, "You should accordingly treat Major Newman, should he call upon you, with reserve and extend him no special facilities."[82]

As Newman went on the rubber chicken circuit, speaking to rotary clubs and society groups across Britain, he was bedeviled by writers for the *New Times and Ethiopia News*, who turned up at his functions just to tear down his wilder assertions. When Newman portrayed the Ethiopians as primitive savages, the paper informed its readers, "Ethiopia was at the same level of culture as England before the Norman invasion."[83] But Newman was preaching to his own choir, too, and he was never going to turn the tide of public opinion by talking to the Royal Empire Society.

The Italians made better progress with the diplomats. Mussolini kept his eye on his new prize, which was to get formal recognition of his conquest. The previous autumn, he made overtures to Eden through Dino Grandi, his ambassador in London, and more hints through Ciano. But Eden understood the Fascists now; Mussolini had the "mentality of a gangster."[84] The answer was still no. It was no as Mussolini saber-rattled over "rights" and sovereignty issues in the Mediterranean, and it was still no in the summer of 1937, when more divisions were sent to Libya.

But May was a month of change in Britain. The nation officially had a new king and a new prime minister. This was the month for the coronation of King George VI, known within the royal family as "Bertie." He was a shy man compared with his older brother, and he had an embarrassing stammer (which would be explored in the Oscar-winning film, *The King's Speech*). Britain now thankfully had a monarch who wouldn't play up to Hitler. Unfortunately, it now had a premier who would let both Hitler and Mussolini have their way.

To almost everyone, Neville Chamberlain looked to be the obvious successor for the retiring Stanley Baldwin. He was the only Chamberlain left in the news— his half-brother, Austen, had died two months before seeing him move into Number 10. Neville had run things when Baldwin was ill the previous year, and like a bulldozer on a slow prowl, he was determined to get where and what he wanted. But his personality and lack of charm was a disaster for a prime minister. Alec Douglas-Home, his parliamentary private secretary (and later briefly PM), once lured him into making an effort to come socialize in the Commons smoking room. Almost all conversation came to an embarrassing halt.[85]

As a prime minister, he was an autocrat. He didn't trust his Cabinet colleagues, and ordinary voters, he thought, were hostages to emotion. During his tenure, there would be journalists who became teacher's pets, given special briefings and information, while the more critical vets of Fleet Street were left out. And when it came to international affairs, Lloyd George grumbled that Chamberlain "saw foreign policy through the wrong end of a municipal drain pipe."[86]

He was the perfect PM for Mussolini, who realized he didn't need to go through Eden anymore, simply around him. Grandi was sent off to see the war secretary, claiming the Duce thought London was preparing for war. He even suggested a mutual disclosure of military preparations, a ridiculous idea that actually earned serious consideration by the War Office.[87] Finally, in a private meeting, Grandi asked Chamberlain directly for legal recognition of Italy's conquest. Chamberlain, without bothering to consult his own foreign secretary, decided on the spot to write the dictator a warm, personal message. Worse, he admitted later in his diary, "I did not show my letter to the Foreign Secretary, for I had the feeling that he would object to it."[88]

For more than seventy years, Neville Chamberlain's image has been of a weak-willed appeaser, a king of fools who caved to pressure and waved a useless document in the air. But there was a "streak of ruthlessness" to the man (which is how Eden later put it) that gets little attention in any documentaries on the inter-war era.[89] Chamberlain relied on a former MI5 section chief, Sir Joseph Ball, who had no reservations at all about using intelligence techniques for political ends. His targets were often Cabinet colleagues, and it was in 1937 that Chamberlain ordered Eden's phone to be tapped. Ball was also used to make overtures to Mussolini's officials, who were relieved at last that Eden was no longer running foreign policy.[90] Chamberlain was a man they could do business with.

Chapter Twenty

EDEN BOWS OUT

In Addis Ababa, a new regular spectacle was held in the marketplace. A large gallows—one on which ten people could be hanged—was erected at the spot where the capital had its largest flow of traffic. And the authorities waited to conduct their executions at the busiest time of day.

It was not enough to merely hang individuals. The soldiers fitted them, just like store window mannequins, with their rifles and other arms to demonstrate they had been secretly storing or using weapons. The crime of each victim, "conspiracy against the Italian empire," was written in Amharic on a placard under his feet. The corpses were often left to dangle for as long as two days and nights, guarded by a patrol of more than eighty soldiers (whose real purpose seemed to be to dissuade any photos from being taken). In a macabre effort to drive the lesson home, the gallows was even lit up at night by two large electric lights.[1]

The Hungarian doctor, Ladislas Sava, noted that Fascist officials "did not notice the moral effect was quite different" from what they intended. Ethiopians would come to the gallows in ritual mourning dress and plant themselves in silent prayer for as long as the bodies were displayed. "What the Italians intended to be a deterrent became a pilgrimage . . . In the houses of the town, wherever dark people lived, prayers were said every night for the salvation of the dead, and for the approach of the day of justice."[2]

Still hunting for the would-be assassins of the viceroy, Italian military intelligence put together a highly speculative report that claimed the monks of the Debre Libanos monastery were involved in the grenade attack. True, Abriha Deboch and Moges Asgedom had stopped at the monastery for a short time on their way out of the capital. This hardly implicated the monks, of course, but evidence wasn't paramount. What mattered was getting their hands on the suspects. Graziani needed little to be convinced. He had no compunction about executing Ethiopian clergy—he'd done it before, and he despised them as much as he hated soothsayers and witch doctors. But his political star had sunk to the gutter in Rome. If he was going to act, he had to act now and justify it later.[3]

On May 18, Italian soldiers arrived at the monastery grounds. Instead of throwing their weight around, they managed to persuade about two thousand Ethiopians there to pack into the Church of St. Tekle Haymanot, where they were held prisoner overnight. The next day, they were all moved to a temporary detention center, where the monks, church officials, and monastery residents were separated from ordinary visiting Ethiopians. Then a couple of days later, on May 21, there was another trip, a final one for many. The captives had no choice but to obediently climb into a set of military trucks. Those who were too sick or too lame, or perhaps too defiant, were shot on the spot. The trucks started their engines and lumbered along in a convoy to a place called Laga Welde. The vehicles parked close to a ravine—distant, isolated, convenient. The passengers were told to get out, and then the machine guns roared and sprayed their deadly fire.

The slaughter was so extensive that in the 1940s, after the war, when travel writer David Buxton visited the area, he still found remains. "Here were innumerable bones and skulls—bones in bags and bones in boxes, bones lying in confused heaps, awaiting burial . . . They will eventually be packed into the crevices below the cliffs, and sealed up with stone and mud."[4]

As the corpses lay in the ravine, a second group of several hundred deacons was transported overnight to a spot called Ingecha, about seventy-five miles north of the capital. On May 26, their bullet-riddled bodies were dumped in mass graves. A thousand more Ethiopians from Debre Libanos, as well as from other monasteries and churches, were rounded up for what had become a horrific ritual—the unbearable truck journey to the hell that was Danane.[5]

* * *

Lekelash Bayan, the female guerrilla leader known as *Strike him*, had kept on the move all this time, occasionally switching to different Patriot groups with her husband as they harassed the Italians, carrying her daughter on her back and sometimes lugging the prize of a captured machine gun. She could hold her own and was respected for her strong leadership, her cunning strategy, and her good fighting skills.

On August 10, the Italians hit her guerrilla cell hard. The firefight was intense, and Lekelash was separated from her husband, as both were shooting away for their very survival. "I could see him firing behind a growth of tall grass," she recalled later to historian Tsehai Berhane-Selassie. "Suddenly he waved to me and fell. I went over to his side, leaving my position."

She rushed to her husband and found that he was dead.

But this was not the moment to grieve.

"Enemy soldiers were close by on the other side of the river. Before I started to pull away, I fired across the river and killed three men. I then took his body and his gun and withdrew. The rest of my men were safe. I went back to camp, and the following day I buried him at the church of Dirma Gabriel."[6]

And then she had to find the reserves of strength to get on with the job. There would be more battles, more straggling through the countryside to look for shelter and food, and of course, the regular domestic chores she performed every day (she used to spin clothes and give them to different Patriot leaders). But now there was no longer the comfort of having a partner, a provider, a lover. The responsibilities remained. At one point, she was charged with taking care of one thousand rounds of ammunition for pistols and machine guns. Now, when a man's voice called out to her in the night, it often belonged to a wounded or dying guerrilla unable to get back to safety. Lekelash Bayan did her share of saving them.

The Patriot cells often couldn't—and didn't—communicate with each other. They could be disorganized and unpredictable. They had new leaders that the Italians didn't know and sometimes had never heard of before. They were just as poorly armed—sometimes worse off—than the old traditional standing armies, and yet often they were arguably *doing more damage*.

All this was pretty amazing in retrospect. The Fascists used to know their enemy. They once congratulated themselves as they bribed the more pliable nobles or listened in on wireless messages. Now they were bottled up in the capital and larger towns, and as word spread about the Graziani and Debre Libanos massacres, it outraged Ethiopians who already resented the foreign regime. Many decided to fight. Those who couldn't fight gave sanctuary and food to guerrillas or passed along information. In Begemder, the Patriots and remaining minor nobles controlled the region so well that they instituted their own tax collection.[7]

But the same lack of unity that could be a strength was also an inherent weakness. Rival leaders were as ready to attack each other as they were to go after the Italians. A secret meeting was held in Shoa when the Patriot leaders struggled to organize themselves, forming a Committee of Union and Collaboration. The story goes that the ever-mercurial Abebe Aregai stood watching some of them and grumbled, "How am I going to control these savages?"[8] In Gojjam, two dejazmaches, Mangasha Jambarai and Negash Bezibeh, harassed the enemy but also regularly provoked each other; both had family connections to Hailu and once held high office in the provincial civil service.

There was no coherent political philosophy for any of these cells—their main job was to fight, period. But as the Patriots grew in confidence, it was perhaps inevitable that there would be new political and cultural stirrings. Their Emperor was far away, the feudal hierarchy was being wiped out or undermined by the enemy. Men who braved machine gun fire and fought in the hills decided they were just as entitled to confer a title as any noble, and so Abebe Aregai was suddenly a "ras." Another new ras was Gurassu Duke, an imposingly tall Oromo fighting in Shoa who was once a member of the crown prince's bodyguard. The lowly born Belay Zeleke was scornful of this conceit. When his men tried to call him a ras, he told them, "The name my mother gave me was Belay—it is enough." Belay in Ethiopian means "above all."[9]

The Emperor stayed in contact with some Patriot leaders, but this didn't mean they were all his supporters. Whether they believed in him or not, they felt they were on their own. When they won, they could figure out *then* who should be in charge, whether it be another Emperor or representatives of a republic.

It was enough for now that they could decimate the Italians almost at their leisure. In September, when a major contingent of Italian troops was sent north of Fiche, the Patriots knew it and prepared an appropriate welcome. The Italians were moving into Merhabete, near Debre Libanos, when they were surrounded by thousands of Ethiopians. At the front and leading the Patriots was Kebedech Seyum, Aberra Kassa's widow, fierce and proud and wearing one of her men's uniforms, out for another helping of vengeance. Then Abebe Aregai's forces joined the attack, relying on Italian rifles and machine guns captured in previous raids. Two more Ethiopian armies arrived, but less equipped, most of their warriors using swords.

Time turned backward, and it was a bloody, hand-to-hand struggle for hours until, according to the *New Times and Ethiopia News*, "the Italians gave way and retired in such disorder that it was practically a flight."[10] The paper may have exaggerated the victory, conceding that there were "heavy casualties on both sides," but it was a resounding success in terms of the resources. It was well-coordinated, well-planned, well-executed. Even the arrival of men armed only with swords or clubs suggests someone, probably Abebe Aregai, had thought things through. This time, the poorer-armed warriors were *not* sent out as sacrificial cannon fodder to make a confusing mess. They were used more as mop-up units.

In early October, the rebellions intensified across the country, so that "whole detachments of troops, most of them askaris," were obliterated in areas the Italians had considered completely under their control.[11]

* * *

The Patriots were using their captured guns, taking the fight to the invader, but ordinary villagers out in the rural areas were also carrying on a campaign of passive resistance; there were plantation fields left fallow for two whole years. Wheat and flour had to be imported, which, of course, was expensive. Exports like coffee slowed down to a crawl. The *New Times and Ethiopia News* reported that the currency crisis was so bad that the Gondrand trucking firm was idle while "hundreds of Italian employees are loafing about in the hotels." The company had no cash to pay them—or to get the spare parts it needed to repair trucks damaged by a Patriot raid on the road to Dire Dawa.[12]

If Mussolini thought a "bread and circuses" approach would keep working, he now had to face the fact that his empire was all circus and no bread. So he decided to shake things up, starting at home. In November, he took over the colonial ministry himself. Now he was running five ministries out of fifteen. Under-Secretary Alessandro Lessona, the great political schemer, was given the boot and had to settle for the intrigues of academia, chairing the colonial history department at the University of Rome. In his place, Mussolini put a nondescript loyal lapdog, General Attilio Teruzzi.

The biggest change was a new viceroy for Ethiopia. Graziani was mercifully replaced by the king of Italy's cousin, Amadeo Umberto, the Duke of Aosta. Aosta, as he became known, remains an elusive figure to this day. A giant at six feet, six inches tall, he was thirty-nine, handsome, and a military hero. Though he had an impeccable family pedigree, he chose to enlist in the army as a private and earned a medal for valor at nineteen years old during the Great War. For all of his climbing of the ranks, however, he was still slumming. Fluent in multiple languages (as expected of nobility), he had a rich man's tastes—he played polo and went yachting, liked hunting and skiing. He married his cousin, a princess. In an age when being a pilot was still thought of as a dashing, gentlemanly pursuit, he flew his own plane from Massawa to reach Addis Ababa.

Why did Mussolini put him in charge? Perhaps he genuinely thought Aosta was qualified for the job—or at least loyal. It was reported years later that Aosta was always a firm Fascist. If the dictator was going to elevate a cipher like Teruzzi, he was just as likely to reward the duke. Aosta knew Africa quite well. He had traveled along the River Webbe in Ethiopia with his uncle, the Duke of Abruzzi, and he'd worked for an Anglo-Belgian company in the Congo for a year. And whether Aosta was a Blackshirt at heart or not, he seemed to at least be an imperialist.

One brief story provides a clue to the man's character. Aosta once dined with a British High Commission official in Cairo, and the British naturally liked Aosta immediately. Part of the man's education was at Eton, after all. When it came to Italy's conquest, Aosta remarked, "Supposing you had shoved all the scum of London's East End into Ethiopia and let them run wild, you can imagine the sort of thing that would have happened. That's just what we did, and I have to clean it up somehow."[13]

In Aosta's mind, it wasn't a case of whether Italy was entitled to an empire or not—it was. He was a veteran of Graziani's brutal campaign in Libya, one of the air commanders who drove the Senussi to scramble from their homeland to Egypt. And when it came to Italian Africa, the duke felt it should be run and populated by those of good breeding and administrative skills, instead of the riffraff. Aosta is remembered in history as a kind of "good" Fascist, and to his undeniable credit, he would change many of Graziani's policies in Ethiopia and free many from the concentration camps.

But at the end of the day, his job was to keep Ethiopia Italian, and new policies had less to do with compassion than with finding what worked best. Summary executions stopped, but not all executions. Captured rebels were still branded under the law as bandits and were hanged accordingly. Soon after the "good Fascist" took up his new job, in fact, he ordered planes to drop new leaflets on Patriot-held areas. "If you . . . hasten to deliver up your arms to our military chiefs, you will be pardoned, but if you do not do so, I shall cause terror to rain down from the sky upon you, your goods, and your kindred, who will necessarily include women, children, and old men, and I shall destroy you all."[14]

* * *

Mussolini wasted no time in abusing his new, friendlier relationship with Neville Chamberlain. He was confident he could achieve his military objectives in the Spanish Civil War with London none the wiser. The British suspected that planes flying out of Palma attacked a British tanker, and soon Italian submarines were going after British destroyers. Anthony Eden was annoyed with the complacency of his colleagues, especially the stupidity of those who argued that bringing in more vessels from the Home Fleet would only give the enemy more targets to shoot at.

Eden was never known as a hawk, but by this time, he was no longer a dove. He spent more time these days with Winston Churchill, who would come to see him in the years of World War Two as his heir apparent. In September, Eden had outfoxed Mussolini by brokering a new naval front to ensure security in the Mediterranean; the smaller powers like Greece and Yugoslavia were happy to let the British and French patrol their backyard waters, as long as the Russians were shut out and the Italians kept at bay. Their deal struck in Switzerland was a success. But when Eden returned to London, Chamberlain offered him only perfunctory congratulations and then tried to sabotage his planned appearance at a Conservative Party meeting in Wales.

Any other power outmaneuvered by the British would have gone away to retool and rebuild. Mussolini lost prestige over the new naval unity in the Mediterranean. He had the advantage, however, of knowing Chamberlain would let him have his African province. So just before Christmas of 1937, Italian Chargé d'Affaires Guido Crolla was back, looking for legal recognition of Italy's conquest. Eden was in no mood to entertain the idea. Aside from the attacks on British vessels, Italy was still sending troops to Spain, building up its garrison in Libya, and producing noxious propaganda directed towards the British and the French. Crolla, like all Fascist diplomats before him, expected a concession without offering anything in return. Eden told him in so many words that the Italians would have to give something to get something.

But Eden had few allies in a government growing sick and tired of having Ethiopia on its hands. By late November of 1937, there were 6,180 Ethiopian refugees in Kenya, another 1,348 in Somaliland, and 32 in Aden.[15] About sixty Ethiopians—a mix of nobles, officials, and their servants—had made it to Palestine, many coming over with the Emperor when he escaped Addis Ababa. All these scattered souls made Ethiopia a headache not only for the Foreign Office, but the Colonial Office as well. The colonial secretary at the time was William Ormsby-Gore, who came from banking and looked at the refugee problem as he would a balance sheet.

When Haile Selassie hoped to send aides to the various colonies to meet with the refugees, officials worried the price tag might go to their departments. The high commissioner for Palestine didn't want to pick up the tab for the Emperor's junket, or, for that matter, the Ethiopians staying there. Neither did Ormsby-Gore, who wrote that he saw no justification "that these refugees should be maintained at the expense of the Government of Palestine."[16] As his under-secretary put it, "the burden on public funds should be defrayed by His Majesty's Government . . ."[17] But that wouldn't sit well with that other great minder of budgets, Neville Chamberlain.

All this time, Sir Sidney Barton had done his best to find out what had happened to several high-profile Ethiopians. He was so persistent that Whitehall civil servants were annoyed by his efforts. Barton had sent a letter to the acting consul-general in Addis Ababa, and this, of course, got back to London. Victor Cavendish Bentinck—later an ambassador, but then a senior official at the FO—was moved to write a dyspeptic confidential memo in early November. Barton's latest inquiry was "the culmination of a series of interferences" and "hardly a visit of his to the Egyptian Department (and they are frequent) passes without his flaring up at some real or supposed injustice done to these wretched natives."[18] He presumed any information Barton might receive would find its way into the *New Times and Ethiopia News*.

Consular staff, knowing already that Barton was on the retirement list, had decided on their own to take a policy of benign neglect over his questions. They wouldn't even bother to tell him he should talk to the Foreign Office. This wasn't good enough for "Bill" Bentinck, who sensed how stubborn the old diplomat could be and insisted the consulate maintain harmonious relations with the Italians. "If we make any effort at present to moderate Sir Sidney's general zeal," he wrote, "I fear that we shall be running into trouble. Sir Sidney may burst out into the press and may become still more active on behalf of the Ethiopian refugees." Instead, it was "preferable" that Barton be kept in the dark over Ethiopians who are relatives or "members of the Emperor's suite or regarding those persons who have been imprisoned or executed."[19]

Mulling it over some more, Bentinck scrawled below his typed draft, "If we are a little cold and return laconic replies to his letters, his zeal may gradually damp down."[20] He didn't have the measure of the man, and he was very wrong.

* * *

More than one thousand Americans sent letters and Christmas cards to Ethiopia's Emperor in exile that winter. A sign of his continuing international popularity was that CBS Radio arranged for him to deliver a holiday broadcast to listeners. He would speak as usual in Amharic, with Edward R. Murrow delivering the English translation. Murrow was now based in London, working as the director of European operations for CBS. After talking at length in homily fashion about Christ, the Emperor finally got to the political substance of his message, mentioning the League of Nations and how "the spirit of the wicked continues to cast its shadow on this world." War, he told Americans, was not the only means to stop war. After wishing them a merry Christmas, he said, "I plead with you to remember in your prayers all those weak and endangered peoples who look to the flags of free nations with confidence, hoping to discern the star which will announce their peace and future security."[21]

The Emperor's Christmas broadcast nearly didn't happen at all. He had come by train to Paddington Station with his aides, but on the cab ride over to the studio, there was a serious collision, and his knee was fractured. He was in severe pain, and his aides wanted him to cancel and go back to Bath, but he insisted on giving his speech. After it was done, someone called a doctor in Harley Street, who wasn't home. Then they tried Sidney Barton; no luck there either.

Finally, Emperor and entourage did the proper, logical thing and went to London's Hospital for Sick Children (since renamed Great Ormond Street

Hospital). Haile Selassie's daughter, Princess Tsehai, was there training as a nurse, and the hospital invited the Emperor to attend holiday celebrations with the staff.

*   *   *

Ethiopia . . . Spain . . . and now the Japanese incursions into China. After constant bombardment, Shanghai had fallen in early October, and in mid-December, the Japanese would commit the Rape of Nanking. Germany grew ever more sinister under Hitler's fist. In Washington, Franklin Roosevelt read the shrill headlines of the latest outrages, and having won his second term, he knew he could be more daring in his foreign policy. He had a plan for world peace, but its success hinged entirely on British cooperation.

Roosevelt's point man for his proposal was Sumner Welles, a man he was far more comfortable with than Cordell Hull. Hull had won his position through politics. Welles was from the same aristocratic stock as Roosevelt, a son of privilege with family links to the Astors. At the age of twelve, he was a page at FDR's wedding, and after he graduated from Harvard, it was Roosevelt who steered him into the Foreign Service. Welles knew art and economics, and in the Roaring Twenties, no one minded if you didn't learn Spanish before you took a posting in Buenos Aires—he learned it on the job.

Roosevelt liked him, trusted him, and Cordell Hull couldn't stand it. Welles was a closet bisexual, and two years later, when he tried to pick up a black Pullman car porter, Hull learned about it and tried an elaborate smear. Welles, however, had someone come to his rescue, the most unlikely ally of all— the greatest extortionist of American politicians, J. Edgar Hoover, head of the FBI.

But all that was in the future. In early 1938, Welles was a relatively new undersecretary of state, at the height of his influence. And on the night of January 11, he strolled along Massachusetts Avenue N.W. over to the Queen Anne-style mansion that housed the British embassy. He couldn't leave his task to messengers or aides; he had to physically put a letter from his president into the hands of Ambassador Ronald Lindsay.

Roosevelt's vision for peace was bold, sweeping, and it would be offered in the form of an appeal to be made on November 11, Armistice Day. He would tell the nations of the world that they must come to an agreement on "principles of international conduct," arms reduction, ways to promote mutual economic security and stability, and in cases of war, "respect for humanitarian conditions." Each item on this wish list was the sort of thing that should have been settled by the League of Nations, but by now the organization had lost all credibility. It had done nothing for Spain or the latest victim nation, China.

FDR's advisers—aside from Welles—were "almost hysterically opposed" to his peace proposals. They insisted he get British and French support because the two countries may feel it competed with their own negotiations.[22] Roosevelt was going to do this anyway. He was concerned most about what was happening in the Pacific, but he wanted support from European nations that didn't have an interest in the region. His great plan had a breathtaking scope: Japan wasn't the only threat, of course, because Greece feared Italy, Yugoslavia dreaded the shadow of the Soviet Union. Hitler hoped to gobble up Austria. Not everyone would come to the table, but maybe an impressive bloc of united countries would form. Combine that with a rising tide of public support in the United States and parts of Europe, and a *moral* momentum could build. Germany and Japan might think twice.

Welles explained to Lindsay that his president needed Britain's prime minister onboard by January 17. Roosevelt would then sketch out the main ideas of the plan for France, Germany, and Italy in confidential messages. Lindsay endorsed the scheme as "a genuine effort to relax the tension of the world."[23]

Ethiopia was never part of this grand vision. Roosevelt couldn't turn back the clock in Africa; he could only set the alarm for Europe and the Far East. But it was Ethiopia's situation that would ultimately decide the fate of the plan. Students of history often think of Ethiopia's conquest as merely the first crumbling pillar for the League of Nations—with Spain as number two, and for number three, Japan's relentless invasion of China. But the truth is that the League's ducking of responsibility over Japan was far less important that winter than the unique opportunity offered by the American president.

Once again, Ethiopia's fate was about to decide the fate of the world.

* * *

Abebe Aregai was the leader the Italians needed to beat. He would confound them for years, attacking their convoys, sneaking out of their traps, mocking them with his plain survival. He also had the infuriating habit of announcing his imminent submission . . . only to change his mind. It was a game the Italians had taught the Ethiopians, and like Haile Selassie toying with Rome's peace overtures, Abebe Aregai told them one thing and then did another, playing them for fools. He wouldn't yield, even after his own son was taken prisoner.

Abebe had put him in the field at the ripe old age of fifteen, telling his boy, "I expect you to set an example to my men."[24] But Daniel Aregai barely got a chance to prove himself as a warrior—he was wounded in his first battle and about to be killed by dubats when white Italian soldiers intervened. Carted off to a prison in

Debra Berhan, he saw both sides of the Italian character tested by the challenge of power. One general barred him from receiving medical treatment until his foot was "a mess of blood and pus."[25] He likely would have died from the infection, but Enrico Cerulli—the African Studies scholar turned colonial official—was horrified at the boy's condition and drove him personally to a hospital. After he recuperated, Cerulli took him home and treated him like an adopted son, even giving him an allowance of fifty lire a day.

Cerulli's influence, however, could only go so far. After Abebe Aregai tricked the Italians once again, the authorities in the capital decided to take it out on his boy. Daniel was picked up and arrested, and then, with that unique touch of Fascist sadism, informed he would be hanged in the morning for the sins of the father. He wasn't. At first light, they put the boy on a white horse and sent him off on a mission: go try to talk his father into giving himself up.[26] This, Daniel actually did. But Abebe Aregai still wasn't interested in submission.

Having seen what happened to the Kassa brothers and others, he must have marvelled at how the *ferengi* could take him for a fool. The cat-and-mouse game would go on, but his son would be at his side again.

*   *   *

Now it was 1938. That January, Anthony Eden took a holiday in Grasse on the French Riviera. He played tennis, went for swims with his sons, and had lunch with Winston Churchill and Lloyd George, where the three hashed over the troubles of Europe. Eden thought there was nothing remarkable in the friendly conversation, except that both veteran politicians were vehemently opposed to recognizing Italy's conquest of Ethiopia. Then he got a phone call from Lord Halifax, who had been left to mind the store at the Foreign Office—Eden was badly needed back at his job.

Eden had to make the trip in horrible weather; no planes could fly, and his Channel boat smashed into the pier at Folkstone, delaying him even more. While he sat on a train to London, reading telegrams and getting brought up to speed by his aides, he didn't know his prime minister was singing solo again. Neville Chamberlain had fired off a response to Roosevelt without a call or cable to Eden, or even a word to the rest of his Cabinet.

There might be "some improvement in the immediate future" to the world situation, he replied in his telegram to Roosevelt, explaining loftily, "His Majesty's Government . . . have realized that if such appeasement is to be achieved, it will not be upon the basis of bargaining in which each side seeks to weigh up what it will get against what it will be asked to give." The word *appeasement* didn't have its pejorative connotations yet; Chamberlain's actions would ruin the word forever. But it was in the thick of a densely worded third paragraph that Chamberlain left his real bombshell: "In the case of Italy, His Majesty's Government would be prepared . . . with the authority of the League of Nations, to recognize *de jure* the Italian conquest of Abyssinia (by which Signor Mussolini sets great store)."[27]

Summing up, Chamberlain wanted the president to consider "whether there is not a risk of his proposal cutting across our efforts here." The Fuehrer and the Duce, he argued, might turn down talks with Britain if these were going to be superseded by American negotiations. Could Roosevelt hold off for a while?

Eden—left out—was naturally outraged when he learned about the cable. Like Lindsay and his under-secretary, Alexander Cadogan, he backed the American plan. He was also gravely concerned that in one message, his PM had ruined the good relations developed with Washington over the past two years. He was right to be worried. Sumner Welles thought Chamberlain's answer was "in the nature of a douche of cold water."[28] The Americans were privately furious over the recognition issue. Word came back that Roosevelt was willing to delay his proposal for a while, but that he "felt a little disappointed." A little meant a lot.

In Washington, Welles drafted a formal reply for the president on January 17 to be given to Ronald Lindsay. The British would be told that recognition would have "the harmful effect . . . upon the course of Japan in the Far East and upon the nature of the peace terms which Japan may demand of China." It would hurt public support in America for international policy initiatives. "Recognition of the conquest of Ethiopia, which at some appropriate time may have to be regarded as an accomplished fact, would seem . . . to be a matter which affects all nations which are committed to the principles of nonrecognition."[29]

As for Chamberlain, he wanted his man in Washington to learn as much as he could about Roosevelt's intentions while he maintained a slow-drip strategy of delay, persuading the Americans to hold off and then to hold off again. Ronald Lindsay saw this for the fatal error it was. He went to talk to Welles on February 2 and confided to him that "there was obviously extreme pressure being brought to bear" on Anthony Eden to renew talks with Italy. And it still looked like those talks would be one on one. Eden got on quite well with Léon Blum and Foreign Minister Yvon Delbos, but relations between Italy and France were now so toxic that the two governments weren't on speaking terms.[30]

Welles decided he'd better be frank as well, and he gave Lindsay a synopsis of the talk he'd had with Italian Ambassador Fulvio Suvich (who was pushed to go to Washington after Ciano took over his job as Italian foreign minister). Lindsay couldn't help showing his surprise—the British wanted to talk about divisions in Libya, the Mediterranean situation, and keeping Spain out of the Fascist orbit.

Welles had learned from Suvich that the Italians had only one thing on their shopping list: recognition of Ethiopia's conquest.

All of this looked ominous for Chamberlain's negotiations, let alone advancing the president's peace initiative. Then Lindsay let Welles know there were British plans for concurrent talks with Germany. The Americans didn't need any more hints. Obviously, Chamberlain never wanted them involved. On February 9, Welles invited Lindsay for another visit; Roosevelt was willing to grant another delay until a new, rapidly unfolding "acute situation" in Germany appeared "a little clearer." But the president had every intention of going ahead with his initiative in the "relatively near future" and would send word later to London.[31]

The "acute situation" wasn't developing so much in Germany as in Austria. Hitler wanted it, and he was determined to get it.

It hardly mattered what events put the plan on hold; the initiative was dead. In his book, *The Time for Decision*, Welles wrote, "The full participation by the United States in such a world-wide effort to keep the peace as that envisaged by the President might have given Italy pause. It might have resulted in a radical modification of Japanese policy. Under those conditions, Hitler would have been forced to think far more carefully before embarking on his last moves towards world war." Roosevelt's appeal "might well have rallied a still vocal public opinion in Europe sufficiently to have changed the course of the events of the next two years."[32]

There are a string of "might haves" in there. Still, the case is compelling that had Chamberlain not pinned his hopes on condoning Italy's conquest, war would have been averted. At the very least, the United States could have become an ally sooner than later in any conflict. To Eden, it "became clearer every day that we had discouraged Roosevelt's scheme to death."[33]

After the Second World War, as Anthony Eden sat in the Maryland house of Sumner Welles, the two agreed that no other opportunity ever came after 1938 that could have prevented the approaching inferno.[34]

*   *   *

Abriha Deboch and Moges Asgedom didn't make it to Sudan.

For many years afterward, historians wrote that the pair was killed by shiftas in the middle of nowhere, but the surviving evidence suggests this wasn't true. Their fighting in the ranks of other Patriot bands was forgotten so that in Western chronicles, they've become small-time outlaws who simply made a run for the border and were slain by stupid luck. The truth was very different. Certain Patriot leaders and the post-war Ethiopian government were sure enough of their facts to write about them to Abriha's mother and give an account to the Emperor.[35]

At some point, Abriha and Moges somehow got separated from their unit during a battle in the Begemder region, near Lake Tana. This was dangerous country, mostly held by the Italians and dotted with forts where patrols or passing supply vehicles might easily pick them up. If they couldn't rejoin their unit, they needed to get away—fast. It didn't matter that Graziani was becoming a memory. The hunt for them continued, and the Italians sent out mercenary bands to track them down. When military intelligence put out a circular with the pair's descriptions, it neglected to mention, interestingly enough, that these men were Eritrean or were responsible for the grenade attacks on the viceroy. The cover-up over the details of the conspiracy and the attack had to go on.[36]

Abriha and Moges headed north. It's possible they may have had to defend themselves against mercenary bands. Much later, an Ethiopian government report would mention they "escaped such bands more than once," but if they were not affiliated anymore with a specific Patriot group, how could anyone know this?[37] Still, one or two skirmishes and harrowing escapes seem plausible. Finally, out of food, out of water, and out of options, the pair wandered up to a peasant's hut somewhere in Chilga. They thought they had found shelter, sanctuary—but someone tipped off the Italians based in nearby Qwara.

As usual, the formal issuing of a death sentence was an unnecessary ritual. The method was to be hanging. The story goes that Moges was to have his head first in the noose, but Abriha—quick tempered to the last—snapped, "I refuse to witness the death of my brother. Hang me first."

The Italians were hardly going to leave the choice up to him, so he told them he was the one responsible for the grenade attack in the capital. The Italian commander allegedly flew into a rage, taking Abriha at his word. He pulled out his pistol, raised it, and shot the prisoners on the spot. Then he ordered their corpses to be hanged. But that evening, a Patriot leader named Werqu led a daring attack on the fort, freeing about twenty-five prisoners and killing the commander in battle. There are some problems with this part of the story, because other accounts insist the Italian officer responsible survived. He either got a severe dressing-down by superiors—who wanted the pair alive—or earned a medal from the Duce himself.

Whatever his fate, the Patriots claimed they drove the Italians into retreat. Then the Ethiopians allegedly found the bodies swinging from a tree, cut them down, and gave them a solemn burial.[38]

* * *

Back at the Foreign Office in London, Robert Vansittart's personal bogeyman was always German, not Italian, but he'd been on his own collision course with appeasement, and he was quietly "kicked upstairs" with a promotion to "Chief Diplomatic Adviser to His Majesty's Government." He was going where he couldn't cause trouble. The whispers in Whitehall were that Eden might be pushed aside as well, and the PM would run Foreign Affairs himself with a small handpicked committee. Vansittart himself warned Eden he wouldn't have his job for long.

Chamberlain barely tried to reassure Eden anymore that his post was secure. And he went right on meddling in Eden's department, running his own back channels. Ivy Chamberlain, the widow of his half-brother, Austen, was staying at the time in Rome, and he persisted in letting her convey direct communications from Ciano. Was it completely inappropriate? Yes—he didn't care. Italy's ambassador, Dino Grandi, arranged to have a meeting on February 18 with Chamberlain in Downing Street; it was only thanks to Eden's insistence that he was present at all. As Grandi summarized Anglo-Italian relations, Eden watched, silently appalled, as his PM nodded approvingly. He thought Grandi's account "would almost seem that we had invaded Abyssinia."[39]

Eden hoped that any new bargain with Rome would at least horse-trade the withdrawal of Italian volunteers from Spain. Italy had to offer something big to win recognition of Ethiopia's conquest. Grandi replied that talks shouldn't be held up over the Spain issue—a deft little sidestep. Chamberlain bought it. As soon as Grandi was out the door, he told his foreign secretary that he wanted preparations to begin for the talks. For Eden, the tactics of bluster and rushed timetables were nothing new, and he advised caution. Chamberlain suddenly lost his patience and his reserve.

"Anthony, you have missed chance after chance," he scolded, pacing up and down the room. "You simply cannot go on like this."

"Your methods are right if you have faith in the man you are negotiating with," argued Eden.

"I have," snapped Chamberlain.[40]

Eden went off to lunch with colleagues, now contemplating the idea that he might really have to resign once and for all. He'd always opposed the idea of recognition and would only grudgingly accept it if substantial concessions were granted in return. He argued again with Chamberlain half an hour before Grandi was due to arrive for another talk—but he managed to win one concession. The issue would go to their Cabinet colleagues to decide. When the PM and foreign secretary sat down again with Italy's ambassador, they offered a stiff but united front. Grandi wasn't fooled. Right after leaving Downing Street, he went in a taxi-cab to discuss the same matters with Joseph Ball, who was still acting as the PM's shadowy intermediary.

Meanwhile, Chamberlain began to apply pressure on his foreign minister and gather his own supporters. He soon called Eden to inform him that John Simon agreed with him. Eden wasn't interested. Simon then started a bizarre and futile effort to spread the word that Eden was sick, both physically and mentally; even his parliamentary private secretary should take a leave as well. It's not clear who came up with this peculiar scheme, but it didn't have much success.

Internal fights in politics are the worst-kept secrets of all, and by the next day, Saturday, a crowd was in Downing Street. It gave Eden a cheer as he strolled his way to a crucial Cabinet meeting, but the support stopped at the door. Both Chamberlain and Eden knew this was to be a showdown, and Eden wrote in his memoirs of "deploying" his arguments. Chamberlain put his case first. He began with a curious notion, but maybe it was because he'd been chancellor of the exchequer; rearmament would have a huge financial cost. He wanted to avoid it, hence efforts to placate Italy or Germany, and he came up with a muddled metaphor; he thought of Italy as "a hysterical woman. She felt that we had thwarted her in her assault on Abyssinia and deeply resented it."[41]

He then told the Cabinet that Mussolini had made a personal phone call to Hitler, trying to make him take a more moderate stance over Austria. This was telling. Chamberlain was obviously credulous enough to believe what could only come from an unreliable Italian source—whether Grandi through Ball or Ciano through Dame Ivy. Eden wasn't privy to this information, and his PM now showed the rest of the Cabinet that he'd shut out his own foreign minister.

After Eden got his chance for rebuttal, he realized how alone he was in the wilderness. The objections of his colleagues were so out of touch with reality, they were preposterous. One suggested that he doubted they "should insist upon evidence of goodwill, as this might not exist."[42] Chamberlain won the day. Formal talks with the Italians would go ahead. All Eden could do was make a veiled threat, telling those around the table that he couldn't stand in the House of Commons and defend the decision. The room became still. They all knew what he meant, and perhaps most had expected him to fall into line. As the buzz of surprised conversation grew, Neville Chamberlain remained calm and oblivious at the table. He wasn't going to change his mind.

At his old skiing haunt in Terminillo, Mussolini was calling Rome every hour for updates on the British Cabinet crisis. Ciano confided to his diary, "It may mean peace or war." Though he and his dicator had managed to enlist Chamberlain now as an unwitting co-conspirator in Italian expansionism, Ciano had no grasp at all for the subtleties of British politics. He envisioned a fantastic scenario in which Chamberlain could lose confidence and Eden could win over the Cabinet to take his place. "An Eden Cabinet would have as its aim the fight against the dicatorships—Mussolini's first." He sent a message to Grandi, giving the ambassador permission to use whatever methods he could to "add an arrow to Chamberlain's quiver."[43]

But Grandi didn't have to do anything. While Eden's threat of resignation was picked apart and analyzed in the Sunday papers, Chamberlain was indifferent to public opinion. He wanted the younger man out, and he sent for Eden that afternoon. After the two men talked about how parting was in the national interest, Chamberlain tactlessly remarked that Rome was now willing to accept Eden's formula for calling home the Italian volunteers from Spain.

"Have they, Neville?" asked Eden, irritated over another example of keeping information from him. "No word has reached the Foreign Office, and I am still Foreign Secretary."

Chamberlain, thrown off guard, replied weakly, "I cannot tell you how I heard it, but you can take it from me that it is true."

"This will make no difference to my decision," said Eden. "Anyway, my head on a charger ought to be worth more to you than a formula." Chamberlain gave him a wry smile to this, but no answer.[44] Perhaps he'd already offered the Italians his secretary's head.

On Monday, February 21, MPs entered the Commons with a sense of expectation. Liberal MP Wilfred Roberts asked what proportion of Ethiopia was now effectively controlled by the Italian government. It was John Simon, instead of Eden, who stood up to reply. "So far as we are aware, civil administration is established in the main centres of population," he answered.

Roberts had a follow-up: "Would it be right to think that the Italian government controls, perhaps, half of Abyssinia now?"

"I could not add to my answer," replied Simon.

"Can the noble Lord say what proportion of the British Cabinet is controlled in the same way?" quipped Labour's Seymour Cocks.[45]

It was late in the afternoon when Eden rose to give his resignation speech. He didn't mention Ethiopia once, but hinged his arguments on the issues of Spain, Mussolini's broken promises over anti-British propaganda, and the clashes in the Mediterranean. Had he raised Ethiopia, of course, he wouldn't be able to claim as much of the moral high ground. Nevertheless, though he had left it out, recognition was the bitterest point of contention between him and Chamberlain. And it cost the British government its chance to build stronger ties with Franklin Roosevelt's administration.

About an hour after Eden got to his feet, Chamberlain rose to say that he always thought of Eden as a "friend" and that his differences of opinion with him "have never been exacerbated by hard words, but have always been discussed between us in the friendliest and most amicable manner."[46] After giving his own version of events, he wrapped up his remarks by announcing triumphantly Mussolini's promise to withdraw troops from Spain.

One of the Labour MPs, Will Thorne, interrupted him. "When they knew that the Foreign Secretary had gone!"

When Labour leader Clement Attlee had his turn, he tore into Chamberlain and the government. Eden, who had been "thrown to the wolves," at least had been different from his colleagues for recognizing there should be international law in Europe. Chamberlain had disregarded this entirely. "We shall be told in due course who is to replace the Foreign Secretary—"

"Mussolini will tell him!" shouted one of the Opposition members.

Since this came from his own side of the House, Attlee moved smoothly on. Regarding Eden, he said, "It looks rather curious to us that just when a colleague is being attacked by people overseas, by foreign countries, when, week after week, he is abused in every possible way, his colleagues do not stand by him." And on the issue of Ethiopia, he pointed out that it was "less conquered today than it was a year ago. Italy holds little more than half of that country and then mainly with people behind barbed wire . . . The Spanish war is not proving the success he thought." And *now* was the time that Chamberlain thought he should forgive everything? Attlee was amazed. "Apparently anything is good enough for him."[47]

Opposition MPs hammered away on Ethiopia, Spain, and appeasement well into the evening.

Miles away in Terminillo, a cocktail party was going on that night where Ciano learned about Eden's exit, and the guests drank several toasts and cheered the news. He stepped away to send instructions off to the Italian press. It "should not be too triumphant—we don't want to turn Eden into a victim of Fascism."[48] But the Italian press couldn't help celebrating as well.

After leaving office, Eden took comfort in the fact that he earned letters of support from around the world, from colleagues and constituents alike. King George VI made clear his sympathy and expected he would be back in office soon. And as historian Kenneth S. Davis put it, Eden "stood up . . . in many an American vision, as a lonely heroic figure, a tower of strength and wisdom and virtue raised against the sea of cowardly and perfidious mediocrity that had watched and continued to wash over England."[49]

Some Ethiopia advocates were harsher in their appraisal. For them, Eden had, at best, done nothing to help Ethiopia, and at worst, was as guilty of betraying it as Simon, Hoare, and Chamberlain. The *New Times and Ethiopian News* had regularly targeted him for criticism. But apart from Sidney Barton, Eden had carried on a lone vigil to first, keep Great Britain to its principles and its integrity, and second, defend the rights of the Ethiopians as best he could. True, he shared responsibility for dropping sanctions, but the momentum for this hadn't come from him. In fact, if it hadn't been for Eden's conscience and initiative, there would never have been any sanctions in the first place.

Some critics have argued that his resignation was hardly tied to principles at all, and Eden wasn't far from Chamberlain's position as was portrayed later in the post-war period. Eden himself addressed this in his resignation speech: "It has recently become clear to me, and I think to [Chamberlain], that there is between us a real difference of outlook and method. It may be argued, perhaps I shall be told, that this is not a difference of fundamental principles. Well, in the sense that the objective of all foreign policy is the maintenance of peace, that is, of course, perfectly true. But in international affairs can anyone define where outlook and methods end and principles begin?"[50]

In more recent times, the scales have tipped back to a positive assessment. His biographer, D. R. Thorpe, called Eden's resignation "immensely brave" and pointed out that he was throwing away an almost sure path to the office of prime minister. Eden was the right man in the wrong time, a doomed Galahad perfectly attired in shiny breastplate and resolve, while the rest of the knights were running back over the hill. And they thought shedding their armor would actually keep the dragons from seeing them.

*   *   *

By early April, the British government wanted to hurry things along for formal recognition. To his continued irritation, Neville Chamberlain knew he had to go through the League of Nations, and so a letter was sent by the Foreign Office to the secretary general, which explained that Britain wanted to clarify what it called "the anomalous situation." The situation was that many states, including no fewer than five on the League Council, already recognized Italian sovereignty of Ethiopia. It was a highly cynical rationale—the smaller states had flouted the group discipline, and London was looking for a pretext to do the same. Had Britain and France shown leadership in the beginning, the smaller states would never have drifted from the fold.

But now Britain's ally was neither the France of the double-dealing Laval nor the France of Léon Blum. By the time the League published the Foreign Office note, Radical politician Édouard Daladier was in office as premier, with Georges Bonnet as his foreign minister. Daladier had no illusions about Hitler or Mussolini, and he was eager for a united front with the British. But in the end he would let Chamberlain have his way. Chamberlain was already going alone on a new Anglo-Italian Pact, which was signed in Rome by Ciano and London's ambassador, Eric Drummond, on April 16.

Eden, now a backbencher and outsider, spotted its problems off the bat. The deal didn't immediately come into force, and there was no sign it had to—it came into effect when Italy decided to withdraw its volunteers from Spain. Well, when would *that* be? Italy also agreed to reduce its forces in Libya, which Eden suspected were only there "in the first place for their nuisance value."[51] There was nothing he could do now except write letters to papers like the *Yorkshire Post* and private complaints to his sympathetic friend, Winston Churchill.

Chamberlain moved on with his Ethiopia agenda, at times completely at odds with the Foreign Office. Victor Cavendish Bentinck—the official who priggishly chose to keep Sidney Barton in the dark—suggested going slow; "it would surely be to our advantage not to be in a hurry to grant *de jure* recognition and thus help to bolster up Mussolini's prestige."[52] He wanted a firm stand taken on borders, and if it came to it, Sudan and Kenyan police officers (but not *troops*) should be put next to Italian outposts to make it clear Britain meant business. He soon discovered, however, that the prime minister didn't care what he thought about frontiers, or what anyone else in the Foreign Office or colonial services thought, for that matter. As maps were shown and everything explained, the PM interrupted.

"Oh, no, I don't like that," said Chamberlain. "The British public won't understand that. The British public and the House of Commons are used to frontiers with straight lines in Africa."[53]

"Bill" Bentinck reminded him that colonial officers had spent months surveying the remote ends of Sudan and Kenya, carefully pinpointing where the different tribes could water their cattle and have the safest access routes.

Chamberlain refused to listen. "I can't help it. A straight line."

After lunch, Bentinck went to draft up the minutes of the session and talked about the disappointing outcome with the Cabinet secretary, Edward Bridges. Bridges told him blandly, "Well, Bill, the only thing that matters about this operation is that the Prime Minister should not appear to have talked balls."[54]

* * *

Haile Selassie had endured strafing from planes, attacks of chemical warfare, and bombardments from artillery, but his health had trouble with England's steady drizzle and cooler temperatures. His wife, Empress Menen, had already left in January to stay in Jerusalem a short while because of the English climate. Now seriously ill and wracked by a miserable hacking cough, he made the long trip nonetheless to Geneva to make one last appeal to the League of Nations. France's conservative voice, *Le Figaro*, groused, "Why has Haile Selassie come, if not to embarrass Lord Halifax and M. Bonnet? Geneva today is not only a useless organ, but is dangerous, and is a place where internal policies subversively combine to paralyze diplomacy."[55]

Haile Selassie didn't need to come in person to embarrass the League—his money had done that for him. As April came to a close, he sent a check for one thousand Swiss francs as partial payment for Ethiopia's dues for membership within the League. Instead of cashing the check, the League's administration simply held on to it.

As he left Geneva's train station, there was a crowd of about a thousand well-wishers, jostling the aides and security men as the Emperor made his way to a car to drive him to his hotel. But when the big bronze doors of the Assembly chamber opened for him on May 12, he entered in complete silence.

As he took his seat in the hall, Britain's relatively new foreign minister, Lord Halifax, rose to argue that Ethiopia no longer existed as an independent nation— to the victor go the spoils. "Great Britain's considered opinion is that unless we are prepared forever to live in an unreal world, the fact of the Italian conquest of Abyssinia, whatever our judgment on it, will have to be acknowledged." His government, he said, didn't approve of the methods used by Italy, "but no good purpose will be served by vain lamentations over the past."[56]

Yes, there was resistance in certain parts of the country, he admitted, but it had no central authority or administration, and it had little hope of success. Haile Selassie sat in his chair, listening with his eyes closed, still a fragile, dreadfully ill man.

"Italy's position in Abyssinia can be altered only by concerted military action, which is unthinkable," said Halifax, "and would not be suggested by any responsible person in any country. I realize that many people in Britain and perhaps elsewhere feel that any action to facilitate the recognition of the Italian conquest of Ethiopia impinges on principles I respect, but I do not share their view." He argued that the League's members didn't have to think of recognition as going back on principles at all. No, it would be one of the "practical victories for peace."

Now came the formula to let them all off the hook.

Great Britain wasn't suggesting the Council should impose a particular course of action, said Halifax—on the contrary. Members could "take such action, and at such time, as seems to each appropriate."[57]

This last part was an astounding rationalization. It undermined all that the League stood for and what it was supposed to accomplish. If each nation might as well go its own way over a conqueror's continued aggression, why then have the Covenant? Why bother to meet at all? *Why have a League in the first place?*

Haile Selassie was too ill to take the rostrum. Instead, Lorenzo Taezaz read his address for him, and perhaps because of this, the speech got less play in the newspapers. Had he been in good health, the Emperor could have used all the force of his charisma to ensure another electrifying moment, though his odds of successfully changing minds were as poor now as when he took the rostrum two years ago. His speech, though well-written, didn't carry the same power as the first time and wasn't nearly so eloquent. Many perhaps thought they were familiar enough with his arguments.

Yet there was much in his address that was new and should have given the League members pause. Lorenzo Taezaz went through a detailed account of how the Italians couldn't hold the country: "There is not one Italian governor in Gojjam; in Shoa, Italian soldiers are found only in Addis Ababa, near Ankobar . . ." The Emperor's speech dealt a serious blow to both Britain's and Halifax's credibility.

This wasn't what the Emperor intended. He had to walk a delicate line, given that he was still a guest of the British: "I deeply regret my disagreement with a government which I heartily admire and to which I am greatly indebted." It had shown him "generosity and hospitality at the time of my grief." As a parting shot against Italian propaganda, the speech closed by discussing how the Emperor kept getting letters and expressions of love from his people. Far more powerful and prescient were his remarks earlier in the address:

> Acts of aggression have become rampant. They are multiplying and infecting many. Some governments are engaged in full-scale struggle. Many others feel the threat. Fear reigns the world. Those who already have been prey and those who are being haunted by aggressors, tremble anticipating what is yet to come. They endeavor to maintain their lives by trying to placate the governments whom they consider as their potential assailants. The good work of the League is being destroyed.[58]

Haile Selassie hoped that instead of the League Council deciding recognition, it would be left up to the General Assembly. But no decision over the issue—for or against—was taken at all. The League president at the time, Latvia's Vilhelms Munters, gave his fellow delegates a convenient out. He declared that most of the Council believed states could recognize Ethiopia's conquest if they wanted.

At almost the same time across the Atlantic, Secretary of State Cordell Hull was commenting on the issue. There was nothing terribly provocative in his words. He told reporters that US policy over Italy and Ethiopia remained absolutely unchanged: neutral America would *not* recognize the conquest. Benito Mussolini should have let this go, especially when the other nations of the world had just given him exactly what he wanted. Instead, he decided Hull deserved the full Fascist spectacle.

In Genoa's Victory Square two days later, he told a throng of a hundred thousand people that if the democracies wanted war, "then totalitarian states will close themselves into one block and march to the bitter end." There were boos and catcalls when Mussolini mentioned Hull's statements, and he told his devoted followers that the Stresa Front was dead. The British and French had long known this, but now he didn't need to hide the body anymore. "Today, the Germanic and Roman worlds are in immediate contact. Both revolutions are destined to leave an imprint in the history of this century."[59]

Chapter Twenty-One

A VOLCANO, PERMANENTLY SIMMERING

In July of 1938, readers of the *Pittsburgh Courier* began following the adventures of a new savior for Ethiopia. His name was Dick Welland, a bright young black man who had graduated from Fisk but was having trouble getting a decent job. His best work so far had been as a "redcap"—a baggage porter in Chicago. Then, out of the blue, his oil tycoon uncle conveniently dropped dead and left him playboy rich, which was how he came to be on a quay in Marseilles, where he had the chance to save an Ethiopian princess. Too bad Dick Welland was fictional.

The author's name was given as "Rachel Call," but it was really George Schuyler, the black columnist and iconoclast. His "Revolt in Ethiopia" serial was the second time he devoted a novella to the underdog country. The tanks were barely parked in Aksum in 1935 when his sleuth, Roger Bates, was racing around Harlem trying to exonerate a love interest in "The Ethiopian Murder Mystery" (a prince is killed above 110th Street). Now his new hero, Dick Welland, was off to Africa to find hidden treasure. It was outrageously implausible stuff, with Schuyler borrowing plot turns from John Buchan and H. Rider Haggard. Dick rescues the Ethiopian princess (a supposed niece of Haile Selassie) in chapter one by knocking down a bad guy literally dressed in a black hat and cape (and who later turns out to be a Gugsa-like traitor). Ras Imru makes an appearance as a Patriot leader named "Yamrou." After weeks of installments and adventures, there is even a scene of gratuitous pulp titillation and sadism when Dick and the princess are stripped nude by their Italian captors, and Dick gets bayoneted and whipped.

Good pulp, however, aspires to make a point, and Schuyler used his hero to voice his international consciousness: "Here was a Negro civilization older than any other except India and China . . . Dick wept unashamed. What a pity that this civilization should be destroyed by brutal Fascism. No, he resolved anew, it must not die; not if he could prevent it."[1]

But there were no black Americans left in Ethiopia. The only candidates for heroes were Ethiopians like Lekelash Bayan, still tough and stubborn, leading her guerrillas and fighting skirmishes. In March of 1939, in the middle of Lent, she and her men were slogging their way one night through a light drizzle, anxious to pitch camp after a long journey. They were suddenly attacked by the Italians, but managed to hang on to fourteen precious machine guns. Lekelash was shaken as she came across one of their leaders, who lay dying.

"He told me to go on with the battle, and he told me to take the flag, because the flag bearer, too, was dead," she recalled. "I found the flag as we were about to go away." But the man who was supposed to be responsible for it refused. Lekelash picked up their standard and put it around her neck. As she turned to leave, she saw the man had been killed. "I said, 'Good, you are dead!' By then I was left alone."[2]

She crossed a river to try to slip away, but found herself surrounded by enemy soldiers on all sides. There was nowhere to run—but she could go up. She climbed a tree before she was spotted and hid there for five days, hungry and thirsty, knowing she needed to wait. And wait. At last, she spied through her binoculars a couple of enemy soldiers approaching. She dropped down and ambushed them, eating what they had brought right up to her hiding spot, and then made her way to Ankober to rejoin her group.

* * *

With the Aosta regime trying a new tactic of leniency, Imru Zelleke was among more than a thousand inmates—along with his mother and sisters—released at last from Danane. They had been pardoned. Young Imru's half-brother stayed in prison, but there was nothing the family could do for him. The best thing to do—the only thing—seemed to be to go back to Addis Ababa, to what was left of their home. "We had nothing, everything was gone, whatever fortune we had," he remembers. "Our house was occupied by the Italians, so we ended up in our stables where we kept mules and horses." He laughs at the memory of it. "So we cleaned up that and then started living and just tried to survive."[3]

Fortunately, in their compound was another small house that the Italians had been using as a sort of storage, and they eventually let his family live there. Under Graziani, the Italians were free to take what they wanted, but now, they actually agreed to pay rent for what they were occupying. "Not much, but they paid some rent," he recalls. "So we collected, and we survived on that." The carabinieri were using what was once the family's house as an office, with another part of the compound for living quarters. Imru Zelleke has no illusions about the change in attitude.

"They had their own rules . . . And they wanted to tranquilize the population anyway, because a lot of rebellion was going on left and right in the country, so they had to show people that things were normal, that they accepted us all. It was good politics on their part also to try to keep things quieter."

He was still too young to run off and join the Patriots, and though fluent in French and English, with a smattering of Italian, he had no hope under the occupation of going to university. Instead, the boy would have a different fate—and an unusual benefactor.

A friend of the family was Afawarq Gabra-Iyassus, who with his ever-flexible loyalties had come home to write anti-Patriot propaganda for the Italians. Under his poisonous pen, the guerrillas in the countryside were "wild worms," shiftas plundering cattle, while the Emperor was a lion reduced to a rabbit that "fled for his life."[4] Afawarq never learned. The man who called the occupation the "Era of Mercy" was caught up in the Graziani reprisal and deported into exile to Italy. With the regime change, Afawarq was now home, and he had secured a new position. His title was apt: *Afa Qesar*, which meant "mouth of Caesar."[5]

After visiting Imru's mother, Afawarq arranged for the boy to get a job in an Italian bank as a filing clerk. Imru recalls that its manager was generally kind to him, but the younger staff members who belonged to the Fascist Party did little to hide their contempt, and they often strutted about in their black uniforms, each with a "ridiculous" dagger, when they went parading at Fascist events.

Growing from boy to man, Imru was aware of how the world he'd been born into was becoming extinct. Several histories of the period have harped on the massive infrastructure the Italians brought into the country, from roads to factories. But they had also forced Ethiopia into a cultural revolution. Imru worked at a bank, where he saw firsthand how his country was switching to a cash economy. He was from a family of noble lineage, but that hardly mattered anymore, and his job bumped him down to the ranks of the middle class, which was growing thanks to the colonial housing developments and new private and government ventures. He had always passed Eritreans and white *ferengi* in the streets, but now there were Somalis and Libyans.

His social world was a network of cousins and friends, children of disenfranchised nobles like himself, all knowledgeable, some educated abroad and fluent in European languages. And none rich, not anymore. They walked to where they needed to go, often meeting at the café of Tesfaye Kejela, a jazz musician who had played with his own band in Belgium. The young people talked about all the things young, intelligent people everywhere do—art, music, literature. Politics couldn't be easily discussed, but still, they hashed over the problems in the country. "The notion that we would get rid of the Italians someday had become an act of faith."[6] It was only later that Imru discovered that some of his friends were acting as operatives of the city's underground resistance.

Imru worked for some time at the bank, and when his half-brother was eventually freed, the two went into business together, transporting grains and cereals to market in a couple of used trucks. It was a sign of the regime's growing rot that Imru and his half-brother succeeded in bribing an Italian major to help their business. But after his brother was arrested on suspicion of being a Patriot, Imru couldn't keep the business going by himself, and he ended up as an interpreter for the Italians at the Political Office. He wasn't alone; many Ethiopians were also still working there, in spite of the grenade attack. Imru suspected this was a way for the Italians to keep an eye on them.

As for Afawarq, does he think of him as a traitor? More than seventy years later, Imru Zelleke doesn't hesitate in his answer: "Well, he certainly was siding with the Italians—what would you call him? But on the other hand, I mean he was a nice man. He knew my father very well. He even did me a favor as I said. He found me a job. But he was also torn. I don't think he was disloyal really, but he was also between two cultures."[7]

Afawarq made his final choice of loyalty, and he would have to answer for it. Ironically, the good turn of a traitor put Imru Zelleke on the path of recovery towards a remarkable career—and the young man would stay loyal to the very Emperor Afawarq denounced.

* * *

In London, the International African Friends of Ethiopia had transformed into a new incarnation: the International African Service Bureau. It adopted the motto: "Educate, cooperate, emancipate. Neutral in nothing affecting the African people." For the price of a shilling, you could be a member, but it cost nothing to wander into Hyde Park in 1938 to hear the passionate discussions over Ethiopia and about the labor strikes being waged in the Caribbean. To build its influence and credibility, the organization sent speakers off to groups like the League of Nations Union and the Labour Party, and it claimed it had managed to get twenty-five questions asked in Parliament.[8]

Yet the great brain trust behind the bureau couldn't come to one mind. With such intellectual heavyweights as C. L. R. James and George Padmore, perhaps it was inevitable it focused more on West Indian concerns. In time, there was very little "Africa" getting discussed in the International African Service Bureau. I. T. A. Wallace-Johnson, a son of Sierra Leone, was the bureau's general secretary; the shadowy men who watched the organization for the British authorities assumed the bureau was his creature. It wasn't, though he did have influence. As historians Leo Spitzer and LaRay Denzer put it, "The only time that the bureau concerned itself to any great degree with African affairs was when he was there to direct it."[9]

But like Jomo Kenyatta, Wallace-Johnson was desperately poor in London, without the change in his pocket to even cover train fares. As the months passed, his situation became so dire that he was kicked out of his room for not paying his rent and ended up staying in the Bureau's office.[10] He would eventually help himself to more than just the bureau's digs.

If there was no cohesive unity among the Patriot cells in Ethiopia, there was precious little among the black and white activists in London, either. Padmore had expressed his bitter disillusionment with the left in his book, *Africa and World Peace*, which had come out in 1937. "Not even the organized labor movement of Western Europe—England and France, which is supposed to be passionately anti-Fascist, did more than express pious words of sympathy."[11] There was much truth in this, and Padmore and James liked to go around to meetings of other organizations, such as the League Against Imperialism and the Communist Party of Great Britain, to start debates and cause mischief. Fun is fun, but you don't bite the hands that feed you, and their stunts alienated key groups that had provided them money.

There were clashes, too, within their own ranks, even between the two old friends from Trinidad. Padmore supported sanctions. James, always scornful of the League, envisioned a scheme of "workers' sanctions," which the people themselves would organize. They argued—passionately, angrily, bitterly. Jomo Kenyatta didn't fully trust James. T. Ras Makonnen despised the International Labour Party and was withering over how Padmore liaised with the organization.[12]

Was all of this pointless chatter and coffeehouse smoke? Not all of it. Protests were still held, delegates still sent to conferences. Scotland Yard and British intelligence still took them seriously enough to spy on them. But the organization's dynamics were changing. Wallace-Johnson—destitute, miserable, and living in the bureau's offices—wrote letters to friends that suggest he was borderline suicidal. At his breaking point, he dipped into the organization's funds, and by April of 1938, his fellow members discovered his embezzlement and kicked him out. He went home to Sierra Leone, where it didn't take him long to bounce back and start organizing, writing, and lobbying again. Meanwhile, James was looking to leave, but not for Trinidad. He wanted to move to the United States. Padmore became even more the bureau's indispensable man, finding new offices, securing new funding, launching a new publication.

In the autumn, James boarded his ship to America. By then, publisher Frederic Warburg had brought out the book that was James's pride and joy, his magnum opus. *The Black Jacobins: Toussaint L'Ouverture and the San Domingo Revolution* has stayed in print for more than seventy-six years. James always acknowledged that "by the time I settled down to write, I had reached the conclusion that the center of the Black revolution was Africa, not the Caribbean."[13] The war in Ethiopia and his activist work in London had shaped his book as much as his research in the archives of Paris. And he ended his classic with a valedictory that stands in sharp contrast to Evelyn Waugh's celebration of a reborn Roman Empire.

"Nor will success result in the isolation of Africa," wrote James. "The blacks will demand skilled workmen and teachers . . . Imperialism vaunts its exploitation of the wealth of Africa for the benefit of civilization. In reality, from the very nature of its system of production for profit it strangles the real wealth of the continent—the creative capacity of the African people. The African faces a long and difficult road and he will need guidance. But he will tread it fast because he will walk upright."[14]

* * *

On September 21, British diplomats were led into a hall at the Dreesen Hotel in Godesburg, near Cologne, where a collection of uniformed army soldiers and Nazi elite waited. What began with Ethiopia had the Rhineland and Anschluss as sequels, and now it was Czechoslovakia's turn. It was another made-up crisis over the treatment of the German minority, even though Sudeten Germans were well-treated, well-tolerated, and had full voting privileges in Czechoslovakia.[15] Now, in this hotel hall someone muttered, *"Der Führer kommt."* And the room fell silent, Germans moving back against the walls.

Hitler walked in, and with an SS guard leading the way, ushered Neville Chamberlain up a staircase to a conference room with a green baize conference table. No sooner had Chamberlain given a carefully prepared statement that pretty much gave Hitler what he'd originally asked for than the dictator sat back and told him, "I am very sorry, but all that is no longer any use."[16] Chamberlain was stunned.

Everything Hitler did at Godesburg was out of the Italian playbook. He threw out old demands and made new ones. He interrupted his own translator with tirades. He had an aide come in every now and then with scraps of paper, pretending to bring news of fresh crimes by Czechs against Sudeten Germans. Hitler was so good at the game now that he even frightened his original role model, Mussolini, who didn't want his bluffs called in Europe. But by now, Germany reveled in being the top threat. Its diplomats treated their Italian counterparts with open contempt. After a major event at Berlin's Olympic Stadium, delegates couldn't find their cars during a rainstorm, so a German officer had casually stolen the Italian mission's vehicle to drive home.[17]

At the end of September, new talks were held in Munich, the spiritual home of Nazism. No Czech representatives were present because no Czechs had been invited. Germany would get the Sudetenland in a scheme that was an echo of the Hoare-Laval Plan. There were, of course, three substantial differences besides the lines on a map: 1) it was happening to white Europeans instead of black Africans; 2) it was proudly announced instead of being leaked; and 3) this time, it would make the statesmen popular at home instead of reviled.

The Fuehrer got his way, but he loathed the petty haggling, and he developed a particular contempt for Chamberlain. Now that it was all over, he growled, "If ever that silly old man comes interfering here again with his umbrella, I'll kick him downstairs and jump on his stomach in front of the photographers."[18]

The man with the umbrella flew back to Britain, and when his plane landed at the airport of Heston (a few miles from London), he was greeted by a crowd of thousands. There were film crews and radio reporters and coverage by the fledgling BBC television service, anchored at the time by Richard Dimbleby. Chamberlain reached into his jacket and waved a useless piece of paper in the air, signed by Hitler and himself. Later, back in Downing Street, he made his famous proclamation, "I believe it is peace for our time."*

Not everyone was fooled. Chamberlain's first lord of the admiralty, Duff Cooper, told the House of Commons on October 3 that on his way to a Cabinet meeting, he had been "caught up in the large crowd that were demonstrating their enthusiasm and were cheering, laughing, and singing; and there is no greater feeling of loneliness than to be in a crowd of happy, cheerful people and to feel that there is no occasion for oneself for gaiety or for cheering." He knew that Chamberlain's "language of sweet reasonableness" was not one that the dictators could understand, and so he had to resign.

The next month, European tensions still dominated newspapers, but some news organizations stopped to notice that Britain was at last formally recognizing the Italian conquest of Ethiopia. Britain's ambassador to Rome, Eric Drummond, signed a brief declaration and then presented his new credentials to Ciano.

At the crucial moment, as Eden had always feared, the British didn't even bother to hold the Italians to their end of the bargain. Mussolini had promised to pull ten thousand Italian volunteers out of Spain, but Chamberlain didn't

---

* Collective consciousness remembers this as "peace *in* our time," but that's not how Chamberlain first put it when he spoke in Downing Street.

wait for the full withdrawal because Mussolini had given him "definite assurances" it would be done. When he announced his decision at the beginning of November, he reminded the House of Commons that France had already offered its recognition.[19]

But France had won nothing either. In fact, the Daladier government's latest weakness only encouraged the Duce to demand more, and an old devil's bargain came back to haunt the Quai d'Orsay. Out of the blue, Mussolini declared the private deal he made with Pierre Laval back in 1935 to be dead. Laval had given him a strip of land from Tunisia to add to Libya, but now Mussolini wanted *all* of Tunisia, and while he was at it, French Somaliland, Nice, and Corsica, too. For this brazenness, he dusted off an old favorite, the rationale that Italy had never been fairly compensated for its service with the Allies in the Great War. There were violent and bloody demonstrations against Italy in Tunis and Ajaccio, Corsica. This time, the French government had no problem with telling Rome: *No.*

As much as appeasement is usually associated with Europe, its web genuinely threatened to ensnare all of Africa. Chamberlain—having learned nothing—always hoped to satisfy Hitler by coming to terms over places like Taganyika and Togoland. But Hitler wasn't interested in talks; he expected the colonies to be handed to him on a plate, pure and simple. It was only the Fuehrer's pride, impatience, and obstinacy that got in his own way. Had he practiced any subtlety and opted for negotiation, the colonial map of Africa would have been even more severely changed.

One man who understood the incredible danger was George Steer. As Chamberlain announced recognition in Parliament, Steer flew off to investigate the former German colonies, which were being governed under League of Nations mandates. His book, *Judgment on German Africa*, would come out the following spring, and as Steer's biographer, Nicholas Rankin, put it, he offered one particularly "devastating argument" against handing chunks of Africa to the Nazis. On maps included in Steer's book, the "sinister Axis black arrows threaten all the Allied territories in Africa, including South Africa . . . as well as all their vital Atlantic and Indian Ocean sea lanes and air routes."[20]

What began at Walwal could very easily consume Johannesburg and Nairobi. Steer noted how in South West Africa (now modern Namibia), members of the banned Hitler Youth organization had reinvented themselves as "Pathfinders," and their leaders wore their SS uniforms when no policeman was watching.[21]

*   *   *

In the village of Ginchi—west of Addis Ababa, east of Ambo—a twelve-year-old boy named Jagama Kello from a noble family had once spotted a young man in the road with both his ears pierced and a combed-out Afro, quite the impressive warrior by the looks of it. Jagama was curious and asked about this stranger, and he was told the young man had gone off to Wollega, where he had hunted and killed an antelope. This made a deep impression on the boy. Out in the forests, there were supposed to be antelopes, lions, elephants, and other wild beasts. Slay one, and you'd earn your earrings. From that point onward, Jagama was eager to go.

This was fine by his older sister, who was due to head back with her husband to their land near Wollega, and young Jagama could hunt all the antelope and elephants there he liked. Fate, however, came up with an alternate plan to mature him. Time passed, and his wealthy father died. Suddenly, the boy who wanted to be a hunter was stuck with being a gentleman landowner, responsible for about forty-seven acres, for which he had to collect revenues from tenants and pay taxes. The antelope would have to wait. "Everyone was expecting me to be an aristocrat when I grew up," recalls Jagama. "But ever since I was a kid, I remembered the young man from the market, and I wanted to kill something and become just like him."[22]

When the Italians invaded, Jagama Kello was fifteen years old, a tall, lanky youth. A family friend gave him a new inspiration. "When you were twelve, you wanted to go to Wollega to kill animals. Now we have a worse enemy."

"Who?" asked Jagama.

"These *ferengi*, the white people, Italians—they want to massacre Ethiopians and take our land, nothing else. They don't want to live in peace with us. Instead of going to Wollega and killing elephants, go and kill the Italians."

Becoming a Patriot, however, wasn't going to be that easy. His father had left the responsibility for his wellbeing with an uncle, who just happened to be a noble who sided with the Italians. The conflict in loyalties sometimes made for peculiar adventures with twists and turns. One time, for instance, Jagama went to buy bullets at his uncle's home.

"There were Italians there who knew my uncle and knew me," he remembers. "I bought the bullets from a man outside my uncle's compound who was cooperating with the Italians. But he suspected that I was from the other side after selling me the bullets and started hitting me. I had to jump the fence and run inside." Quickly, Jagama ran inside the house, only to run into another Italian. But this one "knew who I was so he turned away the guy who was trying to kill me—he saved me." That still wasn't the end of it. "In the afternoon, when they were getting water down by the river, I took my uncle's horse, I killed them both, and ran off into the forest."

With a youth's complete trust in his own immortality, Jagama seemed to be naturally brave. "Fear can't save your life," he argues, looking back. But luck, too, seemed to play a role in his success. After all, he would survive *years* out in the field, virtually a self-taught amateur. Another time, he heard the news that the Italians were trying to capture a strategic location. "I mounted my gun on my horse and tried to get there ahead of them on horseback all by myself." But he was promptly ambushed, with three bullets cutting down his animal under his feet. "I fell to the ground along with the horse. I still had my gun though, and when I got up, they started retreating and shooting. One of their bullets ricocheted off my gun and went up. Had it missed it by a little bit, it would have gone straight into my throat." With no time to congratulate himself on the miss, he kept firing and "so they ran away."

He doesn't have a ready explanation for why he fared so well. Even in advanced age, looking back on the boy he once was, he has a soldier's stoicism mixed with the signature piety of many Ethiopians. "God has given me life; I don't know why I survived. For everything . . . in life, to stay removed from evil, to find the good, you need God. It's all God's will that kept me alive. But I faced so much danger in my life."[23]

And as the years passed and the struggle went on, the would-be hunter turned landowner turned soldier was becoming a leader. Still in his teens, according to Jagama, he was leading a Patriot force that by the end of the conflict had thirty-five hundred men.

*   *   *

On New Year's Day of 1939, Galeazzo Ciano recorded in his diary that his father-in-law, the Duce, was "very much dissatisfied about the situation in East Africa and has pronounced a severe judgment on the work of the Duke of Aosta. In fact, Asmara is still in a state of complete revolt, and the sixty-five battalions that are stationed there are compelled to live in [temporary fortifications]."[24]

Aosta tried to put the best face on things when he was summoned abruptly back to Rome in March. Ciano noted that the Duke "spoke with considerable optimism about the condition of the Ethiopian Empire. I must, however, add that among the many people who have come from there, he is the only optimist." Ciano must have viewed this polo-playing dandy as having no credibility anymore, especially when Aosta lectured his colleagues on how they should avoid war with France, which could jeopardize the East African conquest. "I do not quite understand," sneered Ciano, "whether he was speaking as the Viceroy of Ethiopia or as the son of a French princess."[25]

In London, Sylvia Pankhurst capitalized on each and every one of Aosta's failures. It didn't matter how much Neville Chamberlain's government pandered to Mussolini or how often colonial officials socialized with Aosta on visits; her network of informants continued to get a steady supply of information out of Ethiopia. And she dug up an embarrassment that would last for months and demonstrate that the British Empire was far from prepared for war.

As the first weeks of 1939 rolled on, a secret report out of the colonial district office in Hargeisa confirmed what Sylvia and her supporters already knew: "There is no doubt that the information that the Italians are recruiting our Somalis is correct. We have people coming and going between here and Jijiga every day, and they all tell the same story." Before, the British had timidly *asked* the Italians to at least check whether Somalis were born in territories under their protection. "They are not even bothering to do that now." An Italian captain, a lieutenant, and an NCO had all been assigned to Jijiga just for the purpose of recruitment, and it was estimated that between one and three hundred Somalis a day were enlisting. Any ex-askaris they came across, either demobilized or deserters, were also being forced back into service.[26]

The acting governor of British Somaliland, C. H. F. Plowman, wrote the colonial secretary, Malcolm MacDonald, that "it is unlikely that any effective steps . . . can be taken by us locally, there being no counter-inducements to the prospects of good pay and a life which many of our young tribesmen find congenial."[27]

By mid-June, Sylvia was sending letters again to MPs, including the Tory MP for Cambridge University, John Withers, informing them that "the Italians are being allowed by the British authorities to use natives of British territory, and that on a very large scale, to proceed with their war in Abyssinia. I trust that you will take such action as you are able, both in Parliament and out, against this outrage." She finished her letter by asking for financial support for the *New Times*, adding a handwritten line to her typed letter: "We need this very seriously."[28]

Withers did act. He passed her letter along to the Foreign Office, where it failed to set off any alarm bells; not over Italians relying on British Somalis as cannon fodder, nor the idea that these new recruits might one day point their rifles at the Union Jack.

Raising the issue again seemed to only irritate the Foreign Office's Cavendish Bentinck, who wrote in a memo, "I understand the Somalis do not care whether they are serving us, the Italians, or the French . . . If anything, they are at present inclined to prefer the Italians, whom they regard as easier to deceive and as giving better pay." Like officials in the protectorate, he "thought it impossible to prevent" the nomadic Somalis from enlisting for Italy if they wanted. Not much thought was apparently given to offering them an alternative. Bentinck dismissed the whole matter by recommending that "we should insist on the Italians going through the form" of getting some guarantee that a recruit wasn't from the protectorate: in other words, the status quo charade of before. "This would improve our position if the matter were raised again in Parliament."[29]

By the end of June, he claimed this was the policy that had been adopted in the field.[30] It was business as usual in London two months before Adolf Hitler set Europe ablaze.

* * *

In Paris, however, it was a different story.

Back in March, the minister of overseas France and her colonies, Georges Mandel, had faced a shadowy senior operative of the *Deuxième Bureau*, the country's version of MI5 that fell under the military. "Why the devil are you delaying?" snapped Mandel. He was impatient because war was inching ever closer, especially now that Czechoslovakia was lost.

"My plan is ready, sir. I wait for your green light."[31]

The plan had to do with Ethiopia, and the senior operative was Raoul Salan, a figure so slippery and elusive that he's somehow escaped most English histories of the Ethiopian War, often leaving no more than a single line of reference or a footnote. And yet his career was epic. At nineteen, he was under fire at Verdun, and he ended up battling river pirates and warlords in Indochina while mastering Laotian. His soldiers and associates whispered everything about him from claims about his politics to accusations that he'd been a drug trafficker while in Asia.[32] If Mandel wanted to go behind German and Italian backs to help the Ethiopian Patriots, Salan was the perfect shadow.

So Salan began recruiting a team. He enlisted three Italian anti-Fascists, veterans of the Spanish Civil War who had been stuck brooding in the French Pyrenees after it was over. He found a former prospector who knew Eritrea, as well as the former director of the Franco-Ethiopian railroad and a skilled pilot. And his point man for the mission was an interesting reserve officer, a Frenchman who had also fought in Spain. Even the explosives were requisitioned and put aside for the operations to come.

But then Mandel got cold feet. After accusing Salan of delays, here was the minister fretting that maybe there was a last chance for peace. Mandel had come into politics from journalism, and he'd once worked side-by-side with Emile Zola at the great writer's newspaper, *L'Aurore*, over the Dreyfus Affair. He hated Fascism, had detested the Hoare-Laval Plan, and yet Mandel thought maybe, just maybe, France could find a last-minute ally in Stalin.

"Let's wait for the month of August," he told Salan.[33]

So the great plan was stuck on amber, still waiting for green. But in late August, Mandel got his answer over the Russians—Stalin threw in his lot with Hitler for their non-aggression pact. Raoul Salan's point man was already in London, seeing if the British would join the operation. Officially, the answer was no. Unofficially . . .

* * *

For years, editorial writers and commentators talked about a possible "second World War." In September, they could finally capitalize all three words—Germany invaded Poland. In Pomerania, a cavalry brigade made an utterly futile attempt to charge forward, their lances held high, against the tanks of the German Third Army. It was pathetic in its medieval valor, but then the world had forgotten how spears had pried and hammered two-seater tanks at Dembeguina Pass in Ethiopia. That seemed a lifetime ago.

As Anthony Eden walked to the House of Commons with Duff Cooper, air raid sirens blared over London. Britain finally had to declare war on Germany, and Neville Chamberlain wanted Eden back in government—but only as dominions secretary. It was a far step down from the Foreign Office, but for Eden, it was either serve behind a desk or put on a uniform as a middle-aged officer with his old regiment. He tried the uniform—briefly—and decided on the desk. Ever the skilled diplomat, Eden was good at handling dominions, and this status kept him politically insulated from Chamberlain's dithering War Cabinet, which had only one star: Winston Churchill as first lord of the admiralty. After Hitler's Panzers steamrolled through Belgium, Holland, and Luxembourg in May of 1940, the complete failure of Chamberlain couldn't be denied, and Britain finally got the right prime minister to save it. Churchill made Eden his secretary of state for war—then kept most of the responsibilities for himself.

Everyone knew the war would go far beyond Europe. George Steer had gone to Guernica, to Tanzania, to Finland, chronicling how Nazism and Fascism spread like a cancer. Even after getting engaged to Esmé Barton, he couldn't settle down. Now he brought together two of his close friends, Haile Selassie's loyal aide, Lorenzo Taezaz, and Robert Monnier, who had fought for the Republican Basques in Spain while secretly in the pay of the *Deuxième Bureau*.[34] Here was Raoul Salan's point man. Monnier was a decorated war hero and an unusual character, reckless and irreverent; he joked to the Basque leader, José Aguirre, "in war, you have to shoot people; if you cannot shoot the enemy, then you must shoot some of your own side."[35] Helping to liberate Ethiopia was the kind of crusade that appealed to him.

Monnier took Steer back with him to Paris and into the French Ministry of Colonies, playing "fixer" and securing the finances for their secret crossing into Ethiopia. In London, the Foreign Office kept Steer cooling his heels over a permit to cross Sudan, and in the end, instead of crossing a border, Steer walked down a church aisle to kiss his new bride, Esmé. He would stay behind.

But Salan, who had married recently himself, couldn't resist the action. He concocted the thin excuse that he had to be close to direct his operatives, and so he reappeared in Cairo with other members of his team as "Raoul Hugues," a journalist with *Le Temps* who supposedly couldn't fight because of health concerns. Packed in their luggage were small explosives disguised as quinine capsules in tubes. Meanwhile, Lorenzo Taezaz, Robert Monnier, and the three Italian anti-Fascists headed to Sudan to assess the military situation.

After reaching Khartoum, they avoided the British authorities and took a train to Gedaref, riding camels across the porous border with the Ethiopian frontier. But Monnier and Taezaz had a falling out over how and where to proceed and parted ways. The Frenchman caught malaria and sent off only a handful of reconnaissance reports before he died in November. An Orthodox priest sympathetic to the Patriots buried him in Aussa, "crusted in the decorations that they found in his luggage."[36] One of the group—it might have been an Ethiopian or one of the Italian anti-Fascists—had been lost in a river accident, and it's unclear what became of the Italians, whether they went with Monnier or Taezaz or split up. Lorenzo Taezaz journeyed back to Gojjam, bringing communications from London and stashing letters for the Emperor that he would have to smuggle back to Khartoum. George Steer wrote that the "volcano permanently simmered, and Lorenzo's coming gave it a poke."[37]

It was simmering, yes, but not really boiling over. Not yet. Both the Italians and Ethiopians had exhausted themselves into a stalemate. Rome kept pouring money down the sinkhole of its colony, refusing to admit failure. But worn-down peasants were also losing sympathy for the rebels. Some Patriot units had to resort to looting. And the constant running, bloody fighting, hiding in remote, unforgiving, harsh terrain—being tired, cold, miserable, half-starved most of the time—was naturally wearing down the fighters, too.

In Cairo, Raoul Salan, like others, wouldn't learn of Robert Monnier's death for several weeks. Salan was busy chumming around with correspondents who were none the wiser, hitting the casino, and visiting mosques. He was something of a thrill-seeker with a mercenary's flexible morals, and few back then probably knew how this shadowy war hero would unconsciously play a small part beyond Ethiopia to shaping our own grim modern world of surveillance and security.

But at the moment, he was content to play spy. On a trip to Alexandria, Salan briefed Britain's commander of the Middle East forces, General Archibald Wavell, who told him bluntly, "You are right to undertake this kind of work, but don't cause a scandal. We are not ready to handle the resulting Italian reaction."[38]

Here were the old roles reversed. The French, who had proved so maddeningly difficult in the long diplomatic saga, were daring to strike at last while the British worried over fallout. Salan flew back to Cairo and sent an encoded telegram from France's embassy to Mandel; the British, he warned, were concerned about timing.

Still, Salan would go ahead with his own plans, heading to Khartoum and rendezvousing with Ethiopian Patriots at a local hospital. After a couple of days, he met them again and gave them the cash they needed to help move stockpiled arms and supplies into Ethiopia. Then, like a plot turn in a thriller novel, Salan discovered he hadn't quite pulled off his masquerade. Italian officials in the region and, no doubt, OVRA agents, were apparently growing suspicious over this peculiar reporter. Salan decided it was time to retire his role.

Before leaving for Cairo, however, he had a visitor on the night of October 16. By a bank of the Nile, not far from his hotel, Salan met in secret with Daniel Sandford, now a colonel with the British army.[39] Sandford, of course, knew Ethiopia well and was the man who once told reporter Geoffrey Harmsworth how its people were "tough as nails." He informed Salan that, thanks to French cash and covert arms, the Patriots had managed to hit a few Italian convoys in raids. Success!

But the French mission was a one-off. Monnier was dead, and Salan's departure meant no more money from Paris into Khartoum. French assistance for the Patriots stopped before it really got started, and it would be many months before Ethiopia received proper help again.

Salan, taunting fate, traveled through Italy on his way home to Paris. His cameo for the Patriots was brief, but he wasn't finished with Africa. Years after the Second World War, Raoul Salan would preside over the French military's fading presence in Vietnam, and then in December of 1956, he would become the new Commander-in-Chief of forces in Algeria. He was only days into his new appointment when French *pieds-noirs* tried to kill him with a bazooka. Charles de Gaulle claimed in his memoirs that "there was something slippery and inscrutable" in the man he called a "beguiling figure."[40] This was convenient hindsight. Salan would support him, but de Gaulle would reward this loyalty by plucking his general from his all-powerful command in Algiers and putting him out to pasture as military governor of Paris.

In 1957, Algerian radicals fighting for independence shot any European man on sight, but they had certain rules; they didn't shoot women or children or old men. The *pied-noir* terrorists decided to strike back, and they didn't care about such distinctions. On August 10, 1957, their bomb exploded in the famous Casbah of Algiers, killing seventy Muslim Algerians, including many women and children. The Algerian radicals soon decided to use bombs of their own. And our age of modern terrorism was born.

And later, Raoul Salan—the man who played secret agent and arms trafficker for Ethiopian Patriots, the general slighted by Charles de Gaulle—became the titular head of the OAS, the infamous terrorist organization of French extremists in Algeria.

* * *

Back in 1937, the New York *Amsterdam News* had run an article by Adam Clayton Powell, Sr. It was an obituary of sorts for Marcus Garvey's old organization, the Universal Negro Improvement Association: "With Garvey's exile he became a black Trotsky to the Negro masses . . . Except for isolated chapters, the UNIA is finished." Black nationalism should wait its turn anyway, Powell argued, because now the great priority was for "the union of all races against the common enemy of Fascism."[41]

The black Trotsky in London could no longer hold a crowd. Amy Ashwood Garvey spotted her former husband one Sunday in Hyde Park, stooped and relying on a walking stick, trying to rally onlookers at Speaker's Corner, but "the old fire was gone."[42] It was common for him to be hissed and hooted off his platform. African students wouldn't forgive him for criticizing Haile Selassie, and no one else wanted to hear strident racial politics as the Allies took on Hitler. By late January of 1940, Garvey suffered a stroke that paralyzed his right side. He couldn't write, and he couldn't speak.

The months passed, and then on Saturday, May 18, he read one of the newspapers shipped in from America. There, in the pages of the *Chicago Defender*, was not merely an obituary for his organization like Powell had written, but an actual obituary for himself—and written by one of his old enemies, George Padmore, who was the *Defender's* correspondent in London. Padmore had no love for Garvey, but he seems to have acted in haste more than malice, rushing to get his story out and not bothering to check his facts. It was picked up by other papers, and many of them evaluating Garvey's career were hostile. His secretary did her best to keep the more caustic ones from his sight, but Garvey perused many clippings, shocked and depressed by the collective assessment of his life and work.[43] He died that June of 1940 at the age of fifty-two.

The newspapers were premature in writing him off. Bombastic, combative, self-aggrandizing, egomaniacal, sometimes brilliant, sometimes deluded, Garvey had made himself the focus of his movement, and yet *some* of his message would survive him. In 1938, he had sailed to Canada, where he spoke first in Toronto and then made a significant stop in Sydney on Nova Scotia's Cape Breton Island. Even many Canadians aren't aware that Nova Scotia has the oldest indigenous black population in all of North America; some families go back to the British Loyalists fighting American revolutionaries. Blacks in Canada in the 1930s were treated hardly better than their American counterparts. In Halifax, they were exiled to the balconies of movie houses, and many were stuck in the infamous Africville district, where they had no garbage service, no electricity, no public transit, and lived in desperate poverty—yet were still required to pay taxes. To many of them in Nova Scotia, Garvey was still a hero.

In Sydney, he had spoken to supporters at Menelik Hall, and the war in Africa was not far from his mind. "Every race has to look after its own affairs," he told his audience. "You have formulated no legal or moral claim. That is why people are taking away Africa today, just how Mussolini took away Ethiopia because he thought the Ethiopians had no use for it. One man used his intelligence and knocked out, while the other tried to pray." The reference to Ethiopia has often been ignored or forgotten, because a couple of minutes before it, Garvey offered a phrase in that same speech that was to have more lasting power: "We are going to emancipate ourselves from mental slavery because whilst others might free the body, none but ourselves can free the mind."[44]

More than forty years later, Bob Marley set Garvey's words to a tune he played on an acoustic guitar. He made them live on in a new classic, *Redemption Song*.

* * *

On June 10, 1940, the day that Garvey died at his desk in Beaumont Crescent, George Steer was three Underground stops away at his house in Chelsea, where he turned on his radio at six o'clock in the evening to listen to the BBC News. For anyone else, the broadcast that night might have proved depressing, but Steer recognized an opportunity. Mussolini was throwing in his lot with Hitler, officially declaring war on Britain and France.

France, of course, had to worry about Germans more than Italians at the moment, and its Third Republic, now in full retreat in Bordeaux, had less than a month left. But that was the whole point of the Duce's latest safe gamble. He had told Badoglio: "I only need a few thousand dead so that I can sit at the peace conference as a man who has fought."[45]

In Woodford Green, the Pankhurst family was having a pasta dinner with several Italian refugees. When the announcement came over the radio, it was a cause for celebration. "These words struck guests and hosts like an electric shock," recalled Richard Pankhurst, "which gave way to a feeling of relief and hope for the future."[46] It also provided a boost for the *New Times and Ethiopia News*, which was in a publishing limbo as far as its overseas readers were concerned. From September of 1939 onward, the British government had stopped its shipments abroad to avoid offending the Italian regime.[47] At long last, offending it no longer mattered. Not long after word was out over the declaration of war, angry mobs went on a tear through Soho, breaking the windows of the neighborhood's Italian restaurants.

In Chelsea that evening, George Steer had three distinguished guests come around, including the Emperor, who was staying at the Great Western Hotel in Paddington. Haile Selassie had been at St. Paul's Cathedral only a couple of days before to put a gold cross around the neck of Steer's baby son at his christening. A couple of old friends and allies hadn't lived to see this day. Heruy Wolde Selassie had died a couple of years previously in the Cotswolds. In New York City, the overworked Malaku Bayen had ended up in a sanitarium and developed lobar pneumonia. He died—having just passed his fortieth birthday—on May 4, missing the good news by only a few weeks.[48]

Another guest that evening for Steer was his father-in-law, Sidney Barton, now firmly retired from the diplomatic service. Philip Noel-Baker had also shown up. Noel-Baker was a tweedy, spectacled academic turned Labour MP who was a friend of the cause. The son of a Canadian Quaker, he had gone from being a track star and then an Oxford don to being one of the early policy brains at the League of Nations. Appalled at how the grand vision was crumbling, he'd written several books on disarmament. One day he would have the unusual distinction of being the only person to win both an Olympic medal and a Nobel Peace Prize.

The little group already knew what had to be done; they had talked about it right after the christening in the Canon's study two days before. None of them were prepared to sit on their hands and let events take their course. Certain regions of Ethiopia were still resisting, and a general revolt across the country would be useful to the Allied war effort. The Emperor should lead it. "The alternatives," wrote Steer, "would have been to give the revolt no leadership at all, in which case we would have thrown away a valuable weapon . . . To have played kingmaker to any one Ethiopian would have riled every other Ethiopian chief and have turned the revolt into an Ethiopian civil war."[49]

Haile Selassie had already written to the foreign secretary to say he was ready to act. Eden would have been glad to make use of him, but it was still Lord Halifax in his place—Winston Churchill had kept him on after he took over as prime minister. Halifax hadn't bothered to reply to the Emperor's offer. Now the little group decided they each had to lobby the Foreign Office from different angles. Barton took charge of the correspondence drafted for Haile Selassie, and with his typical short temper, he objected to the flamboyant prose written up by Lorenzo Taezaz and other Ethiopian aides. Noel-Baker set up a meeting for Haile Selassie with the ministry's under-secretary. And Steer worked his contacts in the Foreign Office, building support for the idea of the revolt.

It wasn't easy. Ever since Haile Selassie escaped Addis Ababa, Italy's propagandists spread the fiction that he'd emptied his nation's bank accounts to enjoy vast wealth in exile. His people supposedly hated him. Enough time had passed that these lies had some traction, if not among the Ethiopian people, then at least with the officials in the Foreign Office. But after being an embarrassment to the British government for four years just by his mere presence, Whitehall now decided the Emperor could be useful. After making a couple of broadcasts to rally his people, he would be sent back. Haile Selassie was going home.

Chapter Twenty-Two

DAY OF DELIVERANCE

Four days after Italy joined the war, Nazi soldiers took control of Paris without having to fire a single shot. France had collapsed. During his time out of office, Pierre Laval had become a media baron, but it was a means to an end to return to power. As Paris was taken, some government officials and hundreds of French journalists were in Clermont Ferrand. Laval tried to justify his past policies to the reporter, Pierre Lazareff.

"Throughout this entire conflict, I have never ceased maintaining contact with Mussolini and with Franco," said Laval. "They were neutrals, weren't they? What I tried for many years to accomplish was the creation of an effective opposition to Germany's might by the formation of a confederation of the great Mediterranean states. My dream has now been drowned in blood." He blamed Britain. He blamed anyone but himself. "She has always thwarted my plans for controlling the Mediterranean." And the United States? "The Americans don't know anything about anything."[1]

The man who displayed such talent for betraying allies now betrayed his own country. He became a key figure in the Vichy regime, responsible for some of its cruelest excesses. France would discover the realities of occupation that Ethiopia had endured for close to five years, right down to concentration camps, deportations, summary executions, and mass hunger.

In the midst of all this, a former "enemy" switched sides. As naïve and politically ignorant as she'd been about Ethiopia, at least Josephine Baker was not a hypocrite. French entertainers like Maurice Chevalier adjusted their consciences and cozied up to the Nazis to save their skins. When Josephine downed drinks and batted her eyelashes, it was all an act. She hid members of the French Underground in her château in the Dordogne and helped them get passports for their escape.

Because her past comments on Mussolini put her above suspicion, Josephine was a very successful spy, operating in Paris, Lisbon, and Marseilles.

As her biographer, Lynn Haney, brilliantly put it, "Josephine flitted from one embassy party to another, playing the sexy dingbat, all the while eavesdropping on the conversations of high-placed diplomats who found it hard to talk about anything except the war. Afterward, using invisible ink, she made detailed notes on her sheet music."[2]

In fact, it was because of her old remarks that she was asked to work her charms on those in the Italian embassy in Paris.[3] When Italy entered the war, there were those in the Underground who already knew the details, and they knew them because *La Bakaire* had smiled and giggled and slipped away with valuable information.

"The destiny of our Allies and consequently the Free French," declared one Résistance fighter, "was written in part over the pages of 'J'ai Deux Amours.'"[4]

By the time she was back performing in America at the dawn of the 1950s, the old stain on her record over Ethiopia was gone. Forgiven, she would become active in civil rights, and when close to three hundred thousand African Americans stood in front of the Lincoln Memorial for the March on Washington in 1963, she was on the same platform as Martin Luther King, Jr.

* * *

George Steer was going back with the Emperor, not as a journalist this time, but as an officer for the British army, in charge of propaganda services. Esmé, he confessed in print, "quite frankly hated my going and said that I would never get other countries out of my head."[5] In this, she was correct. But the solemn departure of the Emperor and his supporters did have one or two light touches of farce. Steer and Esmé managed to intercept their maid and prevent an embarrassing scene—the woman was about to serve part of lunch on the imperial dessert plates, ones the Emperor had given the couple as a wedding present. On the secretive drive out of London, Steer's job "for about eight hours was to look behind and see if we were being followed by any waiter from Soho."[6]

They weren't. A flying boat from Malta whisked the group into Egypt, and when it reached the oasis of Wadi Halfa, "the surprised Government of Sudan kept us for a week wondering what on Earth they were to do with us."[7] Sudan's governor-general, Sir Stewart Symes, was not happy to see them—he had an Italian wife and was one of the British elite completely won over by the charming, Anglophile Aosta.

At last, a welcome old friend arrived, Colonel Daniel Sandford, who was to be the military liaison to the bands of resistance in the country. Steer described him as "myopic, optimistic, hairy, and hale," a man close to sixty who had worked in both government and private business, who "rode long distances ahead of his caravan and slept alone under haystacks, walked booted into the Emperor's study to shake hands and to talk."[8] Sandford's role in the Liberation would be pivotal, and he called his operation "Mission 101"—named after an army fuse that triggers large explosions.

After drinks on the afternoon of June 28, Sandford slapped his files down cheerfully and briefed the arrivals on what they had to work with. The Emperor and his supporters were in for a rude shock. There was no artillery. The Emperor could have four mortars, which each had one hundred shells. Twenty anti-tank rifles brought in from Cairo would have to do against forty-five Italian tanks and armored cars in the area of rebellion. When Sandford mentioned that the Patriots might use two thousand Italian rifles captured in Libya, another familiar face, Andrew Chapman-Andrews (now posted to the British embassy in Cairo), piped up quickly, "They're bloody rusty, sir."[9] While they could get their hands on more rifles, there weren't more Ethiopian hands to fire them. Fewer than two thousand refugees were available in the frontier to start a revolt against three hundred thousand Italian troops. About two hundred Italian planes could bomb and gas them as they pleased, just as the planes had devastated the armies of the rases five years before.

Haile Selassie was so deeply upset that he struck the side of his head several times with his hand. "It would have been better had I never left England," he muttered.

The army command in Khartoum agreed. They considered his presence an imposition, and one official told Sandford, "You must advise the Emperor to return to England or to enter his country as a fugitive."[10] The Emperor would do neither.

By evening, he'd recovered from Sandford's disillusioning figures, and now composed again, made notes on a small card. "I am grateful," he told George Steer, "for the aid which the British Government is willing to extend Ethiopia, and I quite understand the burden which is borne by Britain at this moment." This was gracious. Then he said with admirable understatement: "I must, however, point out that the material quality of your aid is far from what I expected."

He laid out his case logically and reasonably. He had told his people, after all, they would get the same aid as other Allies. "My people, as soon as they know that I am in Ethiopia, will leave their homes to get arms against the common enemy," he argued gently. "If they see me with empty hands they may well lose the faith that has sustained them during the last five years and become unconsciously the instruments of the enemy." He had promised they wouldn't attack the Italians "naked as before," but with the same arms that had been used against them. He was still prepared to lead the revolt, but he wanted a "more serious effort made."

All the Ethiopians who had fled to Djibouti, Jerusalem, and Kenya with arms should come to Sudan to be at his headquarters. And he wanted to discuss figures for arms and supplies as soon as possible, with a "note of my requirements which I trust will be sympathetically considered."[11]

Steer was just as disappointed over the sorry lack of preparation. In time, he realized that all of Europe had been asleep, but in that moment, he took this state of affairs personally, just as the Emperor did, crestfallen that Britain seemed to be failing Ethiopia all over again.

The irony was that miles away, the disgruntled consul-general and head of the Blackshirts in East Africa, Arconovaldo Bonacorsi, was fuming over his own lack of supplies and support. Bonacorsi didn't care for Aosta's great experiment in relative leniency, and he didn't see any results. Nor did he like how the army was starved for resources. Equipment, he complained, was in a "lamentable state." There were soldiers going without water bottles and askaris reduced to rags. There was a lack of sandals, a lack of ammunition, seemingly a lack of everything except Ethiopians who wanted to kill them.

Only a few weeks before, Bonacorsi had written in a report, "Throughout the Empire, there is a state of latent rebellion which will have its final and tragic denouement when war breaks out with our enemies. If at any point whatever of our Empire a detachment of English or Frenchmen were to enter with banner unfurled, they would need little or no troops, for they would find the vast mass of the Abyssinian population would unite to that flag of combat and eject our forces. In the case of such an emergency, we should find ourselves unable to withstand the enemy, given the state of unpreparedness and the lack of equipment of our forces."[12]

And that was exactly what was about to happen.

* * *

But the British forces in Sudan needed encouragement—and they badly needed supplies and reinforcements, too. The entire annual budget for British Somaliland, for example, was less than £900 ($3,600).[13] The commander of the Middle East forces, Archibald Wavell, was a Sandhurst graduate whose sympathies were always with men in the infantry. He cabled London on July 4 with a long shopping list. There was only one armored division for his entire command, and it wasn't even fully supplied. Two divisions were incomplete, with another that could only be useful for policing tasks. Wavell needed anti-tank guns and artillery—urgently. This was a hard sell to a Britain facing the greatest threat of invasion since French and Spanish ships sailed to Trafalgar.

The same day that Wavell telegraphed London, the Duke of Aosta took the initiative and sent his forces to attack Anglo-Egyptian Sudan. He managed to drive the British out of their garrison at Kassala and to capture Gallabat.

When Britain's Secretary for War Anthony Eden got back to Wavell on July 8, he had little to offer, but he did have one suggestion: "An insurrection in Abyssinia would greatly assist your task. No doubt every effort is being made to further this, despite difficult weather conditions." Yes, the rain did make things difficult, Wavell cabled back, but his forces could hold on while those at home defeated the Germans.[14]

If Wavell couldn't send in men and tanks, there was one front where the battle could still be fought. Late in the month, RAF planes buzzed over Kassala to scatter a snowfall of fifteen thousand leaflets, along with a hail of bombs. The leaflets were in Amharic, and they bore a long-absent but familiar seal at the top of each paper—the symbol of a lion. Men wept, bringing the pages to their foreheads. This is what they read:

> Ethiopia raises her hands to God!
> Haile Selassie the First
> Elect of God
> Emperor of Ethiopia
>
> People, Chiefs and Warriors of Ethiopia!
> Your courage and your tenacity in confronting the enemy with an implacable resistance during the last five years have won you the sympathy and admiration of all free peoples. Your sufferings and your sacrifices, your heroism and your hopes will not have been in vain.
> The day of your deliverance has come.
> From today, Great Britain grants us the aid of her incomparable military might, to win back our entire independence.
> I am coming to you . . .

This was an *Awaj*, a decree; Haile Selassie and Lorenzo Taezaz collaborated on the text. It was typed out on an Amharic press from Cairo and then reproduced through a laborious printing process by the Sudan Survey Department. "You know what you have to do," the leaflet informed its reader. "Those among you who have submitted to the enemy must redeem themselves at once by deserting the Italian ranks and uniting with the Ethiopian forces. Let none of them be the enemy's instruments, either by action or by word."[15]

It says something about the power of this simple leaflet that the Italians would execute any man they discovered reading it. Carabinieri rushed to gather the falling scraps of hope before the pages fluttered into brown and hungry hands. But just as the *Awaj* said, those who did manage to read them knew what they had to do. Desertions rose among the ranks.

The call for "uniting forces," however, created new logistical problems. George Steer observed, "No arrangements had been made for the refugee influx" into Sudan.[16] The authorities decided the best thing to do was to arrest the new arrivals at the train station and put them up in jail, where they at least got food and shelter. As their numbers increased, they were relocated to the Defence Force's Animal Transport Lines, and an enterprising intelligence officer boosted their morale by organizing modest marches in step. When a superior wanted to know what he was up to, the officer told him that "it was just boy scout stuff."[17]

Just as the war in 1935 galvanized the most fascinating public figures and activists, so the Liberation now attracted a unique cast of characters. The explorer Wilfred Thesiger was back, joining the Sudan Defence Force and impressing everyone with how he could live off the land without rations and bathe in freezing streams. He had grown to hate the Italians and spoke decades later of how Ethiopia "was the one great emotional cause of my life." This had been his home, "the country of my childhood being raped—and England did nothing. It was heartbreaking."[18] But now, at last, something *was* being done. And he could help. Thesiger held the rank of *Bimbashi* in the Force, which sounds exotic but was another name for major. As an old friend of the imperial family, he went to lunch with Haile Selassie and his sons, and the Emperor asked politely about his mother. Oblivious to color prejudice, Thesiger preferred to lead Ethiopian, Nigerian, and Sudanese soldiers "rather than white troops if there is fighting."[19]

Then there was Laurens van der Post, a "rosy-cheeked, mild-voiced, and rather plump" captain and Afrikaner. He would become famous for writing about the Kalahari Bushmen and for his bestselling travel memoirs and novels. They were heavily influenced by Carl Jung—which appealed to those with a spiritual bent before there was even a category for "New Age" at the bookstores. A charismatic storyteller, van der Post would later spin yarns about his time as a POW in a Japanese prisoner of war camp and would hobnob with Margaret Thatcher and Prince Charles. It turned out after his death, however, that he had a bad habit of making things up. A critical biography of him came out in 2002, and the words "secular saint" were soon replaced with the labels "fabulist" and "liar."

If van der Post couldn't be trusted when it came to Africa, there was one of his fellow soldiers who could: Lieutenant—later Captain—W. E. D. "Bill" Allen. On the surface, he was a former Tory MP for West Belfast who used to run a

poster company. His short bio at the back of his book mentions that he was educated at Eton, that he had been a correspondent and a historian of the Georgians
and Ukrainians . . . and left out the less appealing fact that for a while, he was one
of the cronies of Oswald Mosley and the British Blackshirts.

Back when MI5 kept tabs on Italian deposits to the BUF, Allen was one of
those who had signing authority over the bank account in Charing Cross.[20] He
drafted regular anonymous articles for the Blackshirts' newspaper and wrote a
laudatory book about Mosley and his party in 1934.

But by 1938, Bill Allen had broken with Mosley completely; whether it was
a philosophical split or a personal one is unclear. For a former supporter of an
anti-Semitic bunch of hooligans, he ironically wound up serving in Palestine.
MI5 didn't trust him, and his CO, a Captain D. A. Young, was briefed about his
old political activities. Young sent his evaluation to MI5 on May 6, 1940: "Allen
is an adventurer of no morals or stability and might do anything. I believe he is a
loyal Briton and might be useful, though I would never trust him very far." Some
weeks passed, and MI5 checked with Young again. Allen was behaving himself,
so it decided he was "cleared."[21]

This must be why he was accepted as a volunteer for Mission 101, and his
chronicle of the Liberation, *Guerrilla Warfare in Abyssinia,* is an insightful, balanced account. The closest one gets to Allen being an "unstable character" is his
self-confessed scheme to talk his way over friendly drinks into becoming a pay-
master for Sandford's outfit—but then, everyone hoped to be in Sandford's unit.
Allen would end up in a very different one with van der Post, seeing the kind of
action that "unstable" adventurers relish.

As for the Ethiopians, he thought "they are a weird people. The pride of very
ancient days and things clothes in a hierarchic nobility the lords of a few grass
huts. The thin air of great altitudes, a diet of extremes of abstinence and excess,
the pellucid sunlight, the long months of dreary rain have bred a delicately balanced type, small-boned and lively, with quick movements and quick minds,
voices and souls pitched high."[22]

Allen's book appeared as one of Penguin's modest paperbacks in 1943 while
the war was still going on; historians still rely on it.

*   *   *

Back in London, Charles Martin met with one of the US embassy's representatives, doing his best to get arms for the Patriots from a still officially neutral
America.

Just as he had tried with the British, Martin brought up the idea of a loan and dangled a few carrots: "facilities . . . would be granted for trade, for mineral and oil exploration, and Tana Dam concessions."[23] But he got no encouragement from Herschel Johnson, a son of North Carolina who worked as the embassy's counselor. He only told Martin that he would pass on the offer to the US ambassador. Ethiopia wouldn't have mattered in the least to America's top man in London that season. This was Joseph Kennedy, who despised Jews, liked Hitler, and was rapidly losing interest in his job, confident that Britain would lose the war and that whatever happened, America should stay out of it.

From Washington, the adviser on political relations, James Clement Dunn, wrote Herschel Johnson back in August to tell him, "There is no need to go into the political aspects of this matter because, for all practical purposes, no arms could be supplied." Britain, Ireland, and Canada were all bidding the War Department to get the few surplus arms left, a supply that was "practically exhausted." Ethiopia, first invaded, was now at the back of a very long line. Dunn also poured cold water on Martin's idea of a loan, because the collateral "would be quite nebulous."[24] He and Johnson couldn't know that in the post-war world, Ethiopia would become one of America's key allies on a volatile continent.

But that time hadn't come yet, and so Martin went away emptyhanded. He'd told the Americans he was speaking with the full knowledge and authority of Haile Selassie, but he wasn't really—and he didn't know it. His relationship with the Emperor was now so poor that when Haile Selassie left for Khartoum, he didn't confide in his ambassador to Britain. For his part, Martin was busy trying to leave for India; his financial circumstances were so dire that he had to rely on the gift of £1,000 from an "anonymous donor" to pay for his passage.[25] But he still required the Emperor's formal permission to leave his service, and it was a shock to discover that Haile Selassie had flown the coop.

What could Martin do? He was left to gently confront an embarrassed Empress Menen and her eldest son, telling them "that since I had been treated in such a shabby way, I must leave for India as soon as I can get away."[26] Two months later, with bombs dropping on London in the first weeks of the Blitz, Martin managed to leave, taking with him his four youngest children and one of his nephews.

* * *

By that summer of 1940, Shawaragad Gadle was out of prison and back home. And the resistance fighter was about to earn her nickname as "Ethiopia's Joan of Arc."

Exile hadn't tamed her. Once back in town, Shawaragad sold off her father's land and used the profit to buy clothes, guns, ammunition, medicine—whatever the Patriots in the hills near the capital needed most. They were watching her, the Italians. She could get around that, and she did. She made contact with Ethiopia's consul in Djibouti, who sent her stationery with the Lion of Judah crest; in turn, she sent out letters to the Patriot chiefs, claiming they were from the Emperor. Their basic message was, "Britain is helping, but you must be patient."[27] She was running guns to the north and tracking down hidden arms caches. One of her operatives ran a coffee shop; that was his day job. By night, he slipped through the barbed wire around the capital to deliver cartridges and occasionally take part in raids.

She told others to be patient, but now that the British were in the war, she grew bolder. About thirty miles to the west of the capital lay Addis Alam. Two different guerrilla bands were hammering away at the Italians there, and she was in contact with their leaders. Now she asked them to work together for a united attack. She found allies among the Ethiopians working at the town's fort and prison, and she enlisted the help of Jagama Kello, the tall and skinny boy commander with a pensive face and a black cloud of an Afro. When the time came, they would take the fort.

She was more propagandist and cheerleader in some ways than fighter, though she fought, too. It was important to raise hope. "Whenever planes came over I always announced that they were English, even if they were Italian. When Italian mines exploded in the distance, we used to say that the British were bombing Addis Ababa. It kept up everyone's spirits, and many joined us."[28]

Fortunately, the British *were* coming—at last.

* * *

On August 6, 1940, a tight unit that was a mix of British officers and the Emperor's representatives crossed the Kenyan border at Doka into Ethiopian territory. Led by Colonel Dan Sandford, the unit had a wireless operator, medical men, about a hundred refugees turned guerrillas, and pack animals loaded with supplies to last them a month. But they hadn't come to fight—not yet. They were on a mission to make contact with the Patriots, which meant crossing vast and hostile ground all the way to their target destination of Gojjam, the province where they felt geography and the insurgents would both be on their side.

If they ran into trouble, there was a good chance they would wind up dead or in a concentration camp. And the Italians knew someone was coming. An Australian tracker, one who often filed pieces for the *New Times and Ethiopia*

News, had been intercepted by a patrol before he could link up with Sandford's group. His papers were taken, and he disappeared, likely shot. If his presence didn't tip off the Italians, they could also rely on the Gumuz people in the Qwara region, hunters of the bush and scrubland who had been enslaved by the Amhara and were happy to act as paid scouts and spies. In the early weeks of Mission 101, Sandford kept radio silence and typed up messages for Khartoum. Incredibly, messengers who relied on the ancient method of jogging across the country—with the written word clipped in a forked stick—managed to get to Sudan's border.

Sandford and his men zigzagged across the terrain, and they were helped by monks at the Mahabar Selassie monastery. These same monks, prompted by the Christian spirit of their order, had once saved an Italian crew when their plane crashed nearby. The Fascists rewarded them with a bombing and then raiding the monastery, killing several of them and burning out the building.[29] The monks told Sandford that his unit could safely make it to Sarako. They did.

But by the time they arrived, the Ethiopians were all sick with malaria. Sandford's wireless operator had a fever, and many of the mules and donkeys were either sick from disease or exhausted and broken from their labors. Their journey was far from over. They would cross eight flooded rivers and march up a terrifyingly steep slope that was called the Escarpment. By that time, they were down to eleven weary mules. Sandford and his men kept ditching items to lighten their loads. They had to get to a place called Zibist, where they had an ally, Fitawrari Ayellu Makonnen. But before Sandford and Ayellu could even meet, an Italian plane swooping overhead figured out what the unit was up to.

Sandford found himself "running down a cliff . . . sweating into his spectacles while machine gun bullets whistled round him at 400 yards range."[30] Then Ayellu and his Patriots suddenly appeared, coming to their rescue—but from a distance. Ayellu's snipers fired away, holding off an Italian column while Sandford and his men scrambled to a cave eight hundred feet below the lip of the Escarpment. It was a chase, a marathon, and a desperate climb all in one. The Italians, commanded by a colonel named Torelli, were thundering down on Ayellu's meager forces. They had already raided his village and burned his house.

Sandford's men had to get down as quickly as possible, but their guide lost his way.[31] They were, as Sandford's wife later put it, "slipping and clambering down three or four thousand feet of rock so steep that none of them would have tackled it in cold blood." They made it to the ground, but they weren't out of danger. For the next hour, it was a wade through the water of a nearby river. Torelli's soldiers couldn't find them, so they took out their frustrations on the nearby villagers, confiscating their grain and supplies.

Then on September 15, Ayellu's direct superior and one of the strongest Patriot leaders, Dejazmach Mangasha Jimbari, answered Sandford's request for help and sent an escort to bring the unit safely to his camp at the Little Abbai River. That same day, the unit sent a coded message on its wireless back to Khartoum. They had made it to Gojjam.

After all these exhausting trials, the *real* work started. Throughout October, Sandford met with leaders of the resistance. The challenge wasn't simply getting them to team up and follow an overall strategy. He also had to persuade top rival dejazmaches like Mangasha and Nagash to stop attacking each other. Sandford's basic argument, put in his chipper, English way, boiled down to this: Gentlemen, it would be ever so helpful if you remembered *the enemy is the Italian*. Quit squabbling among yourselves. Quit taking potshots at each other. He made them literally seal the deal, with seals on a document that locked them into certain obligations. One of them was that they "refuse to accept a [Patriot] who deserts and goes to the other."[32]

Sandford had other homework. He knew troop movements and plans were still leaked to the enemy far too often. With the incestuous web of family feudal politics, spies and informants were hardly ever punished. There was no way around this, so he factored it in. If leaks were to happen, let them be leaks of *their* choosing. So far, so good. But there was still the occasional embarrassment for the unit. When Sandford ran out of cash, he had to borrow three thousand thalers from Nagash to keep his operation going.

It wasn't until many years after the war that a picture emerged of underlying tensions in Mission 101. The Emperor's representative, Kebede Tessema, had brought a proclamation from Haile Selassie and a memo of orders that seemed to put him on an equal footing with the colonel—at least in Haile Selassie's and Kebede's minds. But out in the field, Sandford made it clear that Kebede must follow his orders. This was the British army's show. On the surface they cooperated, but Kebede began to deeply resent "this Englishman," as he referred to him in a memoir.[33]

Sandford had left Khartoum, thinking he'd convinced the Emperor to stay put and wait until after the rains. His sales job was only half effective. "The Little Man," as the Westerners affectionately called him, was getting restless, and George Steer had the unenviable job of keeping the monarch busy. Steer, who soon had the rank of acting captain and general staff officer for the military intelligence branch, decided in September that it was high time to make Haile Selassie useful, and more importantly, make him *feel* useful. Time for a royal visit to Gedaref in Sudan. Steer escorted him in a Vickers Valentia troop-carrier, and it didn't matter that the plane was creaky and obsolete—it was big and impressive.

In Gedaref, the district commissioner set up a tent and produced an Ethiopian flag he had sewn in secret. Anti-aircraft Bren guns stood "like praying mantises in the tall vivid grass." As the Emperor took his place in the tent, hundreds of refugees from Gojjam rushed up to him in a devotional frenzy, bragging in falsetto about their heroic feats and tossing onto the carpet their captured spoils—Italian spurs, epaulettes, stars from uniforms. They had grown their hair long, refusing to cut it until their Emperor's return or the country's liberation. "We are your servants and your slaves, you are our umbrella!" they cried out happily. And as women "loo-loo-looed" in the background, there was an insect-like drone of Orthodox priests, muttering prayers and praise "like bees at honey."[34]

For the refugees, this was the greatest day of their lives. But Steer's bit of stagecraft had an added benefit. All this time, some in the Foreign Office and the military had accepted the idea that the Emperor wasn't wanted back home. Now the British in Gedaref saw for themselves how wrong they had been; it was "a revelation."

* * *

If they were rejoicing in Gedaref, there was little good news from other spots of the East Africa campaign.

That same month, General Guglielmo Nasi swept into British Somaliland with twenty-five thousand troops in the tried and true three-column advance. Winston Churchill flew into a volcanic rage when he learned how light the casualties were for the retreating British, as if getting wounded and dying in great numbers proved anything. But his Middle East commander in Cairo, Archibald Wavell, stood up to him. He had no time for being second-guessed from London. After Italo Balbo and his plane crew were fatally shot down by ship gunners from their own side, the Butcher of Fezzan was put back in charge of Libya. And on September 13, Graziani took eighty thousand soldiers and three hundred tanks to plow into Egypt.

It didn't matter that Egypt was technically neutral, and as it happened, King Farouk leaned in sympathies towards the Fascist powers (so did army officers Gamel Nasser and Anwar Sadat). But there was a reprieve; the Butcher paused on September 16 at a town called Sidi Barrani close to the Mediterranean Sea. The move didn't make a lot of sense. It was ostensibly so he could fortify his position. But he could have swept east towards Alexandria and made himself a hero by threatening, perhaps even capturing, the Suez Canal. Instead he lingered. And Churchill gambled and sent Wavell reinforcements, despite Britain being in the fight of its life against Germany.

What did all this mean for Ethiopia? It meant that it was still an afterthought. There were deadly stealth games for British ships and Italian submarines in the Mediterranean. English soldiers and Italian Blackshirts were playing tug o' war over parts of Sudan and border towns of Kenya. And Graziani in Libya would get a hard shove back in a couple of months by British and Commonwealth forces. Ethiopia would just have to wait its turn.

One sign of how casual things were was that a subaltern instructor in Sudan apologized sheepishly to soldiers because he had so little wisdom to pass on for their demolitions course—he'd only just taken it himself. Not that it would help, because the area the troops were heading for had no railways and only two bridges. "We were shown one or two tricks which might have raised a laugh in Dublin twenty years ago," recalled Bill Allen, the devout Ulsterman. "But still, playing around with explosives is always an entertaining way of passing an idle morning."[35]

Back in London, they wanted to get more out of the effort than a couple of laughs. So War Secretary Anthony Eden flew out to assess the situation and spent much of October traveling around parts of Egypt and Palestine, evaluating British forces. On a plane to Siwa, a military policeman offered him a pistol, which he turned down with cavalier bravado—then regretted the moment the plane hit the clouds, realizing that if it was shot down, he would be defenseless. But Eden made it safely to Siwa and to all his other tour spots. He also paid keen attention when a local commissioner told him that "Arabs had no cause to fight for and regarded this war as no affair of theirs. Egypt gave no lead."[36]

Eden asked the man a question: how about if we say publicly we'll try to free Libya? Would that help? It certainly would.

On October 28, he was in Khartoum, where it was too hot to sleep in the rooms of the palace rebuilt by Kitchener, so he slept on the roof instead.

He was here to meet with the brain trust of the East Africa Campaign, which naturally included the top commander, Archibald Wavell; General William Platt, who commanded the Sudan Defence Force and enjoyed the peculiar Arab title for his position of "the Kaid"; Lieutenant-General Alan Cunningham, who was taking over East Africa operations from another general in Kenya; and Field Marshal Jan Smuts, who at long last had stopped making panicky comments about race war and thought South Africa must come to the rescue of Britain. He believed this despite the grumblings of neutralist Afrikaners. They were all there to talk strategy, and Smuts advanced a proposal for taking Kismayu, a port city in Italian Somaliland. But that would have to wait until after the rains.

The general idea was to kick the Italians out of East Africa—*not* for the sake of liberating these territories for themselves, but to free British forces for operations elsewhere. Eden, perhaps, might have been the sole person at the table who cared what happened to Ethiopia itself, never forgetting how his government had failed it. He thought maybe a little psychological boot in the rear would help motivate some people for its cause. So after dinner on October 29, he and Wavell blasted Platt, the Kaid of Sudan, for dragging his feet over helping the Emperor, the Ethiopian refugees, and Mission 101. Eden remembered it as a "stormy affair," with Wavell leading the attack and Eden choosing to be provocative. "I fear that they must all have regarded me as intolerable, but there are times when it does little good to sit down to a pleasant evening party, and I deliberately wanted to stir our folks up."[37]

Eden planned to make Britain help the Emperor "without stint."[38] It was just a question of timing. Haile Selassie, of course, could hum this tune from memory; he'd heard it all before. He also wanted to go to the front, wherever the front might be, and he was tired of waiting at his headquarters. He had traded a country house in Bath only to find himself in a country house on the outskirts of Khartoum, a place called the "Pink Palace." Eden still urged caution. If the Italians managed to crush a revolt launched too soon, it would ruin the effect of the Emperor's presence.

And all too soon, there was a disaster to serve as a handy example.

Brigadier General William Slim, who would achieve his highest fame later in the war in Burma, had put the finishing touches on a major push out of Sudan. Slim was a burly career officer who was wounded at Gallipoli in the First World War and once led the famously tough Gurkhas. He planned down to the last detail how the Tenth Indian Infantry Brigade would recapture Gallabat on November 6. It was a great scheme, bold in its vision and its objective. Why, it would clear open the whole caravan route for Sandford and the Patriots from Sudan to Gojjam! Too bad the attack was cursed. Six hardy and much-prized tanks broke down in the fighting, and when an ammunition dump blew up, English soldiers ran for the hills while their Indian counterparts kept their discipline. When the Italians took back Gallabat, Slim had to let them keep it and pulled out.

"What I needed was an English officer who would work in close contact with the Emperor and act as his staff officer," Eden wrote later. "Then an active column working in concert with Haile Selassie might achieve something."[39]

Once he was back in Cairo, Eden took up the notion with Wavell, who had just the man for the job.

* * *

For years, the British, especially their military, had been under the spell of Lawrence of Arabia. They looked for his reincarnation in every guerrilla war theater where "primitives" might be led by the dashing White Man. His ghost, wrote Bill Allen, stalked through "Gordon's city" (i.e., Khartoum) and "checked the elbows of tough Canadians and Australians and Kenya settlers gathering for the kill."[40] Lawrence—who died from a motorcycle accident in Dorset in 1935— was brilliant, stubborn, flamboyant, and maybe a little bit mad. Maybe another madman was just what Ethiopia needed. Whether it did or not, it got one, and as a matter of fact, this one was a distant cousin on his mother's side to T. E. Lawrence.

He was a commander of an anti-aircraft unit in his late thirties who regularly bellyached and moaned about the "military ape" and the stupidity of certain army practices. But he wrote an insightful memo on North Africa that caught Winston Churchill's eye. The word went out: let's use this young man for something. And so Orde Wingate, whose big mouth and cantankerous ways had steered him into the purgatory of a London suburban army base, was plucked from obscurity and sent off to Cairo. Wingate did some homework. After reading up, he knew with every sinew in his body how to win Ethiopia for the Emperor. He went off to Khartoum with a kitbag full of ego and a suitcase packed with one million pounds sterling from the British Army to finance the mission. No sooner had he arrived than he insisted on learning "how precisely and how many times he should bow when he entered the presence of Haile Selassie."[41]

Ethiopia wasn't his first windmill. Wingate was the product of religious fanatics, and though he wasn't Jewish, he became such a sympathetic Zionist while serving in Palestine that his own commanders thought he was a security risk. The fascinating thing, as Wilfred Thesiger discovered, was that Wingate was bullied as a child, and so he identified with the Jews as underdogs. He taught Moshe Dayan a thing or two about night raids in the 1930s, and when he came to Ethiopia, he managed to bring along his old aide from his days in Palestine. Never mind that Abriham Akavia was a civilian. The rules didn't always apply to Wingate, and he made Akavia his de facto chief of staff.

George Steer thought Wingate "was something of a showman" and noted how he could discuss with "icy gusto" hunting hyenas by moonlight with pistols. Like a true eccentric, his odd behavior came naturally and wasn't an affectation. He discussed plans with officers while lying naked on his hotel bed and brushing his body hair with a toothbrush, and he regularly carried around an alarm clock tied to his hand. But he also liked to deliberately antagonize people, ignoring the fact that his stunts damaged his reputation. There were many who loathed him, while others swung around in time to grudging admiration.

Ever the zealot, he insisted on describing the Ethiopian guerrillas as Patriots. It's the word that in English has worked well enough, but the Ethiopians already had their own word for patriots: *Arbegnoch*. And Steer understood the Ethiopians far better than Wingate did:

> The Ethiopians who had been out against the Italians for the last five years were indeed patriots of the highest kind, whose sufferings will never be recorded. But the word, *patriot*, conjures up for us the picture of somebody going to the execution block with his head held high because he had blown up a power station single-handed, or running to his death against machine guns. The Abyssinian who was called a patriot was far more subtle and tentative than that. He seldom took risks, he slid out of gunfire; his chief service to his country's independence and to the British cause was his invisible ubiquity, the complete uncertainty about what he was going to do next because he did not know himself, and the hypnotic consequences that this had upon the Italian army. [42]

Wingate, however, had his own fixed ideas about guerrilla warfare. Sandford's way—arming Patriot bands and trying to coordinate their efforts—had made some modest gains so far. But Wingate was deeply critical of the older man's methods. When Steer asked him later to describe his principles, Wingate had them already outlined on a piece of paper.[43] The "Wrong Method" went like this: after a commander hands over a certain portion of weapons, argued Wingate, he'll wait for results. But there are none. Meanwhile,

> The patriot argues thus: "This person evidently needs my (very inefficient) help; so much that he is willing to part with arms he must know I have only the most rudimentary idea of how to use. Ergo, he has no one better to use them. He evidently has no one to fight for him, and so is prepared to give me this substantial bribe. Therefore he must be in a weak position and may well be beaten. If that happens, I shall be in the soup. That is an argument for not fighting, but no argument for not taking what he offers . . . Why should I die without hope of victory?

The "Right Method," according to Wingate, was for a commander to enter an area with "a small but highly efficient column with modern equipment and armament, but none to give away." The commander makes a point of *not* asking for the Patriot's help and then conducts a successful night attack.

Next day comes the patriot saying, "Why didn't you tell me you intended to attack? I could have been of great help to you."

"Oh, well, you have no arms, and you're not a soldier. And after all, why should you get killed? This is our job."

"But I am a soldier and have been fighting the enemy for years. Only tell me what you want me to do, and I will show you we can do it."

"But you have no arms or ammunition, and I have none to spare."

"It is true that I have very little ammunition, but what I have I want to use in support of my flag."

He concluded that "the essence of the lesson is that to raise a real fighting revolt, you must send in a *corps d'élite* to do exploits and not peddlers of war material and cash . . . We can hope that the rare occasional brave man will be stirred to come to us and risk his life to help our cause . . . All the rest—the rush of the tribesmen, the peasants with billhooks, is hugaboo."

Steer absorbed this and concluded, "That was Wingate: brilliant, certain, and half right."[44] Yes, the rush of tribesmen might mean little in the tactical sense, but to the Italians, these Patriots—with their rags, their wild Afros, and their determination—were a frightening apparition.

After he was confirmed as overall commander of the guerrilla operations, Wingate dubbed his tiny army "Gideon Force" after the figure in the Bible. He had only about seventy British commandos and eight hundred men from the Sudan Frontier Battalion, matched by about eight hundred Ethiopian Patriots. But he had a plan, and he got it approved.

Forget the Emperor leading a large army. That was a sure way to get him killed, especially from bombers above. Instead, Wingate organized a set of units that he dubbed Operational and Intelligence Centers. Each centre would have 150 Ethiopians led by a British officer and four NCOs, and it would be equipped with a radio, an interpreter, and mules. Wingate was smart enough to know he should go see the fields of battle for himself, and he wanted to consult Sandford. But he carried the baggage of his own ideas and often didn't listen to others. He presumed that guides might turn out to be spies, and he didn't want to rely on any roads. Wilfred Thesiger thought these notions ridiculous. He respected Wingate's enthusiasm up to a point, but he was soon longing to serve under Sandford, too.

So on November 20, Wingate went off to Gojjam to consult the man who knew the country better than anyone else. He traveled by air in a rickety Vincent biplane with a soon-to-be-boiling oil gauge (his first idea of parachuting in was thrown out). RAF pilot Reginald Colis surprised everyone with his amazing flying skills, including himself. He used glider techniques to get over the Escarpment at Sekala, which was close to the banks of the Blue Nile, and landed on a hastily-made airstrip ninety-seven hundred feet in the air. To him, Wingate in his tropical uniform, his pith helmet, and his thick beard looked like a Baptist missionary. Their hosts were an equally astonishing sight—noisy and excited Ethiopians with their rifles and spears, growing their hair in large Afros that they hoped would frighten the Italians. For them, the plane was a sign of the air support that was to come.

Wingate laid out for Sandford his scheme for taking back Ethiopia. His operational centers would spread out in the field to help the ragtag insurgent forces, relying on machine guns, mortars, and the important news that the Emperor was coming. When enough progress was made, the Emperor would cross over and establish a base, which would serve as a beacon for the Patriots. The strategy had to tie in with the plans for the rest of Italian East Africa. While the insurgents harassed the enemy in Gojjam and softened him up, Platt and several divisions of the Indian army would bulldoze their way into Eritrea and Tigray. Meanwhile, there would be an impressive juggernaut from the south: about forty thousand native soldiers from Nigeria, Kenya, Rhodesia, and other British colonies, along with twenty-seven thousand white South African troops. These would all be led by Cunningham, who would push up from Kenya. All the while, the job of Gideon Force was to spread mayhem and chaos, tying up resources and terrorizing the Italian soldiers.

After a couple of days, Wingate was ready to take his little group "home" to Khartoum. Reginald Collis had done a fancy trick of landing, but now he had to pilot the Vincent off a spit of land that ended in a straight drop into a chasm. There was barely enough ground for takeoff. On the second attempt, Wingate—who had managed so far to hide his intense fear of flying—called out in a panic for him to brake. Muttering words about God and the perils of flying, the terrified major asked Collis what he planned to do. "Well, that made a nice change," thought Collis, "the aircraft captain making decisions rather than his passenger."[45]

The flight for the day was scrapped, and as Patriots cleared the primitive runway of rocks, Collis ditched everything in the plane that could make a difference in weight, from the radio to the long-range fuel tank. He even considered tossing out the machine gun in the rear cockpit, but decided to keep it. The next day, another attempt: the biplane made a squeaker of a takeoff, but soon it was free and clear. When the adventure was over, Collis and his navigator, Frank Bavin-Smith, would both get the Distinguished Flying Cross.

At the plane's stop in Sudan in the oddly Portuguese-named town of Roseires, Wingate rushed into the office of the base's commander, a colonel, and demanded, "I want 20,000 camels, and I want them right away."

The colonel told him there weren't that many camels in the whole province.

"Don't bore me with the difficulties," snapped Wingate. "Just get on with the job."[46]

This is not the way to talk to a superior officer, and it's a small miracle he didn't find himself booted out of the colonel's office or worse. But the madman got his way again, with seventeen thousand camels delivered. Still, he made a serious mistake. From the plane, he presumed the terrain around Belaya and west of the Escarpment was flat land, and he ignored the warning from others that it was, in fact, a series of lava ridges covered by bush. Definitely *not* camel country. By year's end, only fifty-three of the poor animals survived the highland climate and rough geography to reach Ethiopia's capital, and of those, forty-nine were suffering and had to be put down.

Time and again, Wingate also bombarded Mission 101's signal operators, oblivious to the fact that they had to painstakingly decode his long messages. He was critical of Sandford, too, for giving out Springfield rifles when they might not end up being used. But this hardly mattered—the weapons were inferior to anything they already had or had swiped from the Italians. And as Thesiger would point out, Sandford relied on the guns to win the Patriots' trust and support.[47]

Wingate had done a better sales pitch in Sekala than anyone expected. Sandford was now convinced that the madman with the alarm clock and the rough edges should be in charge of the fighting. Despite outranking him, he let Wingate have his way as so many did, and the cheerful colonel eventually went where he would be happiest, as a political adviser to the Emperor.

* * *

It was in November when the Patriots decided the time was right to launch their attack on the fort at Addis Alam. Shawaragad Gadle and her forces broke into the prison there and freed its inmates, and by her count, her soldiers killed 114 Italians and took eighty prisoners. The boy commander, Jagama Kello, also took part in this raid and remembers more than 120 Italian soldiers were killed while his Patriots captured three thousand guns.[48] But whatever the actual hard numbers, the raid was clearly a success. Jubilant, Shawaragad and her men considered attacking Addis Ababa, but wisely decided it was too soon.

They set out on the Jimma road to join Geressu Duki, another popular and fiercely courageous Patriot leader who had apparently been holding the Italians at bay for a couple of months. But their own numbers were down, and the enemy hit them in a surprise attack. They held out for four hours. "I fired as long as I could but was finally taken prisoner," she recalled. "My woman assistant was killed in front of me."[49]

Shawaragad was taken to the garrison at Dibella, where she was tortured again. The guards tied her hands behind her back, good and tight with wet rope. She couldn't sit. She couldn't stand comfortably. Then began the questions. She asked to speak to an officer. "I think they thought I was going to give away an important secret and an officer was brought. I said, 'You say you are a civilized people, but you treat prisoners in a barbarous way.' He was very angry and told them to take off the cords and put on manacles and anklets."

The chains were attached to the wall, and the manacles were so tight on her wrists that blood came out from under her fingernails. She had to endure this treatment for twenty-five hours. Later, a shifta said in her presence, "The Ethiopian flag will be flying over Addis Ababa in a month."

An Italian colonel asked what the man had said. Shawaragad told him, and the colonel had her manacles tightened even further.

The next morning, she was taken off to a prison in the capital. Her mornings and afternoons were punctuated by interrogation sessions; wasted time, since she refused to tell them anything. "They asked me why I had gone as a rebel, and I replied, 'The lion prefers the forest to the house.'"[50]

For more than a month, she practically starved in her cell, close to death and so weak there was no point in bothering to question her anymore. And the shifta had turned out to be wrong. The British and the Patriots would need more than a month to take Addis Ababa.

* * *

While all the planning and deployments went on for the British Army, the propaganda office in Khartoum was a hive, buzzing furiously as if swatted with a stick. George Steer compared it to the happy bedlam of American newsrooms. Perhaps when he was back in London, he'd gone to the pictures to see *His Girl Friday*, with Cary Grant and Rosalind Russell trading rapid-fire zingers. Today, it's a classic, but it came out in January that year. It certainly sounds like Steer's office had borrowed a few absurd moments from the movie. While his colleague, Perry Fellowes, was figuring out how to slip equipment out of the office without authorization, the secretary couldn't dig up what Steer had misfiled, and their Greek-Eritrean printer chose this moment to bring in his group of children, all sipping lime juice.

At the end of the long, hot room, Steer sat shirtless and hogging the one electric fan as he interrogated an exhausted deserter, but his interpreter wouldn't translate what Steer told him. Old manual typewriters used to make a din like a Tommy gun, and as he pecked away with the vagabond granules of Sudan soil crackling in the machine's guts, he suddenly stopped, looked up, and realized his deserter had vanished. "He has had enough of it, so he is sitting under my table."[51] Three more deserters waited to be questioned.

Each week, the unit produced *Banderachin*, which Steer proudly considered "the first airborne newspaper of the Axis war," dropped along with bombs on RAF raids. The name was inspired by something that deserters had told him, that they wished to die *Negusachin Banderachin*—"for our King and our Flag." In the beginning, the RAF gave *Banderachin* little respect. The plane crews wanted to drop bombs, not "waste paper," and it took time to bring them around. But Steer was doing more than publishing pamphlets, and his interviews with deserters proved invaluable when it came time to lead his Forward Propaganda Unit. Once upon a time, he was the journalist who tried to counter lies and rumor. Now he was a pioneer—almost completely self-taught—of psychological warfare.

"Propaganda is a weapon of cooperation or of exploitation," he realized.[52] Who better to understand the mindset of the enemy than those who had just *fled* the enemy? Like de-programmed victims of a cult, no one had better credibility to persuade those still in the fold. Moreover, a deserter turned propagandist taught himself again and again the virtue of switching sides.

Instead of settling for the frightened misfits dumped on him, Steer rebuilt his unit with the bravest men well-suited for a fifth column. His Patriots would be climbing mountains and crossing rivers, lugging a portable printing press and bottles of colored inks. He understood the power of symbols, and he proposed that attacks carry the Ethiopian flag, a point that prompted only a smile in the early days from General Platt. In time, however, he would get his way, and the RAF blanketed parts of the country with small versions of the Ethiopian green, yellow, and red. Steer was working out principles. If you were going to drop leaflets, you had to drop bombs, too. The bombs destroyed material, and the leaflets drove your lesson home; if you dropped the paper by itself, the enemy sneered at the gesture, and this boosted his morale.

Steer also pioneered the loudspeaker as an effective propaganda tool. It could either assault or manipulate. When the speakers played vintage songs, the music poignantly reminded Italian soldiers of home, "but these did not appeal to the British artillery behind them, who asked them to shut up."[53] What the artillery thought was less important than the fact that on the very first night, sixty deserters crossed over. The loudspeakers defied conventional thinking. Instead of them becoming targets, a clever broadcast of music and talk prompted lulls in the fighting, with Italians eager to listen. And more men gave themselves up.

The speaker talk and the pamphlets didn't always tell the truth—sometimes there were skillful lies. Steer thought it was nonsense to keep propaganda strictly accurate: "Where does truth or untruth lie in saying boo to a goose?"[54] Months later, he would make a point of libeling a Colonel Orlando Lorenzini as a "skunk and a coward." Lorenzini helped slaughter the Senussi of Libya—that made him fair game in Steer's book. He knew askaris followed the "leadership principle" like everyone else, and that "when a man is afraid he always wants to attribute his fear to someone else."[55] Though Platt in Khartoum understood and gave his support, the point was lost on London and Cairo, where lying about the enemy was bad form; one divisional commander was especially furious. Steer didn't care. After Lorenzini was killed, Steer thought that if "such a story could have passed a British censorship, I would have announced that he had been shot in the back by a deserting Eritrean askari."[56]

For Steer, the ends justified the means, and at one point, he forged the Emperor's signature for a leaflet on uniting factions. All of his principles and techniques have made for a dubious legacy, becoming standard in what today is called PSYOP, Psychological Operations. British troops relied on deserters to turn insurgents in post-war Malaya and Kenya.[57] More than 400 million leaflets would be dropped on Vietnam during US involvement in that long, bloody war. In 1989, when American troops wanted to dislodge Manuel Noriega from his refuge in the Vatican's embassy in Panama City, they blasted hard rock music around the clock. And during the first Gulf War and more recently in Afghanistan, leaflets and loudspeakers were used to persuade enemy soldiers to surrender.

* * *

Guglielmo Nasi, a friend of Aosta and considered one of the more moderate Italian commanders of the occupation, was becoming concerned. True, the British were proving so far to be less formidable than expected, especially if Italy's cakewalk into British Somaliland was an indication. But Mangasha and Nagash . . . oh, they were hitting Gojjam hard. Desertions were rising. The insurgents were getting supplies. Nasi was a seasoned African commander who had served in the 1935-'36 war. He decided now was the time for a pay hike for the soldiers, and it wouldn't hurt to toss a few baubles and money packets at the bande leaders. Gojjam and Gonder were his responsibilities, so he decided on a shrewd ploy—he would make Ras Hailu Tekle Haymanot governor of Gojjam.

This was fine by Hailu, who, of course, had oppressed Gojjam before and called it governing. Now past sixty with his hair dyed black, the ras sweet-talked the smaller leaders into submitting to the Italians, and the Patriots pleaded with Sandford to do something about him. He and Hailu knew each other from the old days, but the ras never responded to his letter. The Italians were taking a risk in using a man that—as Christine Sandford put it—"had been a double-crosser all his life."[58] Such was his power that Haile Selassie had even written to him from exile, asking him to switch sides. It was no good. While both sides courted Hailu, he played on the fears of those sick of war in Gojjam, promising he was the only one who could prevent them from being gassed by the Italians.

Aosta, not to be outdone, sized up what George Steer was doing and decided to turn British propaganda to his advantage. He had counterfeit versions of the leaflets made, complete with a phony version of the imperial seal and an old shot of Haile Selassie as well. Then he put out a fake announcement to cause mischief. It announced that Mangasha would be made Negus, a reward for his service. The point was to drive a fresh wedge between Mangasha and Nagash and unravel everything Sandford had accomplished. Steer himself conceded this was brilliant, but it had no real impact because the Italians didn't back it up with any proper military momentum.

But the Italians did persuade almost everybody—including the British—that if Haile Selassie was restored to power, there would be reprisals and massacres worse than those under Graziani. At the same time, they spread the contradictory lie that the Emperor was dead, for as George Steer put it, "They resembled lawyers in their calm preparation of alternative defenses."[59]

The Americans easily bought the first one. Off in Rome, US Ambassador William Phillips cabled Cordell Hull: "There is deep concern apparent in Italian circles with regard to the situation of Italian women and children in Italian East Africa now unable to leave the country."[60] In Sekala, even Wilfred Thesiger was convinced there would be bloody vengeance, and had told Sandford so. Sandford doubted it. George Steer thought the idle speculation should be fought with an imperial pardon issued for collaborators, but Haile Selassie held off. He knew that if he issued a pardon from Khartoum, it would alienate the Gojjam Patriots. Once he was in the province, they would accept this gesture in passing as they celebrated his return.

That is, if he ever did return. Eden *still* didn't want to put him in harm's way and recommended keeping him on ice for a few more months. Winston Churchill had never been a friend to Ethiopia, but he responded with a Churchillian snort of mild impatience and appeal to common sense: "One would think the Emperor would be the best judge of when to risk his life for his throne."[61]

When finally came. The geography of the British Empire surrounding Italy's conquests had formed a gigantic fist, and it was beginning to close.

In Egypt, Wavell's forces took back Sidi Barrani in spectacular fashion on December 9. The news hit Rome "like a thunderbolt" according to Ciano, writing in his diary. Mussolini took it calmly enough, but grew increasingly annoyed by the stream of paranoid and panicking telegrams from his general in the field, Graziani, who had never fully recovered from the grenade attack in Addis Ababa. One of his cables harangued the dictator "for never having listened to him, and for having pushed him into an adventure which leads us beyond human possibilities into the realm of destiny."[62] Mussolini read all this out to Ciano and said, "Here is another man with whom I cannot get angry because I despise him."[63]

Graziani was close to another breakdown, sending his wife his will and asking through *her* for German air support in Libya. Weeks later, he made wild accusations to his liaison officer about Badoglio and claimed the only reason he hadn't committed suicide was his strong desire to get back at his old rival. Badoglio, however, had problems of his own. The war was going so badly in Greece that he soon had to quit his position as head of the armed forces. With Graziani summarily yanked out of Libya, it would be Rommel and the Germans who would give the British their worst fights in North Africa.

But long before that, more bad news was on its way to Rome. Brigades of the Indian divisions under Platt took Kassala in the north on January 19 and chased them back to Eritrea along the roads sown with mines and spikes.

The next day, on January 20, the Emperor and his entourage flew to the border spot of Um Idla in two Hurricane fighters, courtesy of the South African air force. His retinue included his two sons, as well as Ras Kassa and Lorenzo Taezaz. Wingate greeted him and made sure there was suitable pomp and ceremony, a speech made, a bugle call, and the imperial standard run up a pole.

For the first time in five years, Haile Selassie stood on Ethiopian soil as the colors of his nation flew proudly overhead.

Chapter Twenty-Three

CHAMPAGNE AND JAZZ RECORDS

Lekelash Bayan couldn't enjoy the happy news that the Emperor had returned. She likely didn't know, and it wouldn't have made much difference anyway. The desperate Italians had hit back hard against the Patriot groups, driving many into the lowlands. And she and her guerrilla fighters were dropping one by one from starvation and disease. "I was so ill that I did not distinguish between day and night," she remembered.[1] Her men carried her, cared for her, but she ended up alone in a hut in February of 1941 as Italian soldiers took out her comrades in a hopeless last stand. Grenades burst, the door was burned open, and then the *ferengi* were hovering over a listless and sick woman who couldn't flee.

"One of the men hit me with the butt of his gun on my shoulder because he thought I was feigning sleep," she recalled. "I was thus taken prisoner with my child."[2] The men captured with her were shot dead or hanged, but she was treated fairly well. In the midst of barbaric Fascist cruelties, the Italians could often be moved to act chivalrously towards Ethiopian women. The attitudes were never consistent throughout the occupation—Shawaragad was tortured, Lekelash was not. She was fortunate. She received medical treatment and respect, no doubt some of it earned by being such a brave foe. But for her, like Shawaragad, the war was over. She would not see freedom until Ethiopia was liberated.

That day was fast approaching.

* * *

The Italians decided to make an example of stubborn courage at one of their familiar launch points: Keren, in Eritrea.

Here, geography was very much their ally. The garrison was surrounded by mountain peaks, and General William Platt and his Indian soldiers spent weeks—and sometimes only hours—taking, losing, and taking again mountain strongholds. The decisive battle dragged out over two months, but when it was done, the Italians were running back to Asmara. Units of the French Foreign Legion, loyal to a Free France, cut off the road behind the town and captured more than a thousand Italian soldiers. Keren is less than sixty miles from Asmara, and it was only a handful of days before the British were walking freely around the capital of the Italians' East African Empire. Meanwhile, General Alan Cunningham and his forces swept up from Kenya and captured Mogadishu on February 24. Italian forces actually *fled* from Cunningham's juggernaut, which had to struggle to keep pace with those running away.

On paper, the Allied push gives the impression of a *deus ex machina*: "Then the British showed up and saved the day." It's true that in many cases, the Ethiopians appear to be offstage for the big show. You can read in different history books all about Wavell, Platt, and Cunningham, about their valiant Sikhs and South African Rifles, all without a single reference for pages and pages to Ethiopians.

But all of this—all of it—was only because the mortars and shelling and big explosions were the finale to the drama that had been playing out for five years. The truth is that the Patriots had worn the Italians down and reduced their whole enterprise to a nervous wreck. The occupation was a battle-fatigued soldier with many faces—Graziani showed one, offering masks of rage and frustration. More often lately, the patient stared out the window in a self-pitying stupor. Sometimes he rallied, but he didn't like the weather much when he stepped outside. At the garrison of Dangila, Colonel Adriano Torelli made forays with a battalion and bande groups, only to get harassed by snipers.

Wingate's Gideon Force was about to finish what the Patriots had started.

The Italians were so desperate that they even abandoned part of their public relations narrative. A new decree was made by the command in Kaffa province, and the correspondent for the *Daily Telegraph* in Sudan got hold of a copy and promptly reported it. "Prisoners taken from forces operating against Italian garrisons in Abyssinia may freely be enslaved and sold or otherwise transferred without any legal hindrance."[3] So much for the Civilizing Mission.

In late February, two days after the British took Mogadishu, Aosta made Ras Seyum the Negus of Tigray and sent him off with three thousand rifles and title deeds to his province. Not being a fool, Aosta made sure he was watched at the garrison in western Tigray. It hardly mattered. Seyum had gone through the pantomime of submission, but his loyalties were always with the Emperor, and he still managed to smuggle a few rifles off to the Patriots.

* * *

After the speeches and pomp at Um Idla, it was time to make the slow way to Belaya. There was Wingate, members of his Gideon Force, the Second Ethiopian Battalion, plus the Emperor, of course, and a modest retinue bringing up the rear.

Bill Allen was with Laurens van der Post's Op Center, and they "found themselves in a strange world as we rode up the highland valley walled in by forested ridges which rose to a broad flat peak five thousand feet above the plain." Allen felt like he had dropped into *King Solomon's Mines*, and he was moved by the geography and people: "For how many thousand years had this people been stranded in these untrodden uplands while the world and its changing races went through the vicissitudes of history . . . These homespun kings and barefoot nobles with the courtly ways of decadence had race-memories of old empires like Aksum and Meroe and Sheba; their life was ancient already when the ancient dynasties ruled Egypt."[4]

As usual, Wingate ignored what natives told him about an easier camel track to follow. Instead, he urged his forces and the Emperor's party to follow along his own chosen route, which led at one point to "a pool where the elephants drink." The trucks broke down frequently, but they eventually made it to the target camp, marked by piles of elephant dung. The Emperor surprised them by explaining that there were fish in the nearby pool; he proved it by dragging the water with his own personal mosquito net, treating the grateful camp to an evening meal of thirty fish.

Lieutenant Colonel Hugh Boustead had been allowed to take his men along the easier route and was already waiting for Wingate. When the leader of Gideon Force finally trudged into Belaya, he at least had the decency to say, "You were right, and I was wrong."[5]

After reaching Belaya, Wingate took time out to fly back to Khartoum. He went to Sudan a major and came back an acting colonel, now with the security that he was overall commander of British and Ethiopian forces in Gojjam. Sandford was bumped up to brigadier, which prompted bitter envy on Wingate's part. His resentment of the older man never ceased, and he would keep complaining about Sandford to HQ for the rest of the campaign.

When van der Post's Op Center linked up with Wingate's main force at Matakel on February 28, Bill Allen got another chance to glimpse ancient practices seemingly frozen in time. The Emperor held a reception for Patriots from the surrounding hills, and warriors came down to boast their achievements and to slaughter bullocks for the feast. The soldiers of the Op Centers were grateful for the rich meal and the tej. Afterwards, Haile Selassie sat under a tree at a camp table covered in a red plush cloth, lit by one candle lamp. Allen thought he looked frail and ill from the hard journey in; it hadn't occurred to Wingate to *fly* the Emperor into Belaya when he himself could hop-scotch back to Khartoum to meet his superiors. Still, Haile Selassie spoke like a host to guests, talking in French and letting the British officers fill up on whiskey, Turkish delight, and pistachios. The next morning, it was back to the grind of climbing the Escarpment.

The key to Wingate's plan was an incredible bluff. The Italians knew the British were coming in force. They expected them in force. Wingate wanted to use guerrilla tactics to make the Italians believe they were bigger than they were, as if they were forward units of a massive army. In Gojjam, he divided his forces in two. A smaller one—what would be called Begemder Force—would cut the road from Gonder to Dessie to contain the Italians in the north. The larger half would seize a bridge over the Blue Nile at a place called Safertek in the south. It was the only route for the Italians over the river, and this would foil their retreat, as well as cut off Debra Markos, the provincial capital, from Addis Ababa. Meanwhile, Wingate would drive the Italians to distraction with a series of night raids. In theory, all of this sounded brilliant, as imaginative strategies always do. In practice, it would be harder than all that.

Belaya was the first major port of call, and supplies had to be rushed up for a long wait through the rainy season. The camels suffered in the rough and barren lava ridges. They broke their legs. They starved in long stretches where there was nothing to graze. They were pushed to their limits and collapsed in exhaustion. One day Haile Selassie counted fifty-seven of these beasts either dying or dead on the road, and he pointed to a heap of bones for one animal and said, "He died for Ethiopia."[6]

Over the first half of February, the RAF bombed Italian positions to the east at Dangila and Burie, but the planes were soon needed at Keren. Still, this did the trick, and soon the Italians were pulling out of the region. Wingate hoped to attack Dangila, but the fort's seasoned commander, Colonel Torelli, was convinced because of the air raids that a whole British division was on its way. So he ordered his soldiers with their ten thousand horses and artillery to retreat to Bahr Dar, to the northeast. There had been a similar withdrawal of forces from the garrison at Enjibara. Mangasha Jimbari and his Patriots had an actual picnic—they raided the tinned foods the Italians left behind and drank their Chianti.

Perhaps it was just as well that Gideon Force didn't see action for a while. At the tail end of February, the fifteen hundred men of the Second Ethiopian Battalion and the battalion of Sudanese regulars were slogging along on night marches to avoid being bombed during the day. But things soon devolved into farce. It was cold and dark, and the Ethiopians had no training for night maneuvers. Men fell asleep on their feet from exhaustion while others got lost. After they were sent out to gather wood for fires and light guide beacons, they did it so well that they lit up the countryside, making their positions easy targets—and here they were, less than five miles from an Italian command center. Wingate decided to switch to a system of low whistles and using flashlights so that units could recognize each other. One problem: the Ethiopians didn't know how to whistle.

There is a long list of historians stunned by Wingate's unbelievable luck. In all this chaos of flashlights blinking away, whistles tweeting over hills, blazing fires of tinder and brush, it's a small miracle the Italians didn't irritably jump out of their beds and go massacre the column on the spot for disturbing their sleep. Yet this noisy arrival of what was supposed to be a "stealth" force might have actually helped. The Italians assumed the big, bad British army was on its way.[7]

All these clumsy errors prompted Wingate to break the forces up into smaller units, ones easier to manage. His new, slimmed-down teams now went to cause havoc at various Italian outposts nearby, like Mankusa and Dambacha. They made their nightly raids on outposts from Burie to Debra Markos, using mortars to cause terror and chaos, resorting to sniper attacks to make the Italians grind their teeth and lose more of their jangled nerves. His grand bluff seems even more incredible given that many of the native soldiers were learning their craft as they went along. Wingate discovered in a raid, for instance, that one of his men, Makonnen Desta, needed training on the mortar—while they were under enemy fire.

As time went on, the British officers grew in many ways to resemble the Ethiopian Patriots. They couldn't have the big black halos, of course, but they were a shaggy bunch in their thick beards and scruffy hair, their clothes pricked and torn by thorn bushes and coated in dust. Wingate seemed to make a personal point of not washing and offended many of his fellow British soldiers with his lack of hygiene.

Like the Ethiopians, he was also learning on the go. For the Italian garrison at Mankusa, he tried the experiment of a coordinated attack with both his troops and Patriot bands. Mankusa was a special key—it protected the main road for the other forts at Dambacha and Jigga to Debra Markos. It also served as the Italians' major supply line and path to retreat. But after he gave the order to attack, the Patriots stampeded so recklessly ahead that they were hit by the Sudanese mortar shells. These wild Ethiopian guerrillas, decided Wingate, should be left to operate on their own.

He got mixed results, too, when he asked the RAF to make a raid on Burie, which stood between his forces and the true prize waiting, Debra Markos. One of the two planes sent out was shot down. But the presence of air support was more encouragement for the Patriots—and a bad sign to the Italians. At Burie, Colonel Leopoldo Natale knew his retreat might be cut off by the great, big (and fictional) British army on its way, plus there was a local Ethiopian leader just *itching* for a sign to change allegiances and use his warriors on Natale's men. So he decided to get out while the getting was good, evacuating his garrison. On March 4, an hour before dawn, there were trucks and armored cars, cavalry, and bande all on the road and heading in retreat—and right through Mankusa.

Wingate and his small force were still busy there with an attack, and they were caught completely by surprise. He and his merry band soon realized they'd better run for their lives as the enemy swelled in numbers—an enemy in retreat, yes, but large all the same.

As Wingate climbed a ridge, he came across Hugh Boustead, who was having his morning meal. Boustead was yet another odd duck for Gideon Force, a small man with a face tanned and creased like a walnut. Back in the Great War, Boustead had actually deserted his Royal Navy ship in a safe, comfy South African port to go fight for France (he was later decorated *and* pardoned by George V). He had even seen action with White Russian armies, and he normally would have outranked Wingate. But Boustead wasn't the one entrusted with command of Gideon Force.

Now Wingate, in one of his Tasmanian Devil tizzies, demanded to know why Boustead hadn't rushed to the rescue with his Sudanese fighters.

Boustead pointed up to the Italian planes swooping over the open countryside. "Because," he said, "there would then have been no Gideon at all. Have some breakfast."[8]

* * *

It might have been a good thing that Boustead wasn't in charge. Wilfred Thesiger liked him well enough, but recognized that he didn't have Wingate's imagination. While Gideon Force had its setbacks, the strategy was proving effective—but not without a cost.

In early March, the Second Ethiopian Battalion was taking potshots at the enemy in Dembecha, helped now and then by Patriots led by Haile Yusuf, a small, delicately featured aristocrat. Sandford had vouched for his fighting skills, but the British took to calling him "Highly Useless." Wingate sent Thesiger to be Gideon Force's liaison, and Thesiger was with the guerrillas as they attacked a village and drove off the Italians' cattle and mules. Then on the night of March 5, the Patriots noticed in the distance a black mass of soldiers heading their way. Thesiger sent a runner to warn the battalion.

The battalion was camped right where the highway to Dembecha met the Charaka River, which turned out to be the worst possible choice. The idea was to stay hidden in shoulder-high elephant grass, but the seven British officers and three hundred Ethiopians snoozed away that night on ground that sloped *down* away from a ridge, with the river between them and the Italians in Dembecha— which is where they assumed the enemy still was. Unfortunately, the six thousand Italian soldiers under Colonel Natale were barging their way south. They were about to catch the battalion on the wrong side of the river, plus they would cut off its access to the camels, which were grazing on the other side of Charaka's bridge. Natale's bande cavalry would rustle them soon enough.

The battalion's commander was a 40-year-old major, Ted Boyle, who used to work for a liquor company in Nairobi. Boyle would earn a lot of heat for his location choice later, but he and his men had been out of touch with Wingate for close to a week. They had no idea that out of the blue, Natale was trying to cross the eleven miles to the fort at Dembecha, eager to get away from Hugh Boustead's snipers. Just as the light was coming up at dawn, the Italians spotted one of the companies of the battalion.

Boyle and his men recovered from the shock just in time. They were setting up breakfast. The battalion had never been under fire before, but they put up fierce resistance. One British sergeant shot away at askari troops with a Lewis gun that kept jamming, and he had to dig his penknife several times into the breach like a frantic dentist, yanking out cartridges while machine guns blazed away in his direction. Fortunately, the askaris in the elephant grass wore red epaulettes—they might as well have had targets on them. Lieutenant Michael Tutton, an Oxford scholar with a side interest in bees and bugs, compared the horrible odds and the four-hour battle to the Spartans at the Hot Gates. He kept firing his rifle while bleeding from grenade splinters in his leg. At one point, another grenade smacked him right in the thigh . . . and failed to go off. An Ethiopian sergeant major scooped it up, pulled out the pin that was still in it, and hurled the grenade back at the enemy.

While one Ethiopian pitched cricket with grenades, another played rugby with other weapons. A lance corporal, Wandafrash Falaka, made a mad dash across the road with a Boys anti-tank rifle, a beast at thirty pounds with a thirty-inch barrel. British soldiers treated it with scorn because it couldn't punch a hole in heavily armored tanks, but Wandrafrash either didn't know this or didn't care. He blasted away, and as machine guns tore up the hillside around him, he calmly changed magazines and took out two armored cars. Job done, he ditched the Boys, knowing the Italians couldn't use it if they picked it up—he'd run off with the rifle bolt.

From a hilltop, Haile Yusuf watched the carnage below, and Thesiger thought it looked like a battle from Napoleon's time. Later, the British were furious that "Highly Useless" had apparently lived up to his nickname again, but Thesiger was on his side. He argued in his autobiography that the guerrillas kept pressure on the Dembecha garrison and its nearby village—the soldiers there couldn't rush to the Italian column's rescue and attack the battalion's rear. As it turned out, the mere presence of the guerrillas on the ridge was pivotal. Natale had overwhelmed Boyle's three hundred, but fearing the Patriots might join the fight, he withdrew his forces. He abandoned the hulks of armored cars and plunged on to Dembecha while the guerrillas ran down and plundered the dead bodies of soldiers on both sides. This only angered the British more, cursing them as shiftas and vultures.

Historians have criticized the Patriot looting, and David Shirreff, who served in the campaign, considered it "inexcusable."[9] Thesiger, always the Ethiopian advocate, saw things differently and pointed out that Hailu Yusuf and his men made sorties to harass the Italians as they moved on. The skirmishes might even have helped push Natale to give up Dembecha as well, which he soon did. If Shirreff could argue that the guerrillas weren't anxious to be killed at the last minute, Thesiger could turn this accusation back on itself. He reminded any and all that the Ethiopians had put in five long years of fighting with *no one* risking their lives for them.

At the end, Tutton's analogy to Spartans didn't fit (after all, the Spartans were obliterated). The battle was more like an Ethiopian Agincourt. Natale's army limped away with 122 native soldiers killed to only twenty-one Ethiopians lost out of the three hundred. More than two hundred Italian troops were wounded, ten of them officers, while the Ethiopians were bandaging only forty-eight of their own, plus two British soldiers. One British officer was captured, but he would have to endure only two months of captivity as the Liberation neared its climax. True, Natale had bulldozed through and slipped away, but making the Italians scamper off was supposed to be the whole point, wasn't it?

Blunders and all, Charaka gave ample proof that Gideon Force was getting the job done. In a mere two weeks of fighting, the Italians had practically abandoned all of western Gojjam.

* * *

But there were problems, and serious ones at that. After Charaka, more than one hundred soldiers of the Second Ethiopian Battalion mutinied. The Ethiopians could put up with a lot, and they had adapted to harsh British discipline; Thesiger flogged soldiers for looting. But the men of the Second had reached their limit of being slapped by their white officers, including Major Ted Boyle. Another officer had made them give up a freshly dug grave for an Italian instead of one of their own. Boyle was fired and left to command a Somali Scout battalion.

In terms of nasty treatment, Wingate was guilty himself—he once slapped his interpreter. Yet despite all his bluster and moods, the leader of Gideon Force was genuinely concerned for the people he was fighting for. He later annoyed Boustead (again) when he wrote somewhat dismissively of a young British officer's death, arguing the man had "died to put right a wrong done in 1935 and also, which is probably more important, to give the black races of Africa a chance to realize a free civilization."[10] It was this attitude and more that earned him the lasting admiration of some Ethiopians. Ayana Berre, a captain who fought at Mankusa and in other battles, recalled that Wingate "was so friendly towards me [and] made me proud and fearless, even of death." His theatricality may have irritated some British, but when combined with his courage, it impressed the young Patriot. Someone once told him to get down, and Wingate answered, "I do not fear death! Because even if I die, my name shall not."[11]

The debate goes on over Wingate and Sandford. Who did more for the Liberation? Who had the superior strategy? On it goes. And these are the *wrong* questions.

Because at the end of the day, *both* men's strategies made the Ethiopian a subordinate cog in the British military machine. Yes, Sandford championed Haile Selassie leading his own army, but he also allegedly put Kebede Tessema in his place. As for Wingate, he didn't trust the Patriots with the heavy grunt work of fighting. Moral support? Yes. But their fighting value? To him, negligible. His one coordinated raid with the Patriots had been a disaster, and he never tried another.

So the real question is: if the Patriots were so instrumental in damaging the enemy before the British arrival, and if they were still useful to Mission 101 later, why couldn't the most reliable guerrilla bands be trained and evolve into Op Centers? In spite of Hailu Yusuf and Mangasha's moods, there were Patriot leaders who were dependable, who could have been trained with mortars, given anti-tank guns, and trusted to carry on the fight. Ras Imru, Lekelash Bayan, and Shawaragad Gadle had already set heroic examples. True, these leaders were in prison, yet there had to be others.

When it came down to it, the British didn't have faith that most of the Ethiopians could change or receive advanced training. There was the Patriot who could be left to do his own thing and cause trouble for the enemy, and there was the Ethiopian who could be trained like any nineteen-year-old white private from the Midlands—and then used as cannon fodder. But there was no middle road where he got to be an equal partner in Wingate's grand plan.

Once again, it was George Steer who cut to the essence, the truth about the campaign that spoke to more than just the moment, but to our own modern era.

The Ethiopian patriot movement that we fanned with our propaganda is a small candle held to the bonfire that could be raised in
Europe by the combination of small *corps d'elite* [Wingate's princi-
ple] and propaganda contact with oppressed populations. We would
probably find a large proportion of the latter as pusillanimous as were
many Ethiopian patriots, but they give us a weapon which handled
coolly could tie down the enemy everywhere in Europe, while we
fight our Keren against him on our own chosen ground. Modern
guerrilla war is not the wild rush of the tribesmen or the peasants'
billhooks; it is the idea of fear, of revenge in the dark, the unwillingness to abandon this or that territory for reasons of prestige until the
opportunity to do so without disgrace has passed—it is these things
all combined that paralyze an enemy and spread-eagle half his fighting forces to the ground.[12]

These words are from his book on the campaign, *Sealed and Delivered*. It
was in bookshops in 1942, while the war was still very much on. The French
Résistance at home was barely organized. The Americans had just entered the
fight and were getting bloodied and beaten back by the Japanese. Read his words
again: "the unwillingness to abandon this or that territory for *reasons of prestige
until the opportunity to do so without disgrace has passed . . .*"

Here is the theme that would haunt the French in Algeria, both the French
and the United States in Vietnam, the United States in Iraq, and the Soviets and
Americans in Afghanistan.

* * *

General Guglielmo Nasi was so incensed by Natale's retreat that he fired him
and brought in a replacement: Colonel Saverio Maraventano. Maraventano
was from Sicily, a man who could have had a promising career holding a violin
bow instead of a rifle. In the Great War, he was decorated for valor fighting
the Austrians and then was taken as a POW. He was not a fool, and as a commander, he preferred moving forward to backward, unlike Natale. Unfortunately
for Maraventano, the British were still closing in on all sides of Ethiopia. There
was nowhere to run anyway. Nasi tried to use this truth in a motivational talk to
soldiers at the Debra Markos garrison. He informed them "it was a long road to
Rome."

Maraventano now had the thankless mission of trying to take back what his
predecessor had given up with barely a fight. A Sudanese platoon had moved in

and grown comfortable at one of the abandoned garrisons, Emmanuel, on the road to Debra Markos. Maraventano launched a full-out assault on March 19, sending planes, artillery, and two battalions—a swatter far too big for the fly. As it happened, Wingate wasn't caring about Emmanuel because he already had Debra Markos in his sights. By then, he was in the Gulit Hills, overlooking the garrison there, sometimes crawling on his belly along with his men up to the wire, preparing to toss grenades.

Then all of a sudden, it didn't matter what countermeasures Maraventano had in mind. Aosta pulled the plug. He had no other choice, as one look at a map showed how hopeless his situation was becoming. By the early morning hours of March 27, Platt had a Union Jack flying over Keren, and that meant Asmara and Massawa would soon fall. Cunningham had snatched British Somaliland back out of Italian hands. For six years, Caproni bombers ruled the skies above Ethiopia's mountains, but in a single raid, South African planes soared over Addis Ababa and decimated thirty of their aircraft peacefully parked on the airfield.

Yet even at this point, victory wasn't assured. It could all come to nothing, because Aosta, for all the criticisms coming from his Duce and Ciano in Rome, *did* know how to look at a map. And he saw something that must have made him smile.

Aosta told Maraventano to evacuate his forces—twelve thousand strong—and take them across the Blue Nile Gorge through Shoa, where the local Muslim peasants would be less hostile to his army in retreat. Maybe they'd get lucky, and the Muslims would stay out of their way. The Italians would settle in at Gonder and even give up Addis Ababa for a while. The summer rains were coming— stalemate. The British would be stuck before they could take it all. What Aosta had in mind was a shrewd gamble that someone else would come to clean up his mess. That someone else would be Erwin Rommel.

The German panzers that steamrolled through France hadn't tipped off the British yet to just how formidable an opponent they had, but they were about to find out. They knew Rommel was now in Libya, preparing a major assault, but they were convinced he wouldn't be rumbling onto their ground until after summer. And that's exactly what his own commanders in Berlin wanted. They told him wait where you are, stay put. Rommel didn't. Churchill, hearing about this German general's tentative approach to British lines at El Agheila (five hundred miles east of Tripoli), sent Wavell a message: "I presume you are only waiting for the tortoise to stick his head out far enough before chopping it off."[13] Churchill presumed too much, and his generals off in North Africa did, too. The tortoise was actually a fox in the desert. Rommel, flouting his orders, sent his tanks rolling in a blitzkrieg on March 30, plowing his way toward Benghazi and Libya's port city of Derna.

Why should any of this matter to Aosta? Because he knew that deep down, the British cared far more about Egypt than Ethiopia. And he hoped they would pull their division out to run to Egypt's rescue, abandoning the defense of Gojjam. Between the rains and Rommel, maybe Italy could keep one foot planted in their hard-won colony.

Wingate had already sent Thesiger to join Belay Zeleke and his Patriots for an attack on Maraventano's column before it slipped across the Blue Nile Gorge. But Belay Zeleke, riding a caparisoned black mule, was in no great hurry. Thesiger was eager to get into position, but he and his men couldn't go on ahead—they relied on the Ethiopian guerrillas for their food. By April 5, word came that the Italian forces in retreat had made it into Shoa as planned. It turned out later that Ras Hailu had persuaded Belay Zeleke to drag his feet by offering him the chance to marry his daughter.[14] Once again, the old feudal politics ruined the chance to hurt the enemy. Still, Sudanese soldiers and Patriots buzzed like hornets around Maraventano's column, pricking and annoying it as it kept moving.

The good news was that when Wingate did finally reach Debra Markos, he had the chance to pull off one of his signature bluffs. An American foreign correspondent, Edmund Stevens, was tagging along that day, and as they roamed the abandoned garrison, they heard a field telephone spring to life—the line connected the garrison to another one along the Blue Nile. "Ha," said one of Wingate's British officers, "that's the Italians. Apparently, they don't yet know we're here."

Wingate suddenly dreamed up a bit of mischief. "You speak Italian," he said to Stevens. It didn't matter to him that Sevens was supposed to be a neutral on two counts—one, as an American, and two, as a journalist. "Call them back and tell them that a British division, ten thousand strong, is on its way up the road." Wingate even had a lie prepared in case they asked Stevens who he was (he was to pretend to be the camp's physician, who had stayed behind).[15]

Stevens cranked the handle of the phone, yelled *"Pronto!"* down the line and then gave the switchboard operator at the other end Wingate's message.

The operator panicked. "What shall we do?"

"If you want my advice," replied Stevens, "clear out quick as you can."[16]

The trick worked. Hours later, seven hundred Ethiopians captured another abandoned fort, thanks to a little American help.

In abandoning Debra Markos, Maraventano left the irregular soldiers to their fate under Ras Hailu. Hailu knew it was all over, but he still thought he could buy himself time. The British officers sent word that RAF planes would bomb his citadel to rubble if he didn't surrender. Then grenades were hurled at the palace of his daughter, who wasn't home. It was no good. Hailu wouldn't budge; he still wanted to haggle. The last weapon he had left was the bluff of his own majestic presence, and it worked up to a point. His cousin, Makonnen Desta, kissed the traitor's hand and his knees in a revolting gesture of fealty. It was typical of Hailu that his first order of business was to get an assurance that his own property wouldn't be looted. He made it clear that he would only submit to the Emperor.

Haile Selassie's view was, "You want me, here I come." On a new makeshift road that was an impressive feat of Sudanese labor, a British convoy of trucks climbed the rugged terrain in early April. The Emperor was chauffeured in a truck by the French-Canadian manager of Renault's plant in Ethiopia. Hailu didn't endear himself by showing up twenty minutes late, and when the Emperor gave a speech to the troops, the traitor was properly ignored.

When Belay Zeleke showed up outside Debra Markos, oblivious to the fact that he could be seen as a collaborator, Wingate informed him that if he came near the town, he'd be shot. He argued over Belay with Haile Selassie, who insisted he had to see him. Wingate had no choice but to let the appointment happen, but he arranged for four machine guns to be stationed around the throne, their sights set on Belay.

For all their plots, neither Hailu nor Belay fared well afterwards. Belay Zeleke ended up an outlaw and swinging from a noose in 1945. Hailu, who would be forced to go back to the capital with the Emperor, would never see Gojjam again—still a noble, but powerless. Off in Harar, another traitor, a fitawrari who traded his loyalty to the Italians to be a dejazmach, committed suicide.

* * *

In Rome, Mussolini was realizing that his prestige had been built all this time on a sandcastle. The African ants had swarmed their way in and made it crumble, and now the British tide was washing it away. Members of his own inner circle were telling jokes about him. Marshal Emilio De Bono, who never forgot the snub of being relieved of his command, told a good one in the presence of a journalist—and right in the anteroom of the Italian Senate. "Hitler and Mussolini met at the Brenner Pass," said De Bono, "in the usual private railroad car . . ."

After their conversation had gone on for a bit (the joke went), Hitler excused himself to leave for a couple of minutes. Mussolini noticed a bottle of champagne, but when he tried to open it, the cork shot into his face and gave him a black eye. Hitler walked back in, took one look at the bruised Italian dictator, and shook his head. "Duce, Duce, if I leave you alone for a minute, you get beaten up!" The senators "roared with laughter" just before they filed into the chamber and made the usual obligatory cheers for their dictator.[17]

The joke was being told all over Rome, but De Bono had made a dangerous mistake in telling it. More than anything, dictators *hate* to be laughed at.

* * *

For Ethiopians in Addis Ababa, the mood was euphoric. They knew their Emperor was coming. The Italians were so afraid they would fall into the hands of Patriots instead of the British that they sent petrol to the British army units stationed at Awash. Some Patriots had already managed to slip into the capital, and Imru Zelleke recalled that "with their big Afros and beards and tattered clothes and their bandoliers and guns hanging from their shoulders, they were indeed a scary lot."[18] But these stragglers didn't do anything. The Emperor's prohibition against reprisals held.

There would be bloodshed all the same.

Imru recalls that when the Emperor's arrival seemed imminent, he was wandering the streets with his close friend, Hailu Gebru, who knew English and had once worked as an interpreter for foreign correspondents during the invasion. Several Ethiopians—including prominent members of the underground resistance—planned to meet in a restaurant in the Mercato, the popular marketplace, to discuss what to do once the war was over. Hailu Gebru wanted to go. Imru thought his mother and the rest of the family might worry if he stayed out, so he decided to head home.

At the restaurant, there was a heated debate, plus one very unwelcome visitor: Ras Getachew Abate. He had followed Haile Selassie into exile in Jerusalem, but eventually decided to come home and submit to the Italians. A known collaborator, he turned up now on the regime's orders to try to quell the meeting. Why he would still want to help them in their intrigues remains a mystery, given that the Emperor and the British were due to arrive soon. But no one wanted to listen to him anyway, and after a few minutes, he left.

Then Italian soldiers arrived. They sprayed the restaurant with machine gun fire, wounding many of the patrons. But there was only one fatality.

When Imru got word of the shooting, he rushed over to the Lambie Hospital,* but there was nothing he could do. The doctors told him that Hailu had been practically cut in half by the machine guns. The first days of liberation for Imru Zelleke would no longer be full of pure joy. Now they were colored by the

---

* It was later renamed the Pasteur Institute.

heartbreaking tragedy that his friend was gone and would never live to see the free Ethiopia, mere hours away from being reborn.

* * *

South African forces captured Addis Ababa on April 6. Heroes like Shawaragad Gadle and Lekelash Bayan were soon released, telling their stories, reuniting with friends. But Lieutenant-General Alan Cunningham, still fearing a massacre, did all he could to throw up delays to the Emperor's arrival in the capital. Strict orders came out of Khartoum to Daniel Sandford that the Emperor was "not to be allowed" to enter Addis Ababa. The British finally wrapped up their security measures by the end of April, and the date was set for the Emperor to come home: May 5, the day the Italians had captured Addis Ababa.

In the capital, Ethiopians painted their flag on their houses and made garlands of flowers. Thousands of Italian residents wisely chose to stay behind doors. But for all the British paranoia over the natives on a rampage of rape, Italian women billeted at the Hotel Imperiale didn't complain about Ethiopians—it was a group of British junior officers who molested them, and an armed sentry had to be posted.[19] There were moments when the Italians tried crude appeals to racial solidarity, which failed completely with George Steer, the liberal South African: "They whose countryman was Machiavelli asked me how we English, who prided ourselves on our fairness, could stoop so low as to use a native potentate against fellow whites."[20]

Not everyone was as enlightened as Steer. Captain Michael Tutton was disgusted by the warriors who were "ferocious looking savages with huge mops of filthy black hair" and whose faces "appeared to be stamped with every vice under the sun, cruelty, greed, cowardice, cunning, lechery, and ignorance . . ." He confided to his diary, "It horrifies me to call these brutish savages our allies against a white race for whom I once had some affection."[21] But Tutton was another one of those walking British contradictions of the war, just like Bill Allen and his discarded Fascist sympathies. Tutton, who had always enjoyed the devotion of his Ethiopian fighters, would die six months later from a shot to the groin; he would urge his men to go on fighting as they carried him to safety.

On that morning of May 5, about fifteen thousand Patriots of Abebe Aregai's forces marched into the city, triumphant in their wild Afros and rags. There were women warriors in men's clothes, carrying rifles. A few Italian prisoners were paraded in chains. At around noon, Steer's loudspeaker van drove through, then South Africans on motorcycles and in armored cars. A pack of journalists rode in a couple of Italian fire engines. Orde Wingate, having shaved his beard but keeping his pith helmet, held a leather whip as he rode a white horse. The horse was originally meant for Haile Selassie, but the Emperor was saddlesore and chose instead to be chauffeured in a black Ford convertible. The sight of the Emperor was electric. Ethiopians prostrated themselves and threw flowers and rushed the car in a joyful surge, which frightened three police horses into throwing their riders. Wingate himself had to keep a tight hold on his reins.

Cunningham, who had forced the Emperor to wait weeks, now had to exercise his own patience as he stood with an honor guard at Menelik's old palace. When the Emperor finally mounted the rostrum, his speech included a predictable reference to the Bible: "On this day Ethiopia, indeed, stretches out her hands to God, shouting and telling out her joy to her own sons!"

In the afternoon, a rain shower fell and seemed to wash away the colors of the capital, leaving it a temporary gray. George Steer stepped up to a window of Menelik's audience hall, and as a small boy would do, pressed his nose against the cold pane to see. Haile Selassie was inside, drinking champagne with British officers. At four o'clock, the Emperor went back to his Little Gibbi. Steer checked his watch and thought of the vanity of men's ambitions, how it was so much better to "live peaceably, and humbly, and read a book and go for a walk with one's wife and drink with the friends of one's youth and let sleeping dogs lie."[22] He remembered how General Pietro Badoglio had driven past the gates of the capital at the same hour five years ago, expecting the Italian Empire to last forever.

Steer felt good about what had been accomplished. "We had freed the first of the cruelly treated nations," he wrote in his memoir of the campaign. "Our forces could now be sent to other fronts . . . Whatever the future, the Ethiopians were happy."[23] The daughters of Charles Martin—Sarah and Elizabeth, the wife of his friend Yilma Deressa—invited him to come to a dance. It was the first dance held since the Italians had arrived through the dust clouds of their deadly convoy. Sarah had been collecting American jazz records since her release from prison, and someone else brought the old vinyl records of tunes before 1935. Steer ended his book on this scene, with the moving prose that had become his signature:

> Everybody there except me, the only Englishman, had lost a brother or father or cousin under the Italians. But something made them forget it. They were dancing. Tasfai sat against the wall. "Come on, Tasfai," we said, "show us the steps of your youth at Mon Cine and the Perroquet in the old days." That was the last time Tasfai had taken the floor. He smiled and got up in his English pinstripe suit and

carefully selected his partner; a little rusty on his feet he seemed, after those many weary months.[24]

*　*　*

The rest was a mop-up operation. Before he'd left for his triumphant entry into Addis Ababa, the Emperor had gotten in touch with the Patriot leaders in Shoa. And Abebe Aregai was ordered to send troops north to help the British finish off Aosta. A fitawrari was sent to keep herding the enemy that retreated southwest. When it was time to sweep the Italian hold-outs from the countryside west of the capital, Haile Selassie put himself under fire once again, though the danger by then was likely minimal. What is more interesting, as Dan Sandford's wife, Christine, noted, was that Amharic, Oromo, and Gurage* people fought side by side.[25]

Not everyone took their marching orders so well. While they were getting flushed elsewhere, some Italian units had apparently dug in around Gonder and Jimma, managing to destroy the bridge over the Gibe River. So Haile Selassie put the Patriot leader, Geressu Duki, in charge of prying Jimma away from the enemy. The story goes that Geressu sent word back, asking, "Please send Jagama Kello down to help our efforts here." This was reasonable, and so the Emperor promptly wrote the young general a letter, summoning him to go help Geressu. "But I refused and threw away the letter," says Jagama. What was this Emperor to him? How could he give him commands? "He doesn't know me."[26]

This, of course, did not go down well with the King of Kings and Elect of God. Fortunately, another Patriot stepped in to smooth things over: Shawaragad Gadle.[27] She and Jagama, of course, had worked together before, most notably in the raid on Addis Alem. She had heard that he was refusing the orders, but informed Haile Selassie ever so gently that Jagama Kello, after all, was quite young and that "all I needed was a little coercing."

The Emperor—who by now had needed to smooth the ruffled feathers of many a Patriot leader—wrote to Jagama again. *He* would come to Ginchi, Jagama's home base, and the general should wait for him.

It must have been quite a first meeting. There was Haile Selassie, the tiny Emperor, meeting a tall youth barely out of his teens who had behind him thirty-five hundred men, all with Afros and braids. The Emperor inspected Jagama's army, then had the young general accompany him back to Addis Ababa to further report on his activities. He clearly liked what he heard, because he gave Jagama

---

* An ethnic people from the southwest of Ethiopia.

twenty-five thousand thalers—and then sent him off to finally help Geressu push the Italians out of Jimma, which they did.

In fact, according to Jagama, while Geressu's army was stuck at the Gibe River, he and his men found a detour and confronted the Italian forces. He captured two air force commanders, arranged a surrender, and then Geressu's army finished things off by seizing the Italians' weapons and property. "And that was the end of the Jimma war."[28]

It wasn't the end, however, of Jagama Kello being stubborn. Shortly afterwards, he fell sick with malaria and returned to Addis Ababa to check into a hospital. But a British doctor informed him that unless he cut his massive Afro (presumably on an excuse of hygienic reasons), he wouldn't be admitted. Jagama refused. Once again, Haile Selassie had to pay a visit to the boy general, coming around to his house. "You better cut this," he was told. And by now it was understood that when the Emperor said *you better*, it amounted to an order. Jagama duly had a haircut—and his life was saved.[29]

* * *

Colonel Saverio Maraventano put up an impressive fight with his column all through April into May, fending off Sudanese and Ethiopian forces. Wilfred Thesiger, now in charge of an Op Center, was determined to force his surrender, but his unit got a bad thrashing when the Italians tried one of their cavalry charges, managing to kill the brave Wandafrash Falaka. Then Maraventano dug himself in on a miserably cold mountain, Addis Dera, more than nine thousand feet high. Ras Kassa's Patriots were with Wingate, who decided they would be the perfect instrument for a final bluff.

Wingate sent Maraventano word that if the Italians didn't give up soon, he would pull out his British officers and men and leave them to Kassa's Shoan warriors. "If you refuse this last offer, control passes out of my hand."[30] Maraventano didn't buy it, though he was terribly low on ammo and food. It was just as well, because if he decided to push his way out, Wingate would be in genuine trouble. He had even less.

Maraventano blinked first. He gave up on May 23, and thousands of soldiers dumped their rifles in a pile near a squad of machine-gun-toting guards and marched down to a valley. Only then did they see that they'd been conned. Wingate and Kassa had very few men under their command.

A similar scene had played out days before on May 19 at Amba Alagi. This was where Aosta had fled after leaving the capital. His gamble on a German distraction had failed miserably. After the Italian wounded were taken out of the deep caves in the mountain, about forty-five hundred soldiers began marching down while British pipers played. No sooner were they rid of their guns than all the bravado was dropped. Some Italians made for the field kitchen to have a cup of coffee or went to bathe in a nearby stream.

There was an honor guard waiting for Aosta to inspect before he surrendered to an Indian officer. At the end of all the pomp, he shook hands with General William Platt, and then it was another trip, a long one, to Eritrea. British officers saluted the duke as he left, and Aosta called out in English, "Good luck!"

He reminded his soldiers before they surrendered that the war wasn't over, and perhaps he believed it. But the war was definitely over for him. Aosta spent the rest of his days in a prisoner of war camp in Kenya. He died less than a year later of tuberculosis—which happened to be a common disease at Danane and Nokra.

When the Emperor decided to hold a parade of prisoners, Colonel Maraventano complained to Wilfred Thesiger that this wasn't civilized. "It's barbarous to humiliate prisoners so."

Thesiger, the white Ethiopian, snapped coldly, "Don't dare to speak to me about barbarous treatment of prisoners." He rattled off a list of Italian atrocities, including the massacres in Debre Libanos and Addis Ababa. "Now you have the effrontery to stand there and talk about barbarous treatment of prisoners. A few days ago in Agibar, I found photographs of your officers holding by the hair the severed heads of Abyssinians, with their feet on the corpses. Perhaps you yourself took part in the Roman triumph which Mussolini held in Rome at the end of the war, when Abyssinian prisoners were paraded. Now it's your turn."[31]

Maraventano and his men could either march or be driven by Ras Kassa's warriors, and Thesiger "didn't care which." The next day, the parade was a solemn affair, with Kassa riding on a mule and the Emperor watching with sad eyes. The ordinary people betrayed nothing of what they felt, neither anger nor grief.

Chapter Twenty-Four

"THAT WAS ANOTHER WAR"

During the heady, ecstatic days in May after his arrival in the capital, Haile Selassie was looking for new friends, because he was soon disillusioned again with his old ones.

His country was being subjected to humiliating conditions as if it were a newly conquered land instead of a liberated one. Even the name for the temporary administration was an insult: the Occupied Enemy Territories Administration. As the Emperor himself pointed out, Ethiopia was not "occupied enemy territory" at all, but a reclaimed sovereign nation. But the British were throwing their weight around and had even installed Ras Seyum as governor of Tigray without his permission—and without the crucial, face-saving gesture for all of submission first to the Emperor.

It would be many years, too, before the truth emerged over the war's shameful aftermath. Sylvia Pankhurst found parts of the puzzle in the 1950s and disclosed them in *Eritrea on the Eve*, but her revelations made little impact. And she didn't find the whole picture—that would have to wait for decades until her investigation was picked up and completed by her historian son, Richard. In the National Archives at Kew, he discovered how the British had plundered everything they could get their hands on from the land they had liberated.

Mere days after Italy's surrender, the East Africa Command and the War Office decided to help themselves to goods and industrial works built up in the colonies; everything from railway construction goods to a brick factory to an oxygen plant, all resources and materials Ethiopia could have used for rebuilding itself. Michela Wrong, a journalist who has written powerful accounts of overlooked aspects of Africa, summed it up well: "Like an acquisitive mother muttering, 'oh, he'll only break it' as she snatches a gift from her bawling infant, the British told themselves such munificence would only go to waste in a backward nation."[1]

They first promised to compensate Ethiopia, then broke their word—then lied about ever giving it. As grateful as Haile Selassie was for the Liberation, he couldn't passively watch as his allies stripped the country back to a landscape of tukuls. At last, in February of 1942, he told officials in Jimma to keep the British from dismantling a rope factory and shipping it south to Kenya. The situation was tense and might have ignited an international incident, but the British backed down. They could afford to—they had taken away, by the Ethiopians' reckoning, 80 percent of equipment the Italians had brought in for their occupation.[2]

And yet, having packed all the baggage they could, the British weren't really leaving. Their soldiers looked very much like they would stay a while, an impression that wasn't lost on the Opposition back in Britain. They still cared, even if the world seemed to be falling down around their ears. The Luftwaffe had bombed the House of Commons chamber into kindling and ash on the night of May 10, so MPs had to meet for the rest of the war in the untouched House of Lords and Church House, off Parliament Square. On May 14, 1941, Geoffrey Mander, a prominent Liberal MP (he later defected to Labour), asked Anthony Eden whether it was time to extend full diplomatic status and representation to Haile Selassie's government.

Eden was six months into a second term as foreign secretary, a role he knew well and where he excelled. On this matter, he essentially ducked the question, answering that all aspects "were being considered." Mander wouldn't let the matter drop, pointing out that "surely it is not possible any longer to speak of him as merely having a claim to the throne. He is well seated upon it."

"I think I made the position clear last February," replied Eden, "when I pointed out that while military operations are going on in Abyssinia, parts of the country will require temporary measures of military guidance and control, and I must adhere to that."

American diplomats in London were paying close attention. It sounded to them as if "the British Government still considers [Haile Selassie's] restoration to the throne as in the nature of an experiment."[3] A Foreign Office official confided to them that they hoped to "use the Emperor as an instrument of authority in a part of Ethiopia," making it clear to Haile Selassie as he unpacked in his reclaimed palace, "that he must act only by and with British consent."[4] This kind of arrogance irked the Americans, but they listened and kept silent, made their notes, and then waited for the right time to make a cameo in the drama.

In 1943, Roosevelt made an offhand, polite remark that he would like to meet the Emperor, and Haile Selassie dropped broad hints for the next two years through his people that he was quite willing to oblige the president.[5]

* * *

The Emperor also wrote to Orde Wingate about the attitude of the British authorities, but Wingate, while sympathetic, could do nothing to help.

Cunningham blamed him for letting the Emperor get back to his capital, and he suspected his volatile officer might get himself mixed up in politics again as he did in Palestine. So Wingate had been unceremoniously and rudely dispatched off to Cairo—do not pass go, do *not* return to Addis Ababa. And while they were at it, the command dropped him back to major, rescinding his temporary promotion to colonel.

It was shabby treatment for a man widely considered by his peers to be the genius behind the Liberation. With little to do in Cairo, Orde Wingate stewed in his own bitterness and wrote a long memorandum that recklessly blasted high-ranking officers and lowly NCOs, using his favorite expression, "military ape," to knock Cunningham and Platt.[6] And then, not caring that this amounted to career suicide, he sent it off to the general headquarters. Wavell summoned him, argued with him, but let him off the hook for his gross insubordination because Wingate was obviously a mental and physical wreck. What no one knew at the time was that his brain was being eaten away by parasites of malaria.[7]

Career suicide had failed, so he tried the real thing—he stabbed his throat twice and bled all over his hotel room's bathroom. He was saved only because a colonel in the next room heard him collapse to the floor.

Wingate recovered in a hospital, later blaming his suicide attempt on a sense of personal failure over Ethiopia. As he convalesced in London, he was sounded out by Americans for a possible book deal. For once, Wingate checked his ego; he didn't have the writing skills of T. E. Lawrence, and he knew it. Months later, Wavell sent him to Rangoon, though Wingate would have far preferred his beloved Palestine. But both Churchill and Wavell hoped he could do for Burma what he had accomplished in Ethiopia.

He died in a plane crash in northeast India in 1944.

* * *

In the middle of February, 1945, the world was still talking about Yalta, but after the conference was over, Franklin Roosevelt left to meet Haile Selassie at the Suez Canal. It would be quite a meeting—the New Dealer and champion of democracy face-to-face with the tiny Emperor and self-proclaimed Elect of God.

Haile Selassie, with Ras Kassa and a small entourage of aides, was whisked off in a US Air Force plane, and it was another sign of the crumbling relations with London that British Minister Robert Howe wasn't even informed. As the *USS Quincy* was docked in Great Bitter Lake at the canal, the Emperor—wearing a military uniform and a bulky greatcoat—was led up to salute an honor guard of marines and sailors. Roosevelt sat waiting for him in a wicker chair with his daughter, Anna, standing by his side; with his disintegrating health, the president couldn't even put on the masquerade anymore of standing for the movie cameras. Over tea, the two icons spoke in French, and when things got down to brass tacks, the Emperor reverted to Amharic and used an interpreter, sometimes reading from notes in English prepared in advance for him.

He hoped to discuss Eritrea and the Ogaden, the newborn United Nations, and what Ethiopia could do for the broad strokes hammered out at Yalta. Roosevelt, who apparently did most of the talking, was more interested in griping about the French and how they no longer deserved Indochina. He did, however, ask at one point whether Italian Somaliland had ever belonged to Ethiopia; Haile Selassie claimed it had.[8] At one point, the Emperor presented Roosevelt with a small, crudely made, but twenty-four-karat gold globe; Roosevelt, in turn, gave the Emperor four command cars.

There was little tangibly accomplished, yet the meeting was hugely significant. Its meaning was made all the more clear after Winston Churchill decided he'd better assert Britain's role and have his own hastily prepared meeting with the Emperor. A British aide asked Haile Selassie what matters he wanted to talk about with Churchill.

"None," replied the Emperor.[9]

When the Lion of Judah met the English bulldog, it was to prove disappointingly anti-climactic. Haile Selassie put out a feeler over the Ogaden, which only prompted Churchill to ask in a murmur to an aide where the Ogaden was. Then the prime minister tried to top Roosevelt's command cars by giving Haile Selassie a Rolls-Royce.

The British were ruffled by the Americans suddenly competing on their "turf," but they didn't learn from the experience. They soon wanted to rearrange the Horn of Africa one last time, assigning part of Eritrea to Sudan and donating the Ogaden to a "Greater Somalia." And while this predatory scheme started under Churchill and the Conservatives, it went beyond party lines. As negotiations dragged on for years, British soldiers would stay on Ethiopian soil, while Tories and Labour changed places in power and then switched back again. The Union Jack would only be lowered for good in the Ogaden in 1954.

* * *

Any war crime trials for Italy wouldn't lack for evidence. As Gideon Force had gained ground in the Liberation, its members had confiscated photo souvenirs from Italian regular troops and Blackshirts alike, and George Steer catalogued in *Sealed and Delivered* the kind of grotesque scenes these men carried around with them: "an Italian soldier standing guard over a mass of dead Ethiopian civilians after the Graziani massacre of February 1937; six Ethiopians swinging on a gibbet; proud owner sticking a bayonet into an Ethiopian corpse or pointing a knife at a severed Ethiopian head; another severed head of an Ethiopian Patriot, executed at Debra Brehan, being carried round on a plate with his severed right hand set alongside the head in a mock salute."[10]

What's important to remember is that all this was being discovered before 1941 even reached the halfway mark. Reports of the *European* death camps didn't hit Western newspapers until the autumn, and didn't really have much impact until the spring of 1942. Roosevelt had always casually lumped Mussolini in with Hitler as an architect of genocide. He insisted in a telegram to Churchill that "the Head Devil should be surrendered together with his chief partners in crime." In private to his War Cabinet, Churchill declared that he didn't care much whether Mussolini was shot on the spot or locked away until the end of the war. "Personally, I am fairly indifferent on this matter, provided always that no solid military advantages are sacrificed for the sake of immediate vengeance."[11]

That sounded simple enough. Unfortunately, as Italy's defenses crumbled against the Allied onslaught, the top Fascists in Rome did something that would have been unthinkable, even impossible, in Nazi Germany.

They fired their dictator.

They put him under arrest as if he were a CEO who had been caught embezzling the pension fund. And the man they chose to replace him was the second-most-hated Italian in Ethiopia, Marshal Pietro Badoglio.

Suddenly, the Allies were having second thoughts. After all, if Mussolini was out, it could only mean his replacement wanted to surrender. Churchill was no longer blasé. Roosevelt changed his mind, too. The goal, after all, was to take Italy out of the war, and the "devils" could always be rounded up later—if they were rounded up at all. Even Anthony Eden suggested that Italy didn't need a military occupation and should be "run for us, as far as possible" under a sympathetic Italian government.

The problem was that others annoyingly kept remembering events from another era. Only two days after the arrest of Mussolini in Rome, Leslie Carruthers of the *New Times and Ethiopia News* wrote to Eden, hoping to get a commitment from the British government that it would have no official dealings with Badoglio. Instead, he hoped the government would "exact his extradition to Ethiopia, to be tried for his violation of the International Gas Convention." Eden also had to face questions in the House of Commons over Badoglio. But how could peace with Italy be negotiated with all this talk of shoving its new representative in front of a tribunal?

There was also the embarrassing fact that Neville Chamberlain gave Mussolini's rape of Ethiopia a diplomatic seal of approval in 1938.

So the Foreign Office got to work with its broom while it looked around for a place under the rug. It wanted to tell the world that Ethiopia had been another war, a separate war. And yet there was China, lobbying for prosecution of war crimes by the Japanese going all the way back to 1931. If China would be heard, then surely Ethiopia was entitled to court cases over Yekatit 12 and Debre Libanos. The bigger question, some asked, was what had been the whole point of the war if it wasn't to make thugs like Badoglio answer for their crimes against humanity?

The Foreign Office couldn't hope to win that kind of debate, so it needed to cut off the discussion altogether. And in October 1943, it decided on a tactic that came right out of the Fascist playbook: the Ethiopians simply shouldn't be allowed at the table. Officials decreed that because Ethiopia had been liberated so early, it didn't fall under a narrow definition set for membership on the War Crimes Commission: a country that "should be actively fighting the Axis Powers and should have 'suffered' at the hands of the enemy."

Ethiopia, however, still had friends to make its case, and on November 3, Labour MP Emanuel Shinwell demanded to know what was being done. Shinwell had spent his boyhood in Glasgow, the working-class son of Polish Jews. "In view of the use of poison gas by the Italians against the Abyssinians," he asked the Commons that afternoon, "would it not be an act of justice to hand over Italian war criminals to the Ethiopians?"

It was left to an under-secretary of foreign affairs to answer, Richard Law, the son of the one-time British Prime Minister Andrew Bonar Law. The younger Law was as different from Shinwell as could be; he was educated at Oxford, with libertarian principles and a safe Tory seat in Hull. Now he stood up and blandly told the Opposition, "That was another war."[12]

When MPs across the aisle wouldn't let the matter go, another Tory, Herbert Williams, openly sneered at Ethiopia's right to join the Commission. "Can the Right Honorable Gentleman say on what fronts Ethiopian troops are now engaged in capturing any of these prisoners?"

The truth was that the Allies had turned down Ethiopia's offer of troops in other theaters of the war.

*   *   *

In January of 1944, two of the major actors in the drama met their end, but it was Mussolini who exacted vengeance. This was after he'd been rescued by the Germans in a daring raid, and Hitler had installed him as the puppet leader of the short-lived Italian Social Republic. Emilio De Bono and Count Galeazzo Ciano were both on the Fascist Grand Council that had ousted him, and at Hitler's urging, the Duce had them shot by a firing squad. Graziani had stayed loyal. He would, in fact, keep fighting up until the very end.

When Allied troops swept into Rome, Badoglio was replaced by the white-bearded, old, anti-Fascist Ivanoe Bonomi, yet the British still treated Badoglio as a statesman worthy of respect and their agent of change. Churchill fired off a secret cable to his ambassador in Rome, telling him, "You are responsible for the Marshal's safety and sanctuary in the British Embassy or in some equally safe place to which he can be removed." After a reminder that Badoglio had signed a treaty with the American and British forces, he wrote, "A man who has signed such documents could only be brought to trial by the conquered Italians with the approval of the United States and United Kingdom Governments . . ."[13] For Churchill, "military honor" was involved.

By late January of 1945, the Ethiopians lost their patience. If the British were so afraid of embarrassment, it was time to put some blush in their cheeks. A diplomat at Ethiopia's embassy in London vented to the *New York Times*. Ethiopia, he told reporter Sydney Gruson, had submitted a list of Italian defendants to the UN War Crimes Commission through the British legation in Addis Ababa. But London refused to hand over Badoglio or any of the others, because "apparently, personalities entered into the decision to take no action."

Gruson's brief story had just enough details to push the Foreign Office into a tight corner. "It is known that a formal request has not reached the commission itself," wrote Gruson, "and that the commission was never asked to consider the cases of Italian criminals named by Ethiopia."[14] The Foreign Office stubbornly kept to its position: the Ethiopians were complaining about another war that happened a long time ago, and they shouldn't be on the commission anyway.

Months passed, but the Ethiopians weren't willing to give up. Neither was Sylvia Pankhurst, who published a pamphlet in April of 1945, titled *Italy's War Crimes in Ethiopia*. It included several lurid photographs of beatings, hangings, and mass graves. It quoted a letter home by John Melly that described the gassing and bombing of women and children. It quoted a letter Charles Martin had received from his Islamic servant about people who were gunned down as they entered a church. Pages were devoted to the Graziani Massacre, quoting Ladislas Sava's reports, and the slaughter at Debre Libanos.

After quoted testimony and photos, the pamphlet urged, "We submit that the atrocities committed by the Italians in Ethiopia must be laid before the War Crimes Commission, upon which Ethiopian representatives should be invited to take their seat among those of other injured peoples."[15]

The pamphlet was successful enough to go into a second printing. But still the Foreign Office wouldn't budge.

*   *   *

All the while, Benito Mussolini stewed and brooded in a villa on Lombardy's Lake Garna. He was now a ruler in name only, a puppet for Hitler and giving in to self-pity. He told a reporter in January, "Seven years ago, I was an interesting person. Now I am a corpse." He resented being a spectator while his nation was in chaos; much of Italy's south had been liberated, but the Allies were still fighting Germans and pro-Fascist holdouts in the north. "I await the end of the tragedy," he informed the magazine's reporter, claiming that he felt "strangely detached from everything."[16]

The end would come soon enough. Mussolini was captured by Communist partisans, and the next day, April 28, he was shot dead as he stood on a lonely, isolated patch of ground in front of the low wall of an isolated villa. What happened afterwards has become much more famous than his final moment. The bodies of Mussolini and his mistress, Clara Petacci, were hauled away in the middle of the night and dumped the next morning in Milan's Piazzale Loreto in front of an Esso gas station. The sight of the bloody, limp frames prompted a spectacle of vengeance like no other. People spat on the bodies, hitting and kicking Mussolini's corpse so hard that his lifeless skull fractured and an eye was dislodged. One woman fired shot after shot from a pistol into his head while another used her turn to hike up her skirt and urinate on his face. A man tried to shove a dead mouse in the dead Duce's slack mouth while chanting with spiteful fury, "Make a speech now, make a speech."[17] Partisans shot into the air and firemen sprayed water at the mob to restore order, but neither of these tactics worked.[18]

Then the news spread around the world. Winston Churchill was at Chequers when he was told of the Fascist leader's end. He promptly announced it to a room full of dinner guests: "The bloody beast is dead." But his self-righteous bloodlust soon changed when a famous photograph was printed in newspapers far and wide showing Mussolini's and Petacci's mutilated bodies hanging upside down from meat hooks with those of other Fascists. To Churchill, Petacci didn't deserve to be cruelly dispatched with the rest, and to him, shooting the couple was now "treacherous and cowardly." Others celebrated. Wilfred Thesiger, who found plenty of evidence of Italian atrocities, felt "savage satisfaction" over Mussolini's brutal end.[19]

By the time Churchill was dictating his account of events for his six-volume history of *The Second World War*, he struck a note of civilized statesman's detachment above it all: "But at least the world was spared an Italian Nuremberg."[20]

* * *

Those in the Piazzale Loreto had vented all this rage on a corpse because in the end, Italians were his last victims just as much as they were his first. But Italians had also been his supporters, his fans, his devoted worshippers and backers. They had cheered him on, and some had committed horrific crimes in his name.

The Ethiopians had already proved they had a greater capacity for forgiveness than their occupiers. In his speech on May 5, 1941, Haile Selassie told his people, "Do not reward evil for evil. Do not commit any act of cruelty like those of which the enemy committed against us up until this present time. Do not allow the enemy any occasion to foul the good name of Ethiopia. We shall take his weapons from the enemy and make him return by the way that he came."

The temptation might be to dismiss this as rhetoric, but it was followed for the most part. It was a spirit of forgiveness that the world wouldn't see again until the astonishing proceedings of the Truth and Reconciliation Commission in South Africa fifty years later. But while Ethiopia hoped for reconciliation, it still wanted a Nuremberg.

Unfortunately, the Allies had lined up Italy to become a backdrop on the chilly front of the new Cold War. Extraditing war criminals would only enrage a weary Italian population that could veer hard to the left. The shadow men in Britain's Foreign Office kept saying it plainly. "Justice requires the handing over of these people," wrote one senior civil servant, "but expediency, I fear, militates against it."[21] It didn't take long for the administration in Rome, calibrated to London's and Washington's interests, to figure out the charade. Italy's post-war prime minister, Alcide de Gasperi, went through the motions of a war crimes investigation. "Try to gain time," he wrote his officials in 1948, "avoid answering requests."[22]

* * *

Meanwhile as the years passed, Haile Selassie's government adjusted its own war narrative for political purposes.

In 1955, Imru Zelleke was thirty-two years old, a young ambassador with the Ethiopian embassy in Bonn, West Germany, after having already served as chargé d'affaires in Paris. And he got the bright idea to make a documentary film about the Patriots. While home on business, he struggled to advance his labor of love, and he did his homework. He submitted a full script, managed to find a producer, figured out the budget, and could virtually guarantee the film wouldn't cost the government anything but "good will and cooperation." The film would actually cost *him*—he had taken out a personal loan of $25,000 to get the thing started.[23]

But he discovered that the idea was doomed from the get-go. First, it had to be vetted by "a committee of people who hadn't a clue about the movies." The head of Ethiopia's Ministry of Information told him frankly that there was no great urgency for a film about the Patriots. On the other hand, if Imru wanted to make a movie about the Emperor, he could have all the funds he wanted. He realized he had to drop the matter . . . and that he had been naïve.

In the first few years after the Liberation, there had been a power struggle between the Patriots on one side, many of whom never forgave Haile Selassie for fleeing the country, and on the other side, those who had followed him into exile like Ras Kassa. The Patriot faction lost. Haile Selassie preferred the company of those who had lived abroad with him, not men who had carried on alone in the hills, some of whom had changed and matured in their political thinking. To make a film, even a patriotic film about war heroes, would be to stir up a few very old and bitter spats.

*   *   *

Back in 1949 and 1950, Ethiopia's Ministry of Justice had tried one last time to force the issue of war crime trials by publishing two volumes' worth of damning material: *Documents of Italian War Crimes Submitted to the United Nations War Crimes Commission.*

Anyone now could read the telegrams sent by Mussolini and the orders given by the Butcher of Fezzan. The volumes made for nice doorstops, but achieved nothing else. There would be no Nuremberg for Italian war criminals. Alessandro Lessona, who had been Mussolini's minister of the colonies, lived a long life in freedom, dying in 1991. Badoglio, having ingratiated himself with the Allies, walked away and worked in business until his death in 1956.

Rodolfo Graziani would pay, but not over war crimes in Libya or Ethiopia, and not by much. He was convicted in a separate trial for his collaboration with the Germans and sentenced initially to nineteen years in prison. But he was let out the next year—and soon got involved with the neo-Fascist Italian Social Movement. He also got to take his last breath in free and open air, dying in 1955. Of all of the figures Ethiopia most wanted to put in the dock, Graziani was the worst, and more than half a century later, he would come back to haunt Ethiopians in the most shocking and appalling manner.

* * *

In 1944, at sixty-two years old, Sylvia Pankhurst got on a plane for the first time in her life and flew to the country she had written so much about, but had never seen. Haile Selassie's private secretary greeted her with an armful of flowers, and she was assigned a car with a chauffeur. A villa was provided for her stay. And it got better. She discovered a street had been named after her. The Emperor presented her with the Patriot's Medal and with the Order of Sheba, a distinction usually reserved only for foreign queens.

Her legacy, as to be expected, is a controversial one. Historians and her biographers point to her intellectual blind spot, how the country and its Emperor could do no wrong in the pages of the *New Times and Ethiopia News*. She spent her last years in her home in Addis Ababa, surrounded by eucalyptus trees. True, she saw Africa in its primary colors without the complex brushstrokes, and she often made mistakes in facts and let passion win out over logical argument. But there was much she got right. She clung stubbornly to her conscience and showed it off when so many were shedding theirs.

When she died at seventy-eight in 1960, her state funeral was held in the Holy Trinity Cathedral and attended by thousands, including Haile Selassie. The Ethiopian Orthodox Church didn't know the peculiar name of "Sylvia," so they interred this fiery agnostic suffragette as "Walata Krestos," which means "daughter of Christ."[24] Her grave, which you can find just outside the cathedral, is in ground set aside for Ethiopian Patriots, which no doubt would have pleased her, as would her status as an "honorary Ethiopian." She is the only foreigner ever given such a privilege.

* * *

Evelyn Waugh went on to write more books, including the classic *Brideshead Revisited*, and add to the list of people who violently despised him. After the war, he declined into a drug- and alcohol-dependent state of poor health before he died in 1966. But his books have survived.

Herbert Matthews wrote more books, but at heart, he was really a foreign correspondent, a journalist who belonged in the field. His choice of life had its costs. "I actually don't even remember my father when I was a child because he was always off to some war or other," recalls his son, Eric, a respected entomologist living in Australia. As for Matthews' early faith in Fascism, his son declares, "The Spanish civil war cured him of any lingering sympathies that way. Politically I would say that he was an idealist (left-leaning, as I am) and considered naïve by hard-headed people." [25]

Matthews earned lasting recognition in journalism when he went into the mountains of Cuba to interview a young revolutionary named Fidel Castro. Once again, he got too close to power, becoming openly sympathetic to it, and once again, another medal was pinned to his chest. But this time, hate mail at home followed, along with vicious attacks in the leading American news magazines. The reporter would have to defend himself against criticism for decades until his death. [26]

David Darrah unfortunately never became a lasting name on bookshelves or in journalism schools. Neither did Geoffrey Harmsworth. Instead, Harmsworth became a discerning art collector, amassing an impressive collection of items from Renaissance drawings to rare photos. As for Ladislas Farago, he went on to write highly successful works about espionage and the Second World War, particularly biographies on Patton.

George Steer's propaganda methods had proved so successful that he was headhunted by several different commanders. He developed propaganda units for Madagascar and then India and Burma. His life was full of promise. He had published several books, fathered two children (Esmé had given birth to a sister for little George, named Caroline), and had lived more adventures than even many foreign correspondents. All this he accomplished by the time he was thirty-five.

On Christmas Day of 1944, Steer, now a lieutenant colonel, was in the village of Upper Fagu in remote northern Bengal, an exotic region of forests where elephants blustered and tigers prowled. He was there to develop more forward propaganda units. Though regulations barred officers from driving without permission, Steer wouldn't wait for a driver and got behind the wheel of a Jeep to drive a group of soldiers to a sports event being held for the men. It remains unclear what happened, but the Jeep went out of control and pinwheeled through the air, crashing off the road in some tea bushes. Several men were injured and killed. Steer was found with his skull crushed.

Friends were stunned, with one of his oldest complaining in angry grief to Sidney Barton, "What a fucking stupid way to die." The Emperor sent word that his death came as a shock and that Steer was a "loyal friend to us and to Ethiopia," while *The Times* of London called him "one of the adventurers of this generation." [27]

Historians ransacked his books, plundering all the rich color and detail, and more often than not, they left Steer out of their stories and banished him to their footnotes. Perhaps because he was a journalist, they dismissed him as a mere observer. He might have been forgotten altogether, but then Nicholas Rankin—a writer, producer for BBC World Service, and a seasoned, adventurous traveler in his own right—was making a documentary about Guernica's bombing. Intrigued by Steer, he wrote a biography on him, *Telegram from Guernica*, and almost singlehandedly saved him from obscurity. In 2006, Guernica unveiled a bust of Steer and named a street in his honor. In 2010, another street was named after him in Bilbao. He would have enjoyed these tributes, but as a writer, he might have been glad most of all that today, Faber & Faber is offering three of his titles in print again: *Caesar in Abyssinia*, *Sealed and Delivered*, and his classic, *The Tree of Gernika*.

As Rankin points out, had Steer lived, he could have easily gone in many different directions for his career. He had a prose style that would have worked brilliantly for fiction, and he "would have been in his element reporting the end of empire and the movement towards independence."[28]

In terms of Ethiopia, his destiny and the country's were intertwined. It boosted his profile as a reporter, and he paid it back by helping to free it. His innovations in propaganda and psychological warfare have had a profound and lasting effect. But Steer was an individual of deep-seated conscience. He saw past the charade and convenient bluff of objective reporting and tried to give stories an added dimension; when the time came, he signed on to serve in World War Two less out of allegiance to Mother England than to avenge an African nation he had grown to love.

If the war in Ethiopia changed the world, then George Steer was one of those courageous voices that tried to warn the world what was coming.

* * *

In the aftermath of Allied victory, Pierre Laval fled France but could find no safe port in the storm. Spain didn't want him. In Austria, he was quickly discovered and hauled back to Paris for his treason trial. At Fresnes Prison, he managed to take a cyanide capsule as his final escape, but it had lost its strength. His stomach was pumped and it took two hours to revive him, only so he could be half-carried without his shoes and strapped to a chair before his firing squad.[29]

Ethiopia was more forgiving to its traitors. Getachew Abate was arrested during the Liberation but was allowed to live out his life in exile in the remote locales of Jimma and Arsi. Haile Selassie told him, "I pardon you, but I do not know if God will."[30] The writer and diplomat Afawarq Gabra-Iyassus, who ping-ponged back and forth between sides, was tried for treason and sentenced to death, but this was later commuted to life in prison. After having been the "mouth of Caesar," he spent his final years in one last confinement in Jimma, blind and alone and dying in 1947.[31]

The missionary traitor, Thomas Lambie, wasn't welcome, of course, but Haile Selassie was willing to forgive Feodor Konovalov, who ended up living in Ethiopia all the way to 1952 before finally settling in South Africa.

*   *   *

The Brown Condor never flew in combat after the Ethiopian War. When John Robinson tried to serve his country, he faced discrimination—but not over his race. The Army Air Corps told him that at thirty-eight, he was *too old* to fly. Still wanting to be useful, he became an instructor of aviation mechanics at Chanute Air Base in Chicago.[32] Then in 1943, Ethiopia decided to revive the dream of a national air force, and Robinson was invited back. This time, he returned with a group of black pilots that became known affectionately as "the brood." And by 1946, he helped negotiate a deal with TWA Airlines to provide Ethiopia with technical personnel and flight crews into the country.

Life for a while was good. He lived in a villa, was a person of importance who did what he loved, and his best friend was the Duke of Harar. Robinson made another close friend in Charles Martin, now back in the country. For a while, Martin repaired his strained relationship with the Emperor, but it wasn't long before he fell out of favor at court again over financial affairs. The elderly doctor ran something of an informal salon out of his house. Guests of all sorts—from British diplomats to medical men to "the brood" of African-American pilots— regularly dropped in for dinner or were brought over by his children. Robinson often looked for counsel from the older man, and Martin's son, Yohannes, told historian Peter Garretson that the pilot "was quite a character. He was a nice guy . . . He was a very, very close friend of the family."[33]

In 1947, however, there was an ugly episode with, of all people, another legendary veteran of the war.

In 1936, Count Carl Gustav von Rosen had left, but when the Second World War was over, he came back to serve as a major in the Ethiopian Air Force. That meant Robinson, once again a colonel, was his superior officer, and von Rosen apparently grumbled to anyone within earshot that he wasn't happy to be outranked by a black American. Things came to a head when Robinson chose von Rosen as the best qualified co-pilot to fly with him on a twin-engine transport plane to Addis Ababa. Von Rosen told him that "he wasn't about to fly second seat to an American nigger."[34]

Robinson, being a professional, ignored the insult, flew solo in a plane that normally needed a two-man crew, and arrived in the capital without incident. But von Rosen wouldn't let the matter drop—he reportedly stormed into Robinson's office and started a new argument. As Robinson's biographer, Thomas E. Simmons, put it, "Robinson broke von Rosen's jaw and evidently the pride of Sweden."[35] After von Rosen went to the hospital, the Condor went to court. He faced serious charges of assault and battery.

But Robinson's behavior made sense. This Swedish major had called him the worst name in the book, and the man came looking for trouble at the office, perhaps using a few more racial slurs. It's von Rosen's racism that is a shock. He had risked his life for Ethiopians, but perhaps like Jan Smuts, he viewed black people with paternalistic condescension. Here was a black man—and an American, to boot—who was his professional equal, his superior in rank and maybe even in the skies.

Whatever his attitudes, von Rosen was regarded as a valuable contact in terms of economic development from Sweden, which might turn off the tap on a considerable amount of aid flowing into the country. Ethiopia simply couldn't afford to offend it.

The matter seems to have been quietly dropped, with von Rosen placated by taking over the air force, while Robinson was allowed to go free. He still had enough friends at court to keep him out of prison, and he could still help Ethiopia's air development, but now as a private citizen. With his old friend, the Duke of Harar, he founded a modest new air service, Sultan Airways.

Then in 1954, he was making a mercy flight when his plane went down outside the capital in a ball of flames. The Italian engineer died in the crash, while Robinson crawled free but died later from his injuries in the hospital. Haile Selassie gave him a state funeral at the Holy Trinity Cathedral. Robinson got an obituary in newspapers in America, but faded into obscurity, forgotten for years just like the Tuskegee airmen of the Second World War. Then, a fellow native of Mississippi, flying enthusiast, and businessman, Thomas E. Simmons, became intrigued as he ran into references time and again to this self-effacing pioneer, and thanks to diligent research and historical detective work, he revived wider interest in the career of John Robinson.

Von Rosen survived the Condor by many years and went on to new war zones and other thrills. At the height of the Nigerian Civil War, he was entering his sixties and was a grandfather "with greying hair and deep-sunken blue eyes," but he was determined to fly in combat again.[36] In Ethiopia, he had seen the ruthlessness of a better equipped enemy. Now his view changed. It was no longer enough to bring in food and supplies. With a bit of import-export sleight of hand and the complicity of Tanzania, von Rosen arranged for two-seater MFI-9B planes to be repainted in camouflage colors and outfitted with *rockets*. As foreign correspondent John de St. Jorre put it, von Rosen, with his makeshift air force for Biafra, "knocked out half the jet-studded Nigerian air force with an aeronautical equivalent of an Austin Mini."[37]

When the Nigerian Civil War was over, he could have easily retired to a quiet life at his seventeenth-century castle in his native Sweden. Another Ethiopian conflict pulled him back into the battelfields. One last adventure, one last thrill.

During the Ogaden War with Somalia in 1977, he made relief flights for refugees. He was killed—not in the air, but on the ground when the Somalis attacked near the town of Gode.

* * *

In 1955, Winston Churchill finally handed Britain over to his political heir apparent, Anthony Eden. Eden quickly made sure in a general election that he had the people's blessing to be PM, as well as his mentor's. Then, in one of the cruelest of political ironies, he was completely undone by events on the stage he knew best: foreign affairs. And events from twenty years before were significant in deciding his course of action.

Egypt's dictator, Gamal Nasser, nationalized the Suez Canal in July of 1956, and Britain and France chose military intervention. But that is not the whole story. Nasser was far from simply a heroic nationalist taking on cold and corrupt imperial powers. Britain had already signed a deal two years before to withdraw its troops from the Canal Zone. After the soldiers were gone in 1956, Nasser waited all of six weeks to break international agreements. It was his payback to Britain and the United States for yanking their funding of the Aswan Dam—a bloated colossus of an engineering project. Nasser then promptly closed the canal to Israeli shipping and blockaded the Straits of Tiran, Israel's only way to the Red Sea.

For Eden, this was all too familiar, right down to the bellicose propaganda speeches over Egypt's government-owned radio station. His primary concern, however, was making sure Britain got its badly needed oil from the Middle East. The French had their own reasons to detest Nasser, who was providing support to the Algerians in their long war for independence. The French, in fact, came up with a devious scheme to strike back, for which they needed British help. At the end of October, the charade unfolded. Israel crossed into the Sinai and made quick work of Egyptian army posts, while under the pretext of intervention, the RAF bombed Egyptian airfields and the British and French moved in to capture Port Said.

Eden had kept the Americans apprised of developments and had even told the US president in writing that he was "ready, in the last resort, to use force to bring Nasser to his senses."[38] Months later, Dwight Eisenhower would lie to the American public on TV and claim he'd been completely in the dark over what Britain was up to. For his administration, the enemy wasn't Nasser, but a Soviet Union that would love to play a proxy war in the Middle East.

For all the casual similarities, Suez was *not* Ethiopia. And Nasser, though cynical and self-serving, represented the future of emerging states that would play the superpowers off against each other.

As the Suez Crisis grew worse, there was financial pressure on the British pound, and the United States made it clear that it wouldn't help. Treasury Secretary George Humphrey even told Chancellor of the Exchequer Harold Macmillan that Britain wouldn't see a dime until it left Suez.[39] Eden was forced to announce a ceasefire, and though his actions over the canal had been popular early on with British voters, Suez became a divisive issue on the home front. He ultimately had to resign. While UN peacekeepers watched the Sinai, Nasser delighted in a massive public relations windfall, and he would take this as encouragement to become more provocative.

Eden had made his decisions over Suez in a period of debilitating illness and when he was close to exhaustion. His health was certainly a factor, but not the *only* factor, and even battling fatigue and sickness, he was a man who would naturally stick to his world view shaped by important events. He made this clear himself in a 1967 interview that was only to be published after his death: "I am still unrepentant about Suez. People never look at what would have happened if we had done nothing. There is a parallel with the Thirties. If you allow people to break agreements with impunity, the appetite grows to feed on such things."[40]

Support for Eden over Suez has risen or fallen depending on the era. Only a couple of years after the crisis, a chagrined Dwight Eisenhower told congressmen that his administration had made a mistake in not backing the British. Political weather never stays the same, of course, so more critical appraisals came in the years ahead. They unfairly painted Eden as the last defender of an antiquated and crumbling British Empire, when he was nothing of the kind. His latest biographer, D. R. Thorpe, has corrected some of the old presumptions, noting, "Had the Anglo-French venture succeeded in 1956, there would almost certainly have been no Middle East war in 1967, and probably no Yom Kippur War in 1973 also."[41]

Retired from politics, Eden had one enduring friend from the old days of Ethiopia and the League of Nations: France's delegate, René Massigli, who once shared his frustration with the double-dealing Laval. Three decades after the two men failed to push the League into action, the Edens would have Massigli and his wife as house guests, where the retired British statesman could offer, appropriately enough, a vintage wine from the 1930s.

*   *   *

C. L. R. James was eventually deported from the United States for overstaying his visa by ten years. Forced to come home to his native Trinidad, he was disillusioned over political infighting and left for good. He spent his final days in London, in the district that was to become synonymous with Afro-Caribbean aspirations in the city: Brixton.

Years and distance had gnawed away at his friendship with George Padmore; old arguments, old slights, and personality differences. The glory days of feverish lobby work in cramped flats were long gone. Padmore had moved to the newly independent Ghana being run by his old comrade, Kwame Nkrumah, and had quickly discovered it was no worker's paradise. In less than a year, he wanted to leave for the Caribbean, but Nkrumah convinced him to stay. Months later, Padmore was dead from cirrhosis of the liver, and Nkrumah was eulogizing him over national radio.

Nkrumah's halo as an African icon was soon tarnished as he made Ghana into a police state, and in 1966, his government was overthrown in a coup while he was off visiting North Vietnam and China. T. Ras Makonnen—Padmore and Nkrumah's old associate—became collateral damage and was put under arrest. It was only thanks to the efforts of American actor and fellow radical Julian Mayfield that he was let go, and Makonnen packed his bags for Kenya, where another old friend could get him a government job: Jomo Kenyatta, who by then was that independent country's first prime minister. [42]

Kenyatta was earning his own controversial reputation and mixed political legacy. And the very first head of state the prime minister welcomed to his nation was Emperor Haile Selassie of Ethiopia. Today, Kenyatta's son, Uhuru, is a controversial political figure in his own right, and it remains to be seen what his future will be.

*   *   *

Mussolini thought of himself as a new Caesar, and every Italian boy knew from his school lessons that the ancient Caesars were often elevated to the status of gods. He would have been either horrified or amused to learn that his great enemy, a tiny bearded man who once hid from his bombs in a cave, was considered by a whole sect in Jamaica to be the reincarnation of *the* God.

It was a role that Haile Selassie himself never openly sought or was comfortable with, as it offended his piety. The problem was that after being restored to the throne, Haile Selassie might as well have been a god to his people, so absolute was his authority. The 1955 Constitution declared, "By virtue of His Imperial Blood, as well as by the anointing which He has received, the person of the Emperor is sacred, His dignity is inviolable, and His power indisputable."

The young regent who had used all his cunning, all his statecraft and micromanaging to fend off rivals and intriguers in a feudal state, had now become the greybeard monarch who couldn't change his old habits of survival. He ruled; there were so few left who had been groomed to manage government affairs and who might have nudged him, or even pressured him, towards new ideas and reforms. By slaughtering a generation of educated elite and intellectuals, Mussolini and his Fascist occupation blew up the delicate, swaying bridge between an ancient kingdom and a country's modern potential.

It would be naïve to think that Haile Selassie sponsored the Young Ethiopians to "take over" or share what counted most in terms of power; his parliament before the war with the Italians was a rubber stamp, and these progressives were to help him, not to be constitutional equals. But over time, their influence could have broken the ground for a more open and moderate government that could evolve towards democracy. Yes, the bridge had been blown up, but Haile Selassie failed to rebuild it when he came back to the rubble.

Even friends from the old days in Bath and London weren't immune from court intrigues. Lorenzo Taezaz was sent out of sight and out of mind to be an ambassador in Moscow, where he died of illness in 1947. The Emperor outlived his beloved wife and was cursed to outlive many of his children. His second son and favorite, Prince Makonnen, the Duke of Harar, died in a car crash in 1957. As time passed, he was surrounded ever more by the corrupt and conservative. The head of state who banned *Macbeth* from being performed in Ethiopia (because of its assassination plot) gradually turned into a lonely Shakespearean figure.

A disturbing anecdote goes that the Emperor went one day to visit Tekle Hawariat Tekle Mariam. This was years after the war, and the old diplomat had come back from Madagascar to settle on a farm in Hirna. The two argued, with Haile Selassie telling his former adviser, "You keep on saying 'Ethiopia,' but Ethiopia is nothing without me. Her fate is tied up with mine. I am her destiny. Do not imagine that Ethiopia will exist without me."

"How can you think like that?' replied a shocked Tekle. "Ethiopia is eternal. We shall all pass away, but Ethiopia will remain forever."[43]

* * *

Having watched the British loot his country after the Liberation, Haile Selassie was determined to get one very big piece of real estate to compensate him, one he would acquire through a stealth raid of his own: Eritrea.

When the United Nations decided in late 1950 on an ambiguous federation scheme for Eritrea, Haile Selassie's knee-jerk reaction was to say no. He wanted it all. Never again would he allow himself to be vulnerable to invasions from the north, plus his nation would finally get what it always wanted: a precious sea view.

To be fair, Eritrea at this time had many advocates who wanted to be united with Ethiopia, while a substantial portion of Eritreans felt the opposite—they felt it was time to stand on their own. But the camp for independence never got a fair fight. One of Britain's diplomats in Asmara was merrily working away to derail its efforts by playing on religious divisions, all while doing his best to make sure UN commissioners only heard the "right answers."[44] And when the federation solution was put forward, it was doomed out of the gate.

"The Ethiopians did not want federation of any kind, they never believed in any of it," John Spencer told journalist Michela Wrong. "The Emperor really pushed our hands, he was all for taking Eritrea immediately. He said, 'I insist on the full return of Eritrea to Ethiopia.' I told him, 'No, you have to ease into it, you can't grab it all at once. Even if you want nothing to do with the Federation, you will have to slide into it, gradually bit by bit."[45] Acting in bad faith from the very start, Spencer proceeded to use all his lobbying and legal skills to undermine Eritrea's self-determination at the international level. The Emperor's top officials handled the rest.

Below on the middle rungs was Imru Zelleke, who had become a young diplomat and official. As Eritrea was about to be absorbed, he was one of those assigned to work on drafting a revised constitution for Ethiopia. The political reasons were obvious. Yes, Eritrea was a former colony, but it already had democracy's moving parts; its political assembly, the Baito, had elected officials, unlike Ethiopia's club of feudal favorites. And now it was hitching its wagon to what everyone knew was an autocratic state.

As the secretary for the board working on Ethiopia's constitutional revisions, Imru was sent one day to consult with Ras Kassa, who casually ordered, "Tell them to make it like the British Constitution."

Imru had to explain patiently to a shocked Kassa that there was no such thing as a *single* British constitutional document. The pious old ras didn't really believe him. Later, he told Imru, "Don't waste your time on this affair anyway. Whatever change is going to be made will never be implemented."[46]

Disillusioned and growing ever more frustrated, Imru watched while the whole process was cynically undermined from the top down. There was never going to be any liberalization in post-war Ethiopia (or in Eritrea, for that matter). "Genuine liberals," he noticed, "were excluded from any role in government," while those already in the system "were accused of some vague fault or another and sent abroad or given demotions." Imru's own turn in the wilderness waited in the future.

As for Eritrea, the Baito soon became a shadow of itself, and the Eritrean flag abruptly gone. The country's single independent newspaper was shut down. Ethiopia took over Eritrea's crucial port customs and kept most of the money for itself. Business and official communication could no longer be done in Tigrinya and Arabic, only Amharic. The state was whittled away, its shavings swept up and absorbed into Ethiopia, all thanks to broken promises from a royal court, and the complicity of many Eritrean officials who either didn't want to face the truth or who had their palms greased and their jobs secured.[47]

In 1962, there was no need for pretense anymore. Haile Selassie simply annexed the whole country and got rid of the Baito.

By then, a small army of Muslim Eritreans, armed with Kalashnikov rifles, had formed the Eritrean Liberation Front and had started raids to try to win back their country. In seeking compensation for war with Italy, the Emperor had set things in motion for one of the longest, bloodiest wars in Africa.

* * *

As historian Bahru Zewde wrote, Haile Selassie's "greatest crime was that he ruled for far too long—and he was not aware of it."[48]

A cadre of the Emperor's own imperial bodyguard pounced to take over while he was on a state visit to Brazil in mid-December of 1960. In their proclamations, the coup leaders talked about the country's widespread deprivation and lack of development, but their *putsch* was doomed to failure. They had done little to win over the rest of the army, which stayed loyal to the Emperor and would prove it with battle in the streets. And Haile Selassie had powerful friends. While the Americans posed as a neutral party and tried to broker a ceasefire, they were busy letting him use their military listening post in Eritrea and their air force facilities in Liberia to coordinate his return to power.[49]

As tanks smashed through the gates of the rebel-held palace, the conspirators stood in its Green Salon and sprayed their machine guns at their prisoners. They wanted to literally kill the past. Ras Seyum was murdered. So was Abebe Aregai. So was a long list of government ministers and officials.

But when it was over, life in the country went back to its depressingly stunted routine. Instead of answering the wake-up call over the country's bleak economics,

Haile Selassie merely raised the pay of army soldiers, knowing he had them to thank for keeping his place. By 1969, there was still only 10 percent of the population of Ethiopia that could read, and the annual wage for most of its citizens was pitifully low, $65 US.[50] That same year, student radicals managed to close down high schools and bring classes to a halt at the university named after him.

It wasn't only the young who demanded change. For years, one man kept telling the Emperor to go—as impertinently, defiantly, and brazenly as only he could. The irascible Patriot veteran, Tekle Wolde Hawaryat, kept doggedly trying to kick him out of power, but his plots came to nothing, and he was tossed into prison again and again. In November of 1969, Tekle and a small group of conspirators attempted to assassinate the Emperor by detonating a land mine under a bridge, one Haile Selassie often used for weekend trips. The plot was uncovered, and Tekle barricaded himself with a machine gun inside his house when the police came for him. He was killed in a macabre, frontier-style shoot-out, and the national media left out the details of his final defiance when they announced his passing.

* * *

A new storm was gathering force, and the 1970s oil crisis and economic stagnation whipped it up further.

Imru Zelleke, by then in his fifties, brooded over a government "entangled in endless intrigues by sundry interest groups wrangling for position in palace politics." Everyone was criticizing the government, including the officials themselves. Imru watched how the new professional class cared only about its own welfare—owning a house and Mercedes, marrying well and defending their turf. "Although many of them were highly qualified, their ability to implement new measures was limited by the concentration of power in the Emperor, and also by the back-biting that prevailed among them. This was exacerbated by the Emperor's manipulations when he would make a decision by addressing directly a particular official, which made others insecure over their positions."[51]

When the Wollo region suffered crippling drought in 1973, the BBC's correspondent, Jonathan Dimbleby, contrasted footage of starving Ethiopians with shots of what looked to be a luxurious feast in the palace. Overnight, Haile Selassie was viewed as no better than a post-colonial despot. But Wilfred Thesiger argued in his autobiography that the report was highly misleading—the feast was a rare state banquet, and most of the time, the Emperor and his family ate meals that were quite humble, practically ascetic.[52] The massive public relations damage, however, was done.

Whether Haile Selassie ate humbly in his own home cannot excuse how many of his subjects didn't eat at all. Scholars still debate how much he knew, but Imru Zelleke is one of those who believes that officials at court were guilty of keeping the Emperor in the dark over the extent of the famine. Whatever the truth, the country was imploding. When the new prime minister announced reforms in early 1974, it was already too late.

There was a general strike in March, and in April, when Imru's eldest daughter married, the celebration was a subdued affair. The money that might have been spent on the happy couple's nuptials went instead to famine relief. Imru's daughter, Adey, passed along an interesting comment made by the Emperor. As Haile Selassie blessed her marriage, he told her, "I hope that your father will forgive me for all the wrongs I did to him."[53]

The malevolent storm finally broke in September of 1974. It was called the Derg, the name for a small committee of military officers.

Haile Selassie found himself under house arrest and a prisoner in his own palace. Then officers came to bundle him off in the back of a Volkswagen to keep him in a small hut at Menelik's gibbi. The Derg recycled the old Fascist line that he had moved a fortune to Swiss bank accounts, and as the car drove by, crowds jeered the Emperor, shouting, "Thief! Thief!" Legends surround even the grim drive in the Volkswagen. One story goes that the Emperor berated his captors as insolent. Thesiger recounted another version, that Haile Selassie told one of the officers, "If this revolution is for the good of the country then I am in favor of the revolution."[54] He would be held as a prisoner for close to a year.

The most menacing thundercloud in the storm was an ambitious sociopath named Mengistu Haile Mariam. It's unknown how the Emperor actually died, though it's widely believed that Mengistu may have murdered Haile Selassie himself. An attendant found the elderly ruler dead in his bed, probably strangled after he was sedated.[55] Another rumor is that Mengistu indulged himself in a demented private joke by ordering Haile Selassie's corpse buried under some palace toilets. He presided over a new, nightmarish era for his country of repression, war, and famine.

For the second time in his life, horrific events drove Imru Zelleke out of his country, only this time he could at least choose his own destination and was able to leave under his own free will. He fled to the United States. A friend and fellow exile delivered a perceptive judgment on the Derg's darkness: "Everything we considered bad, ugly, and evil has been given free license in our country."[56]

* * *

There is a shabby footnote to the Derg revolution and Haile Selassie's murder. *Jet*, one of the most popular magazines for African Americans at the time, reported in a November 1974 issue that Hubert Julian—by then in his late seventies and having reverted back to his real name—was planning to rescue Haile Selassie. Could anyone take seriously the idea of this elderly, gaunt black man sitting in a cockpit again for a last dangerous adventure?

The FBI could. Despite his age, they monitored his activities because he'd reinvented himself as an arms dealer, brokering shipments through the 1960s to Pakistan, Haiti, and the Congo. By 1974, he was involved in so many shady deals—including gold and diamond smuggling—that both the FBI and US Customs were breathing down his neck. Somehow he escaped arrest and settled for the occasional interview for articles that presented him as a daring rascal.

In a brilliant book review essay for the *New York Times* in 2007, Clive James wrote of Leni Riefenstahl, "She lied about everything. She just went on lying until people got tired, or old, or died." The same can be written of the infamous Black Eagle.

Hubert Julian finally passed away in the Bronx in 1983, old and forgotten, having not left his own house for the final five years of his life, and it took reporters more than half a year to notice he was gone. But his last wife insisted years later to David Shaftel, a journalist for *Air & Space* magazine, "He didn't want any reporters swarming the house. He just told me to keep it peaceful, he'd had enough of it all."[57]

At the very end, Hubert Julian might have at last told the truth.

* * *

After Haile Selassie was dead, a small hand grenade of a book was released in 1978 by the Polish writer, Ryszard Kapuściński. It was called *The Emperor: Downfall of an Autocrat.*

Kapuściński claimed that he traveled to Ethiopia to get an insider's view of Haile Selassie's decline and fall, interviewing servants and those close to the Emperor. The book created a fantastic portrait of a paranoid megalomaniac who needed pillows slipped under his feet and who began his daily routine by listening to informants' reports. "F," one of Kapuściński's mysterious sources, suggests a small dog named Lulu "was allowed to sleep in the Emperor's great bed. During various ceremonies, he would run away from the Emperor's lap and pee on dignitaries' shoes. The august gentlemen were not allowed to flinch or make the slightest gesture when they felt their feet getting wet."[58]

Kapuściński's book was translated into more than a dozen languages and sold around the world. Jonathan Miller directed a London stage adaptation, and while he was still alive, Kapuściński's writing was heaped with literary prizes. After he was dead, the tributes flooded in from critics, associates, and admirers, including Salman Rushdie, Gabriel García Márquez, John Updike . . . and even Bill Deedes.

But little by little, it's become clear that Kapuściński was an imaginative and talented liar. He spun *The Emperor* out of the ether, and he probably invented several of his other journalistic accounts. He encouraged a legend that he was friends with the independence leader Patrice Lumumba, but Kapuściński only visited the Congo in 1961 a month after Lumumba had been assassinated. Those who defend his work often claim it was intended to be allegorical, because Kapuściński couldn't write the truth about his own native Poland under Soviet repression. It's a defense that rings hollow, especially since it turns out that he worked for a while as a Soviet spy, and his job involved snooping on certain intellectual expatriates and occasionally destroying their reputations. Whether it was meant to be allegorical or not, *The Emperor* is still in print and still sits in *non*fiction.

Kapuściński didn't count on or simply didn't care about who knew East Africa, the *real* East Africa. The writer and anthropologist John Ryle, a co-founder of the Rift Valley Institute, wrote a lengthy piece for *The Times Literary Supplement* in 2001 and took apart *The Emperor* with almost surgical skill. He noted that Kapuściński's alleged sources at court remain, for the most part, conveniently anonymous. And the obsequious titles they use, like "His Most Virtuous Highness," don't match anything that fits the Amharic language or that are familiar to those who were actually there.[59] Critics of Kapuściński's work have tallied long lists of factual errors—and not mild, inconsequential ones, but basic and important ones. They confirm, as one of them put it, that Kapuściński simply hadn't "the energy to do more reading, more research, more checking."[60] It was easier for him to make things up.

In Addis Ababa, an art gallery owner, Barbara Goshu, met Kapuściński and was at first charmed by him, only to be astonished by the fabulous inventions of *The Emperor* when the book came out. She later confronted him and recounted to Kapuściński's biographer, "I told him at once that it was dishonest, and that he had presented an unfair picture of the wonderful man Haile Selassie actually was." Kapuściński made a face like a naughty boy caught in the act and "then quickly changed the subject. Never before or later did he ever say what he thought about the Emperor or about Mengistu."[61]

Kapuściński's book and Jonathan Dimbleby's report on the Wollo famine were successive blows that severely damaged the Emperor's reputation. Dimbleby, a respected reporter, diligently pursued facts; Kapuściński didn't care. Their mediums and methods were worlds apart, but these two works of controversial journalism, one after another, have clouded any accurate portrait of Haile Selassie and make it difficult to assess his true legacy.

Reformer and reactionary, modernist and relic—the debate goes on over the lion's legacy. For decades after the Ethiopian Revolution and to this very day, scholars and historians have rattled the imperial bones, wondering what new patterns of insight can be made out in the cast-off dust. Ethiopia's historian Bahru Zewde, noting how foreigners have been "practically mesmerized" by Haile Selassie, asked with ample justification, "Will we ever see the day when Ethiopian rulers will be viewed as human beings who operated within the context of their times rather than as demi-gods or monsters?"[62] Another noted historian and the daughter of a brave Patriot, Tsehai Berhane-Selassie, put it just as pithily to this author: "We Ethiopians live off our own history, and some of us tend to over- or under-cook the past in order to suit the political time of our day."[63]

Haile Selassie might have thought his reign was ordained by God, but he was a mortal with all the failings and conflicted drives of human nature. If he ever thought of his subjects as children that needed his centralized, firm control, they fulfilled Oscar Wilde's maxim; first, they loved him, and as they stepped out of the medieval age of spear and shield and infallible gold cross into the harsh glare of the modern world, they judged him. We must wait and see if they will forgive him.

*   *   *

Consider these famous words: "That until the philosophy which holds one race superior and another inferior is finally and permanently discredited and abandoned; That until there are no longer first-class and second-class citizens of any nation; That until the color of a man's skin is of no more significance than the color of his eyes . . ." These lines were spoken by Haile Selassie in a speech to the United Nations on October 6, 1968, but we are more familiar with them today because they were borrowed for a pop tune. The cadences are almost impossible to hear now without recalling the music to Bob Marley's *War*.

They are worth examining now because when Haile Selassie spoke them, he repeatedly invoked his unheeded call decades ago to the League of Nations. "In 1936, I declared that it was not the Covenant of the League that was at stake, but international morality," he reminded the Assembly. "The Charter of the United Nations expresses the noblest aspirations of man," such as assurance of human rights and freedom and international security. "But these, too, as were the phrases of the Covenant, are only words; their value depends wholly on our will to observe and honor them and give them content and meaning."

As the Emperor offered his lecture, students back home, of course, were frustated over the lack of rights and the pitiful state of their country. Many Eritreans could find a malicious irony in the speech. Putting these issues aside, there is still the value of perspective in what the delegates heard: "The authority of the Organization has been mocked, as individual member-states have proceeded, in violation of its commands, to pursue their own aims and ends. The troubles which continue to plague us virtually all arise among member states of the Organization, but the Organization remains impotent to enforce acceptable solutions. As the maker and enforcer of the international law, what the United Nations has achieved still falls regrettably short of our goal of an international community of nations."

As it still does to this day. The question of the UN's legal and moral supremacy over conflicts is with us still. The Ethiopian War has given the world important lessons that it still refuses to learn and questions that still need to be resolved. In 1999, it was not the UN that finally stepped in to stop bloodshed in Kosovo, but NATO. And as this chapter was being drafted, the news was full of reports over the controversial arms ban regarding the civil war in Syria.

* * *

The Emperor's remains were discovered in 1992 after Mengistu had been ousted and had gone into exile in Zimbabwe. But *where* exactly they were found hasn't been disclosed. Then there were tedious politics over what to do with them; the new regime didn't want to be seen endorsing any old royal institutions. Finally, on Sunday, November 5, 2000, a private ceremony was allowed for a burial instead of a state funeral.

It was a long, complicated affair, spread out over four locations, and at each spot, thousands came out to watch. At the capital's Bahata Church, women walked in a circle, weeping, "Our master, our master . . ."[64] A truck carried the Emperor's coffin with an escort of four bodyguards to Meskel Square, each man in traditional robes with a lion's headdress, carrying a spear and leather shield. The cortege moved on later to the Holy Trinity Cathedral, where drums beat and a bell tolled to mark its arrival.

A British chartered surveyor named Andrew Hilton happened to be in town on business that weekend. He was curious and, knowing it was a moment of history, he took a cab down to the cathedral. Wading his way through the thick crowd, he "managed to get swept up in the swirl of people flowing through the gates and past the policemen, now swamped in their hopeless task of ticket-checking."[65] Hilton couldn't see a thing from the back of the throng, but then an old thin man in white robes guided him to the front, calling out, "Let him through, he's a *ferengi*, and he's got a camera!" It was not enough for the Ethiopians to know this day had happened; others must see it, others must be told.

Hilton was fascinated by the spectacle: the blowing of bugles and beating of drums, the representatives of the Orthodox Church in their elaborate finery, the foreign diplomats who had come to pay their respects.

One important guest was Princess Tenagnework, Haile Selassie's eldest daughter and, in the end, his only surviving child. Ethiopia's turbulent history had cost her much. Her husband, Desta, had been killed by the Italians; the Derg had killed her son and put her in prison for fifteen years; she had to learn from a cell how her second husband had died of illness in London. She also lost a daughter and niece in the same year of the revolutionary upheaval. Now she had the chance to say a final goodbye to her father, whom she was said to be close to and very like in character.

And there was an awe-struck Andrew Hilton, who took it all in and realized, "This was not some staged event for tourists, this was a natural outpouring of love and respect, not only for their Emperor, but also for their traditional way of life. Here at the dawn of the new millennium—despite the four-wheel drives and the modern media technology—the scene was timeless; Ethiopia was staking its claim to its traditional roots."[66]

Hilton noticed a group of elderly Ethiopians dressed in different uniforms, some proudly wearing medals. Patriots, all. Having made new friends in the crowd, he was introduced to these veterans, and this particular *ferengi* and the Patriots intrigued each other. Here was a younger man from far away who wanted to know their stories. And it had been so long since they could tell them to anyone. "Under the Derg regime," noted Hilton, "the Emperor's role in the overthrow of the Italian invasion was erased from the national memory and many of those associated with him disappeared, as did so many others, lost without a trace."[67]

But not all of them. Hilton was so fascinated that he decided to collect the memories of surviving veterans, enlisting the help of the Association of Ethiopian Patriots, Richard Pankhurst, and a clever young history undergraduate (now professor), Yonatan Sahle, to act as interpreter and interviewer. Men in their seventies all the way up to ninety-one recalled their adventures, remembered songs sung, their deeds of bravery. One passed on before Hilton could bring out a book on their remembrances, but though they were old, fading into twilight one by one, the reclaimed history has been preserved.

It's protected, too, in a house along a dusty road in Addis Ababa, next to a small store and a brief walk from the Swiss embassy. It's where retired Lieutenant-General Jagama Kello lives, and his tidy, pleasant living room is decorated with photos of his honors, his wife and family, and beautiful black-and-white shots of his years in service. Jagama spent his teen years as a soldier, and he would end up spending the rest of his life as one. Having learned his craft in the mountains and making it up as he went along, he had to attend different academies to learn administration and proper army instruction. But it wasn't long before he was a senior commander once again in Ethiopia's armed forces.

Though now in his nineties, his memory seems mostly clear, and he still grants interviews and cheerfully invites visitors to have a whiskey with him. It doesn't take much prompting either for Jagama to suggest taking a drive out to the battlefields, where he once took sniper shots from a rifle at the *ferengi* invaders. The body of the war hero is frail, but the spirit of the veteran soldier is still clearly present.

The story could wrap up there so neatly and cleanly. But it hasn't quite ended, because a simmering, quiet feud goes on over how the war is remembered—when it's remembered at all by the outside world. If anyone doubts the Ethiopian War is still with us and still matters, they have only to take a flight to Italy and visit an austere block of a monument in a small town . . .

Chapter Twenty-Five

EPILOGUE OF STONES

Few people outside of Italy have probably ever heard of the town of Affile. Couched in the hills east of Rome, Affile boasts a population today of only sixteen hundred people, and most of the native sons it calls "famous" on its promotional website are actually quite obscure. There's an ambassador from Roman times, a professor of clinical surgery in the 1800s, and a seventeenth-century organ builder. But there is also Rodolfo Graziani, the Butcher of Fezzan, and the town is defiantly proud of him. "His mortal remains," reads copy on the website, "brought to Affile among a huge crowd of people, rest in the tomb of the old cemetery, along with his family, perhaps too much forgotten, forgotten as it was during his life despite the fact that he paid the price for the good . . . of the country."[1]

Graziani hasn't been forgotten at all here. On August 11, 2012, the town became home to an unusual memorial. It's an ugly, unimaginative block that squats on Affile's tallest hill, and under an Italian flag the words "Patria" (Homeland) and "Onore" (Honor) are inscribed left and right. Here, the Butcher's reputation as a favorite son is kept alive with vintage newspaper clippings and a plaque from a street that was once dedicated to him in the town. The memorial's centerpiece is a white marble bust of its beloved hero. Affile's mayor, Ettore Viri, didn't have to go far to get it. At first, he was cagey with the *New York Times* when it asked where it came from: "The head is a donation of a citizen." Then he quickly explained, "Actually, I had it in my living room."[2]

Viri told the paper that he had contributed large sums of his own money for the upkeep of Mussolini's grave in Predappio. But for the Graziani memorial, it was the town that ponied up $160,000 in public funds. Many of its citizens didn't mind. In fact, roughly a hundred of them were on hand for the memorial's dedication, and a few sported black shirts and carried the flags of extremist organizations. A representative of the Vatican was on hand for the ceremony,[3] which was followed by "a buffet and an evening of entertainment."[4]

Their mayor kept insisting all the while that "Graziani was not a war criminal, and he was not sentenced at Nuremberg."[5] This was technically correct—and completely beside the point. "The council administration simply wanted to honor a distinguished citizen who always had his country close to his heart and whose memory has been unjustly sullied."[6]

It would be grossly inaccurate and unfair to suggest the memorial received only support or indifference within Italy. The National Partisans Association suggested publicly that it intended to sue Viri for an "apology for Fascism [and related crimes]." A Jewish women's group, Binah, sent an open letter of protest to Italy's Jewish leaders. One of the most vocal in his outrage was Esterino Montino of Italy's Democratic Party: "It's as if some little village in some German province built a monument to Goering."[7]

Still, the majority of the criticism came from abroad, and often from familiar guardians of Ethiopia's past. Historian Bahru Zewde called the memorial "shameful," writing, "We in Ethiopia are really shocked that such a thing could be allowed to happen. Even if we are aware of the residual Fascism that has been a feature of Italian political life, we never thought it could go this far."[8] Other leading academics, from Francesca Locatelli at the University of Edinburgh to Oxford's David Anderson, also made condemnations. Haile Selassie's grandson, Prince Ermias Sahle Selassie, wrote an open letter to both Italy's president and its prime minister, demanding that the memorial be dismantled.[9]

Richard Pankhurst—who, as a boy, snapped photos while his mother discussed Ethiopia's future with the exiled Haile Selassie in a garden, who has written so much on Ethiopia's history—was equally, if not more, disgusted. He drafted a speech, and at the end of August of 2012, his wife, Rita, delivered it outside the Italian embassy, which overlooks the green and leafy Grosvenor Square of London's Mayfair district. "Let us make no bones about it," went the Pankhurst address. "Graziani is not simply to be numbered as one of the Fascist invaders who committed war crimes in Africa, not even as one of the principal ones: he was, without a doubt, the most criminal one. Those who, for one reason or another, condone his deeds, are all the more guilty."[10]

It is no accident that the Graziani memorial could be erected and, worse, permitted to stay standing in our own era. For decades, Predappio, birthplace of Mussolini, has been a pilgrimage site for skinheads and right-wing extremists who flock to his crypt, decked out like a shrine. It took until 2009 for the city councillors to finally ban the sale of Fascist merchandise, from swastika-decorated knives to truncheons.

Small towns with lingering sympathy might be easily dismissed, but consider the statement made all too recently by Italy's disgraced former prime minister,

Silvio Berlusconi, in late January of 2013. At a Milan ceremony commemorating victims of the Nazi Holocaust, no less, he told his audience, "Obviously the government of [Mussolini's] time, out of fear that German power might lead to complete victory, preferred to ally itself with Hitler's Germany rather than opposing it." He went on to argue, "The racial laws were the worst fault of Mussolini as a leader, who in so many other ways did well."[11]

There was a predictable blast of angry international criticism, and Berlusconi issued a quick statement to clarify his comments. But they were not casual slips of the tongue, nor were they the first time Berlusconi played apologist for the Duce. His political allies, after all, included the "post-Fascist" National Alliance. While still in office in 2003, he gave an interview to Nicholas Farrell of Britain's *Spectator*, in which he called Italian Fascism "a much more benign dictatorship— Mussolini did not murder anyone. Mussolini sent people on holiday to confine them (banishment to small islands such as Ponza and Maddalena which are now exclusive resorts)." Less attention was paid to Farrell's follow-up Diary column, which contained this statement—just as astonishingly provocative and equally wrong—after he quotes the above: "This, though extraordinary, is more or less true. Unlike the Russian communists, the Italian fascists *did not use mass murder to retain power* [emphasis added]."[12]

So it would be wrong to conclude the revisionists for Fascism are only Italian. Earlier that same year, Farrell had brought out a new biography of Mussolini that Tobias Jones of *The Guardian* called "an attempt not at revisionism, but at restoration." Jones noted that "right-wing historians are now openly de-demonising fascism and debunking half a century of 'red' mythology. In the process Mussolini is being once again portrayed as an inspirational leader who, until 1935 (Abyssinia) or 1938 (the race laws), could do nothing wrong." [13]

In *Fascist Voices*, Professor Christopher Duggan makes the point that it's not only historians, but Italian political figures besides Berlusconi, who have pushed this line: "Mussolini had certainly made regrettable errors, they admitted— notably allying with the Nazis and passing racial laws—but overall his regime had been relatively benign."[14]

* * *

The Nuremberg Trials are famous. Their lasting image is one of Goering and other leading Nazis in a dock, each wearing clunky headphones, all guarded by white-helmeted military police. What's hardly ever mentioned is the fact that the entire courtroom was oriented to *view a giant film screen*. The prosecutors at Nuremberg always knew the most powerful, damning weapon in their catalogue of evidence wasn't the vast stock of records that the Nazis kept themselves, or even the survivors who showed up to testify. No, it was the actual footage of the horrors in the death camps. Since everyone knows film footage has to be edited, they wisely pre-empted any accusations of doctoring (even then) and had affidavits filmed and placed at the start of the reels shown in court.

The prosecutors did all this because in 1945, people could hardly believe it had happened. Then the overwhelming evidence forced them to accept it.

Affidavits were signed, too, over atrocities committed during the Italian-Ethiopian War and the subsequent occupation.

But unlike Germany, where to deny the Holocaust today is an actual crime, a state of denial won out regarding Italy that continues to this very day. Even as the bombings and gassings happened, the Italians were given a pass.

Britain's retired general and one of Oswald Mosley's staunch supporters, J. F. C. Fuller, wrote, "More than any other factor, I think, that of the alleged bombing of field hospitals shocked the people; yet I cannot believe that the Italians were so inhuman or so foolish as to select them for targets."[15] While admitting that "thousands were wounded by gas burns," he simply could not believe the Italians were equally capable of bombing hospitals.[16]

American reporter Herbert Matthews was equally incredulous. "Of course, the Italians employed some poison gas," he wrote, "but I cannot conceive how any thoughtful person, using the available facts, could reach the conclusion that the Italians broke the Ethiopian resistance with it."[17] George Martelli, the *London Morning Post's* correspondent in Rome, wouldn't believe the worst either. To Martelli, the deliberate targeting of the British Red Cross hospital in Korem was "not really very plausible." In his book, *Italy Against the World*, he dismissed it as "just a sheer piece of 'frightfulness' with the hatred of the British as an additional incentive."[18]

Decades later, historians poring over records echoed the disbelief of those who walked the actual ground. "It seems difficult to believe that the Italians should be either so inhuman or so foolish," wrote A. J. Barker. "Probably the explanation is simply that hospital tents were placed so close to legitimate objectives that when these were bombed, it was difficult to distinguish between them."[19] This wasn't true—in fact, it's contradicted by the photographic evidence the Red Cross submitted to the League of Nations. It's also contradicted by the Italian air force's own aerial reconnaissance shots.

"It seems difficult to believe . . . I cannot conceive. . . . I cannot believe. . ." The same phrasing crops up again and again. No logical refutation of the facts is offered. The doubters "can't" believe because, emotionally, they don't want to.

A courageous exception has been historian Angelo Del Boca, who at first "could not honestly accept" that Badoglio had authorized the use of gas until he dug deeper. His research prompted him to "state with *absolute certainty* [original italics]" that several regions "were drenched with yperite on several occasions." As Del Boca has argued, it hardly matters how many times gas was used. "That the Italians resorted to mustard gas is the damning fact and nothing can lessen the guilt of the generals and politicians who decided to authorize chemical warfare."[20]

But why should the claims of atrocity be doubted at all? Why were they doubted then? One simple reason that gets little attention—yet is the great elephant lumbering around the room for debate—is race. The Italians bombed and gassed Africans. They bombed and gassed black people, "primitives." That much of the world sympathized with their plight was the greatest shock of all to Mussolini.

Few have ever deconstructed the logic of the denial arguments, both then and now. The reasoning goes that if the Italians bombed Red Cross hospitals—virtually all run by white Europeans—this must have been an accident. If not an accident, the Ethiopians are to blame; they camped too close or misused the Red Cross emblem. The black man is at fault, the white man merely mistaken. If an African makes a claim of atrocity, he must be inflating the numbers. "Possessing a vivid imagination and little power of reasoning," wrote J. F. C. Fuller, "the native is only too apt to exaggerate effects . . ."[21]

Today, it's not so much a case of the African not being trusted with the facts as simply being ignored. And what country likes to be reminded of its past shameful conduct? France has Vichy, Indochina, and Algeria; for five years, it banned the award-winning classic film, *The Battle of Algiers* (made by an Italian director). Turkey has the Armenian Genocide and its law to stifle dissent, Article 301. Japan does not talk about the Rape of Nanking—at all. Is it any surprise, then, that Italy would like to forget how it treated Ethiopia?

Well, yes. Because the amnesia is not the product of time or patriotism in our modern age—it is an actual conspiracy, at least according to some. "An audacious deception has allowed the country to evade blame for massive atrocities committed before and during the Second World War and to protect the individuals responsible, some almost certainly still alive," wrote Rory Carroll in *The Guardian* in 2001. "Of more than 1,200 Italians sought for war crimes in Africa and the Balkans, not one has faced justice. Webs of denial spun by the state, academe and the media have re-invented Italy as a victim, gulling the rest of the world into acclaiming the Good Italian long before Captain Corelli strummed a mandolin."[22]

Still, it is historians with Italian names, Angelo Del Boca and Alberto Sbacchi, who have dug up much of the truth. Del Boca's efforts forced a reluctant Italian Ministry of Defence to admit—but only in 1996—that its planes dropped poison gas on Ethiopia.[23] We know these camps and prisons existed, and one of the internment facilities, Akaki, continues functioning as a prison today, housing those convicted of atrocities during the infamous Derg regime of the 1970s and 1980s.[24] We know some of what was done there from the statements of surviving witnesses. But the numbers for the camps confound us, in part because the records have either not survived or been conveniently "mislaid."

It's unfortunate that by the time that documentary maker Roman Herzog started working on an online oral history archive, so many of the survivors had passed on. But the war—the *whole* war, and not simply its occupation—deserves wider recognition, or we'll merely see the tragedy of the massacres and the camps as just another period when the Africans were victims, infantilizing them once again. The gassings and bombings, the Graziani Massacre, and the camps are all the more poignant because they were preceded by a heroic assertion of independence, by a nation that wasn't so primitive after all, using modern diplomacy first before it was forced to pick up its antiquated rifles.

* * *

The war's legacy for African Americans and Pan-Africanism runs like a distant anthem, the music too far away sometimes to distinguish the lyrics, but perhaps a scrap of the melody can get picked up if you listen hard enough.

There is a lot of conflicting march music and noise to tune out, of course. After all, feelings over Ethiopia in America begin with a Negro spiritual (hands stretching out to God), and somehow along the way, both in American big cities and in London and Paris, they mix with the rousing song for Communists, *The Internationale*. And then horns blast all that away, calling men at last to go fight Hitler, with Mussolini almost as an afterthought. Patriotic African Americans who fought in the Second World War came back and shouted in a loud and clear tone that they were *not* going to settle for the same old conditions as before—their discontent helped propel the first great wave of post-war civil rights activism. Ethiopia was the last thing on their minds.

Then what did the Ethiopian War contribute to the effort? A lot, as it turned out . . . but for the next generations. The wheel would turn full circle. Marcus Garvey may have been disillusioned, but many others were not, and so Ethiopia, wearing all her historic finery again, went on as a beacon for black unity. Meanwhile, the great radical figures in Britain, like Kenyatta and Kwame Nkrumah, came into their own in Kenya and Ghana. For them, Ethiopia lived as a great idea. Each was conscious of how the war with Italy affected their thinking; they all acknowledged the debt of influence. And they would inspire black radicals coming of age in the 1960s, young men and women looking for heroes and examples.

Another souvenir shot: "An Italian soldier standing guard over a mass of dead Ethiopian civilians after the Graziani Massacre . . ." —George Steer

Ethiopian Patriots tied to trees and blindfolded before they were shot dead. This was another photo confiscated from the pocket of an Italian soldier.

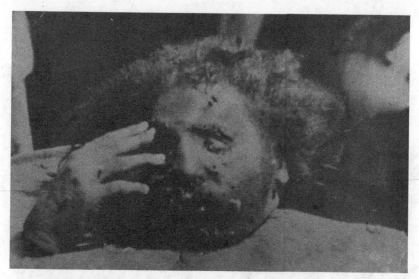

"Another severed head of an Ethiopian patriot, executed at Debre Brehan, being carried round on a plate with his severed right hand set alongside the head in a mock salute." —George Steer

Italian soldiers smile for the camera as one holds up a "spoil of war."

Haile Selassie with Captain George Steer, June 3, 1941.

The Boy General: Jagama Kello, center, with two comrades-in-arms.

Success: Patriots escort the Emperor as Debra Markos is retaken.

Officials of the Ethiopian Orthodox Church waiting for the Emperor's entry into Addis Ababa.

America's Champion of Democracy meets the "Elect of God": Haile Selassie and Franklin Roosevelt on the *USS Quincy* at the Suez Canal, February 13, 1945.

The Tireless Crusader: Sylvia Pankhurst in the post-war period with Haile Selassie.

The Emperor's former palace, now the Institute of Ethiopian Studies for Addis Ababa University. The upstairs floor displays Haile Selassie's and Menen's old bedroom chambers for tourists. The closest set of ground floor white windows are likely where the grenades were tossed at Graziani, with soldiers slaughtering the crowd in front soon after.

The Survivor: Imru Zelleke at age sixteen and modern day as a retired and respected diplomat living in Virginia.

Three Heroes: Patriots at the burial ceremony for the Emperor on November 5, 2000.

The oldest hotel in Addis Ababa, the Taitu Hotel. One of the main hotels where Evelyn Waugh, George Steer, Laurence Stallings, and others would have drank, slept, written dispatches, and competed with each other.

Washa Mikael, outside Addis Ababa. The church was bombed by the Italians then allegedly used later to hide the Ark of the Convenant. Some faithful still visit it today.

One of the rock-hewn churches of Lalibela. Haile Selassie detoured to the town, which remains one of the holiest places in Ethiopia, praying for his country's and his own salvation.

The past endures: people leaving market day near Blue Nile Falls, south of Gonder, 2013. For a good portion of Ethiopia, life is still pastoral and is much as it was in centuries past.

Legacy restored: The stelae field in Aksum, with the Aksum Obelisk back in its proper home.

Just as African Americans in the 1930s looked beyond their shores for inspiration, so a new crop of activists developed an international consciousness. The political theory, the tried and true methods of protest, the sense of collective purpose and racial unity, would all be rediscovered. *Think black, act black, and be black.* That was what Malaku Bayen had urged supporters to do. Then the photos of big Afros worn with bandoliers on mountaintops had been put away.

But now, the Afros were sported proudly in meeting halls in Boston and Brixton. Now independent African nations were the great ideas: Nkrumah's Ghana, Kenyatta's Kenya, Lumumba's brief and doomed Congo . . .

And there were still a few who remembered the Ethiopian War, who were inspired by the original struggle. In 1962, one brilliant activist was at a barracks in Kolfe, a suburb of Addis Ababa, learning guerrilla tactics for the armed wing of the African National Congress. On his road to becoming one of the greatest leaders in modern history, Nelson Mandela first learned how to be a freedom fighter in the land of the Patriots.

*   *   *

Journalists played more of a role in deciding the perception—and ultimately, the outcome—of Ethiopia's war than in any other armed conflict in the twentieth century, right up until Vietnam.

While that might read as a sweeping statement, consider what happened. Walwal began as a postage-stamp item that escalated to front-page news, thanks to the initiative of a few reporters who recognized its significance. It was journalists who ignited the sympathy for Ethiopians and conversely for the Fascist cause, and if the details hadn't leaked to newspapers, the Hoare-Laval Plan would have been a *fait accompli.* A watching world was so outraged that the League allowed the proposal to die. To those who suggest news coverage didn't move delegates enough to act, you could argue that indeed, it did; quick reporting from the front helped create the tragic impression that Italy's victory was a foregone conclusion, ensuring the League acted . . . by turning its back. Foreign correspondents announced the capture of Addis Ababa, and the political and public reaction was that the war must be "over." But of course, it wasn't.

The myth has stubbornly persisted that the whole conflict was a kind of farce, with little relevance to world affairs, aside from the League of Nations. It's presented again and again in books as a tableau in which a group of crusty, bored reporters were stuck in an exotic, backward capital of Africa with nothing to do; they freely invented the facts because, supposedly, there was no "real story" going on.

This is partly because of *Waugh in Abyssinia*, but all the blame can't be laid at one author's door. True, Waugh belittled the war's significance because he left before it actually got going. But to be fair, both George Steer and Herbert Matthews also grumbled as Waugh did about colleagues taking liberties with the facts. Few, if any, specifics were ever mentioned by any of the three, probably because of libel concerns.

The truth is that most of the correspondents probably did their jobs no better or worse than reporters in our era stuck in Cairo, but filing a report on the uprising in Libya. We have phone-in, hotel-room journalism today, and we had it back then. Reporters were often as rebellious over being cooped up during the first Gulf War as they were in Addis Ababa and Asmara. But Steer got into the field. So did Matthews. So did Luigi Barzini, Jr. So did others. And in contrast to the idea that many reporters made things up, there was the reality that sometimes the more diligent correspondents had skeptical editors back home who severely cut or spiked their copy. For Herbert Matthews, the war in Ethiopia "was my first lesson in the difficulty of convincing people of truths that they do not want to believe."[25]

One measure of both the impact as well as the accuracy of the reportage on the war is that the books by Steer, Matthews, and others found enthusiastic publishers in 1935 and 1936, and these books have been heavily relied on as source material for any credible modern retelling. There is a charming familiarity in the urgent "timeliness" promoted on their dust jackets. The generation of the 1930s worried about Ethiopia and Spain; today, we worry about Ukraine and Syria.

Vietnam is widely considered the first "media war" because its horrors were shown on the evening news as Americans ate their Swanson TV dinners. But the pressure by critics and reporters was always on one side; Ho Chi Minh didn't have to care what Morley Safer broadcasted from Saigon. In contrast, both Mussolini and Haile Selassie were deeply invested in how their sides were portrayed and in what went out on the radio and in newspapers the next day, and neither ever had sufficient control over the result.

The Ethiopian War had its unchecked "facts" that created a few great yarns, but it never gave birth to its own legend. And yet the ingredients were all there for the kind of romanticism that would attach itself to the Spanish Civil War: it had a cast of rogues, a reasonable supply of heroes and clowns, battles aplenty, and it even straddled two ages, modern and medieval. It had a genuine bard in Langston Hughes. All of this wasn't enough, and it comes down to a very simple reason. For the Spanish Civil War, *the good guys could show up.*

For Spain, the legend evolved because ordinary people were able to join the conflict. The myth is inclusive. For Ethiopia, those who wanted to fight—African

Americans, black British colonials, and sympathetic whites—were barred from doing so. There could be no great feats boasted or wonderful, half-true stories told at the café tables decades later, because virtually none of the volunteers were allowed to participate. Reporters in Ethiopia wrote colorful copy, but they made those who wanted to join the crusade look down the wrong end of a very long telescope.

It's fitting, then, that some of the most powerful stories of bravery come from the Ethiopian Patriots. The sad thing is that their legend didn't carry the world's imagination like the Spanish Civil War; for a very long time, they were known only by their own people.

The ultimate survivor of the war and its aftermath seems to have been Imru Zelleke, sent as a boy to the Danane concentration camp. He lived. After witnessing the horrors of the Graziani Massacre and enduring the camp, after surviving the occupation, he grew up and married, served his country and his Emperor, had children and grandchildren, and outlived all the heroes and villains, including the ruthless Derg. He built a new life for himself and his family in the United States, where he lives now. So much of Ethiopia's past and its future are woven into the tapestry of his career and personal journeys.

Like Ethiopia, he has endured much, but he has come out the other side. And though the Lion of Judah could not prevail at the very end, the former inmate of Danane has prevailed, living to bear witness.

* * *

Addis Ababa gave a lot of its core to its heroes, many of them foreign nationals who cared and fought passionately for Ethiopia. Besides the street named for Sylvia Pankhurst, there are ribbons of road named for John Melly and Anthony Eden, other streets in the city for Lorenzo Taezaz and for Ras Desta, two long strips for Cunningham and Wingate, and the roll call goes on.

The irony, however, is that except for, say, Churchill Road or a couple of others, ordinary Ethiopians aren't overly conscious of avenue names as they navigate their way around. On the street, you hear the rapid fire shout of *"Bole, Bole, Bole, Bole!"* from the minibuses angling for customers, and as folks pile into the small vans, Addis Ababa is hurtling forward to all the usual curses of modern "civilization." There are satellite dishes sprouting from wretched little sheds of corrugated iron. There are thick clouds of diesel and dust, and always there is the relentless pace of new construction with its preposterous, rickety wooden scaffolds. If you visit the old palace—now the Institute of Ethiopian Studies at Addis Ababa University—you must step inside before you catch a sign that tells you why this place is so important and who once lived here. Out front, thousands were killed long ago, but today it's a parking lot to anyone who casually glances. The actual monument to Yekatit 12 is a distance away.

In the country, much is as it was in Menelik's time. Children will sit by a roadside, working as shepherds for flocks of lamb. Near Blue Nile Falls, tourists must pick their way carefully around the "commuter traffic" going home from market day, which is commonly Saturday. Barefoot men and women in traditional dress, occasionally with a modern-made umbrella, will nudge oxen and mules with sticks along the narrow trails. A woman walks along with a tile of salt that has come all the way from the hot, flat Danakil, transported by camels. It's only since last year that using trucks for salt in the Danakil is now finally becoming a reality.

Ethiopia is an overwhelmingly agricultural nation, and no Western reader should dare to look down on livelihoods involving flocks of sheep and harvests of tef and barley. Imagine, without romanticizing it, how these ways of life could survive so much conflict, so much war and upheaval to our modern day! And so outside of Addis Ababa, it is *ancient* history that still dominates, not the comparatively recent age of Italian invasion and occupation. Those under thirty in Gonder will enthusiastically rave about the courage of Tewodros as if he were a close relative. There's a wonderful statue of him in the center of town. But the young people do not recognize the name of Lekelash Bayen.

In this, they're no different from American or British young people who can't tell you who Omar Bradley or Alan Brooke was. And it's certainly not their fault; it's another legacy of the Derg. In the spirit of Robespierre and the Khmer Rouge, the Derg tried to erase history, and they managed to obliterate quite a lot. But not all of it. There are still those who remember and, more importantly, those who care.

On April 19, 2005, for instance, an Antonov-124 cargo plane flew into the town of Aksum. Aksum today is still small, still a community that relies on the steady pilgrimage of visitors to its holy sites, but of course, today it probably greets more tourists on a regular basis than the faithful. You can check out its best shops and restaurants on its main street in less than ten minutes, and there is never much traffic. But on that day in April in 2005, the town was busy, its people jubilant. As the plane landed, cheers went up from a crowd of officials, priests, dignitaries, and ordinary, interested citizens. At the nearby St. Mariam Cathedral, bells rang in celebration.

Because the plane held a very large, very special piece of their heritage. Ethiopia's Culture Minister Teshome Toga was "excited, overjoyed, and delighted."[26] State Minister of Information Netsannet Asfew told *The Guardian*, "We have waited a long, long time for this. This is a proud moment for us."[27]

Onboard the plane was the sixty-three-ton first section—actually the middle one—of the Obelisk of Aksum. For close to seventy years, the monolith stood far away on the ground of Ethiopia's invader. Its concrete faux windows got a view of the Second World War, the Allied Liberation, the so-called "Years of Lead," and the assassination of Aldo Moro, all the way to the first Berlusconi era and a little beyond. Ethiopians, however, never forgot its loss. More than fifteen thousand people in Aksum alone—a substantial portion of the town's population—had signed a petition calling for the obelisk's return. A lobby campaign went on for decades, and the list of supporters who lent their names to the fight reads like a who's who of distinguished academics, famous writers, and noted figures. Besides Richard Pankhurst, who spearheaded the fight, there was Ethiopian-American scientist, Dr. Aberra Molla. There was Wilfred Thesiger, Germaine Greer, and Rita Marley, Bob Marley's widow. There were experts and historians on Italy and Ethiopia, such as Denis Mack Smith, Angelo Del Boca, Thomas Pakenham, and Richard Greenfield.

At last, it was returned after the seemingly interminable negotiations, to be put back together in a restoration project that cost close to $8 million. Italy agreed to foot the bill. The transport company found the task of moving the huge piece almost as daunting as those who stole it in the first place. The plane was fitted with heaters so the freezing temperatures high in the air wouldn't damage the massive stone, and steel bars encased it to protect it from turbulence.

It took three more years before the ancient stele was upright and cutting into the blue sky of Tigray, but finally, in September of 2008, the ugly scaffold was removed, and a gigantic Ethiopian flag serving as its drape was pulled away. There were thousands, too, that day to cheer.

Today, the Obelisk of Aksum stands in its place of restoration. And Ethiopia, changed by the war with the Italians, but changing the world far more, endures.

NOTES

Introduction

1   Mandela, *Long Walk to Freedom*, p. 292
2   Asante, *Pan-African Protest: West Africa and the Italo-Ethiopian Crisis*, p. 58
3   Franklin, *From Slavery to Freedom*, p. 476
4   O'Kelly, *Amedeo: The True Story of an Italian's War in Abyssinia*, p. 34
5   O'Kelly, *Amedeo: The True Story of an Italian's War in Abyssinia*, pp. 34–35
6   Lamb, *Mussolini and the British*, pp. ix–x
7   Lamb, *Mussolini and the British*, p. 56
8   Thesiger, *The Life of My Choice*, p. 329

Chapter One – The Duce and the Eternal City

1   Darrah, *Hail Caesar!* p. 106
2   Darrah, *Hail Caesar!* p. 103
3   Darrah, *Hail Caesar!* p. 241
4   Darrah, *Hail Caesar!* p. 21
5   Darrah, *Hail Caesar!* p. 23
6   Darrah, *Hail Caesar!* pp. 30-31
7   *Baedeker's Rome and Central Italy*, 1930, p. xxix
8   Darrah, *Hail Caesar!* p. 69
9   Darrah, *Hail Caesar!* p. 63
10 Darrah, *Hail Caesar!* p. 241, p. 272
11 *New York Times*, December 26, 1926
12 Darrah, *Hail Caesar!* p. 272
13 De Bono, *Anno XIII: The Conquest of an Empire*, p. 5
14 De Bono, *Anno XIII: The Conquest of an Empire*, p. 13
15 De Bono, *Anno XIII: The Conquest of an Empire*, p. 15
16 Darrah, *Hail Caesar!* p. 275
17 Darrah, *Hail Caesar!* p. 277
18 Baer, *The Coming of the Italian-Ethiopian War*, p. 53
19 Steer, *Caesar in Abyssinia*, p. 91
20 *League of Nations Official Journal*, February, 1935, p. 259
21 Farago, *Abyssinia on the Eve*, p. 198
22 *League of Nations Official Journal*, February, 1935, p. 264

23 *League of Nations Official Journal,* February, 1935, p. 269
24 *League of Nations Official Journal,* February, 1935, p. 262
25 Mockler, *Haile Selassie's War,* p. 39
26 Steer, *Caesar in Abyssinia,* p. 19
27 Associated Press, December 8, 1934
28 Darrah, *Hail Caesar!* p. 278
29 Darrah, *Hail Caesar!* p. 279
30 Bahru Zewde, *Pioneers of Change in Ethiopia,* p. 55
31 Bahru Zewde, "The Ethiopian Intelligentsia and the War"
32 Darrah, *Hail Caesar!* p. 278
33 Eden, *Facing the Dictators,* p. 4
34 Eden, *Facing the Dictators,* p. 193
35 Eden, *Facing the Dictators,* p. 193
36 Eden, *Facing the Dictators,* p. 193
37 *League of Nations Official Journal,* February, 1935, pp. 272–273
38 *League of Nations Official Journal,* February, 1935, p. 274
39 Coffey, *Lion by the Tail,* p. 19

Chapter Two – The Negus and the New Flower

1 Marcus, *Haile Selassie: The Formative Years, 1892-1936,* p. 99
2 Manchester, *The Last Lion: Visions of Glory,* p. 49
3 Jonas, *The Battle of Adwa,* p. 100
4 Jonas, *The Battle of Adwa,* p. 112
5 Jonas, *The Battle of Adwa,* p. 215
6 Jonas, *The Battle of Adwa,* p. 237
7 Jonas, *The Battle of Adwa,* p. 333
8 Jonas, *The Battle of Adwa,* pp. 276–277
9 Thesiger, *The Life of My Choice,* p. 24
10 Steer, *Caesar in Abyssinia,* p. 26
11 Farago, *Abyssinia on the Eve,* pp. 50–51
12 Farago, *Abyssinia on the Eve,* p. 86
13 Steer, *Caesar in Abyssinia,* pp. 28–29
14 Steer, *Caesar in Abyssinia,* p. 28
15 Farago, *Abyssinia on the Eve,* p. 69
16 Farago, *Abyssinia on the Eve,* p. 69
17 Mockler, *Haile Selassie's War,* p. 11; Marcus, *Haile Selassie 1: The Formative Years 1892-1936,* pp. 92–95
18 Marcus, *Haile Selassie: The Formative Years, 1892-1936,* p. 11
19 Haile Selassie, *Autobiography, Volume One,* p. 98; Marcus, *Haile Selassie 1: The Formative Years 1892-1936,* p. 64
20 Lamb, *Mussolini and the British,* p. 50
21 Lamb, *Mussolini and the British,* p. 51

22   Marcus, *Haile Selassie: The Formative Years*, p. 64

23   *Manchester Guardian*, June 17, 1924

24   Haile Selassie, *Autobiography, Volume One*, p. 136

25   Thesiger, *The Life of My Choice*, p. 93

26   Hastings, *Evelyn Waugh*, p. 235

27   Thesiger, *The Life of My Choice*, p. 92

28   Thesiger, *The Life of My Choice*, p. 235

29   US Diplomatic Papers, 1934, p. 770

30   US Diplomatic Papers, 1934, p. 774

31   De Bono, *Anno XIIII*, p. 116

32   De Bono, *Anno XIIII*, p. 116

33   Baer, *The Coming of the Italian-Ethiopian War*, p. 60

34   Associated Press, January 6, 1935

35   Lazareff, Pierre, *Deadline*, p. 94

36   Laval, *The Unpublished Diary*, pp. 33–34

37   Laval, *The Unpublished Diary*, p. 34

38   Lazareff, Pierre, *Deadline*, p. 96

39   Thompson, *Front-Line Diplomat*, p. 91

40   Thompson, *Front-Line Diplomat*, p. 95

41   Eden, *Facing the Dictators*, p. 195

42   Eden, *Facing the Dictators*, p. 197

Chapter Three – A Silent Room in Stresa

1   De Bono, *Anno XIIII*, p.119

2   De Bono, *Anno XIIII*, p. 118

3   Manchester, *The Last Lion, Winston Spencer Churchill: Alone, 1932-1940*, p. 77

4   Coffey, *Lion by the Tail*, p. 95

5   Eden, *Facing the Dictators*, p. 127

6   Eden, *Facing the Dictators*, p. 132

7   Eden, *Facing the Dictators*, p. 136

8   Waugh, *Evening Standard*, February 13, 1935

9   Farago, *Abyssinia on the Eve*, p. 89

10   Harmsworth, *Abyssinia Marches On*, p. 19

11   Harmsworth, *Abyssinia Marches On*, p. 22

12   Harmsworth, *Abyssinia Marches On*, pp. 26–27

13   Darrah, *Hail Caesar!* p. 286

14   Darrah, *Hail Caesar!*, p. 289

15   *Documents on British Foreign Policy*, Second Series, Vol. XIV, p. 221

16   *Documents on British Foreign Policy*, Second Series, Vol. XIV, p.221

17   *Documents on British Foreign Policy*, Second Series, Vol. XIV, p.221

18   Thompson, *Front-Line Diplomat*, pp. 97–98

19   Darrah, *Hail Caesar!* p. 289

20 Harris, *The United States and the Italo-Ethiopian Crisis*, p. 12, quoting Flandin, *Politique française, 1919-1940*

21 Coffey, *Lion by the Tail*, p. 62

22 Lamb, *Mussolini and the British*, p. 118

23 Darrah, *Hail Caesar!* p. 290

24 Baer, *The Coming of the Italian-Ethiopian War*, p. 128

25 Darrah, *Hail Caesar!* p. 290

26 Thompson, *Front-Line Diplomat*, pp. 100–102

27 Thompson, *Front-Line Diplomat*, pp. 100–102

28 *Documents on British Foreign Policy*, Second Series, Vol. XIV, p. 219

29 Jonas, *The Battle of Adwa*, p. 283

30 Baldwin, *Nobody Knows My Name*, p. 73

31 Simmons, *The Man Called Brown Condor*, pp. 12–13

32 Scott, *The Sons of Sheba's Race*, p. 70

33 Scott, *The Sons of Sheba's Race*, p. 72

34 Scott, "Malaku E. Bayen: Ethiopian Emissary to Black America, 1936-1941"

35 Scott, "Malaku E. Bayen: Ethiopian Emissary to Black America, 1936-1941"

36 Letter from Malaku Bayen to Claude Barnett, January 3, 1935, Barnett Papers, Chicago History Museum

37 Simmons, *The Man Called Brown Condor*, p. 109

38 De Bono, *Anno XIIII*, p. 161

39 Eden, *Facing the Dictators*, pp. 206–207

40 Eden, *Facing the Dictators*, p. 209

41 Ciano, *Ciano's Diary, 1937-1938*, p. 208

42 Eden, *Facing the Dictators*, p. 213

Chapter Four – Bluster

1 Scott, *The Sons of Sheba's Race*, p. 83

2 Scott, *The Sons of Sheba's Race*, p. 84

3 Scott, *The Sons of Sheba's Race*, p. 89

4 Farago, *Abyssinia on the Eve*, p. 185

5 Farago, *Abyssinia on the Eve*, p. 115

6 Farago, *Abyssinia on the Eve*, p. 117

7 Farago, *Abyssinia on the Eve*, p. 136

8 Farago, *Abyssinia on the Eve*, p. 144

9 De Bono, *Anno XIIII*, p. 49, p. 176

10 De Bono, *Anno XIIII*, p. 176

11 De Bono, *Anno XIIII*, p. 176

12 De Bono, *Anno XIIII*, p. 52

13 Mosley, Leonard, *Haile Selassie: The Conquering Lion*, p. 199; Steer, *Caesar in Abyssinia*, p. 145

14 Manchester, *The Last Lion, Winston Spencer Churchill: Visions of Glory, 1874–1932*, p. 830

15 Eden, *Facing the Dictators*, pp. 217–218

16 Eden, *Facing the Dictators*, p. 219

17 Hoare, *Nine Troubled Years*, p. 150

18 UK Hansard, June 7, 1935

19 Darrah, *Hail Caesar!* p. 303

20 Darrah, *Hail Caesar!* p. 307

21 Darrah, *Hail Caesar!* p. 308

22 Harmsworth, *Abyssinia Marches On*, p. 107

23 Harmsworth, *Abyssinia Marches On*, pp. 107–109

24 Harmsworth, *Abyssinia Marches On*, p. 112

25 Harmsworth, *Abyssinia Marches On*, p. 113

26 Harmsworth, *Abyssinia Marches On*, pp. 113–114

27 Barker, *The Civilizing Mission*, p. 108n

28 National Archives, UK, CAB 24/256/21

29 Andrew, *The Defence of the Realm*, p. 174

30 Colvin, *Vansittart in Office*, p. 58

31 Andrew, *The Defence of the Realm*, p. 174

32 Darrah, *Hail Caesar!* pp. 310–312

33 Darrah, *Hail Caesar!* pp. 315–326

34 Chicago *Tribune*, July 6, 1935, p. 10

35 Letter to Claude Barnett, November 21, 1935, Barnett Papers, Chicago History Museum

36 Letter to Claude Barnett, June 3, 1935, Barnett Papers, Chicago History Museum

37 Letter to Claude Barnett, June 3, 1935, Barnett Papers, Chicago History Museum

38 Letter to Claude Barnett, June 3, 1935, Barnett Papers, Chicago History Museum

39 Letter to Claude Barnett, June 3, 1935, Barnett Papers, Chicago History Museum

40 Eden, *Facing the Dictators*, pp. 230–231

41 Baer, *The Coming of the Italian-Ethiopian War*, p. 194

42 Thompson, *Front-Line Diplomat*, p. 103

43 Collier, *Duce!* p. 123

44 Eden, *Facing the Dictators*, pp. 221, 225

45 *Documents on British Foreign Policy, 1919-1939, Second Series, Vol. XIV*, p. 330

46 *Documents on British Foreign Policy, 1919-1939, Second Series, Vol. XIV*, p. 330

47 *Documents on British Foreign Policy, 1919-1939, Second Series, Vol. XIV*, p. 331

48 *Documents on British Foreign Policy, 1919-1939, Second Series, Vol. XIV*, p. 332

49 Collier, *Duce!* p. 121

50 Collier, *Duce!* pp. 122–123

51 Eden, *Facing the Dictators*, p. 225

52 Eden, *Facing the Dictators*, p. 225

53 Eden, *Facing the Dictators*, p. 232

54 De Bono, *Anno XIIII*, pp. 170–171

Chapter Five – Colors of Conscience

1   Bak, *Joe Louis: The Great Black Hope*, p. 90
2   Astor, *And a Credit to His Race*, p. 100
3   Bak, *Joe Louis: The Great Black Hope*, p. 90
4   Astor, *And a Credit to His Race*, p. 105
5   Astor, *And a Credit to His Race*, p. 105
6   Coffey, *Lion by the Tail*, p. 96
7   Coffey, *Lion by the Tail*, p. 96
8   Hull, *Memoirs*, p. 419
9   Hull, *Memoirs*, p. 419
10   Hull, *Memoirs*, p. 419
11   Hull, *Memoirs*, pp. 419–420
12   Hull, *Memoirs*, p. 420
13   US Diplomatic Papers, 1935, p. 747
14   Hoare, *Nine Troubled Years*, p. 154
15   Hoare, *Nine Troubled Years*, p. 154
16   Hoare, *Nine Troubled Years*, p. 154
17   Hoare, *Nine Troubled Years*, pp. 154–155
18   US Diplomatic Papers, 1935, p. 613
19   Eden, *Facing the Dictators*, p. 246
20   Scott, *The Sons of Sheba's Race*, p. 136
21   Harris, *African-American Reactions to War in Ethiopia*, p. 42
22   Scott, *The Sons of Sheba's Race*, p. 65
23   Harris, *African-American Reactions to War in Ethiopia*, p. 43
24   Harris, *African-American Reactions to War in Ethiopia*, p. 43
25   Scott, *The Sons of Sheba's Race*, p. 66
26   *Pittsburgh Courier*, August 17, 1935
27   Lewis, *When Harlem Was in Vogue*, p. 301
28   Harris, *African-American Reactions to War in Ethiopia*, p. 38
29   Scott, *The Sons of Sheba's Race*, p. 136
30   Scott, *The Sons of Sheba's Race*, p. 248n
31   Harris, *African-American Reactions to War in Ethiopia*, p. 51
32   *New York Times*, July 15, 1935
33   *New York Times*, July 15, 1935
34   *Pittsburgh Courier*, July 20, 1935
35   *New York Times*, July 14, 1935
36   Monks, *Eyewitness*, pp. 35–36
37   Monks, *Eyewitness*, p. 36
38   Rankin, *Telegram from Guernica*, p. 7
39   Steer, *Sealed and Delivered*, p. 11
40   Steer, *Sealed and Delivered*, p. 11
41   Steer, *Sealed and Delivered*, p. 11
42   Rankin, *Telegram from Guernica*, p. 12

43   Steer, *Caesar in Abyssinia*, p. 39

44   Steer, *Caesar in Abyssinia*, p. 39

45   Steer, *Caesar in Abyssinia*, p. 40

46   Steer, *Caesar in Abyssinia*, p. 65

47   Marcus, *Haile Selassie: The Formative Years*, pp. 154–155

48   Coffey, *Lion By the Tail*, p. 105

49   Farago, *Abyssinia on the Eve*, p. 214

50   United Press, July 28, 1935

51   United Press, July 27, 1935

52   Ghosh, "Mussolini and Gandhi: Strange Bedfellows"

53   United Press, July 27, 1935

54   Grant, *Negro with a Hat*, p. 439

55   Grant, *Negro with a Hat*, p. 439

56   *The Black Man*, June 1935

57   *The Black Man*, July 1935

58   Associated Press, July 27, 1935

59   *Sunday Times* of London, July 21, 1935

60   *Daily Mail*, July 24, 1935

61   Hoare, *Nine Troubled Years*, p. 160

62   Manchester, *The Last Lion: Alone*, p. 160

63   Eden, *Facing the Dictators*, p. 246

64   Garretson, *A Victorian Gentleman & Ethiopian Nationalist*, p. 215

65   Garretson, *A Victorian Gentleman & Ethiopian Nationalist*, p. 8

66   Garretson, *A Victorian Gentleman & Ethiopian Nationalist*, p. 32

67   Associated Press, July 22, 1935

68   Garretson, *A Victorian Gentleman & Ethiopian Nationalist*, p. 215

69   Peterson, *Both Sides of the Curtain*, p. 113

70   The American Presidency Project, http://www.presidency.ucsb.edu/ws/index.php?pid=14905

71   *New York Times*, August 8, 1935

Chapter Six – The Brink

1   Eden, *Facing the Dictators*, p. 247

2   Baer, *The Coming of the Italian-Ethiopian War*, p. 254

3   Eden, *Facing the Dictators*, p. 244

4   Salvemini, *Prelude to World War II*, p. 256

5   Eden, *Facing the Dictators*, p. 250

6   Eden, *Facing the Dictators*, p. 251

7   US Diplomatic Papers, 1935, pp. 626–627

8   US Diplomatic Papers, 1935, p. 627

9   Thompson, *Front-Line Diplomat*, p. 107

10   Eden, *Facing the Dictators*, p. 253

11   Nugent, *The Black Eagle*, p. 63

12 Monks, *Eyewitness*, p. 50
13 *New York Times*, August 1, 1935
14 Monks, *Eyewitness*, p. 37
15 Letter to Claude Barnett, June 3, 1935, Barnett Papers, Chicago History Museum
16 Scott, *The Sons of Sheba's Race*, p. 90
17 Letter to Claude Barnett, November 21, 1935, Barnett Papers, Chicago History Museum
18 Monks, *Eyewitness*, p. 50
19 Scott, *The Sons of Sheba's Race*, p. 90; Associated Press, August 23, 1935
20 Murray-Brown, *Kenyatta*, p. 183
21 Murray-Brown, *Kenyatta*, p. 362n
22 Murray-Brown, *Kenyatta*, p. 183
23 Murray-Brown, *Kenyatta*, p. 197
24 James, "Discovering Literature in Trinidad"
25 Worcester, *C.L.R. James: A Political Biography*, p. 258n
26 James, "Fighting for the Abyssinian Empire"
27 James, "Fighting for the Abyssinian Empire"
28 Hooker, *Black Revolutionary*, p. 43
29 Makalani, *In the Cause of Freedom*, p. 202
30 Hooker, *Black Revolutionary*, p. 42; Polsgrove, Ending British Rule in Africa, pp. 67–68
31 Makalani, *In the Cause of Freedom*, p. 200
32 *Canberra Times*, August 19, 1935
33 *Sydney Morning Herald*, August 22, 1935
34 *The Times* of London, August 13, 1935
35 Associated Press, August 12, 1935
36 *New York Times*, October 18, 1935
37 *Documents on British Foreign Policy, 1919-1939, Second Series, Vol. XIV*, p. 735
38 Eden, *Facing the Dictators*, p. 255
39 US Diplomatic Papers, 1935, p. 739
40 Steer, *Caesar in Abyssinia*, p. 85
41 Jonas, *The Battle of Adwa*, p. 76
42 Steer, *Caesar in Abyssinia*, p. 82
43 Steer, *Caesar in Abyssinia*, p. 95
44 Steer, *Caesar in Abyssinia*, p. 101
45 Steer, *Caesar in Abyssinia*, p. 102
46 Steer, *Caesar in Abyssinia*, p. 104
47 Steer, *Caesar in Abyssinia*, p. 105
48 Steer, *Caesar in Abyssinia*, p. 107
49 Canadian Press; Havas, August 28, 1935
50 Kertzer, *The Pope and Mussolini*, p. 215
51 Canadian Press; Havas, August 28, 1935
52 Kertzer, *The Pope and Mussolini*, p. 216

53   *New York Times*, June 21, 1931; Associated Press, June 20, 1931

54   Darrah, *Hail Caesar!* pp. 174–175

55   Kertzer, *The Pope and Mussolini*, p. 218

56   Duggan, *Fascist Voices*, p. 253

57   Isaacs, *The New World of Negro Americans*, p. 283

58   *Chicago Defender*, September 7, 1935

59   *Chicago Defender*, September 7, 1935

60   *New York Times*, September 1, 1935

61   *Chicago Defender*, September 7, 1935

62   De Bono, *Anno XIIII*, pp. 147–148

63   Waugh, *Waugh in Abyssinia*, p. 41

64   Hastings, *Evelyn Waugh*, pp. 333–334

65   Hastings, *Evelyn Waugh*, p. 334

66   Rankin, *Telegram from Guernica*, p. 31

67   *Daily Telegraph*, August 31, 1935

68   Hastings, *Evelyn Waugh*, p. 338

69   *Documents on British Foreign Policy, Second Series, Vol. XIV*, p. 555

70   Associated Press, September 2, 1935

71   *New York Times*, September 1, 1935

72   Associated Press, August 31, 1935

73   Hull, *Memoirs*, p. 423

74   Hull, *Memoirs*, p. 424

75   US Diplomatic Papers, 1935, p. 751

Chapter Seven – "I Hope the Organmen Gas Them to Buggery"

1   Harmsworth, *Abyssinia Marches On*, p. 127

2   Harmsworth, *Abyssinia Marches On*, p. 128

3   Associated Press, August 26, 1935

4   *New York Times*, September 8, 1935

5   Associated Press, September 4, 1935

6   Garretson, *A Victorian Gentleman & Ethiopian Nationalist*, p. 216

7   Garretson, *A Victorian Gentleman & Ethiopian Nationalist*, p. 230

8   Monks, *Eyewitness*, p. 30

9   Deedes, *At War with Waugh*, p. 38

10   Deedes, *At War with Waugh*, p. 39

11   Engert, "American Legation Under Fire: Addis Ababa, 1936"

12   Rankin, *Telegram from Guernica*, p. 39

13   Rankin, *Telegram from Guernica*, p. 30

14   Hastings, *Evelyn Waugh*, p. 339

15   Hastings, *Evelyn Waugh*, p. 340

16   Hoare, *Nine Troubled Years*, p. 166

17   Hoare, *Nine Troubled Years*, p. 169

18   *Documents on Foreign Policy, 1919-1939, Second Series, Vol. XIV,* p. 787

19   *Documents on Foreign Policy, 1919-1939, Second Series, Vol. XIV,* p. 788

20   Hoare, *Nine Troubled Years,* p. 166

21   Hoare, *Nine Troubled Years,* p. 166

22   Hoare, *Nine Troubled Years,* p. 171

23   Hoare, *Nine Troubled Years,* p. 171

24   Del Boca, *The Ethiopian War,* p. 24

25   Eden, *Facing the Dictators,* p. 262

26   Tsehai Berhane-Selassie, "Women Guerrilla Fighters"

27   Minale Adugna, "Women and Warfare in Ethiopia"

28   As quoted by Del Boca, *The Ethiopian War,* p. 89

29   Konovalov, Unpublished Manuscript as newly translated by Clarke

30   Konovalov, Unpublished Manuscript as newly translated by Clarke

31   Steer, *Caesar in Abyssinia,* p. 123

32   *New York Times,* October 3, 1935

33   Letter to Claude Barnett, June 3, 1935, Barnett Papers, Chicago History Museum

34   *The Afro-American,* October 12, 1935

35   Scott, *The Sons of Sheba's Race,* p. 75

36   *The Afro-American,* October 12, 1935

37   *The Afro-American,* October 12, 1935

38   Associated Press, September 19, 1935

39   Eden, *Facing the Dictators,* p. 265

40   Eden, *Facing the Dictators,* p. 267

41   *Documents on Foreign Policy, 1919-1939, Second Series, Vol. XIV,* p. 698n

42   Eden, *Facing the Dictators,* p. 270

43   *New York Times,* September 26, 1935

44   Steer, *Caesar in Abyssinia,* p. 129

45   US Diplomatic Papers, 1935, p. 769

46   Haney, *Naked at the Feast,* p. 196

47   Levi, *Christ Stopped at Eboli,* p. 29, p. 133

48   Duggan, *Fascist Voices,* p. 252

49   Duggan, *Fascist Voices,* p. 255

50   Ebner, *Ordinary Violence in Mussolini's Italy,* p. 183

51   Del Boca, *The Ethiopian War,* p. 28

52   Konovalov, Unpublished Manuscript as newly translated by Clarke

53   *Chicago Defender,* October 12, 1935

Chapter Eight — War

1   De Bono, *Anno XIIII: The Conquest of an Empire,* p. 229

2   Konovalov's memoir portion published by Steer, *Caesar in Abyssinia,* p. 318

3   Steer, *Caesar in Abyssinia,* p. 135

4   Steer, *Caesar in Abyssinia,* p. 137

5   Steer, *Caesar in Abyssinia*, pp. 137–138

6   Steer, *Caesar in Abyssinia*, p. 138

7   Steer, *Caesar in Abyssinia*, p. 139

8   Steer, *Caesar in Abyssinia*, p. 139

9   Steer, *Caesar in Abyssinia*, p. 140

10   De Bono, *Anno XIIII: The Conquest of an Empire*, p. 244

11   *League of Nations Official Journal*, November, 1935, p. 1605

12   US Diplomatic Papers, 1935, p. 792

13   Del Boca, *The Ethiopian War*, pp. 59–60

14   *League of Nations Official Journal*, April, 1936, pp. 418–419

15   Baudendistel, *Between Bombs and Good Intentions*, p. 117, Appendices, p. 325

16   *Time*, October 14, 1935

17   Letter to Claude Barnett, November 21, 1935, Barnett Papers, Chicago History Museum

18   *New York Times*, October 4, 1935

19   Eden, *Facing the Dictators*, p. 262

20   *New York Times*, October 3, 1935

21   US Diplomatic Papers, 1935, p. 794

22   Sherwood, *Roosevelt and Hopkins: An Intimate History*, p. 79

23   US Diplomatic Papers, 1935, p. 797

24   US Diplomatic Papers, 1935, pp. 798–800

25   Sherwood, *Roosevelt and Hopkins: An Intimate History*, p. 79

26   Scott, *The Sons of Sheba's Race*, p. 140

27   Nkrumah, *Autobiography*, p. 27

28   Asante, *Pan-African Protest: West Africa and the Italo-Ethiopian Crisis*, p. 130

29   Asante, *Pan-African Protest: West Africa and the Italo-Ethiopian Crisis*, p. 130

30   Eden, *Facing the Dictators*, p. 274

31   Eden, *Facing the Dictators*, p. 275

32   Eden, *Facing the Dictators*, p. 277

33   Eden, *Facing the Dictators*, p. 277

34   United Press, October 6, 1935

35   *New York Times*, October 7, 1935

36   Skidelsky, *Oswald Mosley*, p. 11

37   Pugh, *'Hurrah for the Blackshirts!'* p. 222

38   Sperber, *Murrow: His Life and Times*, p. 80

39   Associated Press, October 11, 1935

40   Sperber, *Murrow: His Life and Times*, p. 81

41   Monks, *Eyewitness*, p. 49

42   Monks, *Eyewitness*, p. 49

43   Steer, *Caesar in Abyssinia*, pp. 181–182

44   Steer, *Caesar in Abyssinia*, pp. 153–154

45   Waugh, *Waugh in Abyssinia*, p. 107

46   Reuters, October 12, 1935

47   Rankin, *Telegram from Guernica*, p. 35
48   Rankin, *Telegram from Guernica*, p. 39
49   *New York Times*, October 18, 1935
50   Associated Press, October 22, 1935
51   Steer, *Caesar in Abyssinia*, p. 170
52   Steer, *Caesar in Abyssinia*, p. 170

Chapter Nine – A Season of Betrayals

1   De Bono, *Anno XIIII*, p. 261
2   Barker, *The Civilizing Mission*, p. 177
3   De Bono, *Anno XIIII*, p. 263
4   De Bono, *Anno XIIII*, p. 264
5   De Bono, *Anno XIIII*, pp. 251–252
6   De Bono, *Anno XIIII*, p. 253
7   Del Boca, *The Ethiopian War*, p. 51
8   De Bono, *Anno XIIII*, p. 267
9   De Bono, *Anno XIIII*, p. 281
10   Steer, *Caesar in Abyssinia*, pp. 162–163
11   Associated Press, October 18, Steer's story, *New York Times*, October 17, 1935; Steer, *Caesar in Abyssinia*, p. 163
12   Associated Press, October 18, 1935
13   Monks, *Eyewitness*, p. 53
14   Monks, *Eyewitness*, p. 53
15   Monks, *Eyewitness*, p. 53
16   *New York Times*, October 18, 1935
17   *New York Times*, October 13, 1935
18   Harris, *African-American Reactions to War in Ethiopia*, p. 45
19   Scott, *The Sons of Sheba's Race*, p. 67
20   Associated Press, October 19, 1935
21   *New York Times*, October 20, 1935
22   *New York Times*, October 26, 1935
23   Coffey, *Lion by the Tail*, p. 199
24   *New York Times*, October 21, 1935
25   *New York Times*, October 21, 1935
26   Associated Press, October 21, 1935
27   Bosworth, *Mussolini's Italy: Life Under the Dictatorship*, p. 368
28   Bosworth, *Mussolini's Italy: Life Under the Dictatorship*, p. 369
29   UK Hansard, October 22, 1935
30   Junod, *Warriors Without Weapons*, p. 15
31   Junod, *Warriors Without Weapons*, p. 16
32   Junod, *Warriors Without Weapons*, p. 26
33   Junod, *Warriors Without Weapons*, p. 28

34 Junod, *Warriors Without Weapons*, p. 29

35 *New York Times*, November 1, 1935

36 Bonham Carter, *Champion Redoubtable*, p. 186

37 Steer, *Caesar in Abyssinia*, p. 172

38 Steer, *Caesar in Abyssinia*, p. 173

39 Steer, *Caesar in Abyssinia*, p. 174

40 Pennybacker, *From Scottsboro to Munich*, p. 89

41 Steer, *Caesar in Abyssinia*, p. 185

42 Steer, *Caesar in Abyssinia*, p. 186

43 De Bono, *Anno XIIII*, p. 297

44 De Bono, *Anno XIIII*, p. 305

45 De Bono, *Anno XIIII*, p. 306

46 De Bono, *Anno XIIII*, p. 310

47 De Bono, *Anno XIIII*, p. 312

Chapter Ten – Schemes . . .

1 Nelson & Sullivan, *John Melly of Ethiopia*, pp. 130-131

2 Nelson & Sullivan, *John Melly of Ethiopia*, p. 131

3 Nelson & Sullivan, *John Melly of Ethiopia*, p. 134

4 *British Medical Journal*, Vol. 2, No. 3902, October 19, 1935

5 Matthews, *Two Wars and More to Come*, p. 33

6 Matthews, *Two Wars and More to Come*, p. 17

7 Matthews, *Two Wars and More to Come*, p. 18

8 Matthews, *Two Wars and More to Come*, pp. 20–21

9 Matthews, *Two Wars and More to Come*, p. 48; The following quotations for this section, unless otherwise cited, all come from Matthews' account, pp. 48–95

10 *New York Times*, November 18, 1935

11 *New York Times*, November 18, 1935

12 Asante, *Pan-African Protest: West Africa and the Italo-Ethiopian Crisis*, p. 106

13 Shirer, *The Collapse of the Third Republic*, p. 243n

14 Steer, *Caesar in Abyssinia*, p. 250

15 *New York Times*, November 20, 1935

16 US Diplomatic Papers, p. 819

17 Hull, *Memoirs*, p. 436

18 Hull, *Memoirs*, p. 439

19 Hull, *Memoirs*, p. 442

20 Associated Press, May 23, 1936

21 Associated Press, May 23, 1936

22 Letter to Claude Barnett, November 21, 1935, Barnett Papers, Chicago History Museum

23 Letter to Claude Barnett, November 21, 1935, Barnett Papers, Chicago History Museum

24 Letter to Claude Barnett, November 21, 1935, Barnett Papers, Chicago History Museum

25 Letter to Claude Barnett, November 21, 1935, Barnett Papers, Chicago History Museum

26 UK Hansard, December 5, 1935

27 Hoare, *Nine Troubled Years*, p. 178

28 Eden, *Facing the Dictators*, p. 298

29 Hoare, *Nine Troubled Years*, p. 178

30 Steer, *Caesar in Abyssinia*, p. 202

31 Steer, *Caesar in Abyssinia*, p. 204

32 Steer, *Caesar in Abyssinia*, p. 204

33 Steer, *Caesar in Abyssinia*, p. 205

34 Junod, *Warriors Without Weapons*, p. 30

35 Junod, *Warriors Without Weapons*, p. 36

36 Junod, *Warriors Without Weapons*, p. 37

37 Nelson and Sullivan, *John Melly of Ethiopia*, p.240

38 Steer, *Caesar in Abyssinia*, p. 205

39 Vansittart, *The Mist Procession*, p. 538–539

40 Vansittart, *The Mist Procession*, p. 539

41 Eden, *Facing the Dictators*, p. 296

42 Hoare, *Nine Troubled Years*, p. 179

43 Hoare, *Nine Troubled Years*, p. 180

44 Hoare, *Nine Troubled Years*, p. 181

45 Peterson, *Both Sides of the Curtain*, p. 117

46 Hoare, *Nine Troubled Years*, p. 179

47 Eden, *Facing the Dictators*, p. 299

48 Eden, *Facing the Dictators*, p. 300

49 Hoare, *Nine Troubled Years*, p. 182

50 Chambrun, *Pierre Laval: Traitor or Patriot?* p. 25

51 Chambrun, *Pierre Laval: Traitor or Patriot?* p. 25

52 Hoare, *Nine Troubled Years*, p. 182

53 Vansittart, *The Mist Procession*, p. 540

54 Eden, *Facing the Dictators*, p. 299

55 Eden, *Facing the Dictators*, p. 300

56 Eden, *Facing the Dictators*, p. 301

57 Eden, *Facing the Dictators*, p. 302

58 Hoare, *Nine Troubled Years*, pp. 183–184

Chapter Eleven – . . . And Downfalls

1 Eden, *Facing the Dictators*, p. 305

2 UK Hansard, December 10, 1935

3 UK Hansard, December 10, 1935

4 *Documents on British Foreign Policy*, Second Series, Vol. XV, p. 448

5   Steer, *Caesar in Abyssinia*, p. 207
6   Steer, *Caesar in Abyssinia*, pp. 208–209
7   Eden, *Facing the Dictators*, p. 307
8   Eden, *Facing the Dictators*, pp. 307–308
9   *New York Times*, December 15, 1935
10   Del Boca, *The Ethiopian War*, p. 74
11   Del Boca, *The Ethiopian War*, p. 74
12   Steer, *Caesar in Abyssinia*, p. 227
13   Steer, *Caesar in Abyssinia*, p. 229
14   *Pittsburgh Courier*, December 14, 1935
15   *Pittsburgh Courier*, December 14, 1935
16   Letter to Claude Barnett, November 28, 1935, Barnett Papers, Chicago History Museum
17   Letter to Claude Barnett, November 28, 1935, Barnett Papers, Chicago History Museum
18   Letter to Claude Barnett, November 28, 1935, Barnett Papers, Chicago History Museum
19   Simmons, *The Brown Condor*, pp. 121–124
20   Simmons, *The Brown Condor*, p. 135
21   Letter to Claude Barnett, November 28, 1935, Barnett Papers, Chicago History Museum
22   *Documents on British Foreign Policy*, Second Series, Vol. XV, pp. 482–483
23   Steer, *Caesar in Abyssinia*, p. 215
24   Monks, *Eyewitness*, p. 46
25   Hoare, *Nine Troubled Years*, p. 185
26   Feiling, *Life of Neville Chamberlain*, p. 274
27   Hoare, *Nine Troubled Years*, p. 185
28   *The Times* of London, December 18, 1935
29   Eden, *Facing the Dictators*, p. 309
30   *League of Nations Official Journal*, January 1936, p. 11
31   *League of Nations Official Journal*, January 1936, pp. 11–12
32   UK Hansard, December 19, 1935
33   UK Hansard, December 19, 1935
34   Sheean, *Between the Thunder and the Sun*, p. 38
35   Sheean, *Between the Thunder and the Sun*, p. 42
36   Sheean, *Between the Thunder and the Sun*, p. 48
37   Sheean, *Between the Thunder and the Sun*, pp. 56–57
38   Bernier, *Fireworks at Dusk*, p. 203
39   Bernier, *Fireworks at Dusk*, pp. 203–204
40   Chambrun, *Pierre Laval: Traitor or Patriot?* pp. 26–27
41   Peterson, *Both Sides of the Curtain*, pp. 121–122
42   Peterson, *Both Sides of the Curtain*, p. 122
43   Taylor, A. J. P., *The Origins of the Second World War*, p. 96
44   Eden, *Facing the Dictators*, p. 297

Chapter Twelve – The Rain That Burns and Kills

1   *Canberra Times*, December 20, 1935
2   Del Boca, *The Ethiopian War*, p. 58
3   Del Boca, *The Ethiopian War*, p. 58n
4   Junod, *Warriors Without Weapons*, p. 38
5   Nelson and Sullivan, *John Melly of Ethiopia*, p. 175
6   Junod, *Warriors Without Weapons*, p. 39
7   Junod, *Warriors Without Weapons*, p. 39
8   Del Boca, *The Ethiopian War*, pp. 78–79
9   Del Boca, *The Ethiopian War*, p. 79
10   Vansittart, *The Mist Procession*, p. 543
11   Eden, *Facing the Dictators*, p. 316
12   Rose, *King George V*, p. 348
13   Rose, *King George V*, p. 340
14   Pimlott, *The Queen*, p. 15
15   Eden, *Facing the Dictators*, p. 317
16   Eden, *Facing the Dictators*, p. 317
17   Baudendistel, *Between Bombs and Good Intentions*, p. 239
18   Baudendistel, *Between Bombs and Good Intentions*, p. 131
19   Baudendistel, *Between Bombs and Good Intentions*, pp. 78–79
20   See Baudendistel's work, pp. 130-132. Not only do photos survive of the camp
     clearly marked, but there is a reconnaissance shot noting the camp and a photo of
     the camp while it is being bombed.
21   Baudendistel, *Between Bombs and Good Intentions*, p. 127
22   Steer, *Caesar in Abyssinia*, p. 243
23   Baudendistel, *Between Bombs and Good Intentions*, p. 127
24   Junod, *Warriors Without Weapons*, p. 48
25   Junod, *Warriors Without Weapons*, p. 48
26   Junod, *Warriors Without Weapons*, p. 49
27   Junod, *Warriors Without Weapons*, pp. 49–50
28   Junod, *Warriors Without Weapons*, p. 47
29   Eden, *Facing the Dictators*, p. 322
30   Baudendistel, *Between Bombs and Good Intentions*, p. 225
31   Baudendistel, *Between Bombs and Good Intentions*, pp. 225–226
32   *Chicago Defender*, January 25, 1936
33   Scott, *The Sons of Sheba's Race*, p. 93
34   Scott, *The Sons of Sheba's Race*, p. 93
35   Arent, "Ethiopia"
36   Quinn, *Furious Improvisation*, p. 70
37   Quinn, *Furious Improvisation*, p. 67
38   Quinn, *Furious Improvisation*, p. 67
39   Del Boca, *The Ethiopian War*, p. 121
40   Steer, *Caesar in Abyssinia*, pp. 245–246
41   Del Boca, *The Ethiopian War*, pp. 50–51, p. 122

Chapter Thirteen – The Old Man on the Mountain

1   *League of Nations Official Journal*, February, 1936, p. 256
2   Eden, *Facing the Dictators*, p. 325
3   Eden, *Facing the Dictators*, p. 325
4   Flanagan, *Arena: The Story of the Federal Theatre*, pp. 65–66
5   Quinn, *Furious Improvisation*, p. 68
6   Flanagan, *Arena: The Story of the Federal Theatre*, p. 66
7   Flanagan, *Arena: The Story of the Federal Theatre*, p. 66
8   Flanagan, *Arena: The Story of the Federal Theatre*, p. 66
9   *New York Times*, January 25, 1936
10 Scott, *The Sons of Sheba's Race*, p. 42
11 Badoglio, *The War in Abyssinia*, p. 11
12 Steer, *Caesar in Abyssinia*, p. 250
13 Steer, *Caesar in Abyssinia*, p. 250
14 Del Boca, *The Ethiopian War*, p. 107
15 Del Boca, *The Ethiopian War*, p. 108
16 Moorehead, *Dunant's Dream*, p. 308
17 Baudendistel, *Between Bombs and Good Intentions*, p. 279
18 Moorehead, *Dunant's Dream*, p. 306
19 Letter from Lambie to Dr. Charles Winckel, Dutch Red Cross, February 21, 1936
20 Letters from Marcel Junod to Dr. Charles Winckel, Dutch Red Cross; handwritten pages, date unclear, and typed letter July 14, 1936.
21 Letter from C. David to Dr. Charles Winckel, Dutch Red Cross, January 28, 1936
22 Report by Dr. Charles Winckel to Dutch Red Cross HQ, February 9, 1936
23 *League of Nations Official Journal*, June 1936, p. 658
24 Moorehead, *Dunant's Dream*, p. 309
25 *Washington Post*, January 10, 1936
26 Bell, *François Mitterrand: A Political Biography*, p. 5; Tiersky, *François Mitterrand: A Very French President*, p. 43
27 Tiersky, *François Mitterrand: A Very French President*, pp. 43–44
28 Del Boca, *The Ethiopian War*, pp. 125–126
29 Del Boca, *The Ethiopian War*, pp. 127–128
30 Del Boca, *The Ethiopian War*, p. 128
31 Badoglio, *The War in Abyssinia*, p. 82
32 Del Boca, *The Ethiopian War*, p. 130
33 Steer, *Caesar in Abyssinia*, p. 262
34 Baudendistel, *Between Bombs and Good Intentions*, p. 80
35 Del Boca, *The Ethiopian War*, p. 135
36 Steer, *Caesar in Abyssinia*, p. 271
37 Steer, *Caesar in Abyssinia*, p. 272
38 Steer, *Caesar in Abyssinia*, p. 273
39 Steer, p. 272; Del Boca, p. 146
40 Del Boca, *The Ethiopian War*, p. 146
41 *League of Nations Official Journal*, April 1936, p. 477

42   *League of Nations Official Journal,* April 1936, p. 477
43   Baudendistel, *Between Bombs and Good Intentions,* p. 229
44   *League of Nations Official Journal,* April 1936, p. 478
45   *League of Nations Official Journal,* April 1936, p. 478
46   *League of Nations Official Journal,* April 1936, p. 478
47   Steer, *Caesar in Abyssinia,* p. 265
48   Steer, *Caesar in Abyssinia,* p. 265
49   National Archives, UK, FO 371/20156
50   Garretson, *A Victorian Gentleman & Ethiopian Nationalist,* p. 216
51   National Archives, UK, FO 371/20156
52   National Archives, UK, FO 371/20156
53   Eden, *Facing the Dictators,* p. 327
54   Eden, *Facing the Dictators,* p. 327
55   Eden, *Facing the Dictators,* p. 328
56   Eden, *Facing the Dictators,* p. 329
57   *Pittsburgh Courier,* February 29, 1936
58   *Pittsburgh Courier,* February 29, 1936
59   *Pittsburgh Courier,* March 7, 1936
60   Del Boca, *The Ethiopian War,* p. 138
61   Badoglio, *The War in Abyssinia,* pp. 93–97
62   Badoglio, *The War in Abyssinia,* p. 95
63   Mockler, p. 105; Steer, p. 268
64   Steer, *Caesar in Abyssinia,* p.269
65   Del Boca, *The Ethiopian War,* p. 140
66   Del Boca, *The Ethiopian War,* p. 141
67   Steer, *Caesar in Abyssinia,* p.269
68   Del Boca, *The Ethiopian War,* p. 141
69   Steer, *Caesar in Abyssinia,* p. 270
70   Steer, *Caesar in Abyssinia,* p. 270
71   National Archives, UK, FO 371/20167
72   Nelson and Sullivan, *John Melly of Ethiopia,* p. 214
73   Steer, *Caesar in Abyssinia,* p. 279
74   Nelson and Sullivan, *John Melly of Ethiopia,* p. 213
75   Nelson and Sullivan, *John Melly of Ethiopia,* p. 217
76   Nelson and Sullivan, *John Melly of Ethiopia,* p. 218

Chapter Fourteen – ". . . If You Think It Better to Come Here and Die with Us . . ."

1   Steer, *Caesar in Abyssinia,* p. 274
2   Steer was likely the first to make this point, *Caesar in Abyssinia,* p. 274
3   Steer, *Caesar in Abyssinia,* p. 275
4   Coffey, *Lion by the Tail,* p. 301
5   Steer, *Caesar in Abyssinia,* p. 275

6   Del Boca, *The Ethiopian War*, p. 154

7   Badoglio, *The War in Abyssinia*, p. 118

8   Del Boca, *The Ethiopian War*, p. 156

9   Shirer, *The Collapse of the Third Republic*, pp. 261–262

10   Shirer, *The Collapse of the Third Republic*, p. 262

11   Steer, *Caesar in Abyssinia*, p. 276

12   Steer, *Caesar in Abyssinia*, p. 276

13   Mockler, *Haile Selassie's War*, pp. 112–113

14   Badoglio, *The War in Abyssinia*, pp. 142–143

15   Spencer, *Ethiopia at Bay*, p. 54

16   Spencer, *Ethiopia at Bay*, p. 53

17   Junod, *Warriors Without Weapons*, p. 57

18   Baudendistel, *Between Bombs and Good Intentions*, p. 275

19   Junod, *Warriors Without Weapons*, p. 61

20   Junod, *Warriors Without Weapons*, p. 62

21   Konovalov memoir portion published by Steer, *Caesar in Abyssinia*, p. 300

22   Konovalov memoir portion published by Steer, *Caesar in Abyssinia*, pp. 300–301

23   Konovalov memoir portion published by Steer, *Caesar in Abyssinia*, p. 301

24   Konovalov memoir portion published by Steer, *Caesar in Abyssinia*, p. 301

25   Steer's story on Harar, *New York Times*, March 30, 1936

26   Eden, *Facing the Dictators*, p. 374

27   UK Hansard, April 1, 1936

28   UK Hansard, April 1, 1936

29   Del Boca, *The Ethiopian War*, p. 157

30   Bahru Zewde, *Pioneers of Change in Ethiopia*, p. 83, p. 180

31   Badoglio, *The War in Abyssinia*, p. 142

32   Konovalov memoir portion published by Steer, *Caesar in Abyssinia*, p. 303

33   Konovalov memoir portion published by Steer, *Caesar in Abyssinia*, p. 305

34   Konovalov memoir portion published by Steer, *Caesar in Abyssinia*, p. 307

35   Badoglio, *The War in Abyssinia*, p. 145

36   Del Boca, *The Ethiopian War*, p. 172

37   Konovalov memoir portion published by Steer, *Caesar in Abyssinia*, p. 313

38   Konovalov memoir portion published by Steer, *Caesar in Abyssinia*, p. 314

39   Badoglio, *The War in Abyssinia*, p. 147

40   Konovalov memoir portion published by Steer, *Caesar in Abyssinia*, p. 317

41   Konovalov memoir portion published by Steer, *Caesar in Abyssinia*, pp. 319–320

42   *League of Nations Official Journal*, April 1936, p. 476

43   Baudendistel, *Between Bombs and Good Intentions*, p. 231

44   Baudendistel, *Between Bombs and Good Intentions*, p. 231

45   Moorehead, *Dunant's Dream*, p. 312

46   Moorehead, *Dunant's Dream*, p. 311

47   Baudendistel, *Between Bombs and Good Intentions*, p. 280; Moorehead, *Dunant's Dream*, p. 311

48   Moorehead, *Dunant's Dream*, p. 311

49   Baudendistel, *Between Bombs and Good Intentions*, p. 281

50   *Une victoire de la civilisation*, as quoted by Del Boca, *The Ethiopian War*, p. 177

51   Konovalov memoir portion published by Steer, *Caesar in Abyssinia*, p. 325

52   Konovalov memoir portion published by Steer, *Caesar in Abyssinia*, p. 327

53   Konovalov memoir portion published by Steer, *Caesar in Abyssinia*, p. 329

54   Konovalov memoir portion published by Steer, *Caesar in Abyssinia*, p. 329

Chapter Fifteen – A King's Lonely Prayer

1   Konovalov memoir portion published by Steer, *Caesar in Abyssinia*, p. 331

2   Konovalov memoir portion published by Steer, *Caesar in Abyssinia*, p. 333

3   Konovalov memoir portion published by Steer, *Caesar in Abyssinia*, p. 334

4   Spencer, *Ethiopia at Bay*, p. 59

5   Steer, *Caesar in Abyssinia*, pp. 8–9

6   Steer, *Caesar in Abyssinia*, p. 342

7   Trotsky, "On Dictators and the Heights of Oslo"

8   Matthews, *Two Wars and More to Come*, p. 140

9   Matthews, *Two Wars and More to Come*, pp. 142–143

10   Matthews, *Two Wars and More to Come*, p. 147

11   Matthews, *Two Wars and More to Come*, p. 147

12   Mockler, *Haile Selassie's War*, pp. 131–132

13   Steer, *Caesar in Abyssinia*, p. 360

14   Engert, "American Legation Under Fire: Addis Ababa, 1936"

15   US Diplomatic Papers, 1936, p. 63

16   US Diplomatic Papers, 1936, p. 64

17   US Diplomatic Papers, 1936, p. 64

18   National Archives, UK, FO 371/20195

19   Mockler, *Haile Selassie's War*, p. 134

20   Steer, *Caesar in Abyssinia*, p. 367

21   Steer, *Caesar in Abyssinia*, p. 368

22   National Archives, UK, FO 371/20195

23   Mockler, *Haile Selassie's War*, p. 135

24   Spencer, *Ethiopia at Bay*, p. 64

25   Spencer, *Ethiopia at Bay*, p. 69

26   Del Boca, p. 203, Mockler, p. 138

27   Gebru Tareke, *Ethiopia, Power and Protest*, p. 165

28   Haile Selassie, *Autobiography, Volume One*, p. 204

29   Marcus, *Haile Selassie I: The Formative Years*, p. 122

30   Steer, *Caesar in Abyssinia*, p. 373

31   Spencer, *Ethiopia at Bay*, pp. 65–66

32   Spencer, *Ethiopia at Bay*, p. 66

33   Steer, *Caesar in Abyssinia*, p. 374

34 Steer, *Caesar in Abyssinia*, p. 375
35 Junod, *Warrior without Weapons*, p. 77
36 Mockler, *Haile Selassie's War*, p. 140
37 National Archives, UK, FO 371/20195
38 Steer, *Caesar in Abyssinia*, p. 376
39 Interview with author, October 8, 2012
40 Interview with author, October 8, 2012
41 Baudendistel, *Between Bombs and Good Intentions*, p. 209
42 Baudendistel, *Between Bombs and Good Intentions*, p. 209
43 Baudendistel, *Between Bombs and Good Intentions*, pp. 210–211
44 Rankin, *Telegram from Guernica*, p. 69
45 Rankin, *Telegram from Guernica*, p. 69
46 Nelson and Sullivan, *John Melly of Ethiopia*, p. 263
47 Nelson and Sullivan, *John Melly of Ethiopia*, p. 267
48 Nelson and Sullivan, *John Melly of Ethiopia*, p. 267
49 Engert, "American Legation Under Fire: Addis Ababa, 1936"
50 Engert, "American Legation Under Fire: Addis Ababa, 1936"
51 Engert, "American Legation Under Fire: Addis Ababa, 1936"
52 Engert, "American Legation Under Fire: Addis Ababa, 1936"
53 Steer, *Caesar in Abyssinia*, pp. 396–397
54 Steer, *Caesar in Abyssinia*, p. 9
55 Quoted in *New York Times*, May 6, 1936
56 National Archives, UK, FO 371/20195
57 Junod, *Warrior without Weapons*, p. 82

Chapter Sixteen – Taken Up to Rome

1   Matthews, *Two Wars and More to Come*, p. 168
2   Matthews, *Two Wars and More to Come*, p. 169
3   Steer, *Sealed and Delivered*, p. 14
4   National Archives, UK, FO 371/20167
5   Junod, *Warrior without Weapons*, p. 83
6   Matthews, *Two Wars and More to Come*, p. 170
7   Matthews, *Two Wars and More to Come*, p. 173
8   Matthews, *Two Wars and More to Come*, p. 173
9   Steer, *Caesar in Abyssinia*, p. 402
10 Steer, *Caesar in Abyssinia*, p. 34
11 Associated Press, May 6, 1936
12 *New York Times*, May 6, 1936
13 *New York Times*, May 6, 1936
14 Mockler, *Haile Selassie's War*, p. 142
15 Collum, *African-Americans in the Spanish Civil War*, p. 14
16 Yates, *From Mississippi to Madrid*, p. 92

17 Yates, *From Mississippi to Madrid*, p. 94
18 Yates, *From Mississippi to Madrid*, p. 94
19 UK Parliament Hansard, May 6, 1936
20 Konovalov, Unpublished Manuscript as newly translated by Clarke
21 Konovalov, Unpublished Manuscript as newly translated by Clarke
22 Steer, *Caesar in Abyssinia*, p. 388
23 Steer, *Caesar in Abyssinia*, p. 389
24 Nelson and Sullivan, *John Melly of Ethiopia*, p. 274
25 Nelson and Sullivan, *John Melly of Ethiopia*, p. 276
26 Baer, *Test Case*, p. 278
27 Konovalov, Unpublished Manuscript as newly translated by Clarke
28 Spencer, *Ethiopia at Bay*, p. 68
29 Spencer, *Ethiopia at Bay*, p. 70
30 Steer, *Caesar in Abyssinia*, p. 404
31 Rankin, *Telegram from Guernica*, p. 74
32 UK Hansard, May 20, 1936
33 Rankin, *Telegram from Guernica*, pp. 73–74
34 Steer, *Caesar in Abyssinia*, p. 405
35 Steer, *Sealed and Delivered*, p. 14
36 Steer, *Sealed and Delivered*, p. 14
37 Steer, *Caesar in Abyssinia*, p. 407
38 Steer, *Caesar in Abyssinia*, p. 407
39 *New Times and Ethiopia News*, April 3, 1937
40 Minale Adugna, "Women and Warfare in Ethiopia"
41 Pankhurst, *Addis Ababa Tribune*, December 7, 2001; Professor Pankhurst introduces an interview with Shawaragad that appeared originally in the *Ethiopia Star*, November 16 and 23, 1941
42 Tsehai Berhane-Selassie, "Women Guerrilla Fighters"
43 Tsehai Berhane-Selassie, "Women Guerrilla Fighters"
44 Tsehai Berhane-Selassie, "Women Guerrilla Fighters"
45 Harrison, *Sylvia Pankhurst: A Crusading Life*, p. 238
46 Pankhurst, *Sylvia Pankhurst, Artist and Crusader*, p. 192
47 Pankhurst, *Sylvia Pankhurst, Artist and Crusader*, p. 193
48 Pankhurst, *Sylvia Pankhurst, Artist and Crusader*, p. 193
49 Pankhurst, *Sylvia Pankhurst, Artist and Crusader*, p. 193
50 *New Times and Ethiopia News*, July 18, 1936
51 *New Times and Ethiopia News*, February 13, 1937
52 Quoted by Fryer, *Staying Power*, p. 342
53 Asante, *Pan-African Protest: West Africa and the Italo-Ethiopian Crisis*, p. 125
54 Quoted by Spitzer and LaRay, "I. T. A. Wallace-Johnson and the West African Youth League"
55 Asante, *Pan-African Protest: West Africa and the Italo-Ethiopian Crisis*, p. 111
56 Fryer, *Staying Power*, p. 342

57   Eden, *Facing the Dictators*, p. 382

58   Jeffery, *The Secret History of MI6*, p. 284

59   Associated Press, May 23, 1936

60   *Chicago Defender*, May 30, 1936

61   Scott, *The Sons of Sheba's Race*, pp. 77–78

62   Letter to Claude Barnett, July 1, 1936, Barnett Papers, Chicago History Museum

63   Scott, *The Sons of Sheba's Race*, p. 146

64   Windsor, *A King's Story*, pp. 298–299

65   Grant, *Negro with a Hat*, p. 440

66   *The Black Man*, May–June 1936

67   *The Black Man*, May–June 1936

68   Thesiger, *The Life of My Choice*, p. 235

Chapter Seventeen – "What Answer Am I to Take Back to My People?"

1   Scott, *The Sons of Sheba's Race*, pp. 94–95

2   Scott, *The Sons of Sheba's Race*, p. 95

3   Matthews, *The Fruits of Fascism*, p. 233

4   Pankhurst, "The Ethiopian Patriots: The Lone Struggle, 1936-1940"

5   Pankhurst, "The Ethiopian Patriots: The Lone Struggle, 1936-1940." See also De Grand, Alexander, "Mussolini's Follies: Fascism in Its Imperial and Racist Phase, 1935-1940."

6   Pankhurst, "The Ethiopian Patriots: The Lone Struggle, 1936-1940"

7   Bahru Zewde, "The Ethiopian Intelligentsia and the Italo-Ethiopian War, 1935-1941"

8   Mack Smith, *Mussolini's Roman Empire*, p. 78

9   De Grand, Alexander, "Mussolini's Follies: Fascism in Its Imperial and Racist Phase, 1935-1940"

10   *New Times and Ethiopia News*, November 23, 1940

11   *New Times and Ethiopia News*, November 23, 1940

12   *New Times and Ethiopia News*, November 23, 1940

13   *New Times and Ethiopia News*, October 5, 1940

14   Feiling, *Life of Neville Chamberlain*, p. 296

15   Feiling, *Life of Neville Chamberlain*, p. 296

16   UK Hansard, June 18, 1936

17   Pankhurst, "Fascist Racial Policies in Ethiopia: 1922-1941"

18   Matthews, *The Fruits of Fascism*, pp. 240-242

19   Duggan, *Fascist Voices*, p. 286

20   Duggan, *Fascist Voices*, p. 287

21   Duggan, *Fascist Voices*, pp. 287–288

22   Shawaraged Gadle interview, *Ethiopia Star*, November 23, 1941

23   Campbell, *The Plot to Kill Graziani*, p. 71

24   Sbacchi, *Legacy of Bitterness*, pp. 208–209, p. 229n

25 Baudendistel, *Between Bombs and Good Intentions*, p. 38
26 Lambie, as quoted by Baudendistel, *Between Bombs and Good Intentions*, p. 42
27 *Washington Post*, December 31, 1939
28 Spencer, *Ethiopia at Bay*, p.71
29 Windsor, *A King's Story*, pp. 296–297
30 Scott, *The Sons of Sheba's Race*, p. 146
31 Spencer, *Ethiopia at Bay*, p. 73
32 *New York Times*, July 3, 1936
33 AP story, *Washington Post*, July 3, 1936
34 AP story, *Washington Post*, July 3, 1936
35 National Archives, UK, FO 371/20167
36 Pankhurst, "The Ethiopian Patriots: The Lone Struggle, 1936-1940"
37 National Archives, UK, FO 371/20167
38 National Archives, UK, FO 371/20167
39 Bahru Zewde, *Pioneers of Change in Ethiopia*, p. 64
40 UK Hansard, December 1, 1937
41 Mockler, *Haile Selassie's War*, p. 163
42 Lentakis, *Ethiopia: A View From Within*, p. 67
43 Mockler, *Haile Selassie's War*, pp. 163–164

Chapter Eighteen – The Pride of Lions

1 Shawaraged Gadle interview, *Ethiopia Star*, November 23, 1941
2 Mockler, *Haile Selassie's War*, pp. 159–161
3 Campbell, *The Plot to Kill Graziani*, pp. 18–21, p. 73
4 Campbell, *The Plot to Kill Graziani*, p. 80
5 Konovalov, Unpublished Manuscript as newly translated by Clarke
6 Mockler, *Haile Selassie's War*, p. 161
7 Konovalov, Unpublished Manuscript as newly translated by Clarke
8 Konovalov, Unpublished Manuscript as newly translated by Clarke
9 Darrah, *Hail Caesar!* p. 336
10 National Archives, UK, FO 371/20198
11 Steer, *Caesar in Abyssinia*, pp. 7–8
12 Rankin, *Telegram from Guernica*, pp. 80–81
13 DePalma, *The Man Who Invented Fidel*, p. 59
14 Clarke, "Feodor Konovalov and the Italo-Ethiopian War"
15 Clarke, "Feodor Konovalov and the Italo-Ethiopian War"
16 Hastings, *Evelyn Waugh*, p. 341
17 Hastings, *Evelyn Waugh*, p. 342
18 National Archives, UK, FO 371/20167
19 Hastings, *Evelyn Waugh*, p. 345
20 Hastings, *Evelyn Waugh*, p. 517
21 Hamilton, *Waugh in Abyssinia*, Louisiana State University Press p. XXXii

22 Russell, *Selected Letters*, p. 342

23 Russell, *Which Way to Peace?* p. 73

24 Russell, *Which Way to Peace?* pp. 154–155

25 Russell, *Autobiography, Volume II*, p. 191

26 Russell, *Which Way to Peace?* pp. 221–223

27 Harrison, *Sylvia Pankhurst: A Crusading Life*, p. 244

28 Harrison, *Sylvia Pankhurst: A Crusading Life*, p. 245

29 National Archives, UK, FO 371/20198

30 Romero, E. *Sylvia Pankhurst: Portrait of a Radical*, p. 225

31 Pankhurst, *Sylvia Pankhurst: Artist and Crusader*, p. 194

32 Scott, *The Sons of Sheba's Race*, p. 173

33 Scott, *The Sons of Sheba's Race*, p. 173

34 Scott, *The Sons of Sheba's Race*, pp. 176–177

35 Scott, "Malaku E. Bayen: Ethiopian Emissary to Black America, 1936-1941"

36 *New Times and Ethiopia News*, September 7, 1940

37 De Grand, Alexander, "Mussolini's Follies: Fascism in Its Imperial and Racist Phase, 1935-1940"

38 *New Times and Ethiopia News*, September 7, 1940

39 Pankhurst, "The Ethiopian Patriots: The Lone Struggle, 1936-1940"

40 Eden, *Facing the Dictators*, pp. 424–425

41 *The Economist* story reprinted by *Washington Post*, October 16, 1936

42 Mockler, *Haile Selassie's War*, p. 165

43 National Archives, UK, FO 371/20923

44 Haile Selassie, *Autobiography, Volume Two*, p. 79; Mockler, *Haile Selassie's War*, p. 167

45 Campbell, *The Plot to Kill Graziani*, pp. 101–103; Mockler, *Haile Selassie's War*, p. 415

46 Campbell, *The Plot to Kill Graziani*, p. 97. Campbell interviewed two key sources who lived into the 21st century; as he put it, "In modern day parlance, Moges was the guru of the cell, and Abriha was the hitman."

47 Campbell, *The Plot to Kill Graziani*, p. 111

48 Campbell, *The Plot to Kill Graziani*, p. 112

49 Campbell, *The Plot to Kill Graziani*, pp. 117–118; Campbell provides a comprehensive list of the prominent nobles and dignitaries who attended Letyibu's meetings.

50 Yates, *From Mississippi to Madrid*, p. 95

51 Yates, *From Mississippi to Madrid*, p. 95

52 Yates, *From Mississippi to Madrid*, p. 96

53 Yates, *From Mississippi to Madrid*, p. 98

54 http://www.alba-valb.org/volunteers/browse/alonzo-watson

55 Collum, *African Americans in the Spanish Civil War*, p. 68

56 http://www.alba-valb.org/volunteers/oscar-henry-hunter; Collum, *African Americans in the Spanish Civil War*, p. 5

57 Greenfield, *Ethiopia: A New Political History*, p. 234

58 Greenfield, *Ethiopia: A New Political History*, p. 235

59 National Archives, UK, FO 371/20923

60 Sbacchi, "Italy and the Treatment of the Ethiopian Aristocracy, 1937-1940"

61 Mockler, *Haile Selassie's War*, pp. 170–171, 414–415n; Mockler argues that Hailu probably didn't know the brothers would be killed and once back in the capital, demanded to see Graziani, presumably to protest.

62 Steer, *Sealed and Delivered*, p. 38

63 Adugna, "Women and Warfare in Ethiopia"

64 National Archives, UK, FO 371/20923

65 National Archives, UK, FO 371/20923

66 Garretson, *A Victorian Gentleman & Ethiopian Nationalist*, p. 224

67 Garretson, *A Victorian Gentleman & Ethiopian Nationalist*, p. 224

68 Campbell, *The Plot to Kill Graziani*, p. 119

69 Campbell, *The Plot to Kill Graziani*, p. 121

70 Campbell, *The Plot to Kill Graziani*, pp. 159–160

71 Quoted by Campbell, *The Plot to Kill Graziani*, pp. 160–162

72 Campbell, *The Plot to Kill Graziani*, p. 155

73 Greenfield, *Ethiopia: A New Political History*, p. 239

74 National Archives, UK, FO 371/20930

75 Del Boca, *The Ethiopian War*, p. 219

76 Testimony of Michael Tessema, Documents on Italian War Crimes submitted to the United Nations War Crimes Commission by the Imperial Ethiopian Government, Extract from Affidavit No. 32 as reproduced on http://www.campifascisti.it/file/media/Testemony%20of%20Michael%20Tessema.pdf

77 Duggan, *Fascist Voices*, p. 288

78 Campbell, *The Plot to Kill Graziani*, pp. 181–182

79 Campbell, *The Plot to Kill Graziani*, p. 186

80 Campbell, *The Plot to Kill Graziani*, p. 191

81 Campbell, *The Plot to Kill Graziani*, p. 195

Chapter Nineteen – Abattoir

1   Campbell, *The Plot to Kill Graziani*, p. 239

2   Campbell, *The Plot to Kill Graziani*, p. 241

3   Poggiali, *Diario AOI*, as quoted and translated by Duggan, *Fascist Voices*, p. 289

4   *New Times and Ethiopia News*, January 11, 1940

5   Testimony of Toka Binegid, Documents on Italian War Crimes submitted to the United Nations War Crimes Commission by the Imperial Ethiopian Government, Extract from Affidavit No. 31 as reproduced on http://www.campifascisti.it/file/media/Testimony%20of%20Toka%20Binegid.pdf

6   *New Times and Ethiopia News*, December 14, 1940

7   Campbell, *The Plot to Kill Graziani*, p. 250

8   Campbell, *The Plot to Kill Graziani*, pp. 251–252

9   Campbell, *The Plot to Kill Graziani*, p. 248

10 Campbell, *The Plot to Kill Graziani*, pp. 254–255

11 Testimony of Michael Bekele Hapte, Documents on Italian War Crimes submitted to the United Nations War Crimes Commission by the Imperial Ethiopian Government, Extract from Affidavit No. 18 as reproduced on http://www.campifascisti.it/file/media/Testimony%20of%20Michael%20Blatta%20Bekele%20Hapte.pdf

12 Testimony of Michael Bekele Hapte, Documents on Italian War Crimes submitted to the United Nations War Crimes Commission by the Imperial Ethiopian Government, Extract from Affidavit No. 18 as reproduced on http://www.campifascisti.it/file/media/Testimony%20of%20Michael%20Blatta%20Bekele%20Hapte.pdf

13 Duggan, *The Force of Destiny*, p. 496

14 *New Times and Ethiopia News*, December 21, 1940

15 Poggiali, *Diario AOI*, as quoted and translated by Duggan, *Fascist Voices*, p. 289

16 US Diplomatic Papers, 1937, p. 680

17 Testimony of David Oqbazqui, Documents on Italian War Crimes submitted to the United Nations War Crimes Commission by the Imperial Ethiopian Government, Extract from Affidavit No. 10 as reproduced on http://www.campifascisti.it/file/media/Testimony%20of%20Blatta%20David%20Oqbazqui.pdf

18 *New Times and Ethiopia News*, December 21, 1940

19 National Archives, UK, FO 371/20937

20 *Pittsburgh Courier*, March 13, 1937

21 US Diplomatic Papers, 1937, pp. 681–682

22 US Diplomatic Papers, 1937, p. 682

23 Personal memoir emailed to author

24 Campbell, *The Plot to Kill Graziani*, p. 271

25 *New Times and Ethiopia News*, January 4, 1941

26 *New Times and Ethiopia News*, January 4, 1941

27 Testimony of David Oqbazqui, Documents on Italian War Crimes submitted to the United Nations War Crimes Commission by the Imperial Ethiopian Government, Extract from Affidavit No. 10 as reproduced on http://www.campifascisti.it/file/media/Testimony%20of%20Blatta%20David%20Oqbazqui.pdf

28 US Diplomatic Papers, 1937, p. 683

29 US Diplomatic Papers, 1937, p. 685

30 Testimony of Toka Binegid, Documents on Italian War Crimes submitted to the United Nations War Crimes Commission by the Imperial Ethiopian Government, Extract from Affidavit No. 31 as reproduced on http://www.campifascisti.it/file/media/Testimony%20of%20Toka%20Binegid.pdf

31 Mockler suggests 3,000 in *Haile Selassie's War*, p. 177; Sbacchi estimates 5,000 to 6,000 in *Legacy of Bitterness*, p. 177

32 Pankhurst, "The Ethiopian Patriots: The Lone Struggle, 1936-1940"

33 National Archives, UK, FO 371/20937

34 Campbell, *The Massacre of Addis Ababa*, forthcoming

35 Campbell, *The Massacre of Addis Ababa*, forthcoming

36 US Diplomatic Papers, 1937, p. 688

37 Campbell, *The Plot to Kill Graziani*, pp. 261–262

38 Del Boca, *The Ethiopian War*, pp. 224-225; Pankhurst, "The Ethiopian Patriots: The Lone Struggle, 1936-1940"

39 Pankhurst, "The Ethiopian Patriots: The Lone Struggle, 1936-1940"

40 Shirreff, *Bare Feet and Bandoliers*, p. 16

41 Shawaraged Gadle, interview, *Ethiopia Star*, November 23, 1941

42 Tsehai Berhane-Selassie, "Women Guerilla Fighters"

43 Haile Selassie, *Autobiography, Volume Two*, p. 170

44 Sbacchi, "Italy and the Treatment of the Ethiopian Aristocracy"

45 Campbell, *The Plot to Kill Graziani*, p. 285

46 Interview with author, October 8, 2012 and personal memoir emailed to author

47 *New Times and Ethiopia News*, February 27, 1937

48 *Pittsburgh Courier*, February 27, 1937

49 *New Times and Ethiopia News*, March 20, 1937

50 Quoted in the *New York Times*, April 4, 1937

51 Ian Campbell, the leading expert on the attack, suggests that given Haile Selassie's contact and coordination with the resistance, "it is probable that although he may not have known the details, the Emperor knew about the plan for a strike on the Governo Generale and approved it." *The Plot to Kill Graziani*, p. 389.

52 Steer's biographer, Nicholas Rankin, thinks it "very possible," given that she was fluent in Spanish and had contacts. See *Telegram from Guernica*, p. 82

53 Rankin, *Telegram from Guernica*, p. 96

54 Rankin, *Telegram from Guernica*, pp. 96–97

55 *The Times*, January 30, 1937

56 Rankin, *Telegram from Guernica*, pp. 99–103

57 Rankin, *Telegram from Guernica*, p. 103

58 *New Times and Ethiopia News*, March 20, 1937

59 Personal memoir emailed to author

60 Interview with author, October 8, 2012

61 Personal memoir emailed to author

62 Personal memoir emailed to author

63 Personal memoir emailed to author

64 Walston, "History and Memory of the Italian Concentration Camps"

65 Sbacchi, Del Boca, Walston all cite Tassemma's Italian War Crimes testimony

66 Walston, "History and Memory of the Italian Concentration Camps"

67 Walston, "History and Memory of the Italian Concentration Camps"

68 Personal memoir emailed to author

69 Personal memoir emailed to author

70 Bahru Zewde, *Pioneers of Change in Ethiopia*, p. 88

71 *New Times and Ethiopia News*, February 21, 1937; AP, February 21, 1937

72 Campbell, *The Plot to Kill Graziani*, pp. 326–353; this account of their flight relies heavily on Campbell's new findings.

73 *The Black Man*, January 1937

74 *The Black Man*, March–April 1937

75   Grant, *Negro with a Hat*, p. 441

76   Grant, *Negro with a Hat*, p. 442

77   Grant, *Negro with a Hat*, pp. 441–442

78   *Chicago Defender*, April 3, 1937

79   Greenfield, *Ethiopia: A New Political History*, p. 242; historian Ian Campbell shared new facts he uncovered during his research in an email to author, January 6, 2013

80   National Archives, UK, FO 371/20923

81   Newman, *Italy's Conquest of Abyssinia*, p. 9

82   National Archives, UK, FO 371/22014

83   *New Times and Ethiopian News*, July 15, 1937

84   Eden, *Facing the Dictators*, p. 451

85   Faber, *Munich: The 1938 Appeasement Crisis*, p. 171

86   Thorpe, *Eden*, p. 191

87   Eden, *Facing the Dictators*, p. 450

88   Feiling, Keith, *Life of Neville Chamberlain*, p. 330

89   Eden, *Facing the Dictators*, p. 555

90   Pugh, *"Hurrah for the Blackshirts!"* p. 267

Chapter Twenty – Eden Bows Out

1   *New Times and Ethiopia News*, October 5, 1940

2   *New Times and Ethiopia News*, October 5, 1940

3   Campbell, *The Plot to Kill Graziani*, p. 314; Campbell writes that Graziani withheld the intelligence report "for several weeks and sent it to Rome only after the massacre [at Debre Libanos] had been carried out."

4   Buxton, *Travels in Ethiopia*, p. 65

5   Campbell, *The Plot to Kill Graziani*, pp. 317–318

6   Tsehai Berhane-Selassie, "Women Guerilla Fighters"

7   Mockler, *Haile Selassie's War*, p. 188

8   Greenfield, *Ethiopia: A New Political History*, p. 245

9   Greenfield, *Ethiopia: A New Political History*, p. 244

10   *New Times and Ethiopia News*, September 11, 1937

11   Del Boca, *The Ethiopian War*, p. 242

12   *New Times and Ethiopia News*, September 11, 1937

13   Mockler, *Haile Selassie's War*, p. 194

14   Pankhurst, "The Ethiopian Patriots: The Lone Struggle, 1936-1940"

15   UK Hansard, November 29, 1937

16   National Archives, UK, FO 371/22009

17   National Archives, UK, FO 371/22009

18   National Archives, UK, FO 371/20923

19   National Archives, UK, FO 371/20923

20   National Archives, UK, FO 371/20923

21   Haile Selassie, *Autobiography*, *Volume Two*, pp. 40–42

22   Welles, *The Time for Decision*, p. 66
23   Eden, *Facing the Dictators*, p. 550
24   Daniel Abebe recounted these episodes personally to historian Angelo Del Boca; Del Boca, *The Ethiopian War*, pp. 243–244
25   Del Boca, *The Ethiopian War*, pp. 243–244
26   Del Boca, *The Ethiopian War*, p. 244
27   US Diplomatic Papers, 1938, p. 119
28   Welles, *The Time for Decision*, p. 66
29   US Diplomatic Papers, 1938, p. 121
30   US Diplomatic Papers, 1938, p. 123
31   US Diplomatic Papers, 1938, p. 124
32   Welles, *The Time for Decision*, p. 69
33   Eden, *Facing the Dictators*, p. 575
34   Eden, *Facing the Dictators*, p. 568
35   Campbell, *The Plot to Kill Graziani*, pp. 352–353
36   Campbell, *The Plot to Kill Graziani*, p. 348
37   Campbell, *The Plot to Kill Graziani*, p. 350
38   Campbell, *The Plot to Kill Graziani*, pp. 352–353
39   Eden, *Facing the Dictators*, p. 582
40   Eden, *Facing the Dictators*, p. 582
41   Eden, *Facing the Dictators*, p. 587
42   Eden, *Facing the Dictators*, p. 590
43   Ciano, *Ciano's Diary, 1937-1938*, p. 78
44   Eden, *Facing the Dictators*, p. 592
45   UK Hansard, February 21, 1938
46   UK Hansard, February 21, 1938
47   UK Hansard, February 21, 1938
48   Ciano, *Ciano's Diary, 1937-1938*, p. 78
49   Davis, *FDR: Into the Storm, 1937-1940*, p. 195
50   UK Hansard, February 21, 1938
51   Eden, *The Reckoning*, p. 12
52   Howarth, *Intelligence Chief Extraordinary*, p. 109
53   Howarth, *Intelligence Chief Extraordinary*, p. 109
54   Howarth, *Intelligence Chief Extraordinary*, p. 109
55   *Brisbane Courier-Mail*, May 13, 2012
56   Australian Associated Press, May 13, 1938
57   Australian Associated Press, May 13, 1938
58   Haile Selassie, *Autobiography, Volume Two*, p. 66
59   United Press, May 15, 1938

Chapter Twenty-One – A Volcano, Permanently Simmering

1   Schuyler, *Ethiopian Stories*, p. 182
2   Tsehai Berhane-Selassie, "Women Guerrilla Fighters"

3   Interview with author, December 8, 2012
4   Bahru Zewde, "The Ethiopian Intelligentsia and the War"
5   Bahru Zewde, *Pioneers of Change in Ethiopia*, p. 57; see also his "The Ethiopian Intelligentsia and the War"
6   Personal memoir emailed to author
7   Interview with author, December 8, 2012
8   Spitzer and LaRay, "I. T. A. Wallace-Johnson and the West African Youth League"
9   Spitzer and LaRay, "I. T. A. Wallace-Johnson and the West African Youth League"
10 Spitzer and LaRay, "I. T. A. Wallace-Johnson and the West African Youth League"
11 Padmore, *Africa and World Peace*, p. 155
12 Makalani, *In the Cause of Freedom*, pp. 209–210
13 Mackenzie, "Radical Pan-Africanism in the 1930s: A Discussion with C.L.R. James"
14 James, *The Black Jacobins*, p. 304
15 Faber, *Munich: The 1938 Appeasement Crisis*, p. 154
16 Kirkpatrick, *The Inner Circle*, p. 115
17 Kirkpatrick, *The Inner Circle*, p. 93
18 Kirkpatrick, *The Inner Circle*, p. 135
19 UK Hansard, November 2, 1938
20 Rankin, *Telegram from Guernica*, p. 155
21 Rankin, *Telegram from Guernica*, p. 154
22 Interview with author, October 20, 2013
23 Interview with author, October 20, 2013
24 Ciano, *The Ciano Diaries, 1939-1943*, p. 3
25 Ciano, *The Ciano Diaries, 1939-1943*, p. 42
26 FO 371/23378
27 FO 371/23378
28 FO 371/23378
29 FO 371/23378
30 FO 371/23378
31 Gandy, *Salan*, p. 64
32 Horne, *A Savage War of Peace*, pp. 178–179
33 Gandy, *Salan*, p. 64
34 Rankin, *Telegram from Guernica*, p. 111; Rankin's Introduction to *Tree of Gernika*
35 Steer, *Sealed and Delivered*, p. 7
36 Steer, *Sealed and Delivered*, p. 10
37 Steer, *Sealed and Delivered*, p. 9
38 Gandy, *Salan*, p. 66
39 Salan, *Mémoires: Fin D'un Empire*, p. 73
40 Horne, *A Savage War of Peace*, p. 180
41 Grant, *Negro with a Hat*, p. 447
42 Grant, *Negro with a Hat*, p. 448
43 Grant, *Negro with a Hat*, pp. 449–450
44 Garvey's speech as printed in *The Black Man*, July 1938

45   Hibbert, *Mussolini: The Rise and Fall of Il Duce*, p. 124
46   Pankhurst, *Sylvia Pankhurst: Artist and Crusader*, p. 204
47   Wrong, *I Didn't Do It for You*, p. 126
48   Scott, *The Sons of Sheba's Race*, p. 177
49   Steer, *Sealed and Delivered*, p. 17

Chapter Twenty-Two – Day of Deliverance

1   Lazareff, *Deadline*, p. 323
2   Haney, *Naked at the Feast*, p. 221
3   Haney, *Naked at the Feast*, p. 217
4   Haney, *Naked at the Feast*, p. 221
5   Steer, *Sealed and Delivered*, p. 21
6   Steer, *Sealed and Delivered*, p. 21
7   Steer, *Sealed and Delivered*, p. 24
8   Steer, *Sealed and Delivered*, p. 25
9   Steer, *Sealed and Delivered*, p. 27
10   Steer, *Sealed and Delivered*, p. 31
11   Steer, *Sealed and Delivered*, pp. 29–31
12   Quoted by Steer in *Sealed and Delivered*, pp. 41–42
13   Manchester and Reid, *The Last Lion*, Vol. 3, p. 158
14   Eden, *The Reckoning*, pp. 125–126
15   Steer, *Sealed and Delivered*, Appendix B, p. 231
16   Steer, *Sealed and Delivered*, p. 47
17   Steer, *Sealed and Delivered*, p. 48
18   Maitland, *Thesiger*, p. 203
19   Maitland, *Thesiger*, p. 201
20   Skidelsky, *Oswald Mosley*, p. 11
21   KV 4/241
22   Allen, *Guerrilla Warfare in Abyssinia*, p. 33
23   US Diplomatic Papers, 1940, p. 522
24   US Diplomatic Papers, 1940, p. 523
25   Garretson, *A Victorian Gentleman & Ethiopian Nationalist*, p. 243
26   Garretson, *A Victorian Gentleman & Ethiopian Nationalist*, p. 243
27   Interview, *Ethiopia Star*, November 23, 1941
28   Interview, *Ethiopia Star*, November 23, 1941
29   Sandford, *Ethiopia Under Haile Selassie*, p. 108
30   *The Abyssinian Campaigns*, p. 58
31   Steer, *Sealed and Delivered*, p. 64
32   Steer, *Sealed and Delivered*, p. 65
33   Shirreff, *Bare Feet and Bandoliers*, pp. 41–43, p. 54
34   Steer, *Sealed and Delivered*, p. 56
35   Allen, *Guerrilla War in Abyssinia*, p. 11

36 Eden, *The Reckoning*, p. 156

37 Eden, *The Reckoning*, p. 164; Mockler, *Haile Selassie's War*, p. 270

38 Eden, *The Reckoning*, p. 164

39 Eden, *The Reckoning*, p. 165

40 Allen, *Guerrilla Warfare in Abyssinia*, p. 17

41 Steer, *Sealed and Delivered*, pp. 104–105

42 Steer, *Sealed and Delivered*, p. 105

43 Steer, *Sealed and Delivered*, pp. 159–161

44 Steer, *Sealed and Delivered*, p. 161

45 Bierman and Smith, *Fire in the Night*, p. 153

46 Bierman and Smith, *Fire in the Night*, p. 154

47 Allen, *Guerrilla Warfare in Abyssinia*, p. 36; Thesiger, *The Life of My Choice*, p. 327

48 Shawaragad gave her figures in an interview for *The Ethiopia Star*, November 23, 1941; Jagama offered his own in an interview with the author, October 20, 2013.

49 Interview, *Ethiopia Star*, November 23, 1941

50 Interview, *Ethiopia Star*, November 23, 1941

51 Steer, *Sealed and Delivered*, p. 99

52 Steer, *Sealed and Delivered*, p. 115

53 Steer, *Sealed and Delivered*, p. 171

54 Steer, *Sealed and Delivered*, p. 129

55 Steer, *Sealed and Delivered*, p. 130

56 Steer, *Sealed and Delivered*, p. 131

57 Rankin, *Telegram from Guernica*, p. 187

58 Sandford, *Ethiopia under Haile Selassie*, p. 113

59 Steer, *Sealed and Delivered*, p. 119

60 US Diplomatic Papers, 1941, pp. 341–342

61 Shireff, *Bare Feet and Bandoliers*, p. 63

62 Ciano, *The Ciano Diaries, 1939-1943*, pp. 322–323

63 Ciano, *The Ciano Diaries, 1939-1943*, p. 323

Chapter Twenty-Three – Champagne and Jazz Records

1 Tsehai Berhane-Selassie, "Women Guerrilla Fighters"

2 Tsehai Berhane-Selassie, "Women Guerrilla Fighters"

3 *New Times and Ethiopia News*, February 22, 1941

4 Allen, *Guerrilla Warfare in Abyssinia*, p. 63

5 Steer, *Sealed and Delivered*, p. 142

6 Steer, *Sealed and Delivered*, p. 144

7 Shirreff makes this point in *Bare Feet and Bandoliers*, suggesting that scouts and spies could have checked the trampled countryside and imagined a much larger force, p. 94

8 Steer, *Sealed and Delivered*, p. 153

9 Shirreff, *Bare Feet and Bandoliers*, p. 118

10 Bierman and Smith, *Fire in the Night*, p. 190

11   Hilton, *The Ethiopian Patriots*, p. 122
12   Steer, *Sealed and Delivered*, pp. 162–163
13   Manchester and Reid, *The Last Lion, Defender of the Realm, 1940-1965*, p. 323
14   Thesiger, *The Life of My Choice*, pp. 338–339
15   *Life*, September 15, 1941
16   *Life*, September 15, 1941
17   Matthews, *The Fruits of Fascism*, p. 290
18   Personal memoir emailed to author
19   Shirreff, *Bare Feet and Bandoliers*, pp. 179–180
20   Steer, *Sealed and Delivered*, p. 194
21   Bierman and Smith, *Fire in the Night*, p. 210
22   Steer, *Sealed and Delivered*, p. 211
23   Steer, *Sealed and Delivered*, p. 212
24   Steer, *Sealed and Delivered*, p. 212
25   Sandford, *Ethiopia Under Haile Selassie*, p. 118
26   Interview with author, October 20, 2013
27   For his interview with the author in 2013, Jagama couldn't recall her name when he
     told this story, but he clearly identified her as Shawaragad when he told the same
     anecdote to Elizabeth Blunt for the BBC in 2009.
28   Interview with author, October 20, 2013
29   Interview with Elizabeth Blunt for BBC World Service, April 2009
30   Bierman and Smith, *Fire in the Night*, p. 214
31   Thesiger, *The Life of My Choice*, p. 351

Chapter Twenty-Four – "That Was Another War"

1   An excellent and detailed account of Sylvia Pankhurst's investigation and Richard
     Pankhurst's findings can be found in Wrong's *I Didn't Do It for You*, pp. 129–142.
     See also Pankhurst, "Post-World War II Ethiopia: British Military Policy and Action
     for the Dismantling and Acquisition of Italian Factories and Other Assets, 1941-2."
2   Wrong, *I Didn't Do It for You*, pp. 142–143
3   US Diplomatic Papers, 1941, p. 348
4   US Diplomatic Papers, 1941, p. 350
5   Spencer, *Ethiopia at Bay*, p. 159
6   Bierman and Smith, *Fire in the Night*, pp. 220–221
7   Bierman and Smith, *Fire in the Night*, p. 224
8   US Diplomatic Papers, 1945, Volume VIII, p. 6
9   Spencer, *Ethiopia at Bay*, p. 161
10   Steer, *Sealed and Delivered*, p. 13
11   Professor Richard Pankhurst has made a detailed study of the whole issue: "Italian
     Fascist War Crimes in Ethiopia: A History of Their Discussion from the League
     of Nations to the United Nations (1936-1949)." This chapter relies heavily on his
     account with his permission.

12 UK Hansard, November 3, 1943

13 Pankhurst, "Italian Fascist War Crimes in Ethiopia"

14 *New York Times*, January 31, 1945

15 Kali-Nyah, *Italy's War Crimes in Ethiopia, 1935-1941*, p. 135

16 Moseley, *Mussolini: The Last 600 Days of Il Duce*, p. 2

17 Moseley, *Mussolini: The Last 600 Days of Il Duce*, p. 314

18 Moseley, *Mussolini: The Last 600 Days of Il Duce*, pp. 313–314

19 Thesiger, *The Life of My Choice*, p. 235

20 Churchill, *The Second World War*, Vol. 6, *Triumph and Tragedy*, p. 461

21 Pankhurst, "Italian Fascist War Crimes in Ethiopia"

22 Pankhurst, "Italian Fascist War Crimes in Ethiopia"

23 Personal memoir emailed to the author

24 Pankhurst, *Sylvia Pankhurst: Artist and Crusader*, p. 220

25 Email to author, July 26, 2013

26 See Anthony DePalma's *The Man Who Invented Fidel* for the full story on Matthews's controversial coverage of the revolutionary leader, particularly pp. 158–159

27 Rankin, *Telegram from Guernica*, pp. 248–249

28 Rankin, *Telegram from Guernica*, p. 250

29 Beevor and Cooper, *Paris after the Liberation, 1944-1949*, p. 175

30 Mockler, *Haile Selassie's War*, p. 391

31 Bahru Zewde, *Pioneers of Change in Ethiopia*, p. 57

32 Simmons, *The Man Called Brown Condor*, pp. 267–268

33 Garretson, *A Victorian Gentleman & Ethiopian Nationalist*, p. 286, p. 297

34 Simmons, *The Man Called Brown Condor*, pp. 280–281

35 Simmons, *The Man Called Brown Condor*, p. 281

36 De St. Jorre, John, *The Brothers' War*, p. 337

37 De St. Jorre, John, *The Brothers' War*, p. 337

38 Thorpe, *Eden*, p. 482

39 Thorpe, *Eden*, p. 537

40 *New York Times* obituary, January 15, 1977

41 Thorpe, *Eden*, p. 603

42 Polsgrove, *Ending British Rule in Africa*, p. 167

43 Bahru Zewde, *Pioneers of Change in Ethiopia*, p. 170

44 Wrong, *I Didn't Do It for You*, p. 165

45 Wrong, *I Didn't Do It for You*, p. 170

46 Personal memoir emailed to author

47 See Wrong's *I Didn't Do It for You*, pp. 177–196

48 Bahru Zewde, "Hayla-Selassie: From Progressive to Reactionary"

49 Wrong, *I Didn't Do It for You*, p. 213

50 *New York Times*, July 9, 1969

51 Personal memoir emailed to author

52 Thesiger, *The Life of My Choice*, p. 437

53 Personal memoir emailed to author

54   Thesiger, *The Life of My Choice*, p. 438
55   Wrong, *I Didn't Do It for You*, p. 245
56   Personal memoir emailed to author
57   Shaftel, "The Black Eagle of Harlem," *Air & Space*, January 2009
58   Kapuściński, *The Emperor: Downfall of an Autocrat*, p. 5
59   Ryle, "Tales of Mythical Africa," *Times Literary Supplement*, July 27, 2001
60   Domoslawski, *Ryszard Kapuściński: A Life*, p. 306
61   Domoslawski, *Ryszard Kapuściński: A Life*, p. 303
62   Bahru Zewde, "Hayla-Selassie: From Progressive to Reactionary"
63   Email to author, February 17, 2013
64   *St. Catherines Standard*, November 6, 2000
65   Hilton, *The Ethiopian Patriots*, p. 11
66   Hilton, *The Ethiopian Patriots*, p. 13
67   Hilton, *The Ethiopian Patriots*, p. 15

Chapter Twenty-Five – Epilogue of Stones

1   Translation of Italian copy from the City of Affile website, www.affile.org, 2012
2   *New York Times*, August 28, 2012
3   *New York Amsterdam News*, September 21, 2012
4   *The Jerusalem Post*, October 8, 2012
5   *The Telegraph*, September 2, 2012
6   *The Telegraph*, September 2, 2012
7   *New York Times*, August 28, 2012
8   Bahru Zewde, www.focusonthehorn.wordpress.com, August 29, 2012
9   Prince Ermias Sahle Selassie, Open letter to Italy's President and Prime Minister, www.ecadforum.com, September 18, 2012
10   Speech by Professor Richard Pankhurst, delivered by Rita Pankhurst outside the Italian Embassy in London, on August 31, 2012
11   BBC News website, http://www.bbc.co.uk/news/world-europe-21222341, January 27, 2013
12   *The Spectator* website, http://www.spectator.co.uk/the-week/diary/11475/diary-83/, September 13, 2003
13   *The Guardian* website, http://www.guardian.co.uk/books/2003/jul/19/featuresreviews.guardianreview3, July 19, 2003
14   Duggan, *Fascist Voices*, p. xvi
15   Fuller, *The First of the League Wars*, pp. 30–31
16   Fuller, *The First of the League Wars*, p. 39
17   Matthews, *Two Wars and More to Come*, p. 119
18   Martelli, *Italy Against the World*, p. 256
19   Barker, *The Civilizing Mission*, p. 243
20   Del Boca, *The Ethiopian War*, pp. 109–110
21   Fuller, *The First of the League Wars*, p. 30

22   Carroll, Rory, "Italy's Bloody Secret," *The Guardian*, June 25, 2001

23   Pankhurst, "Italian Fascist War Crimes in Ethiopia"

24   Roman Herzog interview with Ian Campbell, http://www.campifascisti.it/file/media/Testimony%20Ian%20Campbell.pdf

25   DePalma, *The Man Who Invented Fidel*, p. 53

26   BBC News website, "Obelisk arrives back in Ethiopia," http://news.bbc.co.uk/2/hi/africa/4458105.stm, April 19, 2005

27   *The Guardian*, April 20, 2005

ACKNOWLEDGMENTS

This book is the result of an obsession that has lasted more than a decade. I first tried years ago to write this story as a novel, but the novel thankfully never sold because it was bad, and so I went on (fortunately) to sell slightly better novels and nonfiction books. But I couldn't forget the Italian-Ethiopian War. I was astonished when experts and academics took the emails and calls of a nobody amateur seriously, and if this work has any value at all, it is because of the generosity and kindness of many individuals who have made inspiring breakthroughs and contributions to history and scholarship. It should be naturally understood that any errors are my responsibility alone.

Thanks must go first to Clarissa Eden, Countess of Avon, for granting permissions to quote and cite from her late husband's two memoirs, *Facing the Dictators* and *The Reckoning*. Anthony Eden had such a large role in events that this was vital, and her lovely handwritten note on stationery is now something of a prized possession for me. This wouldn't have been possible without the kind help of Eden's skilled biographer, Richard Thorpe, who granted permission as well for his own book on one of Britain's most interesting political figures.

It was Ian Campbell who generously opened other doors and whose brilliant investigative work on the Graziani Massacre and the Italian Occupation deserves far wider recognition. I owe as much to Richard Pankhurst's graciousness as I do—along with so many others—to the great library of pioneering work he has built in Ethiopian history; he let me happily explore the shelves and rely on his findings. He not only wrote the foreword but inspected the working draft, suggested sources, and offered brilliant advice and photographic material. Professor Bahru Zewde, the other titan of Ethiopia's historical scholarship, also kindly granted permissions. I owe much as well to Professor William R. Scott of Lehigh University, who wrote *the* definitive book on African-American participation in the war. I am grateful as well to Anthony Mockler for his permissions regarding his indispensable volume, *Haile Selassie's War*, and to James Ferguson at Signal Books for his kind help.

Nicholas Rankin gave his time, his encouragement, and his professional judgment, which adds up to a lot. He let me borrow his words and generously negotiated on my behalf for the use of George Steer's words. I must naturally thank as well George Barton Steer for his kind permissions. Nick Rankin didn't stop there, helping me get in touch with Colin Grant, who was just as kind over quoting and citing from his masterly biography of Marcus Garvey. The same generosity was displayed by Professor James Walston of the American University in Rome, who steered me in the direction of other indispensable experts. Professor Tsehai Berhane-Selassie patiently put up with a seemingly endless stream of neurotic questions, offering wonderful and much-needed insights into the Patriots, particularly the women Patriots, and elements of Ethiopian culture in general. I must also thank Rainer Baudendistel, who has written a landmark work with his *Between Bombs and Good Intentions* for his permissions and for supplying rare photos. Thanks must also go to Professor Peter Garretson for permissions over his biography of that amazing figure, Charles Martin, a.k.a. Warqenah Eshate.

Then there are the surviving family members of key figures in the war. Benoit Junod, son of Marcel Junod, was diligent over details and keen to address some controversial contentions in past works, as was Borre Winckel, grandson of Dutch Red Cross doctor, Charles Winckel, who offered me a huge cache of wonderful and much needed photographic, correspondence and report material. Dr. Eric Matthews kindly granted permissions for the books dealing with Ethiopia by his father, Herbert L. Matthews, whose career and writing deserves far more attention. Fortunately, Anthony DePalma's insightful biography has helped redress that, and my thanks go to him for letting me rely on *The Man Who Invented Fidel*. I am grateful to Dr. Matthews as well for making a large collection of photographs by his father available.

And consider the case of serial courage by father and son, the Poggialis. Ciro Poggiali wrote his secret diary and kept precious and damning photos safe, and then in 1971, his son, Vieri, dared to publish it all in Italian in 1971 after his father's death. Vieri Poggiali has been a custodian of history all this time, and I am extremely grateful that he allowed me to bring the material to a new audience. I am just as thankful for the kind permissions of the Sandford family—Stephen Sandford, Philippa Langdon, and Daniel Sandford, the well known BBC correspondent.

Martin Plaut, who has written on the forgotten African soldiers of the Second World War, steered me to his fellow BBC alum Elizabeth Blunt, who interviewed Jagama Kello first. Elizabeth sent along a treasure of valuable links, background information, and contacts. Andrew Hilton enthusiastically lent his support and permissions over his critical work, *The Ethiopian Patriots*, which allows these heroes to tell their stories in their own words. Michela Wrong kindly granted permissions over her book, *I Didn't Do It for You*, a fascinating book on

Eritrea. Jeremy Murray-Brown, who wrote what is an unparalleled biography of Jomo Kenyatta, promptly sent me a reply that he would be glad that his work could be useful to mine. After writing to her about my effort on the Ethiopian War, Selina Hastings emailed back, "What a fascinating subject!" And promptly allowed her permissions from her biography of Evelyn Waugh.

With his southern charm and great sense of humor, Thomas E. Simmons schooled me on John Robinson, saving me from making several mistakes and granting permission regarding his pioneering works, *The Brown Condor* and *The Man Called Brown Condor*. I am deeply grateful to John Stokes for granting permissions over Robinson's letters on behalf of this great hero's family. Professor Christopher Duggan of the University of Reading greeted a quirky Canadian turning up on his doorstep with infinite patience over questions and sent me off with much to think about and a valuable source text. Documentary maker Roman Herzog allowed use of his illuminating website on Italian war crimes and concentration camps, www.campifascisti.it. He did me an invaluable service by performing double-duty as intermediary, helping me to obtain the generous permissions of that giant in the field of Italian-Ethiopian War research, Angelo Del Boca.

Professor Joseph Calvitt Clarke of Jacksonville University removed the cobwebs for me over Konovalov with his brilliant translation, while Boris Gorelik made available a precious copy of Konovalov's original translated draft. Professors Charles McClellan of Radford and Alexander De Grand of North Carolina State kindly passed on works I was desperately searching for and granted me permissions. Professors Robert Hill of UCLA, Minkah Makalani of the University of Texas and Carol Polsgrove of Indiana University didn't hesitate to offer their assistance. And writer Bryan Clough provided me with some fascinating pieces of information on W. E. D. Allen.

Michael Cotter, the publisher of the *American Diplomacy* online magazine, kindly allowed use of a valuable source article on Cornelius Engert, and I was granted kind permission as well by his granddaughter, Jane Engert. Arnold Rampersad was most gracious and generous over his biography of Langston Hughes. My great thanks go as well to Richard Koritz and Open Hand Publishing LLC for granting permissions regarding James Yates's insightful memoir, *From Mississippi to Madrid*. I am grateful as well for the kind permission of Colin Smith, who with the late John Bierman wrote the highly engaging and authoritative biography of Orde Wingate, which brought many new findings to light as well as insights into the man. Lynn Haney's beautiful, evocative biography of Josephine Baker, *Naked at the Feast*, has haunted me for years, first serving as indispensable research behind my first novel and once again proving invaluable for the sections on Josephine for this volume; I can't thank her enough.

In Ethiopia, I met by chance the beautiful and charming Bezawit Asmelash, who sat listening to my hopes of finding retired General Jagama Kello, promptly picked up her cell phone and found me specific directions to his home! Once there, Kimi Sekhon—indispensable travel companion, compassionate gender consultant and tour price haggler extraordinaire—worked my video camera as I asked the general questions on an era now misted over by the ages. I naturally thank General Jagama, a unique character who gave much of his time and who is a national treasure to his people. My one regret is that we didn't have the time to take him up on his offer to go tour his old fighting grounds . . . or to sample his whiskey.

Professor Dickson Eyoh at the University of Toronto took my desperate call about looking for translation help, and he promptly sent my way an exceptional student, Fikir Getaneh Haile, who did a brilliant transcription. I must also thank Richard Hughes, curator of the Documents and Sound Section at the Imperial War Museum for graciously agreeing to trade access to Elizabeth Blunt's interview with Jagama Kello for the donation of mine to the museum.

Talented writer Hamish Copley saved me in the nick of time as I made my clumsy efforts to decode source material on Raoul Salan, while Astrid DesLandes translated correspondence of Marcel Junod. Adey Makonnen went through snapshots of her father and rescued my photo submissions at the last minute. Dennis Chan had incredible patience as he revised designs for his beautiful maps, and Sheng Wang also provided invaluable research assistance.

I have to give huge thanks to Kelsie Besaw at Skyhorse Publishing for accepting my pitch and believing in the material. And kudos to Cat—Catherine Kovach, eagle-eyed editor at Skyhorse, for finishing the job and taking care of "my baby" as if it were her own.

I am, of course, grateful to the staffs of the Public Records Office of the UK, the British Library Newspaper Collections, the Imperial War Museum in London, the Chicago History Museum, the African Studies Department at the University of Toronto, and the Toronto Reference Library.

A great deal of thanks must go to Mr. Imru Zelleke, retired ambassador of Ethiopia and survivor of the Danane concentration camp. Imru offered advice on certain aspects of coverage and saved me more than once from what could have proved to be embarrassing errors. I have for him a great deal of respect—and no small amount of awe—for his patience, charm, and what has been a rich and amazing life.

SELECT BIBLIOGRAPHY

Books

Abebe Hailemelekot. *The Victory of Adowa*. Addis Ababa: Commercial Printing Enterprises, second edition, 2000.

The Abyssinian Campaigns: The Official Story of the Conquest of Italian East Africa. London: His Majesty's Stationary Office, 1942.

Allen, W. E. D. *Guerrilla War in Abyssinia*. London: Penguin, 1943.

Andrew, Christopher. *The Defence of the Realm: The Authorized History of MI5*. London: Penguin, 2009.

Arent, Arthur. *Ethiopia*, stage play, performed at the Biltmore Theater, January 24, 1936.

Asante, S. K. B. *Pan-African Protest: West Africa and the Italo-Ethiopian Crisis, 1934-1941*. London: Longman Group Ltd., 1977.

Asher, Michael. *Thesiger*. London: Penguin, 1994.

Astor, Gerald. *And a Credit to His Race: The Hard Life and Times of Joseph Louis Barrow, a.k.a. Joe Louis*. New York: E. P. Dutton & Co., 1974.

Baer, George W. *Test Case: Italy, Ethiopia and the League of Nations*. Stanford, CA: Hoover Institution Press, 1976.

Baer, George W. *The Coming of the Italian-Ethiopian War*. Cambridge, MA: Harvard University Press, 1967.

Bahru Zewde. *A History of Modern Ethiopia*. Oxford: James Curry, 2001.

Bahru Zewde. *Pioneers of Change in Ethiopia*. Oxford: James Curry, 2002.

Bak, Richard. *Joe Louis: The Great Black Hope*. New York: Da Capo Press. 1998.

Baldwin, James. *Nobody Knows My Name*. New York: Vintage, 1993 edition. (Dial Press, 1961.)

Barker, A. J. *The Civilizing Mission*. New York: Dial Press, 1968.

Barzini, Luigi. *The Italians*. London: Penguin Books, 1968.

Beevor, Antony and Cooper, Artemis. *Paris after the Liberation, 1944-1949* Doubleday, 1994.

Bell, David. *François Mitterrand: A Political Biography*. Malden, MA: Polity Press, 2005.

Bernier, Olivier. *Fireworks at Dusk: Paris in the Thirties*. Boston: Little, Brown, 1993.

Bierman, John and Smith, Colin. *Fire in the Night: Wingate of Burma, Ethiopia and Zion*. New York: Random House, 1999.

Bosworth, R. J. B. *Mussolini's Italy: Life Under the Fascist Dictatorship 1915-1945*. London: Penguin, 2005.

Buhle, Paul, Ed. *C.L.R. James: His Life and Work*. London: Allison & Busby, 1986.

Buxton, David Roden. *Travels in Ethiopia*. London: E. Benn, 1957.

Campbell, Ian. *The Massacre of Addis Ababa*. London: New Cross Books (forthcoming).

Campbell, Ian. *The Plot to Kill Graziani: The Attempted Assassination of Mussolini's Viceroy*. Addis Ababa: Addis Ababa University Press, 2010.

Chambrun, René de and Stein, Elly (Trans). *Pierre Laval: Traitor or Patriot?* New York: Scribner, 1984.

Churchill, Winston. *The Second World War*, Vol. 6, *Triumph and Tragedy*. Boston: Houghton Mifflin, 1953.

Ciano, Galeazzo. Ed. Gibson, Hugh. *The Ciano Diaries, 1939-1943*. New York: Doubleday, 1946.

Ciano, Galeazzo. Trans. Mayor, Andreas. *Ciano's Diary, 1937-1938*. London: Methuen, 1952.

Coffey, Thomas M. *Lion by the Tail*. London: Hamish Hamilton, 1974.

Collier, Richard. *Duce!* New York: Collins, 1971.

Collum, Danny Duncan, Ed. *African Americans in the Spanish Civil War: "This Ain't Ethiopia, But It'll Do."* New York: Macmillan, 1992.

Colvin, Ian. *Vansittart in Office*. London: Victor Gollancz, 1965.

Darrah, David. *Hail Caesar!* New York: Hale, Cushman & Flint, 1936.

Davis, Kenneth S. *FDR: Into the Storm, 1937-1940*. New York: Random House, 1993.

De Bono, Emilio. *Anno XIIII: The Conquest of an Empire*. London: Cresset Press, 1937.

De St. Jorre, John. *The Brothers' War: Biafra and Nigeria*. Boston: Houghton, Mifflin, 1972.

Del Boca, Angelo and Cummins, P. D. (trans). *The Ethiopian War 1935-1941*. Chicago: University of Chicago Press, 1969.

Deedes, W. F. *At War with Waugh*. London: Macmillan, 2003.

DePalma, Anthony. *The Man Who Invented Fidel*. New York: Public Affairs, 2006.

Domoslawski, Artur. *Ryszard Kapuściński: A Life*. Brooklyn, NY: Verso, 2012.

Drennan, James (W. E. D. Allen). *B.U.F.: Oswald Mosley and British Fascism*. London: John Murray, 1934.

Duberman, Martin. *Paul Robeson*. New York: Knopf, 1988.

Duggan, Christopher. *Fascist Voices*. London: The Bodley Head, 2012.

Duggan, Christopher. *The Force of Destiny: A History of Italy Since 1796*. London: Allen Lane, 2007.

Ebner, Michael. *Ordinary Violence in Mussolini's Italy*. New York: Cambridge University Press, 2011.

Eden, Anthony. *Facing the Dictators: The Eden Memoirs*. London: Cassell, 1962.

Eden, Anthony. *The Reckoning: The Eden Memoirs*. London: Cassell, 1965.

Faber, David. *Munich: The 1938 Appeasement Crisis*. New York: Simon & Schuster, 2008.

Farago, Ladislas. *Abyssinia on the Eve*. London: Putnam, 1935.

Feiling, Keith. *Life of Neville Chamberlain*. Macmillan, 1946.

Flanagan, Hallie. *Arena: The Story of the Federal Theatre*. New York: Duell, Sloan and Pearce, 1940.

Franklin, John Hope. *From Slavery to Freedom*. New York: Knopf, 2000.

Fryer, Peter. *Staying Power: The History of Black People in Britain*. London: Pluto Press, 2010.

Gandy, Alain. *Salan*. Paris: Perrin, 1990.

Garretson, Peter P. *A Victorian Gentleman & Ethiopian Nationalist*. Woodbridge, Suffolk: James Currey, 2012.

Gebru Tareke. *Ethiopia: Power and Protest*. Cambridge: Cambridge University Press, 1991.

Grant, Colin. *Negro with a Hat: The Rise and Fall of Marcus Garvey*. New York: Oxford University Press, 2008.

Greenfield, Richard. *Ethiopia: A New Political History*. New York: Praeger, 1965.

Haile Selassie. *My Life and Ethiopia's Progress: Autobiography, Volumes One and Two*. Chicago: Research Associates School Times Publications, 1999.

Haney, Lynn. *Naked at the Feast*. London: Robson Books, 1981.

Harmsworth, Geoffrey. *Abyssinia Marches On*. London: Hutchinson & Co, 1941.

Harris, Brice, *The United States and the Italo-Ethiopian Crisis*. Stanford: Stanford University Press, 1964.

Harris, Joseph E. *African-American Reactions to War in Ethiopia 1936-1941*. Baton Rouge: Louisiana State University Press, 1994.

Harrison, Shirley. *Sylvia Pankhurst: A Crusading Life, 1882-1960*. London: Aurum Press, 2003.

Hastings, Selina. *Evelyn Waugh*. London: Sinclair-Stevenson, 1994.

Haywood, Harry. *Negro Liberation*. New York: International Publishers, 1948.

Hibbert, Christopher. *Mussolini: The Rise and Fall of Il Duce*. New York: Palgrave Macmillan, 2008.

Higham, Charles. *Trading With the Enemy: An exposé of the Nazi-American Money Plot, 1933-1949*. New York: Delacorte Press, 1983.

Hilton, Andrew. *The Ethiopian Patriots*. Stroud: Spellmount, 2007.

Hoare, Samuel. *Nine Troubled Years*. London: Collins, 1954.

Hooker, James R. *Black Revolutionary: George Padmore's Path from Communism to Pan-Africanism*. New York: Praeger Publishers, 1967.

Horne, Alistair. *A Savage War of Peace*. New York: New York Review of Books, 2006 reprint.

Howarth, Patrick. *Intelligence Chief Extraordinary: The Life of the Ninth Duke of Portland*. London: The Bodley Head, 1986.

Hull, Cordell. *The Memoirs of Cordell Hull*. New York: Macmillan, 1948.

Isaacs, Harold. *The New World of Negro Americans*. New York: J. Day Co., 1963.

James, C. L. R. *The Black Jacobins: Toussaint L'Ouverture and the San Domingo Revolution*. London: Penguin Books, 2001.

Jeffery, Keith. *The Secret History of MI6*. New York: Penguin, 2010.

Junod, Marcel and Fitzgerald, Edward (trans). *Warrior without Weapons*. London: Jonathan Cape, 1951.

Kali-Nyah, Imani. *Italy's War Crimes in Ethiopia, 1935-1941*. Chicago: The Ethiopian Holocaust Remembrance Committee, 2000.

Kelly, Saul. *The Lost Oasis: The Desert War and the Hunt for Zerzura*. New York: John Murray, 2002.

Kertzer, David I. *The Pope and Mussolini: The Secret History of Pius XI and the Rise of Fascism in Europe*. New York: Random House, 2014.

Kirkpatrick, Ivone. *The Inner Circle*. New York: Macmillan, 1959.

Knightley, Phillip. *The First Casualty*. New York: Harcourt, Brace, Jovanovich, 1975.

Konovalov, Feodor. Unpublished Manuscript. Hoover Institution, Stanford University. New English revised version by J. Calvitt Clarke III, Professor Emeritus, Jacksonville University, *World War II Quarterly*, 2008 (see Articles). A working draft with citations was also sent to the author. A copy of the original English translated text was provided by Boris Gorelik.

Lamb, Richard. *Mussolini and the British*. London: John Murray, 1997.

Laval, Pierre. *The Unpublished Diary of Pierre Laval*. London: Falcon Press, 1948.

Lazareff, Pierre. *Deadline: The Behind-the-Scenes Story of the Last Decade in France*. New York: Random House, 1942.

Lentakis, Michael B. *Ethiopia: A View From Within*. London: Janus Publishing, 2005.

Levi, Carlo. *Christ Stopped at Eboli*. New York: Farrar, Strauss and Giroux, 1947, 2006 reprint edition.

Lewis, David Levering. *When Harlem Was in Vogue*. New York: Penguin, 1997.

Mack Smith, Denis. *Mussolini's Roman Empire*. New York: Viking Press, 1976.

MacMillan, Margaret. *Paris 1919*. New York: Random House, 2001.

Makalani, Minkah. *In the Cause of Freedom: Radical Black Internationalism from Harlem to London, 1917-1939*. Chapel Hill: University of North Carolina Press, 2011.

Manchester, William. *The Last Lion, Winston Spencer Churchill: Alone, 1932-1940*. New York: Little, Brown, 1988.

Manchester, William. *The Last Lion, Winston Spencer Churchill: Visions of Glory*. Boston: Little, Brown, 1983.

Manchester, William and Reid, Paul. *The Last Lion, Winston Spencer Churchill: Defender of the Realm, 1940-1965*. New York: Little, Brown, 2012.

Mandela, Nelson. *Long Walk to Freedom*. New York: Little, Brown & Company. 1994.

Marcus, Harold G. *Haile Selassie 1: The Formative Years 1892 – 1936*. Lawrenceville: Red Sea Press, 1995.

Martelli, George. *Italy Against the World*. New York: Harcourt, Brace, 1938.

Matthews, Herbert L. *The Fruits of Fascism*. New York: Harcourt, Brace, 1943.

Matthews, Herbert L. *Two Wars and More to Come*. New York: Carrick & Evans, 1938.

Mockler, Anthony. *Haile Selassie's War*. Oxford: Signal Books edition, 2003.

Monks, Noel. *Eyewitness*. London: Shakespeare Head, 1956.

Moseley, Ray. *Mussolini: The Last 600 Days of Il Duce*. Lanham, MD: Taylor Trade Publishing, 2004.

Mosley, Leonard. *Haile Selassie: The Conquering Lion*. London: Weidenfeld & Nicholson, 1964.

Murray-Brown, Jeremy. *Kenyatta*. London: George Allen & Unwin, 1972.

Newman, E. W. Polson. *Italy's Conquest of Abyssinia*. London: Thornton, Butterworth, 1937.

Nkrumah, Kwame. *Ghana: The Autobiography of Kwame Nkrumah*. London: Thames, Nelson & Sons, 1957.

Nugent, John Peer. *The Black Eagle*. New York: Stein and Day, 1971.

Padmore, George. *Africa and World Peace*. London: Frank Cass, 1972.

Pakenham, Thomas. *The Scramble for Africa*. New York: Random House, 1991.

Pankhurst, Richard. *Sylvia Pankhurst, Artist and Crusader.* London: Paddington Press, 1979.

Pateman, Roy. *Eritrea: Even the Stones are Burning.* Lawrenceville: Red Sea Press, 1990.

Pennybacker, Susan. *From Scottsboro to Munich: Race and Political Culture in 1930s Britain.* Princeton: Princeton University Press, 2009.

Peterson, Maurice. *Both Sides of the Curtain: An Autobiography.* London: Constable, 1950.

Pimlott, Ben. *The Queen.* London: Harper Collins, 1996.

Pinckney, Darryl. *Out There: Mavericks of Black Literature.* New York: Basic Civitas Books.

Polsgrove, Carol. *Ending British Rule in Africa: Writers in a Common Cause.* Manchester: Manchester University Press, 2009

Pottle, Mark (Ed.). *Champion Redoubtable: The Diaries and Letters of Violet Bonham Carter, 1914-1945.* London: Phoenix Giant, 1999.

Pugh, Martin. *'Hurrah for the Blackshirts!': Fascists and Fascism in Britain Between the Wars.* London: Jonathan Cape, 2005.

Quinn, Susan. *Furious Improvisation: How the WPA and a Cast of Thousands Made High Art out of Desperate Times.* New York: Walker, 2008.

Rankin, Nicholas. *Telegram from Guernica.* London: Faber and Faber, 2003.

Rey, C. F. *The Real Abyssinia.* London: Seeley Service & Co, 1935.

Romero, Patricia W. *E. Sylvia Pankhurst: Portrait of a Radical.* New Haven: Yale University Press, 1987.

Rose, Kenneth. *King George V.* New York: Knopf, 1984.

Russell, Bertrand. *Autobiography, Volume II.* New York: Little Brown, 1967.

Russell, Bertrand. *The Selected Letters of Bertrand Russell: The Public Years, 1914-1970.* London: Routledge, 2001.

Russell, Bertrand. *Which Way to Peace?* London: M. Joseph, 1936.

Salan, Raoul. *Mémoires: Fin D'un Empire.* Paris: Presses de la cite, 1970.

Salvemini, Gaetano. *Prelude to World War II.* London: Victor Gollancz, 1953.

Sandford, Christine. *Ethiopia Under Haile Selassie.* London: J. M. Dent & Sons, 1946.

Sbacchi, Alberto. *Ethiopia under Mussolini: Fascism and the Colonial Experience.* London: Zed Books, 1985.

Sbacchi, Alberto. *Legacy of Bitterness: Ethiopia and Fascist Italy, 1935-1941.* Lawrenceville: Red Sea Press, 1997.

Schuyler, George S. *Ethiopian Stories.* Boston: Northeastern University Press, 1994. Introduction by Robert A. Hill.

Scott, William R. *The Sons of Sheba's Race: African-Americans and the Italo-Ethiopian War, 1935-1941*. Bloomington: Indiana University Press, January 1993.

Segrè, Claudio. *Italo Balbo: A Fascist Life*. Berkley: University of California Press, 1987.

Sheean, Vincent. *Between the Thunder and the Sun*. New York: Random House, 1943.

Sherwood, Robert. *Roosevelt and Hopkins: An Intimate History*. New York: Harper, 1948.

Shireff, David. *Bare Feet and Bandoliers*. Barnsley, Yorkshire: Pen and Sword Books, 2009.

Shirer, William L. *The Collapse of the Third Republic*. New York: Simon & Schuster, 1969.

Simmons, Thomas E. *The Brown Condor*. Silver Spring, MD: Bartleby Press, 1988.

Simmons, Thomas E. *The Man Called Brown Condor: The Forgotten History of an African American Fighter Pilot*. New York: Skyhorse Publishing, 2013.

Skidelsky, Robert. *Oswald Mosley*. London: Macmillan, 1990.

Sperber, A. M. *Murrow: His Life and Times*. New York: Bantam Books, 1987.

Steer, G. L. *Caesar in Abyssinia*. London: Hodder and Stoughton, 1936.

Steer, G. L. *Sealed and Delivered*. London: Hodder and Stoughton, 1942.

Taylor, A. J. P. *The Origins of the Second World War*. London: Hamish Hamilton, 1961.

Thesiger, Wilfred. *The Danakil Diary: Journeys through Abyssinia, 1930-34*. London: Flamingo, 1998.

Thesiger, Wilfred. *The Life of My Choice*. London: Collins, 1987.

Thompson, Geoffrey. *Front-Line Diplomat*. London: Hutchinson, 1959.

Thorpe, D. R. *Eden: The Life and Times of Anthony Eden, First Earl of Avon, 1897-1977*. London: Pimlico, 2003.

Tiersky, Ronald. *François Mitterrand: A Very French President*. Lanham, MA: Rowman & Littlefield Publishing Group, 2002.

Tissier, Pierre. *I Worked with Laval*. London: Harrap, 1942.

Trythall, A. J. *Boney Fuller: The Intellectual General*. London: Cassell, 1977.

Vansittart, Robert. *The Mist Procession*. London: Hutchinson, 1958.

Waugh, Evelyn. *Waugh in Abyssinia*. London: Penguin Books edition, 1986.

Weber, Ronald. *News of Paris*. Chicago: Ivan R. Dee, 2006.

Welles, Sumner. *The Time for Decision*. New York: Harper & Row, 1944.

Windsor, Edward, Duke of. *A King's Story*. London: Prion Books, 1998 reprint.

Worcester, Kent. *C.L.R. James: A Political Biography*. New York: State University of New York Press, 1996.

Wrong, Michela. *I Didn't Do It for You*. London: Harper Perennial, 2005.

Yates, James. *From Mississippi to Madrid: Memoir of a Black American in the Abraham Lincoln Brigade.* Seattle: Open Hand Publishing, 1989.

Articles

Baer, George. "Haile Selassie's Protectorate Appeal to King Edward VIII," *Cahiers d'Études Africaines*, Vol. 9, Cahier 34, 1969.

Bahru Zewde. "The Ethiopian Intelligentsia and the Italo-Ethiopian War, 1935-1941," *The International Journal of African Historical Studies*, Vol. 26, No. 2, 1993.

Bahru Zewde. "Hayla-Selassie: From Progressive to Reactionary," *Northeast African Studies*, Vol 2, No. 2, 1995.

Carroll, Rory. "Italy's Bloody Secret," *The Guardian*, June 25, 2001.

Clarke, J. Calvitt. "Feodor Konovalov and the Italo-Ethiopian War (Part 1)," *World War II Quarterly*, Vol. 5, No. 1, 2008, (Part 2) Vol. 5, No. 2, 2008.

De Grand, Alexander. "Mussolini's Follies: Fascism in Its Imperial and Racist Phase, 1935-1940," *Contemporary European History*, May 2004.

Engert, Jane M. "American Legation Under Fire: Addis Ababa, 1936," American Diplomacy, http://www.unc.edu/depts/diplomat, November 2006.

Ghosh, Palash. "Mussolini and Gandhi: Strange Bedfellows," *International Business Times*, March 3, 2012.

James, "Discovering Literature in Trinidad: The Nineteen-Thirties" from *Spheres of Existence: Selected Writings*. London: Allison & Busby, 1980.

James, C. L. R. "Fighting for the Abyssinian Empire," *New Leader*, June 5, 1936

James, C. L. R. "Intervening in Abyssinia," *The New Leader*, October 4, 1935.

James, Robert. "Anthony Eden and the Suez Crisis," *History Today*, Vol. 36, Issue 11, 1986.

Mackenzie, Alan J. "Radical Pan-Africanism in the 1930s: A Discussion with C.L.R. James," *Radical History Review*, Fall 1980.

Minale Adugna. "Women and Warfare in Ethiopia," Organization for Social Science Research in Eastern and Southern Africa, 2001.

Pankhurst, Richard. "The Ethiopian Patriots: The Lone Struggle, 1936-1940." *Ethiopia Observer*, Vol. 13, Issue 1, 1970.

Pankhurst, Richard. "Fascist Racial Policies in Ethiopia: 1922-1941," *Ethiopia Observer*, Vol. 12, Issue 4, 1969.

Pankhurst, Richard. "Italian Fascist War Crimes in Ethiopia: A History of Their Discussion from the League of Nations to the United Nations (1936-1949)," *Northeast African Studies*, Vol. 6, Number 1-2, 1999.

Pankhurst, Richard. "Post-World War II Ethiopia: British Military Policy and Action for the Dismantling and Acquisition of Italian Factories and Other Assets, 1941-2," *Journal of Ethiopian Studies*, Vol. 29, Issue 1, 1996.

Rogers, Joel (as Jerrold Robbins). "The Americans in Ethiopia," *The American Mercury*, May 1933.

Ryle, John. "Tales of Mythical Africa," *Times Literary Supplement*, July 27, 2001.

Sbacchi, Alberto. "Italy and the Treatment of the Ethiopian Aristocracy," *International Journal of African Historical Studies*, Vol. 10, Issue 2, 1977.

Scott, William R. "Malaku E. Bayen: Ethiopian Emissary to Black America, 1936-1941," *Ethiopian Observer*, 15, 1972.

Shaftel, David. "The Black Eagle of Harlem," *Air & Space*, January 2009.

Spitzer, Leo and Denzer, LaRay. "I. T. A. Wallace-Johnson and the West African Youth League." *The International Journal of African Historical Studies*, Vol. 6, No. 3, 1973.

Stix, Nicholas. "Forgotten One," *National Review Weekend*, February 3-4, 2001. http://old.nationalreview.com/weekend/books/books-stix020301.shtml

Trotsky, Leon. "On Dictators and the Heights of Oslo," *The New International*, June 1936.

Tsehai Berhane-Selassie. "Women Guerrilla Fighters," *North East Africa Studies*, Vol. 1, No. 3.

Walston, James. "History and Memory of the Italian Concentration Camps," *The Historical Journal*, Vol. 40, No. 1, 1997.

Wilson, Ivy. "'Are You Man Enough?' Imagining Ethiopia and Transnational Black Masculinity," *Callaloo*, Vol. 33, Issue 1, April 2010.

Official Documents

Documents on British Foreign Policy, 1919-1939, Second Series, Volume XIV. London: Her Majesty's Stationery Office, 1976. Medlicott, W. N., Dakin, Douglas and Lambert, M. E., Editors.

Documents on British Foreign Policy, 1919-1939, Second Series, Volume XV. London: Her Majesty's Stationery Office, 1976. Medlicott, W. N., Dakin, Douglas and Lambert, M. E., Editors.

Foreign Relations of the United States Diplomatic Papers, years 1935 to 1942. US State Department, US Government Printing Office.

Hansard, UK Parliament.

League of Nations Official Journal, 1935-1939.

UK National Archives; Cabinet Documents, Foreign Office and War Office files.

Wire Services, Media Networks, Newspapers and Magazines

Associated Press

BBC

Canadian Press

Havas

Reuters

United Press

The Black Man

Canberra Times

Chicago Defender

Chicago Tribune

Daily Mail

Daily Telegraph

The Economist

Evening Standard

The Guardian

Jerusalem Post

Manchester Guardian

New Times & Ethiopia News

New York Times

The Observer

Pittsburgh Courier

Time

The Times of London

The Sunday Times of London

The Times Literary Supplement

Toronto Globe

Washington Post

Unpublished Sources and Correspondence

Personal Memoir by Imru Zelleke

Select papers of Dr. Charles Winckel, courtesy private collection of Borre Winckel

Interviews and Email

Imru Zelleke, Interviews October 8 and December 8, 2012

Jagama Kello, Interview October 20, 2013

Eric Matthews, email correspondence, July 2013

Borre Winckel, email correspondence, September–December 2013

Interview by Elizabeth Blunt for BBC World Service with Jagama Kello, April 2009, Courtesy of the Imperial War Museum, UK.

INDEX

Jeff Pearce

IN MEMORIAM

Richard Pankhurst
1927–2017

Richard Pankhurst wrote the foreword for *Prevail* and was considered the leading authority on Ethiopian history. He was the son of the famous suffragette Sylvia Pankhurst, who lobbied for Ethiopia during the war. In 1962, he was the founding director of the Institute of Ethiopian Studies, and in 2004, he was given the OBE (Order of the British Empire). He was instrumental in the campaign to have the Aksum Obelisk returned from Italy to Ethiopia in 2005. He passed away in early 2017 and was laid to rest at Holy Trinity Cathedral in Addis Ababa.

Photo credit: Indrias Getachew Kassaye